THE POWER OF NEWS

JULIUS REUTER, 1861

THE
POWER OF
NEWS

THE HISTORY OF
REUTERS

SECOND EDITION

DONALD READ

OXFORD UNIVERSITY PRESS
1999

Oxford University Press, Great Clarendon Street, Oxford OX2 6DP

Oxford New York

Athens Auckland Bangkok Bogotá Buenos Aires Calcutta
Cape Town Chennai Dar es Salaam Delhi Florence Hong Kong Istanbul
Karachi Kuala Lumpur Madrid Melbourne Mexico City Mumbai
Nairobi Paris São Paulo Singapore Taipei Tokyo Toronto Warsaw
and associated companies in
Berlin Ibadan

Oxford is a registered trade mark of Oxford University Press

Published in the United States
by Oxford University Press Inc., New York

British Library Cataloguing in Publication Data
Data available

Library of Congress Cataloging in Publication Data
Read, Donald.
The power of news: the history of Reuters / Donald Read.—2nd ed.
p. cm.
Includes bibliographical references.
1. Reuters, Ltd. 2. Title.
PN5111.R4R43 1999 070.4'35—dc21 98–36926
ISBN 0–19–820768–9

1 3 5 7 9 10 8 6 4 2

Typeset by Hope Services (Abingdon) Ltd
Printed in Great Britain
on acid-free paper by
Bookcraft Ltd
Midsomer Norton, Somerset

PREFACE TO SECOND EDITION

REUTERS, the international news and information agency, started in London in 1851. Ever since that period it has been known for its commitment to truth in news. Therefore not surprisingly—but nevertheless pleasingly—when in 1987 I was invited to write the present history, the Reuter management accepted that I must write with a similar unqualified commitment to truth and objectivity. The book, although an authorized account, was not to be a company whitewash; it was to offer a balanced assessment in the light of the evidence.

For this second edition, as for the first in 1992, I have therefore been allowed unrestricted access to the Reuters Archive, apart from personal files of staff and pensioners still alive. And despite sometimes forceful (but usually helpful) comments upon my drafts from Reuter managers past and present, I have been left free to write as I have pleased.

The whole book has now been substantially rewritten. Since the first edition was completed, Reuters has paid for extensive research not only within the United Kingdom, but also in continental Europe, the United States, India, South Africa, Australia, New Zealand, Sri Lanka, Russia, Japan, and Hong Kong. In this wide-ranging enquiry, I was greatly helped by my research assistant (1989–93) Justine Taylor who, in four continents, tracked down Reuter-related material with commendable awareness and persistence.

This new research has produced not only much more factual evidence, but also a deeper understanding of the work of Reuters during nearly a century and a half. In particular, this second edition casts new light: (1) upon the early career of Julius Reuter; (2) upon the role of Reuters as the news agency of the British Empire; (3) upon the questionable contribution of Sir Roderick Jones, the head of Reuters between the wars; (4) upon the formation of the Reuter Trust in contentious circumstances in 1941; (5) upon the work of leading Reuter correspondents during the two world wars; (6) upon the complex personality and career of Sir Christopher Chancellor, the head of Reuters in the 1940s and 50s; (7) upon the response of Reuters to the dissolution of the British Empire, with particular reference to India and South Africa; (8) upon the profitable 1984 flotation of Reuters as a public company; and (9) upon the unsettling impact of such unusual Reuter journalists as Sigmund Engländer, a revolutionary of 1848, J. S. Barnes, a Fascist sympathiser in the 1930s, and

John Peet, who in 1950 suddenly gave up as chief Reuter correspondent in West Berlin and crossed to the East.

For this second edition, I have added a select bibliography, and also unobtrusive referencing. These additions will assist further enquiry. I have also added a list of key dates. The book ends at 1989, a turning-point in history and a year full of news interest. How Reuters has fared since that date cannot yet be considered within a historical perspective.

Both editions have depended heavily upon help from many people in many places. A long list of acknowledgments was included at the end of the first edition; I am glad to repeat here my thanks to those numerous individuals and institutions. For diverse help with this second edition I am indebted to Melanie Aspey, Christine Bolt, Richard Bond, Ludmilla Bonushkina, Doon Campbell, Lee Casey, François Duriaud, Eileen Dwyer, Eamon Dyas, Bernard Edinger, Robert Elphick, Ronald Gladman, Anthony Grey, Gordon Hanson, Jack Henry, Jim Henry, Kyoko Hashimoto, Brian Horton, Galina Ippolitova, Peter Jackson, Aleco Joannides, Dominick Jones, Ken Jones, Jacqui Kavenagh, Adam Kellett-Long, Misha Lavrientiev, Judy Logan, Gerald Long, Clare McDermott, Henry Manisty, Konstantin Mashinsky, Seaghan Maynes, Paul Mindus, Antonia Moon, Brian Mooney, Michael Neale, Michael Nelson, the late Hubert Nicholson, Peter O'Hara, Michael Palmer, John Ransom, Terhi Rantanen, John Rettie, Anne-Marie Schwirlitz, Jacquie Sen, Ron Sly, Stephen Somerville, Gavin Souter, Sir Richard Storey, Gerry Suckley, Geoffrey Taylor, Brian Timms, Konstantin Trifonov, David Ure, Oliver Wates, Mark Wood, Patrick Worsnip.

The help and support I have received from David Chipp, John Entwisle, and Dennis Savage has turned the labour of research and composition into a pleasure. And without the dedicated and cheerful aid of Jessica Harte, I would have had great difficulty in producing a final text. To these four, therefore, I express my particular gratitude.

D.R.

CONTENTS

LIST OF PLATES

LIST OF FIGURES

LIST OF TABLES

KEY DATES

1816	21 July	Israel Beer Josaphat born in Cassel, Germany.
1845	29 October	Came to England as 'Julius Josaphat'.
1845	16 November	Baptized as 'Paul Julius Reuter' at St George's German Lutheran Chapel, Whitechapel, London.
1845	23 November	Married 'Ida Maria Elizabeth Clementine Magnus' at St George's Lutheran Chapel.
1847		Became a partner in a Berlin bookshop, 'Reuter & Stargardt'.
1848	Early	Published political pamphlets.
1848		Fled from Germany. Working in Paris as translator for Havas news agency.
1849	Spring	Started own lithographic agency in Rue Jean Jacques Rousseau, Paris, publishing daily news sheet. Failed in late summer.
1850	January	Reuter running a news agency in Aachen. Agreement (24 April) with Heinrich Geller to supply pigeons for service between Brussels and Aachen. Agency operated for over a year, until telegraph gap closed.
1851	14 June	The Reuters arrived in London.
1851	10 October	Reuter set up office in two rooms at 1 Royal Exchange Buildings, London.
1851	13 November	Cross-Channel submarine telegraph began operating.
1853		'S. Josaphat and Co.'s Continental Telegraph' opened in Royal Exchange Arcade, Manchester—supplying news to local papers. Closed by 1855.
1858	October	Reuter began to supply daily news to London papers.
1859	10 January	First major Reuter news beat—King of Sardinia's speech foreshadowing 'War of Italian Liberation'.
1861	28 March	Julius Reuter presented at the court of Queen Victoria by Lord Palmerston, the Prime Minister.
1863	December	Reuter opened telegraph line from Cork to Crookhaven to speed transatlantic news.
1865	20 February	Reuters Telegram Company registered as a public limited company.

1865	26 April	Two-hour Reuter beat in London giving news of the assassination of President Lincoln on 14 April. Great impact.
1865	Late	Office opened by Reuters in Alexandria, the first outside Europe.
1866	Spring	Office opened in Bombay, the first in Asia.
1866	July	First transatlantic cable completed.
1866	October	Reuter completed his own cable across the North Sea to Nordeney.
1869	August	French Atlantic cable opened, promoted by Julius Reuter and Baron Emil d'Erlanger.
1870	17 January	Agreement signed between Reuters, Havas, and Wolff to establish a worldwide news ring.
1871	Spring	London headquarters moved to Old Jewry.
1871	7 September	Duke of Saxe-Coburg-Gotha conferred barony on Julius Reuter—known henceforth as 'Baron de Reuter'.
1876	November	Cape Town office opened, the first in South Africa.
1878	May	Baron de Reuter retired as managing director—succeeded by his son, Herbert.
1899	25 February	Baron de Reuter died at the Villa Reuter, Nice.
1900	17 May	Reuters two days ahead in London with news of the relief of Mafeking. Great impact: 'mafficking' in the streets.
1915	18 April	Suicide of Baron Herbert—end of the family connection.
1915	6 October	Roderick Jones appointed general manager.
1916	11 December	Reuter's Telegram Company changed into a private company, Reuters Limited. Jones managing director and, from 1919, chairman. Knighted 1918.
1920	1 January	Trade Department created, to spearhead expansion of commercial services.
1922		Reuterian service began—news by wireless in Morse to continental news agencies.
1922	11 November	First agreement to supply news to BBC.
1923		Reuter Continental Broadcasting Service began, delivering price quotations and exchange rates in Morse.
1923	November	Headquarters moved from Old Jewry to 9 Carmelite Street.

1925	31 December	Press Association took majority shareholding in Reuters.
1928		City Ticker introduced in London banks.
1931	March	Reuterian world service of news began.
1938	22 September	Globereuter service began, subsidized by British Government.
1939	July	New headquarters opened at 85 Fleet Street—architect Sir Edwin Lutyens.
1941	4 February	Sir Roderick Jones resigned—Christopher Chancellor his eventual successor.
1941	September	Warner Brothers film, *This Man Reuter*, starring Edward G. Robinson, released in London.
1941	October	Press Association and Newspaper Proprietors Association came together as equal partners in ownership of Reuters. Creation of the Reuter Trust.
1947	Spring	Australian Associated Press and New Zealand Press Association taken into the partnership.
1949	February	Press Trust of India taken into the partnership.
1950	12 June	John Peet, Reuter correspondent in West Berlin, abandoned his post, and crossed to Communist East.
1951	July	Centenary celebrations—Chancellor knighted.
1953	February	Press Trust of India withdrew from partnership.
1956	16 March	Reuters alone with summary of dramatic Khruschev speech denouncing Stalin to Soviet Communist Party congress.
1956	1 November	Chancellor circular to staff emphasizing the need for objectivity during the Suez crisis.
1959	1 July	Sir Christopher Chancellor succeeded as general manager by W. A. ['Tony'] Cole.
1962	27 October	Cuban missile crisis—Reuters praised for delivering, via White House teleprinter, first news to President Kennedy of Khruschev proposal for a deal.
1963	25 January	Cole died in his office at 85 Fleet Street. Succeeded by Gerald Long.
1963	1 June	International Financial Printer operational at Brussels. Direct delivery of information to individual subscribers over wide area.
1964	23 April	Reuters signed agreement with Ultronic Systems Corporation of New Jersey, USA to sell Stockmaster

		outside North America—electronic on-line stock prices by 3-number display. Customer retrieval of information, instead of blanket dissemination. Operational 1 July. Became highly profitable for Reuters.
1967	1 April	End of exchange agreement with Dow Jones. Reuters Economic Services began entirely independent reporting out of North America.
1967	21 July	Anthony Grey, Peking correspondent, under house arrest in retaliation for arrest of Chinese Communist journalists in Hong Kong.
1967	7 September	End of exchange agreement with Associated Press. Reuters started independent general news coverage inside the United States.
1968	2 January	Videoscan introduced in United States. First use of video for textual news display.
1968	22 July	Automatic Data Exchange introduced in London. Computerized message-switching system for faster handling of news worldwide. First use by an international news organization.
1969	4 October	Anthony Grey released by Chinese after 806 days.
1970	February	Videomaster introduced—screen display of stock and commodity prices.
1971	1 December	Reuters launched its own general news service in West Germany for direct distribution to the media.
1972	1 January	Reuters ceased subscribing to Agence France-Presse and began fully separate reporting out of France.
1973	June	The Reuter Monitor Money Rates Service became gradually operational in London. A revolutionary computerized product, devised by Reuters itself. Based upon customer contributed data. Destined to transform Reuters.
1973	17 December	First video editing system started in New York.
1979	1 January	Reuters Economic Services began direct distribution in West Germany, and started independent reporting.
1981	23 February	The Reuter Monitor Dealing Service went live, enabling dealers in foreign currencies to conclude trades over video terminals.
1981	1 March	Gerald Long resigned as managing director. Succeeded by Glen Renfrew.

1982	October	Beginning in United States of direct satellite delivery by Reuters of data by small dishes [SDS].
1982	8 September	Reuter Foundation launched as a charitable body.
1984	June	Reuters floated as a public company, Reuters Holdings PLC.
1985	January	Reuters started news picture service.
1985	October	Reuters took control of Visnews, television news film agency.
1985	October	Japan Financial Service introduced—first internal news product by Reuters for Japan.
1987		First Reuter services launched on Integrated Data Network [IDN]—a global 'highway for data'.
1989	26 April	Conversion of 'A' shares into 'B' ordinary shares. End of privileged position within the company for the Press Association and Newspaper Publishers Association.

INTRODUCTION

THE capacity to communicate with sophistication separates men from the animals. Sophistication of speech and writing was established in ancient times, whereas sophistication in communication at a distance came only in the nineteenth and twentieth centuries with the discovery of electromagnetic induction. This led, first, to the development of the electric telegraph and telephone, and then on to radio and satellite communication. 'News' exists only if it can be communicated. It depends upon command of language, but to be of much effect it also requires to be circulated widely and accurately. For centuries it moved at the speed of the horse. Then in the middle of the nineteenth century came the steam train and the electric telegraph. It was no accident that the London-based news agency which became known as 'Reuters' was started in 1851, and not at any earlier period.

Its founder was Julius Reuter, a German Jew who six years later became a British subject. After a century and a half, the business still flourishes. The name 'Reuter' or 'Reuters' appears daily in newspaper pages and upon computer screens all over the world. Enduring and universal awareness has earned the name 'Reuter' a place in the language as well as in history. The 1982 supplement to the *Oxford English Dictionary* added to its roll the words 'Reuter' and 'Reuters', complete with quotations by way of illustration. The success of Reuters during the century and a half since its foundation in London in 1851 has provided an institutional demonstration of the power of news. People want news, and will pay for it. News informs, news warns, news motivates. Julius Reuter made his fortune by recognizing this power, and his successors have followed purposefully in his footsteps.

For over a hundred years Reuters was a national and imperial institution, the news agency of the British Empire. In the mid-twentieth century the British Empire faded away, and Reuters might have faded with it. Instead, the old news agency saved itself by making a bold fresh start. During the past forty years it has transformed itself from a national into a supranational institution, even while its headquarters remain in London. This transformation has been linked to the revolution in communications technology made possible by the transistor and the microchip. Computerized economic information and data—prices, trade figures, reports, and the like—are supplied on screen to

business people working within a global economy. Reuters has helped to create that economy. Thanks especially to its success in this role, the company's
profits began to grow dramatically during the last two decades of the twentieth century. In 1980 pre-tax profits were £3.9 million: by 1997 £626 million.

Over 90 per cent of current revenue began to be earned not by news for
the media but by products serving the trading community in centres such as
the City of London, New York, and Tokyo. In a sense, the wheel had come
full circle, for in 1850 Julius Reuter had used carrier pigeons to forward stock-
market and commodity prices from Brussels, where the Belgian telegraph
ended, to Aachen, where the German line began. In 1851 he moved to
London, the financial centre of the Victorian world, and there launched his
telegraph agency. By the end of the 1850s he had found success by establishing a high standard for news gathering and distribution. He set out to be first
with the news, and often was. But above speed he placed accuracy, and alongside accuracy he set impartiality in news distribution, which meant that no
subscribers were unfairly favoured. His news services did, however, reflect
the British view of the world. Total commitment by Reuters to objectivity in
reporting, leading to a supranational attitude, can be traced only from the creation of the Reuter Trust in 1941.

A running theme within the present book is the working (or otherwise) of
the Reuter news tradition. How did it begin? How was it developed? Did it
operate when the British Empire was at war? What was the relationship of
Reuters with the British Government? How much conscious or unconscious
bias was there in news selection or presentation? And how well did the old
Reuter tradition survive within the transformed company of the second half
of the twentieth century?

Certainly, the present-day company realizes that worldwide recognition of
the independence of its reporting and management, uninfluenced by govern-
mental or other pressures, is vital for its continuing progress as an international
business. In this knowledge Glen Renfrew, managing director 1981–91, said
firmly: 'in an international company the Reuter people leave their patriotism
at home. The longer they work abroad the more they begin to appreciate all
the countries they work in.' The 1988 edition of the *Reuter International Style
Guide*, produced for internal circulation, spelt out the old tradition to the latest generation of Reuter journalists. It reiterated the continuing need for accuracy, speed, and objectivity. 'Reuters does not comment on the merit of events
. . . one man's terrorist is another man's freedom-fighter.'

Speed with the news has required the ready exploitation by Reuters of the
latest communications technology—overland telegraphs, undersea cables,

radio, and, more recently, satellites. This progression forms a second and major theme within the present book. A third theme is provided by the personal contributions of the long succession of notable Reuter journalists and managers. Julius Reuter and his chief lieutenant, Sigmund Engländer—a revolutionary of 1848—were only the first of many creative or colourful personalities who have served Reuters.

Tradition, technology, people—in addition to these three interrelated themes, another dimension, present only within the history of journalism, adds further interest. The very raw material which Reuters has handled day by day since 1851 has been the stuff of history—news of every war since the Crimean War, statistics of successive trade booms and market crashes, stories of great (and little) deeds and disasters. Reuters has truthfully told what was happening all over a troubled and changing world. In the process, it has itself changed with the times. It could not have survived otherwise. The chapters which follow explain both how Reuters has handled world news down the years, and how its organization and management grew from very modest beginnings into a great business, greater at the end of the twentieth century than at any previous period.

ONE

Julius Reuter: Before and After
1851

They need full epitaph, whose fame
Were else oblivion's easy prey;
'Tis here unneeded, when each day
A myriad prints bear Reuter's name!

(*Punch* obituary of Julius
Reuter, 8 March 1899)

I

THE international news agency 'Reuters' was founded by Julius Reuter in London in 1851. Although unnoticed at the time, this turned out to be a notable event in the history of the worldwide communication of news. The activities of Reuters were to become so necessary—particularly within the British Empire—that the question may fairly be asked why such an important initiative was left to a foreigner, only recently settled in England.

By 1851 news agencies had already been started in Paris, New York, and Berlin; and a second question therefore arises. Why had London waited so long; why had it not led the way in launching an international news agency? Thanks to the industrial revolution, Britain had become the world's leading economic power. It exported its manufactures to all continents, and imported food and raw materials in return. Its merchant ships, protected by the Royal Navy, dominated the seaways. The pound sterling was the world's trading currency, accepted everywhere. All this meant that British merchants and manufacturers in general, and the bankers, brokers, and traders of the City of London in particular, needed the latest news and information from around the world. They were interested in crop and commodity prices and prospects, in stock market reports, in shipping news, and in political news likely to affect trade. Britain's bankers and traders collected as much information as they could from their own agents overseas, but this search was necessarily uneven.

Why did they not organize their own service, perhaps in collaboration with the leading London newspapers? One answer seems to have been that they, and the newspapers, were too much in competition with each other. *The Times*, with a circulation of 40,000 copies daily, the largest in the world, did maintain its own network of correspondents in Europe and elsewhere; but it had no wish to help its rivals by collaborating with them. As will be seen, Julius Reuter eventually checked the dominance of *The Times* by starting to sell his service to the other London newspapers.

Reuter had opened in London, but Paris had shown him the way. From 1832 Charles Havas (Plate 3) had developed a lithographic news service in the French capital. At first, this had simply collected and translated items from the foreign press; but within a few years Havas was employing his own correspondents to report news directly. In 1835 'Bureau Havas' became 'Agence Havas'; and by the end of the decade Havas was offering a range of targeted news services—for French Government Ministers, for departmental prefects, for bankers, and for newspapers. Eventually, he began to sell news to subscribers in other countries. Havas, in short, was the innovator who first organized the wide collection and sale of news as a marketable commodity. Since ancient times, exceptional news had always got through, like that of the Greek victory over the Persians at Marathon in 490 BC, brought memorably by runner to Athens. But from the mid-nineteenth century, less exceptional but still important or interesting news from many parts of the world was made available day by day through the news agencies.[1]

Although Havas could not have succeeded without official backing and subsidy, his agency flourished because his news was usually dependable both in its content and its delivery. For a quick daily service from London and Brussels, he began to employ pigeons. These had long been used by the Rothschilds and others to circulate information faster than was possible by land or sea. Every afternoon, the Paris bourse began to receive from Havas that same morning's London stock exchange opening prices, flown across the English Channel by pigeon.

Even swifter was news transmitted via the overland network of telegraphs. During the 1840s, this network was beginning to spread throughout western Europe. The Government-controlled French system was not made available to the public until 1850, but Havas was allowed to use it from five years earlier. As will be seen, Julius Reuter was to follow the example of Havas by making systematic use of both pigeons and telegraphs.

2

Julius Reuter won fame as a man of business, who built impressively upon the pioneering work of others in telegraphy and journalism. Yet his early years had been unsuccessful. During the 1830s and 40s he had tried to find his way within Germany in a succession of careers; but he did not begin to make lasting progress until after he had changed his name, his religion, and his country. He had been born 'Israel Beer Josaphat' at Cassel in the state of Hesse, near the centre of Germany, on 21 July 1816. The Josaphats were a Jewish professional and business family. At the time of Reuter's birth, his father was acting chief rabbi at Cassel. Israel Beer was the third and youngest son. His eldest brother was to become a notable Talmud scholar; two cousins became university professors.[2]

Other members of the family were in business, and it was in an uncle's office at Göttingen that young Reuter found work at some point soon after the death of his father in 1829. His father had left little money. The uncle was described as a banker, but his main activity seems to have been changing money, which was a necessary function in early nineteenth-century Germany because of the proliferation of local currencies. Understanding of the currency markets was to be vital in Reuter's later success as a vendor of economic data and information.

Further evidence about his career during the 1830s and early 40s is scanty and confused. He seems to have worked in various banks, first in Hanover and then as a managing clerk at Gotha. Yet he was never entirely committed to banking, for he also tried other employment.

While at Göttingen, a university town, young Reuter had become acquainted with the great Professor Karl Friedrich Gauss, who was experimenting in sending electric signals by wire. Reuter may have acted as his assistant. It was afterwards claimed that, although Gauss was little interested in the practical implications of his research, Reuter became aware even at this early stage that communication by electric telegraph would soon be possible. There is no evidence, however, that in the 1830s he foresaw a career for himself in the collection and distribution of news by telegraph.

Was it a feeling of being unsettled which made him change his name? Before 1841, he had already adopted a new first name, 'Julius'. In that year he was registered as entering Hamburg under the name 'Julius Israel Josaphat'. Then in 1845 he took the bigger step of also changing his surname. He now became known as 'Paul Julius Reuter'. Why he chose the name Reuter is not known. It is a common German surname, and therefore a good one to take if he had decided that 'Josaphat' was too Jewish-sounding. Jews were accepted in German business circles, and some had become rich. But strict Jews were still regarded (and regarded themselves) as a separate race. Secular Jews, on the other hand, were relaxing or abandoning their faith. Some of Reuter's relations remained practising Jews, others converted to Christianity.[3]

Reuter himself did the latter. And surprisingly, his conversion was solemnized not in Germany but in London. On 16 November 1845 he was baptized in the name of 'Paul Julius Reuter' at St George's Lutheran Chapel in Whitechapel. He had entered England from Hamburg on 29 October as 'Julius Josaphat'. Was the subsequent double change of name and religion done to please his wife? 'Miss Clementine Magnus' was named as one of his sponsors. And a week later, on 23 November 1845, he was married at the same chapel to the same 'Ida Maria Elizabeth Clementine Magnus', the daughter of a Prussian Government official in Berlin. Why then did the couple not marry in the bride's home city? The reason for their preference for London is not known. Presumably they came to England for reasons of business. But what business? The certificate of aliens called Reuter a 'kaufmann', merchant, a catch-all term. He may have intended to settle in some occupation in London; but if so, he gave up within a few weeks and returned to Germany. The couple's first child, a daughter, was born at Berlin in the following July, but died in August. The Reuters were to have three sons and four daughters, of whom two sons and one daughter reached adulthood.[4]

What Reuter was doing during 1846 is unrecorded. In 1847, perhaps financed by his father-in-law, he became a partner with Joseph Stargardt in the ownership of a Berlin bookshop. Stargardt brought the necessary book-trade experience to the business. Early in the following year—the European 'year of revolutions'—the partners sought to exploit the mood of the time by publishing political pamphlets. These were radical in tone rather than revolutionary. But only a handful appeared. Julius Reuter's own political inclinations were not recorded, either in Germany at that time or in England later, for he was never active in politics. His motivation as a publisher was probably entirely commercial.

Even so, in 1848 he may have found himself under suspicion as a revolutionary, and this may have been the reason why he suddenly quit the firm of Reuter & Stargardt. The Stargardt family always claimed in later years that Reuter decamped from the 1848 Leipzig book fair, stealing in the process the firm's takings of 6,000 thalers (£900). Allegedly as a consequence, the bookshop nearly went bankrupt, and Stargardt suffered a nervous breakdown. A warrant for Reuter's arrest was said to have been issued. If so, it must have been withdrawn, for in the succeeding years Reuter travelled freely about

Germany. Years afterwards, when he was rich, he was said to have offered to repay the money, a gesture rejected by Stargardt in disgust. This episode, if it really happened as recorded, is difficult to reconcile with Reuter's later reputation for honest dealing.

What happened next to Reuter proved to be the turning-point in his career, for he now entered full-time journalism. He became a sub-editor for the Havas news agency in Paris. He seems to have been without any previous journalistic experience, and it may have been simply his command of German, French, and English which secured him the job. He stayed with Havas only long enough to learn about news agency work, and to decide that there was an opportunity for himself as an independent vendor of news.

In the spring of 1849, leaving Havas on friendly terms, he opened his own lithographic correspondence agency in a shabby room in the rue Jean Jacques Rousseau close to the main Paris post office. Havas was nearby. Every weekday, Reuter laboured with his wife and two assistants to send subscribers a bulletin by the 5 p.m. last post. Nearness to the post office allowed just enough time to include bourse closing prices. Reuter's bulletins also carried excerpts from newspaper leading articles, reports of National Assembly proceedings, general news, and a spicing of gossip. He offered this service to newspapers all over Germany at very cheap rates. But there were never enough subscribers to make it viable, and suddenly in the late summer of 1849 creditors seized such furniture and equipment as were worth taking. Reuter and his wife returned to Germany, still sure that there was an opening in the news agency field and determined to try again.[5]

3

Two factors justified a fresh attempt in Germany. First, the Frankfurt parliament had encouraged greater freedom for the press; and secondly, on 1 October 1849 the Prussian state telegraph line between Berlin and Aachen was opened to the public. Bernhard Wolff (Plate 2), a former colleague of Reuter's in Paris with Havas, had already started an agency at the Berlin end; but an opportunity still existed at Aachen, which since Roman times had been a focal point for communications.[6]

From 1 January 1850 Julius Reuter was conducting at Aachen a three-way service for businessmen and newspapers. It delivered news and prices to and from Berlin, Vienna, and Paris, via such telegraph lines as already existed and by the railways and postal services otherwise. Reuter's firm was known as the Institute for the Transmission of Telegraph Messages (Institut zur

Beförderung Telegraphischer Depeschen). *The Kölnische Zeitung* and *L'Indépendance Belge* of Brussels were probably his first newspaper subscribers. The latter's enterprising editor, Henri-Edouard Perrot, was later credited with recommending Reuter to start in Aachen. Reuter's visits to the office of *L'Indépendance Belge* were recalled many years later by Louis Hymans, a Belgian writer and journalist:

> *L'Indépendance* was virtually the only paper to receive correspondents' reports from abroad . . . Telegraphic reports were as yet unknown, and news of stock-market prices from the major European exchanges was delivered by carrier-pigeon. In this connection, I remember having known a long time ago a German who on first acquaintance seemed unremarkable, poorly educated, but astute; he used occasionally to visit the offices of *L'Indépendance* and talk endlessly about pigeons and telegraphs. To judge from his external appearance, he was neither wealthy nor indeed a businessman. I don't remember him ever having said anything of note. He was called Reuter; he must have had truly exceptional qualities and ideas that were both novel and practical, because today he is called 'baron' Reuter . . . I can think of no other example of a fortune amassed so quickly and so cheaply. But to do so, one had to have the insight—which Reuter did—that a telegraph wire could be a source of great wealth, provided one put a journalist at either end.[7]

Reuter probably himself inspired a paragraph in *L'Indépendance Belge* of 27 March 1850, which reported the establishment of 'a general correspondence bureau' at Aachen. It was said to be offering 'at moderate charge, important news and stock-market prices' to the press and finance houses of Belgium, France, and England. This news was being delivered to Aachen by telegraph. Such regular use of the telegraph, claimed the article, distinguished the Aachen bureau from the many correspondence bureaux elsewhere. For subscribers in Aachen itself, the story was later often told (and never denied) of how Reuter locked them in his office when market-moving price information was expected, so that all received the information at the same time.

The *Indépendance Belge* article made no mention of pigeons as carriers of news for Reuter. He began to employ them just a month later. He must have been well aware of their use in journalism—by Havas and the *Kölnische Zeitung* among others. Certainly, Reuter never claimed to have been an innovator in the use of pigeons, except that he had identified a role for them in bridging the gaps within the spreading but still patchy telegraph network.[8]

The French Government did not open its telegraph line to Brussels for public use until a year later, on 15 April 1851. Until then, Paris–Brussels news had to go by train or pigeon. From Brussels, there was at first a telegraph gap of 76 miles to Aachen. Reuter decided to bridge this gap by using pigeons, which could deliver French news to Aachen in only two hours, about a quarter of the time taken by train. On 24 April 1850 he made an agreement with Heinrich Geller, an Aachen brewer, baker, and pigeon-breeder, to provide a total of 45 trained birds for a service between Brussels and Aachen. Twelve birds were to be always available at Brussels; all birds were to be returned by train each day to Brussels, ready to fly back the next day. This pigeon news service was started on 28 April. It obviously worked well, for under a new contract on 26 July Geller agreed to assign all his pigeons (over 200) to Reuter's use.

His care for confidentiality was revealed in this second contract. Geller agreed that the messages, tied in bags under the birds' wings, were to be opened only by himself in his pigeon loft. He was to place the messages in sealed boxes, to be carried by boy runners to Reuter's office. There, the messages were reshaped as necessary into telegram-ese by two clerks, or by Reuter or his wife, and then hurried by runner to the telegraph office for transmission to Berlin. The surviving evidence documents only a pigeon service from Brussels to Aachen (Plate 4); but flights in the opposite direction, bringing news from Germany and beyond, may well have been arranged by Reuter with a pigeon-handler in Brussels.

That Reuter was running some sort of service in the opposite direction (with or without pigeons) was confirmed by a letter in German which he wrote to Rothschilds in London on 27 April 1850, the day before the Brussels–Aachen pigeon service began. He made large claims for what he would be able to deliver to London:

> We can in fact deliver to London *today's* market prices from the Berlin Stock Exchange and *yesterday's* from the Vienna Stock Exchange between 10 and 11 a.m. . . . . At the moment we are only in contact with a few companies, but they are important companies, and convinced of the reliability of our telegrams, as well as the speed of their transmission. Up to now we have made no links with London, and are turning to you first of all—and *exclusively*—because we presume that our proposal will not be unwelcome to you. Should you be inclined to receive the Berlin and Vienna market prices from us, then we would bind ourselves not to make any further involvement in London. Furthermore, we would undertake to compensate you for those telegrams which did not reach you at the stated time. However, in order to give you complete security, we will only require the reimbursement of our outlay and costs to be paid once you have been convinced of the reliability and rapid transmission of our telegrams.[9]

Reuter was offering both news and prices. He was also promising accuracy plus speed, which he was always to promise; and at this date he was prepared to bind himself to exclusivity, whereas in his later career he insisted upon equal distribution to all clients. A same-day service of Berlin prices to London would have been remarkable at this date, bearing in mind the Aachen–Brussels telegraph gap and the lack of an English Channel cable. Perhaps Reuter was contemplating using a second pigeon service across the Channel. There is no evidence that Rothschilds accepted this offer.

The Frankfurt Postal Museum preserves fragments of 10 Reuter pigeon messages, written in German and sent from Paris between 19 August and 5 October 1850. Some gave political and other news, some gave prices. All were published in the *Kölnische Zeitung* within a few days. France was in political turmoil, and the reports quoted newspaper articles and rumours about a further revolution. 'We have just this moment been given the following semi-official manifesto, entitled *What does the President want?*' The manifesto was then quoted at length: 'Public opinion . . . has the right to know what plans Louis Napoleon has . . . He wants no other prerogatives than those which he already has. His only justification is the restoration of order.' Not quite everything in the pigeon messages was politics or prices. Indeed, one item was far-seeing: 'A M. Benoit claims to have invented a portable machine which two people at opposite ends of the globe can use to communicate instantly with each other' (Plate 4).

On 2 October 1850 the telegraph line between Aachen and Verviers was completed. Reuter opened offices as the telegraph advanced, ending up near Qievrain on the French border. Looking for fresh work, he offered the manager of *The Times*, Mowbray Morris, 'to receive and forward to England all despatches which may be telegraphed to Verviers for *The Times*'. Morris promised on 5 December to consider this proposal, but nothing came of it.[10] By 15 March 1851 the Belgian telegraph network reached from Ostend to Verviers, and was connecting with the Prussian network. A month later the final link with the French system was made at Valenciennes.

4

What would Reuter do now? He may have transferred briefly to Brussels. But he knew that, after failures in 1847 and 1850, renewed efforts were under way to lay the world's first undersea cable between Dover and Calais. London would then become linked with the Continental telegraph network. No especial foresight was needed to realize that this would provide an opportunity for a much quicker exchange of both news and prices between London and the political and business centres of Europe.

Yet no British entrepreneur seems to have thought that this was the moment to follow the example of Havas in Paris or Wolff in Berlin. Years later, Werner Siemens, the telegraph pioneer who supervised the construction of many German telegraph lines, claimed that it was he who had advised Reuter to set up in London.[11] An opportunity undoubtedly existed there, but capital would be needed. Reuter seems to have secured backing from the Erlangers, a Frankfurt banking family, Jewish by race but Lutheran by religion, whose activities were extending beyond Germany. In the 1860s, as will be seen, he was to collaborate with Baron Emile d'Erlanger, a son of the family who had set up in Paris. Reuter and his wife landed in London from Ostend on 14 June 1851. His profession was given as 'Director of Electric Telegraph'.[12]

On 10 October he opened an office consisting of two small dark rooms at 1 Royal Exchange Buildings. This was within the heart of the City of London, and near to the main telegraph offices. Cross-Channel telegraph transmissions began a month later, on 13 November 1851 (Fig. 1). Reuter's only assistant was 'Fred', an 11-year-old office boy. This was F. J. Griffiths (1840–1915), who was destined to spend a lifetime with the company.

THE NEW SIAMESE TWINS.

FIG. 1. *Punch*, November 1851: The laying of the Dover–Calais cable

Julius Reuter later liked to tell how on one occasion he had gone to a chop-house nearby, when his young assistant rushed in to say that 'a foreign-looking sort of gentleman' had called to see him. Reuter asked the boy why he had let the man go. 'Please, sir, I didn't,' was the answer. 'He is still at the office. I've locked him in.' Thus was one of Reuter's first subscribers secured. In his later years such enterprise was not repeated by Griffiths. He settled for thoroughness and dedication as company secretary from 1865 to 1890, and as a director thereafter until 1912.

When the Reuter couple arrived in London in 1851 the Great Exhibition was in full swing in Hyde Park. It was a celebration of man's material achievement, with contributions from all parts of the world; but Britain's industrial and commercial supremacy was apparent. This can only have confirmed Reuter in the belief that London was the right place to be. For some time, his main service was to be a twice-daily relay in each direction of prices on the London stock exchange and the Paris bourse. He also received stock market prices from Brussels, Amsterdam, and Vienna, as he had done at Aachen. None of this commercial information was exclusive to Reuter; several established London firms were already offering stock and commodity information from Europe and beyond. But Reuter soon began to claim that, through his expert use of the telegraph network, he was the quickest deliverer of stock market prices, and also that he was collecting the widest range of world commodity prices.

Competition none the less persisted from specialist providers of information about particular commodities, such as grain. And *The Times* remained unimpressed by Reuter's tiny agency. An offer to Mowbray Morris of a service which may have included general news was rejected on 29 December. And on 8 March 1852 Morris declined an offer of European stock market prices.[13]

Yet, by the summer of 1852 Reuter had secured from the Austrian Lloyd's the right to circulate that company's news and market information as received at Trieste by ship from the East. Here was a very important advance for Reuter. It probably required him to visit the port at intervals, and may explain why Karl Marx later described him as 'the Jew from Trieste of telegraphic fame'. The importance of Reuter's coup was shown when on 17 August 1852 Morris reluctantly accepted that *The Times* would in future have to take 'telegraphic news from Trieste' through Reuter's office. But Morris still did not want any other news. On 5 May 1853 he tersely rejected an offer of Reuter's 'telegraphic summaries of foreign intelligence'.[14]

Although the Rothschilds and others employed their own agents to collect stock market and commodity prices, Reuter was confident that he could do

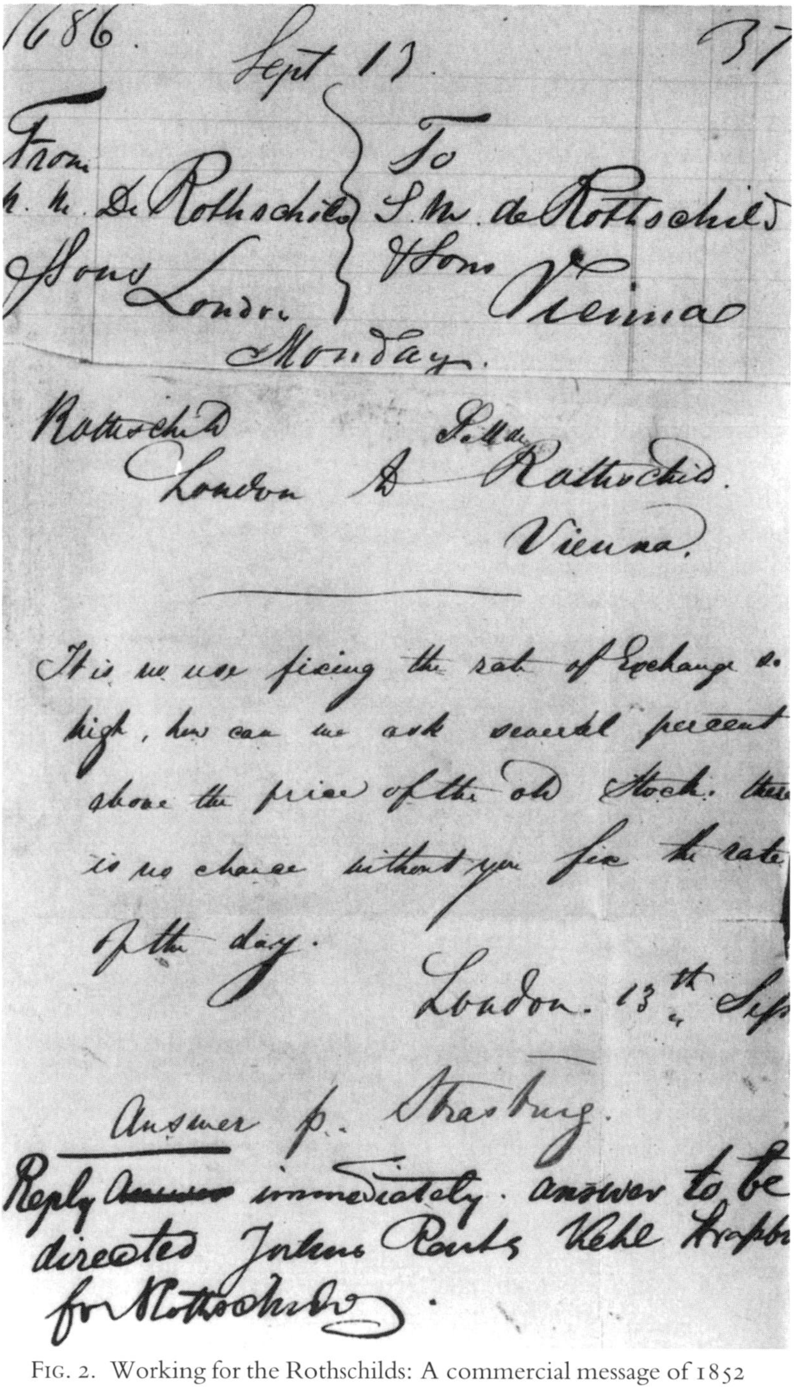
1686. Sept 13. 37

From N. M. De Rothschild & Sons London } To S. M. de Rothschild & Sons Vienna

Monday.

Rothschild London to S. M. de Rothschild. Vienna.

It is no use fixing the rate of Exchange so high, how can we ask several percent above the price of the old Stock. there is no chance without you fix the rate of the day.

London. 13th Sep

Answer p. Strasburg.

Reply ~~Answer~~ immediately. answer to be directed Julius Reuter Kehl Strasbourg for Rothschild.

FIG. 2. Working for the Rothschilds: A commercial message of 1852 better than any business firm. On 19 June 1854 he wrote (in German) to Rothschilds in Paris offering his stock exchange prices. He had enclosed three telegrams by way of free trial: 'nobody in Paris has had these stock-exchange prices so fast or could have had them other than by the measures I have taken through my direct connection with the telegraph and also with the stock exchange so that not a minute is lost.'[15]

Reuter was ready to supply not only market information and general news, but also expertise in working the telegraph network; and this service seems to have been in steady demand during his early years in England. Reuter took commissions to send messages for London firms (including the Rothschilds) via the various Continental telegraphs (Fig. 2). There were not yet any agreed procedures for international telegraphy. The handover of messages between different companies and countries, the correction of errors in transmission, the overcoming of line breakdowns, and the need to bridge gaps in the telegraph network by other means of communication, all required special knowledge and agents at central points.

Surviving telegram books for August to October 1852 show Reuter sending short messages for London firms to Antwerp, Hamburg, Trieste, Stettin, Odessa, Danzig, and elsewhere in Europe. Telegraph charges were high—60 words to Trieste cost £4. 17s. 6d. East European grain prices and prospects were of particular interest to Greek and other merchants in London, at a period when most of Britain's grain imports came from the Black Sea area, with Odessa a key outlet.

Why did Reuter, with so much to offer, make only limited progress in England during these first years? There may have been some prejudice against him as a foreigner or as a Jew by birth. But the City of London accepted Jews readily enough, electing its first Jewish Lord Mayor in 1855. Reuter himself tried to be detached. Although he did business with various Jewish firms, he did not do so on account of their Jewishness. He was himself now a Christian, and the *Standard Jewish Encyclopaedia* (1959) says conclusively that he 'had no connection with the Jewish community'. His difficulty in gaining early acceptance may have been rather more a matter of occupation than of race. He had become a journalist, albeit of a new sort; and journalists (the editor of *The Times* excepted) were still not readily treated as 'gentlemen', entitled to trust. Journalism was only reluctantly acknowledged to be a profession, and, significantly, the very word, taken from the French, was still quite new. *The Newspaper Press Directory* for 1851 was explicit and regretful about this lack of recognition:

> It is a complaint that in England the conductors and members of the press have no recognised standing—no acknowledged place in society; that in fashionable

life they are rather tolerated than admitted on the footing of a recognised social equality; and that they are not distinguished by the government as they are on the Continent and particularly in France, where we find 'journalism', as it is termed, the passport to distinction in society, and to official rank.

If even journalists on well-known newspapers suffered from a lack of trust, it is not surprising that Julius Reuter, the unknown conductor of a small and novel business, found himself granted only reluctant recognition. In personal contact, however, he seems to have usually made a pleasant impression, even if he was obviously not English either in appearance or accent. He spoke English well enough socially; but he preferred to negotiate on the Continent in German, and to address his senior English editorial staff in French. Small of stature, always neatly dressed, with fashionable side-whiskers and wire-framed glasses, he took care to look dependable even if he remained inescapably 'foreign'. In the 1870s, T. P. O'Connor, who was himself destined to become a leading journalist, unavailingly asked Reuter for a job: 'a little, somewhat insignificant man, with a small, deeply-lined and rather shrivelled face, and of a distinctly Jewish type. He was very simple, very pleasant; he was the more impressive from his very tininess.'[16]

What marked out Julius Reuter as truly exceptional was not his slightly exceptional appearance, but his purposeful enthusiasm for the circulation of news by modern methods. He knew that, for his news to be trusted, he himself would have to be trusted. And gradually, undeterred by setbacks, he won such trust, first on the Continent and then in England.

5

The build-up to the Crimean War, and the arduous course of the subsequent fighting (1854–6), was the first big international news story to develop after Julius Reuter's move to London. *The Times* kept a correspondent at the front, the famous W. H. Russell, who wrote long mailed dispatches. These made a great impression by revealing military shortcomings, but they were not intended to give the latest news. Russell sent back only one telegram during the whole course of the war—a description of the defences of Sebastapol after its capture.[17] Only official accounts were transmitted by the military telegraph across the Black Sea to Varna from the Anglo-French lines in the Crimea. But news and rumour from the Russian side, and reports of diplomatic manœuvrings, could be collected in St Petersburg, Vienna, Constantinople, and elsewhere. Havas had agents in these places, and so did Reuter. Many years later, George Griffiths, a Reuter boy messenger at the time, told how he had taken news of an allied victory to the London stock exchange, where the good tidings were received with enthusiasm: 'they took me and placed me on a stool, and I was much satisfied when I was released with about fifteen shillings.'[18]

A biographical article about Julius Reuter in *Vanity Fair* for 14 December 1872 recollected that during the Crimean War 'his news obtained some attention'. How much attention is uncertain. The same article said that in the 1850s Reuter had made three separate attempts to get his news taken by the London press. The first was presumably made when he started in 1851, and was rebuffed by *The Times*, and probably by other papers. Reuter's third attempt occurred in 1858, and was successful. The second attempt seems to have been made in 1853, when he unavailingly offered *The Times* his 'telegraphic summaries of foreign intelligence'. Did any other London newspapers take these summaries? Seemingly not. But for a period from May 1853 telegrams from Reuter started to appear as 'latest intelligence' in the *Manchester Guardian*, *Manchester Courier*, and *Liverpool Mercury*, all of them leading provincial titles.

Here was visible progress. And Reuter no doubt began to hope that the high quality of his news service as displayed in the pages of these Lancashire newspapers would soon attract subscriptions from provincial papers elsewhere, and eventually from the London dailies. Manchester and Liverpool were important places whose lead was often followed, for Manchester had become the world's centre for cotton manufacture and Liverpool was its cotton port. In the event, Julius Reuter's breakthrough into the provincial press was to be disappointingly short-lived. Nevertheless, these were the first credited Reuter telegrams known to have been published in the British press.

From the start, they included Paris bourse closing prices, which reached Manchester by 7 p.m. Other European prices were soon added, along with commodity prices from as far away as Shanghai, Calcutta, and Alexandria. The telegrams also included increasingly full news from Europe and from the East. Reuter was obviously making the most of his exclusive Austrian Lloyd connection. For example, a telegram datelined 'Trieste, May 23'—'the steamer has just arrived'—was published in the *Manchester Guardian* four days later. It gave both general news and commodity prices from Shanghai (30 March) and Hong Kong (12 April), and included the exciting report: 'Japan is to be opened in one year's time. Free ports are being selected.'

Before the start of the Crimean War, accounts of the prolonged diplomatic manœuvring featured regularly. After the landing of Anglo-French forces, Reuter did not claim to have his own reporters at the front. He had to depend upon his agents at Berlin, Vienna, Constantinople, and in the Balkans, and also on the Russian side at St Petersburg and Odessa. These agents provided background news about military and diplomatic developments, not battle-field reports. But with correspondents placed in the Russian capital, and in the Black Sea port of Odessa, he was able to report from both sides, offering for the first time an all-round coverage which he was to repeat more fully in later wars. His Odessa agent was commendably ready to send either good or bad news from the Russian point of view (18 October 1854):

> Our port is not blockaded yet. Neutral vessels are continually arriving and leav-ing. Advices from Sebastapol speak of the despondency in the Russian camp, in consequence of the short supply of water and provisions.

Only occasionally were these telegrams credited in the *Manchester Guardian* to 'Mr Julius Reuter of London'. Mostly, they were ascribed to 'S. Josaphat and Co.'s Continental Telegraph'. The firm was listed in the Manchester directory as possessing an office in the Royal Exchange Arcade, Manchester. This probably amounted to no more than a desk for a Reuter agent within the local office of the Magnetic Telegraph Company. This agent was probably not 'S. Josaphat'. Susskind Josaphat was Julius Reuter's second brother, a schoolteacher in Germany. Why did Julius choose to use his brother's name? Perhaps because he had provided the necessary capital to open the office, while remaining a sleeping partner. In later years, after Julius had made his fortune, he financed his brother's life as a gentleman in retirement in Germany.

Their joint venture in Manchester and Liverpool lasted for less than two years. It collapsed quite suddenly early in 1855, when telegrams credited to either Josaphat or Reuter ceased to appear in the three Lancashire papers. The telegraph companies, whose lines carried all news, seem to have set out to force the provincial papers to take news bulletins compiled by themselves. They may have introduced prohibitive charges for Reuter's telegrams. The *Manchester Guardian*, for example, began from March 1855 to credit its latest intelligence to 'the British Telegraph Company'. Some of that company's telegrams published by the *Guardian* read very like Reuter telegrams. He had probably been left with the choice of either selling his telegrams to the tele-graph companies or not selling them at all. His promising early connection with the provincial press had broken down, and the episode was soon com-pletely forgotten.

6

Fortunately for the survival of his business, Julius Reuter was conducting a successful daily service for newspapers and firms on the Continent. Some subscribers (such as the *Kölnische Zeitung* and *L'Indépendance Belge*) may even have continued through with him from his Aachen period.

Reuter kept up and extended his contacts by frequent travel on the Continent. One visit in August 1857 to St Petersburg was recalled in the memoirs of Paul Usoff, who was starting the first telegraphic news co-operative in Russia. Reuter contracted with Usoff to deliver each weekday to St Petersburg telegrams of commercial information collected from London and the main Continental centres. Reuter's charge was 3,000 roubles (about £375) per month. Usoff noted that on this visit Reuter 'counted every rouble', whereas on a later visit in 1862 he was visibly more affluent.[19]

Although Reuter's main business was with the Continent, he was based in London, and he had become comfortable there, with a growing family. On 17 March 1857 he became a naturalized British subject. His application was supported by four medical friends, who lived near him in Finsbury Square.[20]

By becoming naturalized Reuter was demonstrating confidence in his future in England. Possession of a British passport was also helpful during his travels on the Continent, although it could not conceal his origins. Two years later, the Austrian police files recorded that on 22 May 1859 he used his British passport to cross into Austria. The Austrians were well aware of Reuter's background, and that he was not English-born: 'deserves to be kept under close scrutiny due to his being a naturalised Englishman and due to his provenance.' Reuter was watched throughout his visit, but he was able to show that he had come (as he claimed) to see the Foreign, Interior, Trade, and Finance Ministers. Far from plotting revolution, he was building up his contacts for the collection of official news.[21]

The big news story of 1857–8 for the British press was the bloody outbreak and equally bloody suppression of the Indian Mutiny. The *Annual Register* for 1859 remarked that the 'fearfully-interesting' telegrams from India, 'and the effect they produced on the public feeling and on the money markets made their arrival events of the year'. The Foreign Office received telegrams giving the latest news from India, and it passed these on to the London newspapers and the telegraph companies for publication. On 30 December 1857 Reuter wrote to the Foreign Secretary, Lord Clarendon, requesting to be similarly provided with Indian telegrams. After enquiring about Reuter's business ('He himself is the Continental Telegraph'), the Foreign Office agreed to supply the telegrams for inclusion in Reuter's service to the Continental press. 'I am the Telegraphic Correspondent for almost all the leading papers on the Continent and have to forward to them the London news and Official despatches as soon as possible.' Significantly, Reuter did not claim to be yet serving the British press. At this very period, the manager of *The Times* had again said firmly on 29 December 1857: 'the proprietors of *The Times* are not prepared to enter into arrangements with you'.[22]

A year later, on 15 December 1858—by which time Reuter had at last begun to serve the London dailies, including *The Times*—Reuter wrote to the Foreign Secretary, now Lord Malmesbury, complaining that he had not been sent recent Indian telegrams. Reuter was told that this was because he had published a telegram from Naples which purported to give the gist of a dispatch from Malmesbury to the King of Naples. Malmesbury had found it necessary to issue a denial that he had ever written such a dispatch; and Reuter was refused future telegrams on the ground that the publication of falsehoods confused the public, and 'depreciates the value of the authentic statements with which he is furnished'. The Foreign Office continued hostile to Reuter for some time, probably until Malmesbury left office upon the fall of the Conservative Government in June 1859. On 29 April John Bidwell, a Foreign Office official, asked the editor of *The Times*, J. T. Delane: 'Why do you still give credence to Mr. Reuter's Tels? He is an impostor.'[23]

7

Despite such continuing suspicion in some quarters, the years 1858–9 were to be the period of decisive breakthrough for Julius Reuter. The British press was undergoing a transformation, to which 'Reuters' (as the agency began to be known from the early 1860s) was to make a major contribution.[24]

The repeal of the newspaper stamp duty in 1855 had ended the sales predominance of *The Times*. Penny daily papers now appeared, led by the new (and significantly titled) *Daily Telegraph*. It was selling over 140,000 copies daily by 1861, over twice that of *The Times*. The penny price of the *Telegraph* and other London papers after the repeal of the stamp duty brought about a major redistribution of readers. Many more Victorians now bought their own copies of newspapers for reading on the day of publication. Previously, copies of *The Times* and other papers costing up to fivepence had remained in circulation for several days, being variously resold, hired out, read in newsrooms or coffee houses, or sent through the post, so that each copy might finish with as many as twenty readers. After the introduction of the penny dailies, readers who had formerly secured their first sight of a fivepenny newspaper only on the second or third day after publication, obtaining a handed-on copy for which they might have paid a penny, could now spend that same penny on buying the *Telegraph* on the morning of publication. This change greatly benefited Reuters. Whereas previously hundreds of thousands of newspaper readers had perforce been reading old news, now for the first time they were reading the latest news, which whetted their appetites for more. This novel involvement soon extended to the provinces, where old titles such as the *Manchester Guardian* and new titles such as the *Birmingham Post* began to appear as penny dailies.

In August 1858 the first Transatlantic cable became briefly operational. Reuter had made careful arrangements to exploit the new link. He prepared to receive American news in hours by cable instead of in days by steamer. Writing to Mowbray Morris of *The Times*, he offered to supply a daily American money markets service via the new cable. This time, Morris did not refuse. The saving of money seemed to Morris worthwhile for such routine information, even though it was to be shared with other papers, especially as the accuracy of Reuter's service could be checked in retrospect.[25]

Writing to Usoff in St Petersburg on 4 September, Reuter explained that he had concluded a contract with the Atlantic Telegraph Company: 'on the basis of this I can send you American news for half the cable-rate'. The rate was not yet fixed, said Reuter, but was rumoured to be £2. 10s for a 20-word telegram. Five days later, Reuter wrote to Usoff again:

> the large number of orders I have received from all sides for American despatches has prompted me to set up a central bureau in New York with subsidiaries in all the main cities of the United States, Central and South America. On top of the £5,000 sterling which I am contracted to pay annually to the Atlantic Telegraph Company, this enterprise of mine will require significant capital, not less than £15,000 or £20,000 sterling . . . a large part of which I already have at my disposal.[26]

Reuter invited Usoff to invest £3,000, in return for free delivery of one American news telegram per day. Since one telegram would cost £2. 10s., this offer (Reuter pointed out temptingly) would be worth £900 per annum, amounting to 30 per cent on Usoff's capital.

Reuter's enthusiasm was thus underpinned by financial and organizational awareness. He was a practical visionary. Unfortunately, his Transatlantic initiative came to nothing. The Atlantic cable soon began to fail because of inad-

equate insulation, and it never came into regular use for the transmission of
news. The first successful cable to America was not to be laid until 1866, after
the American Civil War. But Reuter had demonstrated his readiness to 'follow the cable', as he had done in 1851 and was to do again. However, in 1859
his global news transmission plans suffered a further setback, when the
Karachi–Suez cable failed after only a brief life.

Disappointed in America, Reuter continued with his service to the
Continent. He believed that the news he was receiving could be edited to
serve the London press as readily as the Continental papers. In October 1858
he made a fresh effort. He first approached *The Times*, but was rebuffed by
Mowbray Morris in letters of 5 and 6 October. As an inducement, Reuter
seems to have offered the telegraphing of his telegrams by his overseas agents
direct to *The Times* office in Printing House Square. Although this was not a
promise of exclusivity, it would have given *The Times* a start over its rivals,
because they would not have had to wait to receive the same telegrams via
Reuter's office. Henceforward, Reuter was to follow a rule of always distributing his telegrams to newspapers impartially, never allowing priority to any
one subscriber to a particular service.[27]

Reuter next tried the other London daily papers. He first approached James
Grant, the editor of the *Morning Advertiser*. Grant's recollections of their meeting were given in his *History of the Newspaper Press*, published in 1871. Reuter
seems to have particularly emphasized how he was able to gather official news
from Europe. He had, he said, 'formed personal intimacies with gentlemen
connected with most of the European Governments':

> It has occurred to me that I might, therefore, be able to supply, by telegraph,
> the daily press of London with earlier and more accurate intelligence of impor-
> tance, and, at the same time, at a cheaper rate, than the morning journals are
> now paying for their telegraphic communications from the Continent.

Reuter admitted that he had first approached *The Times*, but had been told
'that they could do their own business better than anyone else'. He offered
Grant 'earlier, more ample, more accurate, and more important information
from the Continent' for £30 per month. This was £10 less than the
Advertiser was paying for its own telegrams. Reuter temptingly proposed a
fortnight's free trial. Grant accepted. Reuter revealed that he would not have
persisted if the *Advertiser* had rejected him. In the absence of *The Times*, the
support of all the other leading dailies was necessary to make the service
profitable. Fortunately, the other editors also agreed to trials. They were
immediately impressed by what they received, and soon all had taken out
subscriptions.

The Times was forced to think again. Good though its own news network was, it needed to know each evening what telegrams from Reuter were likely to appear in the columns of its competitors next morning, even though it did not necessarily want to print the telegrams itself. Only a week after his last rebuff to Reuter, Morris noted in his diary for 13 October: 'Saw Reuter about telegrams of foreign news. He agreed to send all to us, and to charge us only for what we publish, for 2/6 for 20 words if his name is quoted, and 5/- if not quoted.'

Thus Reuter was still allowing Morris special treatment, doubly so, in that *The Times* was not required to take out a subscription and yet was allowed to see all the Reuter telegrams. Between October and the end of the year Reuter sent at least 140 telegrams to *The Times*. His first published telegram appeared on 20 October, without a Reuter credit; the first with a credit appeared on 8 December. At the end of January 1859, Morris finally agreed to take out a monthly subscription of £20 per month, therefore paying less than the *Advertiser*. By 1861, after the Reuter service had further expanded and had become clearly indispensable, Reuter was asking £100 a month. Although making his news available to all comers, he had no intention of selling it cheaply. *The Times* always resented the cost and the dependence; and Morris complained at intervals about charges, delays, or what he claimed to be inadequate coverage.[28]

Interestingly, however, at this very period *The Times* of 6 December 1858 had itself explained how important it was for British newspaper readers to be given access to full news from overseas. Britain was the only world power; and how the British public, guided by its free press, reacted to events anywhere in the world could produce significant effects. 'It would be fatal to say', wrote *The Times*, ' "Discuss home matters, but not foreign ones" . . . Every issue of an English journal speaks to the whole world; that is its strength; it lives by its universality; that idea imparts conscious power.'

By accepting the collection of news through Reuters, the rival London newspapers had finally realized that they would be able to receive a much fuller supply of general news and commercial information than they could each collect separately. Yet they remained at liberty to appoint their own representatives in the major news capitals, and they could still send special correspondents to report wars or particular events. Crucially, they soon found that readers did not complain because identical Reuter telegrams were appearing in other newspapers.

What mattered to readers was the interest and trustworthiness of what the unknown 'Mr. Reuter' was reporting. In this regard, Reuter had worked steadily since his time at Aachen to earn a reputation, first, for accuracy and second, for speed. He tried to be ahead with the news; but he made it known that accuracy was even more important to him than speed. The telegraph companies had brought criticism upon the news telegram business by carelessly retailing errors and falsehoods. When Reuter's agents or sub-editors made occasional mistakes, these were admitted and corrections issued without delay.

Accuracy, speed, and impartial distribution to all equivalent subscribers—these became the hallmarks of the Reuter news service in the middle of the nineteenth century; and they have remained so ever since.

8

For important news stories, *The Times* continued to prefer its own correspondents. For example, when its Paris correspondent telegraphed an account of threatening diplomatic language towards Austria used by Napoleon III at a reception on New Year's Day 1859, the Emperor's words were published in reported speech in *The Times* of 3 January. Yet not until next day did Reuters carry the story, and then simply as copied from that morning's *Constitutionnel* newspaper in Paris. This belated Reuter report at least possessed the merit of publishing Napoleon's words to the Austrian Ambassador verbatim, both in the original French and in English translation: 'I regret that our relations with your Government are not so good as they were.' But such a delayed and second-hand report was not, as was often later claimed, the first big beat for Reuters.

What really was the first great beat for the agency came, however, only a few days later. A telegram from Turin, credited to Reuter, appeared in *The Times* on 10 January 1859. It summarized in 146 words the speech of the King of Sardinia at the opening of his parliament. Like Napoleon III's remarks ten days earlier, this speech formed part of the build-up to war in the cause of Italian unification between France and Sardinia, on the one hand, and Austria, on the other. The King's words about what he called Italy's 'cry of anguish' were spoken on the morning of 10 January; and Reuter in London had contrived to receive a telegraphed summary from Turin by 1.30. This was immediately published by *The Times* in an afternoon edition (Fig. 3). The telegram was also republished in the next morning's issue, accompanied by an editorial which did not question the accuracy of the Reuter version. The full text of the speech, 'from our own correspondent', did not appear in *The Times* until 14 January.[29]

The *Manchester Guardian*, now a daily paper, published this same Reuter beat on 12 January, with an accompanying editorial. After printing Reuter

REUTER'S TELEGRAMS.

The following Telegram was received at Mr. REUTER's Office, January 10th, 1859, 1.30 PM.

TURIN, Monday, January 10th.

OPENING OF THE SARDINIAN CHAMBERS.

The following is a summary of the Royal speech.

The King thanks the Chambers for the assistance afforded him during the last session, which consolidated the national policy and the progress of Piedmont. He announces that Government will bring in Bills for judicial administrative and municipal reform. He regrets that the financial crisis and the scarcety of Silk crops prevented a balance in the national Exchequer.

His Majesty says, that the political horizon is not clear, but that the future must be awaited with firmness. The future cannot fail to be fortunate, because the policy of Piedmont is based on justice and love of its country's liberty. Piedmont is small, but great in the councils of Europe, on account of the principles it represents, and the sympathies it inspires. It respects treaties, but is not insensible to Italy's cry of anguish.

The King concludes with the words: "Let us reso-"lutely await the decrees of Providence."

Prolonged acclamations of *Vive le Roi!* followed the conclusion of the speech.

Printed at Mr. REUTER's Office, 1, Royal Exchange Buildings, City

FIG. 3. The first great beat, 10 January 1859

telegrams during 1853–4, the *Guardian* had switched to news supplied by the telegraph companies and by its own correspondents in Paris, Brussels, and elsewhere. But when in October 1858 Reuter telegrams began to appear in the London dailies, the *Guardian* felt free to copy them. This meant, of course, that it was a day behind with Reuter news. Then in January 1859 the 'Magnetic' and 'Electric' telegraph companies jointly contracted to deliver Reuter's telegrams to all towns in the United Kingdom (Plate 6). The companies paid £800 per annum for this arrangement. It involved transmitting Reuter telegrams to provincial newspapers, such as the *Manchester Guardian*. For a few days in January 1859 the *Guardian* gave a revealing double credit: 'The following telegram, received by Mr. Reuter, is communicated by the Electric Telegraph Company.' Finally, from 11 January Reuter was allowed sole credit for his news.

The 'War of Italian Liberation' followed in the summer of 1859, with British public opinion very sympathetic towards the Italians. Telegrams about the war were eagerly read, and Julius Reuter's extensive coverage confirmed him as a major new force in journalism. From the warring capitals (Paris, Turin, and Vienna), and from neutral Berne, his agents transmitted communiqués, gave news of diplomatic manœuvring, and reported rumours. Reuter was allowed to maintain correspondents at army headquarters on both sides. These men were probably nationals of the three countries at war, perhaps serving army officers. They sent early telegrams about the fighting, leaving later and fuller accounts to the newspaper correspondents. This tacit division of labour was to be repeated in the reporting of many subsequent nineteenth-century wars.

News of the decisive Franco-Italian victory at Solferino was reported by Reuter from both sides, first in the form of an official announcement from Paris:

> The following most important telegram was received
> at Mr. REUTER's Office, Saturday, June 25th, 8.30 a.m.
> PARIS, Saturday, June 25th, 7.45 a,m.
> The Emperor to the Empress
> CAVRIANA, Friday evening. Great Battle. Great Victory. The whole Austrian army formed the line of battle, which extended five leagues in length. We have taken all their positions, and captured many cannon, flags and prisoners.
> The Battle lasted from four o'clock in the morning till eight o'clock in the evening.

The next day, Reuter's correspondent at Austrian headquarters in Verona, who wrote without care for objectivity of 'our' troops and 'the enemy', sent an account from the defeated side:

VERONA, June 25th (via Vienna)

The day before yesterday our right wing occupied Pozzolengo, Solferino and Cavriano, and the left wing pressed forward yesterday as far as Guidizoffo and Castellgoffredo, driving back the enemy. The collision of the two entire armies took place yesterday at 10 a.m. Our left wing under General Wimpfen advanced as far as the Chiese. In the afternoon, a concentrated assault of the enemy was made upon the heroically defended town of Solferino. Our right wing repulsed the Piedmontese, but on the other hand the order of our centre could not be restored. Losses extraordinarily heavy, a violent thunderstorm, the development of powerful masses of the enemy against our left wing, and the advance of his main body against Volta, caused our retreat, which began late in the evening.

(The above is official)

Reuter rightly regarded his general news services as running in tandem with his commercial services. He was well aware that reports of battles lost and won, of political crises, or even of bad weather could affect markets; and that, conversely, news of market crises often had political effects. He implied all this in a letter of July 1859 to the Baltic Exchange, in which he described his channels of news collection and mentioned his London breakthrough of the previous October:

> Since the 1st of October I have established a telegraph service for receiving news from all parts of the Continent which I send to all the London papers. I also receive from Liverpool and Southampton by telegraph the arrivals of the American, Brazil and West Indian steamers, the amount of specie brought and all interesting political and commercial news. These messages (which would be of great interest to your members) I am able to give you several hours before they are published in the papers.[30]

Obviously, Reuter did not regard this offer as unfair to his newspaper subscribers. Any news supplied concurrently to newspaper offices and business firms must necessarily have given the latter a start over those who had to wait while the papers printed and distributed the news. As such a difference was unavoidable, Reuter was apparently seeking to use it as a selling point. But seven years later Mowbray Morris of *The Times* repeated (3 December 1866) what he claimed to be a general belief in commercial circles that Reuter deliberately delayed news for the newspapers in order to give his commercial subscribers an advantage: 'such statements are made and generally believed. Their currency is a discredit to your company and an injury to the press.'[31]

These harsh words were a measure of Morris's resentment at the authority given to Julius Reuter by his central position. The speed and accuracy of news from Reuters was being increasingly taken for granted; the more so because when checked from other sources, Reuter reports were usually confirmed. Charges of favouritism in distribution were easy to make and difficult to answer. But no evidence has been found to support Morris's charge. On the contrary, Julius Reuter's contract as managing director of the new Reuter's Telegram Company in 1865 required him 'to communicate the telegraphic intelligence equally and impartially to all the Subscribers . . . without giving priority to any one over any other'.

When at the turn of the century Reuters was selling to commercial firms 'telegraphic bulletins' which provided (in the words of the subscription form) 'a brief summary of news received by the Company calculated to influence the Stock Markets', subscribers were required to engage themselves 'not to publish the same, nor to communicate the intelligence contained therein to any person or persons whomsoever'. The question whether Reuter personally ever made money out of his advance knowledge of foreign stock-market movements or of market-moving news must be left open. He was certainly accused of profiting from his early knowledge of the assassination of President Lincoln in 1865.

9

Karl Marx was living in exile within the London German Jewish community throughout the years of Reuter's rise. The two men may never have met; but Marx had taken notice of Reuter, and disapproved of both him and his right-hand man, Sigmund Engländer. In a letter to Engels on 12 April 1860 Marx gave a garbled account of Reuter's career:

> who do you think is factotum to this grammatically illiterate Jew Reuter?— *Sigmund Engländer*, who was expelled from Paris because, although a spy in the pay of France (600 frs. per month), he was discovered to be a 'secret' RUSSIAN spy. This same Reuter was partner in a Bonapartist lithographic news agency in Paris . . . *Bernhard Wolff*, chief proprietor of the Berlin 'National-Zeitung' and owner of the Berlin telegraphic bureau, is hand-in-purse (partners) with S. *Engländer*, who is at present editing European world history in Reuter's name.[32]

Who then was Engländer? (Plate 5). Sigmund Engländer (1823–1902) had been born into a Jewish family at Trebitsch in Moravia, then part of the Austrian empire. Unlike Reuter, Engländer never gave up his Jewish faith,

although his lifestyle was not characterized by restraint, religious or otherwise. With some justification, he came to regard himself as the co-founder of
Reuters. While Julius Reuter went about purposefully creating a worldwide
news organization, and showing a business judgement which Engländer
lacked, the latter was closer to the news day by day. He served variously as the
first editor of Reuters and as a correspondent and negotiator in Europe. Much
more than Julius Reuter, he was the complete journalist, and he later claimed
to have devised the original format for Reuter telegrams, keeping them
factual and brief. Marx told Engels on 1 June 1860 that Engländer was 'the
heart and soul of the Reuter bureau'. While Reuter secured for his correspondents regular open access to governments, Engländer operated more
behind the scenes. He cultivated contacts all over Europe, and picked up
much early news and rumour. In this regard, Engländer was even compared
favourably by one contemporary journalist with the great de Blowitz of *The
Times*.[33]

Engländer had himself been personally involved in politics. He had been
a revolutionary journalist who fled from Vienna in 1848 under threat of
arrest, although not (as was later said) under threat of death. He went to
Paris where he worked for Havas. He was a man of deep culture as well as
of strong politics, a student of literature who himself wrote novels, a
lover of music, and an engaging conversationalist. In Paris he made the
acquaintance of Heinrich Heine, the German poet, who recommended
him (13 February 1852) as 'one of the best and most intelligent correspondents'.[34]

At Havas Engländer met Julius Reuter, and the two men obviously got
on well, for early in 1849 Engländer left to work in Reuter's short-lived
lithographic bureau. When Reuter set up in Aachen, Engländer probably
served as his Paris correspondent. One surviving pigeon message gave
news of Proudhon, the French political philosopher. Engländer was
himself a Proudhonist ('Property is theft'), and he wrote books about politics in both French and English. The last was *The Abolition of the State*
(1873).

In 1851 Engländer was briefly imprisoned in France for plotting against
the authorities, and in 1854 he was expelled upon the recommendation of
the Austrian Government. Despite his imprisonment, other left-wingers,
including Marx, were sure that Engländer was a police informer for the
French and also a spy for the Russians. The memoirs of Alexander Herzen,
the Russian revolutionary, claimed that Engländer once admitted to being
a police informer because he needed money to support his dissipated
lifestyle. This was presumably a reference to Engländer's involvement with

young women, of whom throughout his life he attracted a steady succession.[35]

Expelled from France, Engländer crossed in 1854 to England. He became a correspondent for several Continental newspapers, as well as being editor of the *Londoner Deutsche Zeitung*. In 1857 he was editor of the *Journal de Londres*, but soon afterwards he joined Julius Reuter as chief editor of his news agency. Engländer was closely involved in the development of the news service during 1858–9, when its quality won over the London press.

Despite his brilliance, Engländer came to be disliked by many of his more respectable English colleagues at Reuters. F. W. Dickinson, himself a future chief editor, remembered Engländer as 'a viveur sans peur and with plenty of reproche'. Dickinson claimed that Engländer only took a wife in 1860 (apparently his second) because Mrs Reuter had refused to receive the girl otherwise. The last straw was probably that she was visibly pregnant, for a boy was born to the Engländers only two months after their wedding. The marriage did not last.[36]

The baby was named 'Julius Sigmund', an indication of the close relationship between Engländer and Reuter. Although there were frequent disputes between them, Reuter remained indulgent towards his old friend, and Engländer was to continue with Reuters until his retirement on pension in 1895. He perhaps came closest to dismissal when on 18 October 1871 the Reuter board questioned him about his involvement in a 'new political and social movement'. Engländer denied any such involvement, which was probably at best a half-truth, for in August he had certainly attended a meeting of British working-class leaders. He was forced to accept that Reuter employees must avoid involvement in politics 'inasmuch as our character for impartiality on which we mainly depend for success' would be damaged by any political connection.

Engländer always felt restless in London, probably the more so as the agency which he had helped to create settled down into a routine as a semi-official institution. In 1877 he left London to become resident correspondent at Constantinople, the capital of the crumbling Turkish Empire, where his talent for unearthing diplomatic and military secrets found fruitful occupation, especially during the Russo-Turkish war of 1877–8. Throughout the later 1880s, travelling round Europe and revelling in news agency politics, Engländer played a leading part in re-negotiating key contracts with Havas, Wolff, and other European agencies.

To the end, he remained one of the most colourful and yet cultured characters in the history of Reuters. When in 1887 at the Constantinople office he received news of the death of Jenny Lind, 'the Swedish nightingale', who had been the great international singing star of his youth, Engländer's assistant noticed that the old man, worldly though he usually seemed, was moved by remembrance of past enjoyment to shed a mourning tear.[37]

10

Engländer was one of several German Jews whom Julius Reuter brought into the agency during its early years. James Heckscher (1834–1909) joined the editorial staff in September 1858. In 1864 he was sent to start an office in Brussels, but was soon transferred to New York to improve coverage of the American Civil War. After the war, Heckscher returned to London, and in 1868 he opened a Reuter office in his native Hamburg. In 1871 he became chief Westminster parliamentary correspondent for Reuters. He won a high reputation for the objectivity of his reporting of British political news, in terms intelligible to Continental readers. Although naturalized British, Heckscher was said to be very German, 'the Bismarck of the Press Gallery'; but he was widely liked, being both cultured and sociable. He retired in 1905.[38]

Another German Jewish member of staff was Emil Wolff (1849–1926). Wolff worked first for Heckscher in Hamburg, and then joined the London staff in 1870. He served as chief accountant from 1888 until his retirement in 1916. Wolff was a shrewd observer, whose unpublished reminiscences complained about the growing influence of Griffiths in the 1870s, 'content to drift along in a sea of formalism without much higher aims than to make the Agency pay a sufficient dividend'.

Julius Reuter made all the early appointments personally. And while welcoming these Germans into the business, he took care to avoid giving an impression of exclusivity. On the contrary, quite soon a majority of the senior editorial staff were British-born. George Douglas Williams (1839–1910) joined the editorial staff in 1861. His steady character, fluent command of French, Italian, and Spanish, and his general culture and intelligence recommended him for a major role in Reuter's European plans. In 1868 he was sent to Florence, the capital of newly united Italy and a centre of major news interest. In 1870 he transferred to Paris, just in time for the outbreak of the Franco-Prussian War. He did well, covering the fall of Napoleon III, the Commune, and other dramatic events. He was dissatisfied, however, with his pay (£400 a year) and prospects, and in exasperation he had even written of Julius Reuter to his fiancée (5 October 1870) as 'a shifty one at the best'. She had earlier exclaimed (20 August): 'you are quite a slave to Reuter's nod. I wonder why your pa did not make you do something else.'

Williams's skill and experience as a journalist was recognized by Reuter when in 1875 he was appointed deputy to Engländer 'for the conduct, supervision and control of the outward and homeward political services'. Two years later, Williams succeeded Engländer as chief editor. He was paid £750 a year, the bare minimum appropriate for such a responsible post. The fact that Reuter salaries were usually marginal was remembered in the autobiography of Williams's son, Valentine, who himself later worked as a Reuter correspondent, before moving to better-paid work for the *Daily Mail*. George Williams retired in 1902.[39]

Henry Collins (1844–1928) had taught Reuter's son Herbert at preparatory school. He asked Reuter for a job, and was given one in 1862 after polishing up his French and German. In the event, he was to work chiefly in the English-speaking British Empire, where he became one of the first of a long line of expatriate managers (Plate 8). In 1866, aged only 22, he was posted to Bombay as first general manager for India; from 1878 until his retirement in 1909 he was general manager in Australia. Collins showed enterprise in his early career and dedication throughout, along with tact in handling people. His reminiscences—*From Pigeon Post to Wireless* (1925)—were factually informative, but very discreet about personalities.[40]

Walter F. Bradshaw (1850–1932) joined Reuters in 1874. He had good command of Spanish and Portuguese, and was immediately sent to Chile to help establish a new South American service. He returned five years later, and became in time a portly figure of more dignity than imagination who succeeded Griffiths as company secretary in 1890. At the very end of his career in 1915 he served uncomfortably and briefly as general manager.[41]

Another recruit in 1874 was Frederic W. Dickinson (1856–1922), who succeeded Williams as chief editor in 1902 and who died in post (Plate 30). Multi-lingual, well informed, observant, sensible, yet humorous— Dickinson became a wise mentor to a succession of young Reuter journalists. As a gesture of encouragement, he displayed photographs of many of them on the wall beside his desk.[42]

The commitment of these early members of staff was demonstrated by their long service—even if, like young Williams, they had sometimes grumbled in private. Williams served Reuters for over forty years, as did Heckscher, Wolff, Bradshaw and Dickinson. They also introduced members of their own families into the agency. About the turn of the century, Griffiths, Collins, Williams, Wolff, Bradshaw, and Dickinson all had brothers, sons, or sons-in-law working for Reuters. In Wolff's letter of appointment on 2 December

1870 Julius Reuter had promised the young man 'lifelong employment'. In other words, late-Victorian and Edwardian Reuters retained something of a family atmosphere, even after it had become a semi-official national and imperial institution.

TWO

'The Great Reuter'

I

O N 28 March 1860 Julius Reuter was presented at the court of Queen Victoria. He was presented, moreover, by the Prime Minister himself, Lord Palmerston. Karl Marx told Engels on 12 April that there were political reasons behind the presentation. Certainly, in terms purely of social station, although Reuter was 'respectable' in the Victorian sense of the word and increasingly prosperous, he scarcely qualified for such elevated attention. The existence of a political dimension would explain why Palmerston was involved. 'Russia has now joined the "Austro-German Telegraphic Union" ', wrote Marx, 'and pour encourager les autres, has got Pam to present her Reuter to the QUEEN.'[1]

Marx seems to have been implying that Reuter was well thought of by the Russian Government as well as by the British. On his 1857 visit to St Petersburg, at the same time as negotiating with Usoff, Reuter had engaged upon other business, probably with Russian Ministers. In every country, he sought to gain recognition for his agency as the preferred outlet for circulating official announcements to the foreign press. About 1860, Reuter had also proposed to the Russian Government the construction of an overland telegraph from eastern Russia to China. With official backing, he sent a 'Mr. Bishop' to explore the route. Reuter's representative successfully crossed the Gobi desert, and reached Peking; but the venture was found to be premature. It was evidence, none the less, of how forward-thinking Reuter was in his ideas for the collection of news. When in 1862 the Russian Government extended its telegraph across the Urals to Tyumen in Western Siberia, Reuter appointed an agent at Peking to organize a weekly service of couriers to take outward news to the new telegraph head, a journey of nearly three thousand miles.[2]

The daily publication of his telegrams in the newspapers naturally provoked the question 'Who is Mr Reuter?'. This was the title of an article by Andrew Wynter which appeared in *Once A Week* on 23 February 1861. The London correspondent of the *Birmingham Journal* had already answered the question on 13 October 1860: 'Reuter is not only the man of the time, but the master of Time.' A piece in the antiquarian journal, *Notes & Queries*, on 3 November had asked who was 'this mysterious person'? A reply by 'J.T.' on 29 December explained that he was a German by birth but naturalized British. He had collected correspondents all over the world. In the London office, continued the article, incoming messages were checked and transcribed by clerks, and then delivered by messengers to the newspaper offices. 'Within the last three years this office has acquired considerable importance.'

The *Birmingham Journal* had still not been sure whether Reuter's news was trustworthy; but Wynter's *Once A Week* article in the following February had commended 'the impartiality and accuracy by which Mr Reuter's telegrams were characterised'. This article contained the first detailed description of Reuter's organization for the collection and distribution of 'electric news':

> all our earliest information from America, India, and China, the Cape, and even Australia, is derived from this gentleman's telegrams. In all these countries he has located agents, who transmit him news in anticipation of the mails. There being no direct telegraphic communication between England and these countries, Mr Reuter avails himself of every telegraphic line en route. Messages from America, for instance, are telegraphed up to the latest moment to the last port in the Atlantic where the steamer touches; they are then landed either at Queenstown, Londonderry, Galway, Liverpool or Southampton, whence they are telegraphed to London . . . All the telegrams first come into the hands of Mr. Reuter, whose day offices are near the Exchange, and whose night offices are in Finsbury Square—thus this gentleman is without doubt, as regards the affairs of the world, the best informed man in it. He gives his political telegrams to the press alone, and never allows them on any account to be communicated beforehand to merchants and bankers for the purpose of speculation.

To reinforce the separation between Reuter's political and commercial services, a day office to handle political news had recently been opened at Waterloo Place in the West End, leaving the Royal Exchange day office to handle commercial information. The Reuter night office at King Street backed on to the garden of Reuter's house in Finsbury Square:

> All the offices are connected by the electric wire, and to still further facilitate the transmission of telegrams to the different newspapers, the wires are being continued from the West End office right into the editor's room of each journal . . . The pedestrian, as he walks along Fleet Street and the Strand, will perceive high overhead what might be termed the political spinal cord of the metropolis.

Young George Williams joined the staff in the same year. He took turns in the night office, where camp-beds were provided so that staff could doze when no news was to hand. In July 1861, he was on duty but asleep when news of the first big battle of the American Civil War at Bull Run arrived by telegram. The telegraph boy failed to rouse Williams from his deep slumber, and had no choice but to leave the message upon his chest. Williams slept on untroubled until, as his son later recorded, 'in the grey light of dawn he was aroused by the spectacle of his employer in his dressing gown and slippers standing over his bed and shaking the fateful message in his face'. Julius Reuter, as was his custom, had come across the garden to check what news had arrived overnight. Reuter forgave young Williams his lapse, which could have cost him his job.[3]

2

During 1859–60, although European news continued to predominate within the Reuter file, material from the wider world was on the increase. In October 1859 Reuter had started a 'Special India and China Service'. Even so, news of the surrender of Peking to British and French troops on 13 October 1860 took nearly two months to reach London. Reuter's report of the sacking of the summer palace—condemned by history as an act of vandalism—was brief and matter-of-fact: 'The Emperor's summer palace was taken and looted on the 6th of October. The quantity of spoil was enormous.'

By 1861 Reuter was publishing telegrams from over a hundred datelines. News from Australia, New Zealand, and South Africa had begun to feature regularly. A lengthy mailed dispatch arrived in Plymouth from Cape Town on 28 September 1861, brought by a Royal Mail steamer which had taken five weeks in passage. Her mails were landed shortly after midnight, and sent on to London by special train. The dispatch included an account of Zulu unrest, news of Dr Livingstone in the African interior, and a report of an injunction 'granted Mr Charles Dickens against the *Eastern Province Herald* publishing his "Great Expectations" '.

Throughout 1861–5 the dominant story came from across the Atlantic— news of the American Civil War. Reuters was the prime supplier of war news to the press of both Britain and the Continent. The war was bloodily excit-ing. It was also significant because of its increasingly explicit moral dimen-sion, for and against black slavery; and it became of direct import because of its damaging economic effects upon the United Kingdom. Cotton supplies from the Confederate southern states were cut off, and the resulting 'cotton famine' brought the Lancashire cotton trade, one of Britain's greatest indus-tries, almost to a halt.

North American news was supplied to Reuter by the Associated Press of New York (AP). In addition, Reuter's New York agent, James McLean did some news gathering himself, as well as gutting the American press for news. Reuter signed a four-year news exchange agreement with AP with effect from the start of 1862, which was probably an expansion of an existing arrangement. AP contracted to send exclusive political, commercial, and other news by every mail steamer out of New York. Each news summary was to fill two printed columns. Late news was to be telegraphed by AP agents in condensed form for putting on board outgoing vessels at 'remote ports' such as St Johns, Portland (Maine), Halifax, Farther Point, or Cape Race. An accompanying 'brief abstract' was to be sent for telegraphing to London from the British port of arrival. The abstracts were to total not less than 2,000 words per week. Reuter agreed to pay $100 per week for these. Otherwise, the agreement was for a straight news swap.

Reuter, for his part, promised to send a news summary from London to New York 'of all important intelligence which may reach him from any part of Great Britain, Ireland, the Continent of Europe, India, China, Australia, New Zealand, Japan, or from any other place'. This was to be sufficient to fill one and a half printed columns. He also agreed to supply a 'brief abstract' with every summary, and to telegraph abstracts of late news to his agents at Queenstown, Galway, and Londonderry for placing on steamers which called there before starting the Atlantic crossing.

The news of the election of Abraham Lincoln as President of the United States was published by Reuter on 18 November 1860. It had been telegraphed to London from Queenstown, where it was taken off the passing steamship *Asia*, which had sailed from New York eleven days earlier. The failure of the 1858 transatlantic cable meant that all American news was still arriving no faster than the speed of steamships. Although major news, such as that of Lincoln's election, could be dropped off in canisters as vessels passed the northern or southern Irish coasts, the news in full had to await their arrival at Liverpool, Plymouth, or Southampton. From there, Reuter agents telegraphed to London the 'brief abstracts' supplied by AP, and then forwarded by train fuller dispatches, plus the American papers. Big news from America therefore broke in stages—perhaps a striking fact first and more facts later, with background and reaction later still. In at least one notable instance, this selection process failed conspicuously. Lincoln's famous Gettysburg address on 19 November 1863 did not feature in the report for Reuters, even though AP's reporter at the ceremony had transcribed verbatim for the American press the President's memorable 272 words about 'government of the people by the people for the people'. The

British papers had to delay until they could copy the famous oration from the American papers.

The arrival of every mail steamer from America was eagerly awaited—for accounts of battles lost and won, for news of cotton supplies and prices, for information about American grain and other commodities, and for New York money and stock market quotations. Reuter distributed this news not only to the British press and commercial subscribers, but also to his European partners, Havas and Wolff, and to his agents and subscribers overseas. Cotton news was of great interest to India, where merchants were poised to make fortunes by selling locally grown cotton to Lancashire in place of the American shortfall.

News of the battle of Bull Run on 21 July 1861 reached London via Boston and Queenstown, with later material added 'by Telegraph to Halifax'. It was published by Reuter on 4 August. This was presumably the telegram which failed to rouse George Williams from his slumbers. The story was told from a northern Federal angle, but no question was left about the southern Confederate victory:

> The Federal army, under General McDowell, has sustained a disastrous defeat. Early on the morning of the 21st the whole of the Federal army advanced on the Confederate batteries at Bull's Run, three miles from Manassas Junction. Great bravery was displayed by the Federal troops, and after nine hours fighting they succeeded in capturing three of the Confederate batteries, but with heavy loss on both sides. At this time General Beauregard is reported to have been reinforced by General Johnstone with 25,000 men. The Confederates then attacked the Union army, and drove them in disorder from the field. A panic from some cause seized the Federal troops, and the whole army fled in open disorder towards Washington . . .
>
> The Federal loss is estimated at from 500 to 2,000 men. Many colonels and officers of all grades were killed. The Confederate loss is also stated to be heavy.
>
> The Confederate army at Manassas Junction is reported to number 90,000 men . . .
>
> The defences round Washington have been reinforced, and are stated to be strong enough to resist any attack by the Confederates. Reinforcements from all parts of the country have been telegraphed for from Washington.
> The repulse has created a profound sensation.

Reuter agents at British ports of arrival were in competition for American war news with representatives of the London newspapers. Although the papers subscribed to the Reuter service, they liked to publish exclusive reports when they could. They started chartering boats to meet incoming American steamers, and a company called Telegraphic Despatch began to meet the steamers at Roche's Point, off Queenstown. This extra-early news was then telegraphed from Cork to London. Reuter found himself being beaten by several hours. In response, never reluctant to act boldly, he discovered a way not merely to match this competition but to overwhelm it.

Four or five hours would be gained if the steamers could be intercepted as soon as they approached the Irish coast. In 1863 Reuter obtained permission to build a telegraph line from Cork to Crookhaven in the extreme south-west of Ireland, a distance of over 80 miles. He formed the South Western [*sic*] of Ireland Telegraph Company Limited to construct and operate the line. One of his partners in the project was Charles William Siemens, the telegraph pioneer. Not all local opinion welcomed Reuter's initiative. The *Cork Examiner* of 23 July 1863 denounced him as a 'clever foreign speculator' intent on 'monopolising the American news'. So he was. But the *West Carberry Eagle* of 25 July reported strong local support for 'this telegraph king', who offered hope for the revival of an area which had suffered severely in the potato famine of the 1840s. In the event, Reuter sold out his personal interest in the company within a year, although his agency continued to use its facilities. No doubt he was aware that the line could have no important function once a transatlantic cable had been successfully laid.

The Crookhaven line was operational from early December 1863. Messages for delivery by the new route were thrown from passing mail steamers in special canisters, which were picked up by long poles lowered from the Reuter steam-tender *Marseilles*. At night the canisters were lit by phosphorous. In rough seas the work could be hazardous, and canisters were occasionally lost. While the *Marseilles* was returning to harbour, Reuter clerks below deck busily sorted the various messages. *The Times* seems to have shared in the venture, for one clerk recorded years later that reports from its New York correspondent came in the same canisters. This would explain how Reuters and *The Times* could each publish their own version of the very first news story sent by this route. Both were described as 'per *Persia* via Crookhaven', and yet were expressed in quite different terms.[4]

3

Much Reuter war news consisted of lengthy quotations from newspapers of both the North and the South. From time to time direct reports came from the South. 'The press in the South is at liberty to discuss public matters freely. Never were a people more cordially united than the citizens of the Confederate States.'

This even-handed approach did not please the United States legation in London. The legation gave countenance to the idea that Julius Reuter was in the pay of the South, a smear for which American historians have subsequently found no evidence. The private diary of Benjamin Moran, assistant secretary at the legation, was tinged with anti-Semitism in expressing a low opinion of Reuter. Moran was convinced that Reuter was consistently slanting the news against the North, even to the length of suppressing or delaying reports of its successes:

> The German Reuter, who now supplies the European press with telegraphic reports has evidently been bought up by the rebels, and he systematically prostitutes the monopoly he holds to deprecate the Union. Some time since he offered to furnish his reports to the [United States] Government, but they were declined, and now he is against us. None of his reports are ever borne out fully by the details given in the journals; but on the contrary, in nine cases out of ten his reports are proved false, or great exaggerations. But the British Press encourages the deception, and there is no way to remedy the business but by buying the fellow up. This I would not do. (26 August 1861)[5]

The legation none the less decided to subscribe for telegrams from Reuter: 'this course', wrote Moran on 25 November, 'will doubtless have a good effect upon him.' But Moran found that there was no change. Such steadiness can be taken as confirmation that the Reuter news file was not open to improper influence. Regrettably, instead of welcoming this, the legation continued to denounce Reuter. 'His rascality in these matters', exclaimed Moran over a year later (26 September 1862), 'is criminal and he deserves to be put in jail.' But Reuter had the consolation of knowing that he was not alone in being unfairly criticized. For example, W. H. Russell's account for *The Times* of the Northern defeat at Bull Run had caused uproar when reprinted in the American papers, and fears were expressed for his personal safety. The Yankees found the truth hard to stomach when they were not winning.[6]

Reuter's Southampton agent, Joseph Sharpe, provided the earliest interview to feature in the news file. The Confederate ship *Nashville* had sunk a Federal steamer, after saving its crew. The men were landed by the *Nashville* at Southampton. 'I immediately went on board,' reported Sharpe on 21 November 1861. He interviewed the captain and some of the passengers, and collected comments about the state of affairs in the South. 'The country, I am told, is prosperous, and the people satisfied of their ability to achieve their independence.' Moran seemed to regard such straight reporting about the South as hostile to the North.

A few days later Sharpe was handling first news of the *Trent* affair. The Confederates had appointed two envoys to Europe—James Mason to

London, and John Slidell to Paris. Reuter had reported in mid–October 1861 that they had run the Federal blockade and reached Havana. They sailed from there on a British vessel, the *Trent*. It was stopped by a Federal warship and the male passengers, including the two Confederate commissioners, were kidnapped. Sharpe took the whole story at Southampton from the mail steamer, *La Plata*, fresh from the West Indies. Julius Reuter then personally conveyed the alarming news to Lord Palmerston, who, on the strength of Reuter's report alone, called an emergency Cabinet meeting.

British public opinion was outraged at this breach of sovereignty, and Palmerston was not disposed to calm matters. War with the North became a real possibility. Palmerston drafted a strongly worded dispatch, which was rewritten by a dying Prince Albert so that, although still firm, it left room for the Federal side to climb down. Throughout the crisis Reuter charted the reactions of both the Northern and Southern papers, and sent summaries of British press opinion to New York. On 20 December the New York office reported that the British note had arrived in Washington, and added: 'if the demands of the British Government for the surrender of Messrs Mason and Slidell are couched in moderate language they will be complied with.'

Reports of the American decision to release the two men were first carried in a Reuter dispatch from Paris on 7 January, quoting two French newspapers. The next day Reuter issued a long report from the United States which included definite news from AP of the release of the pair. On 11 January a further Reuter report gave a partial text of the letters exchanged between London and Washington. The full text of the conciliatory Federal reply arrived next day, a Sunday. Palmerston had not yet himself seen this answer, and Julius Reuter once again personally handed a telegram of very important news to the Prime Minister.[7]

The year 1860 had witnessed the first recorded sports items carried by Reuter. On 15 May a report stated that 'the New York papers teem with accounts of the fight between Heenan and Sayers'. This was the last bare-knuckle fight in England, fought between Heenan, an American, and Sayers, the English champion. It ended in a draw. On 9 April 1862 Reuter reported the arrival at Sydney, 10 weeks earlier, of the first English cricket team to tour Australia. Science, literature, and religion were given regular notice in the news file, on the assumption that readers of Reuter telegrams were people of education with wide interests. One of the earliest telegrams reported in May 1859 the funeral of 'the Nestor of German science, the immortal Alexander von Humboldt'. In July 1862 Lisbon felt it worth while to announce that Victor Hugo's latest work, *Les Misérables*, was selling well in Portugal. The implication was that readers would know the work, and would be interested to be told later that it had been placed on the Roman Catholic Index. The future Cardinal Manning's visits to Rome were reported as news items of general interest, as were Bishop Colenso's disputes with the Anglican authorities at the Cape.

In the spring of 1865 James Heckscher was sent to New York to improve the file from America. The civil war was ending just as he arrived; but he was soon to become involved in covering the most startling American story of this period—news of the assassination of President Lincoln on 14 April. How Reuters reported this dramatic story became itself a story much dramatized in the telling.

About 9.45 on the morning of 26 April the news was taken ashore from the steamship *Nova Scotian* to the telegraph station at Greencastle, near Londonderry, in the north of Ireland. By 11.30 a message—datelined New York, 15 April, 9 a.m.—reached the offices of the London newspapers from Reuters: 'President Lincoln was shot by an assassin last night, and died this morning. An attempt was likewise made to assassinate Mr Seward, and he is not expected to live.' Simultaneously, the news was distributed to Reuter

FIG. 4. Reuter report of the assassination of Abraham Lincoln, published in the *Morning Advertiser*, 27 April 1865

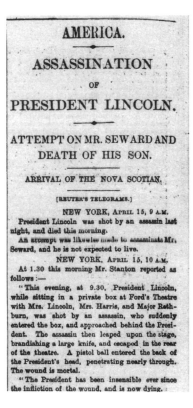

AMERICA.

ASSASSINATION

OF

PRESIDENT LINCOLN.

ATTEMPT ON MR. SEWARD AND
DEATH OF HIS SON.

ARRIVAL OF THE NOVA SCOTIAN.

[REUTER'S TELEGRAMS.]

NEW YORK, APRIL 15, 9 A.M.

President Lincoln was shot by an assassin last night, and died this morning.

An attempt was likewise made to assassinate Mr, Seward, and he is not expected to live.

NEW YORK, APRIL 15, 10 A.M.

At 1.30 this morning Mr. Stanton reported as follows :—

"This evening, at 9.30, President Lincoln, while sitting in a private box at Ford's Theatre with Mrs. Lincoln, Mrs. Harris, and Major Rathburn, was shot by an assassin, who suddenly entered the box, and approached behind the President. The assassin then leaped upon the stage, brandishing a large knife, and escaped in the rear of the theatre. A pistol ball entered the back of the President's head, penetrating nearly through. The wound is mortal.

"The President has been insensible ever since the infliction of the wound, and is now dying.

1865

REUTER'S TELEGRAM COMPANY,

LIMITED.

Incorporated under the Joint Stock Companies' Act, 1862.

CAPITAL £250,000, IN 10,000 SHARES OF £25 EACH.

FIRST ISSUE 4,000 SHARES.

OF WHICH MORE THAN 2,000 SHARES HAVE BEEN ALREADY SUBSCRIBED.

Payment on Application £1, and on Allotment £4 per Share; it is not intended to call up more than £20 per Share. At least Two Months to intervene between each Call.

DIRECTORS.

JOHN DENT, Esq., 35, Grosvenor Square.
SIR JOHN DALRYMPLE HAY, Bart., M.P., F.R.S.
Col. JAMES HOLLAND, Deputy Chairman London and South African Bank.
JAMES SYDNEY STOPFORD, Esq., Director of the Agra and Masterman's Bank.
JULIUS REUTER, Esq., Managing Director.

SOLICITORS.

Messrs. BISCHOFF COXE & BOMPAS, 19, Coleman Street.

BANKERS.

THE AGRA & MASTERMAN'S BANK, LIMITED, 35, Nicholas Lane.

BROKERS.

Messrs. P. CAZENOVE & Co., 52, Threadneedle Street.

SECRETARY (PRO TEM).

Mr. FREDERICK J. GRIFFITHS.

OFFICES:

1, ROYAL EXCHANGE BUILDINGS, LONDON.

This Company is established to provide capital for the purchase and extension of the well-known Telegraphic business of Mr. Julius Reuter.

FIG. 5. The original company prospectus, 1865

commercial clients, and it was from one of these—Peabody and Co., the American bankers in London—that the news reached the Bank of England, and from there quickly spread throughout the City. At first, many believed the story to be a hoax started by stock market speculators, until it was confirmed by a dispatch received nearly two hours later. Myth was to extend the creditable Reuter beat of two hours into an unbelievable one of several days.[8]

4

A few weeks earlier, on 20 February 1865, Julius Reuter had restructured his business. The private firm was transformed into Reuter's Telegram Company, a limited company under the terms of the 1862 Companies Act.

The new firm offered a good investment prospect. It was prospering and still expanding. An auditors' report revealed the profit for 1864 as £8,630. The company was incorporated with a nominal capital of £250,000 (10,000 shares at £25 each); £80,000 capital was paid up. Julius Reuter received £65,000 in cash for his business (worth £2,824,900 at a 1998 equivalent), a figure which for half a century was to be treated as the value of the company's goodwill. Reuter was appointed managing director at a handsome salary of £1,500 per annum, increased to £2,500 in years when a 10 per cent dividend was paid.

The prospectus announced that 'Mr Reuter will continue to have the exclusive management of the Telegraphic Department, which will be conducted as heretofore, with the utmost secrecy, fidelity, and impartiality' (Fig. 5). His contract gave him 'the sole and entire management' of the business, 'and no other Director or Shareholder shall be entitled to interfere'. So Julius Reuter, and his son Herbert after him, were almost obliged to play a dominating part. 'Reuters' was now a public company, but the family was still in control.

The board gave its managing directors steady and apparently uncritical support, although the only surviving evidence is the bland record of the minute books. The board came to comprise just four members, including the managing director. Colonel James Holland (Plate 11) emerged as the first regular chairman, although not given that title until 1868. He had spent most of his military career as a land surveyor and administrator in India. After his retirement from the army, he had become active as a director, and eventually chairman, of three major companies with Indian connections—Reuters, the Great Indian Peninsula Railway, and the Indo-European Telegraph Company. A second director, Admiral Sir John Dalrymple-Hay (1821–1912) had fought in the Crimean War. He sat as a 'Liberal Conservative' Member of Parliament between 1862 and 1885. He was a Scottish landowner, as was his wife's father,

Lord Napier and Ettrick. His wife's nephew, Mark Napier, was to join the
Reuter board when Hay succeeded Holland as chairman in 1888. Hay did not
retire from the chairmanship until 1910, by which time he was sinking into
senility. Another foundation director was James S. Stopford, an East India
merchant, who served until 1880.[9]

The first general meeting of Reuter's Telegram Company Limited was held
on 24 July 1865. The shareholders were chiefly professional men with mainly
London addresses—solicitors, bankers, merchants, naval and military officers, medical practitioners. The 1865 dividend was fixed at 8 per cent free of
tax; the directors announced that they were moving carefully at first.
Thereafter 10 per cent became customary, which was a good return. The best
early annual net profit was £31,939 for 1868. By 1874, however, profits had
fallen to £6,329, as development costs increased faster than revenue.
Expenditure upon 'telegrams and agencies' rose from £27,371 in 1866 to
£59,805 in 1878; annual revenue grew from £49,715 to £79,414 during the
same period. By 1878—Julius Reuter's final year as managing director—net
profit for the year had fallen to £5,627. In 1875 the dividend was cut to 7.5
per cent, which became the norm into the 1880s.

Office accommodation in London was extended as business expanded.
The original two rooms at Royal Exchange Buildings remained in use until
1866. In that year, the headquarters were moved to 5 Lothbury, nearby. But
the rooms there were found to be too disconnected and cramped, and in 1871
a further move was made to a Georgian house at 24 Old Jewry, still in the City
of London. This was destined to be the headquarters of Reuters for over fifty
years. Within a few years, adjacent houses at numbers 23 and 25 were taken.

Although rebuilding was discussed at intervals, these three unprepossess-
ing old properties remained unchanged externally throughout their long
occupation by Reuters. The dining-room at 24 provided the boardroom,
while former bedrooms served as editorial rooms. The atmosphere inside was
purposeful but relaxed. Open fires blazed all day and night; pots of beer stood
on desks; papers were strewn about the floors; and large books of press cuttings, compiled since the early days of the agency, were kept prominently on
hand for background reference.

An article in the *Strand Magazine* for July 1895 described how news was
handled at Old Jewry. The moment a telegram arrived from the cable offices
or elsewhere, it was registered in a book by the timekeeper. The message was
then passed to the senior editor on duty. He had to decide whether to circulate the item, and to which subscribers. By 1859 there were already direct telegraph wires from Reuters into the offices of the main London papers. Charles
Wheatstone's handbook, *The Universal Telegraph*, published in that year, listed

'Mr. Julius Reuter's Establishment' among the users of his 'automatic print-ing telegraph', as well as the 'Houses of Parliament', 'City of London Police Stations', and others. But the apparatus was slow to use, and was suitable only for sending short messages. From 1882 column-printers, capable of 18 words per minute, were put into the London newspaper offices to receive messages from Reuters. The column-printer had a type-wheel which printed words and figures on a roll; these were tapped out on a 'piano transmitter' at Old Jewry by Reuter operators. At the same time, duplicate copies were received on two machines in the Reuter office; these were torn off and the messages summarized—and if necessary translated—for transmission overseas. The column-printer was a major step forward in communications technology, which greatly accelerated the work of news agencies and newspapers.[10]

All outgoing Reuter messages were transcribed by clerks called manifold-ers. At first, this manifolding was done manually by stylus upon thin paper interleaved with black oiled sheets. An expert could make up to thirty-two copies at one writing. Then from the 1880s typewriters were used. Each London newspaper was sent duplicates of all messages already communicated by wire. These 'flimsies' were delivered by Reuter messenger boys.

By the 1890s about sixty-five messenger boys were being employed. They were recruited in their early teens, and most left at eighteen. Their grey—later blue—uniforms had become familiar sights on the streets of central London. From the 1890s some messengers used bicycles (Plate 12). Girl messengers were introduced in 1901 for daytime deliveries (Plate 28). 'A Woman of Experience' complained to *The Times* on 15 November about the moral dan-ger to Reuter girls who ran through the streets, and about the damage to domestic service caused by the introduction of alternative employment.

By the late 1860s Reuters was charging all London newspapers equally. The editors had complained about the repeated increases made as Reuter services extended. Julius Reuter knew that the papers were bound to take his telegrams when their competitors were doing so, and he had felt no hesita-tion in charging accordingly. He was said in one obituary to have often remarked in old age: 'If I did give them something for nothing at the begin-ning, I've made thousands of pounds out of them since.'[11]

Eventually, however, the subscription for the London dailies settled at £1,600 per annum. This was a very high charge (equivalent to about £600,000 a year at the end of the twentieth century). Editors at least had the consolation of knowing that, so long as they paid the price, Reuter telegrams would never be withheld from them. Impartiality in distribution was care-fully written into Julius Reuter's contract as managing director in 1865: 'it shall be the duty of the Managing Director to communicate the telegraphic intelligence equally and impartially to all the Subscribers . . . without giving priority to any one over any other.' This high moral line not only paid in terms of reputation, it also paid in terms of revenue.

Reuter news for the provincial press was distributed after 1868 by the newly formed Press Association. This co-operative had been started by the leading provincial newspapers, exasperated at the unreliable domestic news service offered by the telegraph companies. The PA formed a close relationship with Reuters, exchanging its news from the British Isles for Reuter overseas news, but also paying a differential. This was fixed at £3,000 in 1868, increased to £8,000 from 1881. Because of the PA connection, Reuters never tried to operate as a British domestic news agency.[12]

5

By the mid-1860s Julius Reuter's name and reputation were well established. When on 9 May 1865 Charles Dickens—the great Victorian novelist, who was also a journalist by training—chaired a dinner of the Newsvendors' Benevolent Association, he spoke in humorous vein. He pictured the alarming situation if the newsvendors ever went on strike:

> Imagine all sorts and conditions of men dying to know the shipping news, the commercial news, the legal news, the criminal news, the foreign news and domestic news . . . Why, even Mr. Reuter, the great Reuter whom I am always glad to imagine slumbering at night by the side of Mrs. Reuter, with a galvanic battery under the bolster, telegraph wires to the head of his bed, and an electric bell at each ear [roars of laughter], even he would click and flash those wondrous despatches of his to little purpose, if it were not for the humble, and by comparison, slow activity, which gathers up the stitches of the electric needle, and scatters them over the land.[13]

In these lighthearted terms the great Victorian novelist felt free to joke about the great Victorian telegraphist and his 'wondrous despatches'. The name of 'the great Reuter' was now as familiar as the name of Dickens himself:

ON THE EMINENT TELEGRAPHIST

England believes his telegrams,
Whether they please or fright her;
Other electric sparks are right,
But he is always *right-er*.

(*Punch*, 22 May 1869)

THREE

An Imperial Institution
1865–1914

I

D URING the last forty years of the nineteenth century Reuters news agency functioned increasingly as a semi-official institution of the British Empire. This was a great status for a private company to achieve. It was the more remarkable for a firm started by a foreigner who had not even begun to live in England until the age of 34. Yet during the 1860s and early 1870s Julius Reuter was aspiring to achieve even more than this. He was pursuing a grand design of making Reuters into the predominant world news agency. To this end, he tried a succession of initiatives, each important in itself but still more important as part of his grand design:

1. He sought to establish a major presence in Germany, with offices there linked to England through his own Nordeney cable laid across the North Sea in 1866. He hoped to use Germany as a springboard for expansion eastwards.

2. He became joint sponsor of the French Atlantic cable opened in 1869, and intended to secure for Reuters a preferential link with North America.

3. He sought to gain control of the news agencies of continental Europe, including the two most important, the Havas and Wolff agencies in France and Germany respectively.

4. He opened full-time offices or appointed part-time agents in numerous Asian, African and Australasian outposts of the formal and informal British Empire. Gradually, this imperial initiative began to be pursued for its own sake, but at first it had been only one part of his grand design

The Nordeney scheme was intended to play a key part in the overall expansion plan. One reason for going public in 1865 was to raise capital to pay for this cable across the North Sea from Lowestoft to Nordeney off the north German coast. The necessary concession was confirmed by the King of Hanover on 15 November 1865. Reuter had told his board on 28 September that the benefit to the company would be considerable, 'because irrespective of increased speed and saving of expense, the messages of the Company would then take precedence of all others'. This would be 'the first step towards the development of a very extensive business on the continent of Europe'.[1]

Although Reuter came to be known for 'following the cable' round the world, this had not been his whole intention. He had originally aspired both to build and to own important parts of the cable network upon which he depended to transmit his news.

The Nordeney cable was a year in the making, and was ready by October 1866. In a letter to *The Times* on 15 December Reuter explained that this was not just another line: it had been laid 'to introduce a new system in telegraphic communication—that, namely, of international through [direct] telegraphy'. A direct line, Reuter explained, would reduce delay by taking four wires into north Germany, one of which would reach Berlin.

Reuter's letter made no mention of his hopes of expansion within Germany, and of using that country as a springboard for further growth eastwards. The plans were in danger of disappointment even before the line became operational. The kingdom of Hanover, on the losing side in the Austro-Prussian War, had been absorbed into Prussia. Julius Reuter's letter had been written to emphasize that, contrary to rumour, the Prussians had confirmed the Nordeney concession. So they had—but upon restrictive terms which were intended to prevent Reuters from establishing a strong independent position within Germany. The new agreement denied Reuters an office in Hanover, and also the right to an exclusive line. The 1867 annual general meeting of Reuters was told that this renegotiation had required 'considerable personal exertions at Berlin' by Julius Reuter. At least indirectly, he was dealing with Bismarck; and it may be at this time that he came to know the German Chancellor personally.

Financially, the line was a great success. Traffic became heavy, reaching a level of between 13,000 and 14,000 messages sent and received each month. During 1868 Nordeney revenue totalled £29,744, 'or 19 per cent on the capital invested in the cable and land lines'. The entire cost had been £153,000. But Bismarck was never going to let Reuters compete freely with the Wolff Bureau in its home territory. Significantly, this agency had been refounded in 1865 as the Continental Telegraph Company, with Wolff remaining as managing director but with Bismarck's banker, Gerson von Bleichröder, introduced as chairman.

Reuters might have kept ownership of the Nordeney cable simply as a profit-making venture. Instead, early in 1870 the line was sold off at great gain: the generous buyer was the British Government. Successive British ministers had pursued fluctuating policies with regard to the encouragement of overland telegraphs and undersea cables. By the late 1860s the policy was not to invest in the latter, but simply to provide assistance with marine surveying and to help private projectors in their negotiations with foreign governments. With regard to telegraphy inside the United Kingdom, however, and for 'submarine telegraphy' between the British Isles and the Continent, the British Government had belatedly decided that the national interest required it to take control. The Telegraph Purchase Act of 1868 gave the Postmaster-General power to acquire and work telegraphs. £8 million was allowed for the nationalization of all private inland telegraph companies in the United Kingdom, along with the telegraphic business of the railway companies.[2]

Reuters had petitioned against this measure, and had been represented before a House of Commons committee. But this seems to have been only a stratagem to ensure, rather than to prevent, compulsory purchase. The British Government was not expecting to have to acquire the Nordeney cable at all; but Reuters contrived to demonstrate that interlocking agreements with the Electric Telegraph Company—which the Government intended to buy out, and which provided the land link between London and Lowestoft—made purchase of the Reuter cable unavoidable. And such a purchase was bound to include compensation payment for rights granted by Reuters to the Indo-European Telegraph Company, since one of the Nordeney lines was scheduled to serve as the first leg of the Indo-European's projected route to Teheran.

Having persuaded the Government to accept these commitments, Reuters withdrew its petition. How much should the Government pay? The matter went to arbitration. The ruling was that Reuters was entitled to a price based upon twenty years' profits. This meant that it received £726,000 for an enterprise which had cost £153,000. Julius Reuter had taken an active part in the negotiations. Although his dream of expansion into and beyond Germany was already fading, he had at least contrived to obtain a very large financial consolation prize. The size of the official payout even encouraged the belief, repeated in print, that Reuters had sold its entire business to the British Government, and so become an official organization.[3]

Unfortunately for the future, the Reuter board was overcome by euphoria at this windfall. A substantial reserve fund could have been created, but was not. Reuter himself was given £5,000; the other directors shared £4,000; senior staff split £7,000. £693,000 was distributed to shareholders. Only £7,000 was retained. The agency's capitalization was reduced to £72,000, with £65,000 still credited to goodwill. Late-Victorian Reuters was left to operate as a worldwide organization upon a remarkably narrow capital base.[4]

2

As part of the drive into Europe, the board had voted on 18 September 1867 to spend £20,000 upon establishing new offices on the Continent. A branch had already been started from 1 January 1866 in Amsterdam. Reuters had bought out the existing telegraph bureau of Alexander Delamar, and had installed him as manager. In Brussels, Alexander's brother, Herman, was made manager of a joint office with Havas.

The Low Countries were important for trade and communications; but Reuters also wanted to become established in Germany and beyond. Noticeable progress was made in Hamburg, with its tradition of trading freedom and its distrust of Prussia. Most of Germany's overseas commerce passed through Hamburg, and this gave it a strong interest in commercial information. The Hamburg branch, managed by James Heckscher, opened in 1868. It began to supply a service to local merchants, and also to two of the city's five newspapers. The big breakthrough came when Heckscher negotiated a lucrative contract of 4,000 thalers (£600) per annum to supply a full service of news to the Neue Börsenhalle. This was described by Emil Wolff, who started his Reuter career in Hamburg, as 'a sort of Commercial Club and reading room within the Exchange Buildings'. The Börsenhalle agreed to give Reuters full credit for messages exhibited in its rooms, or when they appeared in its newspapers.[5]

In Heckscher's proposal to the Börsenhalle, the range of news to be supplied by Reuters was described in detail—world political news collected by telegraph or otherwise; fund quotations from the ten leading world exchanges (New York to St Peterburg); corn and flour reports from twenty places; cotton reports from fourteen places; colonial-produce reports from seventeen places; metal reports from eight places; the rate of exchange for bills and discount reports from seventeen places; news of the arrival of transatlantic mails, and of transatlantic specie; freight news; wool reports; petroleum reports.

This Hamburg service included most of the extensive general news and commercial information now available from Reuters. The range was impressive. Havas and Wolff were strong in Europe, but could not match Reuters for news sources elsewhere. 'Its correspondence', claimed Heckscher comprehensively, 'which covers the civilised and partly the uncivilised world, is a tried one and will guarantee to the Hamburg commercial community the quickest supply of any important and noteworthy news.'

Reuter offices were also opened in Berlin, Frankfurt, and Vienna. The Frankfurt and Vienna managers were Reuter's nephews, Robert and Eugen

Salinger. But the Prussian Government ensured that business in Berlin and Frankfurt did not prosper. The authorities favoured the Wolff Bureau by treating its telegrams as priority official correspondence. According to Emil Wolff's recollections, 'democratic' newspapers in Prussia did take the Reuter service; but they could not afford to pay full rates because they were in competition with the subsidized Bismarckian press. One long-repeated anecdote about Julius Reuter said that he secured a personal meeting with Bismarck, the Prussian Chancellor, to protest at the obstacles put in the agency's way. 'Are not', Reuter enquired, 'my telegrams truthful?' 'Certainly,' replied Bismarck, 'too truthful.'[6] On 15 June 1870 the Reuter board studied projected agency profit-and-loss figures for the first half of the year. The German losses were heavy, even at Hamburg (see Table 3.1).

TABLE 3.1 Projected profit-and-loss figures for Reuter offices during the first half of 1870.

	Credits			Debits		
	£	s.	d.	£	s.	d.
Indian Agencies	1,000	0	0			
Brussels	240	0	0			
Dutch	216	6	10			
Constantinople	163	9	11			
Alexandria	43	14	10			
Head Office				675	8	9
Berlin Agency				512	9	3
Frankfurt				375	7	2
Hamburg				203	6	7

When did Julius Reuter reopen a Paris office? At the time of his London start in 1851 he must have employed at least one agent in Paris to send bourse prices via the Channel cable, and to supply London prices in return. By the period of his London breakthrough in 1858–9 Reuter was clearly running a full office in the French capital. His telegrams contained French news almost every day. In 1871 James Grant's history of the press included a description of the Paris office of Reuters in the Palais Royal 'some years ago'. Its chief, wrote Grant, was 'a gentleman alike in manners and education', whose especial duty had been to call upon leading officials, headed by Napoleon III's secretary. A second staff member ran the office; a third searched through the continental

press for news; a fourth wrote the telegrams; and a fifth took them to the telegraph office.[7]

At the other end of Europe lay Constantinople, a centre of dangerous
great-power rivalry as the Turkish Empire slowly disintegrated. This office
opened in 1870 as a major operation; the profit-and-loss account for the year
included 'preliminary expenses at Constantinople' of £766.

In the late 1860s Julius Reuter had been looking west as well as east. He
entered into a second cable-owning venture, this time across the Atlantic.
The first Anglo-American cable had been opened in July 1866, and to
encourage its construction Reuter had apparently promised that his agency
would spend at least £5,000 a year on telegrams. But he became shocked by
the exorbitant charges being levied by the Anglo-American Company. On
25 September 1867 the Reuter board alarmedly compared the costs of its
American service before and after the opening of the cable. During the first
half of 1866 American costs had totalled only £408, whereas for the first half
of 1867 they totalled £2,547.

In July 1868 Reuter and Baron Emile d'Erlanger, the Paris-based member
of the German Jewish banking family, jointly secured from the French
Government the right to form a French Atlantic cable company to be called
La Société du Câble Transatlantique Française. The cable was to run from
Brest on the French coast to the French Island of St-Pierre off
Newfoundland, and from there to Cape Cod. Funds were raised mainly by
sale of stock to financiers in Paris and especially in London. Despite its name,
the working of the cable was chiefly under British management.

Reuter had embarked upon this second cable scheme in the same spirit as
the Nordeney venture, as a prospective heavy user as well as an owner. The
launching of the French Atlantic Company caused a reduction by the Anglo-
American Company from £5 to £1. 10s. per message of ten words even
before the French cable opened for traffic in August 1869. The French
Atlantic Company then adopted this same reduced tariff, announcing that it
would outdo its rival not through further price cuts but by quicker delivery
of messages. Reuters began to use the French Atlantic for many of its
American news telegrams, although not for all. Once again, however, Julius
Reuter's enterprise was destined to be frustrated by the Prussian Government,
albeit this time indirectly. After the Franco-Prussian War, in 1873, the French
Atlantic company was absorbed by its Anglo-American rival to help meet
French war-reparation payments.[8]

3

As Julius Reuter's business expanded, his relationship with Havas and Wolff had required clarification at intervals. Were the three agencies to compete or to co-operate? During the late 1850s and 1860s they fluctuated in their attitudes towards each other, before at last deciding to share the world news market between them.

Reuter seems to have made his first agreement with Havas and Wolff in 1856. This was for an exchange of market prices and quotations. No contract has survived, and perhaps the arrangement was verbal. The first certain tripartite written agreement was a record in French, dated 18 July 1859, of a discussion in Paris between Reuter, Auguste Havas (son of Charles, who had died in 1858), and Wolff. The Reuter service had recently gained acceptance by the British press, and Reuter no doubt wanted to sustain his breakthrough by offering as much news as possible. This agreement covered all types of news, not just commercial. Havas seems to have been already providing Reuter with a service from Paris, for the Frenchman now agreed to send Wolff his telegrams without commission, 'as he is already doing to M. Reuter'. The three men agreed to deliver their telegrams exclusively to each other in their home countries. St Petersburg was made Wolff territory, but 100 francs were to be paid each month to both Reuter and Havas as compensation. It was agreed that any fresh services were to be promoted at joint expense. In general, the aim of the trio was described frankly as both restrictive and expansive: 'to prevent attempts at competition, and to increase the services according to the needs of the public and the development of the telegraph lines.' Reuter was obviously still the junior partner at this point, and Havas the senior. The Havas network in western Europe and through the Mediterranean was mentioned, as was Wolff's network in Germany, Scandinavia, and eastern Europe. No Reuter network was described.

The 1859 agreement was given no time-limit. Yet within three years Reuter was already acting against its spirit. The agreement said that the three parties would 'maintain their services in the status quo in which they are at present'. Nothing had been said about other news agencies in other countries. And in 1862 Reuter tried to buy out Stefani, the Italian agency; the bid failed only because he was offering too little. Italy was supposed to be Havas territory. Similarly, during 1867–8 Reuter tried to absorb the Ritzau agency of Copenhagen, even though Scandinavia had been named as Wolff territory.

By 1865, the agreement of 1859 had clearly lapsed, and a series of interrelated contracts was now signed. On 23 June Reuter and Havas agreed to exchange their news for five years; Havas was to pay £500 a year to cover the extraordinary expenses of the American service. He was allowed a free hand in France, Italy, Spain, and Portugal; Reuter in England and Holland. Belgium was to be shared. The parties agreed not to enter into deals with other news agencies, accepting 'all the duties of an offensive and defensive treaty of alliance'. But Wolff was to be allowed to join the alliance, 'particularly in Europe'.

Wolff duly joined. On 28 December 1865 Reuter agreed to supply him with New York news for one year. However, after the Transatlantic cable had been opened in the following July, Wolff refused to share the very high telegram costs. Instead, Wolff made a deal with the Western Associated Press, a rival of the Associated Press of New York. Reuter was forced to counter by supplying an improved service to AP, in return for AP's news. WAP soon settled with AP to take this improved Reuter service instead of the Wolff service. So Reuters maintained its leading position in the handling of news to and from the United States; but its exposure to competition from Wolff or Havas even outside Europe had been demonstrated. They might try again.[9]

Julius Reuter's response was characteristically bold: he showed himself eager to take over both Havas and Wolff. With regard to Wolff, Bismarck made sure that Reuter did not succeed. In June 1869 the Prussian State Ministry signed a secret agreement with the Wolff Bureau, which granted it a subsidy and priority for its telegrams in return for accepting official control of both its outgoing and incoming news. 'All telegrams of a political nature which the Telegraph Bureau of the Continental Telegraph Company wants to relay are subject to prior control by officials specially delegated by the royal government.' In other words, telegrams to and from Reuters were to be subject to secret censorship.

For several years, Reuters continued under the impression that the Wolff bureau was an ordinary business open to takeover. Only a few months later, Reuters made some such offer, although the details are not known. A letter has survived, however, from Bismarck to Hay, one of the Reuter directors, dated 23 November 1869. In this letter, Bismarck contrived to be both disingenuous in the beginning and decisive at the end:

> In answer to your letter of 26 October I beg respectfully to say that the Continental Telegraph Company [Wolff's Bureau of Berlin] is a private institution. I have therefore to give no permission to sell it to Reuter's Telegram Company and must leave it to the latter to treat directly with the said Continental Telegraph Company. Neither can I hold out any hopes to influence the Continental Telegraph Company with regard to the sale of their

business, as former experience has shown us that it is more expedient to have a North German Telegraph Office which is beyond Foreign influence.

This rebuff left Reuter with no choice but to come to terms. He had to accept that the Wolff bureau was not for sale, and that he could not at present challenge its position within Germany, or hope to compete within its east European sphere of interest. But Reuter took care to acknowledge these realities only on terms which were likely to prevent Wolff making progress in the wider world.

Havas and Wolff had already concluded a deal in 1867 which spelled out their respective spheres of interest. This agreement served as a geographical model for the contract signed in Paris on 17 January 1870 between Reuters, Havas, and Wolff. This was concluded just two months after Bismarck's rebuff to Hay. It was no passing contract, for it was destined to form the basis of the international news agency order until the 1930s. It created a tight ring for worldwide news collection and circulation. And it was to be binding in the first instance for the long period of twenty years.

News was to be exchanged between the three parties mostly without charge. But Wolff agreed to pay Reuters and Havas 25 per cent of its annual profits in return for American news, and also for the abandonment by Reuters of all independent operations in Wolff territories. Reuters agreed to close all its German and Austrian offices except Hamburg. Wolff secured exclusive collection and distribution rights in Germany, Central Europe, Scandinavia, and Russia.

Reuters was given the news monopoly of the British Empire and the Far East. Havas took the French Empire and the Latin countries of the Mediterranean. Provision was made for several shared Reuter-Havas territories, all of them important for news or revenue—Belgium, Greece, Turkey, Egypt, South America. The three principals were to contract with any national agencies within their respective spheres for news exchange with the ring. But the Austrian Telegraphen-Korrespondenz Bureau was permitted to negotiate directly with Reuters, Havas, and Wolff. The circulation of news throughout Europe and the world was now organized as never before. Interestingly, Havas and Wolff telegraphed their news to London in French or German; but Reuter news was translated from English before being sent to Paris or Berlin.

The 1870 annual general meeting of Reuters was told very little about this important contract: only that arrangements had been made 'to avoid expensive competition'. The directors considered it 'unadvisable in the interests of all parties to enter more fully into details'

A fourteen-point informal statement in French of 'Rules for Common Action' supplemented the formal contract. The three parties agreed to keep secret the very existence of the ring. They recognized, however, that there might be need sometimes to reveal to governments how their activities were linked. Governments were to be asked to give the three agencies priority in telegraphing their news—a priority which, as noticed, the Wolff Bureau already enjoyed, but which was presumably not admitted to its allies. An enlarged news service was to be provided at times of crisis. Agents were to be discouraged from merely copying news from newspapers. The market for commercial information was to be urgently studied.

In the case of the Reuter–Havas relationship collaboration had already gone further. On 4 November 1869 the two agencies had agreed to introduce 'joint-purse' working from January 1870. This meant that the total profits of the two agencies were to be shared equally. Here was an important change, and yet Julius Reuter would have preferred an even closer connection. In the previous June he had signed a provisional agreement for a full merger; but difficulties over its acceptability in English law had prevented its implementation. Even so, the wide extent of Reuter's ambition was clear. During 1869 he had sought both to merge with Havas and to buy out Wolff.

The disruption caused by the Franco-Prussian War shook the position of Havas, and Reuter persuaded his board to try again to capture the French agency. In July 1872 he offered on behalf of the company to buy the entire Havas business for 3 million francs (£90,000), on condition that Havas agreed to accept shares for any purchase money not subscribed by Reuter shareholders or by the public. The offer was rejected. Further negotiations none the less followed, conducted at Paris by Engländer. The offer was raised to £120,000, or shares at par. Havas showed interest, but opposition was aroused in France. Engländer told Griffiths on 8 April 1873 that the Reuter bid had been reduced to an offer to buy the Havas foreign telegraph business, and 'not to acquire the French portion of their agency on account of the hostile attitude of the French papers'.

These further negotiations also failed, and the Reuter board finally decided to seek no more than a continuation of the joint-purse arrangement. But friction over finance and over joint operations in South America was already beginning to sour the relationship. In 1876 joint-purse working with Havas was ended by mutual consent.

Until the turn of the century the American news agencies were not treated as equals by Reuters, Havas, and Wolff. In 1870 AP of New York had contracted for a reciprocal news service between Europe and America, with payment of an annual differential of £2,400 by AP. The assumption was that

Europe's news was of more interest to America than vice versa. When this agreement was renewed in 1875, AP agreed with Reuters 'to undertake the Company's Agency at New York for political and commercial news free of commission'. Reuter's agent was immediately withdrawn from New York.

Protection of copyright in Reuter telegrams soon became necessary to prevent unscrupulous editors taking news without payment. In August 1870 Reuter telegrams were formally registered for copyright at Stationers' Hall, London. But protection remained uncertain, and on 6 February 1890 *Reuter's Journal* was started. This daily publication printed a selection of telegrams in the form of a news sheet, which was formally offered for sale at Old Jewry, price 6*d*. *Reuter's Journal* continued publication until 1979.

Although Julius Reuter had failed to take over his French and German competitors, he did succeed in making his editorial office in London the clearing-house for most news originating from outside Europe. He was greatly helped in this by British domination of the world cable network. By 1880 nine cable routes were crossing the Atlantic, and by the 1890s the world was substantially united via overland telegraphs and undersea cables, although the Pacific Ocean was not crossed until the new century. About 60 per cent of all cables were British-owned, and before 1914 an 'all-red route' round the globe, based entirely upon British territory, had been deliberately created for purposes of imperial defence.[10]

The Havas agency in Paris had been the pioneer, but the fact that Reuters was based in London meant that it controlled the supply of much news even for France itself. A report on the French press compiled in 1906 by the British embassy in Paris noted that 'the greater portion of news from the outside world comes to Paris from London through Reuter'. The report added, interestingly, that during both the Boer War (1899–1902) and the Russo-Japanese War (1905–6) the Paris papers, suspicious of British bias against the Boers or in favour of the Japanese, had published Havas telegrams with the attached warning, 'De source Anglaise'. In other words, the French papers were well aware that, under the terms of the news agency ring agreement, much apparently 'Havas' world news was really Reuter news (Fig. 6).[11]

Havas did have its own extra-European territories, including the French Empire; but these were of much less news interest to the world's press than Reuter territories such as India, the Far East, and South Africa. Moreover, Havas and Wolff were known to be Government-subsidized, and this was damaging, as even a German newspaper obituary of Julius Reuter admitted in 1899. 'Not only do they not have such widespread connection as Reuter, but they are not as independent of the Governments of their countries.' Reuters, the German obituary continued, 'has always attached great importance to the

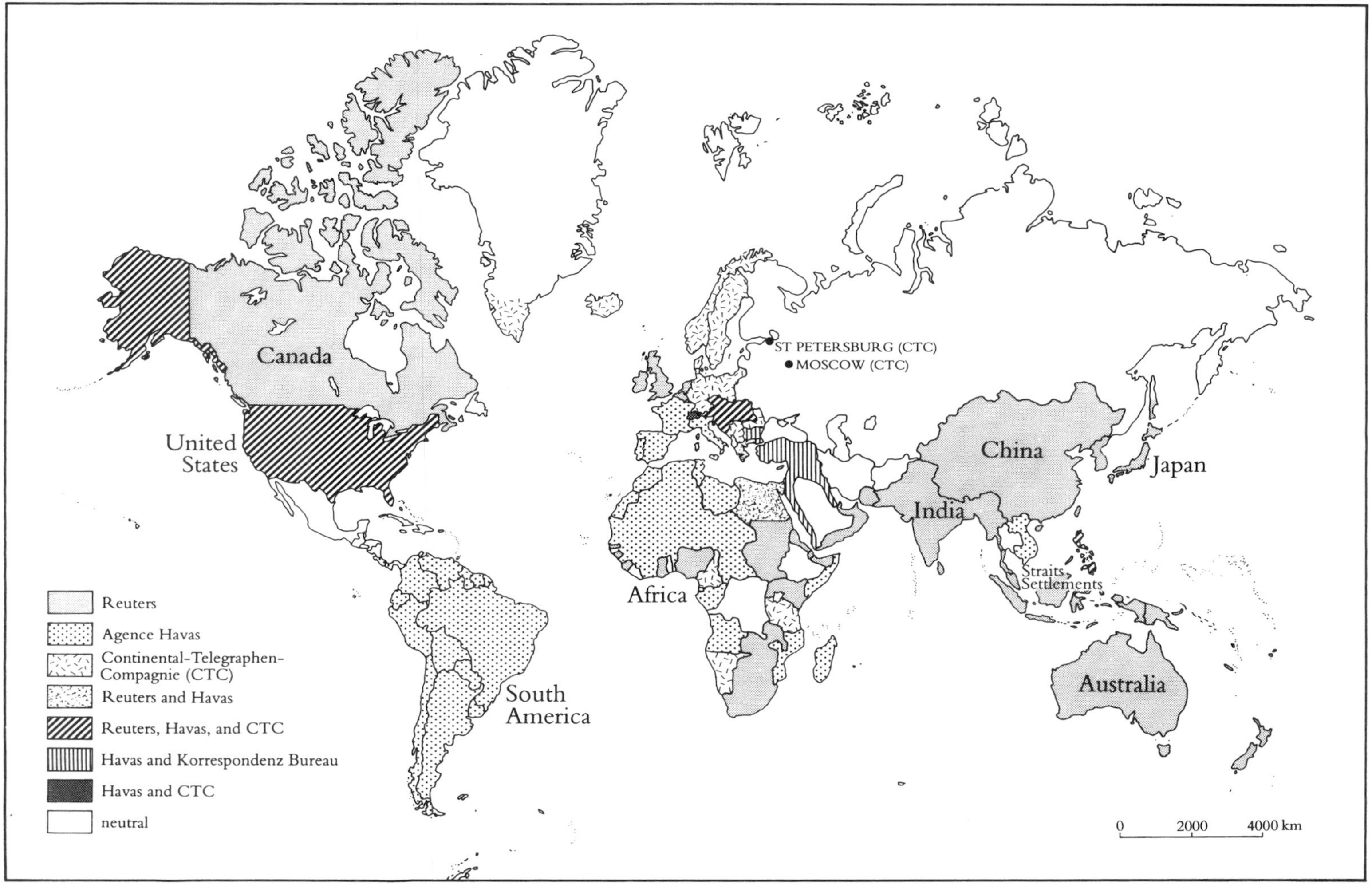

Fig. 6. Territories of international agencies, 1909

Reuters

Agence Havas

Continental-Telegraphen-
Compagnie (CTC)

Reuters and Havas

Reuters, Havas, and CTC

Havas and Korrespondenz Bureau

Havas and CTC

neutral

Canada

United
States

South
America

Africa

India

China

Japan

Australia

Straits
Settlements

ST PETERSBURG (CTC)
MOSCOW (CTC)

0   2000   4000 km

reliability of its news . . . The Bureau has remained faithful to this principle in recent years, when relations between Germany and England, unfortunately, have not always been very satisfactory.' Here was a compliment from a source which might have been reluctant to make comparisons unfavourable to Wolff. But the reality could not be ignored: news from Reuters was more widely circulated and more widely trusted than news from any other news agency.[12]

4

The European manœuvres of Julius Reuter during the 1860s and early 70s had been accompanied by a steady effort to bring the whole British Empire into the Reuter network. This was part of Julius Reuter's worldwide grand design, and it was the part which functioned best. It made Reuters into an imperial institution, and one which was always at work. 'The sun rose as surely everywhere to the click of the electric needle as it did to the tap of the British drum.' So rightly exclaimed one obituary of Reuter in 1899.[13]

The main British possessions in Asia and Africa were linked by cable to London during the 1860s and 70s. The first line between India and Europe opened in January 1865, routed via Turkey. It proved to be unsatisfactory in operation. Julius Reuter complained in a letter to *The Times* on 24 December 1866 that messages took eight to fourteen days to and from India, and that they were often unintelligible on receipt because the telegraph clerks *en route* did not understand English. Charges were very high—£5 for 20 words; and Reuters could not afford to send more than 60 words each day from London, coded for confidentiality.

Two other cables to India were to prove more satisfactory; one overland across Russia (January 1870), the other undersea via Alexandria and Aden (June 1870). Hong Kong was reached from India in 1871, Shanghai and Tokyo by 1873. Australia was linked with India via Ceylon in 1872.

The prestige of Reuters—and also its profitability—came to depend considerably upon its managers and correspondents at work within the white governing and trading communities of the British Empire. By 1871 that empire included some 235 million people, spread over five continents. During the rest of the century it expanded further until about a quarter of the globe was under British rule. Reuters was to report with increasing fullness the many colonial wars and confrontations which accompanied such rapid growth.

Reuter's 1859 agreement with Havas and Wolff had not credited him with any areas of exclusive interest outside Europe. Nevertheless, his telegrams for the year show that he already possessed agents at the Cape, in India, and in the Far East. James McLean, later to be agent in New York, was appointed in 1859 to visit Ceylon 'and divers other places in the East, for the purpose of conducting or managing the telegraphic business'. By the time of Reuter's agreement with AP in 1861, he was claiming agents at the principal ports of India, China, Japan, Australia, and New Zealand, and at the intermediate ports of Point de Galle (Ceylon), Alexandria, and Malta.

Alexandria was a port of call *en route* to India, and also an important marketing centre for Egyptian cotton. The Suez Canal was not completed until 1869, but Suez had already achieved importance as the temporary end-point of the telegraph line from Europe. Egypt was thus a focal point for trade and transport. Not surprisingly, therefore, towards the close of 1865 Reuters opened an office at Alexandria, its first office outside Europe. Edward Virnard was sent out as agent. He seems to have been an experienced journalist specially recruited, whose career with Reuters began well but ended in acrimony. He established the main office at Alexandria, and then added a branch in Cairo. News about Egyptian cotton prices and supplies was in demand both in England and India. And incoming Reuter news was wanted in Egypt, although the local press was weak and could not pay much for it. As well as supplying the press, Reuters therefore published its news directly in the form of bulletins in English and French, delivered by hand. These bulletins were to remain a feature of the Egyptian scene far into the twentieth century (Plate 17). Virnard was dismissed in 1870, when he was sued by Reuters for a £630 deficiency in his accounts. He counter-claimed for wrongful dismissal and libel. Both suits were eventually successful, with the lawyers the only clear winners.

The next man sent east was Henry Collins, aged only 22. He sailed in February 1866 for Bombay 'where the Directors have reason to believe there is a large field for the profitable extension of the system so successfully inaugurated by Mr Reuter'. Bombay at that time possessed no proper European hotel, and Collins set up in a tent on the esplanade until the monsoon. He was assisted by a Parsee clerk and a messenger. One of his first acts was to push circulars about the twice-daily Reuter commercial service through the letter-boxes of Bombay offices. A commercial service started by the newspapers in the previous year was squeezed out, for Reuters was soon found to be indispensable by bank managers, heads of mercantile houses, and cotton traders. Reuter telegrams, wrote Collins in his recollections, 'became the standard on which the local prices of the day were fixed'.

Bombay's cotton season was in full swing when Collins began operations. Buying and selling took place in the open air on the Cotton Green, where bales could be inspected before bargains were closed. Business started at 7 a.m., and Reuter staff had to be there to hand over the latest prices to subscribers, taking care to prevent earlier leakage of incoming news. At one point Collins began to suspect that a leak was none the less occurring. He found that when the cotton prices arrived by telegraph, a Goan clerk would go to the office window. If prices had gone up, he spat to the right; if down, to the left. A watching 'native of the coolie class' would then hurry away with the news.[14]

For nearly a century India was destined to play a central and highly prof- itable part in the Reuter empire within the British Empire. Reuters came to dominate the supply of news not only to and from India but also within the country, to both the English-language and vernacular press. 'In India and Ceylon', noted the annual report for 1868, 'the service is now the counter- part of that in London.' Full-time offices had been opened at Bombay, Calcutta, Karachi, Madras, Colombo, and Point de Galle.

Good relations were soon established with the Government of India at Calcutta. In July 1866 the Viceroy's office agreed to take a 'daily message' from Reuters for R400 (£40) a month. Collins remembered with pride the day in the next year when he was received by the Viceroy himself, Lord Lawrence. This may well have been the first semi-official meeting—the first of many—between an overseas representative of Reuters and a ruler of the British Empire. By an agreement in May 1867 the Reuter agent at Karachi was commissioned to deliver to the Indian Government the telegrams already being supplied to the Indian press. The subscription was fixed at R600.[15]

Point de Galle, at the southern tip of Ceylon, was the end of the cable con- nection with London; and so it was where the mail steamers to and from Australia and the Far East collected and delivered news. Reuter messages were carried by sea to and from Malaya, China, Japan, and Australia. As the cables extended eastwards, Collins went out to open offices and to check agents *en route*, reaching by February 1872 as far as Yokohama in Japan, where Reuters had been represented since 1861. In the previous year Collins had made Shanghai the Reuter headquarters for the Far East.[16]

The Eastern Extension Company began carrying telegrams from Shanghai and Hong Kong via Singapore in June 1871. Initial charges were high. Even dearer was the Great Northern route via Shanghai, using the Russian line across Siberia. This became operational from Hong Kong at the start of 1872. Readers in Britain and Europe began to expect news from China and Japan to reach them in days rather than weeks. Conversely, expatriate readers of English-language papers grew to require similarly up-to-date news from London. Line breakdowns were a recurring early problem, but the news- papers expected these to be circumvented, as the *North China Daily News* at

Shanghai made clear in a complaint on 5 January 1874: 'If Reuters wish to lose all subscribers to their telegrams in Shanghai, they are taking the right way to secure their object. We have not had a word of news for a week. The closure of the Southern route is no reason why news should not be sent by the Northern.'

Collins left India in 1872. After an interlude as Julius Reuter's personal representative in Persia, he went in 1878 to Melbourne as the first general manager for Australia and New Zealand. Despite his efforts, the position of Reuters in Australia was never to match that in India. Most profit was to come from supplying market prices and from running private telegram and remittance services. The Australian newspaper proprietors, tough with each other, were never going to be comfortable customers for news from Reuters.

A cable and telegraph link through Darwin and across Australia to the south was working by October 1872, although often broken. The *Melbourne Argus* and the *Sydney Morning Herald*, the main Australian dailies, had reluctantly agreed to take Reuter news. They paid £4,000 annually, plus telegraph charges. They feared, probably rightly, that Reuters aspired to gain the same dominance over the press in Australia as in India. Lachlan MacKinnon, part-owner of the *Argus*, had initially hoped to draw the press of India and China into an anti-Reuter alliance which would telegraph its own news from London. This attempt failed. MacKinnon also wanted to form an Australian Press Association. 'Without a strong association', he had told the manager of the *Argus* in a letter from Scotland (19 May 1870), 'we shall all of us be in Reutters [*sic*] power.' In the end, MacKinnon wrote (16 June 1871) that he was sufficiently satisfied by the terms agreed with 'the sneaking little Jew'. 'I do not believe that a year ago any reasonable amount of money would have induced Reutter to make the concession he has now made.'[17]

For commercial reasons, Reuters had proved willing to be remarkably self-effacing in Australia. The fresh service was to be known as the Australian Associated Press service, not as a service from Reuters. It was to be handled by Australian editors in London, who were to make their own selection of news for transmission. There was good financial reason for this, quite apart from the Australian desire for independence. The cable rate was 10s. per word, and until charges were reduced the daily file rarely exceeded 50 words, so every word transmitted had to be what Australian readers wanted.

By 1873 John Fairfax of the *Sydney Morning Herald* was grumbling about 'Reuter and all that tremendous expense'. He considered breaking the contract. Instead, it was renegotiated. In 1874 the subscription of £4,000 was maintained for a further year, but was cut to £3,000 for the next year, and to £2,000 for subsequent years. From November 1877 the news service from

Reuters was put on offer to the whole Australian and New Zealand press. The New Zealand Press Association (NZPA), formed in 1878, followed the Australian lead and placed its own editor at Old Jewry. Relations with the New Zealanders were easier than with the Australians. Crises over Australian subscriptions to Reuters recurred at intervals. In 1890 the Australian papers set up their own cable service from London, deliberately reducing their dependence upon Reuters.[18]

In economic terms, South America was part of the informal British Empire in the nineteenth century, and Reuters might have expected to do well there. After the laying of a cable across the South Atlantic in 1874, Reuters and Havas established joint offices in Brazil, Argentina, and Uruguay. Preliminary expenses for the year were as much as £4,250, half paid by each agency. Despite this purposeful start, Reuters never became comfortable in South America. The Spanish- and Portuguese-language newspapers showed more interest in news from Havas, a Latin agency, than in Reuter news. From 1890, South America was left to Havas.[19]

5

To what extent did the close involvement of Reuters with the life of the British Empire bring the agency under the influence, or even the control, of the British Government? Reuters always claimed to be independent of official direction, unlike Havas or Wolff, which became known for receiving covert subsidies from their respective Governments. The Reuter board expressed dismay on 14 December 1870 when Havas—its partner in the joint-purse arrangement—was accused of having accepted subsidies from the former Government of Napoleon III and from the Turkish Government. Havas denied 'emphatically' that it had received a subsidy from Napoleon III, and explained away the Turkish 'payment' as a normal business arrangement.

For Reuters, as for Havas, a test question became 'When is an official payment simply a subscription, and when is it a subsidy?' A subscription at the going rate for an existing service may be acceptable from a Government as from a private firm. On the other hand, an official hand-out accepted as a direct subsidy, or an over-generous subscription taken as an indirect subsidy, necessarily implied some degree of dependence by the agency and of influence by the Government. How many Reuter news services survived only because of direct or indirect official subsidy? How many had been started only because of official inspiration and subsidy? Was the existence of every service

public knowledge? Down the years, despite its protestations of independence, Reuters was to find itself unable always to answer such questions
frankly.

The example of the relationship of Reuters with the Government of India
illustrated how the word 'subsidy' could creep into contracts. This may have
reflected a sense on the Government side that it was not merely buying news
services, but was supporting an essential imperial institution. The 1867
telegram agreement had spoken simply of 'Government subscriptions'; but its
renewal in 1873 saw the introduction of the word 'subsidy'. And when in
1876 Reuters asked the Viceroy for an increase, the letter itself used the word
'subsidy'. Three years later the board minutes of 18 June 1879 noted with satisfaction that 'the subsidy granted to the Company' had been doubled. Did
this progression mean that the Government of India, as it grew to appreciate
the important part played by Reuters, wanted to imply an expectation of
influence over the news services?

Certainly, in later years Reuters began to realize the risk to its good name
of being known to accept payments called 'subsidies' from the British or other
Governments. By the end of the century printed agreement forms were in use
for supplying news from Reuters to officials in the smaller British colonies: the
word 'subsidy' did not appear. 'The frequency and extent of the service', ran
one 1897 Sierra Leone agreement, 'shall depend on the amount of the joint
contributions of the West African Colonies.'

Reuters was unlikely to have been influenced by the small annual 'contribution' of £75 from the Crown Agents in London on behalf of Sierra Leone.
But what about the position in Egypt? Looking back from 1923, Gerald C.
Delany, the local manager, admitted that the whole Reuter operation there
had long depended upon the 'subscription' from the Egyptian Government.
Down the years this had varied between £1,000 and £2,000. The Egyptian
press was too weak to sustain a Reuter presence by newspaper subscriptions
alone. The Government payments had been made since at least 1868, and
probably since Reuters set up three years earlier. 'We took up the role of a
news agency in this country', noted Delany, 'on condition that the
Government would support us in various ways, principally as a subscriber to
our telegrams, and the existence of our organisation in this country depends
upon the continuance of that support.' The Egyptian Government had sometimes reduced the subscription for reasons of economy; but up to 1923, said
Delany, it had never tried to exercise any influence over Reuter news or business because of its payment.[20]

How much then did dependence upon official payments affect the reputation of Reuters for independence? Foreigners simply assumed that Reuters was

a semi-official body, and felt little need to prove the truth of their assumption. In Britain, the perception was more confused. Reuters was regarded as a national and imperial institution, a status which implied obligations towards the British Government; and yet in regularly proclaiming its independence, Reuters was not thought to be disingenuous. This may have been because its independence was treated by Reuters itself as reconcilable with patriotism. Its loyalty was most clearly demonstrated in its coverage of wars, large or small, in which Britain was involved. Reuters reported defeats as readily as victories; but the British cause was always assumed to be 'right', and British troops to be 'ours'.

Its underlying patriotism meant that Reuters could normally expect to benefit from official goodwill. In return, representations from the British Government were usually received sympathetically by Reuters, so long as they did not seem to challenge its independence by sounding like instructions. But how sympathetic was the agency towards the wishes of foreign governments? The limits in this regard were tested during the Franco-Prussian War, when Julius Reuter had a succession of contacts with Bismarck, the German Chancellor. Bismarck understood the importance of news management, and he showed himself ready to manipulate Reuters if allowed.

On 2 October 1870 he sent a news message in German direct to Julius Reuter in London, which was immediately published by Reuters in English translation: 'The report of the conversation between King William and the Emperor Napoleon, given by Dr. Russell, *The Times* correspondent, is founded throughout upon mere invention.' Reuters had not itself reported this conversation; nor did *The Times* publish Bismarck's repudiation. But it was shown to Russell in Paris. He immediately sought an interview with Bismarck, who denied sending the message to Reuters, yet refused to say so publicly. Russell always believed that Bismarck had been upset because the King of Prussia had told his Crown Prince (Russell's unattributed source) more about the conversation than he had told Bismarck. A smoother alternative explanation—eventually accepted by *The Times* itself—was that the message to Reuters had been sent by a member of Bismarck's staff, who had blunderingly turned an intended correction of some of the content of Russell's report into a denial of the whole.

Whatever the truth, Julius Reuter found himself under private attack both from Russell and from Mowbray Morris, manager of *The Times*. The latter asked, with justice, why having published Bismarck's message without hesitation, Reuters had not published a telegram of self-defence from Russell. 'My statement', declared Russell firmly, 'was not founded on pure invention.' The right course for the agency would have been to publish both sides. Had Julius Reuter been too concerned not to offend Bismarck?[21]

Early in 1871 Reuter proposed to Bismarck that official German war telegrams should be sent direct to London from the German headquarters at Versailles. The agency was already supplying Bismarck with a service of incoming war telegrams. Julius Reuter offered to distribute official German telegrams not only to Britain, but also to America, India, Australia, Holland, Belgium, Spain, and Portugal. In return 'for your assistance', he offered to supply German headquarters with all telegrams reaching Reuters out of unoccupied France. Bismarck immediately accepted this proposal. Julius Reuter explained to Bismarck on 11 January that his editors took 'great care' not to use French or Belgian telegrams 'which obviously distort facts'. By way of example, he sent a copy of a telegram from Marseilles which had been suppressed. This telegram, dated 6 January, reported that a letter had been sent by Germans long resident in Marseilles protesting to the King of Prussia against 'the cruel and barbarous war being waged on the French nation'.

Was Julius Reuter undermining the agency's independence in news handling by making such a deal with Bismarck? Not necessarily. The Marseilles telegram had already been suppressed even before the arrangement with Bismarck was concluded. Reuters regarded the telegram as a piece of French propaganda, undeserving of publication. Of course, in drawing Bismarck's attention to this instance of suppression, Julius Reuter was leaving the Germans free to draw the conclusion that he was inclined to favour them. And some others have drawn the same conclusion by mistranslating the word 'Orientierung' in the German of Reuter's letter of 11 January, as meaning not 'for your assistance', but 'for authorization'. Reuter cannot have been proposing to delay publication of all telegrams out of unoccupied France while the Germans censored them at Versailles; he was simply offering to deliver them for information after normal editing in London.

The possibility of foreign censorship or bias colouring the news supplied to Reuters from other agencies in the ring was noticed at intervals. Henry Labouchere, a Member of Parliament and a journalist, complained about this in 1892 to Moberly Bell of *The Times*: 'Reuter "exchanges" with Havas and Wolff, both of which receive subsidies from their respective Governments.'[22]

6

In 1871 Queen Victoria's brother-in-law, Duke Ernst II of Saxe-Coburg-Gotha, had made Julius Reuter a baron, with the title of Baron de Reuter. This, as a short paragraph in *The Times* of 17 October reported, was in recognition of Reuter's services 'to the public in furnishing the Press with telegraphic intelligence'. Such recognition was entirely fitting; but it was perhaps rather surprising, considering that Reuter had separated himself from his German origins and had become a British subject. There may have been an anti-Bismarckian dimension to the gesture by the Duke, who was opposed to Prussian hegemony within Germany. But Reuter may also have been offered the title because the Duke was short of money. It may have cost much more than the 10,000 florins (about £800) required to purchase the necessary landed qualification in Coburg. Appropriately, Reuter chose as his motto the words 'per mare per terras' ('by land and sea'). His arms showed a terrestrial globe between four flashes of lightning.[23]

Reuter had achieved a unique position. He might have now settled for a quieter life. But he was not yet ready for retirement. On the contrary, he next ventured upon a project which, if it had succeeded, would have matched his achievement in creating a world news agency. In July 1872 he secured a seventy-year concession from the Shah of Persia to take over and develop almost the whole economy of the country. Contemporaries were amazed. The scale of the venture was a further demonstration of Reuter's self-confidence. He still regarded himself as an entrepreneur in general, even though he had become a journalist in particular.

Reuter was required to build a railway in Persia, to lay down tramways, to construct roads, bridges, and telegraphs; to work all mines except those for gold and silver; to undertake irrigation works; to establish a national bank; and to manage the customs. He was authorized to raise £6 million on the London market, with the Persian Government guaranteeing 5 per cent interest. As an earnest of good faith, Reuter was required to deposit £40,000 as caution money with the Bank of England.

He told the British Foreign Secretary, Lord Granville (12 September 1872), that he had undertaken 'this gigantic work' in order to improve the social condition of the Persian people, and to open up the material resources of the country for the benefit of the world and especially of Britain. 'I desire to serve my adopted Country by introducing my enterprise under English auspices.' Reuter assured Granville that he did not require financial subsidy or material support; but he did ask for diplomatic assistance if necessary.[24]

The project was probably doomed from the start. There was voluble opposition from Persian religious leaders. The Russian Government was strongly hostile, while the British and Indian Governments remained cool. The story of Reuter's long struggle—first to succeed, and then to secure compensation when he was prevented from succeeding—is not part of the history of Reuters. Suffice it to say that it took many years of intermittent negotiation by Reuter, sometimes guardedly helped by successive British Governments, before a settlement was reached. In 1889 he was given permission to establish a national bank, the Imperial Bank of Persia, in place of his original concession. Julius himself never visited Persia, sending out Henry Collins as his representative and later his second son, George.

This deep Persian involvement drew Reuter's attention away from the news agency. The stress may also have undermined his health, which seems to have been good up to this period. The staff at Old Jewry now saw less of him, although Dickinson, who did not join until 1874, recalled the parties given at Reuter's home. He now lived in a mansion at 18 Kensington Palace Gardens, a fashionable London address, 'millionaires row'. Musical events were a regular feature there, at which leading singers such as Adelina Patti performed. The celebration of the Reuters' golden wedding in 1895, reported *The Queen* (30 November), began with a concert by singers from Covent Garden. 'Following the music and a supper, began the real fun of the evening—a dance to the exquisite waltzes of the Blue Hungarians.' There were also less formal, innocently boisterous parties, much enjoyed by the unstuffy Baron. 'No more comical scene abides in the memory', recollected Dickinson, 'than the spectacle of this Brother Cheryble leading a game of follow-my-leader up and down the stairs and through the spacious rooms of the great house.'[25]

In May 1878 Reuter retired as managing director 'in consequence of failing health'. He was 61. He remained a member of the board, and regularly attended meetings into the 1890s. He died at his house in Nice—the Villa Reuter, 97 Promenade des Anglais—on 25 February 1899, aged 82. He left estate with a gross value of £262,603 (£117,653 net). Julius Reuter therefore died a rich man, although by no means a millionaire at contemporary valuation. In 1902 his career was sketched approvingly in a collection of essays on *Fortunes Made in Business, Life Struggles of Successful People*.

He had deserved his success and his fortune. Although Charles Havas was the originator of news agencies, Reuter was the man who had revealed their full potential. His telegrams had set a recognized standard of trustworthiness. At the same time, he had eagerly 'followed the cable'. As a result, his news agency—soon known simply as 'Reuters'—had begun to deliver yesterday's news of the world to the world, as never before.

Julius Reuter had taken the first step in a progression which was to lead in the late twentieth century to instant news and almost instant public reaction—telegraphs, telephone, radio, satellites; still pictures as well as text; newsfilm; and, finally, television. Arguably, the first stage—the making of news quickly available by overland telegraph and undersea cable—was the most important stage of all, in the sense that whereas the first stage brought about a transformation, everything afterwards, however impressive, has been simply a refinement.

Telegraphy first made possible a daily interaction at a distance, between people and between peoples. Individuals could now send private telegrams to each other: the same people in their millions could read news telegrams in the press. This repeated interplay, public and private, constituted a tremendous new force within society, first released in the mid-nineteenth century.

Railways and telegraphs were closely related in their early stages, not least in terms of their impact. Telegraphs transformed mental communication, while railways transformed physical communication; and in both instances the Victorian first stage was the crucial one. Interestingly, Richard Cobden, the British politician, made this point in 1862 with regard to the impact of railway travel. He had just come by train from London to Edinburgh in ten-and-a-half hours.

> The last time I made this journey without stopping was in 1825, when I rode to London in two days and two nights, which was then considered a marvellously rapid journey . . . *Now* I make the same journey in about a quarter of the time . . . travelling in an armchair in a little carpeted drawing room . . . Our successors can have no such gain on our present travelling even if they are shot like a cannon ball through a pneumatic tube.[26]

Ten years later, a gentle caricature of Reuter appeared in *Vanity Fair*'s 'Men of the Day' series (14 December 1872). The drawing carried the simple but meaningful caption 'Telegrams' (Plate 10). Reuter's air of calm alertness, looking through his spectacles with bird-like eyes, befitted a man in daily pursuit of the news. The accompanying article described his special position: 'he who has the command of telegrams has the command of public opinion on foreign affairs. It is from these pithy despatches that we get all our notions of what is going on abroad.'

The article pondered the wisdom of allowing one man so much influence, but its assessment was reassuring: 'he has never yet been suspected of a conscious purpose to use them for the interests of a particular individual or country'. The article therefore wound up favourably:

> In London he is respected as becomes a man of his power and great wealth, possessing a fine house and wife and always ready to show a magnificent hospitality. Thus moved, Society has used him graciously, and he in return appears to feel a considerable affection for the country whose notions of foreign affairs he holds in his hand.

7

By the time of Julius Reuter's retirement in 1878 his news agency was an established institution within the British Empire (Fig. 7). It was to remain so until the middle of the twentieth century. G. B. Dibblee's short popular book on *The Newspaper*, published in 1913, assumed that its readers would not need telling about Reuters. 'Reuter is so much a household word that an explanation of the function of Reuter's Telegram Company is quite unnecessary.'

Reuters was well known; but its managing director during these years, Baron Herbert de Reuter (1852–1915), was never a public figure like his father. Baron Herbert was educated at Harrow and Balliol College, Oxford, and was thoroughly 'English' in his view of the world. In appearance (Plate 1) his Jewish background was not evident, for his complexion was fresh and his eyes blue; but his accent was guttural. He had dressed in his early days in an artistic manner, befitting a young man whose ambition was to become not a news agency chief, but a professional musician. Despite this, he was appointed 'Assistant manager without salary' in November 1875; and he seems to have been working at Old Jewry for nearly a year before that. At first, he had not given his mind to Reuters. Then one day, as Dickinson recalled, a sudden change occurred. Baron Herbert had fallen deeply in love, and wanted to get married. 'The mop of fair curling hair which he had hitherto worn disappeared, and from that moment he set himself to steady work.'[27]

Baron Herbert soon acquired a thorough knowledge of the workings of Reuters. Although less shrewd than his father as a businessman, he came to understand and oversee the editorial side with a steady affection. He succeeded his father as managing director in May 1878 at the age of 26 and retained the post until his death thirty-seven years later. Although at first the board tacitly placed him under the guidance of Griffiths, the company secretary, Baron Herbert was immediately granted the same 'sole and entire management' as his father. His salary was increasingly generous—£1,000 a year plus commission in 1878, £4,000 plus commission by 1912.

Baron Herbert's commitment was total. Nothing of importance transpired within Reuters at home or overseas without his knowledge. He himself never travelled outside Europe, but wide reading provided him with an encyclopaedic knowledge of countries, languages, and topics. He was particularly interested in mathematics and music, and liked to spend much time solving problems or reading musical scores. He read so much because he slept so little. He suffered from eczema, and could not bear to spend more than a few hours each night in the warmth of a bed. Every morning he sought vigorous exercise on foot or on bicycle, while he pondered the reading of the night before. Unlike his father, he did not entertain at home. Nor did he go into society, not even to concerts, despite his love of music. He was, concluded Dickinson, who had known him since their preparatory schooldays together, a 'sociable recluse'.

As head of Reuters, Baron Herbert kept in personal touch with all his senior staff. He gave luncheon at the City Liberal Club to managers or correspondents going overseas: he gave them lunch again on their return. In this way they were courteously briefed and debriefed. He wrote regularly and fully to his overseas general managers, calling them his 'proconsuls'. Quick with praise, he could be a firm disciplinarian when necessary. In general, he maintained the extended family atmosphere within Reuters which his father had created.

The Old Jewry offices remained the headquarters of Reuters throughout Baron Herbert's time. At intervals, new technology was introduced into the old rooms. The telephone seems to have been installed in 1881, and typewriters came into limited use about the same date. Electric lighting replaced gas in 1890. From 1891 a direct telephone line was connected to Paris, the receiver placed in a special room because messages could be heard only faintly.

In 1919, as part of a history of the agency never published, Charles Marriott of the editorial staff described 'A Day at Reuters'. During the First World War the routine had become much more hectic than in the early days, but the work remained essentially the same. There was now very much more news coming in, without any periods of quiet such as had once allowed young Williams to fall asleep or editorial staff to play chess on duty. All the hours of day and night were covered by four shifts of editors and sub-editors, with supporting tube operators, manifolders, and messengers. Editorial duty rotated so that each man undertook an equal share of day, evening, night, and early-morning duty; but the editors-in-charge for each period were more or less permanent:

> The first impression through the door of the Main Editorial Room is that of machinery; the most prominent objects being the brass tubes through which, by motor suction, telegrams and letters are passed all over the building, and the tape machines. Turn to the right and you are in a low-ceilinged room with a lurching floor divided into three alleyways by two rows of double desks. At right angles to them, under a window, is the more roomy desk of the Editor-in-Charge; its position aptly indicating his only slight detachment from the rest of the staff.

In 1914 this editorial work at Old Jewry was shared between European, American, Asiatic, and Dominion rooms. Offices overseas sent news to

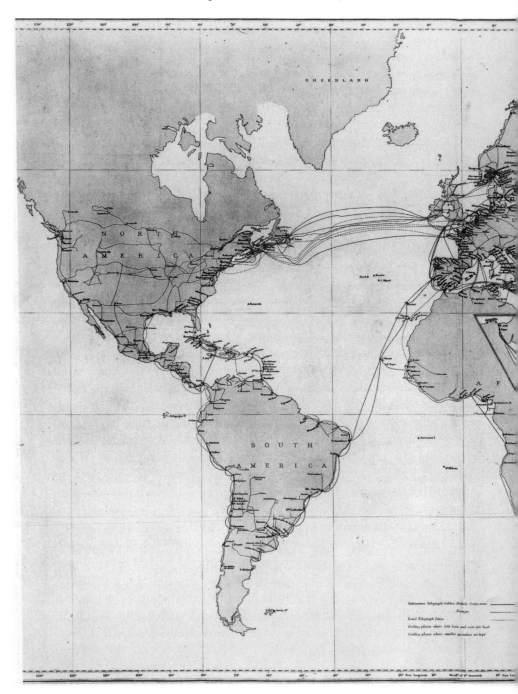

FIG. 7. Contemporary map showing the cable network in the 1880s

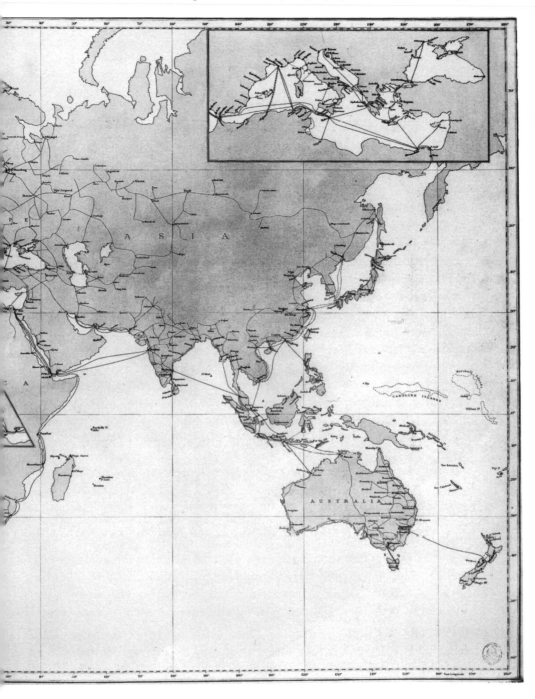

London, and received in return items of world news selected to suit local interests. 'For tens of thousands of scattered Englishmen and Englishwoman', explained Marriott, 'Reuters is the link with home and the only means of learning what is going on in the greater world.'

A chart of outward services, produced for internal information in May 1914 (Fig. 8), indicated the three main channels for circulating Reuter news beyond Europe, other than news to North America handled by AP and to South America handled by Havas:

1. London to Pressreut Bombay—9,000 words per month for India, with a 'small service' on to Rangoon and Bangkok;

2. a bulletin of 12,500 words per month, sent (i) through the Mediterranean to Cairo, Aden, Ceylon, Singapore, Hong Kong, and (ii) to Cape Town, Durban, Mombassa, Zanzibar, the Seychelles, and Mauritius;

3. a 500-words-per-month Pressreut service through Russia direct to Shanghai 'for Far Eastern Stations'.

This wordage, in tight cable-ese and sometimes coded, could be expanded into a much greater number of words in the newspapers.

Much depended upon the skill and willingness of staff in London and overseas. Staff were the basic Reuter resource, masters of the journalistic techniques and of the communications technology used in the collection and distribution of news. In 1914 Reuter staff in London numbered about 150, a comparatively small number for the running of an essential national and imperial institution. Trade unions were not allowed to recruit within Reuters, for union attitudes were regarded as incompatible with the desired family atmosphere. Marriott wrote of 'the invariable cheerfulness with which extra duty is undertaken in exceptional circumstances'. What he really meant was that management invariably assumed such cheerfulness to exist. London editorial staff could normally expect a day and a half off per week. A senior sub-editor was typically paid £400 a year, while an experienced reporter might reach £700. These were the minimum sums acceptable for demanding and responsible work by experienced journalists. But employees' income tax was paid by the company. And in 1881 a life-insurance scheme had been introduced for senior staff, with policies also paid by the company. In 1893 a superannuation scheme was started, with retirement fixed at 65. Senior staff contributed 2.5 per cent of salary, matched by an equal contribution from Reuters. By 1910 this superannuation scheme embraced 182 members, and was described as 'a strong attraction to capable men'. Total salary and wage costs were rising rapidly

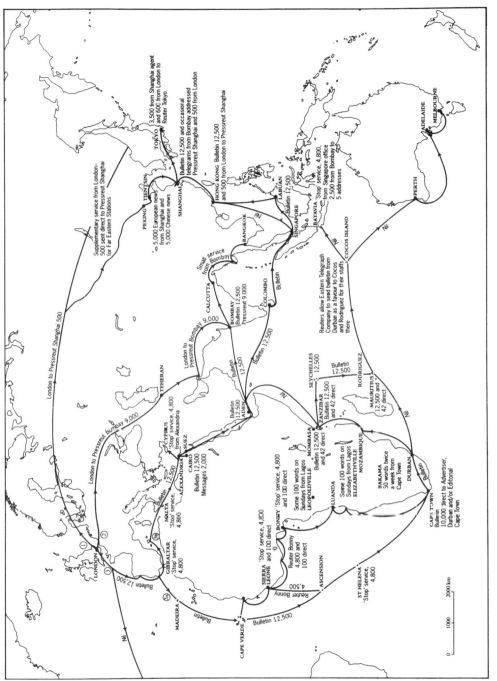

Redrawn from an original in the Reuter Archive

about the turn of the century—approximately £31,000 for 1895, £45,000 by 1902.[28]

The family atmosphere did not exclude recourse to redundancies at times of financial difficulty. A 10 per cent dividend was paid in 1881, but never again for 30 years. The norm now became 5 per cent, and in 1882, 1884, and 1888 the reserves had to be raided to pay even this. Shareholders were told that this tightness was caused by the high costs of war reporting. No dividend at all was paid for 1885, the year of the failure of the Gordon relief expedition to Khartoum.

8

The demand by more people for more news was bringing about a transformation of the British press during these years. In 1860 there had been fifteen morning and evening papers in London, and sixteen morning dailies in the provinces. By the end of the century about 150 papers, London and provincial, were being published. The cheapest were selling at only a halfpenny, thanks especially to a steady fall in newsprint prices. Alfred Harmsworth's new *Daily Mail* of 1896—'a penny newspaper for a halfpenny'—was the most notable product of the new popular journalism. From the start, the *Mail* subscribed to the Reuter general service. The standard printed contract with the *Mail* repeated in print the continuing commitment of Reuters to impartiality in news distribution, 'without preference or priority'.

Sales of the *Daily Mail* touched one million copies per day at the height of the Boer War excitement. The total number of British daily newspaper readers has been estimated to have doubled between 1896 and 1906 and to have doubled again by 1914.[29] And yet despite this great growth Reuters now found it hard to make money overall out of selling its news. The newspapers were reluctant to pay enough to cover the costs of the improved services which they none the less expected. Dickinson, the chief editor, wrote on 15 February 1908 that in the previous year his editorial department 'spent about six or seven hundred pounds more than we gained. The consequence is that economy in every direction is the order of the day.' Such cutbacks were repeated at intervals, but spending upon news collection and distribution still rose almost continuously: 1880, £61,137; 1890, £68,958; 1900 (at the height of the Boer War), £160,993; 1910, £145,192.

The year 1893 saw Reuters falling into the red for the first time, with a net loss of £2,766. Heavy spending upon war reporting and 'the fall in the Eastern Exchanges' were blamed. No dividend was paid for that year, or the next. By

the turn of the century the situation had improved, although the annual dividend was prudently kept at 5 per cent. In December 1904 Baron Herbert
drew the board's attention to the contrast with ten years earlier. Revenue had
almost doubled, from £104,000 to £203,000, while reserves had grown from
only £6,500 to £50,000. By 1912 reserves had trebled to £152,000, with revenue at £257,000. The dividend paid in that and the previous year was back
to 10 per cent. All seemed well. But within two years confidence was to be
severely shaken.

The international community was lurching towards the First World War;
and the chairman complained to the 1909 annual general meeting of 'the
incessant and growing demands of the news department . . . the day appears
to have passed by when it was possible to recoup in quiet times for heavy
expenditure during periods of political activity.' This reality was reflected in
expenditure upon news collection and distribution for the immediate pre-
war years: 1910, £145,192; 1911, £153,018; 1912, £162,158; 1913,
£160,953.

To cover these heavy news costs Baron Herbert had enthusiastically
encouraged a succession of subsidiary activities started over the years. None
was given the status of the news side; but all had been launched in the expectation that they would earn significant profits. Two did. But the last and most
ambitious venture, the bank scheme, was a chief cause of the internal crisis of
1914–15.

The two successful ventures were the transmission of private telegrams by
Reuters and the transmission of financial remittances. To distinguish these
from news transmission, they became known as 'traffic'. The private telegram
service had been started in Julius Reuter's time and prospered throughout his
son's regime. It had begun in 1871 between India and the United Kingdom,
upon the recommendation of Henry Collins, the general manager in India.
Private telegram traffic was subsequently extended to and from the Far East,
Australia, New Zealand, and South Africa. From 1881 the service was using
its own codes, which allowed large savings in wordage, so that Reuters was
able to place telegrams for firms and individuals much more cheaply than they
could do for themselves. The 'Eastern Private Telegram' service was the most
steadily successful, being much used by merchants and shipowners in India
and beyond. Nearly 4,000 Eastern telegrams were passing by 1875. The peak
year for usage was 1912, when 122,692 messages were sent eastwards from the
United Kingdom and 153,503 received in return.

For regular users, one word (it might be 'lion') could be chosen to cover a
whole long address, or even the two addresses of a regular sender and a regular recipient. By 1914 Reuters had as many as 3,000 of such registered clients.

Single words were employed for often-used phrases like 'market rising' or 'market falling'. Sometimes a fourteen-word message could be compressed into as little as three words, and then 'packed' with other messages into one Reuter telegram to or from some faraway and telegraphically expensive place. Large identical code-books became prominent features in Reuter offices throughout the world (Plate 29).[30]

The financial remittance business was started in 1891. As with private telegrams, remittance traffic became important between the United Kingdom and main cities of the British Empire in Asia and Africa. Reuters found that its codes and worldwide network could conduct financial transfers much more cheaply than the banks. People or firms in (say) London or Manchester or Sydney or Cape Town or Calcutta were able to pay sums of money through their local Reuter offices to relatives, friends, or firms in other parts of the world. The land boom in Australia during the early 1890s gave the service an initial boost there, for the local banks became unsafe, and the common instruction was to 'remit everything through Reuters'. £1.5 million passed through the Australian offices of Reuters during the boom. From South Africa, Indian sugar workers usually remitted their earnings home through Reuters.

The service made a profit from the start, reaching about £11,000 a year during the early years of the new century, two-thirds of this from Australian business. By the immediate pre-war years, profitability was falling, although still significant. For the period 1 March 1913 to 31 July 1914 gross revenue from private telegram and remittance business jointly totalled over £36,000 to and from Australia; £15,000 to and from India; and almost £8,500 to and from South Africa. Overall combined profit was £6,542. This was at a time when Reuters was running into serious loss overall.[31]

Unlike the news services, private telegram and remittance business drew the general public into Reuter offices. The two services were sold by clerks at the front counters. A 1910 photograph (Plate 18) showed the ground-floor windows of the Cape Town office carrying publicity for the two services: 'Remittances Forwarded By Cable & Mail To All Parts Of The World', 'Cables Despatched & Coded For The Public. Addresses Registered Etc.' In contrast, the workings of the news side were everywhere invisible to outsiders.

Another venture, started soon after the remittance business, was for the daily publication of the British parliamentary debates. Hansard, the long-standing publisher, had given up the work as unremunerative. Reuters quickly found the same; but not until after money had been spent upon reporters and printers. Only the debates for 1892 were published under the Reuter imprint.[32]

At this same period Reuters was also venturing deeply into an advertising service. Havas had long found advertising to be profitable, and the French example was an influence upon Reuters down the years. In the early 1860s the agency's contracts with newspapers often allowed part-payment of subscriptions through allocation of newspaper advertising space to Reuters. It then sought to sell this space. But there seems to have been difficulty in finding enough advertisers, and the practice was abandoned after the new company was formed in 1865.

A proposal from Engländer in 1876 that Reuters should undertake advertising had been rejected by the board on 22 March as tending to 'lower the Telegraphic Service in the eyes of the press'. Engländer had to wait for another fourteen years. The late nineteenth-century expansion of trade and industry was increasing the need for publicity through press advertising. The chairman of Reuters remarked at a special general meeting on 6 December 1890 that the idea of venturing into advertising had 'long been entertained' by Baron Herbert: 'this Company has exceptional means of establishing an International Advertising business on a large scale . . . we, in fact, seek to create a new business for the newspapers as well as for ourselves.'

The first idea in 1890 had been to operate through a subsidiary company formed with Havas; but the board soon decided that only direct involvement by Reuters would attract sufficient capital. So an arrangement was made to work with a firm of commission and general agents—Gower, Dodson, and Company. Profits were to be shared equally. An advertisement department was opened at 25 Old Jewry. This separate (though next-door) address was chosen in order to underline that advertisers must not expect to influence the content of the news services.

The advertising venture never looked like prospering on the large scale anticipated. Trade depression was blamed; but the management was reckless. Business was undertaken far beyond the placing of advertisements in newspapers. Much attention was given to selling advertising space inside and outside tramcars in provincial towns. Prospectuses were printed for companies which failed to start, or to pay their bills to Reuters. The advertising department believed that it had secured the European monopoly for the circulation of the guidebook to the 1893 Chicago Exposition. Advertisers sued when they found that no such monopoly existed, and that only 2,000 copies had been distributed, not the 100,000 promised.

An attempt in 1894 to transfer the venture to a new company, Reuter's International Agency Limited, failed. Reuters had lost over £27,000 in three years because of these diversions, and in the process had tarnished its reputation for sound judgement. None the less, a small press advertisement department did survive in London, with links across the Empire, most notably in Australia. Reuters arranged the first whole and half-page displays ever seen in the Australian papers.[33]

9

The most damaging initiative resulting from Baron Herbert's search for alternative sources of revenue and profit was the venture into banking. It was probably a bad idea in itself, inappropriate for a news agency: it was certainly bad in the way it came to be conducted. 'He believed that he thoroughly understood finance', wrote Dickinson in retrospect, 'and that he was a shrewd businessman. In both respects he was mistaken.'[34]

The idea had been in Baron Herbert's mind for many years. In 1903 the articles of association had been extended to allow Reuters to engage upon financial business unconnected with telegraphy. In 1908 the articles were again revised. The company was now specifically authorized 'to act as Bankers'. Finally, in 1910 a 'banking department' was opened.

This new department was described by the chairman at the 1911 annual meeting as 'purely subsidiary . . . this business will not be carried on with the slightest risk to the stability and maintenance of the old tradition.' The banking manager was Arnold W. Hajduska, a Hungarian, who had come to Reuters upon the recommendation of Wolff, the chief accountant. Hajduska was said to be an expert in foreign exchange dealing.

In 1912 the capital of Reuter's Telegram Company Limited was increased from £100,000 to £500,000. At the annual meeting the chairman explained how disheartening it was for 'a keen man of business', such as Hajduska, to miss good openings because of lack of capital. An increase in capital would also increase the remittance business by allowing transfer of accumulated funds at remunerative rates. The response to the Reuter share offer was good, and all seemed set fair. On 1 July 1913 Reuter's Bank Limited opened its doors. Nominal capital was £1 million, of which half was issued in fully paid £10 shares—49,795 to Reuter's Telegram Company, 50 each to the four Reuter main board directors (who constituted the board of the bank), one each to five senior Reuter staff. No other shares were issued, and Reuters thus retained control. The first address of the bank was at 25 Old Jewry, but eventually it moved to 43 Coleman Street.

Reuter's Bank attracted very few private deposit customers. It engaged chiefly in foreign exchange dealing, and in negotiating foreign loans. Baron Herbert trusted Hajduska totally. The sceptical Dickinson even began to wonder if Baron Herbert was grooming the bank manager as his successor. Dickinson wrote privately on 4 April 1913 about a Chinese loan scheme which thankfully had fallen through. 'Imagine Reuter lending 25 million sterling to the Chinese Government. It is a bit too strong for me . . . The poor Baron! who has so many projects which very nearly succeed, and produce thousands of pounds, and then just fail, with a loss of some hundreds in preliminaries.' Unfortunately, a risky Mexican loan did go through.

The first annual general meeting of Reuter's Bank Limited was held on 20 May 1914. It was bound to be a formality, given the restricted nature of the share ownership. Profit for 1913 was announced as a 'satisfactory' £20,257, and 6.25 per cent dividend was paid. Had Dickinson been wrong in sensing eventual trouble? Significantly, at the annual meeting of Reuter's Telegram Company, held a week after the bank's general meeting, an experienced London stockbroker, Gerald Williams, voiced doubts from the floor about the running of the bank. He asked for an Englishman to be appointed to the senior staff, 'who will keep you in touch with the banking sentiment of London'. Here was a coded warning.[35]

These first serious public doubts about the bank were expressed at a time when other episodes had already damaged the good name of Reuters. In 1913 a financial publicity department had been started. In October, its manager, W. T. Hedges, distributed a circular to subscribing newspapers which suggested that advertisements placed through this department 'would enable us to make representations for extended editorial reference to your interests'. *The Times* led a press campaign of protest at the suggestion that British newspapers could be thus influenced. The paper announced that it would refuse all advertising placed by news agencies. Baron Herbert had to repudiate the circulars, and the publicity department was closed down. Hedges, who clearly had no awareness of right journalistic standards, was sacked. In June 1914 he committed suicide.[36]

By 1914 two established sources of Reuter revenue were under threat. The private telegram business was falling off, as the cable companies reduced their charges and so made the involvement of an intermediary less appealing. Also, British newspapers were beginning to press for reduced subscriptions, which had remained fixed for over 40 years. Early in 1914 both the *Daily Mirror* and the *Daily Graphic* secured a cut of one-half in their £1,600 payments. The *Mirror* now paid only £800; but in a troubled attempt to maintain the appearance of equal contributions by morning papers, the *Graphic* was persuaded to continue paying £1,600 in return for a commitment by Reuters to supply £800 of advertisements from overseas.

Then there was the Pooley affair. Andrew Pooley, the Reuter correspondent in Tokyo, had bought stolen documents which revealed that Japanese naval officers and officials had been bribed over shipbuilding contracts with several foreign firms. Foremost among these was were Siemens and Vickers, German and British respectively. Siemens was desperate to recover the documents, and Pooley eventually returned them unpublished, after making a profit of several thousand pounds for himself. He gave Baron Herbert a very different account of the affair in a letter of 4 December 1913, implying that it was the Japanese Government which wanted the papers:

> After discussing the matter with the British Ambassador, I decided not to publish the papers and the same have now been restored to the owners on the following terms:
>
> 1. A subscription of £250 to our general service.
> 2. Payment of all expenses.
> 3. Support from the government for our commercial service, when ready.
> 4. An undertaking not to interfere any further with our inward or outward services.

Pooley added that full reports had been sent to the British Admiralty and to the Foreign Office. 'We have dealt the Germans a very hard blow and done Great Britain a very good turn, as the Ambassador has written me.'

Although Baron Herbert expressed satisfaction that the British embassy knew about the affair, he became uncomfortable over the financial aspect, and on 29 December he told Pooley to refund the £250 that had supposedly been paid by the Japanese Government. 'I feel we must forego it because it constitutes part of a bargain which, otherwise unexceptionable, invests it with a flavour of blood money.' Dickinson commented privately on 7 February 1914: 'It is to be hoped that this part of the business won't come out.'

It did all come out. Press reports were telegraphed from Germany to Tokyo about the trial in Berlin of the Siemens clerk who had first stolen the documents and sold them to Pooley. Pooley was arrested on charges of possessing stolen goods and blackmail. The financial agent for Reuters at Yokohama was also arrested, along with two Siemens employees and two Japanese newspaper reporters. Pooley's wife attempted to commit suicide, and one of the Siemens employees succeeded in doing so while in prison. The scandal was extensively noticed by the Japanese press, and there was rioting in the streets. Suspicion centred upon the Prime Minister, Admiral Yamamoto, who was head of the Satsuma (or naval) clan which dominated the Japanese Cabinet. Yamamoto's Government had already been in difficulties, and it fell on 24 March. Pooley received a two-year prison sentence in July 1914. The other defendants were given suspended sentences. The affair was described as the biggest case of bribery ever tried in a Japanese court. Anglo-Japanese relations were damaged. The British Ambassador, Sir Conyngham Greene, had commented severely on 13 May about the enforced retirement of several senior Japanese naval officers favourable to the British side:

> I regret it all the more because their downfall appears to have been largely brought about thro the mischievous activity of a British journalist here, who has thereby not only helped to drag the navy of our ally through the mire, but to injure the reputation of British firms doing business with the imperial government.[37]

Reuters tried to distance itself from Pooley by explaining that he had been acting on his own account, and not in its name. He jumped bail in August, and fled to England.

10

The 1870 ring combination of news agencies continued to function until 1914, and beyond. But there had been prolonged uncertainty and much manœuvring before the first renewal of the ring contract in 1890. For a long time, Reuters was distrustful about the intentions of Havas; and because of this uncertainty, Reuters felt bound to explore alternatives. Abandoning Havas would mean arranging some sort of new deal with Wolff, probably in association with the Italian and Austrian agencies, Stefani and the Korrespondenz Bureau. In 1887 the Italian Government had joined with Germany and Austria to form the triple alliance. Bismarck was trying to draw the British Government into this diplomatic web. And as part of these manœuvres, he and Crispi, the Italian Prime Minister—a personal friend of Engländer—sought to bring Reuters into a parallel news agency alliance.[38]

   Richard Wentzel, the director of the Wolff Bureau, visited London, where he met both Baron Herbert and his father. The fact that the old Baron came out of retirement reflected the strength of his concern about the future. The outcome of the visit was an 'offensive–defensive' alliance with Wolff, signed in February 1887, providing for joint action if the 1870 agreement were not renewed. But after protracted negotiations, mainly conducted for Reuters by Engländer, the ring combination agreement was continued for another ten years from 1890. It was to be twice further renewed before 1914. Havas now gained South America as its exclusive territory, and also Indo-China, which had come under French rule. In return, it gave up its share in Egypt to Reuters. Belgium and Central America were confirmed as shared territories.

North America proved difficult to control during the 1890s. Reuters found itself uncomfortably caught up in struggles between rival American agencies. In expectation of doing a news exchange deal jointly with two new agencies, the United Press and the Associated Press of Illinois, Reuters broke with the Associated Press of New York. Then in March 1893 Reuters signed a long-term agreement with AP of Illinois alone. Reuters had preferred the Illinois body upon the advice of S. Levy Lawson, the Reuter New York agent. In angry response, William Laffan of UP repudiated an interim agreement under which UP news was being supplied to Reuters. AP was not yet ready with its service, and Lawson had hurriedly to open a temporary news office for Reuters in New York—a reminder that at this period no such separate office existed. When AP of Illinois finally took over in October 1893, Lawson reverted, in his own words, simply to 'supervising the service'. In 1900 Associated Press of Illinois was succeeded by the present-day Associated Press, with its headquarters in New York.[39]

The 1893 agreement with Associated Press of Illinois made it a member of the ring combination. It was granted exclusive rights to distribute news from Reuters, Havas, and Wolff throughout the United States, Canada, Alaska, and the Hawaiian Islands. This news was to be supplied to AP agents in London, Paris, and Berlin, who were entitled to receive all agency telegrams supplied to the local newspapers. In return, 'all American or other news' was to be supplied to the agents of Reuters, Havas, and Wolff in New York. A yearly differential of £3,500 was payable by AP, a measure of its still junior status.

But when the 1893 agreement was renewed ten years later important changes were made in favour of the Americans. The differential was cut to £2,400, while Central America, Cuba, and the Philippines were added to the AP sphere. And the news delivery arrangements for Reuters in New York were now put upon the same basis as for AP in London. Under the 1893 agreement the Americans had undertaken to conduct and make the whole service for delivery to the New York agent in New York. Now the news was left for editing by Reuters itself in New York. AP agreed to pay $225 per month to meet the cost of the necessary extra staff for Reuters. From this date, the Reuter presence in North America began to grow.

AP stayed part of the ring combination upon these terms until 1914 and later. However, in 1911 Reuters, Havas, and Wolff considered the possibility of linking up instead with a new American news agency. This was the United Press Associations, started in 1907, and rising fast. But for how long could either AP or UP be depended upon? The head of the Wolff Bureau, Dr

Heinrich Mantler, warned Baron Herbert (2 September 1911) that one day no American agency would want to remain part of the ring: 'all Americans desire to make themselves as independent of Europe as possible. This is the same as regards the United Press as the Associated Press.'

II

The predominance of Reuters within the formal and informal British Empire was destined to be challenged by the Americans during the inter-war years. But the last years of the nineteenth century and the first years of the twentieth were the heyday of that predominance. Baron Herbert wrote regularly to his general managers in India, Australia, the Far East, and South Africa. On 29 April 1908 he told Roderick Jones, the manager at Cape Town, that 'it was a principle of the Company to leave its proconsuls on the spot practically a free hand to safeguard its local interests, and it was only on questions of principle and policy that the head Office was consulted'. This meant, of course, that Baron Herbert retained an active part in explaining and enforcing such policy.

Not all overseas managers proved to be competent, or even trustworthy when they were perforce left in charge of large sums of money. In 1871 E. A. Perkins was accused of misappropriation of nearly £1,000 in Egypt; but as with his predecessor, Virnard, legal action achieved little. The board finally decided in 1875 that all agents should enter into 'substantial' guarantees, and that large cash balances should be remitted to London monthly. Comparative revenue figures showed how much money was being handled (see Table 3.2).

India was the most profitable part of the British Empire for Reuters in this period. It constituted a great market for political news and for commercial information, both incoming and outgoing. Whole pages of the Indian newspapers, English-language and vernacular, were filled with Reuter telegrams. Conversely, news from India, the jewel in the crown of Empire, was in steady demand in England. Edward Buck (1862–1948), who became the Reuter

TABLE 3.2 Revenue figures by territory, 1898–1918. (£)

	Total revenue all sources	UK	Europe	India	Far East	America North	Net profit after tax	% Profit
1898	142,000	54,800	36,155	11,500	5,100	1,200	6,000	4.2
1908	196,500	44,700	29,500	18,400	9,300	600	14,200	7.2
1918	266,300	49,400	31,600	35,200	16,200	800	4,600	1.7

correspondent with the Government of India in 1897, watched each day the doings of the rulers of the sub-continent (Plate 25). Buck's uncle and name-sake had been a senior civil servant in the Government of India, and this helped his nephew to gain entry as a journalist into official circles. In his book, *Simla Past and Present* (Calcutta, 1904), Buck explained that there were two sides, official and social, to life at Simla, the summer capital. 'There are two communities—the bees and the butterflies.' The genial 'Buckie' took care to be well regarded by both. He shared fully in the Anglo-Indian social round, becoming famous for his shooting parties. And his love for India and its his-tory enabled him to maintain good relations with the Eurasians and the Indians. But though he ranged widely, from frontier wars to bazaar rumour, his first responsibility was to report the pronouncements and doings of the Indian Government. From the 1890s to the 1930s he was on personal terms with every Viceroy and Vicereine and their staffs. He secured a steady num-ber of beats, notably his on-the-spot account of the attempted assassination of the Viceroy, Lord Hardinge, in 1912. Buck was awarded an Indian knight-hood in 1929, and only reluctantly retired in 1933.[40]

The Reuter view of what constituted important news out of India included increasingly full reporting of nationalist activity, starting in 1886 with the second and subsequent annual meetings of the Indian National Congress. In 1907 Gandhi, the Indian nationalist, noted with satisfaction that Reuters had sent long reports to the Indian papers about the annual meeting of the Congress; 'This is the first time that the Congress has received such public-ity'. In 1910 a Reuter circular to British newspapers announced that a special correspondent was being sent to the Congress meeting at Allahabad. It promised 'an independent and impartial record'. The British papers were charged an extra six guineas for the service.[41]

Egypt continued to be an important centre for news throughout the late nineteenth century. Reuter headquarters were moved from Alexandria to Cairo in 1879, when Dr Joseph Schnitzler was manager. He served through a turbulent period, which included the bombardment of Alexandria by the British in 1882. He kept in touch with London from a cable ship on station offshore with the British fleet. News of the bombardment was the first impor-tant story to be communicated by telephone to the Press Association from the Reuter editorial office at Old Jewry.

The next manager for Reuters in Egypt, David Rees, served from 1884 until 1914. He was in Cairo at the time of the abortive Gordon relief expedition to Khartoum in 1885. Rees spent much of his time humouring Egyptian politi-cians, whose goodwill was necessary to ensure payment of the indispensable Egyptian Government subscription. He also successfully cultivated Lord

Cromer, the powerful British Government agent; and Sir Herbert Kitchener, the sirdar of the Egyptian army. Cromer was particularly well-disposed towards Reuters. His important two-hour farewell speech in 1907 was telegraphed in full, sentence by sentence, as it was being delivered. The next annual general meeting was told that this had produced the longest message by telegraph ever received at Old Jewry. The episode strikingly illustrated Reuters in action as the busy servant of the British imperial idea.[42]

Egypt was half within the formal British Empire; whereas China—or, more accurately, the main cities of eastern China—constituted an important part of the informal Empire. In 1900 some 20,000 foreigners were resident in China, over a quarter of them British; and over 400 British firms were trading in the treaty ports. Shanghai, where Reuters had its headquarters on the bund, was the chief centre of British commercial activity. Traders there, and in Hong Kong and elsewhere, came to depend heavily and without question upon the accuracy of Reuter commodity prices and stock market information cabled from around the world. In the eyes of both westerners and Chinese, Reuters had an equal standing with the great trading houses such as Jardine Matheson.[43]

The best years for Reuters in terms of revenue from the Far East were to come between the wars; but from 1901 onwards successive annual general meetings were told of the growing importance of China. In 1910 the chairman reported that the number of news subscriptions from both firms and newspapers in north China had much increased. Reuters began to offer three news services—'European', 'Imperial', and 'Pacific'. The Imperial service, started in 1910, delivered 150,000 words per annum to Hong Kong and Shanghai. This was the basic service. The Pacific service, started in 1912, offered internal news to and from China and Japan, supplied by a network of local correspondents.

Japan was awakening much more quickly than China. In 1894 Engländer was instrumental in negotiating an agreement with the Japanese Minister in London whereby Reuters exclusively received all official news issued by the Japanese Government, 'publication of which will be useful to a better understanding of Japan'. In return, Reuters supplied its telegrams to the Japanese Government and agreed to act 'as the intermediaries for the financial and commercial requirements of Japan'. The subscription was set at £600 per annum. This intriguing arrangement was probably Engländer's last initiative for Reuters.

Reuters expanded slightly later in South Africa than in India or Egypt. During the last quarter of the nineteenth century the area was being rapidly transformed from a backwater into an important market for political news and commercial information, both inwards and outwards. This transformation resulted from the great diamond and gold discoveries of the 1870s and 80s. These brought rapid prosperity, but also political tension between Britons and Boers, leading to wars in 1880–1 and 1899–1902. British settlers controlled Cape Colony and Natal; the Boers held the republics of the Transvaal and the Orange Free State. The first full-time Reuter agent, Walter H. Croom 'of the head office staff', was sent to Cape Town in 1876. There had been a part-time agent there since about 1859. The first cable reached Durban in 1879 by a route down the east coast of Africa, and Reuters opened there in 1881. The cable arrived at Cape Town in 1887, which remained the head-quarters throughout the period. In 1895 an office was opened in Johannesburg, the new mining city on the Rand; there was already an office at nearby Pretoria, the Transvaal capital. Reuters was taking care, in other words, to be fully represented on both sides of the British–Boer divide.

Montalt J. M. Bellasyse, an Irishman, became manager for South Africa at the Cape in 1887. He was unfairly dismissed in 1899 soon after the outbreak of the second Boer War. Reuters had been charged by the *Daily Mail* in London with being in the pay of the Boers. This smear was ridiculous, for the agency was simply receiving a normal news subscription of £300 per annum from the Transvaal Government. Reuter telegrams were said by the *Mail* to have shown a pro-Boer bias for several years. Baron Herbert was reluctant to give way to such pressure; but Bellasyse was eventually sacrificed when it was found that H. A. Gwynne—who had been sent as chief correspondent for the Boer War—could not work with a manager who would not take sides. Bellasyse had cultivated good relations with the Boer leaders, who trusted Reuters not to misrepresent them. As a result, at the start of the war W. H. Mackay, the Reuter agent in Pretoria, was allowed to remain and to report under censorship from the Boer side.[44]

Canada was the one major part of the British Empire where Reuters stood back for long periods, although the policy of routing Canada's incoming and outgoing news via AP in New York was questioned at intervals. Finally, under the 1903 agreement with AP, its news for Reuters from Canada was no longer left to be edited for London by AP itself. The New York staff of Reuters took over Canadian editing. The result, Collins assured Baron Herbert on 19 November 1906, was that Reuters now provided from Canada 'an excellent general service to the British press'. Unfortunately, the British public was little interested in such Canadian news; while the Canadians, for their part, were primarily interested not in British news, but in news from the United States. 'In Canada, as in Australia,' admitted Collins (18 November 1906), 'there is a danger of drifting from the old country.'[45]

12

In sending news round the British Empire and the world, Reuters gave prominence to official and semi-official news issued by British Ministers and officials. It also published important pronouncements from foreign governments. So long as such matter was plainly seen for what it was, there was no danger of compromising the reputation of Reuters for independence. But should Reuters go further, and make itself available to circulate news or comments covertly fed to it by the British Government?

Near the end of the century Arnold Gawthrop, the Reuter diplomatic correspondent, was keeping in regular contact with the Foreign Office, and in particular with Sir Thomas Sanderson, the Permanent Under-Secretary. For several years these contacts were put on a formal basis. In July 1894 Engländer had proposed comprehensively to Sanderson:

> That the Company will forward all political telegrams to the person designated by the Secretary of State as soon as they are received.
>
> That in regard to any telegrams of which the correctness may seem doubtful, or the publication inexpedient, time will be given for rectification before they are sent to the press.
>
> That confidential reports of information received from your Agents on the Continent will be compiled by Dr Engländer and forwarded for the Secretary of State's information.
>
> That the Company will publish on its own authority through its Agents abroad any statements or announcements which may be requested by the Secretary of State, strict secrecy being observed as to the source from which they are derived.
>
> The sum to be paid to the Company in consideration of the above to be £500 per annum.

Lord Kimberley, the Liberal Foreign Secretary, agreed to try the arrangement for six months, 'with a further prolongation if it should be found to work well'.

The only known doubts about this arrangement were to come, not from Reuters, but from the British Government. Three years later, Lord Salisbury—who was the Conservative Prime Minister as well as Foreign Secretary—minuted on a Foreign Office internal memorandum, dated 10 August 1897: 'I am sceptical of the advantages of our connexion with Reuter—so is Lord Kimberley to whom I spoke about it.' Francis Bertie, the Assistant Under-Secretary, shared these doubts. Salisbury's private secretary recorded that 'Bertie when in charge is always very much exercised by the frequent visits of Reuter's agent'.[46]

On at least one important occasion Gawthrop provided a link between a foreign Government and British ministers. In September 1899, as the threat of war with the Boers grew daily, Gawthrop had been in touch with Montague White, the Transvaal representative in London. Gawthrop reported to the Foreign Office that White was complaining bitterly about the way Joseph Chamberlain, the Colonial Secretary, was conducting negotiations with the Boers. White would not go to the Colonial Office, reported one Foreign Office official to Lord Salisbury on 23 September, because he believed that he would not be listened to. 'But he is anxious that Your Lordship should be aware of his views on the conduct of the negotiations, which are those of the Boer Government, and he authorized Reuter's man to let this wish be known at the F.O.' Three days later White met Salisbury's private secretary. In a personal letter, dated 30 September, Baron Herbert praised Gawthrop's peace-seeking initiative, only regretting that 'the case is past praying for'.

Four years earlier Baron Herbert had arranged with White for Reuters to handle at press rates all Transvaal Government telegrams between Pretoria and London. South African telegrams at this time could be politically very sensitive. A Reuter telegram, sent by Bellasyse from Johannesburg on 28 December 1895, was used by Dr L. S. Jameson as the pretext for launching his abortive raid into the Transvaal designed to incite a rising against the Boers by the British in Johannesburg. The telegram itself did not take sides, and it carefully balanced hopes and fears:

> Position becoming acute and persistent rumours afloat secret arming mines and warlike preparations women children leaving Rand . . . Political situation talk town and opinion expressed by leading men modus vivendi will be arrived at and wiser counsels prevail.[47]

While Bellasyse was unfairly criticized as pro-Boer, some of his staff were certainly anti-Boer. They supported Jameson and his master, Cecil Rhodes. H. J. Wasserfall, a long-serving member of the South African staff, destroyed all records of compromising telegrams exchanged between Cape Town and Johannesburg before the raid. He did this at the instance of Rhodes. Wasserfall was surprised and relieved not to be called to London to give evidence at Jameson's trial.[48]

The Rhodes group does not seem to have felt any lasting gratitude for this assistance in their cover-up. Like the *Daily Mail*, Rhodes became convinced in the years between the raid and the war that Reuters in South Africa was pro-Boer. Rutherford Harris, Rhodes's right-hand man, wrote to Gawthrop on 21 April 1899 that Rhodes wanted to meet Baron Herbert:

'all of our group are painfully conscious that, in so far as your admirable Services are concerned, you have had no sympathy with us for the last two or three years.' There is no evidence that Rhodes and Baron Herbert did meet.

Reuters never seems to have realized that the Colonial Office shared the doubts of Rhodes and the *Daily Mail* about the agency's patriotism. In May 1897 Reuters offered to improve its service throughout the Empire in return for £500 per annum from the Colonial Office. Chamberlain, the Colonial Secretary, eventually ruled against a deal (16 November 1897):

> I do not like this proposal. The only way in which I think we could enter into special relations with Reuter would be if we wanted fuller Reports of Speeches or Documents sent to the colonies or elsewhere than they would forward in the customary course of their business. But this must be a matter for special arrangement at the time.[49]

In 1911 such an arrangement, but on a regular basis, was secretly negotiated to make propaganda use of the new 'Imperial Service'. Asquith's Liberal Government wanted the circulation of full reports, rather than the usual summaries, of all major speeches made by leading Ministers, such as Lloyd George and Winston Churchill. The Government was prepared to pay secretly for the extra costs involved. Herbert Jeans, the parliamentary correspondent of Reuters, was approached by the Liberal Chief Whip, the Master of Elibank. Eleven years later (19 September 1922), Jeans explained how 'the matter was delicate, for the Opposition might have made trouble, and what Elibank wanted to know was whether I could be trusted to play the game . . . this was the beginning of a long and fruitful association with the Government.' The arrangement became known informally as 'Elibanking'.

Roderick Jones, the general manager in South Africa, had been confidentially forewarned in 1911, along with other overseas managers, that reports of speeches were to be cabled at unusual length. On 4 July Dickinson, the chief editor, tried to reassure Jones about the new relationship:

> it is a great advantage to us to act on these occasions as the hand-maid of the Government. Our doing so strengthens our position in this country very considerably, and, at the same time, it shows to those in authority, who have it in their power to be agreeable or disagreeable to ourselves, that our great organization can be of infinite value to them.

In a letter to Baron Herbert on 3 October 1911 Jones recognized 'the beneficial effect of service so rendered on our relationship in London with the Home Government'. But he obtained permission to cut down the speech reports before publication in South Africa 'if it seriously threatens our prestige on this side or to interfere with our business arrangements with the newspapers'.

Dickinson had discussed with Elibank's private secretary, R. H. Davies, the problem of how to maintain the reputation of Reuters for independence while taking this money. Davies and Dickinson agreed on 11 August 1911 that the attribution 'at the request of a high quarter' should be used; but only 'when criticism has been raised or information asked for by a newspaper'. Davies added that Elibank preferred 'that these extended reports should form a natural part of your service, and not be earmarked in any way'.

Davies did throw in the qualification that secrecy should be observed 'as far as it is compatible with the interests of your Company'. But such a deal, by its very existence, was incompatible with the claim that Reuters always acted freely in its choice of news. Admittedly, the 1911 arrangement did not go so far as that of 1894. Reuters was not now agreeing to publish covert British Government propaganda. The speeches by Ministers were obviously known to have been delivered. But the agreement to give such speeches circulation *in extenso* throughout the Empire was to be kept secret as far as possible. And the payments made were to be kept entirely secret. Reuters was compromised.

This agreement damagingly extended the sympathetic relationship which was well known to exist between Reuters and the authorities throughout the British Empire. Such sympathy could be justified, but only so long as it remained open and informal. When an editorial appeared in the *Nation* on 24 April 1915 commemorating the fiftieth anniversary of Reuter's Telegram Company, the editor looked back over its history with some indulgence, even though the *Nation* was a radical weekly, usually suspicious of official connections:

> The Agency acquired inevitably a semi-official tone. It stood for British interests as the Foreign Office sees them, and in reporting the internal affairs of foreign countries, its bias was usually governmental, though with some subtle variations. Of this it would be futile to complain . . . It was bound to reflect the views here of 'official circles', there of colonists' clubs, and everywhere of the mercantile or governing class. The bias was probably as unconscious as it was inevitable. An Agency which had acted otherwise could never have collected its news.

The *Nation* accepted that Reuters had served effectively as 'our daily periscope' on the world: 'we cannot recollect that it was ever used to further individual views or policies.' But it had not avoided unconscious bias. 'It builds up its own canons of the sort of fact that it is proper to retail':

It was the world as decent black-coated functionaries in banks and public offices would have the masses see it. It reported, fairly enough, as a rule, what men of the same type with similar black coats were saying and doing in other countries, and if strikers or revolutionaries did force their way into its field of vision, it helped us to see them as 'all the right-minded' and 'the compact majority' are wont to see them . . . It is by such means that the compact majority is kept together, and Reuter's was a reliable drill-sergeant, who kept us all to our marching pace, and dressed us efficiently by the right.

FOUR

The World's News
1865–1914

I

T HE completion of the world's first Transatlantic cable was reported by Reuters on 27 and 28 July 1866. A terse telegram in American English (duly translated) from the managing director of the construction company announced:

VALENTIA, July 27.

'O.K.' (All right)

Then at 12.30 a.m. on 28 July came fuller news:

VALENTIA, July 27.

Shore end landed and spliced. Completed at 8.43.
Messages of congratulation passing rapidly between Ireland and Newfoundland. Insulation and continuity perfect. Speed much increased since surplus cable has been cut off.

Equipment failure prevented any news being carried immediately; but repairs were made, and on 31 July a new era began when Reuter subscribers began to receive an unbroken flow of news from across the Atlantic by cable. Admittedly, the first item was hardly momentous:

NEW YORK, JULY 29 (MORNING).

The representative of Tennessee has been admitted to Congress.
Congress adjourned yesterday.

The speed of news by cable compared with that sent by steamship was immediately brought home to newspaper readers. Reuters issued this first cable telegram at the same time as a dispatch datelined 'New York, July 21', brought by the steamship *America* to Southampton, and including New York prices of the morning of 21 July. Suddenly, such delay had become unnecessary and therefore unacceptable. From now onwards the business community expected to receive American stock market and commodity information via Reuters in hours instead of days.

On 1 August the first hard same-day news was telegraphed to London— the resignation of the Secretary of the Interior. Also on 1 August,

Reuters explained to subscribers how transatlantic messages were transmitted:

> The President's reply to the Queen's message left Washington on the 30th July
> and telegraphed from Newfoundland at 3.51 p.m. yesterday, consisting of 405
> letters, making 81 words, at a speed of 7.36 words per minute. Sent by Weedon,
> Newfoundland. Received by Edgar George, Valentia. Message delivered to
> Her Majesty at Osborne at 5 p.m.

In contrast to the twelve days taken in 1865 for news of the Lincoln assassination to reach London, first news in 1881 of the shooting of President Garfield appeared in the British papers within twenty-four hours of the event, as did news of his death after a three-month struggle for life. In consequence, much more extensive mourning was observed in Britain for Garfield than had been shown for Lincoln. There could now be a sense of shared experience, which reinforced the traditional special relationship.[1]

This new immediacy added to the power of news and helped to sell more newspapers. So also did a continuing story. Accounts of Dr Livingstone's appearances and disappearances in 'darkest Africa' recurred in the Reuter file throughout the 1860s and into the 1870s. Livingstone fascinated the Victorian public. On 9 January 1868 a personal letter from Julius Reuter appeared in *The Times*:

> Sir,—I have received the following telegram from Alexandria, dated yesterday—
>
> 'Zanzibar, Dec 1. Intelligence from Keelwa states that Dr. Livingstone, or a person resembling him, was seen travelling towards the West of Lake Tanganyika. You will see that although the news is similar to that already published by her Majesty's Government on Second of November last, the date of the above message is Zanzibar Dec 1.
>
> Supposing the latter date is correct, which I have at present no reason to doubt, Dr. Livingstone must have again been seen east of Lake Tanganyika, which increases the hopes of his safety. It must be remembered that Lake Tanganyika is upwards of 300 miles long.

Julius Reuter was thus circulating this latest news without charge, perhaps out of excitement. It was good publicity.

War news generated continuing interest of another kind. To report the wars of the second half of the century, a new breed of war correspondents emerged, described in *The Times* of 14 September 1870 as 'the accredited messengers of public opinion'. The early years of Reuter's Telegram Company witnessed a succession of highly reportable confrontations—the Austro-Prussian War of 1866, the Franco-Prussian War of 1870–1, the Paris Commune of 1871, and the Eastern crisis of 1876–8.

2

The first colonial war to be reported by Reuters from the front line was the punitive expedition against the Emperor Theodore of Abyssinia in 1867–8. An army under General Napier assembled at Bombay in October, its size and timetable revealed by Reuters without censorship:

> BOMBAY (via Trieste) Sept. 29.—The advance guard of the Abyssinian field force, consisting of about 1,400 troops and 1,000 horses and mules sails on the 5th October, and will be followed a month later by the rest of the expeditionary force.

According to Henry Collins's recollections, Reuters had its own correspondents with the expedition.[2] Who they were is not known; they were probably serving officers, not full-time journalists; but several papers did send professional war correspondents. News of the fighting was carried by military telegraph to the coast, and then by boat to Suez for telegraphing to London. A Reuter correspondent rode with the column which made the final dash to the Emperor's capital (Plate 9), and on 8 May the British newspapers received a Reuter telegram which crisply gave news of total victory:

> HEADQUARTERS, BRITISH ARMY, TALANTA, April 21.—Magdala and its fortifications have been entirely destroyed. The British expeditionary force commenced its return march to the coast on the 18th inst. All well.

The Abyssinian story ended with the arrival of Theodore's son at Plymouth three months later. The local Reuter agent had added a touch of human interest to his report of the formal reception on 14 July: 'He is an interesting little lad, tall for his age (seven years last April), and much delighted with England, exclaiming, "Oh, this beautiful country! I shall never go back." '

By the time of the Franco-Prussian War in 1870, Reuters was supplying a special round-up of news to the Viceroy and Government of India. The telegrams supplied for 1870–1 have survived. Dispatches from many datelines were sub-edited and variously sent by the four available cable routes. War news naturally predominated, but home news was also included. The Queen's speech at the opening of Parliament was summarized at length; debates on matters of concern to India were noticed; the honours list was reported; a strike of Welsh miners was covered. Some news from China was included, and some from the United States. Not least, the beginnings of a domestic service for India were reflected in reports of ship arrivals and departures, and of military and civil appointments.

The results of the Derby and other classic horse-races were also included in the Viceroy's service. In such matters accuracy was especially necessary. Yet this could not always prevent the garbling of Reuter telegrams during cabling, and consequently newspaper sub-editors at the receiving end sometimes had to show ingenuity in restoring the text. For example, the *Japan Weekly Mail* of 18 May 1872 told its readers that a Reuter message had been received which read 'Prince Charlie Cremorne has been appointed a Queen's Messenger'. This, the paper realized, was 'probably an error', and was meant to report the result of the Two Thousand Guineas horse-race, which the paper correctly guessed as: 'Prince Charlie 1, Cremorne 2, Queen's Messenger 3'.

One of the most amusing reporting errors in the whole history of Reuters was given enduring life by Mark Twain in his book, *A Tramp Abroad* (1880). Reuters had received in London a telegram from Australia which read, 'Governor Queensland twins first son'. An editor, having presumably checked that Sir Arthur Kennedy was the Governor in question, expanded this to read: 'Lady Kennedy has given birth to twins, the eldest being a son' (*The Times*, 5 March 1878). This looked like a good example of economy in cabling. But the good news was received with consternation by Sir Arthur's family and friends in England, who knew (or thought they knew) him to be an elderly widower who had not remarried. Reuters had to issue a long apology, which Twain gleefully copied. The telegram, Reuters explained, referred to the construction of a railway line; and should have read, *not* 'twins first son', but 'Governor Queensland turns first sod'.

Thanks to its ties with both the French and German agencies, Reuters received news of the Franco-Prussian War from both sides. But it used its own agents as much as possible. Thus George Williams reported successively from Paris, Tours, Bordeaux, and Paris again. 'Horrible as the war is', he wrote to his fiancée (9 January 1871), 'and weary of it as I am, it is still a harvest time for press men.' Emil Wolff, who had recently started working for Reuters in London, recollected how its reputation was boosted by its war coverage. It did not aim to match the detailed accounts of the newspaper special correspondents, but it did seek to be ahead with the basic facts. Thus Wolff claimed that Reuters gave first news in London of the surrender of Napoleon III and his army at Sedan. Despite the dramatic nature of this item, the telegram from Reuters offered no comment. 'Its brief bulletins,' recalled Wolff complacently, 'without a tinge of sensational prose, were looked upon by the public with absolute confidence.'[3]

3

While Reuter coverage of European news was always comprehensive, news from the formal and informal British Empire grew steadily in quantity as the cable network extended worldwide and as transmission rates slowly fell. And if news from India at first received most attention, South African news came to surpass it for excitement. From the 1870s, Reuters was sending back news of major mineral discoveries in South Africa, first of diamonds and then of gold; it also covered a hard-fought war against the Zulus (1879), two testing wars against the Boers (1881, 1899–1902), and the ill-conceived Jameson raid of 1895.

The Zulu War provided Reuters with a beat which shocked the British people, even though it took twenty days to reach London. John D. Pigott (1852–1923) was the Reuter correspondent, and it was presumably thanks to his enterprise that Reuters got the news first. In London overnight on 10/11 February 1879, Dickinson was the editor on duty. After midnight, he received a telegram from St Vincent, relaying a message from Cape Town. This reported a battle at Isandlwana on 21 January. The message was in code, except for a long list of officers killed. Here was a major disaster, and Dickinson called for relays of hansom cabs to rush the story to the newspaper offices sheet by sheet as it was decoded:[4]

> CAPE TOWN (via St. Vincent), JAN. 27
> On the 21st inst. a British column, consisting of a portion of the 24th Regiment and six hundred natives, with one battery, was defeated with terrible loss by an overwhelming force of Zulus, who numbered twenty thousand.
> A valuable convoy of supplies, consisting of one hundred and two wagons drawn by a thousand oxen, two guns, four hundred shot and shell, one thousand rifles, two hundred and fifty thousand rounds of ammunition, and sixty thousand pounds of commissariat stores and the colours of the 24th Regiment fell into the hands of the enemy.
> The engagement took place about ten miles beyond Rorke's Drift.
> The number of Zulus killed and wounded is estimated to have been five thousand, while our force was completely annihilated.

The Times published this Reuter telegram on the morning of 11 February. It remarked next day that the official dispatch, which was at last to hand, added 'but little'. The *Annual Register* for 1879 noted that this was the most shocking piece of imperial news to hit the British public since the time of the Indian Mutiny. The total number of British dead was above 1,700 officers and men.

Pigott, the Reuter correspondent during the Zulu War, also served the agency during the Afghan, Egyptian, Burmese, and Sudanese campaigns of the period. Several times he undertook long and dangerous journeys to get his messages out. In 1885 he was chosen by his fellow war correspondents to take back news from a tight corner on the Nile. He set off with a local guide, but for a time the two men found themselves lost. The outcome was described in the *Daily Telegraph* thirteen years later (5 September 1898):

> That was the occasion when the guide, with dust on his head, protested that, the way being lost, they should die together like brave men. Pigott replied, 'No, you will die first, and I will drink your blood,' a remark which so frightened the guide that he found the way to Gakdool in an incredibly short time.

Many years afterwards, Dickinson was to recall in the *Reuter Service Bulletin* (January 1918) that, although Pigott had not possessed the literary skills of later war correspondents with greater wordage at their disposal, he had been a well-qualified observer in his time. He had written 'in the plain unadorned English which was suitable to the days when telegraphy was difficult and expensive'.

In 1879, the British public was further shocked during the Zulu War when it heard in June that the Prince Imperial—the son of Napoleon III, and a popular figure—had been killed while attached to the British army in South Africa. This message, via Madeira, took sixteen days to come from Cape Town; but two years later during the first Boer War, when Reuters reported more bad news from South Africa, Durban had become linked to London by cable. As a result, news of the Boer victory at Majuba Hill reached London in less than a day.

The Boers had stormed the hill on the morning of 27 February 1881. The special correspondent sent out by Reuters to cover the fighting (probably not Pigott) had been refused permission by the military to go to the front. Bad communications delayed the news reaching him at Durban. But when he received accounts of the action, apparently written by two officers at the army's base camp, he hurried to the cable office just before closing time at 7 p.m. After sending his message, he took the entire telegraphic staff out to dinner. This ensured that no rival correspondents could lodge telegrams by bribing the staff to reopen.[5]

The economy of words in telling the bad news added to its graphic quality:

DURBAN, Feb. 28 12.15 A.M.
An account of the defeat sustained at Spitzkap says:—
So long as our men's ammunition lasted the loss on the side of the British was very slight.
It was when forced to retreat that the slaughter commenced.

The two companies of Highlanders who were on the summit of the hill remained there throwing stones down on the advancing Boers, and afterwards received them at the point of the bayonet.

The guns from Mount Prospect checked the pursuit of our men by the Boers to a very large extent, doing considerable execution . . .

Another account of the engagement is as follows: —

When the ammunition fell short the slaughter was fearful.

Finally, the British troops made a desperate rush, but too late, the Boers triumphing, and firing with deadly effect.

The 60th fought their way gallantly back to the camp, but were hotly pressed on all sides.

It is stated that only seven men of the 58th Regiment have survived.

The Highlanders were much cut up.

Australia did not generate as much news of interest to British readers as did South Africa or India. There were no wars. But the crimes and eventual capture of the Kelly gang of bush-rangers attracted attention in 1879–80. And tours by English cricket teams received increasing coverage. Ernest Collins, brother of Henry, was in charge of news out of Australia. His full report of the New South Wales budget in 1875—sent in the days before the introduction of a press rate—was said to have been for many years the longest press message ever sent by telegraph, costing £1,200. Collins had overdone the commitment of Reuters to full reporting of important official news.[6]

Protection of the lifeline of the British Empire through the Suez Canal to India and Australia gave the British a permanent interest in the fate of Constantinople, the capital of the decaying Turkish Empire. Britain was prepared to fight rather than to let the Russians take the city. Engländer went there in 1877 to report the war between Russia and Turkey. British warships appeared off the coast, and for a time early in 1878 British intervention seemed to be a serious possibility.

Engländer revelled in the atmosphere of intrigue and corruption which surrounded the Sultan. He knew everyone who mattered at court and among the competing European diplomats. In particular, he established good relations with Henry Layard, the British Ambassador. Queen Victoria, whose office was a long-standing subscriber to Reuters, remarked on 7 February 1878 in a letter to Disraeli, her Prime Minister, that its agent 'generally knows as well as Mr. Layard'. Engländer seems to have acted as a spy-master. Some of his letters to Layard referred to 'the Reporter of Your Excellency'. This person received £50 per month from the British embassy. Such a high retainer suggests that the spy was supplying valuable military and political intelligence.[7]

Engländer's reports to London were almost invariably copied to the Ambassador. In sending material on 29 December 1877 from 'one of my reporters employed by our agency', Engländer asked Layard that it should not be revealed to his competitors. A high Turkish official, codenamed 'the Gentleman in Question', leaked official news and documents. He seems to have been very biddable, for on 9 February 1878 Engländer told Layard: 'I have this morning seen the Gentleman in Question who will draw up a complete account of the negotiations which I shall be able to communicate tomorrow.' The importance of this source was demonstrated when on 21 February Engländer was able to telegraph details of the wide boundaries for the state of Bulgaria being demanded by Russia as a condition of peace. These terms were not acceptable to the other Great Powers.

Engländer was glad to hint at his inside knowledge. In return for supplying Layard with news, he received frequent personal briefings from the Ambassador, and Reuter telegrams gave full prominence to the official British line.

Engländer used various means to circumvent the strict Turkish censorship. He sometimes telegraphed London indirectly by way of Bombay or Odessa, or he passed messages over the Bulgarian border. His assistant and eventual successor, W. H. G. Werndel, recollected years later (21 February 1919) how

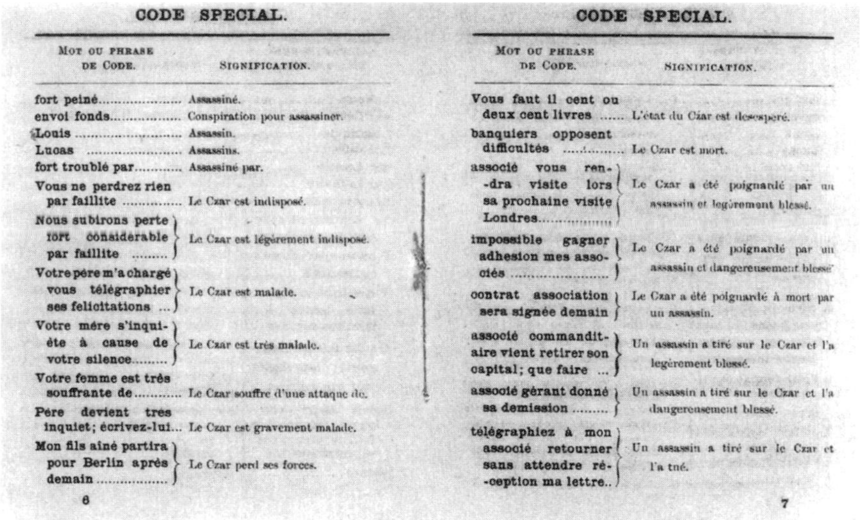

CODE SPECIAL.

MOT OU PHRASE DE CODE.	SIGNIFICATION.
fort peiné	Assassiné.
envoi fonds	Conspiration pour assassiner.
Louis	Assassin.
Lucas	Assassins.
fort troublé par	Assassiné par.
Vous ne perdrez rien par faillite	Le Czar est indisposé.
Nous subirons perte fort considérable par faillite	Le Czar est légèrement indisposé.
Votre père m'a chargé vous télégraphier ses felicitations	Le Czar est malade.
Votre mére s'inquiète à cause de votre silence	Le Czar est très malade.
Votre femme est très souffrante de	Le Czar souffre d'une attaque de.
Père devient très inquiet; écrivez-lui	Le Czar est gravement malade.
Mon fils ainé partira pour Berlin après demain	Le Czar perd ses forces.

6

CODE SPECIAL.

MOT OU PHRASE DE CODE.	SIGNIFICATION.
Vous faut il cent ou deux cent livres	L'état du Czar est desesperé.
banquiers opposent difficultés	Le Czar est mort.
associé vous rendra visite lors sa prochaine visite Londres	Le Czar a été poignardé par un assassin et legérement blessé.
impossible gagner adhesion mes associés	Le Czar a été poignardé par un assassin et dangereusement blessé
contrat association sera signée demain	Le Czar a été poignardé à mort par un assassin.
associé commanditaire vient retirer son capital; que faire	Un assassin a tiré sur le Czar et l'a legérement blessé.
associé gérant donné sa demission	Un assassin a tiré sur le Czar et l'a dangereusement blessé.
télégraphiez à mon associé retourner sans attendre réception ma lettre	Un assassin a tiré sur le Czar et l'a tué.

7

FIG. 9. Reuter code-book: St Petersburg to London, 1889

Reuters employed transmission agents in Bulgaria 'to whom we would address our dispatches, while special codes, worded in homely language, were prepared for the purpose of dealing with any possible contingency'.

Engländer and Werndel seem to have devised these codes simply for themselves. But in 1877 George Williams, the chief editor, had composed a 'Political Code', apparently for general use by Reuter correspondents filing to London. In 1889 a printed code in French was issued, probably in collaboration with Havas and Wolff, for exclusive use between St Petersburg and London. The Tsar had been assassinated in 1881, and other political murders seemed likely. Every possible variation of outrage was covered by innocent-sounding messages. Thus 'Vendez a trente huit' meant that the Tsar had been assassinated by a bomb explosion; whereas 'Annulez commande papeterie' meant that a bomb attempt had failed, with the Tsar unhurt. Other likely weapons and ascending degrees of injury were each coded in combination (Fig. 9).

4

Engländer's transmission costs during the Eastern crisis must have been very high. This was acceptable to Old Jewry only because of the great importance of the news in terms of general European peace or war. However, as telegraphic charges gradually fell, much fuller reporting of less momentous news became affordable. The 1875 International Telegraphic Convention recommended the replacement of 22–word 'telegraphic units' by the more economical method of charging per word.

In addition, extra-low press rates for news correspondents were reluctantly and unevenly conceded by the various cable companies during the last quarter of the century. From the start of 1876, for example, a press rate of 1*s*. per word for uncoded general news was negotiated by Reuters with the Anglo-American Telegraph Company, plus a 12.5 per cent rebate for 'packed work'. In return, Reuters agreed to give its whole North Atlantic business to Anglo-American provided that Reuter messages were transmitted 'at least as well as they can be forwarded by any other route'. Press telegrams took second place to ordinary messages, and sometimes this caused too much delay. Baron Herbert told the 1898 annual general meeting that to keep up with competitors in reporting the recent cricket tour of Australia, Reuters had felt compelled to send many telegrams at the high ordinary tariff of 14*s*. 6*d*. per word, compared with the press rate of 1*s*. 10*d*. per word.

Baron Herbert spoke of 'active competitors'. The growing Victorian demand for news had encouraged the establishment in London of several other news agencies. Some were small and specialist. One rival agency had been started in 1868 by James McLean, who had been the New York agent for Reuters. This did well for some years (see Plate 11); but the most enduring challenge came from the Central News (1871), and the Exchange Telegraph (1872). These were not, however, full competitors, for they were involved only with bringing news into the United Kingdom, not in selling it worldwide. Extel specialized in stock prices and financial information, and it secured the exclusive right to be represented on the floor of the London Stock Exchange.[8]

Both Central News and Extel sent out war correspondents, and they sometimes provided strong competition for Reuters. These rivals were accused, however, of often sacrificing accuracy for speed or colour. In Rudyard Kipling's book, *The Light That Failed* (1891), his fictitious 'Central Southern Syndicate' seems to have owed more to the Central News than to Reuters:

> The syndicate did not concern itself greatly with criticisms of attack and the like. It supplied the masses, and all it demanded was picturesqueness and abundance of detail; for there was more joy in England over a soldier who insubordinately steps out of square to rescue a comrade than over twenty generals slaving even to baldness at the gross details of transport and commissariat.

In the early 1890s, another challenge offered to Reuters was sharp but fairly short. From its headquarters in New York, Dalziel's Agency began to supply cheap and colourful American-centred news. The British provincial press was soon using it heavily. But Davidson Dalziel's greatest coup was to exploit the long-standing reluctance of *The Times* to depend upon Reuters. In October 1890 he secured a contract from Moberly Bell, the paper's new manager; and for a while Dalziel telegrams began to appear prominently alongside Reuter telegrams in the columns of *The Times* and other London papers. Gradually, however, too many Dalziel reports were found to be inaccurate or even untrue; and *The Times* regretfully turned back to Reuters. Bell told Dalziel reprovingly on 25 October 1893: 'Reuters sends us a great deal that we are unable to use, but nothing that would make us absolutely ridiculous if it slipped in'.[9]

The Dalziel challenge helped to encourage a major expansion of the Reuter news service. Some improvements had already been introduced by Baron Herbert in the 1880s. After taking over as managing director, he had come to realize that the service out of Europe lacked freshness and completeness. It depended too much upon news from allied news agencies, many of whom were under the influence of their respective governments. Baron Herbert therefore appointed to the European capitals (in the words of Emil Wolff) 'a number of absolutely independent correspondents, preferably of British nationality'. And to speed up the receipt of news at Old Jewry, correspondents throughout the world were allowed to telegraph directly to London instead of going through overseas Reuter offices.

In 1883 Reuter agents and correspondents were sent the following explicit circular:

TO AGENTS AND CORRESPONDENTS

In consequence of the increased attention paid by the London and English provincial press to disasters &c., of all kinds, agents and correspondents are requested to be good enough, in future, to notice for London all occurrences of the sort. The following are among the events which should be comprised in the service: —

Fires, explosions, floods, inundations, railway accidents, destructive storms, earthquakes, shipwrecks attended with loss of life, accidents to British and American war vessels and to mail steamers, street riots of a grave character, disturbances arising from strikes, duels between, and suicides of persons of note, social or political, and murders of a sensational or atrocious character.

It is requested that the bare fact be first telegraphed with the utmost promptitude, and as soon as possible afterwards a descriptive account, proportionate to the gravity of the incident. Care should, of course, be taken to follow the matter up.

These instructions became famous within Reuters, and were reissued at intervals over the years. They were perhaps written by Baron Herbert himself. Certainly, his correspondence in the 1880s was full of incisive guidance along similar lines. In a letter to W. H. Smith of Associated Press on 21 July 1888, Baron Herbert outlined the Reuter method for reporting set events, such as the recent funeral of the Emperor Frederick of Germany:

one of two things is necessary, either to be first with the news and to receive accounts of the various ceremonies as they take place, or else to wait till the end of the day and send a good descriptive account at the cost of being forestalled. We have always considered the first alternative the more desirable for an agency, and it has been the task of editors in the evening to work up the whole material as best they can.

Three months later on 17 October 1888, at the time of the United States presidential election, Baron Herbert was asking Smith 'to make us a concise and above all prompt service'. Conflicting reports were to be avoided. 'The definitive result should be sent at full rates by both routes in two words thus, "Cleveland elected" or "Harrison elected".'

The assassination of American presidents was even hotter news than their election. A junior sub-editor was said to have spiked a message from New York on 14 September 1901, with the comment: 'These Yanks. They seem to think we're interested in their blooming President's shooting excursions.' The editor-in-charge heard the words and retrieved the cable, which read, 'McKinley shot Buffalo'. This was the first news of the shooting of a third American President.[10]

Engländer, with his strong news sense, became convinced that the improvements introduced during the 1880s did not go far enough. He told Griffiths on 20 June 1889: 'your Editors still shrink from developing any light and colour into the service, and believe the dull skeleton telegrams alone to be acceptable.' Engländer recollected that, thirty years earlier, he had himself inaugurated 'the present service of sober, naked statements of facts'; but now, with much greater wordage affordable, he wanted Reuters to build upon its facts. It must match the 'special telegrams' of its competitors by starting 'special services' of its own, additional to the basic general service.

A joint Reuter/Press Association special service was duly introduced in January 1891, charging extra to newspapers at so much per word used. The special service was described in a circular for correspondents, dated 13 August 1897, as 'a supplementary service of lengthy telegrams of great importance or exceptional interest'. This meant news of military expeditions, of popular disturbances, of 'sensational trials', and of natural or man–made disasters such as major railway accidents or the sinking of passenger ships. 'If the vessel be a great ocean liner, with many British or American passengers on board, or a British warship . . . the correspondent need never stop to weigh the expense of cabling.'

Guidelines for correspondents in the Far East in 1906 reflected the values of the age by suggesting that only the murder of Europeans should normally be reported to London:

> The murder of even an obscure missionary should always be chronicled. . . .
> On the other hand, the murder of one Chinaman by another under the most atrocious circumstances is invested with little or no interest in European eyes and can therefore be ignored. This remark, however, does not hold good in cases where the outrage is of a political character.

The same circular illustrated the distinction between brief general service telegrams and longer special service telegrams. If a gunboat were 'destroyed by natives', the fact should be briefly telegraphed as quickly as possible. Then if the correspondent could collect good eyewitness accounts of the attack, he should telegraph this colour at greater length for the special service.

Another undated circular—in French and apparently for European circulation—drew an interestingly different distinction. The general service, it said, was for educated readers who preferred a sober style: the special service was for the majority with limited education and experience, who liked colourful news and description. By 1907 Reuter special service charges to the newspapers were varying from a ½d. a word for telegrams from Europe to 3d. per word for telegrams from the southern hemisphere and most of Asia.

During the 1890s the expense of fully reporting non-colonial wars forced Reuters to levy extra charges. Subscription agreements with British newspapers came to contain a clause requiring, at one month's notice, an additional £16. 13s. 4d. per month in times of war, civil or otherwise, which involved Britain or any European Great Power or the United States, 'or during any prolonged political excitement, seriously affecting the international relations of any such Powers'. This latter addition meant that, in practice, extra payment was demanded even when only small European states were at war with each other.

For less urgent news, press rates were gradually becoming available by the end of the nineteenth century. A press rate for Australia of 2s. 8d. per word was introduced in 1886, compared with the ordinary rate of 9s. 4d. By 1913 press rates to the British Empire were: Australia 7½d., South Africa 3¾d., India 4d., Canada 5d.

The number of Reuter overseas offices or news bureaux was growing (see Table 4.1), although the bureaux were mostly one-man affairs. Stringers,

TABLE 4.1 Number of Reuter overseas offices or news bureaux

	1894	1906
Western Europe (including UK)	8	10
Eastern Europe	1	3
Africa	2	4
Australasia	6	10
Middle East	2	3
India	5	6
Far East	5	8
North America	3	3

many of them local newspapermen, still contributed vitally to coverage from remote corners of the world.

The end-of-century expansion of services brought good results. Whereas in 1891 the chairman was referring at the annual general meeting to complaints that telegrams from Reuters 'too drily chronicle events', six years later he was telling shareholders that, 'judging from letters received', the news supplied to the newspapers from the recent Ashanti, Sudan, Niger, and Benin expeditions had given general satisfaction.

Yet, characteristically, *The Times* remained quick to grumble. Moberly Bell complained to Baron Herbert on 8 March 1898 that news from the non-civilized world was being automatically charged to the special service. Reuters, Bell argued, ought to have a representative 'in every place from which important news may be expected'; and messages from such stringers should be treated as routine, and be included in the general service. 'If in addition to this you instruct him to wire ornate descriptions of his personal adventures and impressions it is quite right that anyone caring to publish them should pay for the luxury.'[11]

British newspapers were still printing both 'general' and 'special' news from Reuters in telegram form; but the first signs of bolder editing into 'story' shape were evident by the end of the century, with parts of telegrams omitted or material conflated. The word 'story' was first used in this sense in the American press. Newspapers liked to receive their Reuter telegrams in good time for editing. A circular issued on 17 May 1906 told Reuter correspondents that the London morning papers were now printing about midnight, instead of an hour or more later. Consequently, no long telegrams were to be sent to Old Jewry after 10.30 p.m., while between then and midnight 'everything must be rigorously summarised'.

5

The top news story of the 1880s for the British press was the dramatic death of General Gordon at Khartoum in 1885. Here was a story centring upon a national hero which came to a shocking climax with agonizing slowness—in short, an exemplary piece of news. Gordon had featured at intervals in the Reuter file for over twenty years. He personified the Victorian ideal of a muscular Christian, active against the heathen. In the early 1860s 'Chinese Gordon' had been defeating the Taipings; in the 1870s he had been pacifying equatorial Africa, ruling the Sudan, and quarrelling with the authorities in Cairo. Now during 1884–5 he was besieged for ten months by the Mahdi at Khartoum.

As a long-delayed relief column inched its way up the Nile, Reuter correspondents in Cairo and with the army sent back daily reports. Kipling recalled
in *The Light That Failed* how 'it was above all things necessary that England at
breakfast should be amused and thrilled and interested whether Gordon lived
or died, or half the British army went to pieces in the sands'. The hand-to-
hand nature of the fighting, added Kipling, 'allowed of miraculous escapes
which were worth telegraphing home at eighteenpence the word'.

Reuter copy was widely used in the British press; but the first news that
Khartoum had fallen came from official sources in London. The story, however, was not yet complete. No one knew what had happened to Gordon.
There were even rumours that the Mahdi had granted him safe passage. Then
on 9 February Pigott, the Reuter correspondent with the relief column,
telegraphed conclusively but without flourish:

> Korti, Feb. 9, 11.30.
> Sir Charles Wilson and Lieutenant Stuart-Wortley have arrived here from
> Gubat having made the journey in four days.
> They bring intelligence of General Gordon's death on Feb. 4.

Reuters had obtained the beat of the decade, even though next day the date
of death had to be corrected. Gordon had died on 26 January: 4 February was
the day when the two officers had reached Korti.

The British papers printed the bad news on 11 February. Most accepted
that Reuters was correct, although *The Times* began an accompanying editorial: 'A Reuter telegram, which we sincerely hope will not be confirmed . . .'
Not until 14 February was there any such confirmation, when another Reuter
report quoted a dispatch in Arabic found in the saddlebag of a captured soldier. Finally, on 16 February came official confirmation.

Many generals were suspicious of the new breed of war correspondents,
who sometimes wrote as if they knew better than those in command. This
was a temptation felt less by Reuter correspondents than by newspaper representatives who were required to send back long narratives. Lord Wolseley,
the Victorian hero in overall command of the British forces in the Sudan,
showed himself to be quite well disposed towards journalists, but on his own
terms. If necessary, he was prepared to feed correspondents with false
information in order to mislead the enemy. He wrote that it was 'very necessary to *manipulate* correspondents, and to be at all times on the best of terms
with them, but it must be done upon a system'.[12]

The status of war correspondents was ambiguous. They usually had to
make their own arrangements for food and horses. And yet they had to
obtain a licence from headquarters, and to sign a declaration drawn up by

the War Office. They shared with the soldiers many of the risks of death from enemy action, or (more likely) from disease. In May 1885 Frank Roberts, the Reuter correspondent with General Graham's forces in the Sudan, died of enteric fever at Suakin, aged 25. He was the first Reuter correspondent ever to die on duty. Wolseley was chief speaker at the unveiling in St Paul's Cathedral on 16 June 1888 of a large bronze plaque (still in place) dedicated to seven correspondents, including Roberts, who had been killed or died in the Sudan.[13]

Reuters long provided a service of news not only *from* the British army in Egypt, but also *to* that same army. From 1885 a daily telegraphic summary was sent free of charge by the Cairo office, addressed to the 'Army up the Nile'. This service sustained morale by keeping the troops in the desert in touch with the outside world. It continued, with the same address, until after the Second World War.[14]

6

During the Graeco-Turkish War of 1897 Reuters had correspondents on both sides—H. A. Gwynne with the Turks, Kinnaird Rose with the Greeks. 'Taffy' Gwynne (1865–1950) was the outstanding Reuter correspondent of the period (Plate 14). Dickinson described him as 'a man of exceptional physical power, capable of any endurance'. He certainly needed all his strength as a Reuter correspondent while reporting Kitchener's reconquest of the Sudan in 1898, a campaign conducted (as Gwynne later recalled) on the cheap: 'Our daily ration was one pound of onions, a quart of dried beans, occasionally a potato ration, and as much water as we liked to drink out of the Nile.'[15]

Gwynne was said by Dickinson to possess 'moral qualities which gained for him the complete confidence and approbation of the commanding officer wherever he served'. During the second Boer War, Gwynne was the chief Reuter correspondent. He told Baron Herbert on 12 July 1901 that twice a week he was allowed to see Kitchener, who had become commander-in-chief in South Africa. 'One day talking of correspondents, he told me that he would like me as Reuters Correspondent to be the official chronicler in every war so that other correspondents whom he could not trust should not be with the army.' Gwynne took this as a personal compliment. But Kitchener may have wished to favour Reuters because it was a news agency and therefore made its news available to all, in the belief that this was fairer than favouring any particular newspaper, such as *The Times*. Not surprisingly, *The Times* manager, Moberly Bell, always complained vigorously against Reuters being granted any such special recognition.[16]

Gwynne was in charge of over a hundred Reuter correspondents and stringers during the Boer War. None was killed or seriously injured; 21 were awarded the Queen's South Africa Medal. Henry Mockford kept his documents to the end of his life. These included a licence permitting him to 'draw Rations for himself and one servant, and Forage for one horse on payment'. Mockford had accepted the printed *Rules for Newspaper Correspondents Accompanying Troops in the Field.* No ciphers or codes were to be used. 'All communications to the press must be confined to events that have occurred.' Messages must be in English. 'The Press Censor will have full discretionary power.'

Even before the outbreak of hostilities, Reuters showed itself willing to adopt self-censorship. Henry Collins, temporarily in charge at Cape Town, recalled that he had suppressed a report of a consignment of ammunition being allowed to reach the Orange Free State days before the start of the war. Collins did this on patriotic grounds, because 'high official circles' had told him that publication of such a report, even if it explained that the business had been conducted under a binding free-trade treaty, 'would probably have a most disturbing effect in England'.[17]

Although Gwynne, like Collins, was personally a dedicated imperialist, he understood the value of the established Reuter practice of reporting from both sides in wars between civilized states. Gwynne recruited a Johannesburg solicitor, J. de Villiers Roos, to serve as a war correspondent on the Boer side, an arrangement which the Boers accepted even though Reuters was a British news agency. Gwynne outlined to Roos the delicacy of the position (15 September 1899):

> we should be glad to get news from the Transvaal side through you, but you can well understand that it will be a somewhat delicate matter to adjust any disparity in the account of the engagement sent by you and by our special correspondents with your opponents. We are an organisation formed to supply the public with news, and in the capacity of news purveyors we are glad to give every side their say; but we are at the same time a British agency and we would therefore ask you to avoid as far as possible sending us too biassed reports. We do not for a moment expect you to diminish in any way the deeds of the Transvaal forces, but we hope to get from you as impartial accounts of engagements as it is possible for a sympathiser—and probably a combatant—with the Transvaal to give.[18]

The arrangement worked satisfactorily. Roos's reporting from the enemy side was predominantly factual, even if with an underlying sympathy towards the Boers.

Reuters gave particular attention to cabling short first news from the various fronts. The correspondents for the newspapers, on the other hand, were particularly required to supply longer descriptive pieces. Some of these newspapermen were alleged by Gwynne in a private letter (19 December 1900) to have been less than scrupulous:

> One thing this war has done and that is to knock on the head all the romance about war-correspondents. When men have seen such heroes as Bennet Burleigh [*Daily Telegraph*], Melton Prior [*Illustrated London News*] or Pearse [*Daily News*] keep carefully in the rear in reality but blaze forth in their letters and sketches as sorts of leaders of forlorn hopes, they begin to take their proper measure. When we took Bloemfontein I rode in with an Australian the first and I was the first man to announce to Lord Roberts that Bloemfontein had fallen. I am told that Melton Prior in the *Illustrated London News* has drawn a picture of Bennet Burleigh doing this historic action.[19]

When Burleigh died in 1914 *The Times* (18 June) confirmed that newspaper war correspondents of his generation had often been more interested in colour than in accuracy: 'hardy gentlemen of fortune, whose main journalistic asset was robust health, inexhaustible energy, and a picturesque imagination'. Victorian war correspondents for Reuters had likewise possessed stamina and energy; but they had been expected to report with accuracy, brevity, and speed, without 'picturesque imagination'.

The greatest of all Reuter scoops—a scoop rather than a beat, because the agency remained alone with the story—was achieved in May 1900 when Reuters gave news of the relief of Mafeking. The resistance offered by Colonel Baden-Powell's force under siege in Mafeking, although not of great military importance, had caught the anxious imagination of the British public. Some news had come out during the siege, but this had only whetted the public appetite for more. Notably, J. E. Pearson, an American working for Reuters, had avoided the Boer patrols, bicycled to the outskirts, and slipped in and out under cover of night. This gave Reuters a good story from inside the town. Soon afterwards it was relieved. But the British army relief column could only report back to headquarters by mounted messenger. An official announcement was therefore bound to be delayed for at least two days. Fortunately for Reuters, the Boers told W.H. Mackay, its Pretoria correspondent. They presumably assumed that he would not be able to get the story out. Enterprisingly, he saw that he might avoid the Boer censorship by going to the frontier with Portuguese Mozambique. There he handed his message to a railway engine-driver, who took it to the Eastern Telegraph

Company office at Laurenco Marques. Tradition has it that Mackay paid the driver £5 to hide the paper in his sandwiches.

The relief column had broken through on 17 May, and on the following evening Reuters told the world. In a letter to his son, Dickinson described how he was smoking his pipe in the editorial office and watching a game of chess being played by two sub-editors, 'the news being rather slack for the moment', when a telegraph boy appeared with a telegram:

> I opened it, gave such a yell of delight that everybody knew what the news was, sent the chessmen flying and in two seconds had started the glad tidings on its career round the whole habitable globe. I opened the telegram at 9.16 p.m.; by 9.17 the news was in every newspaper office in London; by 9.18 it was telephoned to the Lord Mayor and to the House of Commons; and by 9.20 it had gone to the Queen, the Prince of Wales, the Viceroy of India and the War Office, to say nothing of every Australian colony, China, Japan, the West Indies, West Africa, North and South Africa and every corner of Europe; and by 9.30 an immense crowd, shouting and waving flags, was rushing through the city.[20]

Queen Victoria asked to see the original telegram. The Lord Mayor of London read out the news from the steps of the Mansion House. The country went wild, and the verb 'to maffick' was coined and soon entered the *Oxford English Dictionary*. The Reuter report was not confirmed from army headquarters in South Africa for another two days, but the agency was everywhere trusted; and answering a question in the House of Commons A. J. Balfour, the First Lord of the Treasury, accepted that, although the telegram was unconfirmed, there was 'good reason to think it may be true'.

It was dramatic in its meaning, but not in its wording; and Reuters in London had attached an explanatory note:

> PRETORIA, Friday
>
> It is officially announced that when the laagers and forts around Mafeking had been severely bombarded the siege was abandoned by the Boers. A British force advancing from the south then took possession of the town.

Reuters explained what this meant:

> From the wording of the above telegram, and notably the use of the word 'laagers', it may be inferred that the British relief force vigorously attacked the Boer laagers and forts around the beleaguered town, and compelled the Boers to raise the siege.—Reuter.

The *Daily Express* of 19 May splashed this telegram in the middle of its front page, under the ecstatic headline: 'When Shall Their Glory Fade?' (Plate 15)

7

Typical Reuter news telegrams were much less exciting than the Mafeking example, although all sought to be interesting to newspaper readers in different parts of the world. A few copies have survived of Reuter news bulletins supplied to *Bangkok Times* subscribers in 1894. These bulletins contained a mixture of British, world, and local news. News in March of the final resignation of W. E. Gladstone as British Prime Minister, for example, appeared alongside local news of the sinking of a Thai rice-boat. A telegram telling of the assassination of President Carnot of France in June 1894 rated a whole bulletin to itself.

Copies have also survived of Reuter telegrams in the form of handwritten news-sheets on sale in January 1901 to passengers aboard liners passing through Port Said. The Boer War was still being reported in detail; but the main news was of the final illness of Queen Victoria at Osborne House on the Isle of Wight. 'The Queen is suffering from great physical prostration accompanied by symptoms that cause anxiety' (Plate 16).

Reuters was expected to report wars which the newspapers left alone. Shareholders were told in 1903 that in covering the Somaliland expedition 'the expense in camels, servants, runners, and supplies of all sorts, has . . . been out of all proportion to the amount of intelligence received.' But the cost had perforce been borne because most newspapers were depending entirely upon Reuters for Somali news. The chairman told the 1904 annual general meeting that the Russo-Japanese War was making heavy demands, financial and otherwise:

> as European are not able to subsist on the fare provided for Japanese troops, the different correspondents have been obliged to make arrangements with a contractor to 'furnish cooks and to provide and prepare each day three good plain meals of European food'. Interpreters are also indispensable, because messages sent over the Japanese field wires must be written in Japanese.

The long voyage of the Russian Baltic fleet to defeat in the Far East led to a most serious case of misreporting by Reuters. In October 1904 the Russian ships had fired on British fishing vessels off the Dogger Bank in the North Sea, believing that they were Japanese torpedo-boats. One trawler was sunk; two fishermen were killed, and many injured. British public opinion was outraged. Early in 1905 an international inquiry was convened in Paris. At its conclusion, a Russian diplomat revealed to a Reuter reporter what the diplomat claimed to be a summary of the forthcoming judgment; this exonerated the Russians. Reuters published the leak without giving a source. In fact, the judgment, when announced a few days later, said quite the contrary to the leak; the Russians were censured. Reuters had unwittingly helped them to put up a smokescreen.[21]

In 1912 came the almost unbelievable news of the sinking of the 'unsinkable' *Titanic* on her maiden transatlantic voyage. Reuters was two hours ahead in London with a report of the liner hitting an iceberg at 10.35 on the night of 14 April. When the flash came through, one of the night telegraph operators at Old Jewry was asleep, and the other was occupied. A young messenger boy, Leslie Smith, was left to tap out the startling news to the newspapers. Reuters had its beat; but thereafter came uncertainty. This reflected the confusion in New York, where news about the fate of the vessel was being collected. For example, *The Times* of 16 April contained one Reuter telegram which reported dramatically but reassuringly: '*The Titanic* sank at 2.20 this morning. No lives were lost.' But the same issue carried another Reuter telegram, which was nearer the grim truth: 'The White Star officials now admit that many lives have been lost.'[22]

If Reuters was contradictory, the Central News was worse. It published a colourful description of the supposed rescue of passengers from the sinking liner by other ships. In reality, no vessels reached the scene before the *Titanic* sank.

8

Public interest in sport had become intense throughout the British Empire by the turn of the century. The cost of sports reporting in detail was high. Reuters devised codes especially for each cricket tour by the English, Australian, or South African teams. One cabled word, such as 'AHYAYBITEV', for example, would reach Old Jewry from Cape Town. The sports sub-editor would then refer to the codebook, and produce the following interesting report:

> Nourse [coded as AH] was out one short of his century [YA was code for 99].
> The Natal captain was run out when he tried for the single and Bardsley [YB]
> at mid-off [IT] fielded smartly and threw down the wicket.

Cricket was important in cementing imperial unity, but for many newspaper readers boxing was even more interesting. From the earliest days, Reuters had reported professional bouts, and by 1899 the special service was carrying a 1,400–word round-by-round account of 'The Great Glove Fight in America. Tom Sharkey v. Kid McCoy'. Association football, Rugby Union football, and horse-racing also featured prominently in the Reuter file. A system was devised for cabling the weekly British soccer results to colonial newspapers. Only the figures of goals scored were telegraphed; these were then compared at the receiving end against the known fixture list.

When the first modern Olympic Games were held at Athens in 1896, results and descriptions came from Reuters only irregularly, apparently at the whim of a local stringer. In contrast, by 1912 when the games were held in London, Reuters was providing complete coverage. The commitment of Reuters to accuracy and speed was a strong recommendation in its sports reporting. Both for itself and for its competitors, Victorian and Edwardian, Reuters had set a high standard. But the 'Great War' of 1914–18 was to test the agency as never before.

FIVE

Wartime Reconstruction
1914–1918

I

O N 22 January 1915, six months after the outbreak of the First World
War, Baron Herbert de Reuter wrote to Roderick Jones in South
Africa about the character of the conflict . Despite the German ori-
gins of his family, Baron Herbert wanted a total British victory:

> We here who have professionally to watch and follow, and, for the proper con-
> duct of the Reuter organisation, interpret the meaning of all that unfolds itself
> to the eye of the observer, are staggered by the energy, resources, organisation,
> and skill with which the Germans entered into, and have conducted this stu-
> pendous conflict. Every day I realise more deeply the colossal task before us,
> and the necessity of sparing no sacrifice to succeed where failure spells ruin to
> three Empires, and will involve the unspeakable blight of German military
> tyranny over the whole Continent.

Baron Herbert, who was born in London and lived in England throughout
his life, rightly regarded himself as a patriotic Briton. But he bore a German
name. And the question was publicly asked in the early months of the war
whether he could be trusted, even whether Reuters itself was safely 'British'.
Had it been subverted by German influences?

These questions were given focus by the publication in September 1914—
a month after the start of the conflict—of pre-war dispatches from the British
Ambassador in Berlin 'respecting an Official German Organization for
Influencing the Press of Other Countries'. The formation of this semi-official body had been inspired early in 1914 by the head of the German Press
Bureau, who had rallied the support of leading German industrialists. They
wanted to colour the flow of news about Germany sent to foreign agencies
and newspapers. They planned to advertise only in foreign papers which
received their German news via approved channels. The British Ambassador
reported on 27 February 1914 that Havas had agreed to take its news about
Germany only through the Wolff Bureau, which was to be fed propaganda

by the new body. 'The company intends to make a similar arrangement with Reuter's Telegraph Bureau.'[1]

When this report was made public in September it was naturally asked in the British press whether Reuters had made any such deal. In fact, no recorded approach had been made to Reuters up to the outbreak of war; while Havas, for its part, had rejected such German pressure. But four letters from Baron Herbert to *The Times* were needed to establish the innocence of Reuters. At first, he had tried to be dismissive. A *Times* leader on 26 September thought his lack of clarity suspicious. On 27 September a fourth letter from Baron Herbert, drafted by Dickinson, the chief editor, finally succeeded in removing 'the singular suggestion that our news service is used for the purpose of misleading British opinion in favour of Germany'. On the contrary, emphasized the letter, German newspapers were full of rancour at the patriotic handling of war news by Reuters.

The fiftieth anniversary of Reuter's Telegram Company in February 1915 provided a good opportunity to proclaim the Britishness of the agency. A jubilee leaflet, anonymous but written by Dickinson, declared firmly: 'Reuter's Agency has always been recognised as a British institution representing the English point of view.' Baron Herbert was described as 'in all respects an Englishman. The Directors, the Editorial Staff, and the correspondents are British pure and simple, and so, with the exception of a score, are the 1,200 shareholders.'

This last point needed to be emphasized because rumours had circulated soon after the start of the war that Reuters—with its German name—included a large number of enemy citizens among its shareholders. The British Foreign Office went to the length of analysing the shareholder list, and satisfied itself that this was not the case. An article in the *National Review* for October 1914, which counted 146 holders of 100 or more Reuter shares, found only about ten German surnames, addresses or institutions among the number. Yet the *Review* still described the ownership of Reuters as 'curiously cosmopolitan', and asked suspiciously: 'Are its numerous German shareholders participating in the distribution of its ample dividends?'[2]

This question implied that Reuters was flourishing. In fact, it was not. Throughout 1914 its reputation and its finances were under increasing pressure. Reuter shares, which had stood at £12 each in 1912, were down to £5 by March 1915. The advertising fiasco had damaged the good name of the agency, and Reuter's Bank was in difficulties. The war immediately added another problem when, for security reasons, Reuters was told to stop using its codes. This made both the private telegram and remittance services uneconomic. Many Reuter 'traffic' staff in London and throughout the British

Empire had to be given notice. The British Government was told that whereas the two services had made an estimated profit of £6,542 for the last 17 months before the war, they had lost £17,346 during its first 17 months (August 1914 to December 1915) because of the coding ban. Early in 1916 Reuters asked the British Government to advance £50,000 on easy terms in part compensation. In the event, this request became forgotten when Reuters was reconstructed with Government backing later in the year. Not until after the return of peace in 1918 was Reuters allowed again to use its codes.

2

Worry about losses on 'traffic' was adding to the pressures upon Baron Herbert during the first months of the war. These pressures included family problems. He was estranged from his only son, Hubert, who had disappointed him by working only briefly for Reuters. By temperament, Hubert, although literary, was not a journalist. He wrote poetry. His idealism was to lead him to volunteer for the British army early in the war, and to die a gallant death as a private soldier in Flanders in 1916.

Baron Herbert had reproached Hubert for enlisting against his mother's wishes when she was fatally ill. She died on 15 April 1915. Three days later, a Sunday, Baron Herbert shot himself at his country house near Reigate, outside London. He left a letter addressed 'To the spirit of my dear wife Edith': 'Death shall not separate us for we will repose in the same grave.' So ended, suddenly and sadly, the involvement of the founder's family in the management of Reuters.[3]

Senior staff mourned their chief sincerely. He had been in charge of Reuters for thirty-seven years, much longer than his father before him or any successor since. But for several years the opinion had been growing, inside and outside the company, that Baron Herbert was losing his grip. At the next annual general meeting on 3 June 1915 discussion of the severe difficulties now facing the company led to revelations about Baron Herbert's recent mishandling of the business.

The Hon. Mark [Francis] Napier (1852–1919) was in the chair at this tense meeting (Plate 23). He had become chairman in 1911, in succession to his uncle by marriage, Sir John Dalrymple-Hay. Napier had served on the board since 1888 without making much obvious impact. But, thanks to his character and connections, he was destined to play a vital part in the reconstruction of Reuters during the next few years. A younger son of a Scottish landed family (Lord Napier and Ettrick), he was a lawyer by training, and had shared chambers in the 1870s with H. H. Asquith, who was now the Liberal Prime Minister. Napier had himself been briefly (1892–5) a Gladstonian Liberal Member of Parliament. In retrospect, Asquith described Napier's career as 'haphazard', for he 'did not really care much for the law'. On the other hand, Asquith remembered his friend as 'one of the most lovable men I have known', with variously 'a shrewd native intelligence, infinite courage, fine old-fashioned manners, quite exceptional physical courage and agility, a great aptitude for the mechanical arts, such as carpentry, and imperturbable sang-froid'. This combination of attractive qualities predisposed Asquith to respond favourably in his official capacity when in 1916 Napier made representations for help on behalf of Reuters.[4]

With the death of Baron Herbert, Napier was left as the most senior Reuter director. Two others had become board members in 1912. They were George Grinnell Milne, and the Hon. Edmund W. Parker, a businessman with New Zealand connections. The third member was Gerald W. Williams, a leading stockbroker, who had joined the board in February 1915 to become chairman of Reuter's Bank. He was the most weighty businessman on the board, well respected in the City of London. His stockbroking firm had raised large subscriptions when new capital was being sought for Reuter's Bank in 1912, and he had expressed concern about its management at the 1914 annual general meeting. He was suspected, probably rightly, of aspiring to displace Napier as chairman of Reuters.

Williams seconded the adoption of the report and accounts at the 1915 annual general meeting; but he did not pretend that all was well, either with the news agency or the bank. Napier had already admitted as much in moving the adoption. He spoke of the interruption to the flow of news and trade caused by the war, and the associated breaking of contracts. He mentioned the losses caused by the ban upon the use of codes. He regretted that a major fraud upon the Sydney branch had cost the company at least £29,000. He reported that Hajduska, the Hungarian manager of the bank, had been on leave in Austria when the war broke out, and had been called up to fight on the enemy side. This was not, in fact, correct, for throughout the war Hajduska was stranded in Holland. An Englishman had been appointed in his place. Napier admitted that Baron Herbert had allowed Hajduska 'a too wide discretion' to invest in schemes 'which involved the locking up of part of our capital which would have been better left liquid'. Although company profit for 1914 totalled £35,725, Napier warned that this would all be needed to meet current difficulties. No dividend was to be paid.

Williams, in his seconding speech, was more directly critical of Baron Herbert, even while describing him as a man of 'singular charm':

He had a grave defect as a Managing Director of a Bank, and that was that he knew very little about banking. His brilliant idea of adding a banking branch to the business was remarkably sound, but he put the wrong man in command of that branch, and when he had put him there he backed him up through thick and thin.

Worse still, concluded Williams, was the fact that Baron Herbert had left his fellow directors in ignorance about what he was doing. Williams did not reveal that he had himself threatened—only a few days before Baron Herbert's suicide—to resign from the bank chairmanship and from the Reuter board, if the managing director made any more bank loans upon his own initiative.

This belated frankness by Napier and Williams was not enough to satisfy many of the shareholders present. From the floor, one businessman share-holder, Brodie James, delivered a strong attack upon the board for trying to place all the blame upon Baron Herbert and Hajduska. James quoted some of the large promises about the bank's future made by Napier at the 1912 and 1913 general meetings. The directors had now admitted the slackness of their supervision: 'you have forfeited the confidence of the shareholders and must go'. James demanded a poll for the re-election of Napier as chairman. There was never any danger to Napier, for the directors had some 1,500 proxies in their pockets. He was re-elected by 1,762 votes to 626. Nevertheless, this sig-nificant minority vote—a large majority of those present—constituted a warning that the board must quickly put its affairs in order. The death of Baron Herbert had removed one obstacle to reconstruction; if he had lived, could he have survived much longer as managing director?

3

Who would now succeed him? Dickinson, the chief editor, was sure that it ought to be Roderick Jones, the successful general manager in South Africa. For several years Dickinson had been encouraging Jones's ambitions. He had written to Cape Town on 5 December 1913 about the prospects for 1914: 'One wonders each time that the year goes up a tick what is in store . . . all sorts of things may happen in a very short time. We sadly need some young blood.' Jones, aged 36, did not disagree. After the war had started, and with problems for Reuters becoming threatening, Jones wrote to Dickinson on 4 January 1915 about the company crisis. 'There are not so many gentlemen in the Service [Reuters] . . . and there is a danger of a brood filling the bill who in the end will not exalt the Agency's name.' Interestingly, Jones himself had been born scarcely a 'gentleman'. And his struggle throughout life to improve his social standing shaped his character, which in turn determined his impact upon Reuters.[5]

[George] Roderick Jones (1877–1962) had been born near Manchester. His father—about whom he rarely spoke—was only a hat salesman. His mother, by contrast, was distantly related both to a Victorian Archbishop of Canterbury, and to the ancient Scottish Earls of Cassillis. His mother's father was a cotton agent, a job of higher standing than that of a salesman. In other words, Jones's mother had married beneath her. This may explain why the wedding took place only five weeks before his birth. The social position of the Joneses may have been further damaged in the following year by the crash of the Bank of Glasgow, in which Jones's mother was said to have lost all her money.

This insecure early background marked Jones for life. It meant that he could not attend a fee-paying 'public school', or go to university. His maternal grandfather helped to educate him soundly in Christianity and the 'three Rs'; but Jones knew from childhood that he would have to make his own way in the world. As a young man, he continued his education through wide reading. Fortunately, he was intelligent and energetic. Unfortunately, he overcompensated for his modest origins by acting too emphatically as if he came from a 'good' family and had received a 'good' education. He dressed with excessive correctness. He never missed a chance to make money, much of which he spent while head of Reuters upon living in conspicuous style, both in a London mansion at Hyde Park Gate and in a country house at Rottingdean on the south coast. Perhaps Jones's assertiveness and display owed something to the fact that he was only five feet five inches tall. For years, his passport claimed his height as three and a half inches more, thanks to built-up shoes. His marriage in 1920 at the age of 42 was a 'society' event. His bride, Enid Bagnold—later celebrated as the author of the best-selling novel, *National Velvet*, and of successful plays—alone knew of the vulnerability beneath Jones's grand manner. She passed him a revealing note when he was presiding at a public dinner in 1933: *'Darling.* You sit there looking so real, so humorously critical, so (fallaciously) good tempered—so clean cut, such an intelligent gentleman, that you *can't* be so dissatisfied with yourself as you sometimes seem. You are an ass, Darling, about yourself.'

Jones was pretentious, but he could also be engaging. His appealing eyes were often remarked upon, while his voice has been remembered as unusually compelling. His intelligence and his strength of purpose were readily apparent. Subordinates were shown this strength without hesitation. Among social equals or superiors, Jones was gentler but always purposeful. He impressed by the fund of knowledge and experience, tempered by good sense and good humour, which he displayed in conversation. He was under 30 when he became general manager in South Africa, and looked even younger. Yet leaders of local politics and business were soon asking for his views, and exchanging their own in return.

Jones explained in his reminiscences, *A Life in Reuters* (1951), how he had entered journalism as a step towards becoming Prime Minister of a united South Africa. He was soon to abandon these adolescent political ambitions under the spell of journalism for its own sake. He had been sent in 1895 to live with his mother's married sister in Pretoria, the Boer Transvaal capital. Emigration overseas was of course a traditional way for young Englishmen of no fortune to seek advancement.

Jones started work as an assistant reporter on the only daily newspaper in town, *The Press*. He made rapid progress. He wrote well, whether in simple factual or colourfully descriptive style; and he added greatly to his local usefulness by learning to speak and write Afrikaans. On 2 January 1896 the Boer authorities allowed him, as a favour, to conduct the first press interview with Dr Jameson and two senior colleagues, who had just arrived under arrest at Pretoria railway station after the failure of their raid into the Transvaal. Jones's report was published by Reuters in its special service. 'They were very reticent, but informed me that the attack had failed owing to the absence of the support which they had expected' (*The Times*, 8 January 1896). In the same year, Jones first met Louis Botha, the future Boer leader; and two years later he came to know Jan Smuts. Following the outbreak of the Boer War in October 1899, Jones had to withdraw to Cape Town. After a spell as a 'travelling correspondent' for the London *Times*, when his pass from the censor said that he was 'not to accompany troops at the front', he became chief subeditor on the *Cape Times*, and chief cable correspondent for Reuters. Finally, in the spring of 1902, with the war at last ending, he sailed back to England. He had been recommended by the general manager in South Africa, J. A. Barraclough, to take charge of the new South African section in the London newsroom. Jones rightly saw this as a good career opportunity, despite a drop in earnings. His salary was £400 a year, increased to £500 in 1904. In South Africa since 1895 he had worked only partly for Reuters: now at last he was a full-time Reuter journalist.

Jones successfully developed the Reuter service from London to meet the growing expectations of the South African press. He was soon a favourite with Dickinson, the chief editor, and eventually became on good terms with Baron Herbert himself. In May 1904 an article by Jones, entitled 'The Black Peril in South Africa', appeared in *The Nineteenth Century*, a leading monthly.

Baron Herbert read the article, and summoned Jones to discuss it. Jones had urged Britons and Boers to unite against 'the oncoming hordes of superficially civilised blacks'. Thereafter Jones was invited for frequent talks with his chief.

This intimacy bore fruit when in the autumn of 1905 Jones was appointed general manager in South Africa. His salary was to be £600 a year, plus 10 per cent commission with a £400 minimum. He eventually became sufficiently affluent to invest profitably in the Johannesburg market, with its gold and diamond shares. That market expected speedy news from London, while London was equally eager for news about the South African economy. Reuters dominated this international news exchange, and increasingly also the internal news market. It employed some 250 correspondents and stringers throughout Africa south of the Zambesi. About 100 papers subscribed to local South African news from Reuters.

Some leading South African newspaper proprietors were jealous of this Reuter predominance. In 1908 the *Cape Times*, *Cape Argus*, and *Rand Daily Mail* formed their own organization for the collection of both world and internal news. It was called the South African Amalgamated Press Agency (SAAPA). Here was a major challenge for Reuters, which persisted for nearly 18 months before it was overcome. Jones's policy was to keep the provincial press loyal, while he slowly wore down SAAPA. 'Had we refused to fight,' he later told Napier (19 September 1915), 'or had we failed in the fight or in the subsequent negotiations, we should have been forced to abandon our South African press business.'

South African profits were important to Reuters, and on 2 March 1910 Jones was congratulated by the board for his skilful negotiation of a favourable settlement. This contrived to save the faces of the SAAPA newspapermen, while ensuring a virtual Reuter monopoly in news handling. A new South African Press Agency was formed early in 1910, within which Reuters kept a seven-twelfths holding; the three principal newspaper groups shared the rest of the ownership equally. The Boer papers remained apart from the new body, but were allowed equal access to news from Reuters. On 22 September 1913 Baron Herbert praised Jones in high terms for the 'Pax Romana that your skilful diplomacy has established throughout journalistic South Africa'. Profit from the area for 1914 was a healthy £9,381.

Baron Herbert was impressed by Jones's success in raising the prestige of Reuters through personal contacts in the topmost social and political circles. Reuter general managers could usually expect some recognition within colonial society, but Jones won remarkable acceptance for himself. He became, for example, secretary and later master of the Cape Town hunt, which was as much a social as a sporting body. Most leading figures were hunt members.

Lord Gladstone (son of the Victorian Prime Minister), who in 1910 had been appointed the first Governor-General of the Union of South Africa, was made a member; and Jones became a personal friend. He also lost no time in renewing his earlier friendly relations with Botha and Smuts, the Boer leaders. As Prime Minister, first of the Transvaal and then of the newly united dominion, Botha always favoured Reuters. This meant that the agency was often given first news of official announcements. Occasionally, Jones was deliberately allowed to leak inside information—as when he publicized Botha's intention to deport to Britain the syndicalist leaders of the great 1914 Rand strike. Jones subsequently claimed that during his decade as manager in South Africa Reuters was never once beaten on an important story.

He had received tempting job offers while in South Africa, but he had remained loyal because he was genuinely proud to serve Reuters. Before long, however, his pride in good service was translating into high ambition. Jones wanted to become head of the whole agency, preferably at not too distant a date. After his victory over SAAPA in 1910, he revealed his ambition to Dickinson, who promised to listen out for hints of Baron Herbert's intentions about retirement. In 1912, while on a visit to London, Jones boldly spoke openly to Baron Herbert. The managing director was apparently well disposed towards the idea of eventually handing over to Jones; but tantalisingly he did not say when this might be.

4

Baron Herbert's suicide came at a bad moment for Jones. The dead man had done nothing to prepare the ground for a successor. The four Reuter directors, who had the power of choice, knew Jones only by name. The candidate they knew best was Walter Bradshaw, the veteran company secretary. Jones did not dare to challenge Bradshaw outright. Instead, on 20 April 1915—only two days after Baron Herbert's suicide—he sent Bradshaw a carefully worded cable, and also a letter: 'failing yourself I should wish to press my own claims strongly upon directors in view my admitted services and assurances Baron gave when last in London.' Next day, Jones wrote to Napier, the chairman. asking for his claims to be considered, and for his letter to be read to the board. He was prepared, he told Napier, to sail home at short notice.

On the same day, Jones confessed confidentially to Dickinson that he was willing to serve as deputy to Bradshaw, with the right of succession. Jones sent Napier typewritten copies of letters of commendation which he had received at intervals from Baron Herbert for his work in South Africa. These included a letter (28 April 1908) from Baron Herbert to Rudyard Kipling, copied to Jones, in which the managing director had said that Jones 'unites in his person to an eminent degree the almost mutually exclusive capacities of a journalist and business man, both of the best type'. As further evidence of his suitability, Jones told Napier that he had been 'repeatedly' entertained and consulted by successive Governors, and also by Botha and Smuts.

All this was to no avail in the short term. The board appointed Bradshaw as general manager, although not as managing director. Given the bad state of the company's affairs, the directors announced their intention of taking a more active part than in Baron Herbert's day.

Bradshaw quickly proved unable to cope. He was a natural lieutenant, not a leader. The board was soon thinking again, and Jones's hopes revived. Lord Gladstone, who had returned in the previous year from South Africa, had already been prompted by Dickinson to write to Napier on Jones's behalf. Although this intervention had come too late to prevent the appointment of Bradshaw, Gladstone's continuing support was to be important. Napier and Gladstone were old political colleagues, members of a network of leading Liberal families connected by marriage and friendship—Napiers, Gladstones, Asquiths, Tennants. This network was to play a key part in the restructuring of Reuters. Jones took care to commend himself, directly or indirectly, to these influential people.

The agency's losses were continuing. The board was told on 28 July that these were estimated at £6,652 for the first half of 1915. The Newspaper Proprietors Association, representing the London papers, was also alleging a decline in the quality of the news service. At last, Jones was recalled for consultation. Within days of landing on 31 July, he met Napier. The chairman was soon convinced that Jones, although young for the job, was the man to lead Reuters.

Napier was not all-powerful, however. The other directors might prefer an outside candidate. The only other internal aspirant was Samuel Carey Clements (1866–1947), the assistant manager. He had been close to the centre for many years, having joined Reuters in 1884, becoming assistant secretary in 1890. Clements was a competent administrator and ambitious; but he was not a journalist. Jones was similarly ambitious and a proven manager; he was also an experienced journalist. Moreover, he possessed a certain personal magnetism which Clements lacked. Throughout his life Jones tried to attract people likely to be helpful to him. His attempts did not always succeed; but he had won over Napier. And Napier now gave him a good chance to reveal his quality to the board.

Jones was asked to write and to present a report about Reuter problems and prospects. He was good at written analysis and exposition. His six-page document, dated 20 September 1915, was a model of clarity and conciseness. It recommended, first, that the bank should be entirely separated from the news agency, and if possible sold off. Jones had found that the commercial and advertising departments were still showing a profit; but that the private telegram and remittance services were losing heavily. He therefore recommended immediate closure, if the Reuter codes could not be brought back into use. He found that the editorial department, 'in spite of the war, with its impoverishment of newspapers on the one hand, and our special expenses on the other', was still making money, although not enough to balance the losses on 'traffic'. The Press Association subscription of £8,000 per year, unchanged since 1881, was far too low and ought to be increased, especially as the London papers were paying nearly three times as much. However, they were restless, and needed careful handling. Covenants with overseas news agencies were producing a fair return, while some subscriptions with British Empire countries were lucrative. South Africa alone, Jones noted with tacit self-congratulation, contributed as much in annual profit as the PA paid in subscription. India was profitable, but Australia yielded only £2,500, even though it possessed four times as many newspapers as South Africa. Canada contributed nothing in press revenue, 'a truly astonishing state of affairs'. Further economies in staffing at headquarters were possible, concluded Jones; but the editorial department should be protected. 'It is here that the future of the Agency lies. Go where you will, at Home or abroad, the name of Reuter continually confronts you.'

Jones accompanied his submission of this report with a formal application for appointment as general manager. He listed his achievements in South Africa, but he made a virtue of not promising instant success. In his own support he named 'four of my friends, all public men', who would be willing to act as referees. These were Lord Gladstone; Sir Mathew Nathan, a former Governor of Natal; Sir Star Jameson, of 'raid' notoriety, but more recently Prime Minister of Cape Colony; and Sir Lionel Phillips, head of Wernher Beit and Company.

On 6 October 1915 Jones was offered and accepted the post of general manager, at an annual salary of £1,400 plus £400 representation allowance. Almost immediately the agency's fortunes began to improve. Economies, suggested by Clements even before Jones had returned from South Africa, were beginning to show benefits. Undoubtedly, however, Jones's active presence in charge made an immediate psychological difference. By November 1915 operations had moved out of loss overall, and the year eventually yielded a modest net profit of £3,942. No dividend was paid.

Jones explained in his reminiscences that he had entered office with four objectives: firstly, to overhaul the internal running of Reuters; secondly, to rescue it from 'incipient insolvency'; thirdly, to reconstruct the limited company; and fourthly, to deliver Reuters 'into the permanent keeping of the newspapers of the United Kingdom'. Jones recalled that he had found the first two objectives comparatively easy to attain. The staff were 'strong in the Reuter tradition', and eager for a lead. Economies were made, and new sources of revenue were discovered. But he found that the reconstruction of the company presented a much more difficult challenge.[6]

5

Jones hoped to ensure the survival of Reuters in the long term through its transfer into the control of the British press, London and provincial. But what of the short term? As a private limited company, with about 1,200 shareholders whose main interest was dividend, Jones believed that Reuters was wrongly structured, especially for working in wartime. Such a vital imperial institution ought not to be exposed to the whims of a large body of shareholders.

The British Government shared Jones's concern. It was worried about the functioning of Reuters in the middle of a war in which news management had become important as never before. Ministers feared that a majority of shares in the company might fall into the wrong hands, perhaps foreign. Even before his appointment as general manager, Jones was outlining ways in which Government help might be enlisted to prevent this. He wrote a memorandum, dated 14 September 1915, which defined 'the object to be achieved' as 'to prevent the control of the company from passing into undesirable hands'. Jones suggested two possible ways of ensuring this: either by appointing a managing director with full powers for the duration of the war, 'with a guarantee of dividends'; or by creating a new company, 'whose shares should be left in safe hands: the shares to be non-transferable for a period long enough to secure the object above stated'. The first scheme, he noted, would not guarantee the safety of Reuters after the war, nor would it prevent unsuitable people from gaining control. Jones therefore strongly recommended the second approach. As soon as he became general manager, he set out to find ways of implementing it.

Twice he was to be frustrated. His first suggestion was for the existing company to go into voluntary liquidation, and for a new company to be formed. Reuters was to be lent a maximum of £100,000 by the Bank of England to buy out shareholders. The Bank was also to provide a maximum of £50,000 as working capital for the new Reuters. The British Government was to guarantee these advances; repayment was to be made over an agreed period; some shares in the new company were to be held by Government nominees with powers of veto; and directors were 'to be appointed and the management to be effected by agreement with the Government'. Nothing came of this scheme because, according to Jones's reminiscences, Williams mishandled negotiations with potential investors. Further mishandling aborted a second scheme early in 1916.[7]

A third initiative in the autumn of 1916, with Jones and Napier now taking the lead to the exclusion of Williams, was finally successful in reconstructing the company. Jones himself had become one of the largest shareholders, having invested all his South African savings and having borrowed to the limit. In September 1916 Godfrey Isaacs, managing director of the Marconi Wireless Telegraph Company, had started to show an interest in Reuters. Isaacs was regarded in the City of London as a sharp character. He had been involved in the 'Marconi scandal' of 1912–13, when insider dealing nearly destroyed the political careers of Lloyd George, the Chancellor of the Exchequer, and of Rufus Isaacs, the Attorney-General, Godfrey's brother. The official report on the Marconi affair largely exonerated the two Liberal Ministers; but an unofficial report, drafted by Lord Robert Cecil, a Conservative, was less indulgent. It also spoke severely of the evidence given by Godfrey Isaacs as 'not satisfactory'. By 1916 Cecil was serving as Foreign Under-Secretary in the wartime coalition. One of his responsibilities was to promote good overseas publicity for the British cause.[8]

Cecil was determined to prevent the untrustworthy Isaacs from gaining control of Reuters. Rather than allow this, the Government would have intervened openly. It was glad, however, to consider proposals from Jones and Napier which would make direct intervention unnecessary. Fortunately for Jones, his main contact in the Foreign Office was John Buchan, a rising imperial politician and writer, already famous as the author of *The Thirty-nine Steps* (Plate 24). Buchan and Jones had first met at the beginning of the century in South Africa. Jones supplied arguments for a memorandum which Buchan sent to the Foreign Secretary, Sir Edward Grey. This 'provisional plan' still envisaged a continuation of the existing company; but Jones and Napier gradually realized (in the plain words of Jones's reminiscences) 'that the only way to make certain of Reuters' safety, and of our own personal security in Reuters, was to get rid of the shareholders altogether'.[9]

How such a numerous ownership could become an embarrassment was now very apparent. The directors of Reuters might well feel bound to put to their shareholders some tempting bid from Isaacs. He was ready to offer £10 per share. Jones and Napier therefore moved in quickly with a bid of £11 per share. Isaacs was finally given the hint that any still higher offer from him would be blocked by the Government, using its powers under the Defence of the Realm Act. Jones and Napier set out to raise the necessary £550,000. This was a large sum, approaching £17 million at 1998 values. Napier was a friend of the chairman of the Union Bank of Scotland, Lord Glenconner, who was the brother-in-law of Asquith. On 3 October Napier wrote to ask Asquith for an interview. Old friendship and perception of the national interest pointed in the same direction. The outcome was that the Union Bank offered the required money on the security of Reuters as a going concern. So much became public knowledge, because it had to be put to the shareholders. For them, the prospect of a windfall was irresistible. The scheme was readily accepted at an extraordinary general meeting on 30 November 1916. The shareholders were not told that the British Government had guaranteed repayment of the loan within three years.

It was also not revealed that Jones and Napier were set to emerge as equal sole owners of the new Reuters. This might well have provoked jealous resistance. 'It was essential', wrote Jones in his reminiscences, 'that I keep myself out of the picture.'[10] So the formal purchase of the old company was made in the names of Napier and of three public figures above suspicion, who were willing to act as Foreign Office nominees. The three were Lord Glenconner; Jameson; and Viscount Peel, a sometime war correspondent and a grandson of the great Conservative Prime Minister.

The new private company—Reuters (1916) Limited—started with an authorized capital of £200,000 and a share issue of 999 £1 shares. Napier and Jones divided 498 shares between themselves. The Foreign Office nominees held 500 until such time as the bank guarantee was no longer needed. One public policy share remained. This allowed the Foreign Office secretly to nominate one director with powers to veto the appointment of any other director; to veto any share transfer; and to exercise a veto on questions of public policy. In a letter to Napier on 8 December 1916, Lord Robert Cecil defined public policy in both specific and general terms:

> the Foreign Office should be able both to prevent the Company from taking any action which might be contrary to public policy (such as the dissemination of reports prejudicial to the national interest, the employment of undesirable correspondents or other employees, the undertaking or continuation of undesirable contracts with other news agencies, or the admission of undesirable persons as shareholders or directors) and also to secure that the Company's operations and actions are in conformity with the public policy or the national

interest, and that information of national importance is properly collected and circulated.

John Buchan became the first Foreign Office director. The Government's powers of veto were never used, and were given up in 1919.

Jones did well financially out of these manœuvres. He had bought Reuter shares at £6 or less and sold them at £11. After Napier's death in 1919 he held 60 per cent of the new Reuter shares, leaving the Napier family with only a minority interest. In addition, he was paid £5,000 a year as managing director of the new company.

It was only fitting, Jones believed, that his personal interest in Reuters should be rewarded in this way. In 1918 his solicitor, who had also become the new company's solicitor, circulated a retrospective memorandum about Foreign Office relations with Reuters since 1915. Cecil minuted, on a copy returned to Jones, that it was 'right to record' how 'this extremely successful transaction' had depended upon 'the loyal and patriotic cooperation of Reuters and particularly of Sir Roderick Jones'. 'I quite agree,' added A. J. Balfour, the Foreign Secretary.

Reuter's Bank had been renamed soon after Jones took over. It was now known as the British Commercial Bank, to separate it as far as possible from the news agency. But the reconstruction process had still left Jones and Napier as proprietors of the bank as well as of the agency. Jones was sure that the bank should be sold, although only at a fair price. How much was it worth? An auditor's report on 9 November 1916 had summed up its career as 'unfortunate'. No dividend had been paid after its first year. Profits of £35,721 for 1914 and of £12,100 for 1915 were not distributed. Some of the bank's difficulties could be fairly blamed upon the war, for it had conducted considerable business inside Germany and Austria. But it had also advanced £50,630 against Mexican Government bonds of doubtful marketability.

The bank was clearly in difficulties, but it was not bound to fail. The auditors valued the surplus assets at over £45,000. But they reported that £50,000 more capital would be needed to put the business upon a sound basis. In the end, Jones was able to exploit an effect of the war. Clarence Hatry, a financier who later went to prison for fraud, wanted to control a bank. Yet in wartime it was not possible to start a new financial institution. Here was an existing bank, with tempting unissued capital in the form of 50,000 £10 shares. In his reminiscences Jones told a tale flattering to himself of his long negotiations with Hatry during 1917. These concluded in October with the sale of the bank on good terms for Reuters. Hatry paid almost £480,000, partly in cash and partly in guaranteed paper. This substantial price was equivalent to over

£12 million in 1998. All but £50,000 of the loan from the Union Bank was now cleared off. Jones and Napier bought back the frozen foreign investments of the bank for a sum higher than Hatry believed them to be worth. After the war, claimed Jones, he was able to sell these at a considerable profit.[11]

In removing an encumbrance from Reuters, Jones had made good money for Reuters. And, since he and Napier were now the only shareholders, he had made good money for himself.

6

Jones conducted these bank negotiations while heavily engaged upon war work. In both world wars he believed that patriotism required close contact between Reuters and the British Government. The question was: How close could such contact be without undermining the independence of the agency? Such independence was essential for the worldwide good name of Reuters in peacetime. Even in wartime, argued Jones in public and in private, the national interest would be best served by maintaining the reputation of Reuter news for independence. In September 1918 he told the *Reuter Service Bulletin*: 'Our relations with our own and with other Governments have been intimate and friendly but never subservient. Such as they have been they remain.'

Had the relationship really been so clear and so clean? As a British institution, Reuters always sought to follow the patriotic course. Yet under Jones it started to claim none the less that its news reporting was objective in character. Previously, under the management of Julius Reuter and his son, objectivity had not been pursued as an avowed high purpose—to be set alongside the initial commitment to accuracy, speed, and impartial distribution. Jones now added objectivity as a fourth aim.

And yet, at the same time, he contrived to reconcile objectivity with patriotism. He had given his definition of objectivity (which he called 'impartiality') in an interview for the *Observer* on 24 October 1915, at the time of his appointment as general manager: 'We should preserve a cold and judicial impartiality.' This sounded clear enough. But Jones had then added what for him, as for his colleagues in the higher management of Reuters, was a natural gloss. 'At the same time, as a British agency, when we are dealing with international affairs we naturally see them through British eyes.' Objectivity, therefore, did not exclude reporting the news from the British point of view: it only excluded taking sides within the British point of view. And since almost all shades of British opinion supported involvement in the two world wars, Reuters was left free—indeed, was expected—to support the war effort. Thus were 'patriotism' and 'objectivity' reconciled.

A wartime Agence–Reuter service had been started at the end of 1914 by arrangement with the Foreign Office. This service was for the circulation of news and comment to which the British Government wished to give publicity. Agence–Reuter was kept separate from the normal Reuter news services; but even so, it traded upon the good name of Reuters, and was entirely produced at Old Jewry. Its output went to Allied and neutral countries in Europe and the Middle and Far East, and to every part of the British Empire. By November 1917 about a million words per month were being circulated under the Agence–Reuter credit. The cost to the British Government in that year was £119,835. Yet Reuters made a profit of only £8,231 on the service, without allowing for overheads. Here was a patriotically small return.[12]

Jones wrote a description of the Agence–Reuter service in a memorandum for the Department of Information, dated 10 November 1917. The Department had been formed early in the year, with Buchan as its head. Jones was given charge of its cable and wireless propaganda, working part time and unpaid. This enabled him to supervise the content of the Agence–Reuter service when acting as a departmental official, while at the same time overseeing the distribution of the service when acting as managing director of Reuters:

> Its object is to secure that a certain class of news, of propaganda value, is cabled at greater length than would be possible in the normal Reuter service . . . The principle observed in shaping the service is a simple one. While bearing in mind that the proper presentation of the Allies' point of view is the main object of the service, the fact is not forgotten that this object can best be attained by a candid and exact description of events as they occur. A military operation, for instance, in which the Allies have not been successful, is not ignored, but is set out soberly in its proper perspective. Nor are Allied successes made the subject of paeans of enthusiasm. They are recorded in measured language . . . Many years' experience in the handling of news has shewn that these methods provide the best means of creating that intangible atmosphere of confidence which is indispensable if the service is to be trusted.

Notwithstanding the separateness of the Agence–Reuter service, Reuters was placing its reputation as well as its network at the service of the British Government. 'At Reuters', wrote one DOI official revealingly on 11 July 1917, 'the work done is that of an independent news agency of an objective character, with propaganda secretly infused . . . it is essential that independence should be preserved.'[13] The official knew that, so long as Reuters continued to be trusted, even avowedly official news or comment circulated through the Reuter network would be more likely to be believed. On 29 November 1917 the *Daily Telegraph* published a letter in favour of a negotiated peace from Lord Lansdowne, a former British Foreign Secretary. The 'Weekly Agence Report' of 3 December explained that the Agence–Reuter service had 'made it abundantly clear to the Continent and South America that the country does not subscribe Lord Lansdowne's views'.

From early in the war, neutral Amsterdam, Copenhagen, and Berne had been centres for collecting news out of Germany and for feeding propaganda in. The Foreign Office paid for the removal of Reuter news handling in Amsterdam from the control of Abraham Delamar, the Dutch manager, whose family had served Reuters in the Netherlands for fifty years. Delamar had been continuing the pre-war practice of issuing Reuter, Havas, and Wolff material together under one umbrella Reuter credit. The British authorities naturally did not want to give any encouragement to the heavy output of German propaganda coming via the Wolff Bureau. On the other hand, the Reuter office had long functioned as virtually the Dutch national news agency, and the Dutch were neutral. Finally, in June 1915 *De Telegraaf*, a pro-British newspaper, claimed that Delamar had been passing New York stock exchange prices to Wolff ahead of subscribers to Reuters, such as itself. W. J. Moloney was sent from Reuters to take forceful charge, and a second Amsterdam office was opened.[14]

Jones claimed in his memorandum of 10 November 1917 that his cable and wireless section was clearly winning the propaganda war. He quoted an article in the Berlin *Vossische Zeitung* of 15 August 1917: 'We might march into Petrograd or Paris tomorrow . . . If Reuter, the day after, assured the honest neutral that it was of no importance, he would be believed. Reuter rules the market, not Wolff; London makes foreign opinion, not Berlin.' German material, the article complained, was too wordy. Neutral newspapers understandably preferred a few lines from Reuters to a long-winded German article.

The German humorous magazine, *Kladderadatsch*, devoted its whole issue of 31 March 1917 to Reuters, under the title of the 'Reuter (Lies) Number'. The front and back pages each carried full-page cartoons. The front (Plate 22) showed a man in hunting gear striding along the top of telegraph wires. He exhibited the protruding teeth which every good German knew to be the peculiar mark of the Englishman, and from his mouth issued forked tongues which turned into telegraph wires. From a huge cornucopia he was scattering a shower of unpleasant creatures, representing Reuter news. A duck (German 'Ente' means also 'false rumour') followed the striding figure, while below was an observer comparable to Mr Punch. The caption—'Es ist fabelhaft, wie schnell der Kerl vorwärts schreitet trotz seiner kurzen Beine. ('It is amazing how quickly the fellow strides on despite his short legs).' The cartoon on the back page showed a globe grasped by an imp-like figure. From his huge claws sprang lines of cable encircling the world. Underneath came the rhyming legend 'Die Luge ist der Welt Gesetz—dies lehrt das Reuter-Kabelnetz': 'The lie is the law of the world—so teaches the Reuter cable network'.

Alongside the Agence–Reuter service Jones ran an Official Service for the Department of Information (DOI). The Foreign Office had started this service early in the war. By November 1917 it was publishing about 150,000 words per month. It was therefore smaller than the Agence–Reuter service, and also much less effective, because it was more obviously dealing in propaganda. Over half of its material was delivered by cable, but the rest was transmitted by wireless—an indicator for the future.

The overlap between Jones's position at Reuters and his work for the DOI eventually provoked questioning from the Press Advisory Committee. Could he serve two masters? Jones did not doubt that he could, and should do so in the national interest. 'The major portion of the telegraphic propaganda is conducted through Reuters,' he wrote to Buchan on 21 January 1918. 'As long as I remain managing director I can control this side of the propaganda.' When the Ministry of Information was formed early in 1918, with Lord Beaverbrook as Minister, Jones became its full-time director of propaganda. He still refused a salary. Rather than resign as managing director of Reuters, his functions were put into commission. In July 1918 this drew criticism from the Select Committee on National Expenditure as 'on principle open to objection' because the MOI was making large payments to Reuters. Jones was defended in the House of Commons by Stanley Baldwin, the Financial Secretary to the Treasury, and in a letter to *The Times* from Napier. Both men emphasized that Jones had nothing to do with payments to Reuters. It was certainly true that Clements, now the Reuter manager and secretary; Dickinson, the chief editor; and W. L. Murray, the assistant secretary, together conducted negotiations in the summer of 1918 for a formal contract concerning payments from the MOI to Reuters. Hitherto, for the sake of secrecy there had been only a verbal agreement. Yet Jones watched every move from the Reuter side. On 17 June he minuted to Napier, on a copy of a letter from Clements to Beaverbrook: 'Of course this is my letter. I simply got Clements to sign it.'

Jones refused to admit any possibility of conflict of interest between his official position and his position at Reuters. Under continuing pressure to make a choice, he was bound to choose Reuters, where his heart and his future lay. In September 1918 he therefore resigned from the Ministry, ostensibly on grounds of ill health. Beaverbrook thanked him warmly for his services to the nation, which were 'not perhaps the kind of work which most readily attracts public attention'. Jones made sure, however, that they did attract attention after the war by publishing Beaverbrook's letter in the *Reuter Service Bulletin* for April 1919.

Jones had undoubtedly been an effective conductor of British wartime propaganda. In the process, he had exploited the good name of Reuters; but at least he had conducted the Agence–Reuter service separately. He believed that he had kept the promise made when he became general manager—to reconcile patriotism with objectivity. But he had done so only within his own definition of terms.

Once again he received his reward—this time not in money. On 8 January 1918 Jones was gazetted one of the first knights of the new Order of the British Empire. He revelled in his title. Henceforward he was 'Sir Roderick'.

7

The names of 115 Reuter employees who had joined the Allied forces were listed in the *Reuter Service Bulletin* for September 1918. Eighteen men killed in action were eventually named on the Reuter war memorial. All who served were generously granted half pay by the company, and they were promised jobs on return.

Women were recruited for editorial work for the first time. 'Pretty blouses, pretty frocks,' exclaimed the *Reuter Service Bulletin* for October 1917, 'are in these days dotted about the office.' The experiment was successful; but even so, by the last year of the war serious complaints were being voiced about shortage of staff, heavy workload, and a serious reduction in the real value of pay owing to inflation. Reuter wage rates for boy and girl messengers, for girl telephone operators, and for manifolders had all become uncompetitive. The manifolders pointed out that they were working seven days per week because of lack of numbers. And the traffic superintendent, F. J. Griffiths, reported on 4 June 1918 that the only boys now offering as messengers were 'not of the best'. In September the messengers even threatened to strike unless they were granted a basic wage of 15s. per week. 'I am afraid we shall have to give in,' lamented Griffiths to Jones,' . . . now that the police have set so bad an example [by striking] we must not be astonished at anything.'

Senior staff shared in the concern about the erosion of the real value of earnings. In his 1917 end-of-year message Jones reminded them that Reuters still paid income tax on salaries, despite the very great increase in tax rates. The same message also reminded staff that they and their families were now insured by the company, free of charge, against death or injury caused by German air raids. These raids sometimes interrupted work at Old Jewry, although never for long. As a precaution against being bombed out, plans were made in September 1917 to continue editorial work from the basement of the British Commercial bank in Coleman Street. At this time, Jones took the chance to strike a patriotic note:

> it is well to complete all preparations in order that the work of the Agency should not be interrupted for want of foresight on our part, and in order not to give cause for rejoicing to our enemies, who have a particular dislike of Reuter and all it stands for.

SIX

War News

1914–1918

I

WHAT qualities have been required of Reuter war correspondents in the twentieth century? Although needing to show the same stamina and enterprise as their Victorian predecessors, their attitudes towards the news were to change markedly by mid-century. But they had not much changed by the time of the First World War. In nineteenth-century wars in which British troops were involved, Reuter correspondents had never forgotten that they were writing for the news agency of the British Empire. The call of patriotism was strong. It remained strong during the First World War, even though Jones adroitly contrived to reconcile patriotism with his own version of objectivity.

Dickinson, the chief editor, writing to the general manager in India on 26 June 1917, explained what such reconciliation meant in practice: 'the man who at the present time and in existing circumstances can give a plain and impartial record of the world's events must possess exceptional qualities.' Dickinson conceded that 'the aspect which reaches us of the battles on the different fronts is necessarily British. Latterly we have purposely refrained from quoting German communiqués because they were often so entirely irreconcilable with those of the Allies.' In other words, the chief editor was sure that Reuters must publicize the Allied line above all else. 'Whenever, however, a positive German claim is made we always telegraph it.'

The outbreak of the First World War had not been foreseen by Reuters, even though its European correspondents had been busy reporting the tensions of the immediate pre-war years. The Archduke Franz Ferdinand, heir to the Austro-Hungarian throne, was assassinated at Sarajevo on 28 June. This proved to be the trigger for general war. The first message about the assassination came from Havas, telephoned to Old Jewry from the Paris office of Reuters. Havas reported tersely: 'Sarajevo Ferdinand Deste Assassiné.' That was all. The Reuter sub-editor who took down the call was awaiting the result of the Paris Grand Prix horse-race. Too readily, he assumed this message to be the one expected, and he prepared a report on the lines of: 'The result of the Grand Prix at Paris this afternoon was 1. Sarajevo; 2. Ferdinand; 3. Assassiné'. Fortunately, before this ludicrously mistaken version was circulated, a more senior editor intervened and realized that in fact the report told of the assassination of the Austrian Archduke, whose full territorial title in French was 'd'Autriche-Este'. Within a month, Europe was descending into general war.

The announcement of the British entry into the war caused unexpected difficulties for Reuters. During the last hours of peace on 4 August 1914 the British Admiralty was intercepting wireless messages to German shipping warning that war with Britain was imminent. The Admiralty wrongly interpreted these signals as meaning that the Germans had anticipated the expiry of the British ultimatum by themselves declaring war. The British Foreign Office therefore issued a statement, which Reuters published at 11.45 p.m.: 'Germany declared war at 7 o'clock to-night.' The Foreign Office soon discovered, however, that it had blundered, and that Britain was being left to declare war upon Germany. Soon after midnight Reuters corrected itself by issuing a fresh Foreign Office announcement: 'a state of war exists between Great Britain and Germany as from 11 p.m. on August 4th.' Reuters was unfairly blamed for confusing the public over the details of one of the most momentous news reports in history (Plate 19).

2

Marriott's unpublished typescript history of Reuters, written soon after the end of the war, discussed the major part played by the agency during the conflict. 'Its world-wide service of news', concluded Marriott, 'has tended more than any other influence to keep alive the spirit of imperial unity, from the beginning of the war to the end.' For example, the famous speech by Sir Edward Grey, the Foreign Secretary, to the House of Commons at the start of the war, justifying British intervention, had been cabled in full by Reuters to all parts of the British Empire. 'Scene Commons unparalleled in British history also dense cheering crowds outside.' In Marriott's words, 'it was the very understanding of the true position as set forth by the Foreign Secretary which kindled at once a glowing fire of indignation against the aggressor'.

Reuters quickly found that the same fire could be fanned by specific news items. An early wartime report, from Paris on 14 October 1914, showed Reuters willing to give countenance to a piece of anti-German propaganda, without going quite so far as to confirm the truth of the claim: 'The latest example of the contempt of the Germans for the laws of war is contained in intelligence from Braisne (Aisne) which states that the Germans systematically shelled a Red-Cross hospital, killing two British nurses.'

At first, there had been disagreement about just how much the public should be told about the fighting, apart from the official communiqués. During the years before 1914 it was already becoming clear that the heroic age of war reporting was over. Throughout the Russo-Japanese War of 1904–5, and the Balkan Wars of 1912–13, special correspondents were kept under tight control by the combatants, who did not want their actions to be closely scrutinized. Many generals and some civilians said that war correspondents should never again be allowed to play an active part, for fear that their unofficial reports would reveal military secrets to the enemy, as had allegedly happened during the Boer War. Charles Whibley, a respected journalist and man of letters, argued in a letter to *The Times* on 1 September 1914 that 'the case presented by history against the war correspondent is overwhelming'. He was replying to a letter from Sir Henry Norman, MP, who had contended four days earlier that the creation of a 'people's army' required the presence at the front of war correspondents whose first-hand stories would encourage recruitment. Only reluctantly was this argument accepted.

From the experience of previous wars, Reuters knew that reporting costs would be high; and on 30 July 1914 it introduced a charge to the British press of 1d. per word for a special service of war news. This was changed to £5 per month from 1 June 1915, after the opening of additional fronts in Italy and the Dardanelles.

By that date, news coverage of the war by Reuters had settled down; but the early months from August 1914 had been uncomfortable. First, cable communications round the world had been suddenly interrupted by the Admiralty; and secondly, censorship by the Government Press Bureau began clumsily. Marriott's unpublished history rightly complained that at the very time when the agency's unrivalled network was most needed to circulate news of the spread of war, 'down came the hammer of the Censorship and broke up the entire scheme of things'. In despair, on 3 September 1914 a circular was sent by Reuters to its representatives worldwide asking them to post duplicates of all dispatches telegraphed to London, because so many were being stopped by the censor. Reuters asked to be told the number and content of all messages suppressed, so as to be able to make representations. The suppression of a telegram for Reuters from the official news agency at St Petersburg, which admitted the total defeat of the Russians at Tannenberg, provoked particular protest. A censor had released the news to a rival, but not to Reuters, because (said the censor) 'if Reuters published the news it would be believed and the public is already discouraged enough'. The chief of the Press Bureau promised not to repeat this perverse compliment.[1]

Reuters remained liable to be blamed for deficiencies in news coverage which were in fact the result of censorship. When German communiqués began to have some of their content silently removed by the British censors, before being passed for publication, Reuters circularized the London newspaper editors on 7 October 1915 to explain that it was not responsible for such mutilation.

3

During the course of the war Reuters appointed special correspondents jointly with the Press Association to report the fighting on all the main fronts—not only on the western front in France and Belgium, but also in Italy, at Gallipoli, at Salonika, in Palestine, and in East and South-West Africa.

The western front was, however, always the chief centre of public interest; and two men reporting from France were to emerge as the leading Reuter war correspondents. These were Lester Lawrence and Herbert Russell. Other Reuter correspondents were covering other fronts, but none reported so continuously. Lawrence and Russell were read almost every day, even if they were not necessarily credited in the newspapers by name. For readers of the provincial and colonial papers, in particular, which could not afford war correspondents of their own, Reuters supplied the most widely published accounts of the fighting, though reports from the Central News and the Exchange Telegraph were also used. The Fleet Street dailies naturally gave preference to stories from their own correspondents; but even the nationals used Reuters for additional material, not always credited.

After the end of the war, an article in the *Reuter Service Bulletin* for February 1919, probably written by Dickinson, the chief editor, described the impact of Reuter news from the front:

> Take, for instance, Mr. Lawrence's admirable war despatches. Nowhere, probably, has their craftsmanship won keener appreciation than in our own editorial office in Old Jewry, but one examined them professionally . . . The full significance of what he was telling us, week after week, month after month, did not come home to us—could not come home to us—as much as to those fathers and mothers and wives and children who read those vivid telegrams with beating hearts, without a thought for their literary merit, intent only on the moving and exciting news they contained.

1. *top of page* Founder and son: Julius and
Herbert, *c.*1870

2. *above* Bernhard Wolff

3. *right* Charles Havas

4. Pigeon messages: Aachen, 1850

5. Sigmund Engländer, revolutionary and reporter 1845

6. The new hub of the world: The offices of the British and Irish Magnetic Telegraph Co., 1859

7. Siege of Paris, 1870: Balloon message from Havas to Reuters and the world

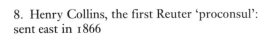

8. Henry Collins, the first Reuter 'proconsul': sent east in 1866

9. Storming of Magdala, Abyssinia: the first colonial war for Reuters, 1868

10. *Vanity Fair*, Men of the Day: Baron Paul Julius Reuter, 1872

11. The telegraph pioneers: Julius Reuter and James McLean (*top pair*), Colonel James Holland (*top right, with beard*), 1883

12. Reuter messengers, 1896

13. Pretoria office, 1900

14. The stars: Boer War correspondents Perceval Landon (*The Times*),
H. A. Gwynne (Reuters), Rudyard Kipling, Julian Ralph (*Daily Mail*)

Daily Express

NO. 23.   LONDON, SATURDAY, MAY 19, 1900.   ONE HALFPENNY.

WHEN SHALL THEIR GLORY FADE?

HISTORY'S MOST HEROIC DEFENCE ENDS IN TRIUMPH.

THE BOERS' LAST GRIP LOOSENED.

MAFEKING AND BADEN-POWELL'S GALLANT BAND SET FREE.

15. *Daily Express* highlights the relief of Mafeking, 1900

REUTER'S TELEGRAM COMPANY, Ltd.
Port Said Branch
TELEGRAMS: (*All Rights Reserved*)

London 19ᵗʰ Janry:

Bulletin noon: The Queen is suffering from great physical prostration accompanied by symptoms, that cause anxiety. The Prince of Wales who intended proceeding to Sandringham today has left for Osborne. ——

16. The end of an age: Port Said telegram, 1901

17. Reuter bulletin-seller, Port Said, 1938

18. Cape Town office, 1910

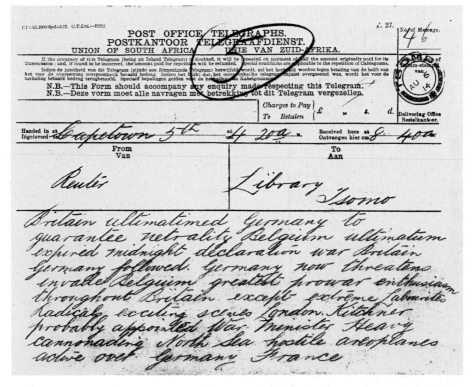

19. 'Hostile aeroplanes active': Reuters tells the Empire of the outbreak of war, 1914

20. Herbert Russell
presented to King
George V, France, 1917

21. Lester Lawrence,
Gallipoli, 1915.

(AWM G1411)

22. German wartime propaganda: 'Reuter(Lies)Number', 1917

23. Mark Napier, chairman 1910–19

24. John Buchan, board member 1916–17 and 1919–35

25. Servants of the Raj: William Moloney, Roderick Jones, and Edward Buck, 1924

26. Commercial services pioneer: Dorothy Nicholson with manager James Lelas and Karachi staff, c.

27. Delhi office, c.1920

28. Messenger girls, *c.*1920

29. The code-books in use: London private-telegram department, 1923

30. Frederic Dickinson, chief editor 1902–22

31. The new editor-in-chief: Bernard Rickatson-Hatt with assistants, 1932

Lawrence and Russell were both experienced journalists, but neither had previously served as war reporters. Lester J. H. Lawrence (1877–1933) had joined Reuters in 1902. From 1909 until the outbreak of war he was the Reuter correspondent in Berlin, one of the most important postings especially so at a time of uneasy relations between Britain and Germany. Every year Lawrence had covered the German army manœuvres, and this was said to have given him an insight into military matters. At the declaration of war, he withdrew to Holland on the British Ambassador's diplomatic train. His opening war reporting assignment was to cover the German advance into Flanders, where he was allowed just one forward tour of the British lines. Even this was a concession; at first, the news agencies and newspapers were expected to be satisfied with publishing the military communiqués, and with official reports written by retired officers, bylined 'Eyewitness'.

Lawrence was eventually transferred to the Mediterranean, where in February 1915 he reported the bombardment of the Dardanelles from the deck of a British battleship. Then on 27 April he described the first Gallipoli landings:

> Your correspondent was on board a battleship, whose special business was to conduct the landing of 750 men at De Tott's. As we closed in with our attendant trawlers, several battleships were pouring a terrific fire into the shore . . . The sight and sound of this stupendous expenditure of destructive energy were overpowering—to the layman, at any rate . . . Most of the boats reached the shore soon after seven o'clock. The enemy had a trench to the left along the shore of Morto Bay, but this was well battered by the battleships, and was carried at the point of the bayonet immediately after a landing was effected. Five Turks were captured; the rest bolted.

Lawrence was not allowed to land with these first troops; he only went ashore some weeks later. But he never sought to avoid danger. 'You never know where or when a shell will fall,' he wrote dismissively from one beach on 4 September. He was an unobtrusive but dedicated journalist, who never gave up. He became friendly with Charles Bean, the chief Australian correspondent at Gallipoli. Bean described Lawrence as 'a game little chap who will carry on a friendly argument—and a most illuminating one in which he is obviously interested—for hours any day you wish'. In a photograph taken at the time by Bean, the bespectacled and slightly bent Lawrence looked positively academic, even while wearing war correspondents' uniform—an officer's tunic with green armbands—but incongruously also a trilby hat (Plate. 21).[2]

Censorship and communication delays, always problems for war correspondents, were especially so from Gallipoli. A full-column report, datelined

'At the Dardanelles, August 10th (via Alexandria, August 24th)', illustrated the difficulties. This report described three landings at Suvla, which Lawrence summed up as 'a successful operation characterised by speed in execution and profound secrecy'. His optimism may have been justified by first impressions. The snag was that Lawrence's account was not published in England until over a fortnight later. In the *Western Morning News* of 26 August 1915, alongside this full-column report for Reuters, appeared a half column from the Government Press Bureau, issued the previous day. This admitted that, in the fortnight since the landings, all had not gone to plan. Consequently, Lawrence's optimism now seemed misjudged.

Much Reuter coverage of the Gallipoli campaign had to be compiled from Egypt, without using Lawrence at all. For example, wounded soldiers were often interviewed in the hospitals there. Lawrence was himself eventually invalided back to Egypt with fever. He recovered, and in the summer of 1916 he was sent to represent Reuters with the French armies on the western front.

4

Herbert W. H. Russell (1869–1944) was the son of Clark Russell, a best-selling author of sea stories. He himself wrote about the sea, and he was praised in the *Reuter Service Bulletin* of August 1916 for possessing 'a literary style which recalls pleasantly what may be termed the sea-breeziness of the family'. Russell's copy was commended by Marriott, the Reuter historian, for avoiding repetition even while describing trench warfare of attrition, which varied little from battle to battle. Russell, claimed Marriott, had found 'new and apt phrases for every incident of warfare'.

Russell was connected throughout most of his journalistic career with the *Western Daily Mercury* at Plymouth, eventually merged with the *Western Morning News*. In June 1915, upon the recommendation of the Press Association, he was seconded by the *Mercury* to serve as naval correspondent for Reuters and the PA in the Dardanelles, replacing Lawrence who was now ashore. Then at the end of the year Russell took over as correspondent with the British armies in France (Plate 20). He succeeded Douglas Williams—a son of the former chief editor—who had volunteered to join the army. Since May 1915 Williams had been working as one of the original five officially approved war correspondents. These five, after persistent pressure from the newspapers and news agencies, had been given belated permission to go forward to report regularly from the British front line.[3]

Despite uncertain health, Russell remained to cover the British front for the rest of the war, with hardly a break. When home on a month's leave in 1917, he was called back after only eight days because of the start of the battle of Cambrai. Whereas correspondents for individual newspapers wrote to fixed deadlines, news agency correspondents were required to produce almost continuous copy. Unlike their newspaper colleagues, they could rarely find time for a break in Paris or Boulogne. They were expected to file separate reports each day for both the British morning and evening papers; and they were told to serve the Sundays with especial care because these had not been allowed reporters of their own at the front. In return for tailor-made reporting, J. L. Garvin, editor of the *Sunday Observer*, promised Jones (20 February 1917) 'to hoist Reuter's name up to the top of the Column, "From Reuter's Special Correspondent" instead of the modest italic at the end'.

Russell and Lawrence came under severe family as well as work pressure. Russell's son and two of Lawrence's brothers were killed in France. Russell's son had previously been gassed. Russell told Dickinson (20 April 1918): 'his philosophy is that he has bought a revolver during his convalescence and does so want to try its qualities upon the Huns.' In the same patriotic spirit, Russell kept on filing unquestioningly. After the war, he was rewarded for his services with a knighthood. He returned to peacetime journalism in the west country, and wrote more novels. In 1944, depressed because he could not contribute during the Second World War as he had done in the earlier conflict, he committed suicide.[4]

By 1917 Russell's reporting from the western front was earning him widespread notice. He was thanked by the Press Association on behalf of the provincial press, and he was praised by the Australians and South Africans for his full reports of Dominion troops in action. Imprecisely but approvingly, Jones described Russell to the general manager of the PA (3 May 1917) as 'far and away one of the best correspondents we ever had'. Jones had just visited the British lines, and had been impressed by the good reputation which Russell had won for himself at the various army headquarters. 'In few tasks', wrote Jones to Russell a week later, 'could the personal equation be of more importance.' In other words, Russell got on well with the military authorities. He did not regard it as part of his function to be critical. Twenty years later, in a letter to Jones offering his services in the Second World War (5 October 1939), he summed up his First War role as 'telling a picture story without giving anything away'.

This meant that self-censorship had often anticipated official censorship. Russell reminded Dickinson (12 April 1918) that 'it does not follow because a War Correspondent does not say a thing he does not know it'. Russell and his fellow First World War correspondents won the approval of the authorities by not causing trouble. They settled into a routine. On the day of a British attack they drew lots to see who would cover which sector of the front. Each then set out in a chauffeur-driven car, accompanied by a conducting officer. They went as far forward as possible without being reckless, and watched the opening bombardment, preferably from positions with wide range of vision. Their reports were necessarily similar in outline; but they achieved variation by adding their own impressions formed by talking to resting troops, walking wounded, and German prisoners.

Such work was demanding and sometimes dangerous. But it did not produce objective reporting. Many correspondents admitted after the war that they had misled their readers by exaggerating successes, minimizing failures, and never speaking of defeat. A striking example of this was Russell's coverage, from July to November 1916, of the bloody and futile battle of the Somme.

5

For the first time in the war British correspondents were fully briefed about what was intended for the opening day; and they were allowed to view the battlefield from points of vantage. What they witnessed turned out to be a traumatic experience in the history of the British Empire. Britain's enthusiastic new volunteer army was wasted to no purpose. And yet in Russell's reports this reality was never to be admitted, or even hinted at.

He began on the first day, 1 July 1916, with a telegram full of hope:

> British Headquarters, France, Saturday, 9.30 a.m.
> At half-past seven this morning a vigorous attack was launched by the British army. The front extends over about 20 miles north of the Somme. The assault was preceded by a terrific bombardment lasting about an hour and a-half. It is too early as yet to give anything but the barest particulars, as the fighting is developing in intensity, but British troops have already occupied the German front line. Many prisoners have already fallen into our hands, and as far as can be ascertained our casualties have not been heavy.— Reuter's Special.

On the same first day Russell mailed back an overview which ran to more than a column in the *Manchester Guardian* of 3 July. It read easily, and contrived to be encouraging in its matter while taking care to seem judicious. This was typical Russell. His writing drew readers into the action, but left them excited rather than fearful or depressed. By this technique, good news achieved maximum effect, and bad news was cushioned. The overview began with four paragraphs of optimistic background:

> British Headquarters, France, Saturday.
> The secret has been well kept. The weeks of essential preparation and concentration have passed without attracting the least degree of suspicion . . . Down to quite lately I had heard officers seriously discussing the improbability of an offensive of any sort by our army this year . . . The offensive which is now in progress is, roughly, on a scale about three times the magnitude of the Battle of Loos, the previous greatest British effort. The concentration of artillery is literally appalling. Every species of weapon, from the gigantic 15 in howitzer to the quick-rattling Stokes trench mortar, is pouring thunderous avalanches upon the enemy positions. The work of the men and women at the benches is at last nobly supporting the efforts of their brothers in the trenches. The opening moves in the terrific drama had been played with great strategic skill. Periodical intense bombardments along the line, any one of which might have been the preliminary to a great offensive, left the Germans doubtful as to where the real blow would fall.

Russell then moved into a lyrical description of the high summer scene at the start of the battle. The *Manchester Guardian* headlined this 'The Thunder-Burst at Sunrise':

> At six o'clock this morning I stood upon the brow of a ridge overlooking the much 'strafed' town of Albert. The sun had not yet risen high enough to eat up the dawn mists which hung on the slopes and in the valleys. July was being ushered in with true summer tenderness . . . a deep azure sky, delicately mottled with fleecy traceries, and a soft warm breeze coming from the west, the quarter which makes the Boche regret that he ever started importing the use of gas into warfare at all. Several kite balloons already floated placidly on high . . . Even as I stood there, with the larks singing overhead and the cattle browsing in the foreground unconcernedly as though nothing else on earth mattered, the desultory crackling of the guns began to take a more rapid and deeper note. With amazing rapidity the devastating chorus swelled (for the time-table of the momentous day had now been reached) until from horizon to horizon the uproar rolled in a ceaseless rataplan of thunder. Several times I tried to count the pulsation of this inferno, but it was a hopeless task. I do not think I exaggerate in the least when I state that the shell-bursts often reached 500 in one minute along the length of the front commanded from the vantage point upon which I stood. From the slow, deep crash of the great howitzer to the malignant treble of the trench mortar, which showers its projectiles at the rate of one every two seconds, the overture to the mightiest battle which the British army has ever yet fought rolled its deafening diapason.

After this enthusiastic description of the bombardment, Russell excused himself from saying much about the success or otherwise of the subsequent infantry attack. 'It takes days to collect and piece into a coherent whole the story of such a far-flung struggle.' He ended by expressing suitable caution, but caution which was subtly coloured by optimism:

> if under the pressure now being thrown by our army upon the enemy and by the French on our right the assaulted front crumbles, then great events may follow. But let us wait for these before clearing our throats preparatory to shouting.

Russell had followed his opening telegram on 1 July by another timed at 1.15 p.m. It talked about 'good progress into the enemy territory beyond the front line . . . So far the day goes well for England and France.' Yet on this first day alone the British suffered nearly 60,000 casualties. Russell could not have known this grim truth immediately; but he could never admit that, in spite of a final total of half a million British killed and wounded, there was no Somme victory.

Week after week Russell dwelt upon local successes, and insisted upon the good spirit of the troops. He told the following story on 9 July:

> The captain of one of the companies had provided four footballs, one for each platoon, urging them to keep up a dribbling competition all the way over the mile and a quarter of ground that they had to traverse. As the company formed on emerging from the trench the platoon commanders kicked off, and the match against death commenced. The gallant captain himself fell early in the charge, and men began to drop rapidly under the hell of machine gun bullets. But still the footballs were booted onward . . . when bombs and bayonets had done their work, and the enemy had been cleared out, the Surrey men looked for their footballs and recovered two of them in the captured traverses. These footballs will be sent to the regimental depot as trophies worth preserving.

Russell clearly found this 'match against death' a matter for admiration. As the weeks went by, he remained buoyant. He never quite claimed that the Germans had been defeated, but he began to suggest that they were slipping into defeat. 'The German army in the West', he asserted on 20 September, 'is now fighting a slow rearguard action.' By this stage, the implication was that the Somme had always been planned as a battle of attrition, with no expectation of a breakthrough—at least not until the Germans had been worn down.

Lester Lawrence—recently arrived in France as Reuter/PA correspondent with the French armies—claimed explicitly in a dispatch from French headquarters on 30 September that the Allies were fighting a war of attrition. 'It is not merely a question of taking villages on the Somme or of breaking through to the Rhine in a few weeks . . . the main factor of the great encircling offensive up to the present is the damage done to the German army, its loss in men and material.'

The inordinate cost in lives was only conceded by implication. By the end of the battle the Reuter correspondents were claiming that the British and French commanders had learned from experience how to minimize casualties. It was asserted comprehensively on 9 October that 'each big attack is less costly to us than its predecessor . . . we are perpetually getting still greater results at a diminishing cost.'

By Christmas Eve 1916 Reuters was admitting that the battle of the Somme was over, but in language which still suggested almost a victory:

> The Somme offensive has been a prodigious tonic, for whilst our troops never doubted themselves during the two long years of defensive waiting, they now enjoy the consciousness of proven power to win. 'Peace or war we shan't be here next Christmas' is the confident philosophy of every man along our hundred miles of front, which means that if the Germans have not gone back voluntarily they will have been driven far beyond that skyline which in so many places has remained unchanged since the great dig-in which followed the battle of the Marne.

This last remark was an unwitting admission that the battle of the Somme— begun so cheerfully on a beautiful summer's morning six months earlier—had achieved nothing of significance on the ground. As for any 'prodigious tonic', suggesting that such a supposed boost was a sufficient return for so much sacrifice—the very idea was an insult to the dead.

6

Two years after the battle of the Somme the war in France was still dragging on. In a letter on 18 July 1918 to Lester Lawrence with the French armies, Dickinson, the chief editor, praised what he called Lawrence's 'masterly efforts of the last few days'. 'What I always admire about your telegrams is the technical military element. It suggests, somehow, a lecture from a master of strategy to a listening public. Apart from this quality, your messages tell their tale easily and most lucidly.'

The chief editor was content that Lawrence, who looked like an academic, should sometimes read like one. Certainly, his sentences could be long and his content didactic. The following, dated 31 March 1917, showed Lawrence offering instruction:

> With the French Army, Saturday.
> Hindenberg will fight in the open, but with his flanks protected by the bastions
> of Arras and Laon, which he thinks cannot be turned, and his new line within
> easy reach in case he should be threatened with the rupture of his front.
> Meanwhile, the battle in the open is developing rather more quickly than the
> German Staff seems to have anticipated. The French advancing from Soissons
> and Noyon undoubtedly overtook the retreating enemy before he was pre-
> pared for them, with the result that the whole Lower Coucy Forest had to be
> relinquished . . . The next thrust of the French will doubtless bring them up to
> the edge of the Upper Forest here as well as further north.

This topographical explanation was neutral enough in tone; but Lawrence
felt it necessary to end on the customary cheerful note. 'The troops and horses
are admirably fit after ten days hard marching and fighting in the open in spite
of the cold damp weather.'

News delivery from the western front remained uncertain until the very
end of the war. In June 1918 some messages from Lawrence were taking over
twenty-four hours between sending from France and publication in London;
but most seem to have got through within twelve hours, which was slow, but
just fast enough for publication in the next day's papers

The Germans read Reuter reports in British newspapers which reached
them via Holland. A message from Amsterdam to the *Rheinisch Westfaelische
Zeitung*, dated 12 May 1918, dismissed Lawrence as an optimist, 'who slaugh-
ters German troops by hundreds of thousands in nearly every despatch'. In
reality, Reuters did not knowingly tell factual untruths. But it did maintain a
steadily optimistic tone, whatever the facts.

For his war services Lawrence was made a CBE (Commander of the Order
of the British Empire) in 1920. In the previous year he had played a leading
part in reporting the Versailles peace conference, after which he became assistant to Dickinson, the chief editor. Jones's expectation was that Lawrence
would eventually succeed Dickinson. A year's experience on the editorial
side convinced Lawrence, however, that, while he enjoyed reporting on his
own account, he was unsuited for supervisory journalism. He resigned from
Reuters, and went to Berlin as correspondent for the *Morning Post*.

7

Reuters played its part in publicizing and encouraging the war effort throughout the worldwide territories of the British Empire. Notably, the close relationship between Reuters and the Indian authorities enabled Edward Buck,

the agency's correspondent with the Government of India, to arrange a service of stories about loyal Indian support for the war. This propaganda service used the Reuter name, but was paid for by the Indian Government. It started in November 1914. 'Buck will from time to time cook up suitable telegrams for transmission, through Reuter, to all parts of the British Empire.' So explained one Indian official plainly.[5]

Buck was not interested in objectivity. For example, on 10 November 1914 he sent the following to London:

> War has united Hindus and Mohammedans in one great body determined to lay down their lives for Empire and to sacrifice everything for ultimate victory of England . . . The small section of seditionists about whose activities much was heard prior to the war has receded into the background. Meanwhile Moslem messages of disgust at manner in which Germany has duped and misled Turkey into disastrous war.

In 1917, a supplementary Imperial Service was started from Old Jewry, subsidized by the British Government through the Department of Information. An editorial order on 19 March explained that the intention was to stimulate the interest of different parts of the Empire in each other, and 'in the continued vigorous prosecution of the war'. At intervals, the chief editor received summaries of telegrams circulated:

INTER-EMPIRE ITEMS

SYDNEY SCOTSMEN URGE FORMATION OF KILTED BRIGADE
(Sent to Canada) 23/6/18

LLOYD GEORGE, SPEAKING AT WELSH BAPTIST TABERNACLE, SAYS THE WORLD MUST BE MADE FIT FOR EVERYBODY—THERE MUST BE NO ROOM FOR MILITARISM, MAMMONISM OR ANARCHY.
(Sent to America, Canada, India, Far East, South Africa and Australasia)
23/6/18

Lloyd George, the British Prime Minister, was well aware of Reuters. In September 1917, as reported with satisfaction in the *Reuter Service Bulletin*, a Reuter ticker had been installed at Number 10 Downing Street. Previously, the Prime Minister's staff had been left to wait for delivery of the newspapers to find out what Reuters was reporting from overseas.

News about the attitudes and actions of the United States assumed increasing importance as the war dragged on. The Allies needed American munitions, and preferably American entry into the war. The Reuter manager in New York, Levy Lawson, collaborated closely with E.M. Hood of AP, who had good contacts with Woodrow Wilson's administration. Hood supplied Reuters with early inside news. For example, Jones told Garvin of the *Observer*

(19 February 1917) that Reuters was 'miles in front' with news of the United States breaking off diplomatic relations with Germany. Wilson's speech of 2 April 1917, asking Congress to declare war, was cabled as it was being delivered via a prearranged 'clear wire' to London. This Reuter report was accepted worldwide as sufficient evidence that America was at last joining the Allies. But Reuters was not infallible. In 1916, when Wilson was narrowly re-elected, it rushed to a conclusion without waiting for the returns from California, and got the result wrong: 'MR. HUGHES ELECTED'. Wilson's famous '14 Points' speech to Congress, laying down his programme for future world peace, was initially reported by Reuters as containing only 13 points.

Reuters appointed a correspondent, H. F. Prevost-Battersby, to cover the American front in France. In the last days of the war he was severely gassed. His telegrams were available to AP; but the Americans depended mainly upon their own correspondents in France. By the end of the war, because of heavy official traffic and inadequate cable maintenance, press messages were taking up to forty-eight hours to cross the Atlantic.

8

As the Americans were entering the war, the Russians were withdrawing from it. The Tsarist Empire collapsed, and two revolutions in 1917 were followed by civil war.

The Reuter correspondent at Petrograd since 1904 was Guy Beringer. He had been appointed after the ending of official obstruction to collecting news and to telegraphing it out. Beringer's greatest pre-war coup had been to obtain the text of the 1907 Anglo-Russian agreement several hours before it was officially released. During 1917–18, Beringer carried on undeterred by personal danger or by food shortages. He was eventually arrested by the Bolsheviks, and spent six months under threat of execution in an over-crowded prison. Although he continued to work for Reuters after the war, his health never fully recovered. He died in 1926, aged 53.[6]

While covering the first revolution in March 1917, for several weeks Beringer enjoyed a virtual monopoly of reporting to the West, to the great advantage of Reuters:

March 16, 10.14 a.m.

> Three days' silence from Russia has been broken by a despatch from Petrograd dated 13th instant describing a revolution which resulted in the Duma, aided by the Army, assuming the Government and the arrest of reactionary Ministers and ex-Ministers whom the people have long suspected of pro-German sym-

pathies which are responsible for the lack of food and lack of enthusiasm in conducting the war. Popular discontent smouldering on the 10th, flamed up on the 11th, and became a conflagration on the 12th, when there was fighting in the streets in which soldiers fought soldiers and people. The fighting ended in the troops, including the Guards and the Navy, joining the Revolution.

March 17, 3 p.m.

(Petrograd).—The Tsar abdicated at midnight on Thursday on behalf of himself and the Tsarevitch in favour of the Grand Duke Michael. The latter abdicated on Friday afternoon and the Government is now vested in the executive of the Duma and a National Cabinet.

The British Government opened a propaganda bureau in Petrograd, but Jones assured Beringer on 16 July that the Reuter service to Russia would continue to be recognized as 'paramount'. The official service through the bureau, Jones explained, was to be only supplementary, started for the purpose of conveying matter ('special pleading and so forth') which Reuters could not handle 'without injury to the Agency's reputation for detachment and impartiality, which reputation it is in the Government's interest, quite as much as Reuters' interest, to preserve'.

Clements was sent to Russia, China, and North America to assess the prospects for the future. He seems to have established good relations with the new Russian Government; but the position of the agency again became uncertain after the Bolshevik takeover in November. The Bolsheviks now controlled Vestnik, the Petrograd news agency with which Reuters was allied. Jones told the Reuter board on 12 December 1917 that the relationship was delicate: 'but our policy was to maintain it, at least for the present, and avoid a rupture, in the national interest.' Vestnik gave Reuters a beat in London with the terms of the armistice agreed by the Bolsheviks and the Germans on 16 December 1917. Jones told Beringer on 21 January 1918:

> The official service from Petrograd has continued unimpaired, and it has been well supplemented by your own telegrams. On this side we were told more than once that your telegrams were thought to be reflecting overmuch the Bolshevik view, but our opinion is that this notion arose mainly out of a natural misconception in London as to what the actual situation in Petrograd was.

Jones congratulated Beringer on 'the adroitness with which, while avoiding anything calculated to affront the ruling party, you act as a commentative chorus upon events in Russia'. At this period, the Bolsheviks were usually referred to by Reuters as 'Maximalists', meaning supporters of the maximum socialist programme:

Nov. 8, 9.25 p.m.

Reuter has received telegrams from the official Petrograd Telegraph Agency, which is now in the hands of the Maximalists, stating that they hold the City and have arrested the Ministers. Lenin, who is the leader of the movement, has demanded an immediate armistice and peace.

Nov. 13, 9.34 p.m.

Trotsky has issued a proclamation as follows: —History will record the night of November 12th . . . The sailors, soldiers and workmen of Petrograd know how to impose, and will impose with arms, the will and power of democracy. The Bourgeoisie endeavoured to separate the army from the revolution, and Kerensky attempted to break it by violence and Cossackism; both efforts have failed.

Vestnik outlined its news needs in a service message to Reuters in London on 17 December:

Please greatly reduce reports speeches newspaper articles stop Substitute short news of more general character for long accounts speeches stop We particularly interested know how various classes receiving successive stages events and peace steps also facts about labour movement.

A Reuter editorial order warned two days later that, although Vestnik had asked for the views of the Labour papers, 'we must not on any account be led into playing into the hands of the peace party'. Articles and speeches in favour of peace 'must be carefully eschewed'.

Early in 1918 internal chaos caused a breakdown in communications; and this led Beringer to withdraw to Finland. Soon, however, he returned to Russia to report from Moscow, now the capital, even though communications were still bad. Personally, Beringer was strongly anti-Bolshevik, and he was at great risk. In a private letter to Jones on 22 June 1918, almost certainly read by a Bolshevik censor, he claimed that the Red Army was a 'rabble' and that 'the Bolshevik bubble' was on the point of bursting.

Beringer realized that many of his telegrams were not getting through. He was reduced to sending batches of them with his letters, which took as long as two months to reach Old Jewry. The British newspapers could only use these telegrams in retrospective accounts of the civil war. The last telegram mailed to London was dated 8 July 1918. Beringer was presumably arrested on that day or soon afterwards.

9

The beginning of the end of the war came in the Balkans, where the conflict had started. W. H. G. Werndel, a veteran Reuter Middle East hand, secured a three-hour beat from Salonika with news of the Bulgarian surrender on 29 September 1918. In contrast, the German surrender on 11 November was preceded by several days of tantalizing uncertainty while negotiations continued. Reuters found itself misled, just as it had been at the start of the war. On 7 November it circulated a wrong report to the London evening papers saying that 'according to official American information, the armistice with Germany was signed at 2.30'. In reality, a German armistice did not come into effect for another four days. Reuters conducted an immediate inquiry into this damaging mistake. Fortunately, on this occasion (unlike 1914) Reuters had covered itself by giving a source. It 'killed' the report within a few minutes. But the Director of Public Prosecutions seriously considered prosecuting Reuters because of the loss of industrial production caused by circulation of this false report, which brought the factories to a halt.[7]

When on 11 November Reuters received the official announcement in London that all fighting was to stop at 11 a.m., it responded energetically. The good news from Old Jewry reached many parts of the British Empire well ahead of any British Government communication (Fig. 10).

For four years one topic had dominated the Reuter file, and the volume of words published by the agency had reached unprecedented levels. The Agence–Reuter and other services for the British Government were alone

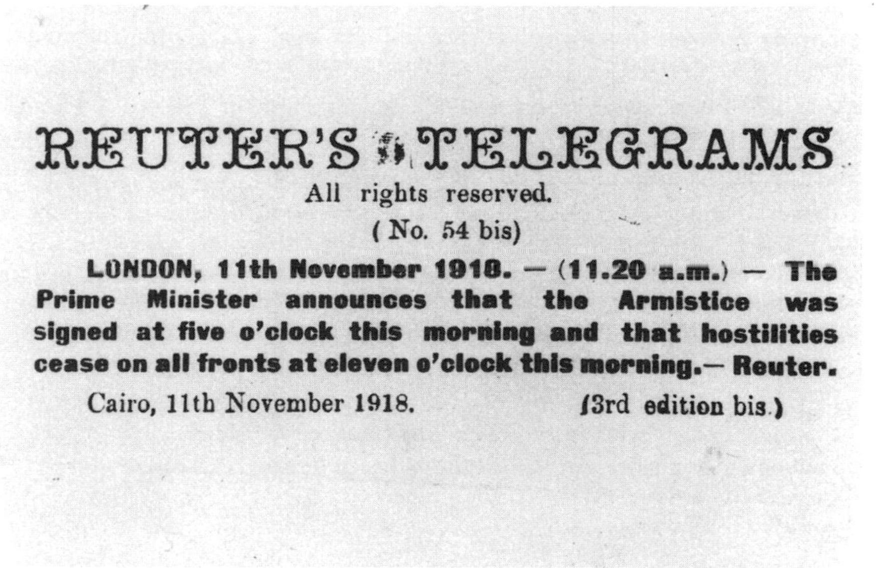

REUTER'S TELEGRAMS

All rights reserved.

(No. 54 bis)

LONDON, 11th November 1918. — (11.20 a.m.) — The Prime Minister announces that the Armistice was signed at five o'clock this morning and that hostilities cease on all fronts at eleven o'clock this morning.— Reuter.

Cairo, 11th November 1918.   (3rd edition bis.)

FIG. 10. Reuter reports the armistice, 11 November 1918

estimated to have added 10 million words to the file. However, not quite everything was war news even in the midst of war. Commercial news and information had still been circulated by Reuters; and some lighter items—such as sports or social news—were regularly included.

It had been a 'good war' for Reuters. In 1914 the agency had been facing serious difficulties, financial and otherwise. By the war's end these had been overcome, and its reputation as the news agency of the British Empire had been restored. But had this really been 'the war to end war'? Would Reuters find no more wars—or, at least, no more major wars—to report? Only nine days after the armistice, Dickinson was writing to Prevost Battersby with suitable caution: 'I do not entirely accept the theory that war has ceased in the world for ever.'

SEVEN

The Autocracy of Roderick Jones
1919–1934

I

SIR RODERICK JONES ran Reuters as an autocracy. This had been his style in South Africa, and it was still more his style as head of Reuters between the wars. At first, Dickinson, the chief editor and Jones's early mentor, remained to influence him. In 1918 Jones made Dickinson a director. But in 1922 he suddenly died. Mark Napier, the chairman, had already died in 1919. Jones, the majority shareholder, with a 60 per cent holding, then became chairman as well as managing director. Henceforward he was the unquestioned head of the news agency, in the eyes of its directors, its staff, and of outsiders. Even after the reconstitution of the ownership in 1926, giving the new board a majority of PA representatives, Jones was left with a free hand. Into the 1930s he continued as before, unchallenged, always smoothly courteous to his fellow directors, but keeping control of policy and management in his own hands.

Jones liked to present himself as successfully continuing in the dynamic spirit of Julius Reuter. He certainly continued to conduct Reuters as the news agency of the British Empire (Plate 25); and he also tried to maintain the international ring of news agencies which Julius Reuter had helped to form. But in both connections the policy of Reuters was no longer dynamic: it was defensive. Between the wars Reuters encountered increasing difficulty in protecting its position throughout the world. In particular, it found the challenge of the thrusting American news agencies hard to meet. The weakening position of Reuters in the world mirrored the weakening position of the British Empire itself. Jones was well aware that he was entering into a period of imperial exposure and prospective change. He wrote to his wife on 19 February 1924 from Government House, Madras, of the pomp and circumstance 'of a system which soon may pass away, or at least be modified, under the democratic influences of the time'. Yet Jones felt no desire to separate the fortunes of Reuters from those of the formal and informal British Empire.

How far, then, should Reuters be associated with the British Government in protecting or promoting British interests worldwide? In peacetime should there be any association at all? Here was the question which had posed itself before 1914, and which had troubled Engländer and Dickinson surprisingly little. Jones had been more circumspect, even during the war. After the war he repeatedly declared in public and in private that Reuters was, and must remain, independent. 'We are not suppliants in any sense', he told the Foreign Office on 2 April 1925. Nevertheless, Jones always emphasized that Reuters could choose to make contracts with the British Government so long as the terms of such contracts did not allow any official control. In other words, Reuters was willing to work closely *with* the British Government in peacetime, but was not willing to work meekly *for* the British Government. This distinction was sufficient, in Jones's view, to leave Reuters independent.[1]

Such an attitude was certainly convenient, since throughout the period Reuters needed Government subscriptions to help balance the company's books. The British Government, for its part, was inclined to accept Jones's logic, since it realized that a Reuters proclaiming itself independent was much more likely to be useful than an obviously subsidized mouthpiece.

At the end of March 1919 the wartime Agence–Reuter service was closed down. Jones had argued strongly against closure, because of the need to compete with angled news from France and America, which was circulating in Europe, the Far East, and South America. Instead, an agreement was made with the Foreign Office for Reuters to send specific messages overseas upon instruction. The Foreign Office agreed to pay the costs of such extra wordage, which often consisted of speeches by Ministers. The contract, renewed in 1921, declared that Reuters would distribute only news 'consistent with their independence and their obligations to the newspapers'. This agreement, and a similar one with the India Office, remained in force throughout the inter-war years.[2]

The British Government did not depend solely upon Reuters for circulating favourable news and comment. The Foreign Office decided in 1919 to continue the British Official News Service, which had been started during the war. This now became known as the British Official Wireless (BOW). In the opinion of Jones, this service constituted unfair and unnecessary competition for Reuters because overseas newspapers could print its official material without payment. Jones was the more irritated because he had himself built up the service during the war.[3]

He pressed repeatedly down the years for control of the BOW to be handed over to Reuters; but the Foreign Office would not contemplate this, because it believed that the agency was not always reliable in its handling of news. For example, the pre-war suspicion persisted in British official circles that the alliance of Reuters with Havas and other agencies meant that all news received by the British agency from Europe was being given a foreign colour at source. This discounted the explanation that Reuters remained free to collect other news from its own correspondents and stringers in each country. During the immediate post-war years Havas certainly held a dominant position in the supply of news to and from continental Europe, and this particularly worried the Foreign Office, which now regarded the French as rivals rather than allies.[4]

The pre-war news ring agreement between Reuters, Havas, Wolff, and AP had been renewed in 1919—with the sphere of Wolff confined to Germany. In quick succession, the news agencies of all the smaller European states, old and new, became allied with Reuters and Havas. Even Rosta (later Tass), the news agency of Bolshevik Russia, became associated with the ring through a contract made with Reuters in 1924. But this Russian connection remained uneasy. Because of the heavy censorship, Reuters did not send a resident correspondent to Moscow. Instead, it kept a correspondent in Riga, the capital of independent Latvia. First news of the banishment of Trotsky in 1928 came via Riga.[5]

2

John Buchan's involvement with Reuters during the First World War has already been noticed. Throughout most of the inter-war years he was available to make representations in official circles on behalf of the news agency. In June 1917, when he became head of the Department of Information (DOI), he had resigned as the Government-nominated director on the Reuter board . The DOI had financial dealings with Reuters. Buchan was reappointed a director in 1919, and served as deputy chairman when Jones was away on a world tour in 1923–4. Before Jones sailed, Buchan had praised him at a company dinner as 'one of the whitest men God ever created'. Jones, for his part, confidentially recommended Buchan as his successor 'in the event of anything happening to me'. Whether Buchan, with his many literary and political commitments, would have accepted the job must be doubtful; but he was a firm believer in Reuters as the news agency of the British Empire. He remarked in the *Reuter Review* (January 1938) that the agency was 'far more than a mere commercial organisation, and every member of it can feel he is in the fullest sense a public servant'. Buchan was elected a Conservative Member of Parliament in 1927. He finally resigned from the board of Reuters upon becoming Governor-General of Canada in 1935.[6]

The death of Dickinson in 1922 necessarily brought changes in the editorial department. Douglas Williams was offered the chief editorship, but preferred to stay as manager in New York. In the absence of a more enterprising candidate, Herbert W. Jeans (1873–1931) was appointed. He had joined the agency in 1898 from the *Manchester Guardian*, eventually becoming the respected chief of the Reuter parliamentary staff at Westminster. Although he claimed in 1924 that Reuters now published 'human interest' stories, the news file under his editorship remained heavily political and official.[7]

A lighter touch was needed, even while traditional standards were being maintained. When Jeans died in post in 1931, Jones installed a much younger man as his successor with the task of modernizing the handling of news. This was [John] Bernard Rickatson-Hatt (1898–1966). Hatt had joined the editorial staff straight from the army in 1923, upon the recommendation of Buchan. He retained a military appearance at Reuters. He was always immaculately dressed, usually wore a guards' tie and sported a monocle (Plate 31), and outdoors he wore a bowler hat and carried a rolled umbrella. And yet there were oddities. His complexion was abnormally pink and white, 'no stranger to cosmetics' said some; and he was suspected of wearing a corset. Hatt often came to the office bearing a small poodle dog. All this suggested a need to put up a façade, conventional and idiosyncratic at the same time. Hatt's nerves had been shaken by his wartime experiences. He was gassed, and after the war he was involved in army intelligence work at Constantinople, about which he never revealed anything. He declined an invitation to write his memoirs, on the grounds that 'he knew too much'. Hatt found relaxation in reading the Greek and Roman classics in the original; and at his death his collection of pornography was said to be one of the best in the world.[8]

Another influential but less colourful figure between the wars was W. L. Murray (1877–1947). Murray had joined Reuters in 1899. He served as a correspondent in Europe during the pre-war years, notably as the discreet Reuter royal-watcher who accompanied Edward VII on his annual trips to take the cure at Marienbad. At the outbreak of the First World War, Murray became liaison officer for Reuters with the official Press Bureau. By 1923 he was company secretary, and in 1932 he was made European manager. He had a sharp eye for economy, but there is no evidence that he possessed vision. He retired in 1937.[9]

J. H. B. Carter (1897–1964), a cousin of Dickinson's, came into Reuters straight from the army in 1919 as private secretary to Jones, who treated him as a senior office boy. Carter was never expected to have ideas of his own, and throughout his career he was regarded within the company as a yes-man. From 1932 he combined the job of personal secretary to Jones with that of company secretary. In a careful letter asking for a salary increase (5 January 1929), Carter remarked that, while it was a privilege and a pleasure to work for Jones, 'it would be idle to pretend that it is an easy or a simple job, calling as it does for exceptional tact, discretion, energy and equanimity'. Jones crossly underlined the word 'simple', and scribbled in the margin: 'if it were, I should have a woman secretary at £6 a week!' But Carter did get a £50 increase on his £800 salary. After Jones's departure in 1941, Carter continued more comfortably as company secretary until his retirement in 1959.[10]

The demanding routine which Jones's secretarial staff had to endure was later described by James Lees-Milne, who in 1935 served briefly as a third private secretary. Lees-Milne recalled that Jones required his desk to be arranged each morning with total exactitude. 'If the softest of the three india rubbers was not found on the left-hand side of the row on the allotted tray and adjacent to the red (not blue) sealing-wax, Sir Roderick's displeasure could be terrible.' Lees-Milne took his revenge by observing his employer's appearance unfavourably:

> He was in stature a little undersized. He was spruce, and dapper, and perky. I would describe his appearance as that of a sparrow were it not for his waist which, instead of being loose, was tight, pinched in by a conspicuous double-breasted waistcoat which he habitually wore like a corset. This constrictive garment gave him the shape of a magnified wasp. His face too resembled that of a wasp seen under a microscope. It was long and the bulbous nose was proboscis-like. His small eyes darted rapidly in his head in the manner of that insect. They never rested on their victim, yet because of a feverish activity missed nothing. His mouth too was sharp and vespine. His sting was formidable and unlike the bee's could be repeated.[11]

As third secretary, Lees-Milne took down and typed only the less important letters. If Jones found that a single word had been rubbed out and retyped, he sent the whole page back, complete with four carbon copies, to be done again. No deviation was allowed from the page layout chosen by Jones for all typed letters sent under his signature.

Each night Jones used to phone down to the editorial floor to ask how the news was going. The senior editor on duty was expected to provide a brief verbal overview. Some editors found this an ordeal, although others recalled that Jones was usually satisfied once he was convinced that everything was under control.

Jones justified his insistence upon the highest standards of performance by emphasizing how Reuters depended especially upon its staff. 'We have no tangible machinery, no equipment,' he wrote in his 1938 new year message: 'just men and brains.' At that date Reuters employed over 1,000 people worldwide, about 370 of them in London. The London editorial department consisted of 12 senior staff and 120 others; the commercial department employed 4 seniors and 86 others.

Jones once described to a would-be recruit his selection policy for those who wanted to become overseas correspondents, and who might later become managers. The qualities needed, he wrote, were a mixture of those expected by the Civil Service and those necessary for a business enterprise. Recruits must show themselves to be hard-working and healthy, good at languages, good with people, prepared to travel, and ready to commit themselves wholeheartedly to Reuters. Some experience of newspaper work was regarded as useful because it produced an awareness of the market for Reuter news. But many years of newspaper employment was not a recommendation; for Jones liked to encourage young men, remembering his own early progress. Older men were rarely brought into Reuters.

Jones was often accused of having a snobbish preference for public school recruits (especially Old Etonians), with Oxford or Cambridge degrees and with private means. Yet snobbery may not have been the whole reason for the noticeable influx of public-school trainees during these years. They were thought to be most likely to possess that social polish which Jones and Hatt felt to be essential. Reuter correspondents and managers were expected to mix easily with top people in every country.[12]

Women had been taken into the editorial department during the First World War, but few were recruited after the war. Muriel Penn, who joined in 1931, was the exception—a formidable personality who flourished within Reuters and stayed for thirty-eight years. She was engaged as a sub-editor, and became at various times a foreign correspondent, a fashion reporter, and a copytaster. Unimpressed by seniority, she insisted upon the highest standards of crisp accuracy. Women staff at all levels were expected to retire upon marriage. Ellen Baylis, who began as a messenger girl during the First World War, and became a parliamentary correspondent during the Second, was the first woman to be allowed to stay with Reuters after marriage. The terms of employment for Reuter male employees still required them to ask permission to marry.[13]

Jones liked to speak of Reuters as a 'service', whose correspondents and managers were its 'officers'. These official-sounding terms had first been used in Baron Herbert's time. Jones also liked to describe the Reuter staff as a worldwide 'family', of which he was the head, many of whose members were in lifelong employment. In this spirit, during the 1920s he and his wife attended Reuter garden parties hosted by the Napier family at Puttenden Manor, a visible expression of a tacit feudal relationship. Jones also gave his support to a staff social club, to a literary and debating society, and to the Reuter cricket club. He was said always to partner the prettiest girls at Reuter dances. Yet junior staff who encountered him by chance at work were usually terrified of him, fearful of instant dismissal. Only a few knew that if cases of sickness or misfortune came to his notice he could be constructively kind.[14]

At a time when a single week's paid holiday was regarded as generous, Reuters allowed even juniors a fortnight. Pension arrangements were also well ahead of their time, and the rest of the British newspaper industry did not catch up with Reuters and the Press Association until after the Second World War. On the other hand, trade unions were not permitted to make demands about holidays or wages. In 1934 Jones did enter into what he called a 'gentleman's agreement' with the National Union of Journalists to pay at least the union minimum rates; but he refused to sign a formal agreement. He told the union secretary on 14 June that 'nobody at home or abroad could ever say that they had turned to me in vain'. For that reason, he 'was not prepared to allow any outside organization, whether the NUJ or another, to come between me and my people'.

But holding out against the unions was becoming increasingly difficult by the late 1930s. In 1939 Reuters reluctantly joined with other agencies in recognizing the National Society of Operative Printers and Assistants (NATSOPA). The board was told on 6 June that the extra cost in wages would be about £1,000 a year. In September 1940 Reuters signed an agreement with the National Union of Press Telegraphists (NUPT). Job descriptions, wages, hours, overtime rates and holiday entitlements were now all spelt out in agreements. The 'family' atmosphere was being qualified: labour relations were coming in.

3

Economy drives at intervals during the 1920s and 1930s caused redundancies, which conflicted with the 'family' image. Strict economy was necessary at all times because Reuters was never comfortable financially. Payment of income tax upon the salaries of management was abandoned in 1920. In 1921 there were actual salary cuts—10 per cent off top salaries, proportionately less for lower salaries. These reductions were gradually restored during the mid-1920s.

Revenue and profits were never sufficient to pay for all the development desirable to meet growing competition (see Table 7.1). Jones's speeches at annual general meetings between the wars voiced a recurring theme—that

TABLE 7.1 Revenue and profit figures between the two world wars. (£)

	Total revenue	Revenue from largest territories					Net profit after tax	% Profit
		UK	Europe	India	Far East	N. America		
1918	266,300	49,400	31,600	35,200	16,200	800	4,600	1.7
1928	382,500	62,400	32,800	81,500	66,400	2,400	27,000	7.1
1938	517,800	145,000	42,400	126,300	73,200	1,700	117,100	22.6

the subscriptions from the British newspapers, London and provincial, were much too low in relation to the costs of the extensive services provided. These costs, Jones explained in a briefing paper for a director (20 April 1931), were four times as much as the newspapers were paying. Ten years later, after Jones had left, the general managers reminded the board (8 September 1941) that the revenue from India alone was greater than the revenue from the entire British press. 'Newspapers abroad are being disproportionately taxed to provide a service cheaply for the British newspapers.'

Yet London morning newspaper subscriptions remained unchanged at £2,400 per annum throughout the 1920s and 1930s. Reuters feared that any attempt to increase these charges might lead the London newspaper groups to cancel their subscriptions, and to make more use of other agencies, British or American. The provincial newspapers in the PA were no more accommodating than the nationals. The PA differential during the 1930s—the difference between what the PA paid Reuters for its overseas news (£36,000) and what Reuters paid the PA for British news (£22,000)—was only £14,000.

In 1925 Price Waterhouse, the accountants, produced revenue and expense figures for the previous five years. The performance of the various departments within Reuters was compared. The news side had failed to improve its margins; the advertisement business was still profitable; but private telegram and remittance traffic, once the financial mainstays, had fallen into loss. In contrast, the contribution of the new commercial department was becoming significant (see Table 7.2).

Reductions in charges by the cable companies meant that it was no longer worth while for customers to code their telegrams through Reuters. The service closed in 1926. The remittance service lingered on in parts of the Empire, the end not finally coming until the closure of the Bombay remittance office in 1954. The London advertisement department was shut down in 1942, and the Australian advertisement service was sold off in 1945.

TABLE 7.2 Comparison of departmental revenue and
expense figures for 1919 and 1924. (£)

	1919	1924
News subscriptions at home and abroad		
Revenue	199,000	208,000
Expenses	131,000	134,000
Commercial and trade service		
Revenue	15,000	72,000
Expenses	8,000	55,000
Private telegram and remittance traffic		
Revenue	35,000	35,000
Expenses	29,000	37,000
Advertisements		
Revenue	13,000	18,000
Expenses	8,000	10,000

4

Old Jewry had been overcrowded for many years. At last in November 1923
the senior London managers (now known collectively as 'the
Administration') and the news staff were transferred to 9 Carmelite Street, off
the Embankment, and nearer to Fleet Street. This was a long narrow building with some pretensions to architectural style. The move cost the noticeable sum of £4,195, and required careful planning to ensure that services were
not interrupted. Douglas Williams wrote lightheartedly to Jones (30
November 1923), who was on a world tour:

> Mr. Jeans brought the Baron's bust down in his car . . . then they found that all
> the men had gone to lunch and there was no one to take it in. So for ten min-
> utes the poor Baron sat forlornly on the pavement with Mr. Carter's bowler on
> his head, much to the joy of the passers by . . . The editorial looks most impres-
> sive and they have six lovely big new oak tables and a new bookcase with a table
> under it, and the gallery looks much better than was expected but the staircase
> up to it is so steep that it is easier to fall down than walk down. I don't think
> Mr. Kemp is very happy—he likes a mess, you know, and he can't throw his
> tea leaves on the floor . . . The Editor-in-Charge sits with his back to the fire-
> place, with the Dominions on his left and the messengers on the right, and on
> the other side is the French staff and all the rest.

Space at Carmelite Street totalled just over 12,000 square feet, still not enough
to house all departments, some of which remained at Old Jewry.

All floors were linked by a small lift. The arrival and departure of 'Sir Roderick' each day via this lift were occasions of some tension, for Jones did not expect to wait. Bells rang to announce his coming and going. His personal messenger boy was in attendance to operate the lift. To speed his evening departure, another boy was sent to press the pneumatic pad which controlled the nearby traffic-lights, so that Jones's Rolls-Royce would not be delayed.[15]

The first story on the wire from the new Carmelite Street headquarters was about the appointment of a fresh German Chancellor. This news had been telephoned from Berlin. By the 1930s, important news from most parts of Europe was being telephoned. A special continental bell rang with the noise of a fire alarm so that correspondents were not kept waiting. Stenographers took down the messages, which were simultaneously recorded on dicta-phones.

Reuters prided itself in the 1930s upon receiving or sending news by teleprinter across the world in a matter of minutes. Four machines were involved in each news chain—one at Reuter headquarters, one at the cable office in London, one at the receiving cable office, and one at the overseas Reuter office. When Amelia Earhart flew from Honolulu to California in 1935, Reuters had the news distributed in London within nine minutes of her landing. The message had crossed America, been edited by Reuters in New York, cabled to London, and put out to the newspapers.[16]

Such news for the London papers, and for the provincial papers via the PA, was delivered on Creed machines. These typed capital letters on foolscap paper at sixty-six words per minute, or faster at risk of breakdown. As each letter was being typed in Carmelite Street, it appeared simultaneously on machines inside the newspaper offices. These Creed machines, successors to the old column printers, had first been installed in 1928. Urgent news could be dictated directly to the Creed operator. A light or buzzer then gave special warning in the receiving newspaper offices.[17]

Baron Herbert had been very interested in wireless developments. As early as 1903 he told the annual general meeting that some transatlantic steamers were being supplied with the latest Reuter intelligence by Morse code. During the First World War wireless made great progress. With all their cables cut, the Germans could only send news overseas by this new medium. The British Official News Service was transmitted by wireless from Hornsea Island and Caernarfon, and after the war from Rugby. Jones was well aware of wireless developments, British and foreign, through his work at the Ministry of Information. In his news agency role, he was particularly con-cerned that the Marconi Company, which had tried to buy Reuters in 1916, would be left to offer strong competition in peacetime. Under the protection of the Admiralty, Marconi had secured a wartime monopoly of news received by wireless. This had given Marconi's Wireless Press an advantage, since it could pick up enemy news directly from the Continent, whereas Reuter journalists had to send the same news by cable.

After the end of the war, Jones campaigned hard and successfully to prevent Marconi being allowed to continue combining the functions of a news agency with those of a major wireless carrier. Havas and AP conducted similar campaigns in Europe and the United States. Jones argued that the free flow of news might be endangered if any channel of communication were controlled by any one news provider, which naturally had an interest in being first with the news. The days when Julius Reuter had aspired to be a cable-owner as well as a cable-user were long past. Reuters did not now want to control either the old cable network or the new wireless stations.[18]

But Jones did want Reuters to make full use of wireless for the transmission of news. In this purpose he was fortunate in finding a young man already on the Reuter staff who combined enthusiasm for wireless with business sense. This was Cecil Fleetwood-May (1893–1971). During the inter-war period, Fleetwood-May made a double contribution. He both developed the circulation of news by wireless, and at the same time he modernized and greatly expanded the Reuter commercial services. His enterprise was to prove vital to the finances of the company.[19]

Fleetwood-May had joined as a sub-editor in 1917. By 1930 he was both the wireless manager and chief of the commercial services. He revelled in these dual responsibilities. In his prime Fleetwood-May was a likeable and yet purposeful personality—genial, boisterous, hard-working, a little man with large but practical ideas. As European manager after the Second World War—in which his only son was killed—he was unfortunately no longer so innovative. His younger colleagues found it hard to credit the story that his fluency in French and German had been acquired in his youth while playing the piano in taverns on the Continent.

The commercial services required the speediest possible delivery of price and other statistical information. This had led Fleetwood-May to explore the possibilities of broadcast wireless telegraphy. Reception points across the world might be able to receive messages in Morse code by wireless simultaneously, instead of by the usual series of cable relays. Although Julius Reuter had early recognized the desirability of delivering commercial information simultaneously, cable relays had necessarily meant that some places received information ahead of others.

Fleetwood-May applied to the British Post Office for a licence 'to study the application of wireless to news dissemination'. This professional application was rejected. Fortunately, he was able to make some progress early in 1922 through listening as an amateur to the various experimental wireless emissions being broadcast in the London area at that time. But he quickly ran short of money to buy equipment. He plucked up courage to ask Reuters for £30 to acquire more. He was called upon to explain his ideas to a meeting of senior managers. Most were unimpressed. Fortunately for Reuters, Jones overruled his doubting colleagues, and money was allocated to set up a more sophisticated listening-post. Fleetwood-May's suburban London home was connected to Old Jewry by a telephone line, which was joined through a transformer directly to wireless sets at Reuters.

Fleetwood-May described years later how difficult it was at first to persuade the editorial department that any news 'picked up' by wireless could be authentic. The newsroom would not accept the result of a football match in Paris until it had been confirmed by cable. However, successful experiments by German and Swiss agencies in using wireless to broadcast commercial information soon changed attitudes at Old Jewry. To meet this novel competition, Reuters negotiated with the British Post Office for a service of long-wave transmissions—'circular toll broadcasts'—in Morse from Northolt, addressed to news agencies on the Continent. The new service went out under the address 'Reuterian'.[20]

So began an association between Reuters and the General Post Office which was to give a lead to the world in the exploitation of wireless for news circulation. In 1923 the Reuter Continental Broadcasting Service began to deliver price quotations and exchange rates at set hours seven times per day. Frequently expanded, it remained Europe's leading commercial service up to the time of the Second World War. In November 1929 the Post Office offered the use of a powerful short-wave transmitter at Leafield. The charges were reasonable, and Reuters started to employ this outlet for sending general news as well as commercial information to Europe.

A novel form of news transmission by wireless was introduced in 1935 which soon took over much of the service to Europe. This employed a type of wireless tape-machine, developed in Germany by Dr. Wolff Hell and known as the Hellschreiber. Electrical impulses, transmitted via Leafield, sent words and numerals from Reuters to Hell-receiving machines throughout Europe. Incoming news was printed on narrow paper tape at the rate of sixty-six words per minute. The limitation was that in bad atmospheric conditions Hell messages could become garbled.[21]

Reuters wanted to reach subscribers more quickly throughout the world, not just on the Continent. At Rugby, the powerful long-wave transmitter built by the Post Office for the Admiralty during the war lay idle for much of the time. Its facilities were offered to Reuters. The minimum charge for start-ing up was £5, even for a message of a few words. But Morse signals from Rugby could be heard in Reuter offices all over the world, and also by over-seas newspaper subscribers. The 'Reuterian' world service began in March 1931. A coding system made key words unintelligible to eavesdroppers. By 1938 this service was being directed to 26 destinations—along the fringes of Europe; over the Middle and Far East, including India; to Africa; and to South America.

By the late 1930s about 90 per cent of Reuter news was being delivered by wireless, notwithstanding occasional periods of atmospheric blackout. Fleetwood-May, steadily backed by Jones, had overseen a transformation in the way the world was supplied with news. Outward cable messages were now confined mainly to items of special interest to particular countries, which made them unsuitable for broadcast distribution by wireless. The formation of Cable and Wireless Limited from 1929 brought the British Empire's com-munications network under unified control.

With the introduction of wireless transmissions in Morse, many Europeans came to prefer their news from Reuters in English rather than in French, so avoiding the delays and pitfalls of double translation. Wireless was here work-ing to the advantage of Reuters. The British Empire press rate also benefited Reuters, allowing news by wireless cheaper than by cable. In 1930 the com-parable rates per word were:[22]

	Cable	Wireless
Australia	6*d.*	4*d.*
South Africa	2¾*d.*	2½*d.*
India	3*d.*	2½*d.*
Canada	2½*d.*	2½*d.*

State-subsidized foreign agencies—French, German, Italian, Japanese—were also setting up world or regional wireless propaganda services. And throughout the inter-war years these determined competitors had much less need than Reuters to count the cost of exploiting the new medium.

5

Under the skilful direction of Fleetwood-May, the commercial services offered by Reuters grew impressively between the wars. They became important to the economic life of both the formal and informal British Empire, and of Europe.

A prices service had continued from Victorian times, run by a handful of staff. But Fleetwood-May, who had acquired experience on trade journals before joining Reuters, soon realized that much more could be offered, since commercial information could be collected through the existing network at little extra cost. During 1919 he began to press to be allowed to explore the possibilities. Jones interviewed him on 4 October and authorized him to make a start.

Within only two months a printed circular was announcing 'a special service of industrial, commercial, and financial messages', to be known as 'Reuter's Trade Service' and opening on 1 January 1920. The service was to be available in London on free trial for four weeks; subscriptions varied from £15 to £200 per annum. At first, information was circulated only through printed weekly and monthly bulletins. Within a few years, however, using cable and wireless, the commercial service (as it became known) was providing information not only in London, but throughout much of Europe and Asia. Jones told the 1928 annual general meeting that the service—'easily the largest, the most widely distributed, and the most trusted in the world'—had become a 'touchstone' for bankers, brokers, dealers, and businessmen. A story which Jones often repeated told how business on the Shanghai stock exchange was once completely suspended for over a day because a communications breakdown had stopped the inflow of world prices from Reuters.[23]

Fleetwood-May eventually recruited a London staff of about ninety clerks and financial writers, special market reporters, engineers, and telegraph operators. By the end of 1930 a weekly total of 737 commercial messages, containing 6,100 words, was being transmitted to Europe; and 459 messages, totalling 10,620 words, were reaching Egypt, India, the Far East, Australasia, and the West Indies. Fleetwood-May informed Jones with satisfaction in July 1934 that a one-minute cotton service was now operating from New York, via Liverpool, London, and Rugby, to Bombay—at the rate of twenty-two messages per day. In Bombay, when the Washington cotton-crop reports were due, Reuter subscribers were locked into a room to receive the information on equal terms, just as subscribers had been confined by Julius Reuter at Aachen.

At successive annual general meetings Jones was able to describe how the commercial services were sustaining the editorial side. For example, in 1933 the profit made by selling commercial information totalled £23,600 overall. Commercial subscriptions from the Far East alone earned £59,000 in that year, and this was £11,000 more than all home newspaper subscriptions. And yet—despite the profitability of the commercial services, and despite strong backing from Jones—the general news staff looked down upon their commercial service colleagues as merely second-class journalists, if journalists at all.

The introduction in 1928 of the City ticker service to private firms in London constituted an important breakthrough. It was the first printer service for the delivery of Reuter prices. Jones told the 1934 annual general meeting that tickers were now placed in seventy-five banks and business houses in the City, including the Bank of England, 'at first a rather shy recruit'. Shanghai had followed London with a ticker service in 1930, and then India, South Africa, and Egypt.[24]

6

When under pressure to resign in 1940 Jones marshalled his defence in a hand-written *aide-mémoire* to himself entitled 'What I have done for Reuters'. The second item read: 'Preserved it for the newspapers of this country, in particular for the Press Association, when I could have cashed out on far better terms.' Jones always asserted that he could have floated Reuters as a public company, and thereby made much more money for himself than he did by selling out privately in two stages to the PA in 1926 and 1930.

A public flotation would have exposed Reuters to the danger of control by undesirable shareholders, the danger which had threatened in 1916. Jones was undoubtedly sincere in his wish to protect the future of the agency by selling it to the British newspaper groups. There is more question about the financial terms which he exacted. His critics were later to contend that he obtained a very generous price in return for following the public-spirited course.[25]

The idea of a co-operative news service for Britain, run by the newspapers themselves, can be traced back at least to an article in the *Nation* of 24 April 1915, published after the death of Baron Herbert. Jones later claimed that at the time of the 1916 reconstruction he was himself already looking forward to transferring the ownership of Reuters to the British press; but that such a big change was not practicable in wartime. In March 1922, during the course of a long conversation with Jones, Lord Northcliffe offered his support for the idea of the ownership of Reuters by the British press; but he died four months later. Jones, however, had other influential contacts, notably Lord Riddell, owner of the *News of the World*, and J. J. Astor, chief proprietor of *The Times*. After Jones's return from his 1923–4 world tour, he set out to test the reactions of members of the NPA, representing the London newspaper groups, and members of the PA, representing the provincial papers. An extra impetus had been added to these discussions by the formation of the first Labour

Government in January 1924. Jones and others in Reuters feared that Labour wanted to interfere with the press, and they believed that there would be greater safety under co-operative ownership.

Discussions started in earnest in May 1925. Jones prepared documents for the NPA and PA which presented the position of Reuters in a surprisingly favourable light, given that he had told Northcliffe in 1922 that profits were 'poor, if not non-existent'. The annual report for 1923 had declared a loss of £3,927. Yet in 1925 Jones was able to convince two firms of auditors—first, Deloittes, called in by himself, and then, Price Waterhouse, called in by the NPA—that Reuters had been continuously profitable since the war. Jones's final 'proposal for sale' to the British press, dated 2 November 1925, based upon the auditors' reports, showed an average net profit of between £25,000 and £26,000 per annum.

Sir Andrew Caird, the representative of the Northcliffe–Rothermere newspaper interests, seems to have been unimpressed by Jones's optimistic presentation. In an effort to satisfy Caird and other critics within the NPA Jones modified his original proposals considerably. He offered the newspapers 40,000 'A' preference shares in Reuters at £4 per share, the NPA and PA to have 20,000 each. These 'A' shares were to enjoy the same voting rights as the remaining 35,000 'B' ordinary shares, held by Jones and by Napier's two sons.

However, a majority of national newspaper proprietors within the NPA showed themselves unwilling to accept equality with the PA in the ownership of Reuters. In the end, Jones's scheme had to be used as the basis for an agreement with the PA alone. Jones was encouraged to settle for this by Lord Riddell, who had despaired of his NPA colleagues. Jones still hoped that the national newspapers would one day take a stake in Reuters through the NPA. Until they did so, the risk remained that some British papers might become partners with one of the American news agencies to the detriment of Reuters.

The PA paid Jones and the Napiers, as private owners of Reuters, the £160,000 which Jones had previously asked from the PA and NPA together. By an agreement of 23 March 1926 issued capital of 75,007 shares in Reuters was split into 50,000 'A' shares, 25,000 'B' shares, and 7 'C' (directors') shares, all of £1. Jones and the Napiers contracted to sell to the PA 31,250 'A' shares and 8,750 'B' shares, all at £4 per share. The agreement gave the PA the option to buy the remaining Jones–Napier shareholding by 31 December 1930 at £4. 10s. per share—18,750 'A' shares and 16,250 'B' shares. This was duly done at the end of 1930 for a price of £157,500. So in total the PA paid £317,500 for Reuters. Assuming that Jones was entitled to 60 per cent of this sum, he must have received £190,500 from the sale, equivalent to over £5 million in 1998.[26]

Jones was allowed to retain a nominal holding of 1,000 shares until his retirement. He had made his continuance as managing director a condition of entering into the negotiations, and he was able to secure generous terms for himself. He signed a ten-year contract at a salary of £300 a year as chairman, £4,200 as managing director, plus £2,000 representation allowance, and commission of 10 per cent on profits over £13,000.

So, notwithstanding the financial tightness of Reuters during these years, Jones prospered greatly. But his skill in drawing money to himself was not what he wanted to be noticed. What Jones wanted to be recognized was his achievement in at least partly realizing his 'vision' for Reuters—putting it safely into the co-operative ownership of the British press.

Not that the six directors now appointed by the PA to constitute a majority on the Reuter board were to think of their involvement in purely supportive terms. On the contrary, they voted each year to pay the PA comfortable dividends. By 1940 these payments had totalled nearly £300,000. A history of the Press Association, written for internal circulation in 1946, described the Reuter dividend as a 'vital element' in the PA's finances.[27]

After 1926, in negotiations with Kent Cooper, the general manager of the Associated Press, Jones liked to emphasize that Reuters was now as much a co-operative news agency as AP itself. And yet in discussions with Karl Bickel of the United Press, AP's main American competitor, which was run as a profit-making organization, Jones claimed an affinity with UP rather than with AP. Bickel recalled in a 1943 letter to Cooper that Jones 'always insisted that inasmuch as we were a "dividend" conscious group we understood each other better than Reuters and the AP'.[28]

7

As head of Reuters, Jones regarded himself as one of the great servants of the British imperial idea. In this role he undertook between the wars five visits of inspection or negotiation to main overseas centres of the Reuter empire within the British Empire. The fatigues of travel were eased by the fact that, as head of Reuters, Jones could expect to stay at Government House in each territory.

Seven Reuter general managers were in post overseas during the 1920s—at Shanghai, Bombay, Cairo, Melbourne, Cape Town, New York, and Ottawa. Europe was managed from London, as was South America and much of Africa. Connections between Reuters and the Dominions—Canada,

Australia, New Zealand, and South Africa—had been established before 1914. The strongest link was with South Africa. By far the weakest was with Canada, where Jones met with only limited success in his attempts to strengthen it. This was mainly because of Canadian satisfaction with the service received from AP, but also because of the Canadian newspaper proprietors' suspicions that Reuters was willing to accept compromising subsidies from the Canadian Government. A visit to Toronto in 1920 to attend the Imperial Press Conference gave Jones the opportunity to meet the Canadian newspaper proprietors, and also the managers of the co-operative Canadian Press (CP) news agency. CP took all its foreign news from AP, although some of this originated with Reuters. From 1921 Reuters sent a 600-word daily service for Canada channelled through AP's New York office. This contained British and imperial news intended to be of interest to Canadians. In 1923 CP opened a London bureau within the Carmelite Street headquarters.[29]

In 1926 Jones visited Australia, where the position of Reuters as an indirect supplier of world news to the Australian press had always been difficult. By the early twentieth century two cable news organizations were in competition, backed by rival Sydney and Melbourne newspapers: the Australian Press Association and the United Cable Services. Their usually intense rivalry did not stop them, however, from forming in 1926, in preparation for negotiations with Reuters, what Jones described to Clements on 31 July as an 'offensive and defensive alliance'. In response, Jones blandly claimed that it had always been his wish to deal with the two bodies together.

The Australians and New Zealanders had been paying only £6,000 sterling per year for news from Reuters and wanted (according to Jones's recollections) to pay even less. Instead, under a new deal signed on 31 July 1926, they agreed to pay £11,000 for five years, and £12,000 for 10 years thereafter; less £4,000 paid by Reuters for Australian and New Zealand news and office accommodation. Unfortunately for Reuters, Jones concluded the contract in pounds Australian instead of pounds sterling. By 1941 this had cost Reuters over £14,000 sterling, which meant that on balance the Australian and New Zealand papers had not really been persuaded to pay much more for their news. Like the Canadians, the Australians opened a bureau at Carmelite Street.[30]

Complaints were also coming from South Africa, where feeling was growing among both the English-speaking and Dutch South Africans that the internal news service should be in local ownership, not controlled by Reuters. In 1938 Jones made his last overseas journey to negotiate a new relationship. He decided that the prudent course would be himself to assist in setting up a co-operative, non-profit-making organization, a South African Press

Association (SAPA). The South Africans were glad to have the benefit of his experience, and invited him to chair the committee which produced a charter for SAPA. Reuters relinquished the production of internal news, while retaining the exclusive right to supply SAPA with world news. In his *aide-mémoire*, 'What I Have Done for Reuters', Jones drew attention to the payment of £21,000 by the South Africans for goodwill, 'which nobody else possibly could have obtained'. The fact remained that this payment was simply a sweetener. Importantly for the future, however, Reuters did retain full ownership of its expanding South African commercial service.[31]

At the other end of Africa, Reuters had been established in Egypt since the early days. During the inter-war years the long-standing yearly payment of £2,300 by the Egyptian Government continued to be vital, since the Egyptian newspapers were still too weak to sustain a Reuter news service through their subscriptions alone. Gerald C. Delany (1885–1974), the Reuter general manager between the wars, was a ubiquitous figure who had won the goodwill of the Egyptian politicians, including the nationalists. At the same time, he kept on usually good but sometimes questioning terms with the British High Commission. His independence of mind was helped by the fact that he was not English, but Irish. In 1922 he was made an OBE 'for services in connection with Egypt and the Sudan'. The local head of Marconi's wireless was Delany's brother, Arthur, who smoothed the way for Reuters in the spread to and through Egypt of its global wireless news services.[32]

In 1931 Dorothy Nicholson (1894–1994) was sent out to expand the commercial service to Egypt. She was doing well until the Finance Minister suddenly told Delany that the service must be abandoned because it encouraged gambling, which was against the teaching of the Koran. Miss Nicholson recalled many years later how she persuaded the Minister at an interview 'that we were doing exactly the opposite, as now everyone received the prices at the same time—all private cables had stopped and no one did any business until they received the authentic Reuter Prices'.

The resourceful Miss Nicholson had earlier helped to develop the commercial services in India (Plate 26). She went on to set up similar services in Australia and South Africa. These were greatly helped by the introduction of the Reuterian global wireless service of prices. Dorothy Nicholson retired early from the commercial service in 1947, destined to live on in South Africa to become the first Reuter centenarian.[33]

8

During the 1930s India emerged as the leading overseas profit centre, after trade in China began to be affected by war. Profit on Indian press business alone—over £17,500 in 1935—more than counterbalanced the loss on press business at home. In addition, profit on the expanded Indian commercial service averaged about £7,500 annually.

A new Reuter generation had come to the fore in India, led by W. J. Moloney (1885–1968), the general manager from 1923 to 1937 (Plate 25). Moloney—an Irishman, as was Delany—contrived to gain acceptance by the white expatriates and in official circles while maintaining a sympathetic attitude towards the Indians in general and good contacts with the nationalists in particular. He returned to London in 1937 to serve as a joint general manager. Moloney was a man of many talents, apart from journalism—a classical scholar, a linguist, a delightful conversationalist, a connoisseur of fine wines, and a skilful woodworker. At the time of his retirement from Reuters in 1944 he asked for (and was given) 'the best set of wood-working tools that can be got in wartime'.[34]

In an autobiographical note dated 11 July 1944 Moloney listed the most important features of his work in India:

(1) 'The closer association of Indians with the management of the branches (there were no Indian managers in Reuters on my arrival in India).'

(2) The merging of the staffs of the Eastern News Agency and of Reuters, which led to great economies.

(3) The supplying of Reuter news to the vernacular newspapers.

(4) 'Successful resistance to the tendency to sell out in India as we had done in Australia, Japan and South Africa.'

This last achievement was indeed noteworthy. In India between the wars the Reuter rearguard action was entirely successful, although it remained a rearguard action. Reuters restructured its organization but held its ground. It continued to supply India with most of its world news, and it continued to dominate the collection and supply of internal news.

The Eastern News Agency, started by Reuters in 1910, had absorbed the Associated Press of India (API). API had been launched by Indians as a domestic news agency to collect news about India for the Indian press; but it was never financially viable. Its moving spirit, K. C. Roy, was an able journalist, and a nationalist who advanced his cause through charm and moderation.

Roy joined Reuters at the takeover, and became head of the news department. He served loyally, without compromising his opinions, until his death in 1931.[35]

The API kept use of its own name within the Reuter organization. It gave full coverage to the nationalist movement, while at the same time reporting all official news. A conflict of loyalties was avoided because API did not add comment. None the less, through the steady circulation of much nationalist material the cause of self-government was well publicized. Neither Jones nor Moloney was expecting a self-governing India to be an India without Reuters. Their aim was to secure the agency's long-term internal and external position by making it indispensable to the Indian press.

In 1937 Moloney was succeeded as general manager by John Turner (1901–70), who had gone out to India in 1930 as chief accountant. Turner was widely liked by the Indians, and it was at his prompting that Gandhi gave API exclusive rights to his personal news. Turner returned to England in 1952, and retired as chief accountant in 1961.[36]

When he became general manager in India, Turner was already thinking about a future without British rule. He warned Jones on 6 December 1937 that 'British control in India is being relaxed . . . We are not in favour of unduly emphasizing British or Empire news at a time when Indian Nationalists are taking an ever increasing share in the Government of this country'. Even so, Jawaharlal Nehru, the nationalist leader, remained critical. He complained (15 June 1939) that Reuters sent too much European news to India—'what Herr Hitler says and what Mr. Neville Chamberlain denies'—and too little from other Asian countries such as China, 'except that an air raid has taken place'.[37]

Reuters, claimed Nehru, still thought that Indians 'wait eagerly for the golden words that fall from the mouths of the big officials of the India Office'; The agency's close and remunerative relationship with the Government of India and with the India Office had certainly continued throughout the interwar years. The three main Indian Government news subscriptions were worth R2,600 (about £200) monthly. In London, the India Office paid 7d. a word for extra news transmitted at its request, reduced to 6d. when cable charges were lowered in 1927.

The Indian Government's subscriptions were described as 'handsome' by J. S. Dunn, the South African general manager, reporting to Jones on 27 April 1923. Dunn had been sent to assess the Indian situation after the death in a railway accident of A.H. Kingston, the manager in India. Dunn found that Kingston had neglected his work, and had become 'sexually unhinged . . . He mixed with the wrong people . . . None of the people who should have been

Reuters' friends in Bombay would know Mr. Kingston socially.' Dunn welcomed the appointment of 'a man of the charm and social status of Mr. Moloney'.

9

China was the part of the world outside the British Empire where Reuters was most prominent during the inter-war years. It supplied not only world news to the Far Eastern press, but also a regional service from local correspondents, called Reuters' Pacific Service. Chinese-language papers such as the *China Times* were required to pay monthly for their news from Reuters; only British-owned titles, such as the *North China Daily News*, were allowed more generous credit. The high status enjoyed by the agency in China impressed Jones on his 1923–4 world tour. In *A Note on Reuters*, which he seems to have written for internal circulation after returning to London, he rejoiced that Reuter price quotations and Reuter political news and commercial information were 'paramount' on every stock exchange throughout the Far East.

William Turner (1881–1965) was appointed general manager in the Far East in 1920. Jones had known Turner as a journalist in South Africa, and in 1915 had put him in charge of the South African service from London. In a memorandum of 25 June 1921, Turner warned Jones that the main challenge to the British position in China was coming from American, French, and Japanese competition both in trade and in supplying news: 'the quiet British atmosphere of the treaty ports is being rapidly effaced by a restless internationalism, in which commercial jealousy, and jealousy of the British especially, plays a leading role.' Despite this, the Reuter commercial service expanded rapidly under Turner's direction during the 1920s. As a result, Far Eastern revenue more than quadrupled, growing from £16,200 in 1918 to £66,400 in 1928. In 1932 Turner became overseas general manager in London, retiring in 1941.[38]

During the 1920s the main challenge to Reuters in the Far East was coming from the United Press. The other American agency, AP, was still a member of the news ring. Nevertheless, it complained increasingly about the quality of Reuter news from the Far East. This was said not to match that from UP in suitability for the American market or in colour. Equally, AP complained that news about the United States circulated in the Far East by Reuters on behalf of the ring dwelt too much upon the seamy side of American life, highlighting the activities of gangsters and film stars. In 1919 the American State Department had secured for AP the use of the United States navy's radio link across the Pacific. This link was made available, and at cheap rates, expressly because the State Department regarded the favourable cable position of Reuters as prejudicial to American interests.[39]

Quite apart from any specific complaints, there was an underlying desire within AP—strongly promoted by Kent Cooper, its general manager from 1925—to quit the news ring, and preferably to break it up. Cooper wanted free competition in news worldwide. What did Reuters want? When Jones spoke at the Royal Institute of International Affairs in 1929 about 'The Control of Press News in the Pacific' his discomfiture was apparent. He knew in his heart that the news ring—and the leading position of Reuters within it—could not last much longer. AP would not allow it:

> Americans and other people talk a great deal about the 'Reuter monopoly' . . . The Americans realize that the presentation of news from an American angle, not only American news but news of the world generally, is calculated to create a state of mind more favourable to American trade in the Far East than the state of mind created or maintained if the people of the Far East are dependent in the main upon a service which either is British in its substance, or, in so far as the substance is foreign, British in direction.

In response to AP pressure, a Reuter American Service had been started in 1924. But Jones admitted in his lecture that this service out of London had still not satisfied the Americans: 'even if Reuters were as fair as the Recording Angel, they still do not want the Far East to get its American news from Reuters, because it is handled by Englishmen. I do not blame them. If the position were reversed I should say the same thing.'

Jones explained that Reuters had added a service of news direct to the Far East from San Francisco. Although AP-originated, Reuters would have been entitled under the ring agreement to label this news as its own. Jones had decided, however, to call it 'the Associated Press Service'. In other words, Reuters had not dared to assert its rights. Even so, why should AP not circulate this news for itself? After sixty years the old news share-out system was looking increasingly artificial.

If China was unsettled during the 1920s, it became even more so during the 1930s when Japanese aggression was added to internal conflict. Reuters had prospered during the troubles of the earlier decade, because its good name made it acceptable to all parties. But in the 1930s it became more vulnerable, although it still made an overall profit throughout the region as a whole. Far Eastern revenue rose from £66,400 in 1928 to £73,200 in 1938.

The young man chosen by Jones to be William Turner's successor in handling this increasingly difficult situation was Christopher Chancellor

(1904–89). Chancellor came from a Scottish landowning family, and had been educated at Eton and Cambridge University, where he took a first-class degree in history. He went into business, but in 1929 found himself suddenly without a job. His wife, Sylvia, wrote in desperation to Jones, whom she had known since girlhood. She was by birth a Paget, one of the influential families cultivated by Jones. He interviewed Chancellor, and made him a trainee in the editorial department. Jones claimed in his reminiscences to have spotted immediately that Chancellor possessed an 'executive outlook'—quick intelligence, plus energy, toughness and patience.[40]

After mastering the editorial routine in London, Chancellor was sent to report from the League of Nations at Geneva. Then in January 1932 he took over as general manager for the Far East at Shanghai. Jones had boldly decided that his protégé was already qualified for top management. Although not himself a regular journalist, Chancellor soon showed that he could control a staff of journalists. He ran the organization efficiently, while at the same time representing Reuters to the outside world with polish and tact, as befitted the son of a colonial governor. His diplomatic skills were more than ever needed after the Japanese entry into China in 1937. The respect for him among the Japanese was increased because they exaggerated his aristocratic connections. They were also sure that he was working for the British intelligence service as well as for Reuters. Chancellor and his wife became leading figures among the social elite of Shanghai, where he cut a handsome figure. Yet at all times he kept a cool head for business, disconcertingly cool for some. In 1939 he was recalled to London to serve as a third general manager alongside William Turner and Moloney. Chancellor, in other words, was being groomed by Jones for the succession.

During the late 1930s business in China was declining fast. Far Eastern commercial subscriptions fell from over £70,000 in 1935 to less than £50,000 in the following year. At the 1938 annual general meeting Jones summed up the overall position of Reuters in the Far East rather optimistically as 'no longer undisputed' but 'still supreme'. Chancellor admitted in a 1939 lecture on 'The New Order in East Asia' that the British were trying to maintain their large commercial presence in China by a mixture of bluff and compromise, 'without power to make our will felt'.

10

In Japan the Reuter bluff had already been called. Here was another country where Jones found himself forced to sell out, asserting by way of consolation that the terms were good. As he wrote in 'What I Have Done for Reuters', 'I got £20,000 out of the Japanese merely for the right to exclude Reuters name from Japan. It is secured to us by a Debenture on the whole undertaking of the Japanese Agency, on which Debenture we draw 5 per cent—a steady £1,000 per annum.'

But the withdrawal of its name amounted to a major climb-down for Reuters. This was the more serious in a country where 'face' mattered greatly. Japan had been Reuter territory since the early days of the news agency ring, and Reuters had largely controlled the supply of news into and out of the country. The first significant change had occurred at the end of 1913, when a Japanese agency, Kokusai, had been started. From 1 January 1914 Reuters was associated with this national agency, whose first managing director, John Russell Kennedy, was also the local Reuter agent. All Kokusai's world news came from Reuters, which held exclusive rights to Kokusai's Japanese news.

After the war Japanese national assertiveness was growing while British influence was declining. The name of Reuters counted for less, and Kokusai wanted to remove any attribution to the British agency even while continuing to take news from it. At the end of 1923 Kennedy was succeeded as managing director by a Japanese, Yukichi Iwanaga. At this point, Jones arrived in Japan on his world tour. He landed just after the disastrous Tokyo earthquake, which had dealt a severe blow to the business of Kokusai. According to Jones, Iwanaga had not expected to pay Reuters any compensation for the withdrawal of the Reuter credit; but Jones insisted upon a payment of £20,000 (equivalent to about £500,000 in 1998). He had urged Iwanaga to take a different course of action: 'Of the two alternatives before you I suggest you would be wise if you chose that of keeping the Reuter name and saving your twenty thousand pounds.' But the Japanese were adamant, even though financially hard-pressed. Jones then suggested the twenty-year debenture scheme as a means of easing payment. The Japanese agreed, and these payments lasted until Japan entered the Second World War in 1941. From 1 February 1924 the Reuter credit disappeared from general news distributed in Japan, although it was retained for commercial information.[41]

In May 1926 Kokusai was absorbed into a co-operative of Japanese national newspapers known as Rengo. In the same year Kokusai had opened a London bureau, housed at Carmelite Street, and the bureau chief began to advise on the Reuter service to the Far East. Reuters next allowed Rengo to send news direct to Shanghai for distribution to client Chinese newspapers. This concession, although small in itself, meant penetration by the Japanese of previously exclusive Reuter territory in China.

From 1926 Reuters also allowed AP to supply news directly to Rengo, even though the terms still recognized the primacy of Reuters. In his reminiscences, Jones dismissed this shift as 'no more than consistent with conditions in the Far East'. But consistency with the new realities was becoming uncomfortable. Jones kept his concession secret from Havas and Wolff. In the following year, Reuters, Havas, and Wolff agreed to cancel the differential which AP had always paid to them within the ring arrangement. AP's news out of America was now accepted as worth just as much as the news about Europe and elsewhere delivered to the United States in exchange.

Even so, AP remained restless. In 1930 Iwanaga of Rengo and Kent Cooper of AP agreed in principle to enter into a full exchange of AP news for Rengo news once Rengo's current contract with Reuters expired in the middle of 1933. Rengo's home rival, Dentsu, was doing well because of its links with UP, AP's chief rival in the United States. AP and Rengo needed to mount a counter-attack.

AP was feeling less and less inclined to humour Reuters. The American agency was now strong enough to stand alone anywhere in the world, and it intended to become a truly international news agency. As a co-operative, it possessed a powerful home subscriber base serving a population of 100 million which could not be threatened by any rival. Cooper was particularly keen to sell AP's news directly everywhere in the Far East. Conveniently, he was able to promote these materialistic purposes by talking not of profit and influence but of freedom in news. His reminiscences, *Barriers Down*, published in 1942, claimed that he was pursuing 'practical idealism in international news relationships'. The idealism was the more sincere because it paid off for AP.[42]

Cooper had written to Jones on 15 February 1930 telling him plainly that AP 'must have a free hand in the Far East'. At the end of the year AP gave a year's notice of withdrawal from the international news ring. Frank Noyes, the AP president, wrote to Jones on 26 December 1930 to explain the American agency's position. Noyes said that AP did not want a complete break with Reuters and the ring, only a less restrictive relationship: 'Conditions have changed materially in forty years.' AP wanted free entry into China. Noyes contended that his agency would be competing there to supply American news to the Chinese rather than with Reuters in supplying non-American news. Jones had already half conceded free entry in a letter on 17 November: 'Come in by all means.' But he still wanted 'a working agreement of some kind on the spot. After all we are allies, not rivals.'

With regard to Japan, Noyes argued that Rengo ought not to be denied the natural right of choosing AP rather than Reuters as its main partner, if it so wished. Jones countered that Reuters had 'carefully nursed the Japanese field' in the expectation of 'a legitimate reward' once the Japanese press became stronger.

UP was well aware of these growing strains, and in April 1931 Edward L. Kean, its European manager, asked Jones whether Reuters would be free to deal with UP in the event of a split with AP. Jones said yes. He wanted to keep the UP alternative open as a bargaining counter, even though he regarded its treatment of news as too sensational. The snag was that Cooper was ready to risk Reuters doing just such a deal.

On 30 June 1931 the Reuter board discussed the coming crisis. Jones asked whether, 'if the Associated Press took up too strong a line', Reuters should stay with AP and break with the continental agencies, or stay with the Europeans and break with AP. He inclined towards the latter course. In the short term, a breach was avoided. In April 1932 a new agreement was signed between Reuters, AP, Havas, and Wolff. Cooper now assumed that his intended news-exchange deal with the Japanese would not be open to question. Jones, on the other hand, still thought that—since the 1932 agreement was supposedly a continuation of the old friendly relationship—AP would never push to the point of directly threatening an established Reuter interest. In a long letter to Jones, quoted in Cooper's book *Barriers Down*, the American gave his own version of news-agency history in Japan:

> for twenty years the Associated Press has deferred to Reuters as respects Japan. But the Associated Press has denied itself meeting its own necessities as long as it dares . . . I was astonished to learn that you are opposed to the Associated Press sharing equal responsibilities and financial returns with Reuters as respects relations with Rengo. It is due you, therefore, as an ally and friend that you know how fairly we feel we are dealing.

Cooper was here being disingenuous, for he had just signed a contract with the Japanese without involving Reuters in the negotiations, and without telling Jones of his intentions. This contract, concluded in May 1933, did permit the Japanese to make a subsequent deal with Reuters, but it did not require them to do so.

Jones was furious, not only because the AP–Rengo deal removed Reuters from its position of primacy, but also because of the way Cooper had acted. Guided by Jones, the Reuter board gave AP formal notice to terminate the 1932 four-party agreement, with the object of renegotiating the whole relationship. He now demanded payment of a £10,000 differential for the Reuter service: this would have been a humiliating step back for AP. Jones claimed in his reminiscences that the demand was not made without consideration.

Havas and Wolff expressed their support for the move, as did Turner and Chancellor, the past and present Far Eastern managers.

The decision to break with AP was made at a special meeting of the Reuter board on 30 June 1933. Jones spelt out the situation as he saw it: 'Mr Kent Cooper is deliberately intriguing against us in the Far East, if not elsewhere.' The Americans were trying to undermine the whole British business position in the Far East, and AP was joining in the attempt. As for the AP–Rengo contract:

> it places Rengo in the position of being able to put a revolver to our head if we are weak or foolish enough not to call their bluff . . . I would like to have authority to give notice to the Associated Press to terminate our Treaty with them. I am of opinion that the best defensive is the offensive.

In answer to a director's question, Jones expressed confidence that the serving of notice would bring the Americans and Japanese to heel: 'Both the Japanese Agency and the Associated Press will take our action as a sign of strength.' Jones was sure that the outcome would be an offer of favourable terms for Reuters in Japan. He admitted, though, that Cooper's attitude posed a problem. 'I have never liked the man,' commented Buchan. 'He is a low stamp of American, of a different class altogether from the old Associated Press men.' The discussion then concluded with a formal resolution, carried unanimously, 'that the matter be left entirely in the Chairman's hands'.[43]

The outcome was not as Jones had forecast. Cooper made it clear that AP could do without Reuters anywhere in the world. Could Reuters, with no full service of American news of its own, really do without AP? Could Reuters hope to compete successfully with a hostile AP, which would be able to spend heavily to promote its services? Would not a new relationship—partly of association under contract and partly of friendly rivalry—be more comfortable for Reuters than total war? In the end, such a new relationship was negotiated. But to achieve it, Jones had to climb down a long way.

The PA directors on the Reuter board had not fully realized the implications of what they were doing. AP's American news suited the British provincial press; UP's lighter approach would not suit as a substitute. Cooper wrote to the general manager of the PA, H. C. Robbins, telling him what was happening. 'I would be glad indeed', the American remarked cunningly, 'if a way could be found to have a direct relationship with the Press Association, although I fear that Reuters would not permit that.'

Robbins was horrified at the prospect of losing AP's news. He convinced the PA board that negotiations must be started to prevent this happening. Jones's 'offensive' had obviously failed, and the PA representatives on the

Reuter board now wanted peace. This was the first time that they had ever asserted themselves against Jones on a matter of importance. Ever adroit in adversity, Jones seems himself to have drafted a conciliatory cable for Robbins to send to Cooper: 'Wishful as we are that the two American British co-operative enterprises Associated and Press Association should continue together instead of being in opposition we prepared use our influence with Reuters.' The cable concluded by offering a meeting in New York 'to clear up all causes of misunderstanding'. Jones, in other words, was now prepared to cross the Atlantic on a journey of appeasement.

He sailed for New York in February 1934. Cooper later admitted that he forced unequal terms upon Reuters. He began the negotiations by saying that he was only interested in a contract with the PA. Eventually, Jones had to take whatever else AP would offer. In exchange for the Reuter service of world news, plus the PA service of British news, Reuters had to accept, not the equivalent AP world service, but only its North American news. This was designed for the American press, and was not an appropriate service for Reuters.

Admittedly, Reuters was now allowed to sell its news directly to the American papers, and Jones claimed this as a breakthrough. But few American editors were interested in buying news directly from Reuters. AP, meanwhile, was left free to compete vigorously with Reuters anywhere in the world, including the British Isles. In addition, a direct contract was signed between AP and the Press Association, without involving Reuters.

The division of the globe into exclusive news-agency territories had gone for ever. Cooper was well satisfied. 'The bubble of Reuters domination has burst.' This, he declared in *Barriers Down*, was the climax to his career in journalism.

Jones summed up very differently. 'We had given new life to an international league', he claimed in his reminiscences, 'which, if not radically reformed, very soon would have broken down.' Yet, in truth, what was completed in 1934 was much more than a radical reform of the old news order: it was the destruction of that old order. Jones's talent for self-deception, here exemplified, was to contribute to his eventual downfall.[44]

EIGHT

The Decline and Fall of Roderick Jones

1934–1941

I

ODERICK JONES spent his last year and a half as the head of Reuters working in brand-new headquarters at 85 Fleet Street. The building was opened in July 1939, only weeks before the outbreak of the Second World War. The new structure, although owned by the Press Association, was the physical expression of Jones's idea of Reuters as the news centre of the world. For years he had talked about the need for such a building. But the long process of construction during the late 1930s was to produce noticeable friction between Jones and some of his fellow Reuter directors from the Press Association. This contributed to a growing climate of tension, which finally brought about his downfall in 1941.

The new building was intended for joint use by Reuters and the PA, but with Reuters requiring the greater space. Jones had hoped to keep the land and the building under Reuter control through a very long lease; but instead the property remained clearly under PA ownership, with Reuters involved simply as main tenants on seven-year lease. The Reuter board had agreed on 11 December 1934 that Jones should submit a written plan to the PA. But a PA board meeting on 11 January 1935 did not accept his idea of a long lease for Reuters, and eventually decided to go ahead with the scheme as a purely PA-financed venture. The PA board meeting was attended by the same five men as had attended the Reuter board on 11 December. They had listened to Jones at one meeting, and had turned him down at the other.[1]

Jones was thus rebuffed early. None the less, his enthusiasm for the project never diminished. He was appointed chairman of a joint PA–Reuter building committee. This involved him in much extra work during the next four years, the more so as he was the only member resident in London. He visited the site at weekends, climbing ladders energetically to check progress. The final total cost of about £450,000 (equivalent to nearly £13 million in 1998) was far in excess of the original estimates of about £140,000. This cost was all charged to the PA. Some hint of the accompanying boardroom tension was given by Jones in a letter to Buchan on 27 November 1937:

> There is an underground tendency in certain quarters to treat the structure as a Press Association building, quite as much as a Reuter building, if indeed not more so. This is due partly to a complex of senior PA executives, and partly to the fact that new PA directors, who do not know the early history of the enterprise, year by year come on to the Reuter board to take the place of older directors well acquainted with its origins.

Jones was still trying to pretend that the venture was chiefly a Reuter concern. Here was another instance of his capacity for self-deception. The new directors were doing no more (but no less) than taking the fact of PA ownership as they found it.

Jones ran into difficulties over the choice of architect. His nominee was his friend, Sir Edwin Lutyens, the man who had designed New Delhi and who had also lavishly reconstructed the interior of Jones's London house at Hyde Park Gate. The PA–Reuter directors were not so sure about Lutyens. They were concerned about the day-to-day internal working of the building at least as much as about its exterior grandeur. In the event, a compromise was reached. Lutyens was made responsible for the structure, including the outside appearance and the decoration: Smee and Houchin, who had recently designed the inside of Bush House to much acclaim, prepared the working interior.

Lutyens's first proposal was too elaborately expensive even for Jones. A second version, which became the basis for the completed building, was rather more restrained. It sought to overcome the constriction of the narrow site, and to blend with Wren's church of St Bride's, whose famous wedding-cake tower stood only a few yards alongside. At a late stage, the upper levels of the new building had to be cut back to meet a complaint from the Dean and Chapter of St Paul's that the top would obstruct the view of the cathedral from Fleet Street. The outline fell gently back from pavement to cornice, the facing blocks of Portland stone being cut at a slight angle. This, in Jones view, avoided ostentation while achieving distinction. Pevsner's authoritative *Buildings of England* London volume seems to agree, drawing attention to the doorway 'surmounted by a circular window with a bronze figure of Fame. The rest seems straightforward until one looks steeply up and discovers the fun the architect has had at the very top: recessed structure with concave front and crowned by a broad circular drum without a dome.'[2]

The new building contained eight floors to be shared with the PA and with other tenants, linked by four 'fast' lifts of which Jones was very proud. Reuters rented almost 40,000 square feet out of the 72,000 available. Jones professed disappointment when the PA insisted upon charging a full economic rent for this modern new accommodation. Eventually, £20,200 annually was agreed, plus half-rents of £600 for the basement and £500 for the restaurant. Departments were transferred from Carmelite Street in stages during the first half of July 1939, the Reuter editorial staff moving into their part of the fifth floor on Sunday, 9 July, less than two months before the outbreak of war.

The editorial layout was more spacious than at Carmelite Street, but the routine was similar. For incoming news, a pneumatic tube ran from the Post Office headquarters at St Martin's-le-Grand; five teleprinters were linked to receive news from the cable companies; and there were seven sound-proofed telephone cabinets. Outgoing messages prepared by the General News Desk were typed in sextuplet on flimsies, and each sheet from these 'sandwiches' went to a separate destination. The top copy was transmitted by teleprinter to the London newspaper offices.[3]

2

When in 1951 a centenary history of Reuters was published its coverage of the recent past was deliberately limited. In particular, the forced retirement in 1941 of Sir Roderick Jones was not explained. Jones had himself told the author, Graham Storey (17 February 1951) that the time had not yet come to reveal the whole truth. Jones added that he had been ejected because of 'the personal equation', which 'was responsible for poisoning the minds of some members of the Board'; intrigues had created 'really wicked misgivings and suspicions of my dealings with the Government that were wholly unjustified. The craft of Iago was child's play by comparison'.

The crisis was not ended by Jones's departure in February 1941. Some of the directors who had clashed with him then clashed with each other soon afterwards. Jones's successor as chairman, Samuel Storey (no relation to the Reuter historian), was forced to resign in October after only eight months. Like Jones, he never published his version of events.

Was Jones treated unfairly? Or was his removal necessary for the sake of Reuters? What were the motives of his opponents? Was it entirely a clash of personalities (as Jones said), or was there a deeper clash of principles? In particular, had Jones sacrificed the independence of Reuters by making a compromising deal with the British Government which he concealed from the board? Was the Reuter Trust, which was created after Jones's fall, an effective instrument for protecting the independence of Reuters in the future? Why did Samuel Storey argue vigorously otherwise? Why was he in turn ejected from the chairmanship? In answering these questions, a lively and important story has to be told—lively because of the personality clashes, important because it stimulated searching discussion of the standards which ought to underlie the handling of news and the ownership and management of news agencies.

Whereas the clash with Jones was kept behind the scenes—in discussions variously between Reuters, the Press Association, the Foreign Office and the Ministry of Information—the subsequent clash with Storey became public knowledge, even provoking a debate in the House of Commons. In this second phase, the national press barons played a key part through the Newspaper Proprietors Association. How much could they be trusted? This question split the Reuter board, which (after the departure of Jones) was entirely composed of provincial newspapermen from the PA. Storey remained actively suspicious of the NPA; whereas a majority of PA members were persuaded by two other Reuter–PA directors—Alexander Ewing, and William Haley—that the NPA could be safely brought into the ownership of Reuters. Ironically, Jones felt the same. Ewing, Haley, and Storey were the prime movers within the Reuter board during both stages of the 1941 crisis.

Samuel Storey (1896–1978), chairman of Portsmouth and Sunderland Newspapers Limited, came from a leading provincial newspaper family. He served as a director of Reuters 1935–41. Storey had been educated at public school (Haileybury) and at Cambridge University, after which he qualified as a barrister. He farmed extensively in North Yorkshire. He was a Conservative Member of Parliament for two spells, 1931–45 and 1950–66. During his last two years in the Commons, he served as Deputy Speaker. He was created a life peer (Lord Buckton) upon his retirement.[4]

The evidence, written and oral, about Storey's character and motivation is totally contradictory. On the one hand, there has been testimony from family and friends that he was a man committed to the public good, pursuing both his newspaper work and his political career because they provided opportunities for service: service to be rendered with dedication and even determination but without personal ambition. It was therefore characteristic that in politics he was a parliamentarian rather than a party zealot. In both politics and journalism, runs this supportive interpretation, Storey always sought to maintain the highest standards. He believed, for example, that politicians in office should not seek covertly to control or to influence the media. As a director of Reuters, he therefore worked to ensure that it was independent of the British Government, even in wartime. This brought him into conflict with Roderick

Jones, whom he suspected of betraying the independence of the news agency.

Such has been the favourable interpretation of Storey's character while he was serving on the board of Reuters, and later. In contrast, other evidence (not all of it from Jones's papers, an obviously partisan source) has claimed that Storey was an intriguer, an 'Iago', always on the look-out for self-advancement. Notably, his critics within the PA and NPA in 1941 came to the conclusion that his ambition to remain as chairman of Reuters had clouded his judgement, even if they recognized his continuing attachment to the highest principles of journalistic conduct.

Two PA newspapermen of influence gave shape and force to this hostile opinion. They were Haley and Ewing. These two were the Reuter directors who had worked most closely with Storey to secure the removal of Jones.

William John Haley (1901–87) had been born and educated in the Channel islands. He did not go to university, an omission which may have added to the intensity of his character. Instead, after war service as a wireless operator in the merchant navy, he began his journalistic career as a typist-telegraphist on *The Times*. In 1922 he went north to become a reporter on the *Manchester Evening News*. By 1930 he was managing editor, a rapid promotion which recognized his capacity both as a journalist and a manager. The *News* had been bought by the *Manchester Guardian*, and this brought Haley into close contact with John Scott, the *Guardian's* manager and a son of the famous C. P. Scott, whom Haley had admired at close hand during the last years of his great editorship. Haley and John Scott brought the *Manchester Evening News* and the *Manchester Guardian* into successful business harness, and in the process developed a quiet liking for each other. In 1939 Haley became joint managing director with Scott of the Manchester Guardian and Evening News Limited. Haley served on the board of Reuters 1939–43. He went on to become director-general of the BBC (1944–52), and editor of *The Times* (1952–66).[5]

Haley's rise was remarkable. But his critics—'and they were many', as his *Times* obituary (8 September 1987) admitted—never suggested that he was excessively ambitious, or an intriguer in his own cause, as some alleged of Storey. He was charged instead with being difficult to work with, too uncompromising over matters of principle and also in his everyday dealings. Shyness, admitted his *Times* obituary, meant that Haley was 'an embarrassing casual acquaintance'. At his death, the *Guardian* summed him up as 'an arm's length workaholic always under a sense of duty to tell the truth'. His commitment to truth in news certainly made him uncompromising in seeking to protect the independence of Reuters; he was determined to ensure that neither the British Government nor the press barons could gain direct or indirect control. After Jones's resignation, the Reuter Trust was created upon Haley's initiative to act as a permanent shield for Reuters.

Senior to both Storey and Haley was Alexander McClean Ewing (1869–1960) of the *Glasgow Herald*. Ewing had started work in 1884 for Outrams, the *Herald's* owning company, and served it for sixty-six years, during most of that time as a manager or director. Unlike Storey and Haley, Ewing contrived to combine attachment to high journalistic standards with an engaging manner which disarmed criticism and won him many friends. An obituary in *The Times* (29 January 1960), written by Haley, described Ewing as 'a vivacious and charming companion'. 'A careful, shrewd, kindly Scotsman of the old school', continued Haley, 'he combined both vision and caution.' This was very high praise, for Haley was not known to exaggerate. Ewing served on the board of Reuters for an exceptionally long period (1932–45), an indication of the trusted part which he came to play. Haley remarked of Ewing that it was as a director of Reuters 'that he perhaps made his greatest mark'. Such was his geniality and diplomatic skill that, although he played a major part in the removal of Jones, the latter continued to treat him as a friend throughout the 1941 crisis, and for the rest of Ewing's long life.[6]

3

The confidence of the PA–Reuter directors in Jones's judgement had been severely shaken by his mismanagement of the 1933–4 confrontation with AP. Jones had led Reuters into a very weak bargaining position, and had left the PA in danger of losing its preferred source of American news. Henceforward, Jones's colleagues on the board began to be more questioning. Their number now included several provincial newspapermen of high calibre—Ewing from 1932, John Scott (1933–8), Arthur Mann of the *Yorkshire Post* (1934–9), Storey from 1935, James Henderson of the *Belfast News-Letter* (1936–41), Haley from 1939.

By 21 April 1938, in a letter to his friend J. L. Garvin of the *Observer*, Jones was denouncing Storey in an added handwritten comment as a 'reptile'. Clearly, the climate had much changed in the six years since Jones had written (2 June 1932) to a previous PA–Reuter director, Sir Robert Webber of the *Western Mail*, that the PA–Reuter 'marriage' had been 'quite easily the *happiest* achievement of my business life'.

During the middle and late 1930s Reuters was hard pressed. Financial crises recurred, intensified by the cost of reporting the successive wars and crises provoked by the totalitarian states—Italy, Japan, and Germany. In 1936 Hatt instructed Reuter correspondents to cut their wordage by a quarter, 'not by ignoring stories but by covering them more briefly'. There was no margin to meet emergencies. This was demonstrated at the time of the 'Munich' crisis in September 1938, when a great extra reporting effort had to be made. The estimated loss for the month reached £3,861.

In order to counter German and other propaganda by publicizing the British point of view, Jones wanted Reuters to be officially assisted to circulate much more news. The British Foreign Office agreed about the news shortfall, but was reluctant to back Reuters without changes in its management. The Foreign Office had noticed the limited number and variable quality of full-time overseas correspondents for Reuters, and also the uneven distribution of Reuter news overseas, strong in some areas but weak in others. Rex Leeper, the head of the Foreign Office News Department, was a particular critic. He wrote (13 July 1937) that the Government regarded 'the responsibilities of Reuters in the foreign field as no less serious than those of the BBC', and it intended 'to keep a careful eye' on the agency's performance. 'Reuter, the most important British agency', he minuted (15 October 1936), 'is steadily deteriorating under its present management and is serving foreign as much as British interests.' This last was a reference to the way Reuters was still exchanging news with subsidized foreign agencies. Jones always claimed that correspondents for Reuters abroad, and its editors in London, were skilled in spotting any distortions in foreign news exchanged in this fashion.[7]

But the Foreign Office files show that Ministers and officials had begun to work behind the scenes for the removal of Jones himself. Too often he found himself apologizing to the Foreign or India Offices for blunders in reporting. For example, when on 28 November 1936 Anthony Eden, the Foreign Secretary, invited Jones for a talk at the Foreign Office, Eden began by saying that two Reuter reports had recently been discussed in Cabinet—one alleging that the Government was contemplating a naval agreement with Italy; another about naval movements in the Mediterranean. Both reports, he said, were wrong, and had been embarrassing because on the Continent (as Eden reminded Jones) what Reuters published was taken as officially inspired.

Jones had to admit the mistakes. But he then sought to widen the discussion. He told Eden that the maintenance of standards was becoming ever more difficult. Reuters was fighting for survival overseas, where it needed to do well since little more than 10 per cent of its revenue came from the British press. Jones emphasized that Reuters did not want a subsidy, but it did want a 'revised and strengthened' relationship with the British Government. The Germans had feared Reuters in the last war, Jones recalled, and the agency hoped to be no less effective 'next time'. He concluded by asserting that Reuters was getting the worst of all worlds. It was a target for complaints from the Foreign Office, and yet it was not being helped to compete effectively upon the international news scene.[8]

The Foreign Secretary took note of Jones's arguments, although he continued to share the official view that Jones himself ought to retire. Eden submitted a paper to the Cabinet on 'British News Abroad' (8 December 1938). The dissemination of such news, explained Eden, depended upon two outlets—the British Official Wireless, which distributed official material; and Reuters, which handled 'world news through British eyes'. He urged consideration of an indirect subsidy to Reuters, in the shape of low wireless transmission rates to pay for increased wordage. Jones was subsequently interviewed about this proposal by a committee, chaired by Sir Kingsley Wood, the Minister of Health. Jones asked for help to send 6,000 words per day to the Continent, and 6,000 words per day to the rest of the world—a sixfold increase.

Jones had engineered these responses by appealing directly to the Prime Minister, Neville Chamberlain, with whom he had been granted an interview on 17 November 1937. In an *aide-mémoire* sent to Chamberlain next day, Jones emphasized the threat to British news services throughout the world from subsidized foreign competitors. Havas, he explained, was receiving £250,000 a year in subsidy; Deutsches Nachrichtenburo (DNB), the Nazi agency which had replaced Wolff, was probably receiving even more. Although foreign newspapers still wanted to take Reuter news, 'because of its reputation for accuracy and independence', they were being tempted to prefer news from Paris or Berlin 'for which they paid nothing'. Such news was often anti-British in tone.

Jones chose not to regard the acceptance of low wireless transmission rates as tantamount to Reuters accepting money, although Eden described low rates as 'practically equivalent' to subsidy. In an address on 'The Printed Word' to the 1939 annual conference of the Empire Press Union Jones spoke frankly:

> The problem is, how to place British news in foreign countries financially in a position to counteract its competitors without exposing it to the taint of subsidy and to the loss of its reputation for independence. To expect to solve that problem with complete satisfaction to ourselves must seem very much like expecting to get the best of both worlds.

By the outbreak of war in September 1939, Jones believed that he had finally achieved this best of both worlds; that he had negotiated extra payments from the British Government for serving the national interest without sacrifice of Reuter independence.

The Government, for its part, was always keen to get value for money. It wanted Reuters to reform itself. A peerage was hinted at if Jones would retire. But he had no intention of going. He never ceased to believe that the problems of Reuters were caused not at all by his autocratic management but solely by subsidized unfair competition. He was extremely surprised when on 30 March 1938 Sir Horace Wilson, a senior civil servant and confidant of the Prime Minister, pointedly told him in conversation 'that an organisation which had for so long been subjected to such individualistic control might perhaps not be the most healthy organisation having regard to future developments'. Wilson noted that Jones 'seemed shocked at the thought that anybody should have it in mind that he should withdraw from Reuters'. Whereas in 1916 the British Government had worked to keep Jones at Reuters, now it wanted him to quit.[9]

As a consolation, Wilson hinted at the possibility of establishing a Reuter Trust, as an ultimate safeguard, of which Jones might be made chairman. During the next three years, the idea of some sort of trust was to feature intermittently in discussions about the future of Reuters. But in 1938 Jones was not prepared to be sidelined. Henceforward he was on his guard, prepared to negotiate but not to abdicate. When the 'Munich' crisis occurred in September 1938 he asked for, and received, extra Government money to expand the wireless news output transmitted overseas by Reuters—from 1,000 to 3,000 words daily. Afterwards, questions were asked in the House of Commons; and Storey, speaking on 7 and 20 March 1939 as a Reuter director as well as a Member of Parliament, argued the case for a permanently enlarged service. Storey did not regard extra Government payment for extra services as threatening the independence of Reuters, so long as it retained complete editorial control. Reuters, said Storey, wanted targeted help. 'Help or no help, they will continue to fight for British interests. But let us be quite frank. The strain is beginning to tell.'

Storey said nothing to the Commons about the internal running of Reuters. He too wanted Jones to retire. But by the summer of 1939, with war approaching, all parties had resigned themselves to working with Jones, at least for the time being. With the aim of projecting the British case more effectively overseas the Government demanded a speedy expansion of the Reuter network, although it also contemplated backing the Exchange Telegraph, which was seeking to start up outside the United Kingdom.

As an alternative to his own immediate withdrawal, Jones was pressed by the Foreign Office to nominate a prospective successor as chief executive of

Reuters. Christopher Chancellor, the manager in the Far East, was regarded by Jones as his most promising protégé. He would not yet nominate Chancellor as his deputy; but in August 1939 he named Chancellor as an additional general manager in London (alongside William Turner and Moloney), with particular responsibility for contacts with the British Government. On 29 August Chancellor expressed his gratitude in a personal letter. 'You know that you can count on me in double measure—upon my loyalty to my chief and upon my affection for my friend.' During the next eighteen months Jones was to find that these sentiments were insincere on both counts. Chancellor was well-connected in high places. He had, for example, known R. A. Butler, the Foreign Under-Secretary, since they were undergraduates together at Cambridge; and he also knew personally Lord Perth, the Director-General designate of the revived Ministry of Information (MOI). Jones assumed that his personal position would be helped by Chancellor's inside contacts. In practice, Chancellor was soon using his influence to help bring Jones down.

4

The Reuter directors were growing irritated that Jones was retaining total control in practice even while claiming to welcome their full involvement. As was his custom with new directors, Jones had assured Haley on 1 June 1939 that he liked the board 'to know all that we possibly can tell them'. Haley, however, was not to be deflected by such blandness. He was soon asking searching questions, and making it clear that he expected full answers. He emphasized to Jones (11 November 1939) his strong regard for the high reputation of Reuters:

> From my earliest days as a journalist, I was imbued with the tradition of Reuters accuracy. So are most other journalists—to such a point that in the more responsible papers a sensational flash will often be held up a moment or two 'to see if we get confirmation from Reuters'. Such a reputation is the most valuable asset Reuters has. It is above rubies.

The implication here was that this reputation must be protected regardless of personal ambitions or sensitivities. In his 1981 *Dictionary of National Biography* article on Jones, Haley offered his explanation of how and why a man who claimed to love Reuters had none the less lost his way. Because the provincial newspapermen on the board knew little of international news handling, wrote Haley, this had encouraged Jones 'to personify Reuters in himself . . .

Naturally autocratic, he became imperial. Reuters' prime purpose lost his attention.'

Ewing was the most senior PA member of the Reuter board, and as deputy chairman he began to offer a lead in questioning Jones. Before the board meeting on 12 September 1939, the first after the outbreak of war, Ewing circulated a seven-page 'confidential memorandum' to his fellow PA–Reuter directors, but not to Jones. This described in detail how Jones had retained his dominance even while selling out to the PA in 1926 and 1930. 'I have put together a story which will in part explain not only how Sir Roderick Jones came to hold his present autocratic power but his attitude towards anything which savours of encroachment on his privileges.' Ewing gave figures which showed that Jones had sold out on terms very favourable to himself. In return, conceded Ewing, Jones had offered a 'vision' of the great future for Reuters if it ever came to be owned by the whole British press, national as well as provincial. It was not Jones's fault that in the 1920s the national press barons had failed to respond.

Ewing was worried that Reuters was running into the red. 'We have been assured that economies are being effected in the administration, but nothing short of a complete reorganisation of outlook on the part of the Managing Director will save the company, let alone the credit of the Board.' Ewing proposed that the PA–Reuter directors should meet privately, away from London and away from Jones, to discuss what should be done about him—in particular, whether he should be given the required year's notice that his contract would not be renewed when it expired at the end of 1940.

Meanwhile, however, Jones brought important business to the 12 September 1939 board meeting, business important for the present and destined to be crucial in his downfall eighteen months later. This meeting was asked to ratify a contract which Jones had negotiated with the Foreign Office, and with the revived Ministry of Information, for the financing and expansion of overseas news services. He submitted, for retroactive approval, a 'Memorandum of Arrangements relating to the provision of additional services by Reuters at the request of His Majesty's Government'. A contract had been 'finally amended in telephonic conversation' with Sir James Rae of the Treasury on 10 August, and had been confirmed by Rae's letter of the same date. Subsequently, there had been discussions with Lord Perth, the Director-General designate of the MOI, summarized in a 'private and confidential' letter to Jones, dated 24 August, 'setting out certain understandings which, although unnecessary in the formal document, are an integral part of the arrangements'. This became known as the 'Perth letter'.

The letter has survived in Jones's papers, annotated by him at the time. These annotations confirm, what he was always to insist, that he was not prepared to accept all of Perth's glosses. Furthermore, as Jones was also to claim, it is clear that he never even acknowledged the letter. In the hectic last days of peace and first days of war from 3 September, the MOI seems to have simply assumed that Reuters had accepted the letter as binding, even though Perth had ended in terms which required acceptance by Jones and a further letter from himself. 'On hearing from you that you concur in the above I will give instructions for the issue of an official letter inviting Reuters to enter into arrangements on the lines embodied in the enclosed Memorandum.' This was a reference back to the contract already agreed with Rae. That had come into effect, but without Perth's 'understandings'. Perth himself, who was a diplomat by training, had been quickly found inadequate as an organizer of news and propaganda, and on 8 September he was demoted.

The Reuter board meeting on 12 September 1939 eventually accepted Jones's interpretation of the Government contract; but only after very close questioning. Jones pointed out that the package of Government payments would add up to a sound business deal, earning additionally over £18,000 per year. He had earlier spoken of securing a much larger extra sum, perhaps even £100,000; but any more, he now explained virtuously, could only have been obtained by sacrifice of independence in news handling. He revealed that in verbal discussions he had agreed 'that Reuters would bear in mind any suggestions made to them on behalf of H. M. Government, as to the development or orientation of their news service or as to the topics or events which from time to time might require particular attention'. This, Jones explained, was something which Reuters had always done, especially in wartime, but without it affecting the agency's 'absolute freedom and discretion'.

Ewing seems to have been readily persuaded. His recent memorandum to the PA–Reuter directors had revealed his concern about the financial position. 'The contract came most opportunely . . . there was no question of a subsidy; the proposed Government payment would be simply a payment for news services to be supplied.' A 'direct relationship' with the Government, Ewing added, would be advantageous in obtaining 'first-hand information'.

Haley took more persuading. 'He had misgivings', wrote Jones, about the undertaking that Reuters would bear in mind suggestions made to them: 'this might be taken as implying some measure of control.' Jones assured Haley that this commitment was only 'verbally understood', not written into the contract. Storey gave reluctant acceptance, 'along with the Chairman's interpretation of the verbal understanding'. But as a Member of Parliament, he feared that Reuters would be in a difficulty if the arrangement were mentioned in the Commons. Jones thought it unlikely that any Minister would publicly lay claim to Government control. Haley requested that any such attempt 'would at once be reported to the Board'. Jones agreed 'most readily'. The board then ratified the contract unanimously.

Jones's reference to 'private correspondence' was as near as he came to mentioning the Perth letter as a letter. The expression 'Reuters will at all times bear in mind any suggestions', which Jones had read out, came from clause B of the letter; but he did not give the context. Jones marked this clause 'Yes' in his copy. There were four other clauses, none of which Jones thought it necessary to mention on 12 September. Clause C dealt with effective use of transmission time ('Yes'); clause D left the Government free to employ other news agencies ('Yes'). Clause A proposed that an additional general manager be appointed, who would be senior to the two existing general managers. The new man was to be 'in immediate charge' of the new arrangements, and was to be appointed chief general manager within eighteen months.

Jones marked this proposal 'No'. He was agreeable to making Chancellor a general manager, and did so forthwith; but he was not prepared to commit himself further. Very properly, he was unwilling to bind Reuters for the future at Government behest, even though in fact he regarded Chancellor as his ultimate successor.

5

At a board meeting on 3 October 1939 Jones reported the appointment in August of Chancellor as an additional general manager. Chancellor himself was in attendance, and the directors acquiesced. But Jones's statement that he had now 'decided' to make the appointment angered his board colleagues. Ewing was sent to tell Jones that the right to make senior appointments rested with the board, and that he must never again take unilateral action. Ewing also reminded Jones that, under his contract, he would be serving at a year's notice from the end of 1939. In other words, the board could give him notice to quit from the end of 1940. This combined complaint and reminder gave Jones pause. The board was clearly restless. But he was genuinely surprised at the complaint about Chancellor. Jones told Ewing that down the years he had made 'about a dozen' such appointments. In Chancellor's case he seems to have felt no need to report that the appointment had been pronounced by Perth, in a postscript to his letter of 24 August, 'acceptable to His Majesty's Government'. Jones perhaps felt that Reuters was sufficiently protected because 'acceptable to' was not the same as 'confirmed by'.

Chancellor was acceptable to Jones, to the British Government, and also—despite their complaint about the manner of his appointment—to the PA–Reuter directors. Haley, in particular, came to regard Chancellor as a promising prospect. Later, Haley began to stay with the Chancellors at their London flat when he came down from Manchester.

Jones's fellow directors were now determined to maintain a close watch upon their chairman. On 6 November, at their request, they met him at Reuters for an informal meeting. Jones believed that it 'greatly cleared the air'. According to his own account, he came away convinced that 'the Directors had no ulterior motives as regards myself, whether as Chairman or as Managing Director'. Haley made his own shorthand record of 'salient points', a copy of which was sent to Jones. Haley's version showed that in reality Jones had been pressed hard, although courteously. The possibility of giving him a year's notice overhung the discussions. The directors demanded to be told much more than in the past. 'We want bringing up to date', exclaimed Storey, 'and keeping up to date.' Jones responded with characteristic blandness. 'Gentlemen, you are pushing an open door. If only because of my own pride in Reuters I am only too glad to give you all the information I can.' He agreed to produce two monthly reports, one general and one financial. He also agreed to consult in future about senior appointments. He recognized the need to have trained senior men available, 'so that if anything happened to him, Reuters would go on'. To this end, he had prepared written recommendations to be read if he ever died in office. This memorandum (5 December 1939), which in the event was never to be seen by the board, said that it was his expectation ultimately to appoint Chancellor as chief general manager.[10]

Jones interpreted these discussions about what might be done if he died or was incapacitated as meaning that otherwise he was in post 'for life'. He failed to notice the very different tone of Haley's account of the meeting. Haley quoted Ewing as speaking in terms which involved no long-term commitment: 'they proposed to leave everything over for the time being'. On 2 February 1940 Haley wrote thanking Jones for sending a copy of the first monthly report. 'It opens up vistas', commented Haley, 'of a whole world which Directors have never before grasped.' Was there a hint of threat beneath these words of congratulation?[11]

Jones was not aware of this possibility until 19 April 1940. On that morning, suddenly, at a hurriedly called meeting in his office he was told by Ewing and Henderson—'avoiding the armchairs, they sat in straight back chairs which they drew up to my desk'—that he had lost the confidence of the board and should resign. Jones was amazed, more amazed than he would have been if he had interpreted the November meeting correctly. There was now a fresh dimension of dissatisfaction, which Ewing and Henderson did not reveal. The three general managers, Turner, Moloney, and Chancellor, had spoken without Jones's knowledge to three directors—Ewing, Henderson, and Herbert Staines of the *Sheffield Telegraph*, the PA chairman for the year. The three managers had complained that Jones refused to accept advice or criticism, and that his arrogance was becoming more and more damaging. He refused to delegate decision-making. This had meant, in the words of Haley's *Times* obituary of Jones (24 January 1962), that 'a second gap grew between him and his colleagues on the board'.

In an *aide-mémoire*, Jones described the demand for his resignation as a 'bolt from the blue', not to be reconciled with the 'very happy understanding' reached in November. He pressed for reasons; but Ewing and Henderson at first said that they were not free to give any. Jones insisted that he had a right to know. Ewing then suggested, according to Jones, that the reason might be found in the strength of Jones's personality. Jones asked for a more specific reason. Ewing then mentioned the crisis with AP in 1933–4, when Jones had persuaded the Reuter board to give notice to the American agency. Jones's policy had made an enemy of Kent Cooper, the influential manager of AP, 'and his enmity had been very harmful to Reuters ever since'. Ewing added that Jones's preference for 'claiming pre-eminence for Reuters' irritated the other news agencies. Finally, Jones's 'grip' on Reuters had stifled the general managers.

Jones denied all these charges. Firm leadership should not be taken for dictation. He demanded to meet the full board, and this was arranged for the Victoria Hotel on the following afternoon. By the time of this meeting, Jones had discovered, from a source which his notes (12 April) do not reveal, that his general managers had 'played the traitor'. 'The most hurting is Chancellor. I have cherished him and pushed him forward.'

At the Victoria Hotel meeting, Jones defended himself against the charge of being a dictator. Apart from Jones, only Staines (as chairman) and Ewing spoke. According to Jones's account, 'the whole proceedings clearly had been most carefully rehearsed'. Jones told the directors that he was 'completely bewildered'. He referred back to the November meeting, still not realizing that he had then been put on probation. He emphasized that there had been no complaints at subsequent board meetings. Why not, if the directors felt so strongly? Jones paused. No one answered. Jones began to accept the inevitable. The board could insist upon his going, but he would expect its being done in a way and at a time that would not damage his reputation. Staines remarked that he accepted this, but that it was a case of 'the sooner the better—for all parties'. This gave Jones the chance to begin to split the solid front presented by his directors. He refused to be rushed. 'The whole course of my career was at stake.' Ewing remarked that Jones would of course need time to talk matters over with his wife and with his lawyers. 'Ewing was clearly trying to ease the pressure upon me.' Eventually, it was agreed that no announcement would be made until the annual general meeting on 2 July. That was three months away, and was certainly much longer notice than the directors had originally intended. Storey and Haley were present throughout, but both kept silent:

> Mr. Ewing helped me on with my coat, and remarked for my ear only: 'A painful business'.
> I replied: 'Yes indeed—for the victim'.

Jones wondered about taking legal action; but for the sake of Reuters he reluctantly decided to accept retirement, if unavoidable and upon honourable and favourable terms. But, even now, was it unavoidable? Jones decided to sound out Ewing, the most sympathetic of his critics. Jones wrote next day asking to consult Ewing 'as a friend without, I assure you, embarrassing you as a director'. The two men duly met on 19 April, and Jones began subtly to encourage Ewing to have second thoughts. He mentioned the names of several prominent newspapermen whom he claimed as friends— John Astor of *The Times*, Lord Camrose of the *Daily Telegraph*, and Lord Kemsley, who was both a national and provincial proprietor. Although he did not admit this to Jones, Ewing took the hint that these influential figures, who held no high opinion of the judgement of the provincial newspapermen who ran the PA, would be very surprised to be suddenly told of Jones's resignation.

On 2 May Jones was handed by Ewing part of a note which he had circulated to the other directors. Jones's hints had produced the desired effect. Ewing's note said that people in the NPA, such as Astor, Camrose, and Kemsley, would conclude that the PA had behaved badly towards Jones. This would add to their existing distrust, and might affect their willingness to continue taking the Reuter news service. A year later, after Jones's departure, the NPA did indeed react in such a critical spirit to manœuvring by the PA. Ewing's second thoughts were therefore reasonable; but it was remarkable that he should have shown Jones even part of the paper.

Ewing was being won back by Jones. Who else might be? On 6 May Jones wrote to John Scott in Manchester, even though he was no longer a Reuter board member. 'Somebody is trying to stab me in the back! I am confident that, so far as you are able, you will not stand by and allow this.' The two men met for lunch; but Scott seems to have remained firmly behind his

Manchester colleague, Haley, who wanted Jones out. On 7 May Jones received a letter signed by Henderson, as the new PA chairman, telling him formally that his Reuter colleagues had 'lost confidence' in him, and asking for his resignation with effect from the annual meeting.

On that same evening, Jones went to see Ewing at the *Glasgow Herald's* London office. According to Jones's account, Ewing revealed that he did not now want Jones to resign. But only one other director, said Ewing— Raymond Derwent of the *Bradford Telegraph & Argus*—felt the same. 'Storey was the arch-enemy.' Jones remarked that if he were driven from the chairmanship, Storey would get it. Ewing thought that the board would not want Storey. 'Storey had been tiresome re paper position at Newspaper Society that afternoon'; he was 'always destructive'. Clearly, Ewing was already critical of Storey, although he was to become much more so a year later. A note by Jones at that time (8 April 1941) listed a succession of occasions at PA board meetings during 1940 when Storey had allegedly been guilty of intrigue. These included: 'Jockeying to remain beyond his time on the PA board and therefore the Reuters Board.' Exceptionally, in May 1940 Storey's tenure was extended for a further year.

Ewing was making more progress than he had admitted to Jones. He had talked Henderson and even Storey partly round. On the very next day (8 May 1940), Ewing and Henderson returned to Jones, and invited him to retain the chairmanship only, at least until the end of the following year. Haley in Manchester seems not to have been consulted. 'Strongminded, young and revolutionary', as Ewing described him to Jones, Haley would require 'careful handling'. But Ewing thought that he would be able to win Haley (and Scott) over by visiting them in Manchester.

Jones insisted that any announcement at the annual meeting about his retirement as managing director would have to carry 'no faintest reflection on myself'. He was hinting that his NPA friends would still ask awkward questions. Ewing began to wonder if Jones might not best be left for the time being as managing director as well as chairman. In a letter to Staines on 21 May, Ewing suggested that the threat to remove Jones had done good by clearing the air, making it plain that he must go when the board judged opportune, 'and not necessarily when Sir Roderick chooses'. On the other hand, Ewing was still worried that Jones's unexpected and immediate resignation as managing director would seem equivalent to dismissal. 'Therefore his friends will ask what crime he has committed.' They knew that he had planned to continue for several more years in full charge of Reuters. Consequently, 'the attitude of the whole membership of the NPA might become much more unfriendly than it already is'.

Only very reluctantly did all the directors agree to Jones remaining as managing director as well as chairman. Some gave way only because at a meeting on 3 June Ewing threatened to resign. As a respected figure within the PA, his resignation would have made the crisis worse, and left the other PA–Reuter directors with too much to explain. Storey and Henderson were the most reluctant to acquiesce in Jones's complete reinstatement. A year later in a letter to Storey (11 June 1941) Henderson was to recall that what he then dubbed the 'cold feet brigade' had 'frustrated a quick disappearance last summer'.

The collapse of the Allied armies in France during May and June 1940, while this boardroom crisis was continuing within Reuters, only added to Ewing's feeling that now was not the time to put the agency under new management. Another way to strengthen it, he told the 3 June meeting, would be to draw the national newspapers into the ownership. Henceforward, this became Ewing's objective, whether or not Jones remained in post.

On 1 July the directors held a further meeting, and afterwards Henderson came to Jones and asked him, in view of the war situation, to defer matters indefinitely: 'would I just go on as usual?' Jones now felt able to stiffen his attitude. He turned round the complaints made against him. 'If the Directors wanted to be more in the concern, so to speak, let them say so. I saw no objection to that . . . subject to all this I was prepared to say, and did say, "I accept".' On 30 July Jones boldly read the board a written statement, deploring the way he had been treated and insisting upon a 'modus vivendi' for the future. This, he announced blandly, required him to take steps to pave the way for his retirement as managing director. He proposed that in future the general managers should report directly to the board. One of them might eventually be designated chief general manager, and thereafter Jones might hand over to him as managing director, while remaining as chairman. This was an adroit proposal. It partly met the other directors' wishes; but it sought endorsement for Jones to remain in the chair for a further unspecified period. Jones withdrew from the room while the others considered their response. They were adroit in turn. Henderson came to Jones's room and read him a written statement. The other directors accepted his delegation proposals; but 'in view of the complete uncertainty of the national position', the directors declined to accept 'any precise scheme regarding the future central direction and management'. Jones remarked that this left 'everything still in the air'. 'You accept my delegation proposals, but the question of what follows you leave open.' 'You have it exactly,' replied Henderson, with more satisfaction to himself than to Jones.

Next day, however, at least according to Jones's account, Ewing assured him that this meant that he was to continue 'until the end of the war'. Only then would the question of his retirement be addressed. Jones asked if he had regained the confidence of the board. According to Jones, Ewing answered: 'They would not like openly to climb down. But he felt sure that I had the confidence and respect of all—omitting Storey. Nothing I could do probably would bring him over. He was definitely hostile. But the others were all right, and he believed felt thankful that they had been saved from making a bad blunder.' If Ewing really did say all this, the desire to be encouraging had taken him too far. Probably, however, Jones had read into Ewing's remarks too much of the meaning which he wanted to hear.

If the directors had now reluctantly and surprisingly accepted Jones for the duration, they still took care in November 1940 to give him formal notice from the end of 1941. This, wrote Henderson to Jones on 9 September, was to 'regularise the position'. It meant that from 1942, or at latest from the end of the war, the board would be free to replace Jones. He had no choice but to accept this proposal in writing, although in his heart he retained hopes of remaining as chairman for many more years.

6

In his letter to Jones of 9 September 1940 Henderson had spoken of his satisfaction at 'this final disposing of what has been a painful episode for all of us'. In truth, Henderson and Storey were very disappointed that Jones had survived, and so were the three general managers. The managers no doubt knew that Jones had become aware of their campaign against him. Chancellor told Sir Horace Wilson of the Treasury that if it had not been for the war he would have resigned from Reuters. In view of the contrast between his protestations of loyalty to Jones and his actions behind Jones's back, resignation would have been the decent course, wartime or not. Instead, Jones and Chancellor settled to continue working together in outward harmony. When, however, in November 1940 Jones offered Chancellor the post of 'personal deputy', Chancellor declined. He said that he could not conceive of any Reuter business which could not be handled by the three general managers acting as equals. Of course, Chancellor did not admit that he was unwilling to tie himself too closely to Jones. 'I am afraid', he wrote to Jones on 5 November, 'you will consider me ungracious and unappreciative.' 'I do,' pencilled Jones in the margin. Chancellor took care to tell Storey of his refusal.

Chancellor had been complaining strongly about Jones in official circles, sometimes in writing and no doubt more in conversation. One channel was through his brother-in-law, William Elliott, an assistant secretary to the War

Cabinet. Chancellor wrote to Sir Alan Barlow of the Treasury on 10 October 1940 that he had spoken privately to Henderson, the PA chairman. 'I told him something of the position and asked him to be on his guard against attempts to misrepresent H. M. Government's intentions with regard to Reuter.' Chancellor was here suggesting that Jones had exaggerated the official pressure put upon him, in order to gain credit for resisting it. This was a quite opposite charge to the more usual one that Jones was compromising the independence of Reuters under official pressure, a complaint against Jones which Chancellor could scarcely have used to Ministers and civil servants themselves. Moreover, the former line was more serviceable to Chancellor's purpose of advancing his own cause, since it presented him as trying to help the official side in its dealings with Reuters.

Chancellor recommended a meeting between Henderson—'he is discreet, reliable and honest'—and Barlow or Wilson. But Chancellor's plotting had begun to seem too eager even for Barlow. The latter's reply (12 October) advised Chancellor to ease off: 'having done so much as you have quite rightly done to help those in authority, both inside and outside the organisation, to understand the true position and its essential needs as you see it, you should for the time being refrain from further overt action.'[12]

On 6 November 1940 Barlow did see Henderson's ally, Storey, in an off-the-record meeting. According to Storey's notes, Barlow told him that it was impossible to ignore the great volume of complaint about Reuter services from the Foreign Office and from British embassies throughout the world. 'RJ's personal inefficiency and his suppression of the GMs transparent. Large part of trouble probably due to RJ's appointment of correspondents.'

Frank Pick had just been appointed Director-General of the MOI, with instructions from the Prime Minister, Winston Churchill, to improve the Reuter services. Pick was told by Wilson on 10 October that the main need was for Reuters 'to reorganise from within', and 'an essential preliminary seems to be to remove Roderick Jones'. Yet, in a short time, Pick was to form a much more favourable view of Jones than was expected. Indeed, after Jones's fall and after his own brief tenure as Director-General was over, Pick wrote frankly to Jones (12 February 1941). 'I have no doubt at all there was intrigue at work. I confess I was told to see what could be done about you, but in the end I came to the conclusion that you were best where you were. Well, I was outmanœuvred, I suppose, and disappeared.'[13]

Pick had devised a plan for a joint standing committee of control for Reuters. In response, Jones and his fellow directors had agreed that, while a channel for discussion of news problems was acceptable, control of Reuters by a body containing outside officials was not. Pick produced 'Heads of

Agreement', which were discussed at length during November and December 1940. Storey was urged by Ewing and Henderson, after a meeting of the three men in Glasgow, to visit Wilson and Pick. Jones heard about this approach, and was angry. Storey had gone, explained Ewing to Jones (7 December), as a PA director: 'a crafty distinction', noted Jones. Storey reported his discussions with Wilson and Pick to a meeting of directors (without Jones) called at Leeds on 4 December, before the same men travelled down to London by train for a two-day Reuter board meeting on 5–6 December. The Government view, communicated by Storey at Leeds, was that Reuters needed 'cleaning up', and that if the Reuter directors did not do it the Government would do it for them. Ewing repeated all this to Jones three days later. Jones still refused to understand that his whole management was being attacked in official circles. He thought that Storey had exaggerated for his own ends 'idle and ignorant gossip in Parliament and Whitehall'. Nevertheless, Jones admitted to himself that Storey's 'poisonous tale' might have damaged him with the Reuter board.

The specific purpose of the Leeds meeting had been to discuss, in the absence of Jones, the MOI proposals for a joint committee and for a new contract to provide extended news services. In a letter to Ewing on 28 November Jones took credit for having already taken the sting out of Pick's proposals. But on 16 December Pick was replaced as Director-General by Sir Walter Monckton. Haley told Storey on 1 January 1941: 'Pick's departure strikes me as good. He was too much with R.J.' Monckton decided that the proposed 'Heads of Agreement' were unnecessarily elaborate. He told Jones at a first meeting on 3 January that he wanted simply to ensure that Reuters 'performed efficiently what was required of them by the Government'. Monckton was a flexible lawyer in search of a solution.

Haley too was ready to be flexible, for his own reasons. Paradoxically, because of his suspicion of the MOI's intentions, as well as because of his doubts about Jones's trustworthiness, Haley saw some advantage in accepting the proposed joint committee. He suggested to Storey (1 January 1941) that, so long as it was purely advisory and included one watchful Reuter director, it would be 'a valuable safeguard to us that we really do know what is happening'. But Haley was already thinking much more broadly: 'we should not overlook the much larger, and far more important task of reorganising Reuters, its Board, its Executive, its Controls and so on. The sooner we start our ground planning the better.' The implementation of such a wider vision for Reuters, shaped especially by Haley, was destined to occupy the whole of 1941 and beyond. But first Sir Roderick Jones had to be removed.

Haley's vision was discussed at the Reuter board on 7 January. A sub-committee of Jones, Haley, and Storey was appointed to handle both the immediate contract negotiations with the MOI and to consider the reorganization of Reuters. Haley would have preferred separate committees, with Jones not involved in planning for the future.

Ewing (as deputy chairman), Storey, and Haley were also granted, in the words of Jones's private record (7 January), 'a roving commission inside Reuters'. Was this more than a quest for information? According to Jones, Ewing was becoming concerned that he (Jones) was once more coming under pressure. Depressed by the 'steady opposition' of Storey, Henderson, and Haley, and the 'uselessness' of the other PA–Reuter directors, Ewing apparently talked of resignation. That same morning at the PA board, noted Jones, there had been 'another row' with Storey over the new PA tariff; it was, declared Ewing, 'the worst yet'. Jones heard this with some satisfaction. 'I told him in detail Pick's description to me of Storey's visit to Pick and the bad impression that Storey made upon him. But I did not repeat Pick's remark to me, "I would be on my guard if I were you against that gentleman: he wants your job: he sees himself as Chairman of Reuters".'

As background to the contract negotiations, Storey and Haley asked to read the existing contracts with the Government. On 10 January Jones sent them copies of the agreement 'under which we have been working ever since the summer of 1939', plus a copy of the related minute of the board meeting on 12 September 1939. 'Writing on the spur of the moment,' he told Storey in a covering letter, 'I cannot recall that there is anything to add to the Minute in regard to the implications of the Agreement. These are made clear in the Minute, and their significance one way or the other has not been altered since.' In other words, Jones still saw no need to mention the Perth letter of 24 August 1939.

None the less, he now felt under continuous pressure from both inside and outside Reuters. He had won round Pick, but Pick had been sacked. Could he now win round Pick's successor, Monckton? Jones arranged an off-the-record meeting on 13 January and gave Monckton his version of negotiations with the Government since his approach to the then Prime Minister, Neville Chamberlain, in 1937. Unlike Pick, Monckton was not open to persuasion that Jones should keep his job, despite an attempt by Jones to win sympathy through denunciation of Storey. Storey, claimed Jones, had worked up the feelings of the rest of the Reuter board in order to undermine his position as chairman, 'and he had made them fearful of the Government's intentions where there was no ground for fear'. This gave Monckton an insight into the tensions within the Reuter board. He was emerging as the most widely briefed player in the whole game. Monckton wanted Jones to be removed in the national interest: Storey and Haley wanted him out for the sake of Reuters. The four men were about to meet in negotiations over the new contract. Could Jones be isolated and destroyed? Monckton was bland in manner, but sharp of mind. Haley's 1981 *Dictionary of National Biography* article on Jones frankly summed up what happened next. 'The Ministry deliberately betrayed him'.

7

In preparation for their first meeting with Monckton, Jones met Storey and Haley on 14 January; according to Jones's private record, they were 'all affable and smiling'. Yet Jones knew that Storey had just seen Moloney and Chancellor. 'Typical of what goes on between these three "loyal" general managers and directors behind my back!'

Monckton's first standing committee meeting with Jones and Haley took place at the MOI on 20 January—with Storey unavoidably absent, but with Moloney and Chancellor in attendance. Monckton began by referring, apparently casually, to the Perth letter as if it were unquestionably part of the existing arrangements. Did he really believe this? A lawyer by training, he must have understood that the letter was in itself no more than a proposal, which required written confirmation from both sides. There was no such confirmation on his file. Jones and Haley both exclaimed that they knew of no letter. Haley meant that he knew of no letter at all. Jones cannot have forgotten that a correspondence had taken place; but he knew that there had been no final exchange of letters of agreement. By the time of the 12 September board meeting, negotiations with Perth had lapsed. Nothing had been finalized. This was to be Jones's defence throughout what became for him the final crisis in Reuters. Haley and Storey were to persuade their colleagues that his explanation did not justify Jones's failure to reveal the existence of the letter.

At the 20 January meeting, Monckton went on to discomfit Jones further. Under cover of asking if one of the general managers acted as Jones's deputy, Monckton referred pointedly to the prospect of a Reuters without Jones. 'Chairmen and Managing Directors are not eternal. Is there anyone to succeed you?' Haley cut in to answer that the board had the matter 'constantly and immediately before them'. When Monckton suggested that the MOI should be consulted about any appointment, Haley objected to the word 'consult'. 'The Government would be advised beforehand, but it would not be consulted.' Haley was making plain by implication that the tacit alliance of certain Reuter directors with the MOI to eject Jones was strictly limited to that one purpose.

Another meeting was held at the MOI on 24 January 1941, this time with Storey present. Jones's notes agree with Storey's that Monckton again referred to the Perth letter. 'Monckton was still under the impression that I had accepted that letter . . . I still maintained that I had never accepted, or replied.' Jones suggested that the Perth letter could be left aside. 'Monckton was inclined to agree but Storey and Haley clearly wanted to delve into the past, so I said I certainly would see what my file produced.' Storey's version was briefer, but ominously questioning. 'RJ again maintained only drafts had passed and suggested not necessary refer back to these but that new letter should be drafted. Why this desire avoid production of letter or draft?'

Five days later, on 29 January, Jones visited Monckton to (in Jones's words) 'clear up the position'. He explained about the Perth letter. 'There were points in the draft which I wished to alter, including the style of CJC position . . . Meanwhile a week later war was declared, and everybody's idea, both Government and ours, was to get on with the work. The Perth letter was never mentioned again—we all forgot about it. In any case I never answered it, much less accepted it.' Jones told Monckton that on 12 September 1939 he had caused the Reuter directors to concentrate upon the essential question— what the words 'bearing in mind' were to mean with regard to Government suggestions about the news.

After hearing this explanation, Jones claimed in his private record of the meeting that Monckton agreed to start afresh: 'no more wasting time on an inquest.' This was clearly what Jones wanted to happen. But was it what Monckton, sensing Jones's vulnerability, really wanted? At a further meeting of the joint committee on the afternoon of 3 February Monckton was still say-ing, according to Jones's own account, that he was 'not quite clear' what the past relationship had been, 'and deriving from that, what it should be'. In other words, Monckton was keeping the Perth letter at the centre of discussion.

The last stage for Jones had already begun that same morning. Ewing, who was on his way to an appointment with Jones in his office, was hurriedly diverted into a crisis conference with Storey and Haley. These two then arranged, at ten minutes' notice, to see Jones at 11.50 to discuss the minutes of the joint committee meeting of 24 January. This proved to be the decisive encounter. Jones's is the only account; but as it is descriptive, rather than interpretive, there is no reason to doubt its accuracy.

Storey asked about 'these letters covering the Government contract'. Jones replied that there had been only a preliminary letter from Perth, to which he had never replied. Jones handed Storey a copy of Perth's text. Storey and Haley then sat together and read it through carefully. Storey afterwards took the copy away, and Haley made his own transcription. 'They maintained that I should have disclosed paragraph A (CJC etc.) to the Board as well as paragraph B.' Jones answered that he had still been in negotiation. He had not wanted to place Chancellor over Turner or Moloney. 'Also I did not feel we should be left saddled with this and its consequences while the Government had the power to terminate the contract any year . . . I reported to the Board the essential clause B, which was to my mind the essence of the "Gentleman's agreement", and I also at the following meeting reported my appointment of CJC':

> At one stage, after repeated reassertion of complaint by Storey and Haley, I said to Haley, in reply to an invidious remark he made: 'Do you suggest that I deliberately concealed this from the Board?'
> Haley: 'Yes, I do.'
> Jones: 'Then I can only say that I am sorry for you. I did no such thing.'

The breach therefore came over clause A, dealing with the appointment of Chancellor; not over the more important clause B, which had required that 'Reuters will at all times bear in mind any suggestions made to them'.

The loss of confidence between Jones and his two strongest board critics was clearly final. But Jones still seems to have retained the hope that he might isolate Storey and Haley rather than be himself isolated. He told them that the matter ought to be raised with Monckton at that afternoon's meeting of the joint committee. However, as already noticed, Monckton continued to speak at that meeting as if Jones might have accepted the whole Perth letter in 1939. Whether or not Monckton had been told about that morning's confrontation is unknown. In any event, he was never going to help Jones.

Jones now cracked. At the meeting of the Reuter board next morning, 4 February 1941, he quietly submitted his resignation. The recurring pressure had worn him down. He was 63 years old and his health was deteriorating. He explained three years later to Ewing (3 March 1944) that he was 'too tired and disheartened after the harassing events of the previous year, too exhausted and utterly disgusted to do anything but resign'.

German bombing had added to the pressure upon Jones. The later exchanges between him and his fellow directors had taken place while London was under almost nightly attack from the air. Jones's home was too far away to reach in safety from Reuters in Fleet Street, and he had perforce taken up residence at the Savoy Hotel, about half a mile away. Each night Jones had to grope his way through the blackout wearing a steel helmet; 'or at a run, sheltering where possible on the way'. Such nightly exposure would have tested the nerves of anyone. Other board members, who lived and worked in provincial cities which were bombed less continuously, were more fortunate, although their trains to London were often delayed.[14]

In offering his resignation, Jones stipulated that he should be paid his full salary until the end of the year, followed by a half-salary pension thereafter. Acceptance of his resignation upon these terms was proposed by Ewing, seconded by Henderson, and carried unanimously.

If Jones had not immediately tendered his resignation, Haley was intending to demand it. He had brought with him a draft motion in his own hand:

> That his fellow Directors, having heard Sir Roderick Jones's explanation of the circumstances in which when on Sept. 12 1939 he sought and obtained the authority of the Board to enter into the contract of 1939 with His Majesty's Government he failed to disclose to the Board that it was Lord Perth's proposal that the arrangements set out in Paragraph A of Lord Perth's letter of Aug. 24 1939 should be an integral part of the arrangements, are of opinion that this information was material to the Board's proper appreciation of the implications of the Agreement, and therefore that they can have no future confidence in him as a colleague or a representative and Resolve that he be called upon to resign his offices as Chairman and Managing Director forthwith.[15]

Haley was not, therefore—as has usually been assumed—intending to bring Jones down on a charge of having covertly compromised the independence of Reuters. At the last, Jones's critics were taking their stand on lower ground. Haley's wording even accepted that Perth's letter was, as Jones always claimed, no more than a 'proposal', not a final settlement. Haley also accepted that Jones had revealed the crucial clause B form of words to the board on 12 September 1939. Haley's attack was confined to the charge that Jones had not revealed for discussion clause A ('CJC etc.'), and that this clause 'was material to the Board's proper appreciation of the implications of the Agreement'.

Jones's answer was that he intended, in further discussions which never took place, to secure modification of clause A. Jones did a few days later appoint Chancellor as a third general manager; but he was not, as Perth had wanted, made senior to the other two general managers. In other words, far from bending under Government pressure, Jones resisted it as much as he thought necessary.

Was Jones therefore treated doubly unfairly—by Monckton at the MOI for his own reasons, and by his fellow directors at Reuters for theirs? Certainly, all that Jones said about the Perth letter was true. It was a proposal. He had not accepted it as final. He was vulnerable over clause A, not because he had accepted it, but because he had not revealed its purport while it was still unfinalized. In view of the desire of the PA–Reuter directors for greater involvement, this was an error of psychology. Jones was still conducting himself in his long-established lofty way. But the directors did not collectively press their demand for closer involvement until two months later. Moreover, at the next board meeting in October 1939 the appointment of Chancellor on Jones's terms (not Perth's) had been duly reported by Jones. The directors had not been allowed any opportunity to discuss the appointment of Chancellor before it was made, but prior approval had not been customary in such cases. As already noticed, the directors had sent Ewing to insist to Jones that in future all senior appointments must be agreed in advance by the board.

The PA–Reuter directors had ceased to trust Jones. Their sense of distrust was demonstrated in Ewing's memorandum, already mentioned, written within a few days of Jones's resignation and looking back over his career. Ewing summed up why Jones had lost the confidence of the board:

> In entering into an agreement with Government which compromised the company.
>
> In concealing this from his board for more than eighteen months, while maintaining that he was opposed to any Government interference in Reuter internal affairs.
>
> In denying, when challenged, the existence of any documents other than had been submitted to the Board.
>
> And finally, in suggesting that because the Perth letter had first been submitted in draft form to him and been accepted by him, he was entitled to repudiate it on the ground that alterations had subsequently been made on the original, which alterations on his own admission were of minor importance only and in no way affected the spirit of the agreement.

These linked charges demonstrated that Ewing had failed to grasp that the Perth letter had remained unfinalized, never 'accepted' by Jones and never reaching a stage which might have required Jones (in Ewing's words) 'to repudiate it' as compromising.

Of course, leaving aside these particular grounds for removing Jones, in general terms his critics were right to force him out. He had clung on too long. Reuters had fallen behind. Its news services were of uneven quality, and complaints from subscribers had become persistent. A change of men and of methods, starting at the top, had become overdue.

Even so, Jones's fall came as a surprise. Most Reuter staff, and most Fleet Street journalists outside Reuters, as well as the public at large, knew nothing of the long-running internal tensions. Nor were they told anything now. For the sake both of the agency's reputation and of the national interest in wartime, all parties agreed not to publish any explanations, which would inevitably have been contradictory. On 14 February Jones simply issued a paternal farewell address to the staff which outlined the achievements of his period in charge—'the activities of Reuters have been quadrupled in these twenty-five years'; and which expressed but did not explain his 'deep personal regret' at going.[16]

8

If only Jones had retired on his sixtieth birthday in 1937 his period of personal rule over Reuters would have ended in harmony. The tributes upon his retirement would have emphasized how his enterprise had revived Reuters during the First World War; how his patriotic dedication had maintained Reuters as the news agency of the British Empire; and how his determination had made possible the protective takeover of the agency by the provincial press. It would have been noticed that, just as Julius Reuter had used the telegraph and cable to transform news distribution, so Jones had led Reuters in similar fashion to take early advantage of wireless technology. Jones would also have been rightly praised for backing a great expansion of the Reuter commercial service, which had quickly become a source of considerable profit, helping to pay for the general news side. If Jones had departed in 1937, his autocratic style of management would not necessarily have been criticized as damaging. Sir John Reith's management of the BBC in the same period was also autocratic, but Reith left the BBC in 1938 with a high reputation. Interestingly, Jones believed that Reith was much more autocratic than himself. The two men were of course working in different circumstances. Reith was energetically creating a new institution: Jones was seeking to sustain an old one.

Jones was never given the peerage which he long expected would be his reward. His claims were put forward several times by his friends in politics— Amery, Buchan, and others. In 1936 his name seems to have featured in a draft New Year's Honours list, only to be taken out at the last moment. His name was withdrawn perhaps because the Government wished to retain the prospect of a peerage as a bait while pressing him to retire. He had apparently decided to take the title of 'Lord Rottingdean' from the seaside village where he owned a house. His family jested that he would become 'Lord Rotters of Reuters'.

After his enforced retirement in 1941 Jones's friends tried again. Chancellor—a protégé, but not a friend—was asked for his opinion. In an interview in 1976 Chancellor described his response. 'I told them what an awful man he was. How he'd been destroying Reuters, and couldn't possibly get one. He didn't.'[17]

NINE

News Between the Wars

1919–1939

I

BEFORE the First World War, although Reuters had offered worldwide news coverage, important parts of its file had come indirectly from correspondents of other agencies within the ring combination. The costs of news collection and distribution were too great to be carried by one agency alone. Between the wars, reporting by Reuters was even more affected by financial constraints at a time when competition was intensifying from the American agencies, buttressed financially by their comfortably large home market and from state-subsidized agencies in Europe and elsewhere. Jones reminded Douglas Williams on 1 March 1924 that Reuters was held back by 'the unwillingness of the [British] newspapers to pay more. In the last analysis the papers get what they pay for.'

Reuters could never afford to maintain as many news bureaux or to appoint as many full-time correspondents as it needed. In 1923 there were forty-three offices (for news and other services) or bureaux (for news) throughout the world: by 1932 there were only twenty-seven. Reuters had to depend increasingly upon part-time correspondents, who were paid retainers, or upon stringers, paid by wordage published. These were either foreign newspaper reporters, freelance journalists, or local businessmen. Between 1920 and 1932 their numbers more than trebled—from seventy to 234. By 1938 the number of 'resident correspondents' worldwide was 676, 282 of them in Europe. Yet only nineteen of the latter were full-time Reuter staff. There were staffers in 12 Indian and eight Chinese cities; but elsewhere in Asia full-time correspondents served only in Tokyo, Singapore, and Manila. A single Johannesburg correspondent was expected to cover most of Africa. And there were only two staff correspondents in the United States, based in New York and Washington.

Reuters always tried to suggest that it was adequately represented throughout the world. But on 8 December 1923 a well-informed exposure appeared in the *Nation & Athenaeum*, entitled 'Reuter's Monopoly in Foreign News'.

The article was widely noticed overseas as well as in the United Kingdom. Its author was Herbert Bailey, a young foreign correspondent with wide experience as a reporter for various British and foreign newspapers. Bailey pointed out that most foreign news in the British press came from Reuters. Yet, claimed Bailey, its compromising wartime links with the British Government had been maintained. Moreover, because it had too few correspondents of its own to collect news overseas, it was forced to recycle propaganda from the foreign agencies with which it was allied by contract. Many of these agencies were under official influence: 'we are constantly flooded with the views of foreign Governments disguised as pure news.'

There was sufficient truth in the article to make it damaging. Jones was on tour, so Buchan sent an answering letter as deputy chairman, published on 22 December. He insisted that the wartime connection with the British Government had ended. All news from foreign agencies, claimed Buchan, was 'checked and supplemented by the correspondents of Reuters'. A week later Bailey came back strongly. He contended that Reuters simply did not maintain sufficient numbers of British-born staff overseas to check the news as Buchan contended. Bailey asked Reuters to reveal how many 'Englishmen' were employed in each European country. Buchan did not respond. In 1924 Bailey became managing editor of the British United Press. He appointed correspondents worldwide, lightened the presentation of foreign news, and won for BUP a prominent place in the columns of the British newspapers, much to the discomfiture of Reuters.[1]

Not all Reuter correspondents were good journalists. An internal memorandum by A. D. Skene Catling (26 April 1929), who was himself one of the more competent, dared to remark that 'the average recruit appears to have no intention of becoming any sort of journalist'. He instanced 'Messrs. Jesse and Justice—excellent fellows, no doubt, but quite unsuitable'. James Robertson Justice went on to become a larger-than-life film actor. Herbert Jeans, chief editor during the 1920s, admitted in October 1922 that few Reuter men in Europe or elsewhere 'have had actual experience of newspaper work or have been trained to look at matters from the sub-editor's desk in a newspaper office'. They reported facts, noted Jeans, but were often weak on background. Although Reuter correspondents were not expected to comment as freely as newspaper correspondents, 'we can be clearer and more explanatory'. When a big story broke, complained Jeans, many Reuter correspondents still waited for newspaper reaction, and simply reported that. D. C. Pendrigh, the dominions editor, demanded an end to all telegrams beginning with the tired formula from Julius Reuter's day, '*Le Matin* says'.

How far should Reuters go in 'brightness'? Apparently not very far. Jones complained about a Reuter report in the *Observer* of 4 September 1932 which told how the Secretary of State for War, Lord Hailsham, had taken third place in a wild-cow milking contest at a Canadian rodeo. The dignity of Cabinet Ministers, thought Jones, should be protected even against themselves.

The Reuter ideal in news handling was well expressed in the contract made with SAPA in 1938. All news supplied to South Africa was to be 'independent, unbiased and impartial'. It was to be supplied in a form suitable for publication in any newspaper, 'irrespective of the political view of the paper, without modification other than curtailment'. And all Reuter services were to be free from propaganda matter, 'except such as is inseparable from the fair reporting of public utterances by men of public importance or events of general news interest'.

In 1918 Reuters appointed a Labour correspondent. This was Vernon Bartlett, who later became a distinguished newspaper columnist and also a Member of Parliament. Jones had been persuaded by Bartlett that it was desirable to take an interest in left-wing politics. But, according to Bartlett's reminiscences, this was not done to counter the impression that Reuters was merely an official mouthpiece: it was done because the agency hoped to continue in that same role 'after the revolution'. The Labour correspondent experiment did not last long.[2]

2

In 1919 exceptional attention was given to reporting the Versailles peace conference. William Turner led a strong team of Reuter correspondents. The wartime British Press Bureau had been closed down, and Reuters was chosen to supply the British official summary of the peace terms, for circulation to the Empire and the world except North America. The British national and provincial newspapers relied entirely upon Reuters. Early on 7 May 1919 Old Jewry issued the 12,750–word official summary of the peace treaty. This unprecedentedly long message, split into sixty-six sections, was cabled to South Africa in four hours and to India in eleven. 'The handling of the Terms', remarked the *Reuter Service Bulletin*, 'can only be compared to the publication of a book by telegraph simultaneously throughout the world.' Here was a great success for Reuters.[3]

A bound volume has survived of all Reuter telegrams published during 1923 in the Seychelles, a remote British colony in the Indian Ocean. This daily bulletin was compiled by the Seychelles colonial authorities, extracted from the Reuter service to East Africa. The telegrams chosen showed the range of news thought appropriate for an imperial outpost. The file contained a mixture of important international stories, news about the British Empire, and 'home' news from the United Kingdom. Familiar names from the war years—Lloyd George, Lenin, Allenby—continued to feature regularly. But new names were appearing—Mussolini, Mustapha Kemal, Gandhi. Reuters had already begun to notice the potential importance of Adolf Hitler. It gave an up-to-the-minute account, duly included in the Seychelles service, of his abortive Munich beer-hall putsch on 9 November 1923:

> After the dictator Von Kahr had spoken at a large Nationalist demonstration at the Burgenbrauen Beer Cellars denouncing the Marxist principles, the Fascist leader Von Hitler [*sic*] entered with 600 men and announced that the Bavarian Government had been overthrown; he added that the new Government was in the hands of Ludendorff who is commander-in-chief, while Von Hitler will be his political adviser; further the chief of the Munich police, Von Poehner, has been appointed administrator, and General Von Lossow, Minister of Defence. Von Hitler's troops then surrounded the cellars; later troops of the Oberland organisation with the Reich colours occupied a number of places, particularly open spaces; there is no further news from the cellars where it is believed Von Kahr and Von Hitler are negotiating; the attitude of the Reichswehr is unknown; Bavarian police have occupied the telegraph office.

Because the status of Indians within the Empire was of particular interest to the Seychelles, Reuters reported British official policy statements, and noticed related editorials and letters in leading newspapers. Both the Kenya Constitutional Conference and the Imperial Conference on Tariffs were covered in great detail.

British politics received ample notice in the Seychelles service—results of by-elections, House of Commons debates (especially on imperial topics), news of Bonar Law's health and of his resignation as Prime Minister, and of Baldwin's appointment as his successor rather than Lord Curzon. The inconclusive 1923 general election and subsequent negotiations between the political parties were treated in depth. Running stories—such as general election results from the constituencies—were covered minute by minute. The wedding of the Duke of York (the future George VI) and Lady Elizabeth Bowes-Lyon presented an opportunity for descriptive writing; but the Seychelles file did not contain much colour or lightness. An exception was a 200-word story about Christmas Day in England, obviously aimed at expatriate colonial readers.

Most stories were straight reports, clearly sourced; but some merely hinted at official contacts—'Reuter learns', 'a Reuter lobbyist learns'. This last was probably F. W. Emett, head of the intelligence [diplomatic] department. Harold Nicolson, the diplomat and writer, once condescendingly noticed Emett in action, trailing Lord Curzon, the Foreign Secretary. Curzon was departing with his staff from London's Victoria Station to attend the 1922 Lausanne conference, and Emett was travelling on the same train. Nicolson wrote:

> I waited with Allen Leeper on the platform. We were joined by Mr. Emmott [*sic*] of Reuter's. 'Is the Marquis often as late as this?', he inquired. 'Lord Curzon', I answered, 'is never late', and as I said the words . . . Lord Curzon proceeded up the platform accompanied by the police, paused for a moment while the cameras clicked, smiled graciously upon the station-master, and entered the Pullman.[4]

Unsourced interpretive articles appeared occasionally in the Seychelles file. An example, timed 'London 31st August 6.55 a.m.', began: 'The danger of flinging lighted torches in the Balkans was not more dangerous in the days of the Sarajevo incident than today when the Lausanne Treaty has left neither Turks nor Greeks completely satisfied.' The article, probably by Emett, noted that the London newspapers were deploring 'Mussolini's precipitancy' in threatening intervention against the Greeks. 'Soberer commentators believe that Mussolini will not proceed the length of his words.'

The Seychelles file contained reports of horse-racing in England throughout the season, and frequent accounts of boxing matches. The main British sporting-cum-social occasions were covered—the Derby, Wimbledon tennis, Henley rowing. The Oxford and Cambridge University boat race on 24 March was given priority, although a laughable error crept in:

| 6 p.m. | Boat Race: Oxford won by nearly a length. |
| 6.20 p.m. | Boat Race: Official: Distance three quarters of a mile [*sic!*]; Time: 20 min. 50 sec. |

A 200-word description of the race followed at 7.20 p.m. In 1923 the Football Association cup final was played at Wembley Stadium for the first time. Seychelles readers were told how 'pressure on the terraces was so terrific that the authorities had to allow late comers to take positions on the running track whence finally they were swept over the pitch'.

In the same year, the massive Tokyo earthquake destroyed three Reuter offices in Japan, but the agency still got the news out. The commercial manager in Osaka, which was not affected by the quake, managed to collect early news from the Kokusai agency in Tokyo. Kokusai was able to radio its Osaka office via a ship anchored in Yokohama bay. Kokusai Osaka then passed the news on to Reuter's commercial manager, who readily undertook the role of an emergency reporter. Reuters also quoted wireless messages picked up in San Francisco, New York, and Peking, as well as a cable received by the Japanese consul-general at Liverpool. The *Reuter Service Bulletin* claimed that the agency's coverage was so far ahead in London that the disaster became known on Fleet Street as 'Reuter's earthquake'. Jones remarked to Buchan (16 October 1923): 'As you say, we are a set of ghouls. The end of the world would be precious in our eyes as a news item—except that we should simultaneously lose our public.'[5]

The discovery in 1923 of the intact sarcophagus of the ancient Egyptian King Tutankhamun led to a great Reuter beat. Valentine Williams had been sent to Egypt as a special correspondent for Reuters, even though *The Times* had negotiated exclusive rights to the story. Williams contrived not only to obtain news of the discovery within minutes of its happening, but also to get a 'flash' out first to the world. The climax had come on 16 February, when Williams rightly guessed that the final breakthrough into the chamber would be made. Reuters had bought him a new car to speed the news from the Valley of the Kings to the western bank of the Nile. Williams had also hired a boat for the day to take the news across the river. He had arranged for a local car then to carry the news from the eastern bank to the cable office at Luxor. As he waited near the tomb entrance, Williams kept in his pocket two prepared cables, each marked URGENT (triple rates). One read 'Tomb empty', the other 'King's sarcophagus discovered'. Williams told in his reminiscences how he had seized his chance when he saw an Egyptian official leaving the tomb:

> I summoned to my aid one of the oldest devices of the reporter for getting at facts, the pretence of knowledge. I addressed the Egyptian in French, because French is the language of polite society in Egypt and I knew it would flatter him, and I called him 'Excellency' because thereby I implied that he was a Pasha. 'Excellency', I said, removing my sun helmet with a bow, 'is it true that they have found two sarcophagi?' 'No, no', replied the fat man importantly in French. 'Only one.' 'Quite plain, they tell me?' 'No, no', he said again. 'It is magnificently decorated, all blue and gold.'[6]

Williams dared not risk another question. He had his news flash. Within thirty seconds his Egyptian assistant was on his way in the car. The London evening papers put the stop-press news on the streets even before the archaeologists had left the tomb. *The Times* retained its monopoly of subsequent descriptive accounts, but Reuters had alerted the world.

The course of the 1929 Wall Street crash led to intense competition for Reuters in London both from Extel and from the International News Service, the third American agency. The New York office provided fast and colourful coverage, while bureaux in financial centres round the world described international reaction:

> New York Tuesday [29 October]: Wall Street has never witnessed such a wild opening as this morning. Practically all the leading stocks opened with initial sales of from 10,000–15,000 shares, with average decline of up to 10 points . . . the closing gong at three o'clock ended a day of greater pandemonium, apprehension and general uncertainty than any broker has previously experienced.

Two years later, Rickatson-Hatt was among editors summoned to 10 Downing Street on Sunday, 20 September 1931 to be told that Britain had gone off the gold standard. Reuters flashed the news round the world well ahead of its official transmission to British representatives overseas. In India, the Viceroy took the necessary action on the strength of the Reuter report alone.[7]

On the first day of 1931 Jones had nominated for the *World's Press News* 'the ten greatest news stories of 1930'. He explained that his choice was made with the preferences of the British public exclusively in mind. His list reflected Reuter news priorities in a year which had not seen any dominant political story. Consequently, the traditional Reuter interest in disasters featured strongly: six of Jones's stories fell into this category. They were headed by the R101 airship crash, which Jones named as the top story of the year. Amy Johnson's solo flight to Australia came second, and Kingsford-Smith's victory in the race there by air was placed ninth. King Carol's dash by aeroplane to seize the Romanian throne came fourth. Only one other political story was selected by Jones—Gandhi's civil disobedience march in India.

3

The rapid development of broadcasting in the United Kingdom during the 1920s and 1930s presented a challenge to the British newspapers. To what extent should the British Broadcasting Company—given semi-official status from 1927 as the British Broadcasting Corporation—be allowed to transmit news bulletins over the air? The newspaper proprietors feared that such bulletins, especially if broadcast at times when the morning and evening papers were on sale, would seriously reduce their circulation. Therefore, should the news agencies, which supplied the newspapers, be left equally free to supply the BBC? And if they did supply news, should there not be restrictions upon BBC usage? A news agency alliance, consisting of Reuters, PA, Extel, and Central News, was formed to find answers to these questions.

Reuters dominated this alliance. Jones had much in common with Sir John

Reith, the autocratic director-general of the BBC. In their recurring negotiations the two men treated each other with warm but wary respect. Jones wrote in a memorandum on 21 October 1927 entitled 'Sir John Reith and Broadcasting Questions' that Reith had given the BBC a 'holy mission' to raise standards in society. Reith, noted Jones, was an admirer of Reuters; but he had his own ideas about 'what the BBC should do in news'. Increasingly, the initiative was with Reith. The news agencies found themselves fighting a long rearguard action.

The first agreement to supply news to the BBC was made on 11 November 1922. The service was to consist of 1,200–2,400 words per day, supplied by the four agencies through Reuters. Payment was to be made on a sliding scale related to the number of wireless receivers licensed, with a minimum payment of £4,000. There was a verbal understanding that no news was to be broadcast before 7 p.m., and each bulletin was to include the acknowledgement 'Copyright News from Reuters, Press Association, Exchange Telegraph and Central News'.

This formula was eventually reduced to 'copyright reserved'. Jones told the 1935 Ullswater Committee on Broadcasting that the purpose was to prevent listeners from taking down and publishing any broadcast news. He explained that the agencies were really trying to stand on property right rather than on copyright, since copyright related only to the form of words, not to content. The agencies claimed property right so long as an item possessed news value. That right, they argued, was not automatically abandoned on first publication, either in print or over the air. Such a right of property had been established in United States law by a Supreme Court decision obtained by AP in 1918. Between the wars, Jones campaigned unsuccessfully for the acceptance of this right in English law.[8]

In the early years, the newspapers and news agencies were very reluctant to allow the BBC to report events as they happened, by means of outside broadcasts. Meetings of newspaper and news agency representatives with Reith (4 November 1924 and 20 February 1925) insisted that this was 'their province'. Some curious compromises were negotiated:

> Regarding the Derby, the Company could microphone what might be termed natural sounds—the noise of horses' hoofs, the shouts of the crowd, and so forth—and the Agencies would not object to the microphoning also of manufactured sounds, consisting of burlesques by John Henry and other comedians, very much as was done with the Lord Mayor's show.

Such extreme restrictions could not last for long. The first running commentary was broadcast in January 1927.

The general strike of 1926 had given a great boost to the aspirations of the BBC. All restrictions upon the times of news bulletins were temporarily relaxed. The BBC organized an emergency news room, and gathered its own material for the first time. Afterwards it pressed for the right to edit the news supplied by the agencies. It began to complain about both content and presentation. 'In the BBC mind', wrote Valentine Harvey, the broadcasting editor of Reuters, on 30 January 1929, 'the Agencies are no longer "the news" but are merely contributors to a BBC news service.' The agencies formally accepted this new reality at the end of 1929. The BBC then agreed to add an extra £2,000 to the £14,000 annual subscription which it had paid since 1927. In place of a 5,000–word news selection, the BBC was to be supplied with the full agency services to edit as it chose.

From 1927 the BBC was broadcasting to the British Empire. At first, the news agencies refused to allow news bulletins to be included. Here was another extreme and untenable restriction. The agencies gave way in 1930.

In March 1929, atmospherics prevented the BBC from broadcasting live President Hoover's inaugural address. The BBC was forced to fall back upon the news agency summary, which was available only a few minutes after Hoover had finished. Four years later, however, Roosevelt's inaugural speech was successfully broadcast live by the BBC. This new development was described by the Reuter board on 7 March 1933 as 'a considerable threat to newspapers and news agency interests'.

The four agencies long resisted pressure from the BBC during the 1930s to be allowed to take news from the British United Press. Jones made it plain that Reuters would not supply the BBC at all if it took BUP news. The four agencies were facing strong competition from BUP's 'bright' news service, which they claimed was placing speed and sensation before accuracy. BUP, despite its name, was Canadian-owned and under American influence. Jones argued vigorously against such a foreign and allegedly unscrupulous organization being allowed to supply news to the British national broadcasting network.

In 1932 Reith tried to detach Reuters, which supplied most of the BBC's foreign news, from the three other news agencies. He offered a direct news contract. If this had been accepted, he would then have been free to deal directly with BUP. The four agencies had always shared the BBC's subscription equally, even though Reuters provided much more than its proportionate quarter of the wordage. Nevertheless, Jones refused to break with his allies. He told Reith on 16 November 1932: 'Human reasons sometimes weighed in business affairs.'

It was only a matter of time before the BBC began to appoint its own correspondents. Reith wanted to send a man to report the war between Italy and

Abyssinia in 1935. Jones told him on 18 September that it would be a waste of money, since the BBC would be getting 'a splendid service' from Reuters. Reith remarked that the BBC had for some time been collecting its own reports from the main European capitals.

In the following year the BBC appointed Richard Dimbleby and Charles Gardner to report home news stories. An article in the *Newspaper World* for 1 August 1936 anticipated that, with these BBC correspondents starting to give live descriptions of anticipated big events, there was little point in news agency or newspaper correspondents continuing to send back written descriptions. Instead, they would have to abandon their grandstand seats, finding story angles by interviewing people, observing their emotions, and highlighting the human interest side. Each of them would have to become 'a reporter again'.

Upon the outbreak of the Second World War in 1939, Dimbleby was sent to France as the first BBC war correspondent. By the time of the preparations for D-Day in 1944 the Reuter board was noticing with concern that, whereas BBC correspondents were now always sure of facilities to report each fresh military operation, Reuters could not be equally certain of sufficient provision.

The power of the microphone could not be denied. Live reports by radio conveyed a sense of immediacy which newspaper reports could not match. And yet, fortunately for Reuters, the fear that the broadcasting of news would reduce the sale of newspapers—and therefore the demand for agency services—did not materialize. Reuters remained a national institution, despite the fact that the BBC had also become one.

4

In the early 1930s Reuters had set out to modernize its methods of news collection and editing. Rickatson-Hatt's new title of 'editor-in-chief' was deliberately chosen. It was a forceful-sounding Americanism, thought to be more up-to-date than the old title of 'chief editor'.

Hatt quickly produced a confidential report for Jones, dated 11 April 1931, on the reorganization of the London editorial department and of the news services. 'I hope to be able to do great things for Reuters.' Hatt began by complaining about the lack of drive within the old agency. 'Editors have come to regard themselves not as newspapermen or journalists, but as conscientious cable transcribers.' Stories, he noted, were often too long, were issued piecemeal, and lost impact by giving the main point last instead of first. Each must begin with a 'lead'. Hatt praised the dominions department, which sent news to the self-governing parts of the Empire, as 'perhaps the premier standard-bearer' for Reuters. 'Millions of people get their ideas of what Reuter is and what Reuter stands for from the Reuter cables that they read in different parts of the world.' But Hatt castigated Emett's intelligence department as 'an almost contemptible farce', devoid of initiative, and Emett was sent into retirement. Hatt appointed three new diplomatic correspondents, on the understanding that Reuters must cease being 'a mere purveyor of Foreign Office and Embassy statements'. He also confirmed what Bailey of BUP had asserted eight years earlier, that there were 'some terribly weak spots' in overseas coverage by Reuter correspondents, especially in Europe. Correspondents and stringers needed instruction in the kinds of stories now required.

Hatt's report hoped that by 1935 there would be enough suitably trained Reuter correspondents in post. This hope was not to be realized. Throughout the 1930s coverage and performance remained uneven. Reuters was too often behind on spot news. For example, on 30 January 1933 BUP beat Reuters by ten minutes in London with the momentous news of the appointment of Hitler as German Chancellor. BUP also beat Extel and Central News, illustrating how strongly it was competing for primacy. Jones always tried to be dismissive. Seven years later he told Haley (18 January 1940) that 90 per cent of BUP material was not its own but originated with UP, its American associate; and that Reuters possessed 'an overwhelmingly larger world organization than the United Press'. In contradiction, UP claimed to be the world's largest news agency. Its European general manager, Webb Miller, explained in a submission to Sir Kingsley Wood's Cabinet committee (15 March 1938) that UP served over 1,440 newspapers in fifty different countries, and that its news was published in twenty-one languages.[9]

On 1 February 1933 Reuters reported from Berlin: 'There appears every prospect that Hitler will remain Chancellor for a considerable time and that his regime will not bring the disasters which many expect.' The first comment was perhaps permissible as an informed opinion, but the second committed Reuters to a compromising value judgement. This was bad practice—quite apart from the fact that the forecast was spectacularly wrong.

Soon afterwards, Victor Bodker was replaced as chief correspondent in Germany by Gordon Young. Young achieved an improvement in performance, even though at first he was working from Berlin with only one full-time assistant, compared with the four or five full-timers employed by other leading news agencies. By 1938 Reuters was itself basing four full-time correspondents in Berlin. There was also a network of Reuter stringers across

Germany. Hatt told Jones (6 December 1934) that they did good work. 'Harmless stories are telephoned and dangerous copy is mailed.'

Censorship within Hitler's Germany was severe, but no restrictions were placed upon outgoing news. However, if any foreign correspondent filed a story to which the Nazi authorities took strong exception, he was likely to be expelled. Reuters had therefore to walk a tightrope, trying to avoid giving offence without suppressing important but sensitive news. Within many other countries, inside and outside Europe, Reuters encountered direct censorship of its messages to London.

William Turner, the overseas general manager, believed that Hatt achieved more success in reforming the inward news provision for the British press than in improving the outward services. In a report on 'The Inward and Outward Services' (6 October 1932), he argued that overseas newspaper readers were of 'considerably higher' intelligence than British readers. Turner gave examples of what he regarded as good and bad handling of stories for overseas readers. He praised an interview by Bodker with Von Papen, the German Chancellor, describing it as 'a good summing up of the German situation'. This was circulated in cable-ese on 17 August 1932:

> we remain office longtime declared chancellor exclusively reutered von-papen confident his appeal commonsense political parties would successful but should vote noconfidence be adopted government would take action accordance situation cumevery intention respecting constitution . . . declared germanys claim equality with other nations regards disarmament was vital progermany who would unlonger submit discrimination be treated as secondclass power germany still aspires return some her colonies retention whereof was unjustifiable discrimination antigermany which must remedied sooner later hoped nazis unwould resort illegal measures but anycase government unhesitate suppress revolt promptly force arms.

This important interview was of course published in the United Kingdom as well as overseas, and the Reuter editorial log for the day noted that most British papers gave the story prominence. '*The Times*, piqued perhaps by our coup, did not publish a word.'

The *Reuter Review* for January 1938 boasted that Reuters had secured more than eighty major beats during 1937. It did not say whether this was more than BUP or AP had achieved. Was Hatt too ready to settle for trying to be first? He was known on the editorial floor as 'a man of glass'—with a quick news sense, but without much depth of interest to follow stories through. By the late 1930s British journalists were once more complaining about Reuters. In December 1939 the foreign news editor of *The Times* told Turner, the joint general manager of Reuters, that sub-editors on the national papers found its news output too bulky, and preferred BUP's briefer, crisper file. In a report for Jones (30 December 1939), Turner admitted 'that our service is too unwieldy'; it contained much unwanted, under-edited wordage. The Reuter board itself began to question Hatt's effectiveness. Answering complaints about BUP and AP 'space superiority' during August 1940, Hatt feebly admitted in a report on 1 October that 'some of our centres have been weak lately. We have been unlucky, too, in suffering from temporary disadvantages in one or two places. Remedial action has been taken wherever possible.'

Hatt had certainly not achieved all that he had hoped for when he set out full of energy and American ideas in 1931. To achieve more, Reuters needed to invest more. Any extra money could come only from the British newspaper groups, or from the British Government, or from both. Yet the newspapers and the Government remained reluctant to provide further resources, at least while Jones and Hatt remained in charge.

5

The Reuter file was dominated during the 1930s by the activities of the totalitarian regimes in Germany, Italy, Russia, Spain, and Japan. In 1933 Reuters covered the show trial in Moscow of a group of British engineers. These men, who had gone to Soviet Russia to work on various construction projects, were used as scapegoats for shortcomings in Stalin's programme of rapid industrialization. They were charged with sabotage and espionage. The Reuter reporter at the trial was Ian Fleming, who had joined Reuters in 1931, well connected and well recommended. Hatt told Jones on 1 October 1931 that Fleming had made a good start. 'His languages are sound. His appearance is good, and his manners are agreeable.' Also, unlike some other Old Etonian recruits, Fleming was hard-working and could write effectively. His 'curtain-raiser' to the trial (12 April 1933), with its attention to descriptive detail, gave a hint of the writer who twenty years later was to create the fictional James Bond:

> (Moscow, Wednesday)—As the famous clock in the Kremlin Tower strikes twelve the six Metropolitan-Vickers English employees will enter a room which has been daubed with blue in the Trades Union Hall and thronged with silent multitudes in order to hear an impassive voice read for 4 or 5 hours the massive indictment which may mean death or exile. Within the packed room there will be a feeling of the implacable working of the soulless machinery of Soviet justice calling to account six Englishmen to decide whether the Metropolitan-Vickers raid was a vast bungle or a Machiavellian coup.

During the trial Fleming filed up to 2,000 words each day. According to UP's Moscow correspondent, Fleming was usually beaten on timings by UP, notably with news of the final verdicts. The fault, though, was not Fleming's, but that of Tass, the Russian agency, which was responsible for cabling the Reuter reports back to London. Moreover, the high quality of Fleming's writing won praise, even though it did not make money. Total expenses of the special coverage were £634, whereas extra payments by the London papers and the PA amounted to only £511. 10s.

Fleming liked Reuters, but chafed at his low salary of £300 per annum. Jones was keen to keep him, and offered him the post of assistant general manager in the Far East. Jones mentioned £800 per annum 'in the tone of one offering sacks of gold'. Fleming still insisted upon leaving to become a stockbroker.[10]

Foreigners working in totalitarian states have always run the risk of being regarded as intelligence agents. This was especially the case with Reuter correspondents who, like other good reporters, were bound to keep themselves informed by trading information with diplomats and others. Even if they were not employed to spy, did this make them into casual agents? Only if, as well as using the matter themselves for journalistic purposes, they passed it on to British officials, at home or abroad. Ivone Kirkpatrick of the British Embassy in Berlin remarked in 1939 that the Reuter and *Times* correspondents were 'often useful scouts and touts for the Embassy'.[11]

Reuter dealings with foreign diplomats in London required care. Jones claimed in his reminiscences that he had avoided social contact with Von Ribbentrop when he was German Ambassador in London. In fact, Jones had telegraphed his 'very cordial congratulations' when Ribbentrop was appointed (11 August 1936); and the Joneses certainly entertained the Ambassador at their London home. When the Czechoslovak crisis was building up Jones sent Ribbentrop (now German Foreign Minister) a 'personal and confidential' letter on 9 June 1938 which expressed 'very kind regards', and offered to send a senior Reuter representative to interview Hitler.

Jones's wife, Enid Bagnold, visited Germany in 1933, and revealed herself in a *Times* article on 2 June as half-impressed and half-repelled by what she saw of Nazism. Hitler's friend, Ernst Hanfstaengl, who had met the Joneses in London, invited them to attend the 1933 Nuremberg Nazi rally. Jones claimed in his reminiscences that he declined 'without hesitation', because to have attended would have compromised his position as head of Reuters. He did not add that before the war he was equally careful for Reuters not to seem critical of the Hitler regime.[12]

As early as 6 December 1931 Hatt had written to Bodker about complaints from the Nazis that Reuters was giving them inadequate attention. Hatt insisted that Reuter reporting of the rise of Hitler was 'fair and impartial . . . more space has been devoted to the Hitlerites by Reuter than to any other political party in Germany.' In 1932 Hitler himself was interviewed by Kenneth Dickins, a Reuter stringer, based in Munich. Over sixty years later Dickins recalled the exchanges:

> We produced a list of questions which Hitler studied for a moment and then launched into a furious attack on Hindenburg and the Brüning government, which had several Jews in it, including the Minister of the Interior responsible for the police. With some trepidation I asked what his reaction was to a report in a London newspaper that in the event of his becoming Chancellor he would immediately organize a 'pogrom' against the Jews. This brought forth a wrathful tirade which effectively closed the interview. Not a hair of a Jewish head would be touched so long as they lived by the laws of the land. The National Socialist Party was the party of law and order and national democracy. Having delivered himself of these very acceptable sentiments he calmed down and became quite a gentleman, even thanking us for driving out to see him. He added that he could rely on the British press to explain the true situation in Germany with its unfair laws and decrees against his party and himself.[13]

To the end of his life, Hitler seems to have trusted Reuters for the accuracy of its reporting.

6

News out of Italy was more than usually important during the 1930s because of the ambitions of Mussolini. The Italo-Abyssinian War of 1935 received much attention from the press of the democracies. Indeed, Jones complained to Kent Cooper of AP on 11 November 1935 that the news agencies and newspapers were spending far too much money upon the war. Reuters, he wrote, had sent eight full-time correspondents to the various fronts, plus assistants and large numbers of stringers.

Following its usual preference, Reuters was represented on both sides. The invasion of Abyssinia from the Italian colony of Eritrea in the north was covered by Christopher Holme; the invasion from Italian Somaliland in the west by J. S. Barnes. The correspondent based in Addis Ababa, the Abyssinian capital, was Walter Collins (1895–1956), an experienced and well-connected journalist. One of his brothers was chairman of the old-established Glasgow publishing house of Collins; while another, Sir Godfrey Collins, served in the Cabinet as Secretary of State for Scotland. Walter Collins had attended public school, but not university. After war service, he worked as a correspondent for *The Times*, first in Sofia and then in Istanbul. When economies at *The Times* lost him that job, he became in 1933 part-time correspondent for Reuters at Istanbul. In the summer of 1935, with international tension rising, he was transferred full-time to Addis Ababa. A year later, following the Italian victory in Abyssinia, he was appointed Reuter correspondent with the Government of India. After three years, however, he was sacked for being too much of a playboy. His private life was certainly untidy, but he was a good journalist; and he later worked successfully in the Middle East for UP, the American agency. In the process, he finally broke the long-standing Reuter monopoly of supplying foreign news to Egypt.[14]

The great altitude of Addis Ababa made the climate enervating. On arrival, Collins had quickly summed up his surroundings to Jones (2 August 1935) as 'very uncivilised'. Partly for this reason, Collins's claims for expenses were high and sometimes colourful. On the excuse that the local water was undrinkable, he was said to have asked Reuters to pay for and deliver to Addis a crate of the very best champagne.[15]

There were about a hundred reporters from the world's press in the capital. Most of them were packed into the only good hotel, but Collins rented a small cottage to be away from the hubbub. Competition was intense and unscrupulous, and after the end of the war he composed a confidential memorandum (19 June 1936) 'for the use of correspondents covering a war or story on which "hot" competition may be expected':

> (1) It is most inadvisable, unless one has known one's colleagues for years, to ever conclude 'A Gentleman's Agreement' regarding collection and time of dispatch of news. Such an agreement is almost always broken . . . On the other hand, unless one has one or two efficient and loyal assistants it may be advisable to co-operate with one or other correspondent, who represents a newspaper like *The Times* and is scarcely a competitor . . .
>
> (2) Reuter's correspondents cannot bribe, but it is necessary to bear in mind that many of one's colleagues (especially Americans) do so, and it is therefore necessary to watch the local telegraph office. It is no use to hand in one's telegram and then go away. One MUST see that the telegram goes off—in its proper sequence. The same remark applies to incoming wires. One must see (a) that no unauthorised person sees the wire before it gets to Reuter's correspondents, and (b) that it is delivered immediately.
>
> (3) A favourite practice indulged in by unscrupulous competitors is to have a copy made of one's outgoing wires. This was frequently the case in Addis Ababa, so much so that we had to 'picket' the telegraph office to see where they went to and who they talked with.
>
> (4) Another pernicious practice is that of reading telegrams upside down. At one time this practice was so rife in Addis Ababa that we used to have two

Ethiopian boys stand with their backs to the telegraph counter. They stood there until our wire had been passed on to the next room. Before this was done, competitors used to read our wires upside down while the operator was counting the words.

(5) When one is racing a competitor in a motor car to a telegraph office, or elsewhere, one can often gain valuable minutes or seconds by pulling up at the wrong side of the road at one's destination . . . It is also advisable, in extreme cases, to employ a second motor car whose sole job is to block the cars of one's rivals by constantly stopping and also by zig-zagging across the road.

(6) It goes without saying that one always had one's typewriter with one in a car, and I found it useful to have a small packing case in the back of the car. One's machine can be more conveniently used in this manner than if it is perched on one's knee (Plate 32).

(7) In Addis Ababa the telegraph office opened and closed at stated times. This led to much abuse. Directly the office opened, it was essential to have a fast runner to cover the 70 or so yards from the outside gate to the counter. At closing time the question was more complicated. To begin with, some competitors used to bribe in order that their boys could gain admittance after hours. The only way to counteract this was to 'picket' the gate and see who was coming in after hours. This was not always enough, and one had to be ready to take off one's coat and use one's fists against the offender. This occurred on more than one occasion.

Collins insisted that he was not exaggerating. Given his realism in other respects, his assertion that Reuters 'cannot bribe' was surprising. In earlier times Valentine Williams described how he, and his father before him, certainly did offer bribes on behalf of Reuters, especially to telegraph officials.[16]

With competition so strong, Collins found that he had no choice but to send all important news from Addis at urgent press rates of 3–4s. per word. The First World War routine—of telegrams supplemented by long mailed dispatches available only days after the event—was no longer acceptable. Occasional mailers providing background or sidelights were still required; but these were no longer part of the daily file. Telegrams were expected to be fast-moving in content and wording. The days were gone of single sentences from Russell or Lawrence which might fill ten or more lines of print.

Collins's report from Addis Ababa of the response to the start of the Italian invasion on 3 October 1935 was widely published next day in the British press. It built up to include an interview with Emperor Haile Selassie himself:

There was tremendous excitement in the capital when a huge crowd, waving swords and revolvers, hailed with delight the proclamation of general mobilisation which was read out by Ligaba Tasso, Grand Chamberlain of the Court. A roll of war-drums which lasted nearly ten minutes preceded the reading of the proclamation . . . The summons to war is being carried through the country by the sound of drum and the smoke of signal fires and the war fever is spreading with lightning rapidity.

Collins exploited to full effect his interview with Haile Selassie. The first words quoted told arrestingly of an alleged Italian atrocity:

'I have just received news that the first bombs dropped by the Italian aeroplanes at Adowa fell on the Red Cross hospital, killing and wounding nurses', the Emperor declared . . . the Emperor looked fit and well as he sat in a leather armchair on a raised dais in front of an open window. He continued with a tribute to Britain: 'We wish to express to the British people our sincerest thanks for all their statesmen have done in the cause of peace.'

Haile Selassie asked for the lifting of the embargo on the export of arms to his country. 'Italy manufactures arms, but we do not possess one arms factory.'

As Collins realized straight away, the Emperor was the moving spirit on the Abyssinian side, and this justified frequent notice of his words and actions. Collins contrived to be favourable in tone towards Haile Selassie personally without losing overall objectivity. 'The Negus', he noted deftly in the middle of one long descriptive report (6 December 1935), 'is said to have directed the anti-aircraft defence. He himself took a hand, trained a gun on the invaders, and fired it. He exposed himself fearlessly in the palace gardens maintaining absolute composure while bombs exploded within fifteen feet of him, wounding a group of soldiers.' George Orwell was later to say that during the war Haile Selassie had been called 'the Emperor' by his friends, and 'the Negus' by his enemies. But for Reuters Collins employed both titles.[17]

7

While Collins was based at Addis Ababa, [Hugh] Christopher Holme (1907–91) followed the Italian Northern Army into Abyssinia from Eritrea. He subsequently claimed to have been the only correspondent who saw the whole campaign through from the Italian entry into Adowa in October 1935 until the entry into Addis in May 1936. After joining Reuters in 1931, Holme had quickly proved himself to be one of the most cultured and competent of the public school and university recruits. He had been transferred to Eritrea from the Berlin office. His reporting of the 1933 Leipzig anti-Communist show trial, staged by the Nazis following the burning of the Reichstag, had particularly impressed Hatt. After Abyssinia, Holme covered the Spanish Civil War, and then at the end of 1937 he was sent to Austria. During the

Second World War he served as a public information officer in Palestine. Holme spent the second half of his career from 1948 with the BBC, producing some outstanding arts programmes.[18]

Holme's coverage of the Italian invasion of Abyssinia from the north was widely published. Sometimes he found himself more than 100 miles from a transmitting station, and yet many of his stories appeared in the British press on the day after writing. 'I have sent messages by every kind of courier, foot-soldiers, truck-drivers, motor-cyclists, and often Italian military aircraft pilots.' Censorship varied according to the military situation. At first, journalists could go where they liked on the northern front, but official information and transmission facilities were inadequate. In the second phase, when the Italian advance was held up, Marshal Badoglio kept the journalists under strict control. They were not allowed to visit the front for nearly two months. A third phase of officially conducted tours began with the battle of Amba Aradam in February 1936, when correspondents were allowed ringside seats on a ridge. After this major Italian success, which started the Abyssinian collapse, they were allowed to be present at all the Italian victories. Finally, Holme and others drove 700 miles in seventeen days from Asmara to Addis Ababa in a specially organized journalists' column, which accompanied the conquering Badoglio into the Abyssinian capital.[19]

The journey—'proceeding as well as the terrible state of the rainsoaked roads allowed by forced stages'—was something of a journalistic epic. Holme's excited account was read in the British papers on 6 May 1936:

> With the Italian High Command
> In Addis Ababa, Wednesday.

> Marshal Badoglio at the head of an imposing cortege of thirty cars, including his whole staff and Generals Santini and Pirzio, myself and other journalists, who were the first people ever to motor from Asmara to Addis Ababa, entered the capital at 4.45 p.m. last evening . . . We slept only three hours on Monday night, sleeping upright in cars and we did the final 140 miles in two days. After a few mechanised detachments had entered the outskirts of the city, Marshal Badoglio proceeded in an open car to the head of a slow procession past the British Legation, the occupants of which were in the compound watching. The compound, though full of tents, looked refreshingly English after seventeen days trek across Africa. The inhabitants of Addis sat on their doorsteps all showing the whiteflag and all saluting. Some were placid, some grinning, and most frankly curious.

Holme's use of the expression 'refreshingly English' was a reminder that Reuter correspondents still regarded themselves as working for a British news agency.

Yet the loyalty of one Reuter correspondent in Abyssinia was suspect. This was James Strachey ('Major Jim') Barnes (1892–1955), who was a Fascist sympathizer (Plate 33). In 1928 Barnes had established himself as a leading publicist for Fascist ideas when he published a book with the resounding title of *The Universal Aspects of Fascism*. This contained a preface by Mussolini himself, whom Barnes knew personally. Fascism, Barnes argued, had first expressed itself in Italy, but it was destined to become a global force.

Barnes had been born in India, the son of Sir Hugh Barnes, a senior member of the Indian Civil Service. His mother was a daughter of Sir John Strachey, another leading Indian Civilian. Barnes was largely brought up by his Strachey grandparents, who in retirement spent much time in Italy. His schooldays at preparatory school and at Eton were unhappy. In 1914, while at Cambridge University, he became a Roman Catholic; and his religion became central to his thinking. It was for the church, he argued, to declare the moral law, and for the state to enforce it.[20]

During the First World War Barnes enjoyed a varied career —wounded in France, becoming a pilot in the Royal Flying Corps, and acting as a liaison officer with the Italian air force. As a self-avowed expert on Italian and Balkan affairs he secured attachment to the British delegation at the 1919 Paris peace conference. He moved into journalism only gradually. During the first months of the war he had acted as a British newspaper correspondent in Milan. In 1926 he served as locum for the *Manchester Guardian's* correspondent in Rome. Finally, in 1931, he applied for a job with Reuters. In his application he claimed to know personally 'the majority of the Italian ministers', plus the leading Balkan politicians. He joined the editorial department on probation in May 1932. The expectation was that Barnes's expertise and connections could be exploited by Reuters, while his strong opinions were to be held in check, preferably by Barnes himself.

He was sent to India in 1933 to replace Buck. Within weeks, however, Barnes had begun to offend everyone in authority in India from the Viceroy downwards. He was full of his own opinions on all matters, civil and military. He did send back some good stories, commended by Hatt for including helpful background; but after a year Jones was warning (20 August 1934) that 'readiness patiently to listen to the other man without being too vocal oneself, are essential to the successful practice of the Reuter art'.

The outbreak of the Italo-Abyssinian War offered an opportunity to exploit Barnes' Italian connections. He volunteered to cross from India to report the war from the Italian side. The Italians had hinted that he would be given special facilities, and this would obviously be advantageous for Reuters. But were not Barnes's Fascist sympathies so pronounced as to disqualify him as an objective reporter? A letter from Barnes to Moloney on 10 October 1935 ought to have caused Reuters pause. Barnes was scathing about the League of Nations, which was trying to protect the Abyssinians from the Italians. 'It is only unfortunate', exclaimed Barnes, 'that we have allowed the humbug of the League to be erected into such enormous scaffolding.'

The question of Barnes's suitability was even raised by the British Foreign Secretary, Sir Samuel Hoare. Hoare expressed concern to Jones (15 October 1935) 'as to the character of the news he is likely to send'. Jones replied soothingly (19 October): 'I am bound to believe that any correspondent who is not pro-Italian will have such a poor time that he will be quite useless to his employers.' Being acceptable to the Italians, Jones explained, did not mean that Barnes would be allowed to abandon objectivity: 'a specially strict watch will be kept upon his work.'[21]

Soon after his arrival at the front Barnes was allowed to share a reconnaissance flight over the lines with Count Ciano, Mussolini's son-in-law. Barnes's report appeared in the British press on 25 October 1935. It certainly gave an impression of privileged involvement:

I flew today with Mussolini's 'Death or Glory Boys' for 300 miles over enemy country. Led personally by the Duce's son-in-law, Count Ciano, the squadron swooped low over detachments of Abyssinians, opening fire with machine guns . . . The reconnaissance continued in an attempt to discover the whereabouts of Ras Seyum's men. We did not succeed.

Although coloured by underlying admiration, this report stopped just short of open bias. Indeed, Hatt praised it in a letter to Barnes's father (16 November) as an *'excellent* story'. 'We are now issuing under his name all important war dispatches from your son.'

Yet Barnes's judgement soon came into question. On 28 November 1935 he and four French journalists sent a joint letter to the League of Nations at Geneva claiming that the Abyssinians were using illegal dumdum bullets. Jones was much angered by this initiative. 'No doubt', he commented, 'this was inspired, if not organised by Barnes, who is definitely pro-Fascist. I take strong exception to Reuter Correspondents identifying themselves in this way with one side or the other.' Even if illegal bullets were being employed, which was disputed, it was not for Reuters to do more than report the facts. The Italians then exploited this alleged use of dumdum as justification for themselves employing mustard gas against the Abyssinians. In his autobiography Barnes readily accepted this justification. He also never admitted that the Italians had deliberately bombed civilian targets.[22]

Despite Jones's promise to the Foreign Secretary, some tendentious reporting from Barnes did slip through the editorial checks. The nature of this material was not recorded; but a confidential editorial circular was issued within Reuters on 13 December. 'It is a hundred times better to scrap a story from Barnes altogether than for Reuters to carry tainted or biased news. In particular, be on your guard against any suggestions of an *anti-British* nature.' Britain and Italy seemed to be on the brink of war, and Jones minuted alongside this last sentence that 'these must be watched for most vigilantly'.

Barnes afterwards complained that he had become distrusted because he had accurately forecast an Italian victory. He included in his autobiography a dispatch sent by him on 15 December 1935, which had not been published. 'My general impression is that the Italians undoubtedly hold today all the best trump cards.'[23]

Barnes proved to be right in this judgement; but would he have spoken so plainly if the Abyssinians, not the Italians, had held the initiative? He simply did not realize how biased he was. This was revealed strikingly in a mailed dispatch which he posted in February, describing celebrations to mark the birthday of the Fascist militia. 'Please see last paragraph of this effusion,' commented Hatt. The paragraph read:

> I had just got back from the advance to Neghelli where the spirit of the troops was like dry champagne—intoxicating, exciting, electrifying—another side, the side representative of action, of this new Italy which it would be folly to deny is wonderful. But here in the dead quiet of the sand dunes I was led deeper into the hearts of these extraordinary soldiers and I found them most admirably and persuasively generous.

'Barnes off his balance again', noted a sub-editor. The piece was not published. Yet Barnes thought it so fine that he printed it in full in his autobiography.[24]

After the Abyssinian war had ended an India Office official warned Jones at lunch on 22 June 1936 that Barnes's return to India 'would be a very nasty shock for Simla'. He was regarded there as unpatriotic, and had been cut socially. Jones responded with characteristic adroitness. He replied that Reuters could not submit to official pressure; but on that very same afternoon a letter was sent to Barnes from William Turner, the overseas general manager, telling Barnes that his contract would not be renewed when it expired in April 1937, and that if he wished he could leave sooner on full pay.

This letter came as a total surprise to Barnes, for he had felt no sense of his own unsuitability. At an interview on 27 April 1937 Jones explained to him how he lacked the detachment vital for news agency work. Jones claimed that by the end of their talk Barnes had accepted the inevitability of his departure. But Barnes's Italian wife certainly had not done so; for on 15 June 1937, apparently without her husband's knowledge, she wrote to Jones from Rome, complaining bitterly that Barnes had been unfairly dismissed. He no longer wished to live in England: 'he has been driven to it by you and the monstrous behaviour of your noble representatives . . . You will go on living in your beautiful houses and give your children an expensive education, and get a peerage, and you can gain the earth and lose your soul.'

At the end of 1937 Mussolini awarded Barnes the Italian 'Silver Medal for Military Valour'. During the Second World War he broadcast in English from Italy in support of the Axis side. On 7 February 1941 he spoke about Jones's sudden resignation. The broadcast was monitored by the Reuter listening station:

> Sir Roderick's disappearance is the disappearance of one of the most powerful men in England . . . He is a very astute man and probably realises that Britain is a sinking ship and does not wish to remain on board much longer . . . We shall not be surprised if the next we hear of him is in Portugal and then in South America. This is a sign of the times.

Barnes had adopted Italian nationality before the war, and this saved him from being charged with treason afterwards. But for some time he was fearful about his situation, and the Reuter correspondent in Rome reported on 3 October 1946, over a year after the end of the war, that Barnes was still in hiding. Ironically, if (as his wife's letter to Jones had claimed) Barnes had been driven to adopt Italian nationality because of his rejection by Reuters, that rejection had perhaps saved his life. He died at Rome in 1955.

Barnes apart, its correspondents and stringers had served Reuters well during the Abyssinian war. Their reports were widely used, especially by the London evening papers and the British provincial press. Despite Jones's early grumbling about costs, the 'Italo-Abyssinian Exclusive Special Service'—which included material from Rome and the League of Nations at Geneva as well as the war fronts—earned a useful monthly profit, which peaked at £543 for February 1936.

8

Reuters first heard of the start of the Spanish civil war from its resident correspondent at Madrid, John Allwork. He wired London cryptically, using a private code, 'Uncle Charlie dies tonight'. London editorial at first failed to take the hint, and wired back that Allwork was perhaps under the influence of Spanish wine. Four hours later the Republican Government announced the outbreak of a serious army revolt.

By the end of 1936 life in Madrid had become dangerous because of Nationalist bombing raids. On 13 December Allwork interviewed a young married Englishwoman who lived in the capital. She told him that she went out shopping as little as possible, partly because of the danger and partly because other women in the queue were often very unpleasant: 'I cannot go out looking decently dressed because that is regarded as bourgeois.' Some women used fear of air raids to get ahead in food queues. 'One woman starts screaming: "The bombers are coming", and this starts a panic-stricken stampede. Then the woman who has started the scare moves comfortably to the front of the queue. If you are in the open market place when air raids start, the only thing to do is to lie on the ground and hope for the best.' British readers feared that one day they would have to face the same ordeal. Allwork's story was the more effective for giving the reactions of an ordinary woman, especially as she was English.

Worried about costs, Reuters never kept more than four full-time journalists in Spain during the war. They were divided between the two sides. The British First World War method for controlling the activities of war correspondents was copied by the Nationalists. Correspondents were given regular briefings, but they were allowed to make only occasional visits to the front, and always under the supervision of conducting officers. Censorship was rigorous, and those who did not report favourably might be victimized. One Havas correspondent ended up in prison, and another was placed under house arrest.[25]

Christopher Holme's success in Abyssinia meant that he was an obvious man to send to Spain. Despite the intense ideological atmosphere surrounding the war—Communists and other left-wingers outside Spain supporting the Republican Government, Nazis and Fascists backing General Franco, who emerged as the Nationalist leader—Holme was determined to report objectively. This was the harder for him because, after his experience as a reporter in Nazi Germany and with the Italians in Abyssinia, he was strongly anti-Fascist in his personal opinions. His desire for balance had one curious effect, as he explained in an interesting letter to Jones on 4 December 1936:

> I am rather handicapped by my disgust at the selfishness and public irresponsibility of the white [Nationalist] generals and their cold-blooded massacres of working men, women and children, as also by a feeling of helplessness—owing to an unprecedentedly strict and arbitrary censorship—to give proper reminders of the menace to the Empire of German and Italian aggression.

> Owing to the capriciousness of the censorship, I have limited myself to purely
> military news, eschewing atrocities—the only one I know about from personal
> experience are white, so it would be hardly fair to report at second-hand red
> atrocities which have undoubtedly been committed.

In other words, Holme felt that to tell only about one side's atrocities would
leave the Reuter file not merely incomplete but misleading. In this he was
being over-scrupulous.

The first part of Holme's letter to Jones had complained that he was under-
paid—a frequent and often justified grumble among Reuter journalists. He
was competing, Home said, with British and other correspondents who were
earning twice as much. He was receiving £600 a year, and asked for £800.
All he got was a £50 bonus.

Late in 1936 Holme covered Franco's unsuccessful advance upon Madrid;
but after that, with a lull in the fighting, he was recalled to London to save
money. Coverage from the Nationalist side was left to Havas. In February
1937 Holme returned to northern Spain, basing himself in Bilbao, the
Basque–Republican capital, after being refused access to the Nationalist lines.
His objectivity had made him unacceptable to Franco's side. He was about to
become much more so.

On 26 April 1937 Holme was at dinner in Bilbao with three other corre-
spondents—George Steer of *The Times*, Noel Monks of the *Daily Express*, and
Mathieu Corman of *Le Soir*. In the middle of the meal a distraught Basque
Government official rushed in with the news that the small town of Guernica,
fifteen miles away, had been almost destroyed in a German bombing raid. The
four journalists hurried to the scene. Holme's report first appeared in the
London evening papers on 27 April; Steer's fuller account was published in
The Times next day. The published versions of all four correspondents agreed
upon the basic facts—that the planes came in waves, first dropping high
explosive bombs and then incendiaries, and that the town was devastated.
Holme wrote of 'the most appalling air raid in the history of modern warfare':

> German bombers came over Guernica seven at a time in uncounted numbers,
> accompanied by equally numerous fighting planes. The crews leaned out from
> the planes dropping hand grenades. Relays of planes dropped more than a thou-
> sand high explosive bombs. Then came incendiary bombs. By the time the
> planes had finished, Guernica was a mass of blazing, smoking streets.

The impression was given by Holme that Guernica was not a military
target, and that the raid had been solely a practice act of aerial terrorism. In
fact, there seems to have been some military excuse for the raid. Guernica was
a place where the hard-pressed Republican–Basque forces might have

regrouped. Misguidedly, the Nationalists and the Germans began by trying to deny that any raid had ever taken place. This seemed only to confirm the charge of terrorism.

A generation later, when questioned by historians, Holme was still upholding the view that the raid had served no military purpose. However, the effectiveness of his contribution to the controversy had been reduced, even at the time, by a blunder in the Reuter editorial office. In publishing a follow-up report from Holme on 29 April, rebutting Nationalist claims that the raid had never happened—'I myself saw a number of easily recognisable German aeroplanes withdrawing from the bombardment'—slack Reuter sub-editing confused German aircraft type-numbers (Junkers 51 and 52, Heinkel 111) with the totals of the various aircraft actually involved, which were much smaller. The mistake was corrected within the hour; but it enabled the German propaganda machine to dwell upon the unreliability of Reuters.[26]

On 5 May the Nazi paper, the *Völkischer Beobachter*, asserted that Holme was in the pay of the Bolsheviks, and demanded his dismissal. The next month the false story was spread that in the last stage of the battle for Bilbao Holme had fought for the defending Basques against Franco's forces. The British Foreign Office passed this rumour on to Reuters, and suggested that Holme should be careful about his safety. Clearly, he was at personal risk, and was also being misrepresented as a biased reporter. On both counts, the time had come to pull him out. Concerned at delay in doing so, Jones telephoned on 15 June 1937 to the editorial office. 'He is in grave danger. We want a live correspondent, not a dead one.' In the event, Holme eventually got away safely. The Nationalists regarded him as having been expelled.

The British Foreign Office News Department pressed for Reuters to send Holme to Vienna as resident correspondent. Austria was under threat of a Nazi takeover, in contravention of the Versailles peace treaty, and had consequently become a centre of strong international interest. The acting Reuter correspondent, an Austrian Jew, Hugh Kuranda, was an active but unreliable journalist with an intrusive private life. The Foreign Office wanted him to be replaced by a 'good British staff man'. Holme's 'known anti-Nazi tendency', argued Randal Neale, the head of the Reuter Paris office (2 July 1937), would not matter provided Holme was properly briefed, 'and is quietly lectured on the subject of "poise".' This presumably meant that Holme should blandly keep his opinions to himself.

Holme went to Vienna in November 1937, and started well. He successfully developed the Vienna office as a news clearing house for central Europe. On 9 March 1938 he secured a fifty-minute beat with news of Chancellor Schuschnigg's decision to call a plebiscite on the question of unification with

Nazi Germany. This precipitated a German invasion three days later. Holme was now again at personal risk, at least of a beating and probably of arrest. The Nazis regarded him as having been hostile since his time in the Berlin office, a hostility confirmed in their eyes by his handling of the Guernica story and his recent reporting from Austria.

Knowing the Austrian frontiers to be closed, Holme drove by car to Germany and then crossed into Switzerland. For a second time he had quit a totalitarian state in a hurry. In his car-boot he had concealed his Austrian assistant, Alfred Geiringer, who was in great danger because he was both a Jew and a socialist. Geiringer was destined for a long and important career with Reuters.

9

Holme's successor in Spain was R. J. ['Dick'] Sheepshanks (1910–37), an engaging Old Etonian and Cambridge graduate, a particular favourite of Jones's, who had joined Reuters in October 1933. He had served briefly in Addis Ababa during the Italo-Abyssinian War before being invalided home with dysentery. In Addis, Sheepshanks had become acquainted with another correspondent, Evelyn Waugh, the celebrated writer, who used his experiences as the basis for his great novel, *Scoop, A Novel About Journalists* (1938). Sheepshanks may even have contributed unwittingly to the novel, for he revealed some of the ingenuousness about cut-throat competition between war correspondents shown by Waugh's fictional correspondent, William Boot. Sheepshanks—who was clearly a gentleman first and a journalist second—exclaimed to Jones (14 November 1935) that it was 'not a nice sensation to be unable to believe anything that one is told'.[27]

By the time he was sent to Spain in June 1937 Sheepshanks had become more realistic and knowledgeable. While briefly back on leave in October he was even called in by the Foreign Office to give his estimate of Franco's prospects: 'so far as he could judge without intimate knowledge of the Government side, he would be prepared to bet pretty heavily on an ultimate victory for Franco.' Sheepshanks did not agree that the Nationalists were all anti-British, only the Falangists.[28]

Aware of Holme's difficulties, Sheepshanks had set out to cultivate the respect of the Nationalists, albeit on his own terms. 'After two months here', he assured Jones on 29 August, 'I can now say with confidence that Reuter is again persona grata with the Nationalist authorities.' He had been, he wrote, 'definitely suspect at first, and my refusal to send plain propaganda did not please them in the early weeks'. He had declined to take sides; but he had shown himself prepared sometimes not to tell the whole truth. For example, he had not revealed that the so-called Italian 'volunteers', who had participated in the capture of Santander, were in fact regular troops. To have said so, would have got him 'thrown out of the country at once'. Reuters always preferred to maintain a presence in any country, even under censorship, so long as what its correspondents were allowed to report remained truthful, even if selective. But by knowingly repeating an untruth Sheepshanks was going too far.

He was not destined to serve long in Spain. On the very last day of the year, near Teruel, he was killed in a car by the blast and shrapnel from a Republican shell. Sheepshanks was the first-ever Reuter war correspondent to be killed on duty, ending a remarkably long run of good luck. Two American correspondents with him were also killed. A fourth correspondent, Harold Philby, representing *The Times*, escaped with only slight scalp wounds. Philby, unknown to his employer, was already a Soviet agent; and in the 1960s was to be exposed as the 'third man' in the Burgess and Maclean spy ring inside the British diplomatic service. In Spain, Philby had recently been ordered to arrange for Franco's assassination.[29]

Sheepshanks and the two dead Americans were posthumously awarded by Franco the Cross of Military Merit for Meritorious Services. Was the decoration of a Reuter correspondent by one side in a war reconcilable with the agency's commitment to objectivity? Only if Franco was accepting that such a commitment was itself 'meritorious', which was unlikely. But presumably Reuters thought it churlish to refuse. British and Allied awards to Reuter correspondents in both world wars were accepted without hesitation.

In the *Reuter Review* for May 1938 Jones described his ideal in war reporting as a 'combination of dispassionate reliability and vividness'. Sheepshank's successor, Alexander [Graeme] Clifford (1909–52), was to show himself an outstanding exponent of this method as a war correspondent, first for Reuters and then for the *Daily Mail*. Clifford, who had joined Reuters in 1931, was another public school and Oxford recruit. For over six years he had worked capably on the editorial floor, eventually becoming deputy chief sub-editor. Clifford possessed a thoughtful temperament, detached and careful in expression, but always alert. His *Times* obituary (15 March 1952) portrayed him as 'not a man of action but a dispassionate observer with a deep loathing of violence'. Clifford's father-in-law, Robert Graves, the poet and novelist, summed up perceptively:

> when in the Spanish Civil War Reuters sent Alexander Clifford out at a moment's notice to replace a correspondent who had been killed, he went without fear or enthusiasm. Though Spain was to prove only an introduction

to a life of almost continuous adventure and travel, he never allowed himself to derive any romantic excitement from it. His refusal to commit himself emotionally to any religious, political, national, or other cause made him the perfect correspondent: his pride was in drawing up a balanced statement of facts without slant or artifice, and he would never compromise his integrity by accepting any official direction.[30]

Clifford maintained the relationship of mutual respect with the Nationalists which Sheepshanks had established. Indeed, he told Jones on 2 April that 'Franco's people' had helped him considerably. So had the editorial office in London. 'As this is my first assignment abroad I had never realised before how much better Reuters looks after its correspondents than any other organisations do. My service of logs, cuttings and copies is the envy of my colleagues.' This service had been introduced by Hatt. The daily editorial log listed and commented upon each day's main stories.

At the end of 1938 Clifford left Spain to become chief Reuter correspondent in Berlin. He stayed there until the outbreak of the Second World War in the following September. In Berlin, he was in a similar situation to Lester Lawrence twenty-five years earlier. Clifford's high reputation led to his being chosen as the first (and for a month the sole) reporter allowed to accompany the British Expeditionary Force in France. He represented all the press until terms of appointment for other correspondents could be agreed with the authorities. In April 1940 Clifford left Reuters for the *Daily Mail*. He continued as a correspondent for that paper throughout the Second World War, and until his early death in 1952.

Good-quality war reporting did not guarantee profitability. Reuters had made a profit out of its Abyssinian war coverage, but it lost money on its 'Spanish War Special Service' throughout 1937. When in April the loss peaked at £290 for the month, Jones minuted the single word 'dreadful' on his copy of the figures. From October 1937 the Spanish figures appeared alongside those giving the costs of reporting the war between Japan and China, which had started in July. Reuters began to lose money on its service from China, even though it did not appoint any special war correspondents, relying entirely upon its regular staff.

Its managers in Canton and Hankow were there chiefly for the commercial service, but they found themselves reporting the devastating Japanese air attacks upon the two cities, which attracted worldwide attention. The raids on Canton, repeated for sixteen days, were vividly described for Reuters by Alan Hammond:

> It is as if gigantic ghastly abattoirs have been created. Gaps fifty yards wide have been torn in rows of dwellings with scattered human remains protruding from

the debris. I saw one Chinese woman, killed while sitting at her front door, sitting there still, upright and quiet in death. Further on a grim-faced Chinese gentleman raised a piece of matting, showed me the mangled remains, and said simply: 'This is my wife.'

The London evening papers of 23 September 1937 devoted their front pages to Hammond's account of 'the most terrible air raids in history'. 'People Go Mad With Terror', exclaimed the *Evening News*. British readers, fearful of themselves being bombed in a future war, wanted to know the worst. After Guernica and Canton, there was no doubt that the old distinction between combatants and civilians no longer applied. Never again could war reporting be confined to the battlefield.

10

Reuter coverage of the 'Munich' crisis in September 1938 was extensive and expensive. Jones had pressed for Reuters to be allowed to distribute a temporarily enlarged wireless news service overseas, at Government expense. Sir Horace Wilson agreed at once ('World opinion is uncertain, and we must not run any risks'), and the service began the very next day, 22 September. Reuter wordage was trebled, from 1,000 to 3,000 words per day. The extra wordage was given the address 'Globereuter'. Jones virtually took editorial charge during the crisis.[31]

On 12 September Guy Bettany was sent to the Nuremberg rally to hear Hitler's speech. A direct telephone line to London was held open for four and a half hours, and the Reuter report started running only five minutes after Hitler had begun speaking. Chamberlain, the British Prime Minister, had asked for copies of the Reuter tape to be sent to him immediately at 10 Downing Street. A motor-cycle messenger did the round trip from Carmelite Street in twelve minutes, so enabling batches of copy to be delivered at fifteen-minute intervals. Downing Street was extremely pleased with the service.[32]

Gordon Young, the associate editor, led teams of correspondents to cover the visits of Chamberlain to meet Hitler at Berchtesgarden, Bad Godesberg, and finally at Munich. Chamberlain's decision to return to London from Godesberg on 24 September produced a forty-one minute beat for Reuters, and an exclusive statement from the Prime Minister.

Regardless of expense, Reuter correspondents made much use of air travel to and within Germany. During the first three weeks of September this helped them to match the strong competition from other agencies. However, as the probability of a breakdown into war came closer, Jones and Hatt wondered how many men to leave in Germany, or even in Czechoslovakia. If war came, they feared that all Reuter correspondents might be interned, including some of their very best. Nearly all were therefore told to withdraw from Berlin and Prague to Zurich, Amsterdam, and Budapest. The Berlin office was briefly left in the charge of just one correspondent. But when news of the intended Munich meeting came through unexpectedly on the afternoon of 28 September, the policy of withdrawal was abandoned. At such a dramatic moment in history Reuters simply had to report from Germany and Czechoslovakia with as many correspondents as it could muster.

Unfortunately, these comings and goings affected the quality of the Reuter report during the later stages of the crisis. This showed in comparison with the performance of the American agencies, whose correspondents were not at risk. BUP also beat Reuters on major stories. Even the *Reuter Review* later admitted shortcomings. 'At Munich we were compelled to register certain opposition beats, but our sober, full, and accurate report, made in difficult circumstances was eloquent of the work done.'[33]

William Turner, the joint general manager, spoke plainly of 'our failure at Munich' in a report for Jones on 11 October 1938. He blamed this partly upon the failure of DNB, the Nazi German agency, to provide expected 'influential assistance', especially with communications out of Germany. The *Reuter Review* complained that telephone calls had taken up to eight hours to be connected. On 30 September Reuters had secured one late beat, but it came out of London not Germany. The Czechoslovak legation revealed that the Czech Government had reluctantly accepted the Munich terms.

The cost of all this extra Munich activity was over £3,000, all unbudgeted. Afterwards, economies had to be enforced. The result was a poor showing during the early months of 1939. Remarkably, news from Prague, the Czech capital, was left to a single local stringer, despite the continuing tension which led eventually to the German occupation of Czechoslovakia. In contrast, UP kept four staff men in Prague.

An angry exchange in 1939 between Reuter head office and Cornelius Murphy, the Rome correspondent, illustrated the difficulties faced by understaffed news bureaux. Jones had cabled testily on 12 April: 'Disgracefully forestalled Mussolini Greek communiqué imperative you take measures to tighten up service.' Murphy replied equally testily on 17 April that tightening up would require manning the bureau round-the-clock 'as the opposition does'. Reuter staff were too few to do this. 'We are doing our best in the worst equipped office in Rome, consistently working longer hours than anyone.' The particular delay complained of, added Murphy conclusively, was a consequence of a recent instruction that cable tolls were never to exceed £3 per day.

Although other agencies often beat Reuters on spot news, Reuters led on interviews. Its reputation and semi-official status gave its correspondents access to key figures in most countries, for talks on and off the record. Thus during the Munich crisis Young told Jones (19 September 1938) about interviews with the British Ambassador in Berlin, Sir Nevile Henderson. The Ambassador was strong for appeasement. 'Why should a little shyster lawyer (Sir Nevile used these words) like Dr. Benes be allowed to drag Britain into war? . . . I think we shall be all right if only the British Government sticks fast and doesn't get misled by any false prophets like Winston Churchill.' None of this was for publication.

A revealing hour and a half interview was given by Dr Josef Goebbels, the Propaganda Minister, to Young on 12 November 1938, apparently at the request of Jones. Goebbels told Young: 'We desire that England shall take no interest in the way we solve the Jewish question.' A room was set aside in the Propaganda Ministry with two secretaries and a stenographer so that Young could complete his report in time for use by the British Sunday newspapers. Such was Goebbels's desire to publicize his views through Reuters.

Reporting of Nazi anti-Jewish policy was vetted by Jones personally. Young had assured Goebbels during their interview that Reuters would always be 'objective'. What did this mean when dealing with anti-Semitism? Jones explained on 10 February 1939 in a letter to Sir Neil Malcolm, High Commissioner for German Refugees, that Reuters was trying to maintain a balance. 'Horror stories are dangerous, the newspapers rightly are chary of them, and the public do not particularly want to read them. Decrees are in a different category. These and other measures will continue to take their place in the Reuter report.' Jones appended a list of twenty-seven Reuter reports of anti-Jewish decrees issued by Hitler's Government since October 1938.

II

Sport and politics were mixed at the 1936 Berlin Olympic Games. The Germans wanted to impress Reuters, and gave its sports editor, Vernon Morgan, a privileged viewing-box. This did not prevent him from making a dig at Hitler in his report of the opening ceremony on 2 August. 'With one of the shortest speeches of his career Herr Hitler formally opened the Olympiad on Saturday. To bursts of applause from the 100,000 people who packed the stadium, and the firing of a battery of guns, he said simply: "I declare the eleventh Olympiad open." '

Except for the Olympic Games held every four years, Jones had ruled that for reasons of economy Reuters should concentrate upon the sports of widest popular interest—cricket, football, and boxing. Gilbert Mant, an Australian member of the editorial staff, was sent to cover the 1932–3 England cricket tour of Australia. The tour was nearly abandoned because of England's 'body-line' bowling; but Mant respected the Reuter tradition by supplying the scores and a factual account of the play without partisan comment. The word 'bodyline' was coined by an Australian journalist, and Mant recalled in old age that he had been careful not to use it, 'except in parenthesis to denote a sort of dirty word'. The preferred euphemism was 'leg theory'. On his way back by sea, however, Mant began to write a personal account of the tour. Jones refused him permission to publish, on the ground that Mant's contentious opinions might be taken as those of Reuters. Jones likewise refused to allow Gordon Young, the associate editor, to publish a book about Hermann Goering, Hitler's deputy.[34]

The prevention of the separate publication of controversial personal opinions by known Reuter correspondents was justifiable. But what about the withholding of news? Reuters assisted the British press during 1936 in its voluntary blackout of all news about the relationship between King Edward VIII and Mrs. Wallis Simpson, an American. Hatt had served during the First World War with Mrs Simpson's current husband, and their friendship led to Hatt's introduction into the social circle round Edward. Hatt was present at York House in February 1936 when the King first told Simpson that he wanted Wallis to become his wife and to be crowned Queen.[35]

Far from publishing such inside information, Hatt told the editorial staff not to mention Mrs Simpson without clearance from himself, except when she was named in the Court Circular. Damaging stories were circulating in the American press, many of them sent from London by foreign agencies; but Reuters said nothing. When the British papers at last began to write about the affair early in December 1936 Jones personally supervised the handling of the story night by night. Valentine Harvey, the chief parliamentary correspondent, was informed of the King's decision to abdicate on 11 December shortly before the official announcement. Hatt was rumoured to have known sooner still, and to have offended Jones by not telling him.

Jones informed Samuel Storey, the Reuter director, on 10 May 1937 that Reuters had been 'soft-pedalling' on the latest twists in the story of the ex-King (now Duke of Windsor) and Mrs Simpson. They married in June. Newspaper interest in their doings continued, not all of it sympathetic. On

18 May 1938 the Duke requested Hatt's assistance with the press. A dinner-party was being given for the couple by the British Ambassador in Paris, and the Duke asked Hatt to ensure that the occasion received 'good publicity'. Hatt obliged, and subsequently sent the Duke newspaper clippings to illustrate the restrained and extensive coverage in the British papers. The Duke was well satisfied, but not the Buckingham Palace authorities. The Reuter chief correspondent in Paris was summoned to the British Embassy to explain how Reuters had found out the names of the guests. They had been supplied by the Duke himself through his equerry.[36]

Matter of such triviality would soon cease to be worth publishing. War was again approaching.

TEN

War News

1939–1945

I shall never forget the extraordinary sensation of looking down
—I repeat 'down'—on the Heinkels and Junkers as they roared
past the ships and turned sideways to launch their loads.

(Arthur Oakeshott, Arctic convoy to Russia, 1941)

During the night brave Cossack cavalrymen watered their horses
in the Dniester.

(Harold King reporting from Moscow, 1944)

When I left the fighting area I left something behind me — my
face print in the mud of Normandy's beaches.

(Marshall Yarrow, D-Day, 1944)

The Atomic Bomb wiped out over four square miles.

(Jack Smyth covering Hiroshima from Guam, 1945)

I

R EUTERS sent correspondents to all the main battlefronts during the
Second World War. The quotations given above were just a few of the
more striking turns of phrase in their reports.

British censorship during the Second World War was generally more flexible than during the First. It was still tight and sometimes unpredictable, but
it allowed war correspondents greater freedom of expression and movement.
They were sometimes impeded more by bureaucracy than by intention.
Martin Herlihy, the Cairo manager, complained to Storey, the Reuter chairman, on 27 August 1941 that correspondents in the Middle East were sometimes having to submit their copy to one or more of seven separate censors.
And he repeated a complaint heard in every war, of 'messages which were
suppressed in our case slipping through in the case of the Opposition'.

George Orwell, whose wife worked in the censorship, went so far as to claim in 1941 that this was 'the most truthful war that has been fought in modern times'. Was Orwell right, or was the apparent openness more a matter of impression? Official censors worked at desks inside the Reuter and PA newsrooms at 85 Fleet Street. Censorship of news circulated inside the United Kingdom was heavier than for news distributed abroad; the British authorities recognized that overseas competitors, who were not exposed to British censorship, must not be given too much advantage over Reuters. In London, Rear-Admiral George Thomson, the chief press censor, issued a stream of 'D notices' (Defence notices) which gave sometimes oracular guidance on what could not be published, or what should be submitted. The censor blandly enjoyed power without responsibility: 'the fact that matter is passed for publication by the censorship does not mean that it is guaranteed as accurate or that its publication is desired.'[1]

Censorship at source inside 85 Fleet Street saved valuable time. Delay on big stories was further minimized by devising a drill for 'super flashes', which warned the outward radio services when an important message had been handed to the censor. In 1941 a flash of twenty words was taking three minutes fifty seconds to pass through censorship to transmission, but later in the war this delay was much reduced. The censorship at 85 Fleet Street was the more acceptable to all parties because it gave the impression of being almost a voluntary system, appropriate to a liberal democracy at war.[2]

How far the British authorities might seek to manage this system was demonstrated early. Germany invaded Poland on 1 September 1939, and Britain declared war two days later. During the very last days of peace the British Government was anxious that United Kingdom newspapers and news agencies should not publish anything which, by upsetting a temperamental Hitler, might make him decide for war rather than peace. On 30 August Sir Samuel Hoare, the Home Secretary, called in five representatives of the British news agencies to offer them 'guidance'. This was readily accepted by Hatt and Neale, who represented Reuters. 'It was advisable to avoid any personal references whatever to Hitler at the present time.' On the positive side, Hoare suggested that it would be helpful if the news agencies mentioned the perfect calm of the British people; 'and, above all that we were resolutely determined to honour our obligations towards Poland'.[3]

As in the First World War, Reuter correspondents were appointed with both the British Expeditionary Force and the French army. On 9 November 1939, however, Jones cryptically reminded the board of another source of news. 'Reuters have the important direct channel known to the Directors and accessible to nobody else in the British isles.' Was this a reference to information gathered by the British intelligence services? To boost morale at home or to gain propaganda advantage overseas, some of this information may have been fed to Reuters for circulation as its own news. Certainly, evidence has survived of the War Office feeding information to Reuters on at least one occasion, although in this instance it was not material coming from British intelligence. On 18 October 1939 Major Blumenfeld of the War Office sent a story to Hatt 'concocted (for your private ear) in collaboration with Foreign Office': 'we shall be greatly obliged if you can arrange for this to be put out, under a Shanghai dateline as from your own correspondent, for tomorrow's morning papers. Naturally you will not disclose its real source of origin—and we are not giving the cable to any other agency.' The story was issued by Reuters as requested. Hatt agreed to check how much it had been used by the newspapers. He found that it had not been used at all. The piece—headed 'Tommies Defy China Floods', and telling of the resilience of the British army garrison at Tientsin—was obviously judged by the papers to be of little interest. So the War/Foreign Office plant failed, whatever its purpose. But other plants may have been arranged over the telephone, without leaving written evidence behind.

At a meeting with editorial staff on 27 July 1939 Jones had discussed how 'news which impinges on what you might call the official area' should be handled in wartime:

> Reuter must never lose sight of the national interest. Reuter is authoritative, more so than any other British press organ, even including *The Times*, and Reuter is so regarded abroad. This places Reuter under the obligation to observe great prudence in handling any news which may possibly involve the national interest, and to act in close collaboration and accord with Whitehall in this connection . . . On a lower plane, Whitehall is a most important source of news to Reuter, and any failure on Reuters' part to conform to the principle and practice of close collaboration with Whitehall would ipso facto close that source of news to us.

Such a co-operative attitude, Jones decided, was 'perfectly compatible' with independence. 'It is not submission to dictation, but consultation of expert advice.'

A curious episode—barely reconcilable with the Reuter tradition— involved a letter being published in *The Times* of 18 June 1940. This was the month of the fall of France to the Germans. The letter came from Gordon Young, who described himself as 'Reuter's Chief Berlin Correspondent for three years under the Nazi regime', and now special correspondent in Turkey. Jones had approved the letter. Young warned against 'overestimating the power and resources of our enemy'. The policy of Goebbels and the Nazis, he wrote with some truth, had always been to exaggerate their strength. He drew from this the extremely optimistic conclusion that 'our victory may be much less remote than it appears to be'. Clearly, the good name of Reuters was here being used to boost national morale. Even at a time of great danger, ought such a letter to have been written? The answer presumably was that the letter—which was expressing an opinion, and was not trying to present opinion as fact—justified itself under the circumstances.

After the departure of Jones and Hatt in 1941 Reuters sharpened its attitude both towards the collection of news and towards official censorship. Early in the war Reuter correspondents often filed even big stories at cheaper (because slower) rates, and thus were late with the news. Fresh instructions were issued to correspondents on 5 March 1941 telling them to use the fastest channels for hot news. Even so, the American agencies still had more staff in the field; and for over two years, until the entry of the United States into the war in December 1941, the Americans were able to file directly out of Germany, Italy, and occupied Europe.

In 1942 Haley of Reuters and Cooper of Associated Press settled upon an agreed attitude towards censorship. They accepted that in wartime, although their two agencies would insist upon publishing only truthful news, the whole truth could not always be told. 'There is acceptance of the right of government to have us withhold news for the common good, but no acceptance of any right of government to say how we shall word what we do transmit.'[4]

In the same year the War Office produced printed *Regulations for Press Representatives in the Field*, which ran to twenty-eight pages. The foreword emphasized that good relations would depend upon both censors and correspondents acting in a spirit of goodwill:

> The essence of successful warfare is secrecy: the essence of successful journalism is publicity. The above is a bald statement of the respective functions of the soldier and the press-man in time of war . . . No official regulations can bridge the gap between two such incompatible outlooks, unless goodwill and commonsense are resolutely brought to bear by both sides . . . no amount of subsequent denial can counteract the effects of an indiscreet or ill-timed statement once it has appeared in print.

The regulations assumed that war correspondents would accept the need for censorship, provided that it was exercised with discrimination. 'Complete frankness on the one hand, loyal discretion on the other; and mutual co-operation in the great and almost sacred task of leading and steadying public opinion in times of national stress and crisis.'

Yet Reuters knew that its subscribers did not like reports which were too much shaped by official handouts. Good war correspondents have always sought to write distinctively, speaking as far as possible from personal observation and often in the first person. One important story from Reuters, successfully employing this method, was written at the time of the evacuation from France in 1940. Alaric Jacob, just back in England, set his own hectic experiences within a wider context. His report was dated 19 June, 'From Reuters Special Correspondent with the BEF. A South of England Port':

> German motorized columns are today in possession of the French port from which I sailed in a transport filled with British troops . . . We slept like sardines on every available inch of deck space . . . The French army was not prepared to fight a 'war of zones' but only one of lines—and the lines were non-existent since the Battle of France began. I had evidence of this three days ago near Bernay through which I motored looking for British troops. French troops told me that the British were on the left flank but that it was safe for me to go to Brionne as the bridges were blown up there and the Germans could not cross the stream. Taking their word I did so—only to drive straight into a German patrol three miles further on. But turning our cars round at once and speeding off my party managed to make a lucky escape. Between those Germans and the retreating French there was nothing but empty country, not a gun or defensive position to be seen.

Here was a report which gave an honest explanation of the Allied defeat, but which made the bad news more palatable by including personal touches within the overall theme:

> A British major told me that near Rouen he was approached by a French staff officer and given the order to retire. The major demanded confirmation of this and stood by whilst the staff officer telephoned through apparently to headquarters, at which the British officer pretended to be satisfied. But later he traced the call and found that it had been made to a local butcher's shop. By this time the bogus staff officer had disappeared.

Jacob ended with comments which were cheerfully patriotic even while admitting the worst:

> Although our troops were disappointed as they marched to the sea, through a countryside so like Devon or Cornwall, to think that on the morrow Nazi tyranny would sweep forward in their wake, engulfing France, they were not men in despair. They knew the worst. They felt that at last we had touched bottom and that our fortunes, now at their lowest point, must shortly turn. They felt that they were retiring to the last fortress of freedom in Europe to last against the Nazi-Fascist hordes.

The same sentiments had been given expression only a day earlier in Winston Churchill's famous 'finest hour' speech. This report from Reuters left no

doubt that the news agency of the British Empire was in total sympathy with
the defiant mood of the British people.

2

In the victory number of the *World's Press News*, published on 15 December
1945, Christopher Chancellor contributed an article on 'How Reuters did its
Job Right Through the War'. This article included photographs of the twenty
leading Reuter war correspondents, all in uniform. Jacob was not among
them, because in 1942 he had left Reuters for the *Daily Express*. The *Express*
had offered him £1,000 a year, which was £600 more than Reuters paid.

A correspondent who rated particular mention by Chancellor was
Desmond Tighe (1906–85). Tighe had reported conflict on land and sea for
longer than any other Reuter journalist. He had joined the agency in 1930,
and had served throughout the decade in the commercial service, latterly in
Alexandria. He had wanted to transfer to the editorial side, but had not been
allowed to do so, perhaps because he had left school at 17. Tighe's chance
came with the outbreak of war, when he happened to be on leave in England.
He was made a sub-editor at headquarters; and then in January 1940, to fill a
gap caused by sudden illness, he was sent to Finland as a second correspondent covering the Russo-Finnish War. When the Germans were about to
invade Norway in April 1940, he was hurried to Oslo. But he found himself
arriving there on 10 April at the very same time as the German army. He
escaped on the last train to Sweden, under the eyes of enemy pickets.
Chancellor praised Tighe's version of this close encounter as 'one of the most
vivid narratives of the war':

> Standing on the edge of the pavement amid a crowd of Norwegians, I watched
> a column of Germans, about 1,000 strong, march into the centre of the city at
> 3 o'clock yesterday afternoon. Every man, armed with formidable-looking
> rifle or machine-gun, was carrying a bandolier uncovered and glistening with
> bronzed machine-gun bullets ready for immediate action . . .
>
> The city had capitulated an hour or so earlier, after a night and morning of
> terror, during which German planes bombed all military objectives in the
> neighbourhood and machine-gunned the districts round the harbour
> defences . . .
>
> The Oslo station was already heavily guarded by German troops, but the
> only possible means of departure was by train . . . Near the time at which the
> train was scheduled to leave we walked quickly through the streets, now
> thronged with Germans, to the station. On arrival there we walked boldly past

a guard of some fifteen soldiers, armed to the teeth, and booked two tickets to Stockholm for a train packed with evacuees bound for Sweden.

Thanks to this surging crowd we managed to pass undetected and unquestioned. It was about midnight when we reached the frontier . . .
Everyone asked me the same question. 'What is your navy doing? Surely this invasion could have been stopped.'[5]

Tighe's next adventure was to travel from Sweden by sledge to Namsos in northern Norway, where he interviewed the British army commander. From Sweden, he made his way back to England, via Russia, the Balkans, Italy, and France. He remained only a few days in England, before being posted to Turkey on an intelligence-gathering mission, secretly half-paid for by the Ministry of Information. Tighe had moved into the grey area where reporting merged with spying. His 'special task' (as it was called within Reuters) lasted only a few weeks, and by September 1940 he was in Egypt. In October 1941 he was sent to Tobruk, which was under siege by Rommel's Afrika Corps. Tighe's private diary showed how well he possessed the right combination of qualities for a war correspondent under pressure. On the one hand, he never pretended to bravery: on the other, he was a determined seeker after news. 'God, what a place. Those people who write glowing reports and despatches about the tommies liking Tobruk should be shot. It's absolute hell' (19 October). 'One reaches a stage where every noise tends to make one grab a tin hat and lie flat. Bomb happy they call it. Don't think I've quite reached this stage yet' (12 November). After two months, he returned to Egypt: 'written dry on desert.'

At the start of 1943 Tighe joined the Mediterranean fleet as naval correspondent, and covered the war in North Africa, the invasion of Sicily, and in September 1943 the Salerno landings. He thought his problems with communications from Salerno sufficiently interesting to be worth writing about on their own account (18 September). In the absence of air or land links from the beachhead to the censor's office at Malta, all dispatches were sent by sea. But by which ships? Vessels scheduled to leave might remain to continue the bombardment, while other might sail unexpectedly. One solution was to send duplicate copies by several ships, trusting to luck that one would sail to Malta. Unfortunately, a ship which Tighe himself boarded at Salerno for Malta was diverted to Bizerta in Tunisia, and he had to endure an 800-mile sea, land, and air journey. 'From Bizerta I obtained a staff car, and driving through the night to Tunis we crashed off the road into the sand dunes. I hailed a passing American jeep and reached Tunis just in time to obtain a last seat on a courier plane for Malta. But my luck held and arriving panting with despatches, I flew in over the surrendering Italian fleet and was able to jump in on the story.'

The main report of the fleet's surrender was filed by the chief Reuter correspondent in Italy, David Brown, 'representing the Combined British Press'. The news editor of the *Sunday Express* enthused over Brown's report— 'Aboard H.M.S. Hambleton in the Mediterranean'—as 'one of the finest pieces of journalism I have ever put headlines on' (12 September 1943): NAVY LEADS ITALIAN BATTLEFLEET TO ANCHOR UNDER GUNS OF MALTA.

Brown was a good correspondent, but also a difficult personality, often at odds with his colleagues and with the British authorities. He was an American, who had joined the New York office in 1937. As chief correspondent, he grumbled forcefully about slow communications and bureaucratic delays. The head of British army public relations in Italy, Philip Astley, complained about Brown to Lord Burnham, the Director of Public Relations at the War Office in London. Astley's letter (9 December 1944) was revealing not only about Brown but also about official attitudes towards Reuters:

> Brown is a most difficult person, suspicious, provocative, and always ready to find fault, but quite apart from this, I do not think that Reuters best interests are being served by having an American as chief of a British Agency. The chief Reuters representative is naturally one of the most important correspondents here by virtue of his position and is looked upon pre-eminently as an upholder of British interests. I am not suggesting for one moment that Brown is unfair in any way or that in his despatches he ever forgets he serves a British Agency. On the other hand his outlook is totally American as are his methods. This, it seems to me, militates against satisfactory dealings with various British interests.

This letter was copied from the War Office to Chancellor at Reuters. Brown was soon afterwards transferred to the Pacific theatre.

The German press, itself controlled by Goebbels, had no doubts that Reuters was a British propaganda outlet. The Germans sometimes referred back to what they ruefully remembered as the successful propaganda role of Reuters during the previous war. *Der Neue Tag* of 3 October 1939 recalled how 'the poison cooks of Reuters' had functioned then. They had turned the 'fabrications' of Lloyd George and Churchill 'into easily understood "objective "language which, by its pretended nobleness, attained the desired impression'.

The Germans monitored all reports issued by Reuters, and were quick to take advantage. Reuter mishandling of the news of the assassination of Admiral Darlan at Algiers in December 1942 gave them such an opportunity. The facts were published by Reuters, but along with comments which implied satisfaction at the removal of Darlan ('he was a man who had few friends and many enemies'). The British Government had distrusted Darlan, whereas the Americans had been favouring him. The German propaganda machine was able to exploit this difference with help from the Reuter report. A warning instruction was issued to Reuter staff on 31 December 1942. 'Our message was of such a nature that the Germans were able to make insinuations which did not easily permit of a ready rebuttal, and it caused considerable concern in high places . . . in political matters we must never express a view of our own.'

3

In January 1943 Stewart Sale filed a graphic 1,500-word report after flying on a bombing raid over the German capital:

> I saw Berlin burn from the nose of a Lancaster, one of the many scores converging on the city. I looked down on hundreds of points of fire—incendiaries which had just struck and looked like strings of gems, others were already an angry red. There were also dark crimson puff-balls thrown up by the big bombs . . . Most of the pilots, it seemed, thought the flak over Berlin was light. My own captain thought it rather bad. I know it was bad enough for me. We made another run to release our other bombs, among them hundreds of incendiaries. I tensed myself again for the sickening sensation as the nose went down. For a wild moment the redness that masked Berlin seemed to rise until it was in line with my shoulder . . . Looking down on the furnace, I remembered nights on Fleet Street roofs when the bombers were over. By the time the bombers following us were through with it, Berlin too would know what bombing means.[6]

Eight months later, Sale was killed while reporting from Italy. In all, five Reuter correspondents were killed while covering the Second World War. The life of each correspondent was insured by Reuters for £3,000.

Although Sale might fly over Berlin, news from inside Germany and occupied Europe could not be obtained directly by Reuters. Some news from enemy countries came through neutral Sweden and Turkey, but the main source was the monitoring of enemy broadcasts by the Reuter listening station at Gothic House (renamed Radio House) at High Barnet, north of London. This had opened just before the war in 1939. The chief foreign sub-editor of the *Daily Express* told his editor in August 1942 that Reuter monitoring was 'far ahead of any other agency . . . generally first and more accurate'. But not all was praise. The BBC's foreign news editor complained at intervals about allegedly inaccurate Reuter monitoring of German broadcasts, giving examples; he claimed that complaints were always brushed aside.[7]

The most notable of the Reuter beats secured by radio monitoring was first news of the German invasion of the Soviet Union on 22 June 1941. The German Foreign Office had issued a statement saying, 'We are expecting a quiet week-end.' This struck Geoffrey Imeson, the editor-in-charge, as disingenuous, and put him on his guard. Normally, both Reuters and DNB, the Nazi agency, shut down their monitoring about midnight and resumed at 6 a.m. This unofficial truce was intended to allow their translators a rest. On this occasion, however, Imeson asked Nina Gee to stay listening all night— just in case. In the small hours she told Imeson excitedly over the telephone that 'Germany has invaded Russia'. Imeson immediately sent out a worldwide flash. Only after this had been transmitted did Nina Gee explain that all she had heard was an announcement about a proclamation from Hitler denouncing Soviet policy. This was shortly to be broadcast by Goebbels. Did it really mean war? In fact, it did. The reputation of Reuters for speed with the news was boosted; but its good name would have been seriously damaged if the flash had turned out to be wrong. In later years, Imeson was to describe his ten-minute beat as 'ill-deserved'.[8]

In the following April Harold King (1898–1990) was sent to Russia as a second Reuter correspondent. His bylined pieces were soon being widely published, and taken as evidence of the revival of Reuters after the departure of Jones. King had joined Reuters in Paris in October 1939, having decided that in wartime he would find only limited scope for his peacetime work as a financial journalist. He had been born in Germany, and had changed his name from Koenig to King. On appointment as a war correspondent he taught himself Russian, rejected an approach to supply material secretly to the British Embassy in Moscow, and sent back a stream of important reports. In his unpublished recollections King claimed that he was read worldwide in over 4,000 newspapers, 'just because of that tense suspense all over the globe about which side was going to win.'[9]

The *Newspaper World* of 9 January 1943 declared itself 'greatly impressed with the way in which Harold King, with no "dead" periods to ease his task, has supplied graphic news commentaries and spot news. Tribute to his work is reflected in the number of times he has ousted the newspapers' correspondents from their own front pages.' Yet King, though a good searcher after news, was not so capable a writer. Throughout his Reuter career he supplied the essentials to the sub-editors in London, who gave his stories the necessary polish.

In his reports of the fighting King had to build intelligently upon official and semi-official information, for he was never allowed to witness the fighting day-by-day, as did Reuter correspondents elsewhere. The best that

Moscow correspondents could expect was to be taken on guided tours. King's battle of Stalingrad coverage was accepted as authoritative, and yet he was not permitted into the city itself until after the German surrender. He then walked the battlefields for two days, with two Russian officers as guides through the minefields. He heard the story of the battle from General Chuikov personally.

On 7 January 1943 the *Birmingham Post* based a typical page of war news upon a sector-by-sector account from King of the turning tide of conflict in southern Russia:

> The battle for the two main railway lines south of the Don—railways vital to Hitler's communications with his armies in the Caucasus—has begun (Reuter's Moscow correspondent telegraphed last night). Latest despatches from the front show that Soviet forces are pushing forward along both railways in the face of stubborn German opposition . . . At Stalingrad, General Rodimtsev's guards, having fought their way clear of the city, are attacking von Hoth's trapped and exhausted divisions—twenty-two of them—to the west . . . East of the railway, in the windswept barren Kalmuck steppes, fast Russian columns are keeping close on the heels of the Germans falling back from Elista. 'Red Star' reported yesterday that the Russians have broken through the German defences at one point.

In May 1943 King wrote directly to Stalin, and his boldness was unexpectedly rewarded with a long reply of worldwide importance, signed on 28 May by the Russian leader personally, which discussed the recent dissolution of the Comintern. King's question had indicated that British opinion was responding very favourably to the Comintern's dissolution. Stalin answered:

> I feel that the dissolution of the Comintern International is perfectly timely because it is exactly now, when the Fascist beast is exerting its last strength, that it is necessary to organize the common onslaught of freedom-loving peoples to finish off this beast and to deliver the peoples from Fascist oppression.

This letter was taken as evidence that the Soviet Government had abandoned its dream of 'Bolshevizing' the world.[10]

Stalin was now asserting that the Red Army's objective was to clear the Germans out of the Soviet Union, but not to go beyond. He said this not because he meant it, but to lull the Russian people into thinking that their sufferings would end the sooner. Russian censors began to be coy about just how far their armies had advanced. King cleverly got round this by reporting: 'During the night brave Cossack cavalrymen watered their horses in the Dniester'. This meant that they were into Poland.[11]

4

In contrast to King, kept at a distance from the fighting, Alan Humphreys (1908–92) worked close to the action. In 1942 he covered a succession of Commando raids upon the German-held coast of western Europe. Like Tighe, he had joined Reuters in 1930 as a lowly member of the commercial staff; but, again like Tighe, he had aspired to become a general news journalist, and the war gave him his chance. He soon acquired a reputation for lively but controlled writing, appropriate for a news agency war correspondent.[12]

On 19 August 1942 Humphreys watched the biggest raid of all, that upon Dieppe. It was a disaster, although called a success. It was successful only as an example of what not to do when eventually the Allies were ready to mount a second front. Well over half the 6,100 men who embarked ended up killed, wounded, captured, or missing in one day. The public had been told that a raid had begun, but there was a long delay before any news was released about the outcome; and the overall truth, although known to some in Fleet Street, was suppressed until after the war.[13]

Humphreys's report of the raid was held back for two days. Its first part admitted just a little of what went wrong on the beaches:

> On board a Tank-landing craft off Dieppe, Wednesday afternoon

> For eight hours I watched Canadian shock troops, squadrons of Britain's tanks, naval vessels, and an armada of RAF fighters battling in daylight against a concentrated German opposition . . . A 1000 to 1 chance found the raiding craft carrying some of the Commandos being intercepted before they were due to land. One enemy patrol was the cause, with the result that not only were the Commandos' craft severely damaged by the German flak ships and E-boats who held their fire until the landing craft were only about 200 yards away, but, much more important, warning was given to the Germans defending the coastal batteries which were the Commandos' objective . . . The guns—first vital objective of the raid—were never silenced.

In the second part of his report, Humphreys described what he heard by radio from the beach:

> Radio reports from the tanks ashore are still not good. The Casino is proving a strong fortress, and a nearby tobacco factory is very strongly held . . . The tank radio now gives the word everybody has been expecting for some time. The men on the beach and promenade and some way into the town have had a hard fight, but they have stuck to it. They have done magnificently. 'Evacuate,' says the radio . . . 'Evacuate tanks, or destroy them on the beach,' instructs the tank commander. Twenty-five minutes later the beach reports that a tank landing

craft is holed and sinking. The voice which answers this piece of dire news is quite unchanged. 'Can you see anything coming in yet?' asks the tank . . . Four minutes later the radio emits only a heavy burst of machine-gun fire. The end is very near. Another four minutes and I hear: 'I am ready by the centre tank landing craft to upload.' Back comes the imperturbable answer: 'You will see me when the smoke comes in.' Only one more minute—the last. 'I have to upload. My guns are gone. I can do no more good on the beach.' The smoke had come in.

So ended the Reuter report, published on the front page of the *Daily Express* on 21 August, under the headline, 'OUR TANKS RADIO BACK, "WE'RE KILLING GERMANS".' The *Express's* editor sent his congratulations to Reuters. But the truth was that too few tanks had got ashore, and none got back to England.

Humphreys had not been in a position to make any overall assessment; and he would not have been allowed to publish one if he had known the truth. Interviewed over forty years later, he admitted that at the time he had thought the raid to have gone sufficiently well. Eye-witness accounts of battles inevitably tend to tunnel vision.

Later in 1942 Humphreys was sent to cover the Allied landings in North Africa and then in Sicily. Communications from Algiers proved to be especially troublesome. Messages from the front reached there quickly enough, but onward transmission to London was much slower than to New York. Reuters could itself cable via New York, but this was expensive, and meant taking turns with the American agencies, who were then likely to be first with the story. Humphreys told Walton Cole, the news manager, on 25 April 1943 that he was trying to address the 'horror' of the communications situation. Cole responded with concerned service messages—'what route used upward [UP] yesternight eightarmy attack on which we disastrously beaten'; 'view possibility another big story please send first break and descriptive by every route'; 'grateful reply speediest how many correspondents apathy [AP] upwards [UP] have northafrica etof total how many algiers'.

Such pressure from London drove some correspondents to outbursts of anger and even to threaten resignation. Cole answered one such outbreak from Humphreys and his colleague, Denis Martin, with a piece of masterful cable-ese via Algiers on 18 June 1943:

humphreys explanation background recent episode understood completely forgetting it etis between us three so oncarry your excellent work etbe patient etconvinced as eye your future reuters unsurpassed anywhere fullstop when offbrowned offlet steam me etbe unprimadonnaish full stop.

5

Reuters began preparing to report the Allied invasion of western Europe more than a year before D-Day on 6 June 1944. With four correspondents killed during 1941–3, and with others committed to the Italian and Russian fronts, or to the war with the Japanese in Asia, it became obvious that Reuters must find new blood, even though available good journalists were in short supply on both sides of the Atlantic. Cole brought one man from Scotland and another from Northern Ireland, and he recruited five more from the United States and Canada. All proved to be good appointments. Tighe came back from the Mediterranean to cover the naval side of the invasion. Reuters still found itself sometimes outnumbered on big stories by AP and UP, the American agencies, but this was usually masked by high quality reporting.

The youngest of all the media reporters involved on D-Day was Doon Campbell of Reuters. Born in 1920, he came from a lowland Scottish back-ground. Cole had noticed Campbell's good work for the Edinburgh *Evening Dispatch*. He was exempt from military service because of an arm disability, and this meant that he was free to accept a job offer made by Cole on 11 March 1943.[14] In the following November Campbell was posted to Algiers, and next month he crossed to Italy for a first taste of war. His eyewitness account of the blasting of Monte Cassino demonstrated that Reuters had found a first-class correspondent (15 March 1944):

> At 8.30 this morning Cassino sat in the sun, with only an occasional shell-burst disturbing the quiet. By noon it was grotesquely gaping and ugly—like an unearthed ruin, like a second Pompeii . . . Three spouts of smoke went up as the first cluster of bombs hit the southern end of the town. A few seconds later terrific explosions caused the whole countryside to heave. Bombs dropped in layers . . . Cassino (less than two miles from the olive grove where I stood with a British general) was for the moment hidden by a pall of smoke which seemed to spiral almost as high as 5,000 feet . . . The bombardier of one of the planes said: 'Our objective was to get rid of the town—we got rid of it.'

Soon afterwards, Cole decided that his young discovery must join the Reuter reporting team for D-day.

Seaghan Maynes (1916–98), an Irishman, was slightly more experienced than Campbell. He had started as a reporter in Belfast on the *Irish News*, and had moved to the Press Association in London, where he met Cole. Keen to report the war, he asked for a job; and taking a cut in salary he joined Reuters in May 1944, just in time for D-Day.[15]

Cole had visited the United States early in 1944, and while there he had interviewed over forty candidates for assignment as frontline correspondents with the American and Canadian forces. He assured the board sweepingly on 4 February that 'all the recruits are joining Reuters because of their belief in our future and the important role we are destined to play in post-war Europe'. The implication was that these recruits would stay long term. Yet they were recruited on the cheap. Because of the lower cost of living in Britain, Cole persuaded them to accept smaller salaries than in North America. William Stringer, John Wilhelm, and Robert Reuben came from the United States; Charles Lynch and Marshall Yarrow from Canada.[16]

Some fifteen Reuter journalists became directly involved in the invasion coverage, either as correspondents in Normandy or as editors in London. Approximately 800 men and women were accredited from the world's press to Supreme Headquarters. Of these, about 180 reported regularly from the forward areas, and these included some twenty-five who represented the British national papers and news agencies (Reuters, British United Press, and Exchange Telegraph). An article on 'Front-Line Reporters' by Macdonald Hastings, himself one of their number, appeared in the popular weekly *Picture Post* on 14 October 1944. Hastings claimed that the war correspondents were 'better known than most of the generals':

> The press looks to its correspondents, and Parliament and people look to the press, to give a fearless, independent, and accurate account of the state of the nation's affairs in the field . . . the men of this war have done a far, far better job than the war correspondents in the last . . . The reporting of this war, if it's only occasionally been brilliant, has generally been accurate, and nearly always first-hand.

Hastings added one important reservation. 'Where the war correspondents generally have fallen down in this war is not as reporters, but as military commentators. It is hard to think of a single instance where, from direct observation in the field, a war correspondent in this war has foretold with accuracy the future outlook of a campaign.' The article was accompanied by photographs of thirteen leading British war correspondents. Doon Campbell was pictured for Reuters; while two others—Alexander Clifford of the *Daily Mail* and David Woodward of the *Manchester Guardian*—were former Reuter men.

6

Cole and Sidney Mason, the chief news editor, created a system which handled reports from the frontline in Normandy more effectively than any other news agency. From D-Day onwards, Mason based himself with two other Reuter journalists at SHAEF (Supreme Headquarters Allied Expeditionary Force) in London to handle incoming material. Four others were sent to reinforce the Reuter group in a room at the Ministry of Information, which became the conduit for all copy. A mix of material—official communiqués, propaganda handouts, pooled dispatches, stories exclusive to Reuters, and feature articles—reached the Reuter room. An electric switch enabled Reuters to deliver urgent news directly to the London newsrooms of the British national papers. Rival agencies were unable to accelerate their delivery in this way.

Mason gave detailed guidance to his correspondents. 'As a rule,' he warned (25 April 1944), 'censors don't like news, particularly when it is interesting.' He had therefore devised a way to deflect their attention. 'If you find this so, write a general lead and come to the guts of the story apparently casually.' This meant suspending the usual insistence upon putting the main point of every story into the first sentence. Quotation, added Mason, was preferable to paraphrase, or to writing in the third person. 'Quotes tell a story where the third person technique will not. Instance—Eisenhower says "The invading forces are going strongly". This is world news and very different from a reporter saying—General Eisenhower said that our invading troops were doing well.'

Mason's ideal length for most stories was 400–500 words, sufficient to fill three-quarters of a newspaper column. Of course, longer length might sometimes be justified. 'There's only going to be one invasion of Europe. If you have the story of the century about it, then go all out, but first be sure you have.' As for communications, 'find out all you can about them. It is always foolish to go after a big story if you don't know how the hell you are going to shift it.'

Mason reminded his correspondents that they faced strong internal competition from Radio House. And curiously it was not a journalist at SHAEF or in Normandy, but monitoring of German radio which gained Reuters a two-minute beat on 6 June 1944 with first news in London of the invasion—Reuters 06.33, BUP 06.35, AP 06.38. SHAEF had held the news back, but the Germans were not so reticent. As a result, Reuters first heard of the landings from Transocean, the German overseas news agency. The resulting Reuter flash was of dramatic brevity: 'Allied forces began invasion of Europe landing on Normandy beaches today.'

As with the Mafeking scoop in 1900, the military authorities were left to confirm what Reuters had already reported. A public relations officer began a Ministry of Information press conference—at a time when no SHAEF communiqué had yet been issued—by still not announcing the news officially, but by saying: 'We have landed, according to a German radio message picked up by Reuter.' The weekly editorial log for 5–12 June noted that Reuters was ahead of BUP and AP on most of the early invasion stories.[16]

The Reuter team for D-day included eight frontline reporters:

With naval light forces	Tighe
With British land forces	Campbell
With US land forces	Maynes, Stringer, Yarrow
With US air forces	Reuben, Wilhelm
With Canadian land forces	Lynch

The Reuter editorial log for 6–7 June claimed that Tighe 'had the honour of supplying the best published description of the invasion'—the best presumably in the British press. He reported from a British destroyer 8,000 yards off the coast of Normandy:

> Guns are belching flame from more than 600 Allied warships. Thousands of bombers are roaring overhead, fighters are weaving in and out of the clouds as the invasion of Western Europe begins . . . The air is filled with the continuous thunder of broadsides and the crash of bombs. Great spurts of flame come up from the beaches in long snake-like ripples . . . It is now exactly 7.25 a.m., and through my glasses I can see the first wave of assault troops touch down on the water's edge and fan up the beach . . . Conditions are not ideal. A fairly high sea is running, the sky is overcast . . . It is early yet, but so far there has been no enemy air opposition at all. The invasion fleet came over to the shores of North-Western France unmolested . . .
>
> The plans for the invasion of the coastline allowed for four separate phases:—(1) Landings by airborne troops and paratroops in the rear. (2) A tremendous full-scale night bombing by the RAF on the landing beaches themselves. (3) A sea bombardment by more than 600 Allied battleships, cruisers, monitors, and destroyers. (4) Finally, a daybreak bombing attack by the full force of the United States Air Force just after dawn and before the initial landings went in . . .
>
> It is too early to know how the initial landings have gone. But they were made to split second according to timetable.

At first, all invasion stories for the British press were pooled. The above report was bylined 'Desmond Tighe, Reuter's Special Correspondent for the Combined Press'. But pooling was abandoned as unnecessary after a couple of days, and competition between correspondents resumed.

Campbell had landed with a company of Royal Marine Commandos on Sword beach at 9.10 a.m. He was the first seaborne correspondent to land, although several others (including Reuben and Yarrow of Reuters) had already touched ground with the airborne troops. Under fire, Campbell crossed a road, and stumbled into a ditch. He tore a page from an exercise book, and scribbled a few lines from 'A ditch 200 yards inside Normandy'. He handed the message to a naval officer who was operating a shuttle service between the beach and England; but the message was never heard of again, perhaps because the officer was killed.

Marshall Yarrow, with the Americans, sent back a first report highly effective because of its stark economy:

> I landed in Normandy with the first glider forces of the invasion. It was dark, it was deadly, and we landed in a country of stinking swamps and hidden snipers ... I crawled as I have never crawled before. When I left the fighting area I left something behind me—my face-print in the mud of Normandy's beaches.

Although Reuter First World War correspondents were sometimes at risk of being shelled or shot from a distance, they were never as close as this to the fighting.

Two early Reuter messages were successfully delivered from Normandy by carrier pigeon, and served as reminders of Julius Reuter's early days. Pigeons were, however, very unreliable under battle conditions; and Lynch, who landed with a basketful of thirty-six birds, found that they all flew off in wrong directions. Campbell wrote later that he would have refused to have carried a pigeon.[17]

A composite of his messages filed on and since D-Day dominated the front page of the London *Evening News* of 9 June 1944:

> It is a miracle that I am alive to write this story, that I have survived 24 hours on this bridgehead bag of wicked tricks. Bombs, shells, bullets and mines to say nothing of booby traps, make each hour an age of grim experience. The dead lie about, covered by a piece of tarpaulin or half-buried in the sand.
>
> I was pinned down for an hour by a withering barrage of enemy shell fire yesterday. The beached craft got the full weight, but men were also hit. The wounded dropped unobtrusively away the whole afternoon.
>
> Most of my 24 hours have been spent lying flat out on my face burrowing into sand or earth, the good earth. Every forward soldier thanks God for soft earth. It makes him feel safe at least. The front is so fluid, so fluid, in fact, that I crouched for two hours in a sewer—it smelled like one anyway—before realising that I was a good hundred yards ahead of the front Allied trench.

Even in this exposed situation, Campbell remembered to continue the Reuter practice of including mention of particular British soldiers, complete with home addresses to satisfy their local papers. 'Private W. Nicholls, of 80 Chertsey-road, Addistone, Surrey, told me: "They put up a bit of a fight at first, but were not long in coming out, waving handkerchiefs and pieces of white cloth".'

Campbell had developed a technique for getting his stories through with (he hoped) minimum delay. First, he delivered a series of two- or three-line snaps, which focused upon the highlights—'won the battle of the beaches', '7,000 prisoners taken Sunday night', 'German women snipers killed'. Being short, these were likely to be cleared quickly by the censors. Then he sent a full account. And finally he offered an overall lead, ready-made for the tabloid papers.

On D-day plus six (12 June) General Montgomery gave a briefing at his headquarters to nearly fifty correspondents, including Campbell (Plate 39). Campbell's report rightly let 'Monty' speak for himself without comment:

> 'We have won the battle of the beaches. I am very happy and very pleased indeed with the situation so far, but there is a good deal to be done yet. There are no longer any gaps between the British and the Americans—that is good, very good . . . They are confident and have already got the measure of the enemy. The support given to our armies by the Navy and Air Force has been superb—without it we could not have done it.'

Correspondents were still accompanied by conducting officers. Some were helpful; but their presence was felt to be superfluous by many front-line journalists, who often had greater experience than their minders. Relations after D-Day between Reuter correspondents and the censors were generally good. On the one hand, the generals did not make exaggerated claims, while on the other, the censorship was not stifling.

A week after D-Day, Mason congratulated Campbell warmly: 'your copy has reached a level when it cannot go much higher.' Others had also noticed this; and AP tried to lure Campbell away by offering him a starting salary of £25 per week, twice what he was getting from Reuters. But he told his father, a month after D-Day, that he was content to stay where he was. He admitted, though, that the pressure was beginning to tell. He had not washed 'whole body' since D-day. 'I do two things. I scrounge and work. I should do three. I should sleep.' Cole kept a sympathetic eye upon his young protégé, promised him a great future in Reuters, and urged him to take some time off.

Cole had been over to Normandy to investigate why transmission times were slow. The problem was not caused by the censors at Campbell's end; but stories were taking up to eight hours to pass through army signals and SHAEF censors. Cole secured a reduction to two hours.

Seaghan Maynes, the lively little Irishman, rivalled Campbell, the dedicated Scotsman. Mason, the chief news editor, once light-heartedly portrayed Maynes to Campbell (13 December 1944) as 'so small that the opposition is sometimes inclined to overlook his presence with the result that he sometimes gets in first'. In Normandy, Maynes had joined the American 3rd Army on Utah beach. In an apple orchard, General George Patton gave a first briefing to correspondents. 'Our job is to kill, capture and conquer the bastards.' But the killing was always going to be two-way. More than once, Maynes found soldiers being shot around him.

The truth about death in action could be told, but not the truth about total casualties. Nor in either world war could the full reality of life behind the lines be revealed. Only afterwards did Charlie Lynch of Reuters write of finding a queue of GIs outside a brothel, where the madam took his French-speaking conducting officer away for a drink, leaving Lynch to operate the till. In 1992 Canada issued a series of Second World War stamps, which included one entitled 'War Reporting'; this showed Lynch interviewing a wounded Canadian soldier (Plate 41).[18]

Patton's troops could have been first into Paris, and Maynes with them; but they were held back to allow the liberation to be accomplished by Free French troops. So, with the help of the novelist Ernest Hemingway, who had contacts with the maquis, Maynes slipped in ahead of the Americans. He used a French resistance radio transmitter to send a dispatch 'onpass Reuter', which got through. This was technically in breach of censorship, and Maynes was suspended for sixty days.

The abortive Arnhem landings in September 1944—intended to force a crossing of the Rhine—were covered for Reuters by Jack Smyth. He landed by parachute. But he was injured during the fierce fighting, and was captured. For seventeen days he was roughly interrogated by the Gestapo, and was even threatened with death. While a prisoner of war, he sent Cole a card of apology, dated 11 October 1944. 'A fine correspondent I turned out to be! Four days in the field, a solitary despatch and then captured.' Smyth's dispatch, the only press report from the landing zone, had been published in the London papers on 22 September:

> With Airborne Force, Arnhem Area, Sept. 21
>
> On this fifth day our force is still being heavily mortared, sniped, machine-gunned, and shelled by self-propelled guns. But, as their commander says, they are in good heart.
>
> The medium guns of the Second Army have just come into communication, and have begun shelling enemy targets that we have signalled. Maybe the tanks will arrive today. Anyway we are holding out until they do.
>
> These airborne men are magnificent. They fight individually as well as in platoons and companies. When the Second Army arrives and relieves this

crowd, then may be told one of the epics of the war. In the meantime they just go on fighting their hearts out.

7

The final Allied push from the west came with the crossing of the Rhine in March 1945. Doon Campbell crash-landed in a glider, and Maynes dropped by parachute. *Reynolds News* for 25 March carried stories from both men written just before they took off, though only Maynes was bylined:

> Sky Men's Secret Briefing
> by Seaghan Maynes (who dropped with the Airborne Army)

> Now we know where and how we are going to smash into the rear of Kesselring's Rhine army guardians. The young debonair, cravat-wearing airborne General, standing before a mass of maps, aerial photographs, and a large minutely detailed model of the territory we are jumping into, has briefed me behind locked, guarded doors. Every German machine-gun nest, weapons-pit, and gun position has been pin-pointed . . .

> There was an ENSA show on Friday night in the crowded hut. They roared 'Lili Marlene': 'When Irish Eyes Are Smiling' and the Paratroops' song. Among the instructions they've received are: no looting and leave the civilians alone if their behaviour is good. If they interfere with operations and carry out hostile or warlike acts—shoot them . . .

> Everything is ready. The chatter of conversation has died out. Now we are filing into the planes. We are on our way.

Campbell's piece was headlined 'FOUR MEN IN AIR JEEP'. It cleverly built up the tension by mentioning ordinary things:

> We are four men in a jeep inside a glider . . . We are off in 20 minutes. It's a beautiful morning. We rose at 5.30. Breakfast was pineapple juice, steak and jam and fried potatoes and sliced peaches.

> The gliders are stacked nose to tail behind the tug planes. Some of the men had guns, some grenades, some just knives. Shaving cream and packets of cigarettes showed under their packs . . . In our jeep are two Americans, a Londoner, and myself, a Scot . . . Now we are about to take off. In three hours we will be in Germany. Until then, cheerio England—and so long America.

Campbell did not add that gliders were known as 'cardboard coffins'; or that his glider was overloaded, and that he was packed in tight with his arm resting on a box of grenades.

Both Reuter correspondents landed under heavy fire. Maynes picked up a sub-machine gun dropped by a dead German, and fired off bursts of self-protective fire, very conscious that the Germans were unaware of his non-combatant status. His report of the airborne landing did not mention this firing; but he did admit that he had yelled 'hands up', and that five Germans in a machine-gun nest had duly surrendered.

Interestingly, German radio got hold of Maynes's account of the landing, and quoted from it selectively: 'Seaghan Maynes of Reuters at least knows the truth.' The radio repeated Maynes's admissions about difficulties and casualties, but omitted his correct conclusion that the operation had been an overall success. With internal communications to Hitler's Berlin bunker breaking down, the German High Command seems to have increasingly depended upon Reuter reports to help plot the progress of the Allied armies. These reports were probably received by Hellschreiber in the nearby Propaganda Ministry.[19]

Campbell described with powerful simplicity the horrors of the concentration camp at Belsen (20 April 1945):

> Men I saw there a few hours ago will certainly have died by the time you read this. Over 17,000 prisoners, men, women and children, are said to have died last month. I cannot tell the whole shocking story . . . In one hut were 50 men, huddled sore to sore. One seemed to have a rail over his head—then you recognised arms. One seemed just bone—till you went close and saw skin. One with so many scabs, could only see through narrow slits of eyes. One was trying to stand on string-like legs that dangled from a body the thickness of a naval hawser. But they all said 'Hello' and tried to smile.

Reuters enjoyed a notable world beat on 28 April with news of an offer of surrender to the western Allies from Himmler, the Gestapo chief. Another beat, which told about the disintegration of the Nazi leadership, was secured by Duncan Hooper, King's successor as chief correspondent in Moscow. Hooper got news of the suicide on 1 May of Josef Goebbels. A Soviet official had approached Hooper at a party and said: 'It is very sad about Dr. Goebbels.' Knowing nothing, Hooper had responded carefully. 'Very sad.' The official then revealed all. 'They killed the children in the bunker and then killed themselves.' Hitler had shot himself in the same Berlin bunker on the previous day. He did so after hearing, courtesy of Reuters, that Himmler was trying to treat with the Allies. This news had been a last blow. News of the discovery a fortnight later of what the Russians thought to be Hitler's body gave Hooper another beat.[20]

Seaghan Maynes ended the European war back with General Patton's 3rd United States Army. Four days after V-E day, on 8 May 1945, Maynes received a letter of congratulation from the general. The fact that Patton

always said what he meant and meant what he said made it the more acceptable:

> Through the dusty days of last summer and the bitter days of the winter in the
> Ardennes I have seen you in pursuit of the story where it happens. When I
> think of how much of your time you spent with the front line troops I am at a
> loss to understand why more correspondents aren't dead.
>
> The men of the Third United States Army will always remember the war
> correspondents who lived among them so that the people at home might know
> of the daily progress of their men at the front. The immortal fame which these
> men have achieved is due in large part to the faithful and accurate day to day
> recording of their deeds by the front line correspondents.

8

The war in Europe took priority for Reuters—as for the United Kingdom—
over the war with Japan, which had started with the Japanese attack upon
Pearl Harbour on 7 December 1941. Relations between Reuters and the
Japanese authorities had been growing increasingly strained during the years
before the war, even though links with the Domei news agency remained
cordial. On 29 July 1940 Melville James [Jimmy] Cox (b.1885), the chief
Reuter correspondent in Tokyo and a Far East veteran, died in mysterious circumstances while in police custody. He fell from a third-floor window at the
secret police headquarters after being arrested on suspicion of spying. About
ten other British subjects were detained at the same time.[21]

Cox had been questioned for fifty-five hours. Did he jump? Was he
pushed or thrown out? Kenneth Selby-Walker, Chancellor's successor as
general manager in the Far East, had visited Tokyo during the previous May
and had found Cox 'in somewhat of a nervous state'. Cox felt that he was
being watched, which probably he was. Selby-Walker reported to Jones on
14 August, after a visit of enquiry to Tokyo, that Cox 'did take his own life'.
'I feel that, in his nervous state, he decided it was more than he could bear
to go on indefinitely suffering the acute physical discomfort of his surroundings, the indignities of the situation and the mental bullying.' An
American doctor's report, communicated to the British Foreign Office, said
that foul play was not suspected. Cox's injuries were consistent with a fall of
about forty feet. The body was some way forward from the wall, as would
be likely if Cox had jumped rather than been pushed. In 1960 a respected
Japanese newspaper reporter, who had no reason to speak anything but
the truth, told the Japanese Ministry of Justice that he had seen Cox on the

window ledge. 'He looked calmly round him, raised his hands to his face and deliberately jumped.'

Comment in 1954 from a Japanese secret-police commander, who was in charge of the section dealing with Cox, suggested that the police had never wished to murder him, but that they had believed him to be an intelligence gatherer for the British Embassy. Cox's files were found to contain information about the Japanese army and navy. This may have been no more than cuttings and other published material of a kind which any Western journalist would have expected to collect; but even such a collection has always been suspect in totalitarian countries.

Was Cox therefore totally innocent of spying? He left a note for his wife which could be read as meaning that he was about to crack and reveal something, or simply (as Selby-Walker argued) that he was choosing suicide because he could take no more: 'See Reuters re rents. See Cowley re deeds and insurance. See H.K. Bank re balance and shares in London. I know what is best. Always, my only love. I have been quite well treated but there is no doubt about how matters are going.'

In a public statement Reuters made a 'flat denial' of the charge that Cox and other Reuter correspondents had official connections. Reuters did not admit that about this same period the salaries of several of its correspondents in sensitive parts of the world (the Balkans, Ankara, Bangkok, and Hsingking) were being supplemented by payments from the Foreign Office. Interviewed nearly fifty years later, C. R. Graham-Barrow admitted that he had been sent to Hsingking in Manchukuo in 1940 'officially to sell the Reuter service, but (I don't think Reuters would like this) I was loaned to His Majesty's Government for the period to keep an ear to the ground'. The British Government paid Reuters £926 per annum for Graham-Barrow's help. When he was repatriated after the outbreak of war with Japan he sailed on a ship with British diplomats and officials, much to the surprise of other journalists.[22]

The Japanese were embarrassed by the Cox tragedy. Through the Japanese Ambassador in London, Matsuoka of Domei, the national news agency, privately gave 100,000 yen (over £5,800) to Cox's widow as a gesture of sympathy (Plate 36).

Cox's general manager, Selby-Walker, was himself to meet a violent end. Reporting the Japanese advance, he gradually withdrew through South-East Asia at the turn of 1941–2, and after the surrender of Singapore, had reached Java. Reuters in London told him on 5 March 1942 to report from there until the last moment, 'but remember we do not want you be caught'. The warning was already superfluous. Selby-Walker's last message by cable next day said bravely:

eyem afraid its too late stop eyve only myself to blame goodluck hope see you all sooner than you expect.

He tried to escape with three other journalists, but all were presumed drowned when their boat was sunk off Java on 7 March.[23]

Reuters in the Far East took a long time to recover from these shocks, and coverage remained uncertain throughout 1942. When the Japanese conquests were at their greatest extent, the agency was left with correspondents in India and Australia, and at Chungking, the emergency capital of Nationalist China. The Bombay office took charge of reporting from East Asia, but not until Alan Humphreys was transferred from the Mediterranean in September 1943 was Reuters sure of good coverage on the Burma front. Humphreys joined a Chindit expedition behind the lines, watched the Eastern fleet, and was present at the liberation of Rangoon. He finished up at Singapore, reporting the Japanese surrender there.

On 25 October 1944 radio monitoring secured for Reuters one of its most noticed wartime beats when Radio House heard faintly a broadcast by General MacArthur from the Philippines. He was announcing the virtual destruction of the Japanese navy by the Americans in the battle of Leyte Gulf. This decisive news was not immediately received in the United States itself, either by radio or cable, much to the embarrassment of the American authorities and press.[24]

The historic news of the dropping of the first atomic bomb on Hiroshima on 6 August 1945 reached Reuters from Washington where President Truman had made the announcement. Follow-up news was sent on 8 August from Guam by Jack Smyth, who was now reporting from the Pacific after recovering from his six months as a prisoner-of-war in Germany (Fig. 11).

9

The Second World War ended a few days later. Cole had rightly foreseen that some Reuter correspondents would encounter problems of adjustment. A year earlier, he had already been telling Humphreys (28 July 1944) that 'the era of war correspondents as such will end sooner than some of us imagine and those whose only qualification is war corresponding will have to acquire experience of our requirements the hard way'.

Humphreys himself left in 1946 for the *Daily Mail*, although he was to reappear twelve years later to work for SAPA and Reuters in South Africa. Tighe was unhappy to be called back to London at the end of 1945 for a refresher course in commercial service work, prior to returning to Egypt. He felt that

o   8.8.45..

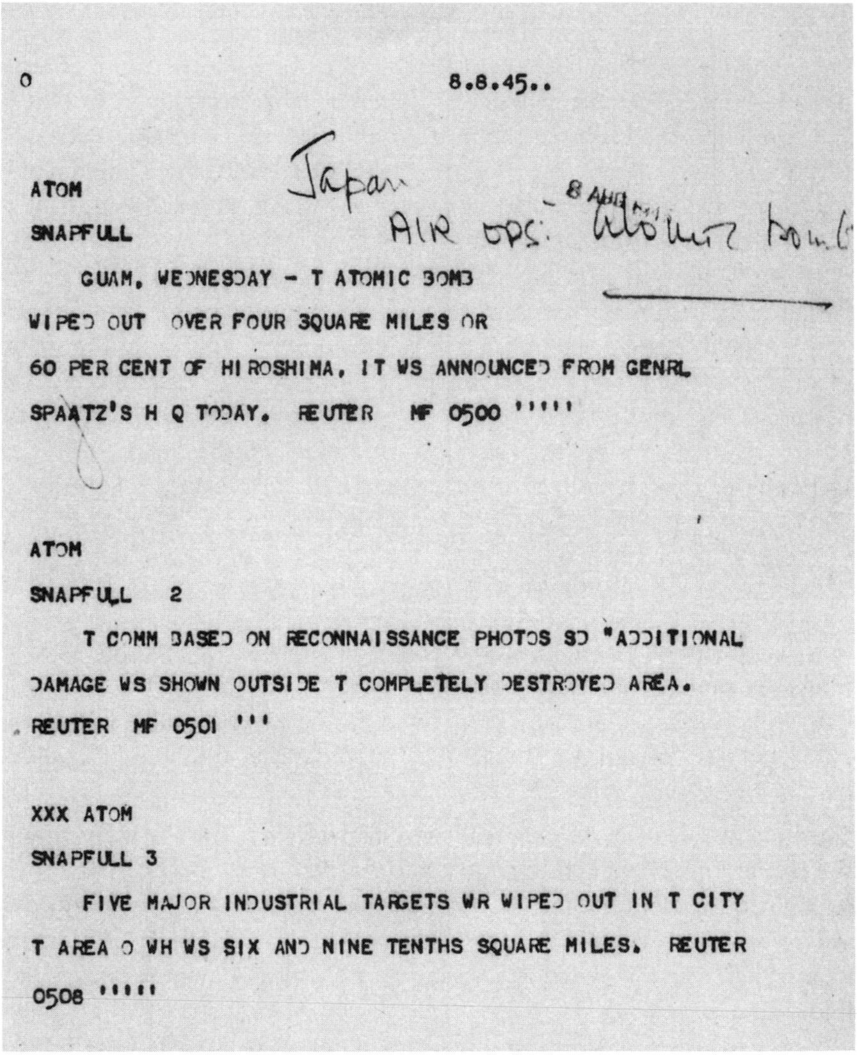

ATOM   *Japan*
SNAPFULL   AIR OPS: *atomic bomb*

GUAM, WEDNESDAY – T ATOMIC BOMB
WIPED OUT OVER FOUR SQUARE MILES OR
60 PER CENT OF HIROSHIMA, IT WS ANNOUNCED FROM GENRL
SPAATZ'S H Q TODAY. REUTER   MF 0500 '''''

ATOM
SNAPFULL   2
T COMM BASED ON RECONNAISSANCE PHOTOS SD "ADDITIONAL
DAMAGE WS SHOWN OUTSIDE T COMPLETELY DESTROYED AREA.
REUTER MF 0501 '''

XXX ATOM
SNAPFULL 3
FIVE MAJOR INDUSTRIAL TARGETS WR WIPED OUT IN T CITY
T AREA O WH WS SIX AND NINE TENTHS SQUARE MILES. REUTER
0508 '''''

FIG. 11. Hiroshima two days after the bomb

he was going back, more than just geographically, to where he had been in 1939, and that his transformation into a successful general news journalist was being disregarded. At a 1946 New Year's Day dinner party at the Chancellors, he got drunk and provoked an 'incident'. He subsequently apologized, but at the same time he resigned. Later in the year he was made an OBE in recognition of his long war service. He afterwards worked for the Arab News Agency, which had close links with Reuters during the 1950s and 60s.

Doon Campbell was mentioned in dispatches for his work as a war correspondent. Although he too encountered problems of adjustment, he stayed with Reuters. As his first post-war job, he was assigned to Chungking, but while there he began to feel restless. He asked for a three-year contract, or to be recalled. These demands caused offence at headquarters. Campbell then explained himself apologetically in a letter to Chancellor on 28 December 1945: 'the binding obligations of a contract seemed the surest instrument of restraint and stability. Since Europe I have come to realise that my greatest problem is myself.' Campbell admitted perceptively that he was 'still going through a process of reconversion from spot news assignments with no restriction on filing to a world market to the no less important but more prosaic static coverage of day-by-day happenings in a national capital'.

Campbell duly learned how to make this transition, and rose within Reuters to serve successively as chief correspondent, news manager, editor, European manager, and deputy general manager. He left in 1973 to become external services manager for United Newspapers. Seaghan Maynes remained with Reuters as a senior correspondent, specializing in Commonwealth and Irish affairs, until retirement in 1978.

10

Even in wartime, many days were not days of excitement. For example, the day-duty log for 15–16 February 1941 began simply: 'There was no big foreign news.' On such days Reuters had to make the most of what news there was. And its editorial staff had always to bear in mind that newspapers in Britain and elsewhere still expected some sports news. Although Malta was under siege by air, Mabel Strickland, the doughty proprietress of *The Times of Malta*, once cabled: 'would appreciate full list of Derby runners as soon as possible'.

In November 1942 Cole had used his contacts to obtain a copy of the famous Beveridge report on social welfare a week before publication. This enabled Reuters to publish a detailed summary as soon as the document was released. Here was a plan for implementation in post-war Britain. But what about post-war Germany? Mason was very interested in the state of German public opinion. At the time of the final push into Germany in 1945, he asked Reuter correspondents for full coverage of more than the fighting:

> The story has still to be told in connected fashion of the life of the Germans under Hitler since 1939, and the angles to this are so many that any correspondent could think up enough to fill a couple of books . . .

> Are the Germans going to be any better in the future than they have been in
> the past? Are they really beaten? Are we going to have to feed and clothe them,
> or are they sufficiently well off?

So Reuters prepared to report the painful return of peace to the world, just
as it had reported the destructive course of war. Despite censorship restrictions, its reputation as a major source of speedy yet accurate news stood much
higher in 1945 than in 1939—just as it had stood much higher in 1918 than in
1914. During each war, the agency had successfully restructured itself,
becoming in the process a more effective news collector and distributor.
Moreover, during wartime people everywhere had read their newspapers
with extra attention; and—as with Harold King's reports from the Russian
front—the name of 'Reuter' became attached to stories of great interest to
readers worldwide.

And yet what perhaps fixed the name of Reuter subconsciously in the
global memory at this period, as much as any war reporting, was a Hollywood
film. In the United States it was called *A Dispatch from Reuters*; elsewhere it was
entitled *This Man Reuter*. The film was released in London in September 1941,
when the United States had not yet entered the war but was sympathetic
towards the British cause. The film was a good piece of pro-British propaganda. Through the example of the career of Julius Reuter, it illustrated the
commitment of both Britain and the United States to freedom in news; and
it showed how, in order to create a news agency which successfully promoted
such freedom, Reuter had chosen to leave Germany and to set up in London.
The geographical moral was tacit but obvious.

The decision to make a film had been taken before the war. Even in peacetime the need to stand up for freedom in news was apparent, in the face of
manipulation of the media by Goebbels and others. But at that point
Hollywood was probably more interested in Julius Reuter because he was a
good subject for historical biography. Films about two other European
celebrities of the nineteenth century, Pasteur and Zola, had been popular.
Several approaches from film-makers had been made to Reuters in London
during the 1930s. These had all come to nothing. But on 6 December 1938
Jones reported to the board that he had settled for a film to be made in
Hollywood by Warner Brothers. Jones had required that the script be
approved by Reuters, which meant in effect by himself.[26]

As finally made, the film was misleading in many details. Julius Reuter was
even shown impossibly addressing the House of Commons from the public
gallery. And to allow room for love interest, the Reuters were portrayed as
not yet married at the time of the Aachen pigeon service, which featured
prominently. *The Times* film critic (22 September 1941) neatly concluded that

'its general account of the rise of Reuters has not quite the reliability of Reuter's daily service'. Nevertheless, the film did succeed in conveying the innovative atmosphere of the early days, as Julius Reuter advanced from small beginnings to international status. Julius was played by Edward G. Robinson, glad to have a rest from his usual gangster parts. He rightly portrayed the agency's founder as cheerfully purposeful.

Jones asked for an epilogue to be added to the film, outlining the later history of Reuters. It was to include shots of himself as a young man in South Africa, and as chairman in London. The implication would have been that he was a second Julius Reuter. A Warner Brothers executive dismissed the idea sharply: 'it STINKS'. By the time of the film's release Jones was no longer in charge of Reuters.

ELEVEN

'In the Nature of a Trust'
1941–1963

I

AFTER receiving Sir Roderick Jones's resignation on 4 February 1941, the Reuter board immediately appointed Samuel Storey as chairman. This was proposed by James Henderson and seconded by Alexander Ewing. Henderson was the current PA chairman, and Storey's ally. Yet Ewing disliked Storey, and it is uncertain why he acted as he did. Probably because there was no alternative candidate of sufficient seniority, given that Ewing felt himself too old for the job at past 70.

Storey accepted without hesitation. He knew that much needed to be done, and he was ready to take the lead. If this was ambition, it was honourable ambition. Eight months later, at the PA meeting on 17 October 1941 which was to precipitate his resignation, Storey explained that he had 'welcomed the chance because although it was a great responsibility it was also a great opportunity'. He added that he had accepted the chairmanship without precise terms of appointment because he had expected full support from his board colleagues. In the event, he was soon to find himself at odds with a majority of them. The charge was quickly being made by Ewing and Haley that Storey was becoming a second Jones, acting as managing director as well as chairman.

Certainly, Storey began to give most of his time to Reuters. He resigned as managing director of his family newspaper group, and cut back his political work. He also arranged to sleep at Reuters. During his time as chairman, outward communications were greatly improved by the introduction of beam radio transmissions to different parts of the world. However, as Jones pointed out, this had been planned before Storey took over.

Ewing, Storey, and Haley had got rid of Jones by exploiting the Perth letter; but they had not got rid of the letter itself. With support from the Reuter board, Storey asked Sir Walter Monckton of the Ministry of Information for Clause A, referring to the appointment of a deputy to Jones, to be withdrawn as no longer applicable. Monckton agreed. But the requirement 'that Reuters will at all times bear in mind any suggestions' was not withdrawn. 'The rest of the letter will stand', wrote Monckton on 27 February 1941.[1]

Ewing had reluctantly recognized this in an important memorandum dated five days earlier. 'Until Monday, 3rd February 1941, I cherished the delusion that Reuter independence was no mere myth. The disclosures of the Perth correspondence proved that since August 1939 at least, the Chairman and Managing Director of the Company had sacrificed much of its claim to complete independence.' Paradoxically, Ewing recommended cooperation 'to the fullest extent with Government', in the hope that this would 'establish such improved relations as might induce them to ignore, if not to tear up, the humiliating and objectionable document'.

If the Perth letter was still a factor, so also was Sir Roderick Jones. Despite blaming him for the letter, Ewing kept in surprisingly close touch with the former chairman after his fall. They regularly dined or spoke privately together. Ewing found that Jones was ready to use his influence with his friends in the Newspaper Proprietors Association to encourage them to accept the idea of a partnership with the PA.

Ewing put his ideas on paper in a memorandum dated 22 February 1941, which was discussed by the Reuter board on 3 March. Ewing formally raised the idea of bringing in the NPA, and also the possibility of some sort of trust for Reuters. In response, Storey showed himself cool about NPA involvement, but interested in a trust without the NPA. 'PA might maintain its ownership', he wrote on his copy of the memorandum, 'but the Board be nominated or appointed by a Trust.'

That same evening, Ewing dined with Jones, who made notes of their conversation. Both men condemned Storey as an intriguer, who was making himself 'a fixture' as chairman. Ewing said that Haley was 'disgruntled' at not being appointed managing director by Storey. The recent allies were clearly falling out. Haley did not say in his diary that he wanted to become managing director, but he recorded on 23 March that he had gone down 'every week' from Manchester to London 'preparatory to reorganising the editorial'. Folk memory within Reuters recalled Haley sitting and watching with sharp eyes how the news was handled.

Two papers written at this period by Jones reflected his activity behind the scenes. One was a six-page discussion paper composed at the end of March for those in the NPA and PA who wanted the two bodies to join in the ownership of Reuters. The other was a memorandum written for his friend Sir Roy Webber, a former PA and Reuter director.

The discussion paper gave Jones's view of how the independence and effectiveness of Reuters might be promoted. The first step towards a more efficient Reuters, he argued, must be to vest the ownership in the British press as a whole; Reuters would then be able to work with the British Government 'without taint or suspicion'. Such consolidation behind one news agency, explained Jones giving numerous examples, had become the practice in many countries.

The centenary historian of Reuters was told by Jones ten years later (29 December 1950) that his authorship of this paper had been deliberately concealed. 'It was sufficient that I provided the powder and shot.' Similarly, Jones's memorandum for Webber (26 April 1941) was written as if it were entirely the latter's work. Its purpose was to influence the wider membership of the PA through Webber, who was a respected figure. The memorandum discussed the negotiations with the PA and NPA in 1925, when the press lords had refused to join in the equal ownership of Reuters. The time had now come, argued the memorandum, for the two parties to complete what ought to have been completed then.

In this way, Jones was able to prompt others; but he received no encouragement to re-emerge as a player on his own account, much though he would have liked to have done so. He even retained the unrealistic hope of returning as chairman of Reuters, in place of Storey. 'I said I would be willing to help out for a year or two if asked.'

Within the NPA, the keenest advocate of a deal with the PA was probably Lord Kemsley, who was a major provincial as well as a national newspaper proprietor. But the man who had to take the lead was the NPA chairman, Lord Rothermere of the *Daily Mail*. On 21 March the NPA formally requested a meeting with the PA directors. This took place on 8 April. Rothermere—heading a five-man deputation, which included Kemsley—read out a long memorandum. This recognized the need to strengthen Reuters, noticing the greatly increased competition inside the United Kingdom from the American agencies. The memorandum followed Jones's prompting by emphasizing that the national news agencies of the Dominions were already in co-operative press ownership. To achieve the same end, the PA was asked to sell half its Reuter shareholding to the NPA.

Most of the memorandum was constructive, but it did contain an element of threat:

> If common agreement cannot be found, we would have to ask Reuters to disclose to us what steps are being taken to organise a collection of news in the present German-controlled countries and elsewhere. Agencies that are now mere puppets of their Governments must be suspect for many years, and we would have to know the sources of foreign news so that we could determine whether we should remain as subscribers or organise our own news collecting

agency, or make other arrangements. We doubt if the provincial newspapers have the experience to satisfy us who have their representatives in all parts of the world.

The danger of the national newspapers setting up their own rival news agency had long been recognized by Reuters.

The PA directors disliked this part of the memorandum, and also Rothermere's brusque manner. They were unsettled by the meeting. The 50 per cent share demand, with an equal number of seats on the Reuter board, was more than the PA wanted to concede. The directors suspected that this was intended to produce NPA predominance. Storey was deputed to visit Rothermere to find out 'what the true objectives of the NPA were'.

At an informal meeting of five Reuter directors at Leeds on 15 April Storey reported that the interview had been unsatisfactory. Rothermere had not clarified his intentions. The five men discussed at length the NPA's threat to form a rival news organization, rival to the PA as well as to Reuters. Haley remarked that he was in a dilemma. He knew how between the wars the press lords had ruined or seized many provincial newspapers. He wanted co-operation with the NPA; but not if 'all the worst features of rivalry, cut-throat competition and "downing the other man" would reappear as soon as the war was over'.

Ewing was eager to do a deal if possible, for the sake of the PA as well as of Reuters. The PA was short of liquid resources to meet impending commitments; a Reuter share sale would ease this pressure. Storey was aware of the financial dimension, but he was already looking for some less risky alternative to forming a relationship with the NPA as a whole. He elaborated ideas for bringing in the NPA's newspaper groups on an individual basis. The five Reuter directors finally agreed to continue the negotiations, but simply in a spirit of enquiry.

At meetings of the PA board and consultative committee on 23 April Storey aired the idea of some sort of trust to protect Reuters, in which the NPA could participate alongside other institutions such as the Empire Press Union and the BBC. Haley supported the trust idea. But the trust which he had in mind was not intended negatively; it was to be more than simply an alternative to the NPA acquiring a half-share in Reuters. Instead, it was to be shaped high-mindedly to stand as an ultimate safeguard for Reuters—whether the NPA became an owner or not. Haley read out 'an outline of a Trust Deed'. Ewing had almost certainly seen this in advance, and in discussion he spoke of the PA's ownership of Reuters as being 'in the nature of a trust'. This formula was to feature centrally in the final trust document.

With the idea of a trust in mind as an ultimate safeguard, it became easier to accept the proposal of an equal shareholding for the NPA. Ewing and Haley were still hoping to carry Storey with them. Indeed, the three men had been appointed by the PA board as a negotiating sub-committee. On 24 April the full PA board held a second meeting with the five NPA representatives. The NPA now demanded not only equal representation on the board of Reuters, but also a full-time independent chairman. This brought Storey's future tacitly into the discussions. The press barons were not prepared to regard him as independent, and they doubted his competence. Ewing supported Storey's claims, but in negative terms: 'if the NPA came in it should be clear that they were not doing so because the present Board of Reuters was incapable of running the business. He personally did not want to embark on the task of looking for a new whole-time Chairman.' The NPA took back for consideration the idea of a 'non-dividend paying trust'.

A three-page handwritten note by Haley, dated 1 May 1941, marshalled his thoughts in preparation for a PA board meeting on that same day. 'Reuters need of new lifeblood and reorganization, the deal the great chance. It threatens to break down over Storey. We ourselves have never come to terms with Storey. But we did begin these negotiations with feeling that whatever happened Storey should be chairman.' Haley supported Storey's continuance in office, although not at the price of a fair deal with the NPA: 'the future of Reuters is bigger than any of us'.

Haley doubted whether in practice Storey could be abandoned. 'If we throw over Storey danger to Reuters. A second immediate shock to a vast and intricate organization. The effect on the General Managers of having a newcomer foisted upon them. The effect on the outside world.' Haley dismissed as 'dangerous' Rothermere's proposal for an independent outsider as chairman. 'To be handed over to a succession of amateurs.' Haley then mentioned his trust plan. 'Reuters regarded as a trust and we don't get rid of the trust when it has ceased to be a PA investment.'[2]

At the PA board on 1 May Ewing reported that in discussions with the NPA he had argued for the retention of Storey as chairman. Storey himself was present. Ewing added the qualification, however, that he would not be prepared to abort the negotiations 'on that point alone'. And for information, Haley relayed the NPA's case against Storey—that as a PA man he could not be independent; that he was 'an unknown quantity'; and that it was usual for a new board to elect a chairman. Storey replied that 'all he wanted was a fair chance to do the job'. The right structure for Reuters, argued Storey, was a 'working Chairman to supervise administrative–editorial co-operation'. In Storey's view, there was 'no room for a managing director at all'.

Up to this point, Ewing and Haley were still standing by Storey; but only just. A 'working chairman' was what Jones had been. They now began to wonder if Reuters needed a chairman at all, apart from someone to chair board meetings. Ewing told Jones on 6 May that four directors, including Ewing himself, were now ready to abandon Storey, 'and Haley apparently being the same way'. Haley may have been still slightly reluctant to break with a colleague with whom he had so recently worked closely. But after a meeting of the PA consultative committee on 6 May he was sent to tell Storey plainly that the PA declined to make his continuance as chairman a condition for agreement with the NPA.

In response, Storey circulated a five-page paper which spelled out his position. He complained that at each meeting with the NPA the PA had given ground. 'Take the Chairmanship of Reuters. You first insisted upon my retention of that office. Then you compromised upon my retention of it for a limited period and with a limited right of a casting vote. Now, some at least of you appear ready to deprive me of it at the dictation of Lord Rothermere and Lord Kemsley.' At a meeting of the PA consultative committee on 12 May Storey demanded that the PA should take a stand, breaking off negotiations unless the NPA accepted him as chairman for a minimum of two years. The press barons should be told that a Reuter Trust was to be created, which would hold all Reuter shares, the income being used to develop an independent British-owned news agency. This would demonstrate 'that you regard your ownership of Reuters as a trust and not as an investment'. The trustees and board should represent a wide range of outside bodies involved with Reuters.

Storey's position was much weakened by the chance that his membership of the PA board had come to an end a few days earlier, although he remained on the PA consultative committee. At the same time, Ewing had become PA chairman, which was another blow for Storey. On 12 May the PA board agreed 'to leave the whole matter of the [Reuter] chairmanship and the administration to the new board'. This was tantamount to rejecting Storey. He was replaced on the sub-committee negotiating with the NPA by Derwent of the Westminster Press group. The other members were Ewing and Haley.

Ewing now revealed his hostility to Storey very clearly. He expressed a wish for Haley to displace the present chairman by becoming managing director of Reuters 'if his company can spare him'. There would then be no need for a 'working chairman'. Ewing and Haley were sent by the PA board to tell Storey that he should give up. He refused. The split was complete.

2

Storey now began to campaign to rally support. He went to Monckton at the MOI, and complained that his critics were seeking to remove him. If Storey expected Monckton to say that the Government would not countenance a second change in the chairmanship, he was disappointed. Monckton offered no comment. Storey also tried to retain the support of Moloney and Chancellor, the two general managers (Turner was about to retire). The managers seem to have worked smoothly with Storey, and they now wrote expressing misgivings about the prospect of his removal, and requesting to address the Reuter board. Ewing and Haley concluded that the managers were being misled by Storey. They must be won back. Haley wrote to Ewing on 23 May:

> We want both Moloney and Chancellor (but Chancellor particularly) to look at this as the biggest opportunity in Reuters whole existence . . . bringing them hope, as giving Reuters its chance, at long last, to fight its rivals on an equal footing, as revivifying the whole organization from top to bottom, and as allowing every man in it the opportunity to do his damnedest without fear or favour, without a sense of defeat or frustration, but with the feeling that to be a member of Reuters is the greatest thing in the world.

Such was Haley's vision. He went to see the two managers together, and he also spoke to Chancellor separately, perhaps to point out his good long-term prospects within a revived Reuters. The two men were persuaded quietly to desert Storey. According to Haley writing to Ewing on 31 May, Chancellor spoke of the new vision as 'thrilling'. The pair withdrew their request for a hearing by the Reuter board.

So Storey's search for backing from the MOI and from the general managers had failed. From this time forward, although he was to fight a long rear-guard action lasting into the autumn, the initiative on the PA–Reuter side lay with Ewing and Haley. Nevertheless, James Henderson—who was a member of the PA board chaired by Ewing, as well as of the Reuter board—kept his friend, Storey, fully informed. Henderson also won over Malcolm Graham of the *Wolverhampton Express & Star*, who was a new member of both boards. Like Storey, Graham deeply distrusted the press barons.

At this point, the members of the NPA were not agreed among themselves, and their differences might well have led to a collapse of the whole negotiation. Lord Kemsley tried to keep things moving; but he was not totally disinterested. Ewing told Jones on 7 July that Kemsley wanted to become chairman of Reuters himself, a move to which Lord Beaverbrook was strongly opposed. For this and other reasons, Beaverbrook's lieutenant, E. J. Robertson, had been making difficulties.

According to Ewing, Beaverbrook was keeping Churchill, the Prime Minister, informed (or misinformed) about the negotiations. But Beaverbrook's was not the only voice. In July Churchill appointed his friend, Brendan Bracken, as Minister of Information. Bracken was himself a successful newspaperman, and he began to take a knowledgeable interest in what was being proposed for Reuters.[3]

'The Reuter deal still hangs fire', wrote Haley in his diary on 13 July. Eight days later, however, he was noting that 'the NPA are biting again'. He repeated to himself the case for doing away with the chairmanship. 'How Storey will like the idea I don't know, but I am convinced it is all wrong and too dangerous for Reuters to be under his or any other person's single control.'

At the PA board on 28 July, with Ewing in the chair, Henderson proposed and Graham seconded that negotiations with the NPA be broken off; but this was voted down by five votes to two. According to Ewing's account to Jones next day, Ewing said that he would now respond speedily to an NPA request for more information about Reuters. To lose the deal, argued Ewing, could be dangerous. 'He hinted at both the Ministry and the PM wanting it.' If disappointed, Ewing feared that the Government might reduce its support for Reuters, and might turn instead to competitors such as the Exchange Telegraph.

Henderson had apparently stalked out of the PA board meeting after being voted down. This did not augur well for the Reuter board meeting next day (29 July), chaired by Storey and with Henderson and Graham present—to face again the five (including Ewing and Haley) who as PA directors had refused to abort the negotiations. A confrontation duly occurred, described by Ewing to Jones and written up by him on 30 July. Storey asked formally, what he must have known already, whether any decision had been reached by the PA about the negotiations. Henderson answered that the PA board had decided to continue the negotiations, although he himself had voted against. 'Storey said emphatically he was of opinion that he, as Chairman of Reuters, ought to have been consulted.' Henderson and Graham supported him. This angered Ewing, 'and the proceedings became so hot that Ewing said there was nothing to do but adjourn the meeting':

> 'Until when?', said Henderson.
> 'Well—until some time tomorrow, or even maybe Thursday if we can't get the
> NPA response in time for further consideration by the PA board.'
> H[enderson]. 'In that case I shall not be able to be present.'

E[wing]. 'That I fear will be no loss—so far you have not assisted the proceedings—quite the reverse.'
(Henderson silent, pale and furious!)

Storey then hurried out of the room. The other directors stood up, and Henderson said:

'Well this is a pretty mess we've got ourselves into.'
E[wing]. 'For which you are mainly responsible—it was you who moved Storey be Chairman, the moment Sir R.J. left the room upon *his* resignation.'
H[enderson]. 'I fear I must admit that—it was an unwise step.'

Jones commented that this was a 'strange admission' from Henderson. But perhaps he was simply regretting that he had let Storey in for so much trouble.

During the next few days, progress began to be made with the NPA. 'At last', Haley wrote in his diary on 3 August, 'we have got the NPA into line, but Storey threatens trouble.' Haley arranged a private meeting with Rothermere. Such informal contacts were important throughout. Gradually, NPA prejudice against the PA's provincial newspapermen had been reduced by personal contacts through the Newsprint Supply Company, a wartime body within which the national and provincial papers had perforce to work together. Haley wrote in his diary on 14 September that he had spent four days in London 'trying to finish up the Reuter Trust', although supposedly on holiday with his family. 'At last we have it all straightened out with the NPA, and it is only a case of waiting to see if Storey will summon a meeting of the members. Even so the thing should go through, and I can take a fair share of the credit for getting the trust into being.'

The three general managers produced a paper for the Reuter board on 8 September which supported the idea of NPA involvement so long as it meant recognition of the agency's importance as a 'great national asset'. At the PA consultative committee on the same day Ewing had claimed that the War Cabinet was keen for the emerging deal to go through. Storey checked with Clement Attlee, the Deputy Prime Minister, who apparently did not confirm the claim: 'a lie', exclaimed Storey.

On 10 September Ewing had written formally as chairman of the PA to tell Storey as chairman of Reuters that two days previously the PA board had decided by five votes to two (Henderson and Graham dissenting) to sell half of its Reuter shares to the NPA. Moloney and Chancellor had attended the PA board by invitation, and had supported the proposal. Ewing's letter to Storey insisted that this was a wise decision: 'and it is equally wise to complete the sale without calling a meeting of members. No member', claimed Ewing, 'could possibly express a useful view without long examination of the numerous documents relating to the safeguards which have been provided.'

This was unconvincing. Ewing was never going to persuade the Storey party to acquiesce without an appeal to the PA membership at large. After some procedural manœuvring, an extraordinary general meeting of the PA was called for 17 October 1941.

3

During the five weeks before this meeting, the arguments for and against the PA selling half its stake in Reuters to the NPA were much rehearsed as both sides lobbied for support. The Storey party did not object to the national press buying an interest in Reuters, only to the NPA as a body being allowed an equal holding. Storey contended that if the NPA obtained half the Reuter shares, it would be in a position of potential dominance, since some of its members already held a quarter stake in the PA through their ownership of numerous provincial newspapers. The commitment of Reuters to truth and independence might one day be sacrificed by the press barons for their own commercial ends. They might ruin Reuters and disrupt the PA. In addition to these fears for the future, Storey and his supporters did not like being told, at least by implication, that they were incapable of running an international news agency on their own.

The Ewing–Haley party answered that the PA urgently needed the money which a sale of half its Reuter shares would produce. They were also concerned about the financial burden for the future if the PA continued in sole ownership of Reuters. They argued that they had devised machinery in the form of the Reuter Trust which would prevent the NPA (or any other interest group) from dominating the agency. Meanwhile, under the protection of the Trust, the modernization of the news side would benefit from the long experience of the national newspapers in the collection of overseas news. In general, the Ewing–Haley party believed that the standing as well as the effectiveness of Reuters would gain from ownership by the whole British press. Not least, it would be better placed to resist pressure from the British Government.

Were Ewing and Haley right in these claims? Certainly, the terms finally agreed were carefully contrived to protect the PA interest in Reuters, while at the same time allowing the NPA an equal shareholding. The NPA's members—with the exception of Beaverbrook's *Express* group—agreed to buy half the issued capital of Reuters at £4.10s per share, the price paid by the PA

in 1930. The NPA therefore paid £168,768 for 37,504 shares. This new holding was designated 'B' stock, the remaining PA holding 'A' stock. The composition of the new Reuter board was to be elaborately balanced. It was to
contain three directors from the PA and three from the NPA; and even if one
or two directors were absent, each side was to retain its right to cast three
votes. No permanent chairman was to be appointed. The directors were to
take the chair in turn at each meeting, and there was to be no casting vote.

Haley, the prime inspiration behind these checks and balances, noted in his
diary on 12 October:

> Chancellor told me Storey is spreading it abroad that I am ditching him so that
> I can get the chairmanship. The complete answer to that is that it is I who have
> destroyed the chairmanship. As I said to Bracken: 'Reuters has been run by a
> Baron. It has been run by a Knight. It is now being run by an MP. It is time it
> was run by some honest-to-goodness newspapermen.' Bracken agreed.

The declaration of trust, as finally settled, expressed itself in language of
some solemnity. The hand of high-thinking Haley was apparent. The preamble referred to the immediate wartime situation:

> The Press Association and the Newspaper Proprietors Association recognising
> that the present national emergency and the uncertainties of the future render
> necessary special precautions to ensure in the national interest that Reuters be
> so established and consolidated that in every event it shall preserve its position
> as the leading world news agency have mutually agreed to enter into this
> Agreement.

Here was shrewd manipulation of the idea of 'national interest'. Far from
denying its relevance in wartime, the preamble simply assumed that the intention to secure the independence of Reuters must be in the national interest.

The main part of the declaration of trust was clear in language and high in
purpose:

> The Press Association and the Newspaper Proprietors Association hereby
> record their mutual agreement that they will regard their respective holdings
> of shares in Reuters as in the nature of a trust rather than as an investment and
> hereby undertake to use their best endeavours to ensure:
> (a) That Reuters shall at no time pass into the hands of any one interest group
> or faction.
> (b) That its integrity independence and freedom from bias shall at all times be
> fully preserved.
> (c) That its business shall be so administered that it shall supply an unbiased and
> reliable news service to British Dominion Colonial Foreign and other overseas
> newspapers and agencies with which it has or may hereafter have contracts.

(d) That it shall pay due regard to the many interests which it serves in addition to those of the Press, and

(e) That no effort shall be spared to expand develop and adapt the business of Reuters in order to maintain in every event its position as the leading world news agency.

The PA and NPA were each to appoint four trustees, under a chairman to be approved by the Lord Chief Justice. The trustees were given a five-year term. Their function was 'to act in a consultative capacity with the Board', but 'in accordance with the principles enunciated in this Agreement'. They were to appoint three 'A' directors from the PA and three 'B' directors from the NPA. The Trust was to last for a minimum of twenty-one years.

On 17 October 1941 the crucial emergency general meeting of the PA was held under Ewing's chairmanship in the conference room at 85 Fleet Street. Over sixty people crammed into the room. The meeting lasted all day. Great strength of feeling was apparent on both sides, but Ewing kept the underlying personal animosities under sufficient control. By the day of the meeting Storey's supporters knew that they were likely to be in a minority, because many of those present had been instructed to vote for the agreement regardless of what was said at the meeting. Nevertheless, Henderson and Storey delivered well-argued speeches. Ewing, who spoke first, was very long, but ended cogently. Haley confined himself to answering specific points, and he thought that he had spoken well. Certainly, the official report of the meeting noted that Haley's speech terminated in applause; but so also did Storey's.[4]

There was much discussion of the NPA's April memorandum. Storey and Henderson argued that its partly threatening language demonstrated that the NPA ought never to be trusted with equal control. Ewing and Haley assured the meeting that they thought the memorandum to be, in Ewing's words, 'a remarkably reasonable statement'. Storey countered that they had not found it so reasonable at first hearing in April. He revealed that Haley had then expressed uncertainty about the NPA's intentions, and had said that any deal would be a gamble. Haley was much annoyed by this awkward revelation. He explained that he was now convinced that the NPA was acting in the right spirit. Storey remained unconvinced. He was also critical of the arrangements intended to restrain the press barons if necessary. As a lawyer, he pointed out—what was not admitted by Reuters for forty years—that the Trust declaration, presented by Haley as sure protection, was in fact no more than a shareholders' agreement which could be undone if the shareholders so decided: 'the shareholders can at any time get rid even of the camouflage of the Trust by putting Reuters into voluntary liquidation.' Even while the Trust was in being, added Storey, the trustees had no teeth; 'although nominally they will appoint the directors they can only nominate those nominated by the shareholders'. Haley's inadequate answer was that the trustees would have the power to remove any directors.

Storey was sure that Ewing, Haley, and Derwent had been tricked by the NPA. Storey reminded his audience of the limerick about the young lady from Riga who went for a ride on a tiger. 'May I carry that tale further: Three men from the Reuter–PA Boards went out for a ride with two Press lords; they came back from the ride, Reuter–PA inside, and smile on the face of the Press lords.'

In the end, a Storey supporter proposed that the sale should not go through; and that instead participation by the national newspaper groups should be sought on an individual basis, which would leave the PA in control. This was rejected on a show of hands by 43 votes to 17. Henderson called for a poll. The proposal was then defeated by 5,024 votes to 2,272. The Storey party always maintained that this majority had been obtained only thanks to votes representing the provincial editions of London newspapers, and of provincial titles within the London newspaper groups. But the official historian of the PA has concluded that, even without such votes, there would still have been a small majority from the independent provincial press against the resolution. Storey maintained, however, that the votes of the *Yorkshire Post* ought also to have been discounted. The *Post's* managing director had worked with Storey to secure the calling of an extraordinary meeting; and yet he was forced to switch sides at the last minute under instructions from his chairman, who was thought to have come under NPA pressure.

Storey made one last effort to stop what he regarded as a disastrous course for Reuters. He feared the NPA even more than he feared the British Government, and he was now prepared to accept official intervention if this would produce different terms for the reconstruction of Reuters. He therefore promoted a debate in the House of Commons five days after the PA general meeting.

Storey began his Commons speech by emphasizing his disinterestedness. He was chairman of Reuters, but he took no salary as chairman. He then restated his case against the proposed scheme—that the NPA might come to dominate Reuters; that what was needed was a 'genuine trust' to represent the various groups interested in its services, without any group gaining predominance. Storey asked Ministers to intervene: 'they must act quickly'. In reply, Brendan Bracken, the Minister of Information, agreed that Reuters could not continue as it was, for during the past dozen years it had lost ground to AP, the American agency, 'in a most remarkable way'. But Bracken did not accept that 'the bold bad barons of Fleet Street' would act unscrupulously if they became equal owners of Reuters. Nevertheless, the Government promised to keep a 'fatherly eye' upon what was happening.

The very next day (23 October) Bracken and Sir Kingsley Wood, the Chancellor of the Exchequer, met a deputation consisting of Ewing, Haley, and Derwent from the PA, and Rothermere, Kemsley, and Astor from the NPA. Kingsley Wood reiterated that the Government did not want to run Reuters itself. It did want an independent outside chairman of the Reuter board, or at least of the new trustees. In other words, the Government was not challenging the new arrangements, but was proposing additional safe-guards. Both sides finally agreed that the chairman of trustees should come from outside journalism, which would underline his independence. Haley accepted this only 'after some hesitation'.

Kingsley Wood also asked for the BBC to be offered a one-third share in Reuters. The idea of BBC participation had been circulating intermittently throughout the year. The Reuter directors were against it; and Ewing was glad to tell Kingsley Wood that the BBC itself was now unsure whether it really wanted to become an owner. Several BBC executives had voiced sec-ond thoughts, in part because some observers thought that Reuters was Government-controlled. Public opinion might therefore consider a link to be damaging for the BBC. Conversely, Reuters opposed any formal ties partly because the BBC was itself widely believed to be under official direction. Bracken closed the discussion by saying that the present was not the right time for BBC participation. On 6 November the BBC board contented itself with expressing satisfaction that the Reuter Trust provisions were promising 'due regard' to the interests of non-press subscribers, such as itself.[5]

On 25 October a letter appeared in *The Times* from Sir Roderick Jones, welcoming the new ownership plan but denying that Reuters had lost ground to AP. Next day a letter from Storey appeared in the same paper, defending the performance of Reuters under his chairmanship.

Storey, as much as Jones, was becoming a man with a past in Reuters but no future. Yet he had still not resigned as chairman. Finally, at the board on 28 October he was formally removed. Immediately beforehand the PA board had met under Ewing and had authorized the transfer back to the PA of Storey's single qualifying share as a Reuter director. The transfer document was tabled at the Reuter board, with Storey himself in the chair. The minutes simply recorded: 'Mr. Storey having thus ceased to be a Director he then withdrew.' That same evening Ewing described the scene to Jones. 'Storey as Chairman said the transfer was in order. He signed it and then said: "Gentlemen, that naturally severs my connexion with Reuters and the Reuter board. Good day."'

So for a second time within the year the chairman of Reuters had been forced out in circumstances of high tension. Who, if anyone, was to blame?

Ewing and Haley, on the one hand, and Storey, on the other, were all men of high principle; and yet they quarrelled in 1941, and were never to be reconciled. Storey deeply distrusted the press barons, which in the light of experience between the wars was reasonable. But his fears about the NPA's intentions were not to be realized. The national press proprietors never tried to exploit their position within Reuters for their own advantage. Indeed, from 1945, three leading NPA personalities—Lord Rothermere, Lord Layton, and Guy Bartholemew—played active and constructive parts as Reuter directors. Christopher Chancellor welcomed their involvement, and only began to complain when during the 1950s lesser NPA figures were appointed. This added to the pressure upon him as general manager caused by the lack of a regular chairman. Over-reacting to Storey's wish to be a 'working chairman', Ewing and Haley had contrived to leave Reuters with no proper chairman at all.

The 1941 Reuter Trust arrangements also proved to be imperfect. This was pointed out in 1950 by Lord Goddard, the Lord Chief Justice. In the 1941 declaration of trust the Lord Chief Justice had been given the power to name the chairman of the Reuter trustees, and to monitor the Trust's functioning. On 12 July 1950 Chancellor communicated to the trustees Goddard's opinion that 'the documents governing Reuters were most peculiar from a legal point of view. There was not a Trust Deed but a Trust Agreement.' Here was a crucial distinction. 'Lord Goddard told him that the documents could in actual fact be changed without his consent.' In other words, the arrangement was, as Storey had said, no more than a shareholders' agreement. Goddard declined to commit any future Lord Chief Justice to involvement with the Reuter Trust.

In 1941 the then Lord Chief Justice had named Sir Lynden Macassey, an arbitration lawyer, as the independent chairman of the trustees. At the end of 1950 Macassey was eased out. Thereafter, the trustees chose their chairmen themselves, without reference to the Lord Chief Justice; and all came with backgrounds in journalism.

No publicity was given by Reuters to the discovery in 1950 that the much-heralded Reuter Trust provisions—proclaimed as a certain safeguard, and as a model for other news agencies—were well-intentioned but flawed. A copy of the Trust document was said to have been always carried in Chancellor's pocket when he travelled to negotiate abroad. In 1941 Storey had voiced strong doubts about the supposed impregnability of the Trust provisions. He had been proved right. Yet Haley kept the credit for a job well done.

4

Under the reshaped board, Christopher Chancellor and Walton Cole led Reuters together throughout the later years of the Second World War and during the post-war period. Chancellor was already a Reuter figure of long-standing: Cole only joined in 1942, but he soon made himself indispensable.

Chancellor's earlier career has already been noticed. He was general manager in the Far East from 1932 to 1939, and he became joint general manager in London from August 1939, just days before the outbreak of the Second World War. In 1944 he was left as sole general manager, when his colleague W. J. Moloney retired. In the face of strong competition, especially from the American agencies, and with limited resources, Reuters under Chancellor was always going to find it hard to gain acceptance as 'the leading world news agency'. Yet he was determined to act as if it could be made so; or at the least, he was keen to ensure that Reuters did not lose more ground. To emphasize the break with the past made in 1941, Chancellor liked to speak thereafter of 'the new Reuters'. Yet one of his successors, Gerald Long, later likened him to Horatius at the bridge, skilful in defence but limited in what he could otherwise achieve.[6]

At the time of his departure from Reuters in 1959 Chancellor remarked that for fifteen years the agency had been 'largely identified in the eyes of its customers and staff with my own personality'. In the absence of a regular chairman, he had been expected to combine a representational role with that of chief executive. This made his considerable diplomatic skills the more necessary. 'His quiet and strangely unvarying tone of voice', noted one obituary, 'was suited to commanding respect, even fear'. Certainly, Chancellor's smooth manner scarcely concealed his underlying firmness of purpose, or his sharp mind. He could swiftly penetrate to the heart of any problem or document.[7]

And yet there was more sensitivity behind Chancellor's surface coolness and rationality than most people realized. Many of his personal letters to Cole showed him looking for emotional support within their working relationship: 'I miss you deeply when you are away and feel quite alone in dealing with all the things that come along' (23 March 1955). Man to man, such intensity of expression may seem surprising. Lacking a chairman to turn to, Chancellor had turned to Cole.

One serious criticism was to recur throughout Chancellor's career. In his dealings with others was he flexible to the point of being 'devious'? Many remembered him so. Someone—perhaps in Australia—dubbed him 'crafty

Chris', at work in tandem with Cole who was labelled 'phoney Tony'. In 1942 the head of the Foreign Office news department, William Ridsdale, minuted acidly: 'we must regard Mr. Chancellor's effort to palm off on the Secretary of State his own suggestion for circulating a note about "the new deal" in Reuters as characteristic of his methods'. Of course, Chancellor's position often required him to face more ways than one, because he was seeking to find strength for Reuters while trying to conceal weakness. A more straightforward personality might have done less well.[8]

As for Cole, if indeed he appeared to be 'phoney' to harsh critics, this was perhaps because he had risen from modest beginnings, particularly in comparison with Chancellor. Both men were Scots, but otherwise their origins were very different. Whereas Chancellor had come from an old Lowland family of landowners, and was educated at Eton and Cambridge, Walton Adamson ['Tony'] Cole (1912–63) had left secondary school in Edinburgh at 15. He first became a junior reporter on the *Scotsman*, and then went to the *Falkirk Herald*, where his 'nose for a story' began to be noticed. In 1935 he moved to London as a reporter for the Press Association. By 1939 he had been made night editor. Cole and Chancellor first met when they became members of the PA–Reuter Home Guard (both were mere privates); and they also came together in the basement of 85 Fleet Street from where during air raids Reuter and PA news was distributed.[9]

In the crisis year of 1941 one problem for Reuters was that it could not find from outside a dynamic new editor-in-chief to oversee the improved news service which Haley in particular was determined to develop. As a last resort, Chancellor himself was made editor in March 1942. He remained also a general manager, and the intention was that he should concentrate upon the news side for only a short time while new blood was being introduced into the newsroom. From 1 April Cole was transferred from the PA upon Chancellor's recommendation to become joint news manager at Reuters. 'He was much more of a professional than I was,' Chancellor recalled in an obituary, 'interested above all in the techniques of journalism.' As early as 16 May 1942 Chancellor was already telling Haley: 'Cole is a winner.' He soon became a dominant figure, working a fifteen-hour day and sleeping at 85 Fleet Street for months on end. By 1945 he had become managing editor, linking through his presence the administrative seventh floor with the editorial fifth. After Cole had established himself, Chancellor was rarely seen at the lower level.

Cole's rapid rise did not mean that he was himself a good writer. He tended to be wordy, and his command of grammar was suspect. His strength was that he could spot a good story, and he could motivate better writers than himself.

He could also organize and re-organize the news services. He was, in short, a great news editor.

Although his approach to journalism was intuitive rather than cerebral, he subscribed enthusiastically to the ideal of truth in news, and he regarded Reuters as having a special mission to promote that ideal. He expected all Reuter journalists to match his own commitment, even though they were being paid less than other journalists. In this expectation his strong personality and 18 stone bulk carried everyone with him, as Sandy Gall (a young Reuter correspondent in the 1950s) recalled:

> The huge figure rose and propelled me by apparent force of personality towards the door. I tried to say something about a rise in pay, but he brushed my feeble attempt aside with what I discovered later was his standard and classic phrase. 'Don't worry about the money now old boy', he drawled, towering over me, although I was just as tall as he was. 'Keep in touch, ole boy . . . so long.'[10]

Cole's huge figure became a trademark for Reuters. Once, when he and Chancellor landed at Cairo airport, the royal guard turned out because they thought that he was King Farouk, then still on the throne. Cole's appetite for food and drink—soda water after he gave up alcohol—was enormous, an intake which he transformed into instant energy. He needed little sleep, and worked all hours, even at home. His intense involvement was at first necessary, but later came to seem excessive. He feared the emergence of rivals who might cheat him of the succession to Chancellor. Though he encouraged others to do well for Reuters, he did not want them to rise too far. He pursued a policy of divide and rule.

Cole's many tours to overseas offices were occasions for developing local contacts and for signing contracts; but at the same time he watched the progress of Reuter people. His visits were occasions of considerable tension. In January 1955 David Chipp—then a South-East Asia correspondent, and later (1958–60) personal assistant to Cole—described in his private diary a visit by 'the great man' to Rangoon and Bangkok:

> Wed. Jan. 19. After days of anxious waiting the great man arrived . . . In great good form and luckily impressed with my airport contacts. Carrying a huge briefcase called 85 Fleet Street . . .
>
> Sat. Jan. 22. Vital day. Clinched deal with The Nation, and laid foundation for economic one with the government. First Prof. Tun Thin who had schedule for Comtel all prepared. Obviously very keen. Thought Information Minister, Tun Win, was going to run out on us, but he saw WAC in end. Latter very tough and impressive . . .
>
> Sun. Jan. 23. Arrived at WAC's room at 06.45 and we got straight down to report. With only short break for breakfast we went on right to lunch.

Tues. Jan. 25. Impressions of Cole—obviously NOT a gent and likes to hear good opinions of himself. Wears made-up bow ties. But he certainly gets things done and is a real worker; a good companion. Completely ruthless, and I found myself going under his spell.

As negotiators, Cole and Chancellor made a contrasting pair: Chancellor cool and slim, Cole warm and large, exuding a rare magnetism. The British manager of the Arab News Agency recalled how Cole could win over initially unsympathetic Arabs 'by some curious radiation of goodwill that seemed to depend little on words or acts'.[11]

Towards Chancellor, Cole was supportive to the point of being deferential. He said 'Sir Christopher', never 'Christopher'. What, in return, Chancellor really thought about his self-made colleague was never quite clear to others, who of course did not see his personal letters to Cole. 'Your companionship', Chancellor told Cole on 20 August 1951, 'is among the few fundamental things that mean everything to me in my life.' Chancellor praised Cole to Sir Keith Murdoch of AAP (9 June 1950) as an 'outstandingly able man' who 'could hold his own in any profession in any country'. Yet Cole was sometimes laughed at by Chancellor in the presence of others. And the general manager was once heard to remark only half-jokingly that 'Reuters isn't quite the place for a gentleman'. Was he here separating himself socially from his colleagues, including Cole? And yet at the same time, was he implying that someone like Cole could be well suited to Reuters even if not a gentleman—acknowledging that what mattered was not the social standing of the two men outside Reuters but their good working relationship within it?[12]

5

As soon as the new ownership had been established in October 1941 Reuters began to seek a fresh relationship with the British Government, a relationship no longer conditioned by the Perth letter. At the beginning of that year the Ministry of Information had tried to prohibit the publication of enemy communiqués in the overseas services of Reuters; but the idea of such prohibition had been firmly resisted. Reuters insisted that it must publish overseas even bad news for the British cause. Monckton, the MOI's director-general, had reluctantly agreed with Storey on 21 February 1941 that 'Reuters are still at liberty to include the substance of enemy communiqués in their service in a form which would exclude propaganda'.

The joint committee of Reuters and the MOI continued to meet. Reuters produced a paper for the committee on 11 February entitled 'Some proposed methods of combating the effect of enemy communiqués other than by suppression'. It recommended 'a persistent spoken, written, broadcast and whispering campaign' to undermine confidence in enemy communiqués. Reuters would continue to publish them, but counter-propaganda from the MOI could be included in the same overseas radio transmission.[13]

The difficulty was that this combination required the submission of every enemy communiqué to the Ministry, in case it wanted to comment. Reuters began to find such delay damaging. On 10 December 1941 publication of a Japanese communiqué announcing the sinking of the British warships *Prince of Wales* and *Repulse*—a major disaster in the new war in the Far East—was delayed for an hour. Meanwhile, AP had sent the news from London to New York. The New York office complained that this delay had given the impression to American subscribers that Reuters was trying to suppress unpleasant news. An explanation on 23 December from Cyril Radcliffe, Monckton's successor, was more alarming than soothing. 'Any other arrangement would leave Reuters in effect in the same position in its relations with the Ministry as any other news agency with which we maintained no special connection. But, of course, we have special connections with Reuters.' Such an answer, if accepted, would have left Reuters tightly bound.

With this in mind, on 27 January 1942 the Reuter directors, plus Moloney and Chancellor, met Radcliffe. Haley presided. The discussion proved to be fruitful. The Perth letter had declared 'that Reuters will at all times bear in mind any suggestions made to them on behalf of His Majesty's Government'. Radcliffe now accepted that Reuters 'would not be expected to include anything in its service as a result of Government directives'. He did ask, however, for more effort by Reuters to understand 'how news which it sends abroad can affect Government policy throughout the world'. On the question of enemy communiqués, the meeting agreed that there must be consultation 'where a major British disaster is in question'. Otherwise, if no speedy comment came from the MOI, Reuters was to be free to transmit a communiqué abroad. In this way Reuters clarified its relationship with the British Government over the handling of news.[14]

On 11 August 1942 Anthony Eden, the Foreign Secretary, lunched at 85 Fleet Street with the Reuter board, and toured the editorial floor. At Chancellor's request, Eden had circulated a note about Reuters to British missions abroad. Chancellor was seeking recognition for what he liked to call 'the new Reuters', but Eden's circular of 20 July was more qualified than Chancellor expected:

> The present management admit that Reuters' standard of efficiency in recent years has left much to be desired and declare their anxiety to improve matters

> . . . Reuters naturally desire that their representatives abroad should receive all
> possible help from His Majesty's Missions . . . While helping Reuters in every
> way, it would of course be unwise to discriminate against competent and well-
> disposed correspondents of other British or American agencies or newspapers.

By 1941 British Government payments for extra wordage in Reuter radio
transmission overseas were running at almost three times the payment to the
British Post Office from Reuters itself—£15,000 per annum from Reuters,
and £44,000 from the Government. Did these large official payments constitute a subsidy? The Reuter board decided that, at least in their existing form,
they did. On 1 June 1943 it therefore resolved 'to complete the liquidation of
the emergency arrangements with the Ministry of Information'. In a letter to
Radcliffe on 22 September 1943 Chancellor included a transcript of this resolution. He explained that it covered all arrangements between the
Government and Reuters 'dating from 1939, details of which will be available
to you at the Ministry'. Thus, in this decisive but unexcited fashion, the provisions of the Perth letter were finally repudiated by Reuters.

Yet the same board resolution promised that there would be no contrac-
tion of Reuter activities. How then were Government payments to the Post
Office in aid of Reuter transmissions to be reconciled with the new spirit of
detachment? At a meeting on 7 September the Reuter board decided that the
continuing need for cheap transmission rates could be satisfied, without hint
of subsidy, if cheap rates were made available to all. A low tariff for every user,
Chancellor told Radcliffe, 'could in no way be called a subsidy to Reuters and
it would be analogous to the Empire press rate'. Yet in practice little changed.
Because the transmission facilities available in wartime remained very limited,
Reuters alone benefited from these low rates. In addition, the British
Government continued to make up the difference between what Reuters
paid and the actual transmission costs—a gap of £80,000.[15]

A really new start was not made until the beginning of 1945. And, paradoxically, pressure for this came more from the British Government than
from Reuters. The very fact that the agency was editorially independent had
led some officials to ask why so much was being spent. 'On the editorial side
the subsidy has brought with it no advantage. Its removal will take none
away.' Sir Alexander Cadogan, the head of the Foreign Office, had expressed
concern to Radcliffe of the MOI (20 January 1944) that 'the subsidy element
in our relations with Reuters . . . does so much to prejudice our relations in
the field of international news with the Americans'. The American agencies
had asked the British Post Office for similar cheap rates to those enjoyed by
Reuters. Reuters could not object. The outcome was a new higher tariff
which left Reuters with extra expenditure of £64,00 per annum.[16]

The British Government remained ready to help by paying generous subscriptions for services. An agreement was made between Chancellor and Radcliffe on 17 February 1945, summarized for the Reuter board on 1 March:

> 1. Existing British Government 'subscriptions', totalling about £15,000 per annum, were to be 'crystallised' as at 25 January, and were to be altered only to meet changes in 'out-of-pocket' expenses of Reuters. But to this end, £10,000 had already been added to the £15,000 from 1 January 1945.
>
> 2. British Government offices overseas were to be supplied with the Reuter service 'for internal use'. This news could be published in some weekly British information bulletins issued locally, but only with specific permission from Reuters.
>
> 3. Reuter and Press Association services were to be provided for use in the British Official Wireless service at a subscription of £4,000 per year.
>
> 4. Reuters was to be paid £6,000 a year for sending the Forcereuter service on the European and Eastern transmitters to British servicemen abroad.[17]

Chancellor explained the new arrangement in a circular sent to correspondents on 11 April 1945. Total British Government payments would, he admitted, be worth approximately £35,000 per annum. But this would not imply any special relationship, because the payments would be subscriptions, such as even the American agencies accepted from various governments. What Chancellor did not admit was that the payments were deliberately very generous.

Against this background, when in January 1946 the American State Department issued a booklet on *The Post-war International Information Programme of the United States*, which claimed that Reuters was still subsidized by the British Government, Chancellor felt free to publish a vigorous denial (4 January 1946), which was widely reported. He expressed indignation that the State Department 'should seek deliberately to smear an organisation which, although it may happen to be British, represents a high conception'.

Three weeks later (28 January 1946) Chancellor spoke in the same spirit to a meeting of journalists at Washington. 'We are British because we are co-operatively owned by British newspapers. But we are not doing a British job. We are doing an international job.' Yet to the British Foreign Office, whose generous subscriptions were needed by Reuters, Chancellor changed the emphasis. On 8 January he had privately told the British Foreign Secretary, Ernest Bevin, that 'it was an essential British interest for Reuters to develop as a great independent world service based upon London, sharply distinguished from British publicity services in every form'.

The Foreign Office remained critical of the performance of Reuters. In 1947 it circularized British missions abroad for comments about the local operations of the agency. Six main criticisms were collected in reply—that Reuters was 'insufficiently represented'; that Reuter management was 'over-cautious in its financial policy', seeking to make a profit everywhere; that it did not cater for the tastes of its customers; that it did not offer foreign language services in certain parts of the world where these were in demand; that its managerial methods were not always up-to-date; and that its news distribution needed speeding up. Chancellor soon got to hear of the survey; but the Foreign Office decided not pass on the collected complaints. One Information Policy Department official concluded (6 October 1948) that he must 'walk warily': 'they are completely independent of Government control, highly sensitive to criticism of any kind . . . we have also to consider the Agency's difficulties (they are largely financial) which at present seem to militate against any radical improvement.'[18]

The Foreign Office had long been particularly keen for Reuters to establish itself in Latin America. The 1927 renewal of the international news agency ring had allowed Reuters right of entry into the area, where Havas had previously been left as the leading European agency. In 1931 Sir Roderick Jones had decided upon a big effort. After a sales-promotion visit to South America, the Prince of Wales had spoken publicly of the need 'to improve the present very inadequate news service in South America'. Here was a challenge to Jones's patriotism. Reuters started to distribute its news in South America through a service centred upon Argentina. But this comprised only 1,000 words per day, compared with between 10,000 and 15,000 daily from the American agencies. After three years, the losses had become insupportable, and Reuters withdrew.[19]

The fall of France in 1940 brought a new opportunity. The Foreign Office asked Reuters to take over from Havas. Chancellor went out in the summer of 1940 (and again in 1943) to organize the service. Initially, this largely meant re-engaging the Havas staff, although most were later replaced. Reuters started with what Jones described to the board on 1 November 1940 as a 'blanket grant' from the British Government of about £30,000 to cover expenditure not met by revenue. Transmission to South America of the Globereuter and other services was subsidized to the extent of 11,000 words daily.

Gross revenue built up well—from approximately £73,000 in 1941 to £108,000 in 1950. These totals exceeded revenue from North America, and made South America in 1950 the third overseas revenue-earner after Europe (£235,000) and the Far East (£127,000). But expenses were always high, and

Reuters could never afford to start a service of Latin American news, prefer-ably in Spanish, for sale alongside its world news. Such a regional service was essential for lasting success and profitability. Instead—for reasons of economy, and to the dismay of the British Government—a policy of concentration upon Argentina, Chile, and Brazil was tried after the end of the war. This amounted to a tacit admission that Reuters could not compete fully with the American agencies. Even in Argentina, Reuters remained only a supplemen-tary service. It could not offer news pictures, such as the Americans provided. The 1951 centenary history expressed surprise 'that Reuters stayed in Latin America at all'.[20]

The policy of concentration eliminated losses from the smaller republics, but the position was never secure. During the 1950s news revenue from the region collapsed, partly because of local currency devaluations. In 1958 the drastic decision was taken to give up supplying general news to Argentina, Uruguay, and Chile, the remaining Spanish American markets. Chancellor told the board, and also the Foreign Office, that Reuters could not run a suc-cessful service within South America unless it received some form of indirect subsidy of at least £100,000 per annum. Perhaps, wrote Chancellor to the Foreign Office (9 July 1958), a Latin American news agency could be launched 'with the support of British interests', through which Reuters might work. How much was to come from British firms and how much from the British Government was left unclear, for the proposal was never a starter.

6

The position of Reuters in North America during the 1940s and 50s was less volatile than in South America, but still difficult. From 1942, a relationship of friendly rivalry was maintained with the Associated Press. The new relation-ship was established by William Haley, who spent from April to June 1942 in the United States and Canada drawing up a new contract with AP. For three weeks Kent Cooper of AP would not meet Haley at all; but Haley waited patiently. He eventually persuaded the distrustful American that the prin-ciples which now guided Reuters were the same as those which Cooper claimed for AP—commitment to 'truth in news', all news being collected without official interference or subsidy.

Haley and Cooper were both men who liked to parade their commitment to the highest principles of conduct. Cooper, who had never liked Jones, was impressed by Haley. They agreed that, for the two agencies in the future, 'the basis covering our relationship should be "Compete and co-operate".'

Co-operation was intended to promote truth in news: competition to pro-vide choice in news.

The outcome of the 1942 negotiations was harmonious, but the Reuter board had been prepared for failure. On 10 March 1942 it denounced the 1934 contract with AP as 'intolerable'. The board was ready for a complete break with AP if better terms could not be obtained. It knew that the alter-native of creating an independent news network out of North America would be very costly, but the board was determined.

In his long report on the negotiations, dated 1 July 1942, Haley described Cooper's recollection of Jones as amounting to 'almost a phobia'. Jones's cold and patronizing manner had made the American suspicious of everything to do with Reuters. On five separate occasions, Cooper told Haley how in the 1920s he had approached Reuters in a spirit of collaboration, and how Jones had rebuked him for his presumption. This personal dislike was joined to the belief that Reuters was subsidized by the British Government. In response, Haley gave Cooper a copy of the new Reuter Trust document.

In this way Reuters and AP became (in Cooper's phrase) 'blood brothers'. New and equal terms were agreed on 24 June 1942. AP was to have full access to the Reuter and PA news service, as delivered to the London papers, for use anywhere in the western hemisphere. In return, Reuters was to have full access to the AP news service, as delivered to the New York papers, for use in the eastern hemisphere. This represented a great improvement upon the 1934 agreement, which had delivered to Reuters only AP's North American news. As before, the exchange of news was to involve no money payment.[21]

Reuters still needed to find new American subscribers for its Globereuter service. In 1942 the *New York Times* was the only paper buying this service. Cole went over to set up a new teleprinter network, and Reuters began to sell its world news to a handful of other leading east coast papers. This was pres-tigious, but Cole wanted wider geographical penetration. And to achieve this he negotiated what came to be recognized as the most remarkable of all his many news deals. In 1944 he signed a contract with the *Chicago Tribune* for delivery of the Reuter service in London and New York. This represented a triumph of personality against the odds, for the *Tribune* was owned by Colonel Robert McCormick, who was well known for his anti-British atti-tudes. Cole succeeded in persuading McCormick, first, that Reuters was not controlled by the British Government; and secondly, that its news service was worth buying.

McCormick sent his news editor, J. L. Maloney, to sit in the London news-room. Maloney was satisfied by what he saw, and the Reuter service to the *Tribune* started on 1 December 1944. The paper paid a total of £7,000 a year

32. Reuter correspondent J. W. Collins, covering the Italo-Abyssinian War, 1935.
His three runners, ready to take telegrams to the post office, are lined up behind

33. James Strachey ('Major Jim') Barnes, Reuter correspondent and
admirer of Mussolini

34. Samuel Storey, chairman, 1941

35. William Haley, author of the 1941 Reuter Trust deed

36. Jimmy Cox, chief correspondent in Japan, Yukichi Iwanaga, President of Domei, and
Christopher Chancellor, manager Far East, and wives, 1939

EDWARD G. ROBINSON in "THIS MAN REUTER" – A Warner Bros · First National Picture

37. The Hollywood view of Reuters, 1941

38. Seaghan Maynes, Normandy, 1944

39. D-Day plus six: General Montgomery briefs war correspondents, Normandy, 1944 (Doon Campbell *extreme left*)

40. The British press: Playing-card issues to German troops, 1942

41. Canada remembers a Reuter correspondent: Charles Lynch, commemorative stamp, 1992. (Stamp reproduced courtesy of Canada Post Corporation.)

42. Cecil Fleetwood-May, pioneer of wireless and commercial services, 1951

43. Hellschreiber in use: Manila, Philippines, 1950s

44. Monitoring the Balkans: Green End Listening Station, 1962

45. 85 Fleet Street: The Lutyens building

46. The editorial team: Sid Mason and Geoffrey Imeson, 1951

47. London editorial: Japan and Pacific desk, *c.*1952

48. Harold King and General de Gaulle

49. Christopher Chancellor
with Walton Cole—and the
Baron, 1951

50. John Burgess (chairman
1959–68) and Cole, 1960

51. John Ransom with Stockmaster, *c*.1966
52. Fred Taylor with Videomaster, 1971
53. Gerald Long with Monitor, 1976

54. A Frankfurt dealing-room before Monitor

55. Dealing-room with Reuter terminals, Canadian Imperial Bank
of Commerce, London, 1987

56. William Barnetson, chairman 1968–79

57. The 1984 flotation: Nigel Judah, Denis Hamilton (chairman 1979–85), Glen Renfrew, and Michael Nelson at the London Stock Exchange

58. Christopher Hogg (chairman 1985–) and Peter Job (managing director 1991–)

59. Reuter Saigon staff at the height
of the Vietnam War, 1969

60. Hala Jaber interviews Lebanese
soldiers on Beirut's Green Line, 1986

61. Angus MacSwan (*left*) interviews
Colonel Ernesto Vargas, El Salvador,
1988

62. Working on a story for the Arabic-language Desk, Cairo, 1989

63. Satellite transmission of news and news pictures: Frederick Neema and Gill Tudor in Liberia, 1990

64. Visnews cameraman Mohammed Amin covering the Tigre famine, Ethiopia, 1984

65. The Berlin Wall comes down, 1989: Reuters news picture

for the Globereuter service to North America, and for the Reuter and PA services as supplied to newspapers in London.

Three months later a second contract was signed with a news syndicate run jointly by the *Chicago Tribune* and the *New York Daily News*. The syndicate agreed to market Reuter news in the American mid-west and south on a profit-sharing basis. In return, Reuters was authorized to sell news from the syndicate throughout Europe, the Middle East, India, and South Africa. Hesitation on both sides had been overcome. Reuters and the *Tribune* issued a long statement explaining to the paper's American readers that the British agency was now acceptable because it was protected by the Reuter Trust. Seven years later Chancellor and Cole reminded the Foreign Office that these arrangements had been made only after 'careful discussion' with the Ministry of Information and with the British Ambassador. The British authorities had been persuaded that Reuters simply could not afford to act alone in North America. Chancellor confirmed in 1951 that, without the McCormick connection, Reuters could never have circulated its news extensively inside the United States, even as a secondary service to AP or UP.[22]

But writing news for American readers required an understanding of their particular interests and attitudes, and also of American English. At first, these were insufficiently understood at 85 Fleet Street, until in 1950 Cole persuaded Stuart Underhill, a Canadian journalist, to join the North American desk. Thereafter, Chancellor liked to introduce Underhill to visitors as 'the man who translates English into American'.[23]

During the rest of the 1950s the Reuter presence in the United States remained limited but visible. This was the minimum for an agency which aspired to be 'the leading world news agency'. Interestingly, Kent Cooper's 1942 book, *Barriers Down*, had more realistically misprinted these words as '*a* leading world news agency'.[24]

The personal relationship between Cooper and Chancellor, although friendly on the surface, was uncertain underneath. Cooper exclaimed in conversation in 1947 that 'he had got very close to Haley and could talk freely with him which he could not do with Chancellor'. These remarks about himself were reported by Chancellor to the Reuter board on 21 May 1947. On another occasion, Chancellor wrote privately of Cooper: 'I don't think it is quite fair to call him a "humbug"—but I am never *quite* sure'.

Early in 1946 Chancellor had negotiated a fresh Reuter–AP contract with Cooper. Chancellor knew that he had no choice but to humour the American, because Reuters needed his goodwill. The outcome was a new contract for a mutual exchange of news in the spirit of 'compete and co-operate'. The centenary history of Reuters claimed that this contract constituted 'the most important agreement for the free and unhindered movement of news in the English-speaking world'.

Yet the spirit of the old news ring was not quite dead. During a visit to the United States in 1948 Chancellor told Cooper that 'it would be essential for the AP to accept Reuters as the paramount agency in certain territories: Reuters on its side would be prepared to accept AP as paramount in other territories'. This suited Reuters, which could not afford to compete everywhere as the equal of AP. Chancellor realized that he was proposing something which, if made public, would be criticized. He told the Reuter board (3 May 1948) that the proposed arrangement was to be a 'strictly private affair'.

Both Reuters and AP were still benefiting from preferential cable tariffs, subsidized by their respective governments. When publicly challenged about this in 1946 Cooper argued disingenuously that United States Government money which reduced the cost of news to AP's member newspapers was subsidizing not the news agency, but the newspapers.[25]

Reuters had to accept a secondary role as a news supplier within North America; but as a world news agency, it was bound to be active in seeking as much news as possible for itself from Washington and from the United Nations at New York, even while it continued to depend heavily upon AP for other American news. Chancellor reported on 6 October 1949 that a quarter of the Reuter file into London came from North America. The necessary organization—comprising three offices in New York and one in Washington—grew during the 1950s into the biggest overseas Reuter operation, with about fifty full-time staff and 150 stringers. The North American radio-teletype circuit to London carried 30,000–35,000 words each day, and another 12,000 words of commercial material were also sent. In the opposite direction, a fast commercial service was received from London. Inside the United States, Reuters leased a 5,000-mile teleprinter network to serve its media subscribers. It had 400 news and commercial service subscribers—still a modest total.

Costs were high. By 1960 $940,000 was being spent anually upon collecting outward news, and upon distributing news within North America. Gross revenue was $655,200. The bigger the North American operation became, the more it lost money. Here was a trading reality which Chancellor and Cole had to accept.

7

Following the success of his 1942 negotiations with AP, Haley was sent at the end of the year to negotiate a new contract with the Australian Associated

Press. The AAP was the successor to the Australian Press Association, which had signed the expiring 1926 contract. Before setting out, Haley wrote a comprehensive report on 'Reuters in Australia' (25 October 1942). He rightly concluded that the history of the agency in Australia was 'the record of an attempt by powerful newspapers acting in combination to keep Reuters from establishing itself there'.

As expected, the negotiations were tough. But Haley was able to establish good personal relations with two of the Australians—Rupert Henderson of the *Sydney Morning Herald* and Sir Keith Murdoch of the *Melbourne Herald and Sun*. Henderson—who was to be involved with Reuters for over forty years—was described by Haley as 'one hundred percent a newspaperman'. 'He has, far more than Sir Keith Murdoch, a genuine apprehension of American influence in Australia after the war. He is determined to combat it, and he feels a Reuter service, provided it is as good as that of its American rivals, is essential to the Australian press.'[26]

The fixing of the amount payable by the AAP was explicitly treated by Haley as a test of whether or not a new spirit had been created. He told Henderson that he was going to name straight away what he thought to be a fair figure, without starting from a higher figure simply for the sake of bargaining:

> Mr. Henderson asked 'And the figure is?'
> I said 'Ten thousand pounds a year'.
> Mr. Henderson pursed his lips, looked at me and said 'You want this to be more than a mere business deal?'
> 'Yes.'
> 'And you want it to be in a spirit above a bargain?'
> 'Yes.'
> A pause. Then
> 'All right. It's done.'

Unlike Jones in 1926, Haley took care to negotiate for pounds sterling, not Australian pounds.

The agreement was for fifteen years from 1 May 1943, but with either party free to give a year's notice on 30 April 1950. For the future, Haley's report on the negotiations (16 May 1943) was hopeful but not unrealistic. 'Experience indicates that the AAP's feelings towards Reuters will always be subject to fluctuations. That is the Australian nature.'

During 1941–2 Reuters had been swept by the Japanese out of a vast area north of Australia. Chungking had become the only Reuter office functioning in the whole of China, and Reuters was the sole western agency still distributing news. The Japanese seized the Shanghai office on 8 December 1941.

Thanks to the personal intervention of the president and general manager of Domei, the Japanese news agency, the British staff there were well treated. The Japanese even allowed a limited local service of commercial and general news to be published during January–May 1942. This excluded any items which 'might give the Chinese people the idea that, although we are winning some victories now, we will lose the war later'. Cromarty Bloom, the manager, was repatriated in August 1942. Nearly all the staff of over 100 were paid off with dollar IOUs, to be honoured (as they were) after the war.[27]

In Hong Kong, a captured British colony, the Japanese attitude was much harder. W. J. O'Neill, the manager, was an Irish citizen, and as a neutral could have been repatriated. But he insisted upon staying with his staff, and was interned in harsh conditions until the Japanese surrender in 1945.[28]

Working for Reuters in London also brought its dangers. Air raids threatened much more serious disruption of news collection and distribution during the Second World War than during the first. Fortunately, the new building at 85 Fleet Street had been built with basement shelters, where alternative editorial and wireless transmitting facilities were available for use during air raids. Fleet Street was several times cut off from incoming news because of damage to cables. The teleprinter system out to British newspapers was interrupted only once—for 3½ hours in the early morning of 17 April 1941, when a landmine dropped by the Luftwaffe became caught in lighting wires strung across Fleet Street, near to the front door of Reuters. If the parachute had not become entangled, enabling the mine to be defused, the Reuter headquarters would have been shattered, perhaps with loss of life.

Such an outcome would have been serious, but not conclusive. For a standby news centre had been set up in a house near Barnet, on the northern edge of the London telephone network. The entire overseas staff became based there during the worst of the blitz in 1940–1. Emergency lines to the Post Office radio transmitters kept the overseas output flowing without interruption.[29]

8

During the 1930s Rickatson-Hatt had improved the handling of news by Reuters in London, but standards seem to have been slipping again by the time he left early in 1941. Upon joining Reuters a year later, Cole set out immediately to make big changes. Interestingly, while still night editor at the PA, Cole had listed what he believed to be the faults in the handling of news by Reuters. Cole's analysis, dated 25 June 1941, written for the editor-in-chief of the PA, was passed to Haley. 'Wordy is the best description for most Reuter stories', complained Cole. On a big story such as the recent German invasion of Russia everything was handled 'from the "historic document" viewpoint', including thousands of words of Nazi propaganda. The PA had 'spiked' at least 10,000 words from Reuters on the invasion.

In general, continued Cole, Reuters lacked awareness of news values; all its stories were published at length, even though many deserved only 'compact form'. There was little attempt 'to present a story in the fashion that it will be published'. Not quite all of Cole's comments were hostile: 'The timing now is good'. But here was a largely unflattering assessment from a main user of Reuter news. This commentary would certainly have been shown by Haley to Chancellor, and it no doubt helped to recommend Cole to both of them.[30]

To help address these defects Cole recruited Sidney J. Mason (1900–65), a forthright belt-and-braces Cockney character, who came in December 1942 from the British United Press to be night editor. Sid Mason was an experienced news craftsman. In 1944 he was promoted to be chief news editor. In this role for more than twenty years, he oversaw the incoming file from correspondents overseas. Most of them came to idolize him. He briefed them carefully on first posting, criticized them sharply but helpfully when they failed on a story, praised their successes warmly in 'herograms', and always defended their interests at headquarters. To Mason, beating the competition with a 'good timing' was perhaps excessively important. 'He made the men on the desk so nervous that they often started up a story before anything had really happened.'[31]

At any one time, about thirty journalists, plus an equal number of typists and wire operators, were at work in the newsroom at 85 Fleet Street. In 1947 this was moved from the fifth to the fourth floor. In that same year, at Chancellor's suggestion, Reuters recruited its first two graduate editorial trainees. These came from Cambridge, his own university. Chancellor told the 1948 Royal Commission on the Press that when he and Cole took over they had been 'startled by the haphazard method of recruitment'. The scheme was some years later extended to include Oxford and other universities. Fluency in at least one language other than English was usually expected, plus a willingness to learn further languages as needed. Not all recruits stayed for long. By 1960, forty-three university trainees had been accepted since 1947, but twenty-three had left. Reuters could not match the salaries offered by the London newspapers or by the American agencies. In 1948 Chancellor admitted to the Royal Commission that even the best Reuter correspondents were receiving only about three-quarters as much as their AP or UP rivals. During the mid-1950s, this meant between £1,000 and £1,500 a year.[32]

By 1945 Reuters was employing nearly 2,000 full-time staff worldwide, the highest total ever. In 1950 large offices were operating in twenty-three countries, and small reporting bureaux, with one or two staffers, in nineteen other countries. News was supplied directly to subscribers in fourteen countries; but in thirty-one other states news distribution was still through the national agencies. Reuter news was received from London by newspapers and radio stations in thirty-five countries, mostly within the British Empire.

The Central Desk at 85 Fleet Street remained the focal point, where all news came for processing. But relevant news also went to a growing number of regional desks—North American, European, Asian, African, and so on (11 by 1961)—each with an editor. On joining Reuters, Cole had been surprised to find that the entire news service was being produced in just three parts—a direct teleprinter service to the London papers and the PA; a general overseas service; and a service to Europe. Through the regional desks, Cole sought to diversify the news services from Reuters. But Geoffrey Imeson, Cole's deputy, recalled in old age that there were never enough journalists to maintain all the desks at proper effectiveness: 'any visitor from the region concerned was duly impressed when shown a desk set-up hastily reinforced for the duration of his visit'.[33]

So the reality did not live up to the ideal. But the ideal was at least being pursued. An analysis of the company's trading account submitted by Chancellor to the board on 10 June 1947 showed him encouraging the directors to recognize the need for wider horizons. He suavely accepted that 'provision of a complete news service for members' was 'the basic activity of Reuters'. Beyond that, however, he deftly suggested that the 'new Reuters' had undertaken an obligation to distribute its news as extensively as possible, because the Trust guidelines required it 'to maintain in every event its position as the leading world news agency'.

Chancellor's report included a financial overview as at April 1947. This showed an annual deficit of £92,000 on news provided for the press of the countries sharing in the ownership of Reuters. The Australian Associated Press and the New Zealand Press Association had recently become junior partners alongside the PA and NPA. The deficit on news for the three 'home' territories was reduced by £70,000 worth of other news revenue, mainly comprising subscriptions from the BBC and the Australian Broadcasting Commission. The deficit on news contrasted with a commercial service surplus of £48,000 worldwide, although this had been costed without charge for use of the Reuter network. Overall, Chancellor estimated a company trading profit for the year of £36,000 before tax.

The newspaper groups which owned Reuters still felt no qualms about taking their news at much below cost. In effect, Reuters was providing an indirect public service to and through the press. On the occasion of the centenary of Reuters, *The Times* of 12 July 1951 published a leader which addressed the question of whether a news agency ought to function as a public service or for profit. The paper concluded that, although service was the higher purpose, profit must also be sought:

> News gathering is a business to the extent that, unless it can be made to pay, it loses freedom to tell the truth, but it cannot be regarded merely as a business. Too much is at stake. Unless the common man, upon whom so much responsibility rests nowadays, knows what is happening in world-affairs, he is a citizen blindfold. He depends on the independent gatherers of news to qualify him to vote and to act with free will . . . What comes from Reuters is a valuable supplement to the truth flowing into newspapers even when they can afford the costly service of a staff of correspondents of their own.

The Times added its satisfaction that Reuters was now owned by the press, and that it was protected by a trust.

9

The Paris office in the Place de la Bourse was the largest overseas Reuter office in the immediate post-war period, with a staff of about fifty. It served as a collecting point for French news; as a distribution centre for Reuter general news and commercial services to French subscribers; and as a retransmission post to London for news collected in many other European centres. During the 1950s the news service for France was redesigned and news distribution reorganized. By 1958 trading profit was £45,922, compared with only £686 for 1949. Reuters now felt more confident in competing on the home ground of Agence France-Presse, the post-war successor to Havas.[34]

On the other hand, AFP had become a strong competitor on the world news scene. At the time of AFP's emergence Chancellor had urged it to become a newspaper co-operative, with which Reuters could 'compete and co-operate' in a friendly spirit as with AP. Instead, AFP settled for a large subsidy from the French Government, although its editorial independence was supposedly maintained. The French Government wanted to re-establish French global influence through the circulation of news. Cole regarded AFP as the most dangerous agency rival for Reuters. He told the board in June 1960 that AFP's annual subsidy totalled about £2 million, which amounted to some two-thirds of its total revenue. This subsidy was not much less than the whole revenue of Reuters.[35]

Just before the war, the news agencies of Belgium, The Netherlands, Switzerland, Finland, Sweden, Norway, and Denmark had come together in the '1939 Group'. This body continued active during the post-war years, pressing Reuters for lower subscription rates. At first, Chancellor and Fleetwood-May, the European manager, responded over-generously, being more interested in consolidating community of interest than in extracting maximum financial return. Eventually, however, rather more realism began to be introduced into contract and other negotiations with the Europeans. The man responsible was Alfred Geiringer, an Austrian by birth, who had started with Reuters in Vienna in 1937 and who had been smuggled out in the following year in the boot of Christopher Holme's car.[36]

In 1944 Geiringer was selected to re-establish the Reuter organization in central Europe, beginning with Switzerland, where he was sent to help modernize the Agence Télégraphique Suisse. He persuaded the Swiss that they could not afford to buy news from more than one world agency, and that they should choose Reuters. He also negotiated a direct contract with the Agence Cosmographique for Swiss rights to the Reuter commercial service.

Geiringer's greatest achievement came in post-war Germany. Gradual relaxation of Allied control of news supply allowed him time to build up a strong organization in West Germany, where Reuters found that it was regarded by the Germans with especial goodwill because of the origins of its founder. Offices were opened in Berlin, Hamburg, Bonn, and Frankfurt. Frankfurt became the editorial point for central, eastern, and northern Europe. From the first, Geiringer realized that the Germans would soon want to establish news agencies of their own; and, wisely, he did not try to resist this. Instead, he took care to ensure that the German co-operative agency—formed by a merger on 1 September 1949 of the agencies in the three Western Allied occupation zones—would be linked to Reuters by a five-year contract. The new German agency was called Deutsche Presse Agentur (DPA).

As with the 1939 Group, Chancellor offered collaboration rather than competition. He told Fritz Saenger of DPA on 1 January 1951 that, because AFP had lapsed into being a subsidized organ of the French Government, DPA could easily become the leading continental agency. 'Reuters needs a strong ally in Europe, and I feel that if we work together each can help the other.' In 1949 a West German commercial news agency had been formed with Reuter support—the Vereinigte Wirtschaftsdienste (VWD). A financial reorganization in 1951 led to Reuters taking a third share.

But VWD proved to be unenterprising, and DPA lost its independence, at least in spirit. By November 1960 Gerald Long, the chief representative for Reuters in West Germany, was pointing out that the development of DPA had 'not followed the lines envisaged' when Reuters had decided to promote a strong cooperative agency as an ally, rather than distribute news directly within West Germany as the American agencies had chosen to do. 'There is in the agency [DPA]', said Long, 'an atmosphere of deference to official wishes which has led to a rather bureaucratic and passive attitude to news.'

At the time, Chancellor's post-war policy for Europe was thought to have done well enough financially. Europe became the main revenue-earning territory for Reuters, following a sharp decline in revenue from India after independence. Revenue from the Far East, especially Japan, also became important (see Table 11.1). Long was less content than Chancellor or Cole with these European figures. He believed that the continentals could be made to pay more for their news from Reuters. And he was sure that, although they had been allowed exclusive country rights to the Reuter commercial service, most of them were failing to sell the service with sufficient vigour. Years later, while accepting that Chancellor could not have taken risks, Long regretted what he described as the post-war one-dimensional attitude within Reuters: 'shared interests, a common concept of press freedom, co-operation among the kith-and-kin, sure contracts, small returns, the whole within the larger myth of the break-even.'[37]

TABLE 11.1. Gross post-war revenue figures. (£)

	Europe (excluding UK and Ireland)	Far East	Indian sub-continent
1945	55,155	10,980	277,090
1950	235,122	126,658	57,635
1960	526,501	368,471	67,088

10

The commercial services, which had been seriously disrupted in Europe and the Far East, slowly revived after the war. In March 1944 Reuters had bought Comtelburo. This was a private company, dating from 1869, which was on the verge of collapse but which enjoyed a virtual monopoly of reporting commercial prices between South America and London. This made it attractive to Reuters, which was trying to break into South America.

On 14 February 1944 Reuters concluded an agreement with the Press Association and the Exchange Telegraph to pool their handling of commercial information in the United Kingdom and Ireland. Comtelburo contracted to provide a 'home commercial service', and also the 'overseas commercial, financial and trade services'. Extel agreed to supply home financial and Liverpool services. London fast-printer services were to be run jointly. In other words, Reuters was seeking to prosper in supplying commercial information, but it was not yet seeking to dominate the field.

The commercial services shared the Reuter communications network with general news, but not on equal terms. Derek Jameson, then a duty editor, recalled how Comtelburo staff at 85 Fleet Street were forever trying to gain access to the wires. ' "Sorry, cock", we would say, "they've just formed their 29th postwar government in Italy. No room for your crap".'[38]

These commercial services were still regarded as subsidiary. Chancellor made this brutally clear in a board paper on 10 June 1947. 'The main activity under the second function (profit-making) is the so-called Commercial Service. This is run for the sole purpose of subsidizing the news service. If it ceased to show a profit we should discontinue it.' In the event, Comtelburo profits doubled during the 1950s—from £68,956 in 1950 to £143,197 in 1959. Without this money, the financial position of Reuters would have passed from being tight to being precarious.

Progress in communications technology had brought important developments during and after the Second World War. Most news from outside Europe was still being carried by the cable companies. But after the war, monitoring of broadcasts from Communist countries became vital when inside reporting was made increasingly difficult. In 1953 a new listening station was opened at Green End, 30 miles north of London, with a staff of nineteen listeners. Monitoring continued there until 1980.[39]

For outward services, Chancellor told the 1948 Royal Commission on the Press that there had been a 'complete revolution in communications' in recent years. In the days of news distribution by commercial cable the emphasis had been upon brevity because charges were related to wordage. Now channels leased by time were used, either land-line or radio. Radio channels were available from the Post Office for twenty-two hours per day, allowing an enormous increase in wordage. Chancellor gave the figures to the board on 21 January 1952—from an average of 115,000 words per month in 1938; through 1,175,000 in 1942; to an average of 6,200,000 words each month in 1951. 'It has altered the whole style of the work, and the tendency is to write the news in London in a much more presentable form.'[40]

High-frequency radio, which had made possible a switch from 'broadcasting' to directional beams in 1941, allowed the distribution of different Globereuter services, with their content selected by the regional desks in the London newsroom. After the war, separate beams were directed towards the Middle East, North America, South America, South Africa, North-East Asia, and South-East Asia. In 1949 a high-frequency radio-teletype service was opened between London and New York. This replaced Morse, and reduced transmission time to seconds. Unfortunately, high-frequency transmissions were often affected by interference, which could block or garble messages. A blackboard, chalked up by hand, showed from hour to hour the wordage being carried on each beam and the backlog. At the end of 1949, the British Post Office at last allowed Reuters to employ its own operators.[41]

Lines were less liable to interruption than radio, and here also big advances had been made. The Globereuter radio service to Europe was replaced in 1949 by a leased-line teleprinter network which provided a two-way link between London and the European capitals. A first stage had been started to Paris in 1947. This European Printer Network (EPN) was financed and operated in association with the European national news agencies. Reuters was following the American agencies and AFP, which had already created their own networks. Cole told the board in February 1950 that Reuter correspondents could now be confident that if they started ahead with a story, Reuters would stay ahead in getting it published.

II

At the end of 1946 the Australian Associated Press (AAP) and the New Zealand Press Association (NZPA) agreed to join in the ownership of Reuters from March 1947. The idea of some sort of British Empire news agency had been talked about between the wars, but without result. The initiative was finally taken in 1946, when the suggestion for a closer relationship between Reuters and the AAP—perhaps to be followed by similar links with other Dominion news agencies—was raised during a visit to London by Sir Keith Murdoch of the *Melbourne Argus and Sun*, one of the leading figures in Australian journalism. Murdoch's suggestion was vigorously taken up by Rupert Henderson of the *Sydney Morning Herald*. The two men eventually secured wide support from the newspaper owners of Melbourne and Sydney. Idealism about Commonwealth unity was spurred by unease at the way the American agencies were threatening to dominate the supply of news to Australia.

Because of the practical difficulties, Chancellor's initial response was cautious, but by 3 July 1946 he was writing to Murdoch encouragingly:

the only way for the Australian newspapers to have their *own* world news service is to take stake in the ownership and control of Reuters. Otherwise they are always in the position of buying a ready-made service in London and New York which has not been built up with any regard at all for Australian newspaper requirements. Naturally from Reuters' point of view I would welcome participation by Australia. This would strengthen Reuters financially and broaden the whole conspectus of Reuters in the editorial sense. It would also enable us, with a wider spread of newspaper ownership, to look the American agencies in the eye and compete with them on a more equal basis.

The practical benefits obviously appealed to Chancellor; but he also described Murdoch's conception as 'thrilling'. This was the same adjective as he had used about Haley's vision for Reuters in 1941.

On 22 July Chancellor wrote to tell Murdoch that the Reuter board had warmed to his idea. He warned that the AAP must not expect a cash dividend on its investment. 'This would not be an ordinary business deal.' The use of such disarming language was characteristic of Chancellor when he felt emotionally involved. 'To a large degree the motive would have to be idealistic . . . designed to widen the ownership and strengthen the competitive power of the only British-owned *world* news service. But it would give the Australian newspapers a *direct* participation in a *world* news service.'

Cole flew out to Australia and New Zealand early in October 1946; Chancellor followed four weeks later. Cole demonstrated to the AAP how it could make economies once it had merged its news gathering outside Australia. Reuters agreed to accept approved Australian and New Zealand journalists as joint (AAP–Reuter) correspondents, especially in the Pacific area. Three Australians and one New Zealander were initially selected. Editorial supervision was assigned to Melbourne, but in practice London retained ultimate control.

In his report to the board (14 December 1946), Chancellor summed up optimistically:

We shall employ Australians and New Zealanders in Reuters and they will be a source of strength to us; but the AAP news organisation outside Australia will gradually be absorbed into Reuters and the basic news service to Australia—to be called AAP–Reuter—will be increased from about 5,000 words a day to 15,000 words a day. This will establish the Reuter name in Australia and New Zealand and make the Reuter service the main news source for the Australian and New Zealand newspapers. And it will relegate the American services to a supplementary service. To my mind this is just as important as the financial terms.

Reuters was none the less glad to receive a substantial cash injection. An additional issue of 37,500 'C' shares was made at £1 par value. This 'C' share issue equalled the number of 'A' and 'B' shares held respectively by the existing owners, the PA and NPA. The AAP took up one-third of the issue at the price paid by the NPA for its shares in 1941—12,500 shares at £4. 10s. per share. The NZPA bought 2,500 'C' shares. The Australians thus paid £56,250 to become part-owners of Reuters, and the New Zealanders £11,250. The AAP was given the right to appoint one director and one trustee. The NZPA was allowed one trustee, and also secured a link with the AAP board.

In place of the 1943 contract, under which the AAP had been a customer, the Australians were to pay an annual assessment of £36,000. This was in proportion to their shareholding, amounting to one-seventh of the total owners' assessment. A rebate of one-third was allowed to cover the expenses of Australian staff in London and New York. The Australians were well pleased by these terms. The AAP's secretary noted on 18 December 1946 that they gave it 'a seat at the Reuter Board table at which all the principal international news agreements must from time to time be discussed'.

The American agencies were less pleased. Cole reported (8 April 1947) that Lloyd Stratton of AP 'thought there had been ultra-smart dealings on our part'. For once, while acting in the agreed spirit of 'compete and co-operate', Reuters had been making the running. It was the more piquant that this new competition was being arranged in the very name of news agency co-operation. Kent Cooper could scarcely complain.

The AAP and NZPA formally became partners in Reuters on 1 March 1947. In the process, Chancellor might have been lost to Reuters, for he was apparently offered a job by Murdoch. It was with Henderson, however, that Chancellor formed the more important relationship. He claimed in old age to have been greatly impressed by Henderson's personality and brilliance as a newspaperman. Certainly, during the next few years he wrote some fulsome handwritten private letters to Henderson, notably when the Australian's term as a Reuter director came to an end in 1950. 'For me the Reuter idea will always be associated with you. You have been the inspiration. I am terribly upset that you are leaving the scene.' In retrospect, Henderson claimed never to have been impressed by Chancellor's protestations. 'He was unscrupulous even to his own people but not to me. He wrote me some unbelievable letters of apology and that sort of thing that you would not expect from a man in his position. He used Reuters for his own good and treated Cole like a dog.'[42]

So the Australian and New Zealand connection was established. What about Canada, South Africa, and also India—now on the point of achieving independence? The Reuter board had agreed to explore the possibility of further widening. But the Canadian Press was rightly regarded as unlikely to be interested, in view of its close ties with the United States. And when Chancellor and Henderson visited South Africa in 1947, they found that Afrikaaner opinion was against any partnership with a British news agency. 'I realised that the spirit of Paul Kruger lived on,' exclaimed Chancellor to the board (6 August 1947).

12

It was fortunate that the South Africans never joined the partnership, and unfortunate for both sides that the Indians did join. The Associated Press of India, a Reuter subsidiary, had been a successful and profitable organization. It was dominant within India, employing about 500 people and controlling about 6,000 miles of leased teleprinter lines. Reuter assets at independence in 1947 (including API) were worth about £100,000. Indian subscriptions were much the highest for any part of the world—£277,090, roughly one-third of which came through as profit. Indian revenue peaked at £330,000 in 1948, but was not afterwards to reach six figures.

On 7 April 1945 the Indian Newspaper Society had resolved to press for a complete takeover of API, and for 'an interest' in Reuter internal services 'with a view to reorganizing them on co-operative lines'. At this stage Reuters was ready to concede no more than an equal share in the ownership of API, and no share at all in the Reuter commercial service. This was earning very good profits of about £30,000 a year.

Cole went to India to examine the situation. He quickly decided that the Indians could not be offered less than sole ownership of API and its internal news service. Terms were eventually drawn up for transferring the ownership of API to a new Press Trust of India (PTI). But the negotiations were aborted when the new interim Indian Government refused to allow Reuters, as a non-Indian organization, rights over internal teleprinter lines.

Early in 1947 a fresh start was made. The new president of the Indian Newspaper Society, Kasturi Srinivasan, who controlled the *Hindu* of Madras, was a moderate nationalist. Chancellor wrote to him on 18 March in conciliatory terms: 'this is not just an ordinary business deal: it is much more important than that.' Similar words had been used by Chancellor in his recent dealings with the Australians, and by Haley in his negotiations with Kent Cooper in 1942 and with the Australians in 1943.[43]

John Turner, the general manager in India, was instructed to explore the ground. A Turner–Srinivisan agreement, dated 1 June 1947, included a formula for sharing profits between Reuters and the PTI. However, in a letter to Chancellor on 2 June Srinivisan looked beyond these 'tentative proposals'. He expressed a desire 'to enter into some relationship with Reuters organisation as the other countries which sit on the Board'. For the Indians, financial concerns were at least as important as idealism about journalistic standards or Commonwealth co-operation. Reuters too had a financial incentive—fear that the American agencies, AP or UP, might sooner or later displace it as the main supplier of world news to India, if the Indians were not tightly bound.

On 19 June 1947 the Reuter directors agreed to invite the Indians to discuss entry into the partnership on terms similar to those agreed with the Australians. By coincidence, this was the very first meeting of the board attended by Rupert Henderson as the AAP–NZPA representative. Lord Layton reminded his fellow directors that they were sitting 'for the first time as a British Commonwealth Board'.

Annoyingly for Reuters, the Indian Newspaper Society now hesitated; and not until May 1948 did a delegation arrive in London. As well as Kasturi Srinivasan, its members were his cousin, C. R. Srinivasan, publisher of a large Madras vernacular newspaper group and a governor of the Reserve Bank of India; Devadas Gandhi, son of the Mahatma, managing editor of the *Hindustan Times*; Ramnath Goenka of the Madras *Indian Express*; and Swaminath Sadanand, of the Bombay *Free Press Journal*. In a note for the board (January 1948) Chancellor warned variously that Devadas Gandhi exploited the prestige of his father's name, but was 'very much a man of the world and a hard negotiator'; that Goenka had 'a somewhat dubious record as a stock exchange speculator'; and that Sadanand was 'entirely untrustworthy'. In 1935 Sadanand had been successfully prosecuted by Reuters for breach of contract.

The objectives of the Reuter negotiators were defined by Chancellor at a board meeting on 11 February 1948. They were, first, 'to retain as high a proportion as possible of the net revenue from India'; and, secondly, 'to keep India permanently as a Reuter territory'. The negotiations in London dragged on from 21 May to 18 June 1948. They quickly came down to questions of money—in particular, to the amount of assessment to be paid by the Indians. 'The basic point', summed up Gandhi, 'was that the Press Trust wanted to pay £35,000 and Reuters wanted it to pay £42,000.' Breakdown seemed likely. But at the last moment heads of agreement, drafted by the Reuter side but approved by the Indian Government, were accepted by the Srinivasans and agreed in principle by Gandhi. At a meeting of the Indian Newspaper Society from 22 to 24 July 1948 Gandhi spoke out strongly in favour of these proposals, while Goenka and Sadanand spoke against. The Society publicly announced its acceptance on 21 September 1948.

The heads of agreement of 18 June proclaimed that the PTI 'will assume the same responsibility as the other owners for the Reuter world service and maintenance of the principles of the Reuter trust'. The PTI was to take 12,500 'D' shares at £4. 10s per share—the same number as the AAP. And, like the AAP, the Press Trust was given the right to appoint one director and one trustee. An Indian desk was to be set up at 85 Fleet Street to take over the work of the Eastern desk. This desk was to serve Pakistan, Ceylon, Burma, Malaya, and elsewhere, as well as India. The Indian news zone was to stretch from Cairo to Singapore, and primary responsibility for news collection in the zone was to rest with the PTI. Four extra correspondents were to be appointed. All zone correspondents were to be known as 'PTI–Reuter' journalists.

On transfer day, 1 February 1949, the entire API organization was handed over intact. The PTI paid Reuters the value of net assets, but without attributing any value to goodwill and with payment spread over five years. The Reuter commercial service was included in the transfer. The PTI assessment was fixed at the same nominal level as that of the AAP—£43,333. 6s. 8d. A 'development rebate' for three years cut this by £13,000. Reuters agreed to meet the costs of the Indian desk in London up to a maximum of £10,000 per annum.

The Indians joined the Reuter partnership for an initial four years. Devadas Gandhi became the first Indian director, and C. R. Srinivasan the first Indian trustee. In the following month, a Reuter 'goodwill mission' flew out to India, consisting of Chancellor plus three directors, Layton, Graham, and Henderson. The quartet toured India for a month, and were well received by Indian newspapermen.

High hopes were expressed about the new connection, not only in India and the United Kingdom, but also in Australia, New Zealand, and the United States. Nehru, the Indian Prime Minister, described the move in a letter to Kasturi Srinivasan on 23 September 1948 as 'another step in our liberation, for a free Press and a free news service are the most vital characteristics of a free nation'.

Chancellor and the Reuter directors were enthusiastic in public, but more cautious in private. Layton told the trustees at their 1948 meeting that he and his fellow negotiators had felt an obligation to back moderates such as the Srinivasans against 'extreme nationalists who were thinking in terms of having a subsidised news agency'. Layton frankly admitted that Reuters itself had been subsidized under the raj. 'It had operated as a protected business in India with big profits.' But now Reuters was looking to a very different future. 'It was important to keep Reuters as the basic news service in India and to find a formula which would cover the difficult first years of Indian independence.' Chancellor warned the trustees that the agreement was 'a sort of trial marriage—with an escape clause for both parties at the end of four years'. He told Harold King (24 September 1948) that India was 'suffering from a hysterical form of nationalism . . . if we can make this partnership work we shall have done something worth doing. But it will not be easy.' By 1951, the centenary history of Reuters was making public this sense of caution. It described the enlarged partnership as 'a move in practical internationalism', which could only succeed 'if, in practice, acceptance of the basic conception of truth in news transcends the fluctuating movements of nationalism'.[44]

13

Publication of the history—*Reuters' Century*, by Graham Storey, a young Cambridge historian—was part of the hundredth anniversary celebrations of the agency. These celebrations cost Reuters some £25,000, in a year which saw an overall pre-tax loss of nearly £23,000. Such large expenditure was defended on the ground that the various events produced favourable world-wide publicity.

A banquet for over 1,100 guests at Grosvenor House, Park Lane, on 11 July 1951 was the social high point, a glittering white-tie occasion which cost nearly £7,000. The guest of honour was Kent Cooper of AP. Other guests were Clement Attlee, the Prime Minister; the Archbishop of Canterbury; press chiefs from over fifty countries, and also Sir Roderick Jones. The menu included delicacies supplied from each of the countries within the Reuter partnership. Cooper proposed the toast of Reuters. Attlee's speech was characteristically brief, saying that his Government was glad to leave Reuters alone, 'except when offered their hospitality'.

Other centenary activities included the symbolic release of 100 pigeons from 85 Fleet Street by Chancellor's daughter (cost of pigeons: £56. 13s. 4d.); and a garden party for Reuter staff at Dane End (cost: more than £3,500). This was the Chancellors' country residence, north of London. They circulated with warm smiles, and conducted countless tours of the old house. To ensure that everyone could attend, before or after duty, the festivities began at noon on Saturday 14 July, and lasted for over twelve hours. Strong drink flowed unceasingly; dancing took place indoors; and a fireworks display provided a climax. This was the last 'feudal' headquarters occasion in the history of Reuters, a final memorable expression of that embracing spirit which went back to the days of Julius Reuter.

To mark the centenary, Chancellor was knighted. That such an honour should have been offered, and accepted, was an indication of how much

Reuters was still seen—and at least on its own terms, was still seeing itself—as 'British'. Chancellor had already accepted a lesser honour (CMG) in 1948.

One Foreign Office official, commenting in that year upon a letter from Chancellor, had complained in revealing terms (2 February 1948):

> Reuters professes to lay such stress on the sacredness of 'news' but it never hesitates to stress or publicise items highly prejudicial to the British cause. It is so British when in difficulties and so 'impartial' and so uninterested in the British cause when prospering.[45]

A more understanding explanation of these contradictions would have recognized that Reuters was in a transitional state; that it had consciously intensified its international awareness, but that it had not yet reached the further stage of seeing itself as supranational. Certainly, 'Sir Christopher' did not hesitate to accept a British title. 'Yes, I *am* pleased about it', he told Henderson in Australia (23 July 1951): 'I think it helps and it does give one a feeling that what has been achieved is worth while.'

14

During the next few years, however, attitudes within Reuters moved on significantly. Notably, the Anglo-French invasion of the Suez canal zone in 1956 provided a striking opportunity for the agency to demonstrate its editorial independence from the British Government, and its commitment to telling all sides of a story with equal detachment. On 1 November Chancellor sent a circular to Reuter staff throughout the world. He began by quoting from that same morning's *Manchester Guardian*. The paper had said how deeply British opinion was divided over the rights and wrongs of military intervention for the purpose of regaining control of the canal. Chancellor continued:

> It is the duty of Reuters, both to itself and to the many newspapers all over the world who rely on the Reuter service, to keep this fact in mind and ensure that it is reflected in the news service—that is, so long as it remains a fact and the nation remains, as it is today, divided on the issue of war with Egypt. Reuters does not represent the British Government. In the strain of the next few days I know the editorial staff will always bear in mind the fact that Reuters must strive to give a true reflection of opinion in this country.

So, although Chancellor's starting-point was Suez in the British context, he was emphasizing also the responsibility of Reuters to newspapers throughout the world, most of which were not British. He knew that the press of the Third World was generally opposed to British intervention. He therefore took care that, although nominally for internal reading, his circular became known in India and elsewhere.

This concern for the wider, non-British responsibilities of Reuters triggered a very important response. Politicians and newspapermen in the Third World, including Egypt, started to react as if Reuters was not merely refusing to take sides within Britain, but was rising above its British background entirely. Reuters began to be widely accepted as wanting to be supranational. Its carefully detached reporting of the Suez crisis is detailed in Chapter 15.

Chancellor's separation of Reuters from the British Government was the more easily achieved because personally he felt shocked by the invasion. He told Laurence Scott of the *Manchester Guardian* on 2 November: 'I have seldom felt more unhappy about England.' The emotional streak beneath Chancellor's cool exterior broke through when Anthony Eden, the British Prime Minister, appeared on television to justify Government action. In anger, Chancellor threw a glass of whisky and soda at the set.

Chancellor was on friendly terms with several leading Labour politicians. including Hugh Gaitskell, the Leader of the Opposition, who strongly opposed the Suez invasion. On 28 September, while the crisis was building, Chancellor had hosted a lunch party at Reuters for two leading Labour journalists, Francis Williams and Kingsley Martin, and two leading Labour politicians, Aneurin Bevan and Richard Crossman. Crossman described the occasion in his diary:

> What has made men like Chancellor so angry is the memory of the off-the-record briefings which the Government gave at the early stages to proprietors and editors, and at which they clearly and emphatically encouraged the press to threaten war against Nasser. A man like Chancellor is quite shocked that Eden should now lie and say that no such briefings were given nor suggestions made. The fact is that every proprietor and editor knows as a matter of fact that these briefings were given for at least ten days. Chancellor on the other hand, seems to me ridiculously pro-Nasser, just because he met him once in March and found him very attractive.[46]

Both Chancellor and Cole were certainly impressed by Nasser. Cole, who had personally supervised the handling of Suez news, visited Egypt in March 1957, when diplomatic relations between Britain and Egypt were still broken off. Nasser granted Cole a two-hour interview, remarking that the Reuter teleprinters at his office and home had been of 'immense value' for watching developments during the crisis.

15

Looking back at the time of his resignation in 1959, Chancellor described the centenary year of 1951 as the culmination of his period as general manager. He believed that soon afterwards Reuters began to lose momentum in its management. He admitted that this may have meant that the time had come for his own departure; but he believed that the slackening was due also to a lessening of interest in Reuters by the national newspaper proprietors. The leading NPA figures who had become Reuter directors in 1945— Rothermere, Layton, Bartholemew—had not been succeeded by men of equal calibre. The board was unadventurous, too readily constrained within a financial straitjacket of its own making. In 1951, 1956, and 1960 there were actual losses (see Appendix).[47]

Problems in the 1950s were not only financial. Indian participation within the Reuter partnership never worked smoothly, and in 1953 the Press Trust of India withdrew after only four years. Several specific causes of tension had fed a growing sense of unease on both sides. The Indian zone arrangement had quickly produced differences between Reuters and PTI. The Indians resented any permanent Reuter correspondents from London being appointed within the zone, particularly to India or Pakistan. The Indians regarded this as a reflection upon their objectivity. By 5 April 1950 Chancellor was complaining strongly to A. S. Bharatan, the general manager of PTI, that it had been 'trying to press the zonal idea unduly and unwarrantably in the direction of "exclusivity" '. This, said Chancellor, was against the ideal of freedom in the collection of news.

The Indian zone included Pakistan (East and West). The historian of the PTI has rightly expressed surprise that Reuters should ever have created a PTI news zone which included Pakistan. Hostilities between India and Pakistan were continuing within Kashmir throughout the partnership negotiations. Chancellor told the Commonwealth Under-Secretary (21 September 1948) that Reuters still hoped one day to bring the Pakistanis into the partnership alongside the Indians. Yet the Pakistanis were offended by the idea of Indian nationals being posted to Karachi or Dacca to report for PTI–Reuter. The Pakistanis demanded separate coverage by Reuters from London.

A British national was appointed as resident correspondent in Pakistan from the start of 1949. He was expected by PTI to report to Bombay under the zone arrangement, but he was also required to report directly to London. John Turner, now joint general manager of PTI with Bharatan, admitted to Cole (22 November 1949) that he preferred not to clarify who was 'primarily to control' the correspondent. Chancellor tried to strengthen the a case for non-Indian appointments in Karachi and Delhi by stressing the wish of the British press and the BBC for Reuters to have London-trained correspondents in every capital.

From 1 January 1949 the Pakistan part of the Associated Press of India was reconstructed as the Associated Press of Pakistan (APP). In the following year Reuters gave up its involvement, and APP became Pakistan's independent national news agency. A Pakistani journalist was appointed to Reuters in London, and a separate radio beam was established to transmit news to the Middle East and Pakistan.

Chancellor spoke plainly to Bharatan of the PTI (5 April 1950) about how its news from Pakistan was not being accepted as objective. The reputation of the Reuter world service was at risk. 'I cannot gloss over this problem.' Another difficulty was that PTI coverage from India tended to dwell upon news which interested Indians rather than being selected for world markets. Some of Nehru's speeches as Prime Minister were certainly of worldwide interest; but PTI was reluctant to condense them. Its excessive wordage became known outside India as 'sacred cow copy'.

By the early 1950s the supportive attitude of Nehru towards Indian participation in the Reuter partnership had changed to suspicion. He had renewed Indian membership of the Commonwealth when India became a republic at the start of 1950; but thereafter the alignment of international opinion for and against India over the Kashmir question drew Nehru towards the Soviet bloc, despite his articulation of a policy of non-alignment. The Indian Government decided that Reuters was still under the influence of the British Foreign Office, which meant in official Indian eyes that it was likely to be anti-Soviet and pro-Pakistani.

The handling of news by the British sub-editors who comprised a majority on the Indian desk at 85 Fleet Street gave credibility to this view. K. Gopalan, PTI's chief representative in London, found that the desk tended, for example, to report speeches by the British delegate to the United Nations at length, while simply saying that the Russian delegate 'repeated the same old arguments' or that 'the Iraqi, Pakistan, Egyptian and Indian delegates also supported the motion'. But Gopalan's complaints were heeded, and he eventually accepted that the Indian desk was achieving more balanced coverage.[48]

In correspondence with the Indians, Chancellor was all patience, whereas elsewhere he complained sharply about what he regarded as their repeated unreasonableness. He also grumbled about the expense of the new relationship. In a note for the board (21 January 1952), he compared Indian payments with Indian costs for the period 1 February 1949 to 31 January 1952. The net return to Reuters had been little more than £10,000 a year. Chancellor and the non-Indian directors came to the conclusion that the Indians were claiming a right to more than equal treatment—both over what they paid, and over their methods of operation.

Devadas Gandhi, the Indian director, had not reported back fully to his constituents. As a result, the strength of feeling among the other partners came as a surprise to the PTI when in 1952 discussions began about renewing the Indian agreement. This was due to expire on 1 February 1953. The Indians sought to renew it more or less upon the existing terms; but the other partners demanded changes which would take account of the difficulties since 1949. A first round of talks in India was adjourned, and a second round began in London in July 1952.

A draft agreement for three years was finally recommended by the Reuter board, and also by the two Srinivasans. But not by Gandhi. This draft accepted that 'the full board of Reuters is responsible for the Reuter World Service'. It recognized the right of Reuters and of all member organizations to send correspondents 'as, when and how they please' to any part of the world 'including the territories of the parties to this agreement'. More than equal treatment for any partner was ruled out. 'The whole is greater than the part and any rights or privileges of one part should not directly or indirectly affect the whole.'

On 17 August Nehru wrote to Kasturi Srinivasan complaining about Reuter coverage of his non-aligned foreign policy, and hinting strongly at the desirability of a break. Nehru suggested that under the draft scheme PTI would become only 'a very junior and ineffective partner'. He said that he was interested, first, in 'the rapid development of a national news agency'; and, secondly, in 'the proper interpretation of our foreign policy in India and as far as possible elsewhere'. The Indian Minister for Information had already warned Srinivasan that if PTI became 'subservient' to any foreign organization, the Indian Government would consider withdrawing 'facilities and co-operation'.[49]

The PTI board met on 20 September 1952. The now inevitable decision was taken to withdraw from the Reuter partnership. Goenka, who had opposed joining in the first place, claimed years later that experience had convinced most of his colleagues that 'the much-vaunted objectivity of Reuters was an exaggerated claim'. He compared the sense of release felt by PTI with that felt by Nehru when India became a republic, freed at last from showing deference to London.[50]

As an alternative to partnership, a 'friendly' contract was concluded between Reuters and the PTI, effective for three years from 1 February 1953.

PTI was granted exclusive rights to the Reuter world service. In return, PTI agreed to use this service as its chief source of world news. It was to pay £32,500 a year for general news and £7,500 for exclusive rights to the Reuter commercial service. In return, Reuters was to pay £10,000 for Indian general and commercial news. Reuters thus settled for a net £30,000 from India. Goenka, as chairman of PTI, had forced the figure right down, letting it be known that he was ready to switch to AFP, the agency subsidized by the French Government.

Business considerations were thus threatening to override sentiment, even though the contract began with a sentence which implied a continuing special relationship, and was followed by a second sentence which recognized that independence, not official subsidy, was the best basis for news agency work:

> Whereas both parties have been closely associated with each other in the past and intend to maintain this association in the future and whereas both parties declare that they are free and independent news agencies concerned solely with the collection and dissemination of truthful and objective news.

The Indian Government had decided at independence that priority in the allocation of internal teleprinter circuits should be given to Indian news agencies and newspapers. This policy was reinforced by a confidential Indian Cabinet decision in 1956 that news could be distributed within India only by Indian organizations. Although this policy blocked Reuters, it also blocked its main rivals, AP, UP, and AFP.

For outward news, Reuters ended up in the 1950s and 60s with just two staff correspondents at New Delhi, plus five stringers elsewhere. As telephone links between Delhi and the rest of the country were uncertain, much had to be left to PTI. Some good reporting was still to come out of India; but the great days for Reuters—great in profit, great in prestige—were over.

The postwar pursuit of an expanding Commonwealth partnership—sought by Reuters for mixed reasons of business benefit and of journalistic and political idealism—had met with only limited success. Canada, South Africa, and Pakistan had stayed outside: India withdrew. Into the 1950s Chancellor tried to be optimistic. He told Rupert Henderson in Australia (23 July 1951): 'despite the ups and downs it is worth doing—a creative idea which will produce something worth while in the end.' In old age, however, Chancellor confessed to ultimate disappointment. 'As I travelled around I found that the supposed community of interest within the Commonwealth was a myth.'[51]

16

On one of these Commonwealth journeys on behalf of Reuters Chancellor made a serious mistake, which attracted wide notice. In February 1956 he visited South Africa, where the Nationalist Government was introducing its policy of racial separation, apartheid—a policy which was coming under increasing attack in the British press. Despite the sensitivity of the situation, Chancellor's visit seemed to have passed off smoothly. A banquet was given in his honour by the South African Press Association, attended by Prime Minister Strijdom. Strijdom spoke of his confidence that 'we can depend on Reuter through its worldwide news distribution to give a true and objective picture of our country as against the sensation hunters'. So far so good. Unfortunately, however, when Chancellor's ship called at Durban on his way home, in an interview with two local newspaper reporters he revealed some of his personal dissatisfaction with the South African Government. His comments ran the obvious risk of being taken as the opinion of Reuters itself, and they ought not to have been made.

Chancellor was reported as saying that attacks by South African Ministers upon the British press had been indiscriminate and counter-productive. He criticized the South African Foreign Minister, Eric Louw, by name. 'Mr. Eric Louw has been particularly guilty in these attacks.' Chancellor was apparently unmoved by the fact that at the SAPA banquet Louw had spoken favourably about Reuters. The outside world, Chancellor continued, believed that the South African Government was seeking 'to muzzle the press'. He did concede late in the interview that the country's problems were complex. 'People should be cautious when writing about South Africa.' Yet Chancellor had not been cautious himself.

The effect of these comments was immediate. Through SAPA, Louw issued a statement which directly criticized Chancellor's personality. 'He is an entirely different type of person from his predecessor, Sir Roderick Jones, whom I knew well . . . by this unfounded and personal attack on members of the Union Government, Sir Christopher Chancellor has not rendered the Reuter organization a service.' Leading English-language and Afrikaans newspapers alike expressed dismay at Chancellor's language and timing. *Die Burger* wrote on 1 March that he was guilty of 'open bias in an argument which he as head of Reuter has nothing to do with'.

When Chancellor's ship reached Dar es Salaam he found himself having to limit the damage. He quickly wrote to Strijdom and Louw, and he issued a public explanation 'to put the record straight':

(1) I thought South Africa had exaggerated the picture of British press hostility. (2) There seemed to be a tendency to generalise unduly about the British press which covered the widest variety and spread of newspapers. I did not, repeat not, intend to refer to Mr. Louw in this connection. (3) I thought that the many attacks on the British and American press and their representatives in South Africa had done South Africa much harm because they had given the impression that there was a desire and intention to intimidate the press and control news. On these matters I feel deeply and sincerely and I think it right for me to express my views. Nothing, however, can mitigate my regret at the form in which my Durban interview appeared as relayed to Cape Town in summarised form.

This explanation was of course not an apology for what Chancellor had said, only for the appearance of discourtesy. And he was seeking to blame such appearance entirely upon 'summarised and telescoped' reporting. Yet at the same time Chancellor emphasized that he 'would not dream of criticising the reporters'. Presumably, he knew that each of his questioners had produced very similar accounts of his words. By implication, he was blaming SAPA's sub-editing. His discomfiture was obvious. That the head of a great news agency should have so mishandled a press interview was remarkable. Beneath Chancellor's smooth exterior lay an emotional streak, which had suddenly revealed itself as he unwound after a testing tour. He did not like the way South Africa was going, and he had gone too far towards saying so in public.

Reuters in London did not publish Chancellor's interview, or his subsequent explanation. Likewise, it did not report comment by Louw in the South African parliament in which he urged the opening of news links between SAPA and an American news agency, as an alternative to Reuters. As a result, SAPA started to take news from AP as well as Reuters.

On Chancellor's return to London, he called upon the South African High Commissioner, G. P. Jooste. Chancellor apparently tried to dismiss the published version of the interview as inaccurate, and blamed SAPA. Chancellor was embarrassed when the High Commissioner made clear his awareness that Reuters had failed to report the interview or subsequent reaction, including Louw's condemnation. The incident came to the notice of the Commonwealth Relations Office. The British High Commissioner in South Africa noted in his fortnightly summary that Chancellor had claimed to have been misreported. 'The damage however has been done, and will not speedily be repaired.'[52]

17

After 1945 the Pacific rim began to gain in importance, and Reuters took care to adjust accordingly. The Singapore office was revitalized by Graham Jenkins on his appointment as manager for South-East Asia in 1955. Competition from AP and AFP was intense. Jenkins—an Australian, rugged and smooth by turns—introduced post-colonial attitudes just in time. He deliberately separated himself from the old colonial ruling circle, now in its last days. Jimmy Hahn, a Korean by birth, who had worked for Reuters in Hong Kong, was made office manager, and new equipment was installed to encourage a spirit of enterprise. In 1964 Hahn was himself to become regional manager, the first Asian to be promoted to such a level.

Singapore was the hub of the Reuter communications network for East Asia. It used Hellschreiber, radio-teletype, and some Morse. Singapore relayed the Reuter service to Hong Kong and Japan, and radiated tailored services throughout the region. Jenkins ensured that they contained plenty of regional news, having decided very early that emerging Third World countries wanted to hear about each other.[53]

After the war, the Japanese (like the Germans) had been keen to restart their own news agencies. In November 1945 two new agencies were formed in place of Domei. One was Kyodo, owned by the Japanese provincial press, and the other was Jiji Press, owned by its staff. Chancellor explained approvingly to the 1951 Reuter annual general meeting that, being a co-operative run by a diversity of newspapers, Kyodo was committed to objective reporting. He had commended DPA, the new co-operative German news agency, in much the same terms. As in Germany, Reuters decided to collaborate rather than to compete, although in the case of Japan action was delayed for several years.

Chancellor told the board in April 1952 that poor radio communications were making the direct Reuter service to Japan very unreliable. Reuters found itself unable to match the American agencies, and Chancellor had concluded that it would therefore be better to operate in Japan indirectly. In 1953 a contract was signed with Kyodo. It took over the Reuter English-language service, and published it under a Kyodo–Reuter credit. A regional desk, targeting news for Japan and South-East Asia, was created at 85 Fleet Street.

Chancellor had written on 12 March 1952 in characteristic terms to Matsukata of Kyodo, revealing once again his liking for beyond-the-ordinary business relationships with other agencies. 'It will be more than just a buyer–seller relationship. It will be a close editorial relationship in which Kyodo will play a constructive part in shaping a basic world service for the

Japanese press.' A complementary contract was concluded with Jiji. This secured a subscription of £24,000, which was about one-third more than existing commercial service revenue from Japan.

A good service from Japan and Singapore was part of the benefit which the Australians and New Zealanders had anticipated when they joined the Reuter partnership in 1947. At the 1948 annual general meeting Lord Rothermere claimed that the accession of the Australians had been 'a complete success'. In reality, the new relationship with AAP soon ran into problems—over the rebate payable to the Australians; over Pacific 'AAP–Reuter' news arrangements; about the absence of promised Reuter credits in the Australian press; about the joint newsroom in New York; and over the high proportion of profit taken by the AAP out of the commercial service. An underlying problem was that the AAP was not fully developed as a news agency. In an undated note for Chancellor, Cole described it as 'an Alice-in-Wonderland operation', not yet ready to play its intended large part within Reuters.

The Australian newspapermen divided their energies between quarrelling among themselves and complaining about Reuters. In exasperation, Chancellor told Cole (4 March 1955) to make clear on a visit to Australia that 'if they were really dissatisfied it would be best to dissolve the partnership'. Perhaps this was over-reaction; but in a paper for the board just before his departure from Reuters (19 February 1959) Chancellor wrote that the Australian connection had ended in disappointment, 'largely because the newspaper leaders have been so unsatisfactory to deal with'. More than once, Reuters had tried to increase the AAP payment of 15 per cent of gross revenue from the commercial service in Australia, pointing out that the rate elsewhere was 30 per cent. In 1959 the Australians reluctantly conceded 20 per cent. AAP profits had more than quadrupled, whereas the payment to Comtelburo had increased only threefold (see Table 11.2).

TABLE 11.2. Gross revenue figures for the commercial service in Australia, 1948–59. (£ Australian)

Revenue		Expenses	Comtel fee	AAP profit
1948	11,756	7,766	1,763	2,227
1959	55,647	40,940	5,348	9,359

18

Fresh from his success in rebuilding the position of Reuters in post-war Europe, Alfred Geiringer became chief of the commercial services in May 1952, and manager of Comtelburo at the end of 1953. Comtelburo profits were to grow steadily during the 1950s, and comparative figures showed how much the loss-making general news services were being subsidized. By 1959 Comtelburo's revenue was amounting to approximately one-third of total company revenue, and profit had more than doubled since 1950 (see Table 11.3).[54] Geiringer brought drive to the running of the existing commercial services; but he could not be expected to foresee the computerized information revolution which was to transform those services and to offer great new market opportunities from the 1960s. On the contrary, he was convinced that, after two world wars and an intervening depression, public opinion would never again leave capitalists free to play the markets and to affect the livelihoods of all the world's population.

TABLE 11.3 Comtelburo revenue and profits, 1950 and 1959. ($£$)

| | | Comtelburo | | |
	Revenue	Costs	Profits	Reuter overall pre-tax profit
1950	336,978	268,031	68,956	17,145
1959	748,201	605,004	143,197	35,871

Geiringer also wrongly believed that Reuters might make money by telling businessmen about new developments and opportunities. An International Business Unit (1955–8) failed for lack of subscribers wanting reports on such topics as the Italian noodle industry, or 'the Market for Beer in Iran'; while a bulletin called *International Business Facts* survived for less than a year (1956–7) because businessmen preferred specialist magazines or financial newspapers. *Business Facts* was quite different from the daily or weekly Reuter bulletins about particular commodities—from asbestos to wool. These were well targeted, and Reuters was publishing eighteen of them by 1961; they earned nearly one-third of the commercial service's United Kingdom revenue.

For Cole the advance of the commercial service came to have a personal dimension. He had been on friendly terms with Geiringer as assistant European manager just after the war; but as Comtelburo manager Geiringer emerged as a competitor for resources. In the end, a confrontation occurred between the two men. Geiringer left behind in his personal papers a hand-written draft note to Cole, undated but from the mid-1950s, which may or may not have been sent. It began bleakly. 'I take our personal frigidity for granted and would like you to do the same.' Despite this frigidity, Geiringer claimed to have been disturbed by 'recent squabbles between us':

> I regard your ultimate claim to the top position in Reuters as amply justified and you have and will always have my complete support and loyalty . . . However, you cannot 'go it alone'. Reuters is too big for that . . . If you want me, I would be happy to plan the rest of my working life to fit into a Reuters going from strength to strength with you at the bridge. But I am no Yes-Man, and never will be.

Always suspicious of possible rivals, Cole would scarcely have been reassured by such a promise of support only on Geiringer's terms.

The conclusive clash between the two men came when Geiringer pressed for a new European communications network to be created for the commercial services, entirely separate from the general news teleprinter network. He promised Chancellor that with such facilities Comtelburo would be able to contribute millions a year in profit. Chancellor had been impressed by Geiringer's previous work in Germany and elsewhere; but after making him Comtelburo manager his increasing assertiveness on behalf of what Chancellor regarded as a subsidiary activity began to annoy the general manager. He turned down the request for a separate network. Chancellor knew that Cole strongly opposed the proposal. In April 1958 Geiringer suddenly resigned in frustration.

Geiringer's longest-lasting contribution lay in the people he left behind him. He had understood the need to recruit and train university graduates to become the managers and correspondents of the economic services of the future. He had sent them abroad to run small offices where they combined the functions of journalists, salesmen, and managers. Thanks to Geiringer, when markets and technology presented novel opportunities in the 1960s, Reuters was unique among the international news agencies in possessing a corps of young men who understood the business of fast economic information. As a result, Reuters was able to transform itself.

In October 1960 Cromarty Bloom—who had succeeded Geiringer as manager—reported that Comtelburo's revenue was being earned chiefly from the sale of fast information 'covering finance in every aspect, commodities of all sorts and freights and shipping'. By this date Reuters was looking well beyond the circulation of stock market and commodity prices; in

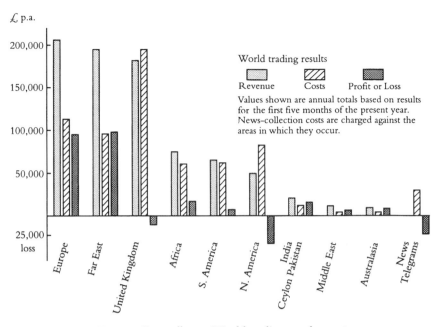

£ p.a.

200,000

World trading results

Revenue   Costs   Profit or Loss

150,000

Values shown are annual totals based on results
for the first five months of the present year.
News-collection costs are charged against the
areas in which they occur.

100,000

50,000

25,000
loss

Europe   Far East   United Kingdom   Africa   S. America   N. America   Ceylon India Pakistan   Middle East   Australasia   News Telegrams

FIG. 12   Comtelburo: World trading results, 1960

addition, it was offering more and more financial news from different parts of
the world. Comtelburo's first head office-trained financial journalist was sent
abroad in 1956—to Paris.

By 1960 Comtelburo was employing 186 staff in London and 282 overseas.
World trading results by region showed large profits from Europe and the Far
East, but losses from the United Kingdom and North America caused by
heavy production overheads (see Fig. 12). Experience had shown, continued
Bloom, that Comtelburo did best when it acted on its own. At the start of
1962 Reuters terminated the arrangement with PA and Extel under which
they had distributed Reuter commercial information throughout the British
Isles apart from central London.

19

Chancellor gave up as general manager in June 1959 at the age of 55. He had
long believed that executives, such as himself, who had reached the top comparatively young, should not remain until retirement age, but should seek
new challenges. He had been strengthened in his determination to leave by

dissatisfaction with the Reuter board during the 1950s. The NPA, in particular, seemed to be no longer much interested in Reuters. One episode had especially discouraged him, as he explained in a memorandum written at the time of his resignation (19 February 1959):

> I know that my own enthusiasm and belief in the future of Reuters suffered a setback when one director (Lord Burnham) vetoed a scheme whereby the PA and Reuters jointly could have entered the television field by performing the functions now performed by ITN. I felt at the time, and still feel, that this was an opportunity that should not have been thrown away.

Chancellor's proposal that Reuters should supply news for the new British commercial television network had been made in 1954. In response, Lord Burnham of the *Daily Telegraph*, who joined the Reuter board in June of that year, immediately began to argue that Reuters ought not to venture into preparing television news programmes. It should seek only to supply news in the usual way. Initially, Burnham gave fear of financial loss as his reason for opposition. He later also began to argue that if Reuters became directly identified with news appearing on commercial television screens 'the Reuter board would be constantly under criticism and attack' (12 January 1955).

The clash with Burnham still rankled with Chancellor four years later. And more recently there had been a difficulty with another director, Cecil King of the *Mirror* group. Chancellor and Cole had insisted upon sending a young inexperienced female correspondent, Elizabeth Bower, to newly independent Ghana. Even the male correspondents found the situation extremely dangerous and King, whose group owned the Accra *Daily Graphic*, had strongly advised against sending a woman; but he had been persuaded against his better judgement to withdraw his opposition. Soon after reaching Ghana, Bower disappeared for four days, much to everyone's alarm, before being found lying at the roadside out in the country suffering from loss of memory. She could well have died. Chancellor bore the responsibility, and the episode reinforced his feeling that it was time for him to move on. The experience also delayed the fuller employment of women correspondents by Reuters.

King wrote to Chancellor (9 January 1959) that it was 'no use either of us crying over spilt milk. We both want to see Reuters on the up and up and this in my view needs fresh thought, fresh enthusiasm and more money.' In the previous July King had argued to the Reuter board that the agency needed an extra £500,000 per annum in order to escape inevitable slow decline, and that only the British Government could provide such backing. When his drastic solution found no support—and irritated also by the Bower fiasco—King resigned from the board in January 1959.[55]

In the next month, Chancellor announced his own intention to resign as general manager. At the time of the ITV clash a director from the PA—John Burgess, chairman of Cumberland Newspapers—had strongly backed Chancellor. Burgess was well regarded for his good sense and good humour. This became particularly important when the Reuter board began to look for a successor to Chancellor. In his resignation memorandum he had written: 'I do not have to stress the desirability, indeed the inevitability, of Mr. Cole's appointment.' But, added Chancellor, Cole would need 'the support, and at times the control and guidance' of a reliable part-time chairman. Either Laurence Scott of the *Manchester Guardian* or Burgess would, in Chancellor's view, be able tactfully to manage Cole, who had great energy and 'remarkable intelligence', but who did not possess all the qualities necessary for sole charge of Reuters:

> I cannot see him acting as the focal point of a board without a Chairman. I am not sure how firm a grip he would keep on the general finances of the Company, and I think occasions would arise when his judgement might falter unless he had someone to consult. He is a bad administrator in the sense that he refuses to delegate. He will now have to organise himself quite differently, and he will need someone who is both sympathetic and strong to help him in this process.

Chancellor's advice was taken. Scott was too busy to accept the chairmanship. So on 1 July 1959, at the same time as Cole became general manager, Burgess was appointed non-executive chairman for three years.

Cole was deeply upset at being given a minder. He saw Chancellor's memorandum. He did not blame Burgess, but he never forgave Chancellor. He never invited his predecessor back to Reuters.

Happily, John Burgess (1912–87) was to prove well able to fulfil the chairman's role designated for him. Although he looked like a simple fresh-faced country gentleman, he was much more than he seemed. He was obviously upright, both in bearing and in mind. This was to make him a good figurehead for Reuters. But as well as an engaging presence, Burgess possessed a clear mind. This enabled him to respond quickly and constructively to ideas put to him. Burgess's responsiveness was to prove of great benefit to Reuters during the nine years of his chairmanship.[56]

20

Soon after becoming chairman, Burgess began to recognize that Reuters would only progress in the face of worldwide competition if—instead of aiming at little more than balancing the books—it committed itself to earning a sufficiently large annual surplus to permit significant investment in development and innovation.

On 7 October 1959 Burgess told the board of his regret that Reuters had been so often driven to making disruptive economies. He added:

> In order that the editorial should work smoothly, it is my opinion that Reuters should always operate on a substantial surplus. This should be a cushion for the unexpected and unpredictable expenditure, but, if this should not be required, the surplus should be placed to reserve for capital expenditure and for financing new services during their early non-productive life.

Burgess admitted that the partners in Reuters might feel aggrieved 'at having to subsidise more than is immediately necessary and then see half of the excess going in taxes'. But such thinking, argued Burgess, would be short-sighted: 'it is in the interests of the owners that their agency should be run efficiently.'

As part of their campaign to persuade a reluctant Reuter board to take long views, financial and otherwise, Burgess and Cole submitted a steady stream of reports and proposals. Cole revelled in pie-charts, diagrams, and maps. For example, in November 1960 the board was shown 'Communication costs at a glance' (Fig. 13); and in September 1962, how the revenue for 1961 had been earned and spent (Fig. 14). Reuters was spending nearly £600,000 a year on communications, compared with editorial costs of £376,300.

The biggest single user of news from Reuters was the BBC. In 1960 the BBC's main news subscription was worth £101,250. No other subscriptions approached six figures: the next three were Kyodo (£48,750), DPA (£40,820), and the Arab News Agency (£29,800); the ANA also paid its transmission costs of £15,000. Long-time subscribers such as the *New York Times*, *France-Soir*, the *Chicago Tribune*, and the main European national news agencies, each contributed sums within the £20,000–£29,000 range.

Since 1944 the arrangement had been that the BBC paid a basic subscription equal to 22.5 per cent of the total PA and NPA assessments. The BBC and Reuters accepted that they stood in a special relationship. At intervals, however, the BBC complained about the increasing sums which it was required to pay under the 22.5 per cent formula. A BBC deputation led by Sir Ian Jacob, the director-general, met the Reuter board on 9 October 1957. Harry Lindley, the Reuter chairman for the meeting, emphasized that the board wanted the BBC to feel that it was 'not just a client and customer but some way to being a partner'. Jacob answered that if the BBC were ever to become merely a customer, it would expect to pay less; but it had decided 'that it was right under the present circumstances to support Reuters as a

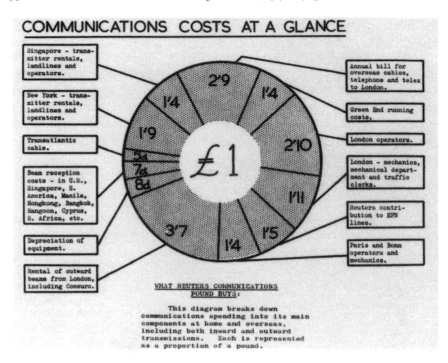

COMMUNICATIONS COSTS AT A GLANCE

Singapore – transmitter rentals, landlines and operators.

New York – transmitter rentals, landlines and operators.

Transatlantic cable.

Beam reception costs – in U.S., Singapore, S. America, Manila, Hongkong, Bangkok, Rangoon, Cyprus, S. Africa, etc.

Depreciation of equipment.

Rental of outward beams from London, including Comeuro.

Annual bill for overseas cables, telephone and telex to London.

Green End running costs.

London operators.

London – mechanics, mechanical department and traffic clerks.

Reuters contribution to EPN lines.

Paris and Bonn operators and mechanics.

WHAT REUTERS COMMUNICATIONS POUND BUYS:

This diagram breaks down communications spending into its main components at home and overseas, including both inward and outward transmissions. Each is represented as a proportion of a pound.

FIG. 13. 'Communications costs at a glance', November 1960

British institution. The two sides agreed that in future the BBC should have access to all essential documents and accounts, and that the director-general should be free to attend Reuter board meetings 'whenever he felt that there was some reason for doing so'. In the event, he never did. But contact on a daily basis was maintained from November 1955 by two liaison editors from the BBC working on the London editorial floor. In his resignation memorandum, Chancellor forecast that 'sooner or later' the BBC's claim to a share in the ownership would have to be met. It never was.[57]

In 1960 the Arab News Agency's £29,800 was the third-highest overseas subscription. This payment was valuable, but compromising. The ANA was covertly subsidized by the British Government; and Reuters knew this to be so. Yet in 1954 it had handed over to the ANA the distribution of its general news and commercial services throughout most of the Middle East. Reuters continued with its own news-gathering network, but the ANA also supplied commercial reports.[58]

The ANA had originated during the Second World War. Because it depended for its existence upon official subsidy, Reuters had regarded it at that period as an unfair competitor, and the board was warned at intervals about its activities. After the war Chancellor complained (8 January 1946) to Ernest Bevin, the Foreign Secretary, about 'sham "news agencies" ' in the Middle East and elsewhere: 'I feel there are cleaner and indeed more effective ways of presenting the British case abroad.' Overseas publicity services, suggested Chancellor, 'can run in parallel with Reuters'.

Reuters did not relish having to compete with the ANA, which charged little for its services, and sometimes even nothing. Chancellor told the board on 26 June 1951 that he saw no hope of extending the Reuter presence in the Middle East. The cost of teleprinter equipment for additional services would be heavy, and translation costs into Arabic would be high. In 1953 Cole was sent to explore the possibility of a handover of Reuter distribution to a projected new Egyptian national news agency, but the project collapsed. 'It was in this vacuum', recalled Cole in 1961, 'that I entered into negotiations with ANA.'

Reuter trading profit from the region had been little more than £1,000 for 1953, and was falling. In this knowledge, Cole negotiated an agreement with the ANA. He did so even though he admitted that the ANA was receiving a large subsidy of about £150,000 a year from the British Government. The agreement guaranteed an annual revenue to Reuters of £28,500 for seven years. In return, the ANA was granted the exclusive right to distribute a

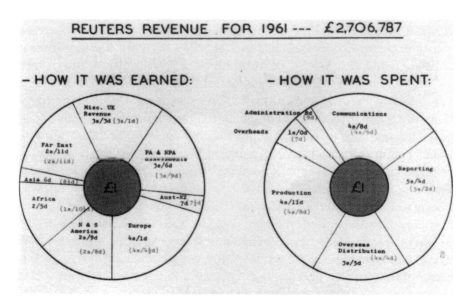

FIG. 14. How Reuters revenue for 1961 was earned and spent (figures in brackets show values in 1960)

Reuter-originated file of world news throughout the Arab countries. The ANA promised to pay Reuters one-third of any new commercial revenues which it collected. And it bought up the assets of Reuters in Egypt.

Such terms had proved irresistible. The board discussed the ANA offer on 14 July 1954. Chancellor described it as financially 'very attractive'. He conceded that 'the objection to the contract was the fact that the Arab News Agency was known to be subsidized by the British Government.' Laurence Scott argued that deals had been done previously with Government-subsidized agencies, and that this did not matter 'so long as the purchaser did not tamper with the service'. Scott failed to recognize that the ANA was not a national news agency. It was a propaganda body, seeking to promote British interests. It had obviously decided that such interests would be served by distributing Reuter news over more than one country in an important part of the world. The ANA's dependence upon the British Government was to remain concealed. Reuters was therefore not only indirectly accepting British Government help: it was also pretending not to know that it was doing so. The board none the less empowered Chancellor to sign the contract.[59]

During the Suez crisis the ANA was expelled from Egypt, its headquarters being transferred from Cairo to Beirut. Looking back with satisfaction in March 1961, Cole reported that the ANA had scrupulously credited Reuter news. He did not add that this was scarcely surprising, since the British Government was seeking to make use of the good name of the agency. Reuters, said Cole, was now 'almost indispensable' to leading newspapers and broadcasting stations throughout the Arab world, 'regardless of the Suez affair'.

Notwithstanding its always tight financial position, should Reuters have kept clear of this ANA connection? Writing to Burgess (29 July 1957), Laurence Scott pointed out how much Reuters still depended upon official help. 'I don't think we can run away from this question. In the Middle East the answer was the Arab News Agency. In Nigeria it was large broadcasting subscriptions. Elsewhere it has been large local subscriptions by the British Embassy. Which of these methods do we approve or disapprove?' Scott did not answer his own awkward question.[60]

21

Burgess told the 1960 annual general meeting that 'the whole of West Africa is alive and tingling'. Reuters, he said, was planning a service of news to and from black Africa 'in the great tradition of the past'. Reuters could not have responded to this challenge without help from the British Government. Ralph Murray of the Foreign Office had told Burgess on 12 November 1959: 'We want more news—more Reuter news—into Africa.' Cole warned Murray on 16 June 1960 that an intensive survey had revealed that 'deficit development' expenditure of about £50,000 would be needed to introduce services into West and Central Africa, including a French-language service. Reuters did not ask for a subsidy as such, but for a large increase in British Government and Central Office of Information subscriptions for delivery of news services to their African outlets. From 1 April 1961 the block subscription on behalf of British Government overseas departments was raised to £70,000 per annum plus £22,120 for the COI, with news delivery charges paid for at cost. This amounted to a total increase of £60,199, which was about half of what Reuters had requested.[61]

With this financial support Reuters launched into black Africa, both English- and French-speaking. The venture was entrusted to Patrick Crosse (1916–93), who in just five busy years spread the name of Reuters across the continent. This notable achievement owed much to Crosse's diplomatic skill. His patrician manner—quietly strong while courteously sympathetic—served him well in dealing with African politicians and newspapermen, who would have resented being patronized and yet needed guidance. Crosse had joined Reuters in India in 1936, where his uncle, W. J. Moloney, was manager. During the Second World War Crosse served as a war correspondent, was captured in Libya, and spent three years as a prisoner.[62]

Crosse was assisted by Shahe Guebenlian, who became manager for East and Central Africa. Believing that Africans preferred to do business face-to-face rather than by correspondence, Guebenlian made hundreds of flights throughout the continent. In the same week he had meetings with two heads of state—Kaunda of Zambia and Banda of Malawi. Crosse and Guebenlian realized that the news needs of each African country would have to be met individually. At the same time, each country would expect to receive a service of news from the rest of Africa as well as from the wider world. Reuters had enjoyed an early success in Nigeria, where Cole had negotiated long-term contracts in 1956 with the Federal Government (£9,000), and three leading newspapers. The policy there, and everywhere, was to work with Governments as the only sure points; and to assist the desire of most African states to establish their own national news agencies. Cole reminded the board in May 1960 that 'Reuters as a matter of principle and of policy does not itself attempt to be a domestic news agency'.

Reuters eventually signed news contracts with thirty-five independent African states. The only exceptions were Gambia, Rwanda, and Burundi. In

February 1965 Long, by now general manager, attributed the success of Reuters in Africa to its whole-continent approach: 'It is through the Reuter report that African countries have news of one another.' He emphasized that news contracts with the African Governments required them to preserve the integrity and identity of the Reuter service when issuing it internally. The name of Reuters now reached into French-speaking Africa, once the preserve of Havas or AFP.

By 1965 Reuters maintained twenty-four correspondents in Africa, plus fifty stringers. Five years earlier there had been just three staff correspondents to cover the whole continent. Reporting costs in the mid-1960s totalled about £215,000 annually. This allowed a clear surplus of revenue over expenditure: annual revenue was £175,000 from English-speaking Africa, £121,000 from French-speaking Africa. Reuters served 132 media clients. Unfortunately, many of them paid their subscriptions only in arrears.

While a new relationship was being opened with Africa, the old Reuter relationship with Europe was beginning to be transformed. A conference of top managers and senior departmental executives had decided in October 1960 that Reuters should plan for the eventual direct distribution of its news services to West European countries. Traditional ties with the national news agencies were to be relaxed. Cole reported to the board on 14 December 1960 that he had successfully resisted a plan by Daniel Ryelandt of Belga, who acted as leader of the 39 Group, to allow only uniform subscription increases for the European agencies and to refuse individual negotiations with Reuters. Gerald Long, the assistant general manager for Europe, told Cole on 20 July that the revenue from commercial news delivery to the smaller Western European countries was 'derisory', bearing in mind that they were advanced economies with high volumes of foreign trade.

Michael Nelson, the young new manager of Comtelburo, argued on 29 October 1962 that Reuters ought to run its own commercial service in Belgium because of 'the growing need to make services on the European level, and the importance of Brussels in this'. Glen Renfrew, another young Comtelburo specialist, was sent to assess the Belgian situation. His report, dated 7 December, confirmed that profits would be doubled by direct management. The energy of the head of Belga's commercial side, claimed Renfrew, 'appears to be totally consumed by the effort of staying awake in office hours'. The whole situation, Renfrew concluded, was typical of what he had found in many other European countries—services badly produced, and with no effort made to sell more.

Against this background, Long proposed and Cole agreed that the Belga subscription for general news should be increased by 20 per cent, and that the running of the commercial services in Belgium should be taken over by Reuters. Ryelandt was shocked; but he found the new purposefulness shown by Reuters impossible to resist. He was described dismissively by Cole in December 1962 as 'capricious'. 'It is imperative that we stand up to Mr. Ryelandt. Belgium is a test case for us.'

Cole was in poor health, and left Long to conduct the detailed negotiations in Brussels. On 25 January 1963 Ryelandt flew to London to continue the discussions. Fog delayed his arrival. Cole, feeling unwell, lay down for a rest on a sofa in his office. When his secretary came to rouse him, she found that he was dead: he had suffered a massive heart attack.

Cole's death made no difference to the Belga negotiations. He was succeeded as general manager by Long, who insisted upon the 20 per cent increase in the general news subscription and upon selling commercial news and information directly. Belga tried and failed to develop a commercial service of its own, based upon AFP's economic service.

22

On 19 October 1962 a wall-plaque had been unveiled at the Aachen inn where Julius Reuter had conducted his pigeon service in 1850. Pigeons were released to race to Brussels as part of three days of celebrations in memory of the founder. The board had met in Aachen that same morning, its very first meeting outside London. Cole was in an expansive mood. '"Stand still" was a phrase unknown to Paul Julius Reuter,' he exclaimed at a luncheon for West European newspapermen. 'It is also unknown for us who follow him in the space age . . . Reuters will follow the new cables, the satellites, the stars, the planets and whatever fresh scientific wonder might come in communications.'

Certainly, Reuters was destined soon after Cole's death to undergo a period of revolutionary change, centring upon the application of computer technology to the distribution of economic data. Had he lived, would Cole himself—outstanding though he was as a general news journalist—have been the man to oversee such a revolution?

TWELVE

Making the New Reuters
1963–1981

The problem with information is the indigestibility
of it . . . Putting that computer at the front end of it,
and retrieving it when you want it, has made all the
difference to our business and will continue to do so.

(Peter Job, chief executive of Reuters, 1995)

I

DURING the decades after Cole's death in 1963 Reuters was transformed. Its commitment to following high principles of conduct in
the collection and distribution of news and information remained the
same; but the process was much altered in practice. What happened was
summed up by Peter Job above.[1]

By the 1980s annual profits were growing into tens and hundreds of millions of pounds. Nearly all of this profit was drawn from services delivered by
computer to traders in the world's financial and commodities markets. To
provide these services, scores of economic journalists were recruited, while
thousands of technical, marketing, and sales personnel joined Reuters who
were not journalists at all. In other words, the staff profile was redrawn. At the
same time, traditional general news services continued to be supplied to the
media, and these old-style services were themselves expanded. Here was an
exciting mixture—a recipe for much public success, and for some private tension. Here was a new Reuters.

A modest annual working surplus, such as Burgess and Cole had begun to
seek, could never have paid for this transformation. To achieve such a major
change, the raising of millions of pounds in investment capital became essential and urgent. The man who persuaded three successive chairmen to guide
a doubting board into countenancing such boldness was Gerald Long, Cole's
successor as general manager.

When Long resigned in 1981, his contribution was summed up by the current chairman, Sir Denis Hamilton:

> Mr. Long's two decades as Chief Executive of Reuters have been of historical importance to the Company. He has maintained and developed the traditional highest standards of integrity and reporting of Reuters as the largest world news service. He has now, after a period of incredible risk taking and technical innovation, built it up into the greatest international service of financial and business information, provided for almost every country in the world.

This high praise was dismissed by some as merely routine farewell eulogy; but in fact it was sufficiently deserved. While others were the creative forces behind particular projects, Long alone was in a position as chief executive to oversee the making of the new Reuters.

Long's appointment as general manager in 1963 had come as a surprise. At 39 he was the youngest of the internal candidates, all of whom were assistant general managers. The others were Patrick Crosse, Stuart Underhill, and Doon Campbell. The only outside candidate to be interviewed was Michael King, the son of Cecil King, the former Reuter director. Michael King, who had worked for Reuters as a diplomatic correspondent, had apparently applied for the job. When asked at interview how he would propose to raise more money for development, he replied that, since the owners declined to provide such vital finance, it would have to be sought from the British Government. As already noticed, King's father had argued the same while serving on the board; but despite this, Cecil King apparently did not endorse his son's candidature.[2]

Among those consulted by Burgess was Christopher Chancellor. At the time of Cole's appointment in 1959, Chancellor had written that Long would be a strong candidate for the top job in the future. Support from such a quarter obviously carried weight, but it was not as conclusive as Chancellor later claimed. Burgess made up his own mind, and played the leading part in deciding in favour of Long. The chairman never doubted that he had made the right choice, although he was to find Long much less easy to work with than Cole. In 1973 Long joined the board as managing director.[3]

Gerald Long (1923–1998) was the son of a York postman. While serving in the British army in post-war Germany, he became involved in setting up newspapers under British military control. In 1948 he entered Reuters as a graduate recruit from Cambridge University, where he had read modern languages. Long spoke both French and German like a native. He possessed a rare, because equal, liking for French and German literature, music, art, and (not least) food and drink. After spells in Paris—where he won over an initially hostile Harold King—and Ankara, Long was appointed chief representative in Germany in 1956. Cole began to ask for his opinions, and to take him on tours. In 1960 he was made assistant general manager for Europe, based in London.

Long's personality was intriguing. His mind was subtle, but not his manner. He had a Yorkshire forthrightness, which many took for brusqueness, sometimes correctly. Yet he could be engaging. His face provided a striking canvas for either humour. His hair was short-cropped, his eye steady, his gesture firm, his voice slow but decisive. It all depended upon the play of expression around the full moustache, sharp chin, and thrusting eyebrows. He could be amiable, or he could be fierce. He was rarely neutral, even when he lapsed into silence, which disconcertingly he sometimes did.

All found themselves at odds with Long sooner or later, even his protégés. The answer was not to let him slip into bullying. He accepted contradiction if it was well-informed, and obviously for the good of Reuters. His concern for the company was undoubted, and his knowledge of its history considerable. Indeed, he consciously set out to become another Julius Reuter, a second founder. He wanted to make Reuters into an aggressive and profitable organization, such as it had been in Julius Reuter's prime. 'I felt I had much in common with him.'[4]

Long was entirely undeterred by charges of arrogance about his own or the company's attitude. He encouraged a strong sense of the specialness of Reuters, and this built up morale. He later explained that his guiding idea had been 'a powerful conviction that if Reuters had survived for 115 years with its central force untainted it had a dynamism which would enable it not only to survive but to adapt and grow'.

Cole had drawn all lines of communication within the top management towards himself, suspicious of direct discussion between senior staff. Long, by contrast, had no fear of cabals. He delegated readily, sometimes out of laziness. And he revelled in free-wheeling discussions. One of the questions asked in these discussions was how best to develop the economic services without causing tension with the general news journalists. No soothing answer was found.

2

Upon becoming general manager Long immediately began to seek better ways of monitoring costs and revenue. He also introduced a comprehensive policy for staff relations. Both reforms were necessary if Reuters was to make best use of its financial and human resources.

During the 1960s the financial position of the company remained precarious, with overall losses occurring in 1964 and again in 1967. The British newspaper groups, the senior partners in Reuters, were themselves hard-pressed, because of competition from commercial television for advertising income. Reuters was now drawing some 70 per cent of its revenue from outside the British Isles, its headquarters territory. It was unique in this regard among news agencies—quite unlike AP or UPI, the American agencies, with their strong home bases; or AFP, which was French Government-subsidized; or Tass, which was the official Soviet news agency. AP revenue for 1964 exceeded £19 million, which was well over five times that of Reuters; AP made a profit on the year of £186,792, Reuters a loss of £57,092. AP could afford to spend £2,678,571 upon foreign news coverage: Reuters only £1,256,000, which was less than half. These comparative figures measured how much Reuters needed to strengthen itself.

Not least, Reuters had to escape from over-dependence upon a few subscribers. The nineteen main contracts running in 1965—each worth £20,000 per year or more—earned a total of £684,525. Reuters could not risk losing any one of these contracts. Clearly, it ought to widen its revenue base. The effects of the devaluation of sterling in 1967 led Reuters to abandon its traditional policy of expressing major contracts in sterling. S. G. Warburg, the merchant bank, advised that the company should have as much as possible of its income expressed or paid in the hardest currencies, particularly in Swiss francs.

Long introduced careful planning. Care meant much more than the making of economies, although economy drives were still attempted at intervals. In July 1971 he defined the company's objectives in a board paper:

> Reuters central purpose is to achieve the highest standards of excellence in the provision of news services and information and communication systems to subscribers throughout the world. To maintain this purpose Reuters must be profitable, since profit is the condition of Reuters existence and the touchstone of Reuters efficiency. The use of profit is to develop Reuters services and to benefit Reuters shareholders and staff.

Long repeated this statement several times down the years. He depended heavily upon the financial expertise of Nigel Judah (1930–91), the secretary and chief accountant of Reuters from 1960. Judah had joined the company in 1955, and had been promoted rapidly. For three decades he was destined to be close to the top, trusted by successive chief executives. His wide range of contacts within the financial world, plus his softly courteous style of doing business, enabled him to secure large loans for Reuters, at a time when its credit rating was indifferent. A key document from Judah, dated 24 June 1966, concluded that the company needed a minimum capital injection of £250,000. He suggested that the owners might themselves put up fresh capital by subscribing for additional stock. They refused to do so. The bold alternative was to borrow. Burgess, the chairman, backed the bold course, but most of the other directors were reluctant. Long made his determination clear. Faintheartedly, the board agreed to borrow.[5] A loan of $430,000 was raised in October 1966 from Morgan Guaranty Trust. A second loan of 4,500,000 Swiss francs (£375,000) came in August 1967 from Credit Suisse of Zurich. This loan was for ten years at 6.75 per cent, subject to a guarantee for both loans from the company's bankers, the Bank of Scotland. The Reuter reserves, worth approximately £350,000, were pledged by way of further guarantee.

The Reuter board was told by Long in June 1967 that the Swiss loan was needed both for immediate and longer-term purposes. Immediately:

1. To buy a computerized message-switching system (Automatic Data Exchange) for conducting the news services more effectively.
2. To fund a United Kingdom overdraft.
3. To buy Agence Cosmographique, which was desirable in order to exploit the strong position of the economic services in the highly profitable Swiss market.

By 1972 investment in new equipment was totalling £1,217,954 for the year. This heavy expenditure was financed partly out of cash flow and partly by an unsecured loan of $864,000 at 5.5 per cent over five years from Morgan Guaranty, in association with the Export/Import Bank of Washington. Judah had been particularly pleased to find this latter source. The loan had to be spent exclusively upon the purchase of equipment manufactured in the United States for export; but this presented no problem, since Reuters was already intending to buy American. At the end of 1973 outstanding borrowing from all sources totalled £1,400,230—only 14 per cent secured.

Turnover was now growing fast. It passed £10 million in 1970, and reached £50 million by 1977. In that year, sixteen countries each contributed over £500,000. Nine were in Europe, plus the United States, Canada, Hong Kong, Japan, Singapore, Brazil, and South Africa. In other words, although Reuters maintained a presence nearly everywhere, its prosperity depended upon the Westernized capitalist world. Its expanding economic services were particularly designed to serve that world.

In 1965 Long introduced comprehensive budgeting into Reuters for the first time. Annual forecasting followed from 1973, which was important to ensure the exploitation of success. A yearly 'budget and plan' document was produced from 1976. At first, this attempted to look five years ahead; but from 1982, after Long's departure, the period was cut to three years in order to concentrate upon achieving early benefits.

Long wanted Reuters to present a modern visual image. Through his friend, Theo Crosby, in 1965 he commissioned a new Reuter company logo for use on stationery, buildings, vehicles, and elsewhere. The result was a distinctive presentation of the word 'Reuters', picked out in dots, a design inspired by teleprinter tape.

Notwithstanding his frequent brusqueness towards individuals, Long was solicitous about the staff in general. He knew that Reuters was a labour-intensive organization, which depended upon retaining a committed trained workforce. During the 1960s staff costs amounted to about half of total budget, and staff numbers were rising steadily, especially overseas. The global total first passed 2,000 in 1976 (see Table 12.1).

TABLE 12.1. Worldwide staff numbers, 1964 and 1976.

	Head Office	Overseas	Total
1964	699	653	1,352
1976	893	1,143	2,036

At the end of 1963 Long appointed a staff manager. The man chosen was Brian Stockwell (1915–89), a quiet but popular figure, responsive without being weak, who could both lead and listen. He was trusted by everyone, from Long downwards. Stockwell's father had spent a lifetime in Reuters. Brian himself joined in 1938, and he had acquired wide experience as a journalist and manager both in London and overseas.[6]

Stockwell began by negotiating the introduction of graded salary structures for all employees. This suited both management and trade unions. By July 1966 Long was telling the board that Stockwell had 'regained in most of our dealings with the unions the initiative which previously lay permanently with them'. He had organized recruitment and training programmes, and had brought staff wastage 'within bearable limits'. An independent outside review of staff employment in London, undertaken in 1969, reported a high level of job satisfaction.[7]

The trade unions within Reuters at this period were active, but they were much more reasonable than those within the Fleet Street newspaper offices. Reuters met no blanket resistance to the introduction of new technology. A crucial success for Stockwell was a 1966 agreement for the joint manning of computer installations. These jobs had been claimed by two unions, and the agreement provided for recruitment turn by turn for all new computer staff, except engineers and technicians. Demarcation disputes, which might have wrecked the new ventures so vital to Reuters, were thereby avoided.

During the 1970s the London press telegraphists were worried at the prospect of visual display units (VDUs) being introduced into newsrooms. Kevin Garry, who was in charge of staff relations from 1974, told a meeting of telegraphists on 19 March 1975 that 'anybody in the Company, whatever union card he held, should be able to use VDUs'. In October and November 1974 national union officials and Reuter union representatives visited Reuters New York at company expense to study video editing in operation. It had been introduced there at the start of the year. Garry hinted that, if London refused to follow New York, the whole Fleet Street editorial operation might be moved outside the United Kingdom. This concentrated union minds. Agreement was finally reached on 2 July 1975. The telegraphists abandoned their right to exclusive control of the transmission of news to line, and in return Reuters offered retraining and redeployment without redundancies, plus phased pay supplements. In the event, the introduction of video editing into London was delayed for technical reasons until the end of 1979. Although the telegraphists had conceded the right of London journalists to input news directly, the journalists demanded extra payment for doing so. Eventually £625 a year was agreed.[8]

Labour problems were to be found during these years not only inside Reuters, but also within the British Post Office and in the electricity supply industry. Strikes in these sectors, or a strike within the London technical centre of Reuters itself, could have cut off the computerized economic services. Customers for price information needed it every second, and Reuters knew that disruption of its economic services would be even more damaging than disturbance in the delivery of general news. This was one reason for the decision in 1979 to establish a second technical centre at Geneva. Switzerland enjoyed good industrial relations as well as good communications. The centre opened in May 1982.

3

Global communications technology was developing very fast during the 1960s. A circular on 'Reuters Communications' from the statistical unit (30 November 1965) began arrestingly. 'By the time you read this note some of the information may well be out of date . . . Reuters watches all new developments, and as soon as they are practicable technically and commercially, uses them to further the basic aim of giving "the world's news to the world".'

Under Cole, Long had been put in charge of communications development, and he continued to take a close interest after he became general manager. In a note for the board in February 1968 he explained how Reuters had recently concentrated upon exploiting the advantages of 'bulk working' in international communications. Wherever possible, it had bought high-capacity circuits 'so to speak wholesale' from the communications authorities. This process had begun in March 1963, when Reuters leased a voice circuit across the Atlantic, and bought terminal equipment to divide the circuit into 22 teleprinter channels. The capital cost of equipment was a modest £5,000, while the lease cost £80,000 a year.

During the 1950s Reuters had worked the transatlantic route exclusively by radio. But radio was liable to interruption, and communication by physical link came back into favour when coaxial cables were developed. Miniaturization techniques allowed the insertion of electronic repeaters into such cables at frequent intervals. In August 1960 Reuters began to lease a circuit in a new Transatlantic coaxial cable for nine hours each day. Within two years, the use of radio across the Atlantic had been entirely abandoned.

Reuters was able to operate these circuits with a new independence. It was no longer just an ordinary customer of the national telecommunications authorities. It lobbied extensively to reduce official constraints upon how it conducted its business; and by the early 1970s Long was able to claim that Reuters was operating the largest and most technically advanced news and information network in the world. The network had two main arteries. One crossed the Atlantic and Pacific Oceans (Tatpac): the other (Europlex) linked the main cities of the Continent to each other and to London. In June 1964 Reuters leased eighteen channels in the new round-the-world Commonwealth cable to Sydney via Canada. Within six years Tatpac had become fully operational, joining London to Singapore and Tokyo through Montreal, Sydney, and Hong Kong. The complementary Europlex system became operational in the summer of 1967, after difficult negotiations with the European communications authorities. Europlex connected London, Paris, Geneva, Frankfurt, The Hague, and Brussels in an eighty-eight-channel ring. This was fed by data spurs and leased teleprinter lines from other major European cities.[9]

At the London heart of the Reuter news service network was a message-storing and switching system known as ADX (Automatic Data Exchange), introduced in July 1968. Reuters benefited from being the pioneer in using such techniques in the news field, although at first the system was inclined to crash at peak times. At full stretch, ADX could process nearly three million words daily for the general news and economic services. ADX made possible the editing of English-language regional services from one central position, the World Desk, rather than from numerous regional desks. Only the French and Western Hemisphere Desks continued.[10]

During the mid-1960s Reuter news was reaching nearly 6,500 newspapers in 112 countries. These papers claimed an aggregate daily circulation of 276,479,000 copies. News was also being supplied to networks claiming to serve 393,678,000 radios and 177,184,000 television sets.

The formation of a General News Division (GND) in July 1967 constituted a major initiative by Long—not only in structural but also in psychological terms. It was intended to reinforce the position of the general news services in comparison with the fast-growing economic side. Long was enthusiastic for the further development of the economic services; but he was himself a former general news journalist, and he hoped that the fresh structure, headed by the editor-in-chief, would help general news to hold its own within Reuters by enabling it to make money in parallel with Reuters Economic Services (RES). In 1962 trading revenue from general news had still been everywhere ahead of revenue from the economic services. By 1970 it was far behind in Europe, and also behind in North America (see Table 12.2). Down the years, different titles had been used for the commercial services in different parts of the world—'Comtelburo', 'Comtel Reuter', 'Reuters Economic Services'. From April 1966 this last title, hitherto confined to Australia, was adopted everywhere. In other words, the Reuter name was no longer kept back from use by the non-media services.

RES revenue overtook that from the General News Division in 1968. Could general news make a comeback? Long was encouraged to believe so

TABLE 12.2. Comparison of trading revenue, 1962 and 1970 (£000)

	1962		1970	
	GND	Comtelburo	GND	RES
Europe	342.2	246.3	644.5	2,962.3
Africa	167.6	71.9	503.6	367.5
North America	209.0	91.7	566.6	694.2
Asia	257.0	37.2	614.3	492.3
Total	957.8	447.1	2,329.0	4,516.5

by a journalist who had trained under him in Germany. This was Brian Horton, a New Zealander with a family background in journalism, who had joined Reuters in 1957. In October 1968 Horton was made editor-in-chief and an assistant general manager, and put in charge of GND. He had already played the leading part in the introduction of ADX.[11]

GND was designated a profit centre alongside RES. This gave the editor-in-chief responsibility not only for the collection and distribution of news, but also for the sale of media products throughout the world. Some senior executives thought this misconceived, that it was like giving the production manager at Fords charge also of selling the cars. GND and RES each employed separate staffs in London, and each ran their own newsrooms. In most Reuter offices throughout the world there were two editors and two budgets. In October 1969 GND maintained 276 staff in London (including 130 journalists), while RES had 233 staff (48 of them journalists).

Horton had cut GND numbers in London to 213 by 1973. As a result, he was able to contain news costs. But he could not generate more revenue by much increasing the price of news from Reuters, because AP, UPI, and AFP were already charging their overseas subscribers far less. In 1968 the general news loss on the year was about £100,000. Inflation and rising communication costs magnified the problem so that by 1978 the annual loss on general news was being estimated at £7 million.

Horton's critics within Reuters contended that he had been at least foolish and at worst arrogant to believe that he could make money overall out of news. The whole history of Reuters demonstrated otherwise. In the executive committee, Michael Nelson, Horton's RES counterpart, was openly critical. Long remained convinced that the GND initiative had been worth attempting; but he reluctantly recognized that Nelson was nearly indispensable, whereas Horton was not. Long had also come to realize that to reveal so plainly the large losses being made on general news was bad public relations.

At the end of 1973 the experiment of making GND a profit centre was abandoned. In its place came Reuters World Service. This was designated a cost centre: Reuters Economic Services remained a profit centre. Reuters Media Services and Reuters North America became other profit centres. Although RES was to buy general news from the World Service, and the Media Services were to sell World Service news to the media, the much greater profit-making potential of the economic side within the new Reuters had now been structurally recognized. Horton resigned.

4

Long's three internal rivals for the top job in 1963—Crosse, Underhill, and Campbell—had all left the company within ten years. Two younger men, Michael Nelson and Glen Renfrew, were rising fast throughout the 1960s. While Long ranged broadly and dealt with the board, Nelson and Renfrew were foremost in promoting the products which brought about the transformation of Reuters.

Michael Nelson was born in 1929, the son of a carpenter. Geiringer had recruited him for Comtelburo in 1952 as a graduate trainee from Oxford University. His first overseas managerial posting was to Thailand in 1954. He gradually became known for his purposefulness. Underhill, who was instrumental in getting Nelson made manager of Comtelburo in 1962, recollected years later 'a slight, red-haired young man, thoughtful in manner', but with 'the toughness, cheek and adaptability of an English sparrow'. Throughout his career Nelson was to be precise, hard-working, acute, strong-minded, far-sighted, usually good-humoured, and sometimes humorous. This strong combination served him well as a manager and negotiator for Reuters.[12]

During the 1960s and 70s Nelson oversaw the introduction of a succession of computerized and other products for the distribution of economic information. These were to earn great profits. Nelson did not himself create these products, although he sometimes suggested improvements. Rather, he carefully evaluated the possibilities, and gave steady support to just a few initiatives. He was being bold and cautious at the same time. He knew that the company was too poor to make expensive mistakes.

Nelson was a good spokesman for his growing band of economic journalists. He insisted upon proper recognition for himself and for his staff; and by the late 1970s, with the demise of the GND experiment, he had gone far towards achieving this. In 1976 he became general manager in succession to Stockwell, and a joint deputy managing director. He was put in charge of company planning, and of the business management and trading of Reuters apart from North America. He also became the channel of communication with middle management. By this date, many both within the company and outside regarded him as the obvious successor to Long.

Also appointed joint deputy managing director in 1976 was Glen Renfrew. Born in New South Wales in 1928, Renfrew had joined Comtelburo in 1952, a few weeks before Nelson. They were destined eventually to compete for the top job. Renfrew was the tenth child of an Australian coalminer, who had left the pit to become a lay preacher. Young Renfrew revealed a talent for languages, becoming fluent in French, German, and Italian. After graduating from Sydney University, he travelled around Europe. He applied to Reuters, and Geiringer eventually appointed him to Comtelburo. More than once, however, during the next few years, he was nearly sacked. Before leaving Australia he had worked at a construction camp where hard drinking and fisticuffs ruled, and he later admitted: 'maybe I still had some of the manner of that place.' Yet there was always much more to Renfrew than 'a wild colonial boy'. He was, for example, an enthusiast for literature and the arts. And although his personality was strong, he was not arrogant. He could listen and learn, and he had a clear mind. Helped by a cheery grin and an Australian accent (gradually reduced), he related with people of all sorts. These qualities enabled him to become an outstanding salesman and negotiator for Reuters.[13]

Very importantly, Renfrew became interested in the new communications technology, to such an extent that in evaluating the great developments of the period he was able to hold his own with the specialists. He kept his colleagues aware of what had become possible, and of what further advances might be made. He believed that only by introducing new technology could Reuters hope to protect its existing contracts, attract new business, and make more money. Throughout his career he dedicated himself to bringing together fresh products, greater sales, and higher profits.

Between 1955 and 1959 Renfrew was in South Africa, where he ended up as manager. He was highly successful in developing the economic services there. In 1960 he was made Comtelburo manager for South-East Asia at Singapore, where again he did what Cole described to the board in July 1960 as 'an outstanding sales development job'. At the start of 1963 he was appointed manager for Belgium. This was his big chance, and he took it. Reuters was breaking its commercial service connection with Belga, and Brussels had become the main administrative centre for the European Economic Community. Long told Doon Campbell (17 January 1963) that Renfrew was to be 'Common Market overlord'.

In July 1964 Renfrew was made manager of the new computer division of Comtelburo. Here was recognition of his interest in the new technology; but it was left to him to make what he could of the job. He began with just a secretary and three technicians. During the next few years his division was to play the key part in introducing computerized Reuter services. Renfrew's drive and command of languages helped him to get on well with equipment suppliers, potential customers, the stock exchanges, and the regulatory authorities. In 1969 he was made Nelson's deputy in Reuters Economic Services. But he was not the man for second place. From the start of 1971 he became manager in North America, one of the most challenging assignments within Reuters.

5

Reuters took up the new information technology not in any spirit of daring, but in a spirit of realism. Long and his colleagues knew that if Reuters did not adopt the latest technology, subscribers would turn to competitors who were willing to do so. Ever greater speed had always been the objective since the time of Julius Reuter's pigeons. But this was to be much more than simply another acceleration. The data-processing revolution was to make possible, first, the circulation of both general news and economic information everywhere at the same time; even while, secondly, it was to lead to the creation of products which allowed subscribers to be selective, to retrieve only the data that they required. In combination, these new facilities—of instant ubiquity and of personal choice—delivered more than improvement. They brought about a transformation.

In July 1965 Long compared the positions of the general news and Comtelburo services. 'Reuters main function in its general-news services is to provide a service, whereas Comtelburo's chief aim is to make money.' Long was here making the same point as Chancellor had made in 1947. Nevertheless, Long's tone in recognizing the dependence of Reuters upon its economic services was not grudging, as Chancellor's had been, but complimentary. He reminded his senior managers on 3 June 1965 that no other firm possessed such a good economic news network and such expertise: 'we must make a great effort to ensure that everyone in the organisation realises how much we depend on these services.'

On 1 June 1963 the International Financial Printer was started in Brussels. It was the brainchild of Renfrew. IFP provided bankers and brokers in Europe with high-speed delivery of general news and economic information. This constituted a significant advance. For the first time businessmen over a wide area could receive a service simultaneously and continuously. Previously, news and information had been first transmitted to Reuter offices and agents; these had then compiled services as quickly as they could for distribution by teleprinter, telex, telephone, mail, or messenger. Direct delivery was to be the way of the future, not only (as here) through printers, but especially through new computer-based products.[14]

Using computer technology, words no longer need be spelt out on printers: they could be processed for retrieval. Nelson had become aware of the rapid development of computerized price-quotation products in the United States. In New York, Reuters subscribed to 'Stockmaster', a computerized product from Ultronic Systems Corporation of New Jersey. This was a new firm, formed by a group of enterprising engineers from Radio Corporation of America. With the encouragement of Cyril Smith, who was the Comtelburo manager in New York, Nelson turned to Ultronic. Its brilliant and businesslike president, Robert Sinn, was a pioneer of the revolution; his young company was ahead of all others in applying know-how about computers. Sinn was invited to London by Reuters where he convinced the top management that he was the man to follow. Long explained to the board on 8 April 1964 that the growth of computer technology had 'brought about a revolution in the technique of dealing with the kind of statistical information which is Comtelburo's main stock-in-trade'.

Ultronic, and its main American rival Bunker Ramo, had moved into Europe early in 1964 to serve a number of brokerage subscribers in Geneva, London, and Paris. But the prospects for Ultronic on its own in Europe were limited. To provide prices at an acceptable speed, Stockmaster needed to employ a wide communication band; yet the wider the band-width the greater the expense. At the same period, Reuters was starting to use twenty-two channels across the Atlantic. The opportunity for a deal became obvious to both parties. A contract with Sinn was signed on 23 April 1964; it was to come into force from 1 July. During the intervening weeks the Ultronic engineers showed their excellence. They worked out how to apply time-division multiplexing to the handling of the large volume of data to be transmitted across the Atlantic from the master Stockmaster computer. Capacity on the Reuter cable was doubled—from twenty-two to the equivalent of forty-four channels.

The Ultronic system fed ticker-tape signals from stock exchanges and other markets into a master computer at Mount Laurel, New Jersey. This processed the material for feeding by line into slave-memory computers. One of these was in London, to serve subscribers in European financial centres. Slave memories were connected to the offices of brokers and other subscribers, who each had a small desk unit which gave them access to the latest information on stock prices simply by pressing buttons. The desk unit produced three illuminated digits and looked like an old-style adding-machine (Plate 51).

This joint venture made the latest technology available to Reuters at minimum cost and risk. It obtained exclusive rights to Stockmaster outside North America for ten years. This meant a free hand in the United Kingdom, continental Europe, Asia, and elsewhere. Ultronic put up all the capital for equipment, the costs being charged against the project over five years. In return, Reuters made available the spare capacity in its transatlantic cable channels, and its understanding of the market. Net costs and profits were shared equally.

If the risk and cost to Reuters had been proportionate to the great opportunity, would the board have taken the chance? Almost certainly not. Reuters was able to begin the transformation of its fortunes upon remarkably easy terms. In January 1969, after five years of operating the joint venture, Long reminded the board of its good fortune:

> Reuters is attempting to achieve a commercially successful operation without that working capital which for most companies is the prerequisite of development. Ultronic, especially since it has become part of the great electronics complex of General Telephone and Electronics, has capital readily available and is prepared to supply it for projects taking Reuters know-how as our contribution to joint investment. The availability of such a partner has greatly helped Reuters to make a transition from obsolescent teleprinter services to electronic systems, especially those of interrogation and display . . . Reuters provides almost all the information apart from US stock prices. Ultronic provide all the equipment including the computers.

Yet the exciting launch of Stockmaster had been followed by several months of worrying difficulty and loss. Faced with new technology, the monopoly European telecommunications carriers had become obstructive or had imposed tariff surcharges. The carriers claimed that—because it was transmitting information which was really the property of Ultronic, or of the stock and commodity exchanges—Reuters was seeking itself to function as a carrier. The concept of a proprietary database assembled from different sources was yet to be recognized.

Competition intensified when Bunker Ramo introduced Telequote into Europe with aggressive marketing. Reuters met this threat by halving the basic Stockmaster subscription from $1,500 to $750 per month. Together with heavy start-up costs, this meant that initial losses were higher than expected. The Reuter loss on the project for the second half of 1964 was about £20,000. Although small in retrospect, this sum loomed large at the time. The very viability of the project came under question.

These doubts soon subsided. Stockmaster made a profit for Reuters every year from 1965, reaching as high as £244,000 for 1968. The traditional economic services had made money but were cheap. Stockmaster, by contrast, was able to charge a relatively high subscription. In addition, traditional services often required only a single installation in each subscriber's office. A Stockmaster sale, on the other hand, which might begin with one or two desk units, could readily grow into an installation of twenty or more, although charged at a lower subscription.

The success of the project meant that the master Stockmaster computer in New Jersey was soon matched by a master in London. This also held prices from European stock and commodity exchanges, which Telequote did not have, and which made the service more attractive both for the original US broker subscribers and for European banks. The network was eventually offering over 10,000 stock or commodity prices at push-button command—at first in fifteen seconds, later in only two seconds.

The demand for Stockmaster became extensive. By April 1969 Ultronic had invested about £880,000 in the project, and Reuters had installed 1,100 desk units in 300 subscriber offices in ten European countries. Telegraphic circuits had been replaced by quicker voice-grade channels. Stockmaster soon reached most of the capitalist world, including Hong Kong, Japan, Australia, and South Africa. Reuters now claimed that material was being fed into the system from all the world's main exchanges. This glossed over the reality that Reuter access to such data long remained uneven. The West German exchanges, for example, agreed fairly quickly to distribution of their quotations outside Germany; but they were slower to give approval for distribution of these quotations in the German domestic markets.

Nevertheless, by the late 1960s the quickest way for a bank in (say) Dusseldorf to inform itself about quotations on the Dusseldorf exchange was through the Reuter network. Reuters—whose business had long been the moving of news and information from one country to another—was now also reaching into domestic markets. This extension was significant and profitable. Two distributors of Reuters Economic Services—Jiji of Japan and VWD of West Germany—had each earned more revenue supplying the RES service to their domestic markets than Reuters itself earned from selling its economic services throughout the world. This imbalance was about to change. Whereas Reuters had received only modest fees from offering its traditional economic services for resale by the national agencies, for Stockmaster those agencies were paid only a commission. Most of the revenue went to the joint venture. Moreover, marketing and servicing Stockmaster gave RES a presence in many European countries, and this made agency collaboration no longer so necessary. In Switzerland, which became the most profitable market for Stockmaster, Reuters bought up the local distributor, Agence Cosmographique, in 1967.

As early as the end of 1965 Stockmaster had become 'the standard tool of the US brokerage industry in Europe'. So wrote Renfrew to Sinn on 5 January 1966. Contrary to a forecast that usage would be limited to the larger American brokers, Stockmaster was now being ordered by the smaller houses. The *Wall Street Journal* of 17 November 1965 quoted comments from brokers describing how Stockmaster had boosted their business. American Treasury Secretary Fowler remarked that, thanks to the new information medium, European investment in American stocks had increased significantly, and this had benefited the United States balance of payments.

The success of Stockmaster and its successors depended heavily upon the expertise of Reuter technical staff, and upon a network of field-service representatives. Together they taught themselves how to create and to maintain the world's first intercontinental real-time information network. Product marketing and selling also became increasingly sophisticated. In 1962 Comtelburo had employed just one salesman, based in London. By 1976 RES maintained eight international and forty-seven national sales staff. These salesmen became skilled at demonstrating to potential subscribers how greatly they needed the new information service, even without needing to understand its technology. Nelson and his colleagues took care to remember that Reuter products must always be simple to operate, highly reliable, and profitable in use.

The prosperity brought by Stockmaster soon changed attitudes within RES, and gradually within the organization as a whole. Salaries began to improve, starting with the marketing staff. Restrictions upon travel and upon making international telephone calls, which had been severe, were relaxed. Money was spent upon product promotion, and frequent demonstration sessions were held in pleasant locations in many parts of the world. Superior accommodation was provided for the computer installations and for the staff involved with them. This was the start of a trend which was eventually to transform the office environment throughout Reuters.

From 2 March 1967 RES ventured upon totally independent reporting out of North America. This marked the end of a thirty-year association with Dow Jones, the New York financial information agency. Since 1937 Reuters had exchanged its world economic news, delivered in London, for the Dow Jones service of North American financial information, delivered in New York. No payment had been made by either party. Although the agreement made no mention of exclusivity, Reuters had not sold its financial information in North America and Dow Jones had not sold its service in the rest of the world.

In 1965 Dow Jones announced its intention of marketing its ticker in Europe, and of ending certain Reuter rights to its material. Dow eventually joined forces with the Associated Press; and their Economic Report started on 1 April 1967. Dow Jones withdrew its ticker from the New York office of Reuters, and Reuters withdrew its City ticker from Dow's London office.

Reuters was very worried about the prospective costs and risks of entering into competition with Dow Jones. Fortunately, Ultronic was again willing to put up money for a joint enterprise—the Reuter Ultronic Report (RUR). This backing transformed a serious difficulty for Reuters into a major opportunity. Leading subscribers were becoming ever more international in their trading; and they expected Reuters to be equally global, capable of collecting all its news and information for itself. RES could never have emerged as a complete world player during the next few years if the cosy link with Dow Jones had been maintained. Reuters needed to be fully independent inside the United States, the hub of the international economy.

The Reuter Ultronic Report was launched at the beginning of 1968. It was a United States business wire of prices and related news, delivered to brokers, banks, and news media by 100-word-a-minute teleprinters; or alternatively by video display. The latter service constituted another major advance. It was the first Reuter service to be sold to subscribers for display on screen as an alternative to noisy and space-taking teleprinter delivery. This important new product, called Videoscan, had been developed by Ultronic at the suggestion of Nelson and Renfrew.

RUR was competing directly with Dow Jones on its home ground. In May 1969, after intensive lobbying by Reuters, the New York stock exchange made it almost obligatory for corporations to file their news to Reuters as well as to Dow Jones. This greatly increased the standing of Reuters, which from the start of 1972 took over the whole enterprise, and renamed it the Reuter Financial Report. By 1974 RFR was operating about 700 installations in the United States, compared with an estimated 3,200 for the Dow Jones Economic Report.

In February 1970 Reuters had introduced Videomaster into Europe from Ultronic. This product displayed seventy-two digits on screen, which was a big improvement upon Stockmaster. Subscribers could select from over 9,500 world stock and commodity prices, and were also offered prompts about related news stories (Plate 52).

In January 1974 Long looked back over the first ten years of the Stockmaster and Videomaster joint venture. He reminded the board that Ultronic had contributed almost all the risk capital of £3.4 million. Yet Reuters had received profits totalling some £4 million—£1,321,000 in 1973 alone. In proportion to the limited original risk, Reuters had been greatly rewarded.

Stockmaster and the other new products and services of the 1960s and early 1970s had begun the making of the new Reuters. In only a few years, RES had gained a dominant position in the provision of real-time information outside North America. Reuters had established the only international network operating such services, and it had created a unique database of world financial and commodity information. It had also developed an effective international technical, marketing and sales organization for such services.

6

The joint venture with Ultronic had been rewarding for both parties. But by the late 1960s Ultronic was losing much of its entrepreneurial zeal, at the same time as Reuters was feeling ready to pursue further initiatives by itself. In 1973 came the launch of another major product—this time without any technical or financial help from a partner. It became known as the Reuter Monitor Money Rates service.

The launch of Monitor was to mark a turning-point in the history of Reuters. The profits were to be immense. And yet, as with the introduction of Stockmaster, the decision to develop the service was as much defensive as aggressive. In December 1971 two American companies—Bunker Ramo and Dow Jones—had announced a joint venture to create a computerized financial news service. They were seeking to leap ahead into a new field. The Swiss banks had similar aspirations. In response, Reuters succeeded in outdoing all its rivals by creating its own brilliant product.

In this process, an important contribution was made by a unique Reuter character, Fred Taylor (1920–76). Taylor was a cockney rough diamond, who insisted upon remaining so. He had started in Reuters as a messenger in 1934, and for many years he reported London prices for Comtelburo. From 1969 he was sales co-ordinator within the United Kingdom sales unit of RES. Taylor had developed a wide range of contacts at many levels within the City of London—contacts whom he occasionally met, but whom he more often questioned confidentially by telephone. Even Taylor felt uncomfortable when he was invited by one high-powered City contact for a yachting week-end. What to wear? What to do? But Taylor went.[15]

Taylor's inside knowledge was invaluable, first in shaping the new foreign-exchange service, and then in selling it. The joke was that Monitor was launched on a sea of lunches. These were held chiefly with foreign-exchange managers. Taylor's manager, Alan Jackson, reported on 3 August 1973, soon after the start of Monitor, that it would have taken much longer to construct the new service but for Taylor's efforts. 'He offers us very lengthy experience coupled with a freshness of approach to problems more often associated with a young graduate rather than a man over 50.' Sadly, ill health forced him to take early retirement only a year later.

Taylor professed to be suspicious of young graduates. Yet, paradoxically, one such graduate, Andre Villeneuve, was the man who gave shape to Monitor. The idea had already been talked about casually within RES, and others were to play vital parts. But Villeneuve was rightly credited by Nelson with making the crucial proposal. He had joined RES from Oxford University in 1967, and the Monitor project gave him his chance to reveal his quality. Villeneuve combined perceptivity of mind and thoroughness of method with charm of manner. In the spring of 1971 he was sent on tour by Nelson to survey the European banking market. The Swiss banks, which were the foremost European customers for Stockmaster and Videomaster, had just announced their intention of creating their own Telekurs service in competition with RES. When this Swiss service was finally launched in 1975, two years after Monitor, it took its American data from Bunker Ramo.

The question in 1971 was—how could Reuters counter this prospective competition and loss of revenue? Villeneuve came up with a proposal for a money-rates service which (he argued) the Swiss and others would find indispensable. He accepted that such a service would be more difficult to conduct than Stockmaster or Videomaster. Their market for stock and commodity prices had enjoyed a physical existence, whereas no physical market-place existed for foreign exchange trading. But Villeneuve concluded boldly that this absence represented not an insurmountable obstacle, but an exciting opportunity.[16]

With the disintegration of the Bretton Woods system of fixed exchange rates, dealing in foreign exchange and money was about to expand rapidly. The problem for banks and dealers was how to receive quotations with sufficient speed. Dependence upon telephones and telex was unsatisfactory, since by the time an answer to a request for (say) a bank's dollar/sterling price had been given and transmitted, that price might have already changed. Seconds could be crucial. Villeneuve conceived the idea of installing computer terminals in the offices of banks and other foreign exchange dealers. Reuters would in this way create its own electronic market-place. Market-makers (contributors) would be able to insert their foreign exchange and money rates into the system. At the press of a button, these rates would become available on screen to interested parties (recipients) such as other banks and international businesses. Reuters would charge both contributors and recipients for access to this interactive system.

Here was the concept of computerized contributed data. Two companies inside the United States already ran share information services on such a basis. But Reuters was to the fore in thinking of bringing contributed data into the field of foreign exchange, a market which functioned between countries and between continents.

How would the London trade unions react to the novel idea of data insertion not by telegraphists at Reuters but by customers? The question was addressed early. David Smee, the staff manager, persuaded the telegraphists that the proposal would not reduce the number of their jobs; and also that if Reuters did not develop such a product, some rival organization, or the banks themselves, would do so.

On 25 February 1972 Villeneuve and John Ransom, the RES development manager, submitted a detailed proposal to Nelson for what they called 'a Forex system'. They noted that foreign exchange and money markets had recently developed in line with the growth of world trade and industrial investment across frontiers, now unimpeded by the Bretton Woods fixed parities. 'As a result industrial and commercial entities are forced to devote far closer attention to foreign exchange and money market operations, and stand to gain or lose considerable sums of money on these transactions.' Here was a new opportunity. 'Our proposed service should fill an information gap.' Reuters would provide the equipment, communications, and marketing facilities; market information would come from contributors. Villeneuve and Ransom admitted that the London brokers had given them little encouragement when told of the idea; bankers had been more interested. The service should therefore be designed especially to suit the banking community, starting in London, Western Europe, and North America.

The proposal explored the technical aspects in detail. The recommended central system used a software processor, even though a hardware processor might have seemed more likely. A working model using modified Ultronic hardware had been designed and demonstrated by Peter Howse of the technical services department; but a software solution was rightly preferred by Peter Benjamin, the technical services manager, as more flexible for the future. Digital Equipment Corporation (DEC), a world leader in computers, was given the order for both the central system and for the desk control units. Reuters itself was left to develop a suitable keyboard and screen. These were pleasingly designed by Kenneth Grange of Pentagram. The keyboard was manufactured by Honeywell, the screen by KGM Electronics.

On 29 February 1972 Nelson submitted a twelve-page formal proposal to Long. It admitted various possible risks. Dealers had never before reported money rates in real-time into a central system, and might not co-operate. The banks might decide to start such a service themselves, or the telecommunications authorities might decide that Reuters could not lease circuits because regulations about third-party traffic had not been formulated to take account of contributed data. Moreover, Ultronic might well claim that the project was an extension of the Stockmaster–Videomaster joint venture; if so, suggested Nelson drastically, 'we could argue that our Master Agreement with them was anti-trust'. Overall, the tone of Nelson's paper was carefully confident. The intention was to launch the service in only ten months time, on 1 January

1973. But what should it be called? 'Forex', the name so far used, was too lim-
iting, since the service would also include other money rates. Long himself
ended the uncertainty with a brilliant choice—'Monitor'. The Roman god-
dess Juno Moneta had given her name to the word 'money' because of the
accident that her temple in Rome had come to house the city's mint.

On 22 June 1972 Long submitted the final proposal to the Reuter board,
comparing the promise of Monitor with the performance of Stockmaster and
Videomaster. In contrast to the three digits available from Stockmaster,
'Monitor will be part of a Reuter system able to display up to 170 words or
1,100 characters at a time on a television screen from a database capable of
expansion to 40 million words. This data will be real-time current information, rarely more than 24 hours old.' Long explained that Monitor would
require heavy borrowing, and he received board permission to secure external finance 'by the best method available'. The great success of Stockmaster
had made the directors more ready to be persuaded. A very large
Eurocurrency facility of £800,000 was arranged with the Bank of Scotland,
repayable over five years. £200,000 was drawn during 1973.

A modular pricing policy was recommended for Monitor. 'We propose to
charge inserting banks per page of information they supply.' The monthly
rental for access to one page of data was fixed at £525 for each contribu-
tor/recipient, £190 for a recipient only. Each additional page cost £70.

Nelson and his colleagues realized that Monitor could only hope to succeed if it was found to function with total reliability. Partly because of doubts
about reliability, and partly because of late supply of equipment, the delayed
launch-date of 1 May 1973 was eventually abandoned. Instead, the system
became operational gradually—still in creditably quick time, given its novelty. It first ran in London for a full working day (08.30 to 18.00 hours) on 25
June 1973. Thereafter, during thirty-eight working days up to 8 August the
system was available for 99.89 per cent of the time. In the first weeks, however, subscriber equipment proved less satisfactory in operation than the central system. The PDP8M mini-computers being used as subscriber processors
suffered from assembly faults, which took time to rectify.

In September Long told the board that the Monitor foreign exchange service had been more widely advertised than any product in Reuter history. Yet
at launch there had been only fifteen contributor/recipients and fifteen recipients. After three months Barclays Bank, one of the first contributors to be
signed up, was expecting the service to collapse. Some banks objected to paying for insertion of their own information. Villeneuve remarked that he had
been told: 'without their rates, we had nothing to offer'. Some banks simply
did not want to reveal too much.

Brokers feared that they would lose business if the new service established itself. One admitted as much to Gordon Linacre, a Reuter director, at the 1974 annual lunch. Linacre wrote to Nelson on 21 June:

> I probed [X's] pride; and as a result, his two marriages, his habits (sporting, cultural and sexual) and his pride in his young lions are memories to me as well as him. He fears that Monitor will rob him of his devious livelihood. I hope you can convince his young partners that they can still get fat with Monitor.

Not until 1977 did members of the London Foreign Exchange Brokers Association order the Reuter service.

A serious problem was late delivery of equipment. This left too few contributors or recipients in the system, and so discouraged others from joining. By the start of 1974, 111 Monitor customers had been signed up, but fifty-nine were awaiting installation. Installations were progressing at the rate of only three or four per week. In subsequent years, late delivery of equipment became an irritating consequence of success, as Reuters sought to buy more equipment than DEC could readily supply.

The forecast Monitor capital requirement for 1974 rose to £734,700, compared with an original forecast of £301,800. Long assured the board in September 1973 that this was really an encouraging sign. 'The further outlook is for a much larger market than we had originally envisaged.' With the service operational, and with abandonment certain to be highly damaging to the reputation of Reuters, Long was being determinedly optimistic. He also contrived to demonstrate that the amount of capital at risk was relatively small. Subscribers were required to sign two-year contracts; yet the capital cost of equipment was covered in about ten months for recipients and in about half that time for contributors. They all paid six months in advance, whereas equipment suppliers gave Reuters credit.

It was a paradox that high activity in the markets at first almost aborted the new service. During the Arab–Israeli War of October 1973, when oil prices shot up dramatically, many contributors found themselves too busy to think of inserting their rates. Yet the flux in the markets and intensifying worldwide inflation made a foreign exchange and money rates service the more necessary.

The breakthrough came between March and June 1974, when Reuters signed 109 Monitor contracts. When Monitor started to attract continental clients, the United Kingdom banks—which at the beginning were the main contributors—saw at last a potential widening of their market, reaching other banks, particularly at first in Italy. By June there were 125 subscribers in the United Kingdom, and 121 in the rest of Europe; fifty-two were contributor/recipients, and 194 were recipients only. Additional recipients gave contributors the incentive to put in better rates: better rates attracted still more recipients. The Monitor range was subsequently extended to bonds (1975), commodities (1977), equities (1978), and US Government securities (1978). In June 1979 the position was:

> Monitor Money Rates—2,130 subscribers, including 358 contributors in 36 countries;
> Monitor Bonds—100 contributors and 569 recipients;
> Monitor Equities—296 subscribers, including twenty-three contributors;
> Monitor Commodities—367 subscribers, including thirty contributors;
> U.S. Government Securities—nine contributors and 204 recipients in the USA and Canada, the service being also distributed to Money Rates, Bonds and Equities subscribers worldwide.

By 1980 the Monitor system was daily averaging 136,800 page updates supplied by contributors, and was handling 840,000 page requests.

In August 1975 a money-news retrieval service, promised from the start, was at last made available. A series of headline pages could be called up, with extra details on offer if wanted. Long told the board in June 1975 that this gave 'uniqueness to the content of Reuter Monitor', and so made competition more difficult. A particular strength was Monitor's expandability, its ability to carry add-on facilities. By the time of the tenth anniversary in 1983, forty-seven distinct local and international Reuter Monitor services were on offer.

One problem of success was that large amounts of capital were becoming locked up in the value of standing equipment. This was threatening to block further progress. The answer was found by Judah. Under agreements made in 1975, some Reuter-owned equipment was leased back, while other equipment became leasable directly. Leaseback continued until 1982.

In the first five years, up to June 1978, Monitor generated gross revenue of well over £30 million, and operating profit of over £11 5 million. This compared with an original profit forecast of just over £1.1 million. By 1983, operating profit after ten years totalled £100 million. Here was a remarkable success, which transformed the face and fortunes of Reuters. Company turnover in 1983 was fourteen times that of 1973 (see Appendix).[17]

Currency movements were, of course, increased in the new situation. But the Monitor Money Rates service did not itself encourage speculation. By making so much contributed data available worldwide, Monitor was simply creating a purer market. How players then conducted themselves remained their own responsibility. 'The purer markets are, the better [chance] the world economy has to grow and to function, and you only get pure markets

by good and fast information.' So explained Nelson when interviewed in
1989.

An article in the *Harvard Business Review* for 1979 noticed with satisfaction
that the Reuter Monitor Money Rates service was enabling quotations to be
obtained simultaneously from twenty-four world markets. Bankers, brokers,
and treasurers of international businesses could now take advantage of varying rates. 'In the broadest sense, we have for the first time a genuine international economy in which prices and money values are known in real time
in every part of the globe.'[18]

7

The option of venturing into a computerized dealing service had been considered when the Money Rates service was under discussion before 1973. A
cautious step-by-step approach was eventually decided upon—with dealing
by dialogue accepted as a next stage, and possibly beyond that 'matching', the
automatic consummation of deals on the basis of requirements stated by subscribers. The paper of 25 February 1972 from Villeneuve and Ransom, detail-
ing what became the Monitor Money Rates system, had explained why they
were not then recommending an early advance into dealing. 'Many banks
want the rates they put on the screen to be indicative only; they do not wish
to feel any obligation to trade at the rates they screen.' Also, noted Villeneuve
and Ransom, a dealing system would be very demanding technically, and
would take longer to create than a money rates system. This indeed proved
to be the case.

Once again Villeneuve pointed the way. He prepared a twenty-six-page
'Reuter Monitor Dealing Feasibility Study', dated 18 April 1975. He reported
that a simulated dealing facility had been demonstrated to thirty-seven Reuter
customers in the United Kingdom and Western Europe. Interest had been
shown by thirty-one, and enquiries in North America had shown similar
interest there. Most subscribers to Monitor Money Rates regarded a progression to dealing as logical. 'Our presentation stressed that the objective
involved no change in current market practice. Personal contact, a sensitive
subject among dealers, would not be undermined by the proposals. Dealers
would continue to use the telephone. There was no attempt to create a
matching system.'

Villeneuve emphasized that a lasting commitment by the banks to the
proposed service needed to be ensured. He suggested offering them close
involvement, either through equity participation, or through some less

formal association. This would prevent them setting up a dealing service of their own. Nelson was cool about the equity proposal, and Renfrew hostile, feeling that it would unnecessarily complicate the development of the project.

In a paper dated 1 May 1975 Nelson recommended that a dealing project should be promoted; but that it should be financed 'as we did with the Reuter Monitor'. Once again there was a mixture of aggressive and defensive motivation. The hope was for additional profit, but the first aim was the protection of existing revenue. 'We believe that if a successful dealing system were established by another organization it might make the Reuter Monitor redundant.'

Nelson explained the novelty of the proposal:

> A dealing system is different from Reuters present business. It is information handling, but makes Reuters an instrument in the execution of a transaction which we have never been before. At least one senior executive believes that we should not do it because it will affect our relationships with our sources since we shall become a part of the actual trading operation.

In other words, whereas Reuters had traditionally *supplied* economic information, it was now going also to facilitate the *use* of such information. But each decision to deal was to be left entirely to subscribers, and so Reuters could fairly claim to be still sufficiently detached.

In December 1974 Long secured board authorization to study the establishment of 'a money dealing system'. He knew that in the United States such a system had already been started in a small way by Tafex. It failed soon afterwards.

The name of David Ure became closely associated with the dealing project. He had joined RES in 1968 as a graduate trainee from Oxford University. He was a thoughtful Scot, deliberately recruited by Nelson as different from the usual run of graduate recruits, whose social graces (Nelson had begun to suspect) sometimes exceeded their business acumen. Ure trained on the financial desk in Brussels, returning there in mid-1970 as RES manager. Long noticed Ure's high intelligence and wry sense of humour. He became product planning manager in 1974, and at the beginning of 1977 he was made dealing project manager. This was a major responsibility, for the dealing project had emerged as the great hope of the company for future profit. Success was far from certain. Ure persevered in the face of technical difficulties and trade union awkwardness. His progress reports were never misleadingly optimistic.

In May 1976 Long was given board approval to spend £69,000 upon development work. Not until 13 July 1977, and only after clearance had been given by the European telecommunications authorities (PTTs), did Long request and receive final endorsement for the dealing project to go ahead. He was authorized to spend £2,563,000 during 1977–9. There had been serious doubt whether the co-ordinating Comité Européen des Postes et Télécommunications would allow Reuters to run a dealing service at all. After intensive representations the committee had finally agreed to permit Reuters to lease circuits, with charges levied at a higher rate related to the volume of traffic. This was particularly noteworthy because it broke new ground in relations with the PTTs. Instead of having one point broadcasting to all points, the dealing service was designed to place two people in communication with each other. The PTTs had feared that this innovation would threaten their revenues.

Long explained to the Reuter board that the new service would widen the company's revenue base. The now lucrative Money Rates service remained vulnerable because it depended upon quite a small number of contributors. He admitted that there was opposition to the dealing project from foreign exchange brokers, who feared loss of business. On the other hand, 'a strong body of opinion in European banks . . . trusts Reuters'. This opinion, continued Long, 'believes our well-accepted reputation for neutrality and reliability makes us a suitable medium for essential information exchange'.

A succession of promised launch-dates was to come and go throughout 1979 and 1980. Technical difficulties were made the harder to solve because of problems with the workforce, which was split into disharmonious elements. Over a hundred people became involved—far too many for systematic progress. The development of a software multiplexing system (SWM) for the data-communications network was the responsibility of a Reuter team; the development of the dealing equipment was in the hands of consultants. On 3 July 1978 Ure ventured to put a price upon failure. Abandonment at once would leave Reuters with a loss of just over £1 million; if the project collapsed at launch, the loss would be trebled; if the service stopped after six months, assuming only fifty initial orders, the loss would be £3,745,000.

RES pressed ahead with enlisting foundation subscribers. Long reported to the board in December 1979 that 146 contracts had been secured worldwide; the projected number at launch was 160. No more than this were wanted at first, because subscribers needed to be trained in the proper use of the service. Villeneuve reminded Nelson on 30 October 1978 that Dealing was 'the most sensitive product, in market terms, which Reuters has ever launched. The banks are treating its introduction by Reuters with some suspicion. They are particularly suspicious of the fact that Reuters will have control over the pricing of a product on which they will be heavily dependent.'

Nelson demanded heavy final testing during the last months, in the knowledge that this was not a service which could be left to get better by trial and error. Month after month he found himself telling the board that the service was not yet ready. Huge costs were being carried. About £8 million had been invested in the project—double or treble the company profit for each of the years when it was under development.

The Reuter Money Dealing service went live on 23 February 1981 to 145 subscribers in nine countries. By June there were 174 subscribers. This was the biggest project ever undertaken by Reuters, and it had begun cautiously. Nevertheless, the availability of the service was extended rapidly—from the United Kingdom, Western Europe, and North America at launch, to Hong Kong, Singapore, and the Middle East in the next year. The breakthrough came after Dealing had reached Bahrain in May 1982. Oil money now found an easy route into the European banks. The service was renamed Reuter Monitor Dealing.

Bob Etherington had been appointed Dealing market manager in September 1981, with a brief to relaunch sales presentation throughout the world. He emphasized to potential customers the word 'speed'—how the new product offered the opportunity to conclude deals in two to four seconds, compared with up to ten times as long by existing methods. Only through Reuters could dealers communicate with each other at high speed to buy, sell, or lend money through the same screen, taking hard copies of transactions from associated teleprinters. Dealers still had to work out their own deals, since this was not yet 'matching'; but the new service was a great advance.

One Reuter press advertisement showed a frustrated old-style dealer waiting for a response to a telephone call, under the slogan: '30 seconds is a long time in a dealing room'. The advertisement reminded dealers that in such a time 'Cable may then have moved 18 points; and on a £1 million deal that could have cost $1800'. Reuter support staff were on hand both before and after signing contracts to help dealers overcome their 'techno-fear'. Charges at launch were $1,500 per month for first terminals, $850 for second and $500 for third and subsequent terminals.[19]

By the second anniversary in February 1983, the Dealing service had 400 subscribers in twenty-four countries; thirty-seven of the world's top banks were participating; calls through the system were averaging 10,000 per day. Within a further year, calls had doubled again, with peaks of 40,000 in active markets. In May 1984 Renfrew summed up for the board what had become another great achievement. The Dealing service, he wrote, had reached a level of acceptance which made it 'another basic money market tool, like the

Reuter Monitor before it, generating its own growth momentum'. By the end of the decade at least half of all foreign exchange spot transactions in the London market were being done through Reuter Monitor Dealing.[20]

From the 1960s onwards the contribution made by Reuters to the provision of information to the world trading community had been increasingly remarkable. The International Financial Printer had introduced dissemination of information directly to subscribers. Stockmaster had made computerized stock market information available by retrieval internationally, and in seconds. Videoscan and Videomaster had then introduced screen display. Monitor Money Rates had brought contributed data within a computerized market-place. And finally, Monitor Dealing had drawn Reuters into the very process of trading.

Here was an impressive progression, but not an inevitable one. Both Monitor Money Rates and Monitor Dealing might have failed after launch, for both were slow to reach critical mass. They could not have prospered simply because they were technologically advanced. They were grounded upon careful market research; they were promoted by an energetic sales force; and they were reliable and user-friendly in operation. This gave the two products the necessary resilience to achieve ultimate outstanding success.

Reuters was being transformed, but Julius Reuter was not forgotten. In 1976 a bust of the founder was placed in the City of London near where he had opened his office 125 years earlier. Gerald Long, Reuter's successor as managing director, composed the inscription:

> The supply of information to the world's traders in securities, commodities and currencies was then and is now the mainspring of Reuters activities and the guarantee of the Founder's aims of accuracy, rapidity and reliability. News services based on those principles now go to newspapers, radio and television networks and governments throughout the world. Reuters has faithfully continued the work begun here.

THIRTEEN

Achieving Worldwide Presence
1963–1981

I

As well as promoting the computerization of the economic services during the 1960s and 1970s—a purpose in which Nelson and Renfrew briefed him—Long also secured for Reuters an independent worldwide presence in the reporting of news. In pursuit of this liberating purpose, Long needed no briefing, for he was himself an experienced general news journalist.

Until this period, although Reuters had been publishing news from all parts of the globe for over a century, it had remained dependent for important parts of its file upon overseas agencies with which it had made exchange agreements. Foremost among these were the Associated Press in the United States, the Press Trust of India, the Australian Associated Press, and the South African Press Association. The breaking off or dilution by Reuters of its various special relationships with these four bodies was to be a vital act of disengagement.

To achieve his great objectives, Long necessarily depended upon the support of successive Reuter chairmen. In 1968 John Burgess was succeeded by William Barnetson (1917–81), whom Long rated more highly than Burgess. Barnetson—who became a life peer in 1975—was a Scot who had made his way as a busy, genial figure in the world of journalism. From 1966 he was managing director of United Newspapers, then a mainly provincial newspaper group, whose fortunes he revived.

Long said waspishly in retrospect that Barnetson had been a 'a truly modest man because he wanted the approval of everybody'. Yet Barnetson's desire to please all-round was not necessarily a weakness. It meant that he worked steadily to keep Long and the Reuter directors in harmony at a time of great risk-taking, persuading the board to accept Long's proposals for innovation and borrowing—including, most notably, the Monitor project. Instinctively, Barnetson disliked going deeply into debt, and he had said so at board meetings before he became chairman. But Long convinced him that borrowing was necessary to avoid falling behind in the computerized information race.

Long humoured his chairman skilfully, letting him take credit: 'he liked a certain kudos, and I liked a free hand and support when needed.'[1]

2

Expansion under Long's management required much extra working space. By 1977 Reuter operations in London were spread over nineteen different addresses. Most were not in Fleet Street at all, although the top management and the newsrooms remained at number 85 in the Lutyens building. A scheme for the transfer of headquarters to a new block on the south bank of the Thames was actively considered in the early 1970s; but the move was eventually abandoned as not cost-effective. In July 1979 a London technical centre, bringing together the computer and communications operations of Reuters, was opened in Great Sutton Street.[2]

Easier personal communication by telephone and telex, and swifter travel by air, meant that world regional management from 85 Fleet Street was possible by the 1960s. Two men became particularly involved—Patrick Crosse, who was made responsible for Africa (as already noticed), and then for Latin America; and David Chipp, who oversaw Asia and the Pacific.

Latin America was an old problem region for Reuters. In a 1975 report, Peter Job, assistant manager for Latin America, surveyed the position since 1958, the year when Reuters had withdrawn its general news service. Job warned that the Latin American market was both too fragmented and too competitive to yield much revenue quickly. AP and UPI, the American agencies, were strongly entrenched, and they supplied radio-photos alongside their world news, whereas Reuters did not. AFP, the subsidized French agency, offered very low subscriptions, without always requiring them to be paid.

The revival of large-scale Reuter operations within Latin America had begun in 1963 with the creation of a leased communications network. By 1968 Reuters was employing twenty-one full-time general news journalists and managers in the region, plus nine economic journalists and two joint reporters. A Latin American general news service in English and Spanish was revived from 1 February 1964, which was serving some twenty-five subscribers by 1966, including the influential La *Prensa* of Buenos Aires. Even so, the Latin American loss for the year was £18,000 and rising. Crosse—fresh from successfully introducing Reuter news services into newly independent black Africa—was appointed in July 1966 to transform present 'modest success' in Latin America into future major achievement.[3]

The return of Reuters to the region had been covertly encouraged by the British Government. In 1964 Regional News Services (Latin America) Limited was formed as a front organization. This was a twin of RNS (Mid-East), the successor to the Arab News Agency, which since 1954 had collected and distributed news for Reuters. From 1964 to 1971 RNS (LA) paid generous subscriptions of £25,000 or £30,000 a year to Reuters, avowedly for mutual assistance in Latin America.

A regionally owned news agency had been talked about for years. The excessive influence of AP and UPI had aroused resentment among both the governments and the newspaper proprietors of Latin America. Crosse decided that Reuters might be able to exploit this resentment by offering to help start an independent agency. Reuters would then hope to shed its local trading loss by offloading its wholesale news distribution; and also to save outward reporting costs by gaining access to the agency's news file. Such was the background to the formation in January 1970 of a Latin American news agency, Agencia Latinoamericana de Información (Latin) SA.

'Latin' was a co-operative. It began with thirteen newspaper shareholders (*socios*) in seven Latin American countries. The larger shareholders each paid $3,500 per month; others were charged $1,500. In July 1971 Reuters took an 8.5 per cent shareholding, raised in 1973 to 49 per cent, with an option of taking a majority. This greatly enlarged holding was a way of converting Latin's debt to Reuters into equity. By 1975 Latin owed Reuters an estimated £410,000, an uncomfortably large sum.

Crosse had been seconded in 1970 for two years as Latin's first general manager. He was good at negotiating with politicians and newspaper proprietors, less good at day-to-day management. He left Reuters in 1971. Long had been critical of his methods, and was never quite convinced that Reuters was right to join a co-operative rather than to stand on its own. He had told the executive committee on 4 February 1969 that Latin was associated in his mind with 'a defeatist attitude'.

Latin aimed to produce a balanced news file consisting half of world news from Reuters and half of Latin American news. The latter was collected by seventeen staff correspondents based in Latin America or in Washington; most were Reuter-trained. Conversion to satellite communication improved Latin's performance, but also raised its costs. By 1975 it was serving about 130 subscribers. These were located throughout Latin America, except in Cuba where the Communist authorities simply pirated the service.

Despite seeking to meet an important need, the survival of Latin always remained in doubt. Its newspaper shareholders refused to allow subscriptions to be raised in proportion to rising costs, or even to pay what they owed. The

Latin trading loss for 1974 was £103,000, and rising. Yet Reuters could not allow the agency to collapse without risk of damage to its own reputation. Nelson went out in December 1974 to assess the situation. He sought to attract backing from the various Latin American governments. In the end, only President Carlos Andres Perez of Venezuela proved willing to help financially. In October 1975 his Government signed a contract for Latin to deliver its service to forty-three Venezuelan embassies throughout the world, along with a daily bulletin produced by the Venezuelan Central Office of Information. This contract was worth £680,000 to the end of 1976.

The deal with Venezuela prolonged the life of Latin, but failed to save it. The newspaper proprietors, always politically divided, remained uncertain about their commitment. In November 1977 the Latin and Reuter news collection operations were merged. In February 1980 the Venezuelan contract expired. This removed the last obligation to maintain a separate organization, and in May 1981 Latin ceased trading. Henceforward Reuters was to distribute its Spanish services in Latin America under its own name.

3

Like Latin America, North America presented a challenge throughout the 1970s which Reuters actively addressed but did not lastingly overcome. In February 1973 Long explained to the board how, after the collapse of the British Empire, Reuters had turned towards Western Europe and the United States. By 1972 North America was contributing 17.5 per cent of total company revenue. But the position there remained uncertain, for competition was stronger in North America than anywhere else, and Reuters could not make a profit from the region (see Table 13.1). The North American deficit for 1964 was £134,000, and for 1968 £306,000.

The long-standing heavy dependence of Reuters upon Dow Jones for American economic information, on the one hand, and upon AP for

TABLE 13.1. Revenue figures by area, 1964 and 1972. (£000)

	Total world	North America		Europe (excl.UK)		Rest of world	
		Gross	% of world revenue	Gross	% of world revenue	Gross	% of world revenue
1964	3,583	417	11.6	691	19.3	2,475	69.1
1972	13,827	2,423	17.5	5,162	37.3	6,242	45.2

American general news, on the other, was ended in 1967. From that year Reuters began separate reporting out of North America. The credit for insisting upon this bold initiative was Long's. He had recognized that Reuters was never going to become truly supranational until it reported everything for itself; and especially from the United States, which was the world's most important news and information source. Nelson—often a sharp critic of Long's leadership—acknowledged the break with AP as a vital step in the transformation of the old agency. It was, said Nelson, Long's 'greatest service to Reuters'.[4]

There was certainly room for more businesslike provision in some quarters. In later years Nelson liked to tell of a phone call to the hard-pressed one-man Reuter bureau in Los Angeles. It came from the representative of a local company who wanted to communicate his firm's quarterly results. 'Hang on,' answered the wife of the Reuter correspondent, who was perforce helping out in her husband's absence, 'I just have to see to the baby.'

When Long took over in 1963, Reuters in North America was still operating under the constraints of contracts signed a generation earlier. Out of total press revenue from the United States of £207,000 per annum, £42,857 came from the *New York Times* subscription, £21,428 from the *Chicago Tribune*, and £14,600 from the *Chicago Tribune* Press Service. The connection with the *Tribune* syndicate service, undertaken with justifiable satisfaction in 1945, had come to seem restrictive by the 1960s.

The file of news from North America was also unsatisfactory. Under the 1947 agreement with AP, Reuters received AP's 'A-wire' service of American news in exchange for the PA service of British news. As the importance of news from Britain declined, this arrangement had begun to look unequal to the Americans. Long recognized that AP would sooner or later demand payment of a differential. Yet at the same time AP's A-wire service had become inadequate for Reuters.

Long warned the board on 26 May 1965 that this dependence upon AP had become dangerous. 'It is a sword hanging over our heads by a string and no one knows just how thick the string is.' Long described Wes Gallagher, AP's general manager, as 'dour and tough and no friend of Reuters': 'the only safe course is to begin now to build up a news collection network in the United States which will enable us as soon as possible to become independent.'

In September 1966 Gallagher duly gave notice that AP would require payment of a differential from the following September: 'We're trading elephants for apples.' At first, he would not reveal how much he wanted; but he eventually demanded $200,000 per annum. This was, as Long recalled years later, 'a fortune for us at that time'. Stuart Underhill was sent to the United States to assess the situation. After three months, his report concluded that AP would break the relationship sooner or later, even if Reuters paid up now. And he estimated that Reuters could produce its own news service for $225,000 a year—in other words, for not much more than AP was demanding for its inadequate service.[5]

Gallagher would not lower his demand, and his obduracy turned out to be a blessing in disguise for Reuters. Long would have felt bound to settle for (say) $100,000, in the knowledge that the unadventurous Reuter board would have insisted upon paying this price rather than face the risk and cost of going ahead alone. Gallagher simply did not believe that Reuters would be able to compete successfully in news reporting out of North America. He failed to understand that its journalists would not be in pursuit of every small-town story. Reuter customers wanted only selected American news—about events likely to affect their own countries, plus a leavening of gossip about people prominent in politics and entertainment.[6]

Long therefore pressed a reluctant Reuter board into authorizing the creation of an entirely separate news file from North America. As an alternative to AP, the directors would have been ready to make a deal with UPI, AP's rival. But Long was insistent, and Burgess, the chairman, stood by him. Long knew that Reuters had already built up staff numbers to improve the quality of its American news file. In 1965 there had still been only sixty-four full-time Reuter staffers in the whole of the United States and Canada. Five additional correspondents were then sent to New York, two to Washington, and one to Chicago. By January 1968, after the break with AP, 105 full-time staff were in post.

As noticed in Chapter 12, reporting of economic news and information independently of Dow Jones began on 1 April 1967. Reporting of general news independently of AP followed on 7 September. The AP printer in the New York office went dead at midnight—a significant moment in the history of Reuters. Cyril Smith, who had already started the expansion of the economic services in North America, planned the extended coverage of economic news and information. Julian Bates, a journalist with wide experience, organized the independent service of general news. Reuters was now able to claim that it was the only major non-American news organization with an independent American file. Others, such as AFP or Tass, subscribed to the American agencies.

Glen Renfrew took charge of North America in January 1971. Two years later, to achieve greater coherence, he ordered the integration of the general news and economic services. There was to be one news-collecting team, and one marketing and sales force, but still with specialists in general or economic news. Reuters North America (RNA) was incorporated in 1973. The Western Hemisphere desk moved from London to New York in September 1973.

From the start of 1968 the syndication arrangement with the *Chicago Tribune* Press Service was ended. Henceforward, Reuters was free to sell its news anywhere in the United States. Yet for many years this was to remain an untaken opportunity. The American newspaper base actually slumped to a low of only sixteen subscribers, before recovering during the 1980s to almost 100 papers.

By 1980 Reuters had four addresses in New York, plus offices in Washington and six other American cities. New York was the head office, and Washington filed its news through New York editorial, a cause of continuing complaint. The practice was described (23 October 1979) by Ian Macdowall, the chief news editor, as 'an essentially political decision by RNA that Washington should not have direct contact with head office'.

The Washington bureau had twenty-seven staff in 1974, compared with AP's 130 and UPI's 100. Reuters was still treated as a second-class agency by the White House and State Department. This meant that its correspondents were not given equal access with the American agencies to the President or the Secretary of State. From the late 1970s, however, as greater resources became available, Reuters at last began to achieve a strong presence in the political news capital of the Western world. From 1989 it was granted full rights within the White House press pool, including a seat on the presidential plane.[7]

Renfrew divided RNA into five profit centres—brokerage, banking, media, cable, and Canada. The first four corresponded to specific markets at which different Reuter services were aimed. These services, and the technology to develop them further, were Renfrew's particular interest. But shortage of money, and also the restrictions about North American involvement which were built into the joint venture with Ultronic, precluded an early attack upon the main computer information markets. Renfrew looked instead to openings on the fringe, where competition was likely to be less intense. During Renfrew's first year his enthusiasm for cable technology resulted in the creation of Reuters News View, which offered two channels on television screens, one of general news, and the other of financial or sports news. News View was an immediate success.

The United States market remained overwhelmingly domestic in its interests, and this necessarily limited the demand for international material from Reuters. Paradoxically, however, this American concentration of mind proved to be advantageous, because it led the American information providers to remain focused upon their home market. Meanwhile, although still losing money in North America—up to $2 million each year in the mid-70s—Reuters was increasingly prospering elsewhere.

But what would follow Stockmaster or Videomaster? Here was a vital question for Reuters about the time when Renfrew took over in North America. London's answer was the Reuter Monitor Money Rates service. But Renfrew in New York began to search for a cheaper and even bolder product. He launched a technical development programme, which became centred upon a subsidiary company formed in March 1973—Information Dissemination and Retrieval Inc. (IDR) of Farmingdale, Long Island. IDR set out to develop a computerized data system of advanced performance. The aim was for data to be delivered by coaxial cable for display on television screens at more than 400,000 words per minute. Transmission by cable was to be continuous. At the push of a button, subscribers would be enabled to use keyboards to 'grab' material as it flowed by, and to hold it on screen. This 'frame-grabbing' concept—later changed to 'row-grabbing'—led Renfrew into discussions with two small American companies. One of them, owned by Robert Nagel, was working on hardware. Nagel became a partner in IDR. He was an enthusiast, and for a time he carried Renfrew along with him. After a legal action brought by Nagel in 1977, but settled out of court, he returned his IDR shares in return for $180,000 from Reuters. According to Nagel's evidence, Renfrew had told him in 1973 that he was 'by far the most brilliant technical person he had ever met'.[8]

Reuters had put systems together before, and it had written software for them; but this project called for hardware to be made by Reuters itself—and made, moreover, for a revolutionary system. By the end of 1974 a prototype row-grabbing system was on offer to business houses in New York, via Manhattan Cable Television. Long told a press demonstration optimistically that in about a year Reuters would be able to put out news and information cheaply, even upon family television screens. Row-grabbing came to employ a mixture of satellite, cable, microwave, and phone-line relay. Unfortunately, the exciting prospect promised by row-grabbing proved very difficult to translate into a widely available and reliable service. In addition, row-grabbing needed wide-band communication, which was chiefly available in North America. A study at the end of 1975 by David Ure and the technical department in London advised against attempting to introduce it into Europe. It never crossed the Atlantic. Pressed at interview after his retirement, Nelson offered a guardedly critical assessment of Renfrew's alternative approach: 'if the Company had laid down much more clearly a strategy of only going for technical solutions which were clearly applicable everywhere in the world, you might not have done it.'[9]

Long had left Renfrew free to experiment boldly and separately in North America. During the years 1973–83 IDR lost well over $1 million, mainly because of its work upon row-grabbing. But IDR also became involved in other activities. From 1977 it gradually became the main supplier to Reuters of terminals for use as cheap alternatives to DEC models for the Monitor services, both in North America and elsewhere. After a slow start, Reuter Monitor Money Rates operated successfully in North America, using telephone lines rather than cable for delivery.[10]

In 1973 Renfrew promised that Reuters North America would seek to earn profits. But when? He accepted full responsibility not only for revenue growth but also for cost control—insisting that all costs arising within RNA should be charged to RNA. Inevitably, this made the search for profitability much harder. In March 1978 Renfrew had to admit that 'while escalating losses have been avoided, we have not been able to make any progress towards the area definition of area profitability'. During the second half of 1980 RNA finally recorded a profit overall. For 1981–2, the annual profit figures showed all trading areas in profit (see Table 13.2). Critics within Reuters said, however, that RNA's novel profitability was more apparent than real.

TABLE 13.2. Annual trading-area profit, 1980–2.(£000)

	1980	1981	1982
Reuters Europe	4,519	9,498	16,331
Reuters Asia	5,423	10,690	16,836
Reuters North America	(83)	2,036	3,909
Reuters Overseas	(865)	(407)	1,758
(Middle East, Africa, Latin America			

RNA encountered continuing difficulties with its staff as well as with its technology. The Newspaper Guild of New York was a union open to all workers in the industry, except printers and typesetters. Its relationship with Reuters became increasingly troubled during the 1960s, as its representation increased. Some union members believed that Renfrew set out 'to screw the Guild'. Yet in 1971 he decided to accept the Guild's high salary demands in order to secure the removal from the agreement of clauses which would have prevented the introduction of automation. In 1974 a ten-day strike by 149 Guild members (out of 195 North American staff) ended with the union settling for salary increases below those initially offered. This was in exchange for a cost-of-living escalator, which management had originally refused. Reuter executives kept all services functioning with help from about twenty non-striking Guild members. Members of the National Union of Journalists in London agreed not to handle copy from New York.

A strike was narrowly averted in 1977, but RNA management was prepared for a confrontation in 1980. In that year, a new salary structure was offered which reflected market rates, rather than the above-market rates demanded by the Guild. Management knew that the Guild was in serious financial trouble. Jim Bell, the Reuter unit chairman, even began to recommend a switch by Reuter staff to the American Communications Association (ACA), which was an affiliate of the notorious International Brotherhood of Teamsters. Bell contended that Reuter staff would be better represented by a vigorous union than by an almost bankrupt one. The prospect of the teamsters moving into Reuters horrified the management—at headquarters in London as well as in New York.

On 1 November 1979 the ACA filed a petition with the National Labor Relations Board for an election to be held at Reuters to ask staff whether they wanted representation by the Guild or the ACA, or by neither. The Reuter management urged staff to vote 'neither'. On 14 December the ACA suddenly withdrew from the contest. This meant that the Guild retained its place within Reuters, since there was now no opportunity for staff to vote 'neither'.

Negotiations dragged on throughout the first half of 1980. One ingenious union demand was for a staff holiday on Julius Reuter's birthday. On 3 July Reuters terminated the old contract unilaterally, posting new conditions of employment and implementing pay increases. These ranged from 5 per cent for lower job categories to 8.5 per cent for the highest.

In response, the Guild called a strike for noon on 24 July. Telegraphic circuits out of New York and video-editing installations broke down; but the strike proved to be ineffective, even though the Guild received transatlantic support. For the first time in the history of Reuters, journalists in London came out on strike, their sympathy action continuing for eight days. Some clerical and administrative staff joined them briefly. Attempts to spread the strike to continental Europe failed, and editorial operations in both New York and London were maintained by executives. Over a quarter of Guild members remained at work. After twenty-five days the Guild accepted terms less good than those originally on offer.[11]

4

Long told the board in February 1973 that he regarded North America and Western Europe as 'the two pillars' of Reuters. After the Second World War

Western Europe had emerged as the main region for revenue, producing over half the total by the 1970s. In a note for the executive committee (undated, but probably from 1970) Long described his aspirations for Europe. It was 'time for us to pull the disjointed elements of our European activity together into a coherent policy'. He asked how the reputation of Reuters as 'a neutral collector and supplier' stood in the eyes of the European media, RES customers, and European Governments. 'We have in Europe, as elsewhere, tended to increase our acceptability by co-operating with a national partner.' But was this policy, hitherto unavoidable because of financial weakness, still the best for Reuters? The Europeans, Long argued, must now come to accept the right of Reuters to distribute directly. 'We must establish Reuters reputation as a news agency whose domestic area is Europe.'

In Germany, as in the United States, Reuters finished up standing on its own in the provision of news and information. As in the United States, bold decisions were taken with a mixture of hesitation and enthusiasm. A German-language news service, edited in Bonn for distribution to the German media, was launched in December 1971. This followed the ending of the connection with DPA, the German agency.[12]

The initiative for the break came from DPA; and yet Reuters was glad to go its own way. Long's contempt for DPA in general—and, in particular, for its general manager, Wolfgang Weynen—was strong. He believed that DPA was using Reuters largely as a tip-off service, crediting its stories as little as possible. This had caused the virtual disappearance of the Reuter name from the West German press. Long also argued that the revenue coming through DPA was insufficient as an indirect subscription from the whole West German press.

Long reported in April 1971 that DPA had been told of this growing dissatisfaction. Weynen said he still wished to renew the contract, so Reuters offered him terms. Yet on 2 July a letter from Weynen arrived in London saying that DPA had decided to accept another offer. Reuters knew this to be from UPI. Relations were so bad that Weynen had not told Long of his decision, even though they had met at Frankfurt on that same day. Long believed that Weynen had treated the Reuter offer only as a target for UPI to beat. 'I conclude that he never intended to renew the contract with Reuters.'[13]

Manfred Pagel, who had joined Reuters in 1961 as a local correspondent in Bonn, became the German-service editor. German by birth and American by education, he seemed well suited to handle the challenge. Yet the service was slow to take off, partly because its charges were high, and partly because of uncertainty about its objectives. Was it aiming to match DPA in its home territory? Or was it seeking to provide a secondary service for the German market, which meant that it was in competition with AP and AFP, which for many years had sold German domestic news? Clearly, any attempt to displace DPA would be too ambitious. And by the late 1970s Reuters had found that its service of foreign news plus domestic highlights, although sufficient for radio and television, offered only weak competition to AP and AFP within the newspaper market. The Reuter domestic report was therefore expanded to attract more subscribers from the West German press. Even so, during the 1980s about 60 per cent of West German media revenue earned by Reuters still came from radio and television stations.

The decision to break with VWD, the German economic news agency, was influenced by its lack of enterprise. The economic services of Reuters were distributed through VWD, while in return Reuters was granted access to the VWD economic report. But VWD had been slow to start teleprinter services. And when Reuters introduced Stockmaster in 1964, VWD refused to participate in a joint company. Nationalistic protectionism coloured VWD attitudes. For example, all sales interviews for Stockmaster had to include a VWD representative. A new five-year contract between Reuters and VWD was signed in 1973, which at last gave RES a free hand in selling and running its computerized services within West Germany. But in October 1977 Long was still calling the relationship 'uneasy'.

The breakdown came at the end of the following year. Reuters refused to continue paying commission on its computerized services to VWD. At the same time, VWD was wanting to reduce its subscription for Reuter news services. Long explained to the Reuter board in June 1978 why he viewed a break with equanimity. 'In major European countries we must operate retrieval services independently of agencies because of the need for international co-ordination and because such services are too important to our existence and our future to confide them to an outside agent.' In 1980 the one-third shareholding of Reuters in VWD was sold back to the German company for DM1,400,000. A nationalistic article in *Die Zeit* on 11 December complained that Reuters had always exploited VWD, and had now abandoned it when there was no more to take: 'these British gentlemen crucified their German partners.'

Against this background, RES began independent reporting in West German from 1 January 1979. The number of RES journalists was increased from three to seven, and part of the economic reporting operation was transferred from Frankfurt to Bonn to facilitate liaison in producing the German-language service.

Reuters aspired to be strong in France as well as in Germany. The entrenched position of the state-subsidized AFP made this difficult. The

French-language service, produced by Reuters in London, was offered in France, Belgium, and Switzerland. From 1972 Reuters tried working with the second French news agency, Agence Centrale de Presse (ACP) of Marseilles. The ACP file mixed international news from Reuters with its own domestic news. The connection proved to be less advantageous than hoped. The extra play given to the Reuter service in provincial France was limited, and the financial benefit was negligible. Not that profitability was necessarily a priority. Long told the board in October 1977 that media services to Europe now contributed only 9 per cent of company profits.

5

During the 1960s and 1970s—as well as making fresh starts in the Americas and in Europe—Reuters was redeveloping its presence in Asia; where it had once been dominant, but where it had lost much ground after the Second World War with the fading of the formal and informal British Empire (Table 12.2). By 1968 there were 262 Reuter staff in Asia, with the largest offices in Singapore (75), Hong Kong (60), and Tokyo (24).

In India, by contrast, Reuters maintained only a small outward reporting bureau. To supply news internally, it was required by the Government of India to operate through an Indian outlet, the Press Trust of India—the body which briefly (1949–53) had been a partner within Reuters. Even after 1953 the dealings of Reuters and PTI were coloured by a lingering sense of special relationship; by a willingness not always to apply strict commercial criteria on the Reuter side, and by expectation of favour on the Indian side.

The motivation of Reuters was not entirely altruistic, for it was well aware that in the post-colonial era western news agencies would have to act with circumspection. How Reuters treated the Indians would be noticed throughout the Third World. Even so, the responsiveness of Reuter management was soon being tested to its limit. PTI began to demand cheap news contracts which were unrewarding for Reuters, even while retaining the right to criticize strongly. The cost to Reuters of providing services and communications for the sub-continent rose by one-half between 1953 and the end of the decade.[14]

Negotiations for contract renewal in 1956 and 1959 proved to be frustrating for Reuters. PTI had its own financial problems, and wanted to pay not more but less. The 1959 discussions were conducted in the knowledge that AP and UPI, the American agencies, and AFP, the French agency, had each offered tempting terms to the Indians. In response, Reuters was forced reluctantly to reduce PTI's annual net subscription from £30,000 to £24,500. Even so, the clause from the 1953 contract which said that PTI would treat the Reuter service 'as its main source of world news' was dropped. From the start of 1960, PTI subscribed to the AFP service as well as to Reuters World Service.

A board paper in January 1961 graphically illustrated the post-war decline in revenue from the Indian sub-continent (see Fig. 19). Cole, the general manager, told the board despairingly in April 1962 that even Ghana was 'worth more financially today than India'. Each contract renewal, he complained ungrammatically, had been 'epitomised by chisel' from the Indian side. He described as 'ludicrous' PTI's payment of only £7,500 for sole rights to the commercial services, a sum which had remained unchanged since 1953. He compared this with a commercial service surplus of £30,000 from Hong Kong. Cole warned the Reuter board to face the possibility of 'total withdrawal'. He received authority 'to disabuse the PTI negotiators that Reuters

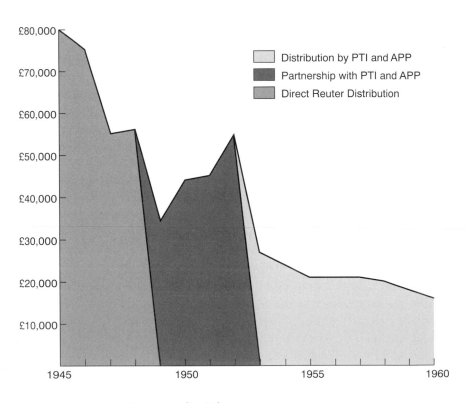

FIG. 15 India–Pakistan revenue, 1945–60

would never be prepared—in the final analysis never be allowed—to break with India'.

Eventually, Patrick Crosse—who had joined Reuters in India before the war, and who understood Indian methods—negotiated a new contract from 1 July 1962. Net revenue from India was raised from £24,500 to £30,000—back at last to the level of 1953, although no more. Crosse had insisted upon an increase, even though the Indians were wanting a further decrease: 'evading (wrote Cole approvingly) the familiar Indian booby-traps to break his nerve—complete inability to make appointments, threats, intrigue, the apparent breaking off of discussions.'

PTI secured the right to make its news and commercial services available outside India. And the sentence from the 1953 contract about close association being maintained 'in the future' was no longer included. The Indians were claiming the right to unqualified freedom of manœuvre. But so also for the future was Reuters. 'Because of the way they have treated us,' wrote Crosse to Cole (14 May 1962), 'PTI can make no claim to loyalty or abiding friendship.' Crosse recommended that in future Reuters should 'maintain an aggressive attitude'.

From 1962 Reuters started to treat PTI as one customer among others—quite important, but no longer entitled to particular indulgence because of past association. PTI's general manager, K. S. Ramachandran, failed to sense this change of attitude. As late as 14 May 1965, in a letter to Long, he was still writing that he had 'no desire to delve into the past but certainly the past forms an essential fabric of our relationship'. In December 1966 the Asian desk in London was absorbed into the Pacific desk, and from April 1967 the editorial office at Singapore took over from London responsibility for making the news services to South-East Asia, India, Pakistan, and Ceylon. India was no longer to be served separately.

Mutual dissatisfaction was now tending to feed upon itself. Reuters had cut back because PTI would not pay more: PTI was unwilling to pay more for reduced services, even if it could afford to pay more, which it denied. In 1971 PTI's chief news editor told Kevin Garry that 'the older generation of PTI subs still revered Reuters, but the younger people had no special attachment to Reuters, and treated it on its merits as against those of AFP and UPI'.

In 1978 Peter Job, manager for Asia, wrote an overview (23 August) which was reminiscent in its tone of Crosse's 'aggressive' recommendations of 1962. Reuters, he wrote, had been treated 'extremely badly' by PTI, and 'taken completely for granted'. Job pointed out that there were now alternative outlets for Reuters within India. 'Our best course remains to stay with PTI and exploit new markets. But we are not I think obliged to do so on any terms.'

Reuters therefore gave PTI notice to end the existing news contract, unchanged since 1968. Immediate payment of arrears—which amounted to a whole year's subscription—was required, plus a 40 per cent subscription increase for the future. Reuters also demanded direct marketing of its economic services, with PTI co-operation. The RES side, Job forecast perceptively, was 'ultimately where the source of our money will or will not be found'. The Indians once more tried delaying tactics. But it was now PTI which had no alternative to working with Reuters, rather than vice versa. No competitor, Job realized, would want 'to rig up an obsolete radio transmission to purvey economic information to badly-paying Indians'. 'Now is the time to strike.' He was right. In 1979 PTI finally agreed to the demand for a 40 per cent subscription increase. This meant a healthy net total of £45,000 per annum. In the same year, the obsolescent Asian radio beam—with its high costs and uncertain reception—was replaced by satellite circuits.

Whereas in India Reuters was required to operate through a national news agency, in Japan, South Korea, and Taiwan it worked through licensing agreements. In June 1969 Long informed the board that revenue from Japan was approaching £300,000 per annum, third only to that from the United Kingdom and Switzerland. Reuters worked with three Japanese partners— Kyodo, the prinicpal general news agency; the *Asahi Shimbun*, the country's leading newspaper (which in 1969 had just passed 10 million for its combined morning and evening circulations); and Jiji Press, primarily an economic news agency. In addition, from 1971 Reuters held a small share in Quotation Information Center (QUICK), which distributed computerized information services for Reuters.

Long remarked in 1969 that relations with both Kyodo and *Asahi Shimbun* were extremely good, less good with Jiji. The latter's president, Saiji Hasegawa, was 'an old-fashioned Japanese nationalist', who denounced dependence upon foreign news sources as 'news colonialism'. He had refused to join with Reuters in introducing computerized economic services into Japan. The Japanese media liked to limit their dependence upon the international news agencies by using all of them a little and none of them very much.

The Tokyo office of Reuters had been transformed by Kevin Garry, chief correspondent 1964–7. He had set out to encourage a strong sense of loyalty to Reuters. He explained his methods to Doon Campbell (20 June 1964):

> I found a very demoralised staff here when I arrived a month ago . . . The general idea seemed to be that they were the 'coolies' for the foreign staff . . . I try to talk a lot about the news to the Japanese staff, and seemingly for the first time, explain why we can or cannot do such and such a thing . . . I am trying to make

life more fun for them—sending them out on their own for small stories instead of relying on Kyodo (which is unreliable) or telephone calls. This costs us nothing but gives them experience, makes them feel responsible for the success of Reuters.

6

Australia continued to generate both problems and opportunities for Reuters. Some senior managers, including Long himself, regretted privately that the board had ever allowed the Australian Associated Press into the partnership in 1947. The Australians, for their part, emphasized how they had injected much-needed capital into the company in 1947; how closely they had worked with Reuters in the Pacific region; and how greatly they were contributing to the expansion of the economic services. They claimed optimistically that by the 1970s—but for the partnership constraint—the AAP would have been offering strong competition to Reuters in East Asia.[15]

Reuters had been seeking modification of the partnership agreement for several years, but AAP had been very reluctant. In particular, Reuters wanted complete editorial control of news from the Pacific area. An informal board committee was formed in April 1965 with the Press Association's 'A' Reuter shareholders and the Newspaper Proprietors Association's 'B' shareholders as members, deliberately excluding the Australian and New Zealand 'C' shareholders. This committee contemplated with equanimity the idea of the Australians leaving the partnership. Burgess even mentioned the possibility of inducing them to quit 'by making the present Agreement unworkable'.

Since becoming partners, the Australians and New Zealanders had been receiving one-third rebate on their assessments; AAP's rebate in 1965 amounted to £33,956. This concession had been intended chiefly to cover office expenses in London and New York. The PA and NPA directors argued that the rebate had ceased to be justified now that the Australians had reduced their staff in London and no longer kept an office in New York. The new Tatpac cable was allowing the AAP easy access to the full Reuter file from London for sub-editing in Sydney.

Conveniently, the rebate arrangement had been found likely to be *ultra vires* in law. This legal opinion was revealed at a meeting of all the partners in London on 8 June 1965. Rupert Henderson, one of the Australian makers of the 1947 agreement, and Duncan Hooper, managing editor of AAP, attended. The discussions were often heated, with Henderson contending that Long and other Reuter senior managers were anti-AAP. He claimed that, as servants of the company, it was 'no part of their task to lay down policy'.

The 1947 agreement spoke of the 'paramount interest' of Australia in the Pacific region. Long insisted that Reuters now had at least an equal interest in news from such an increasingly important part of the world. He refused to accept that the Australians were especially expert in Pacific affairs, or more acceptable in Asia than the British. Although in practice the Australian right to appoint correspondents had often gone by default because of lack of suitable candidates, Long did not like the principle involved. He complained in June 1965 that the idea of qualification by nationality was 'entirely out of place in Reuters'.

AAP and NZPA finally accepted major changes to the 1947 agreement. The new arrangement was detailed in a letter of 10 August 1965 from Henderson to Burgess. The assessment rebate was replaced by a payment which recognized 'the additional financial burden falling on AAP and NZPA by reason of their mode of operation'. New terms for running the economic services were agreed. The Australians and New Zealanders were to be entitled to nominate 'not fewer' than four correspondents in the Pacific area, but editorial control was to be exercised from London. This crucial concession was cosmetically qualified by the creation of a Pacific board, whose functions were deliberately not described in detail. Burgess told Long on 5 November 1965: 'We don't want Frank Packer to say that rule so and so has not been obeyed by the pommy bastards!' Packer, one of the dominant figures in AAP, was a long-time director of Reuters. The Pacific board was never allowed to exercise much influence, and it faded away during the 1980s.[16]

The 1965 agreement had left the AAP responsible for the news service for Reuters out of Australia and New Zealand. Ian Macdowall, the chief news editor of Reuters, reported tartly to the editor-in-chief on 27 June 1973: 'The presentation of the AAP file is occasionally satisfactory and more frequently deplorable.' In 1974 two Reuter correspondents were sent to Sydney, one for general news and the other for the economic services. They received a very cool welcome. Finally, in 1977 Reuters assumed main responsibility for both its general news and its economic information out of Australia.

7

As with India and Australia, so with South Africa, Reuters followed a course of gradually ending the old special relationship. South Africa was facing serious racial problems; and the South African Press Association, the associate of

Reuters, was coming under pressure from the Nationalist Government, which had committed itself to a policy of apartheid. The subsequent racial tension and violence within the country became of great news interest throughout the world; and yet Reuters found that, because of its dependence upon SAPA, it could not always report the crisis fully and freely.

After the Second World War, SAPA had contemplated entering the Reuter partnership on terms similar to those of the Australians. But in the end both Reuters and SAPA were glad for political reasons to let the idea drop. Instead, they concluded a fresh news exchange contract from the start of 1950. Its underlying spirit was still consciously special. SAPA agreed to double its basic annual subscription to £24,000, while Reuters doubled to £3,000 its payment for SAPA's domestic service. African beam radio costs (£17,000 in 1948) were shared one-quarter by Reuters, three-quarters by SAPA. And to improve news file quality, Reuters appointed an editor in permanent charge of the African desk in London. A Reuter board paper (24 May 1949) described SAPA's news requests as 'vigilant and exacting'. But this was accepted as a natural consequence of historically close ties. 'In essence SAPA is treated by Reuters differently from any other customer. The editorial contact is so close.'

The Reuter commercial service in South Africa had remained independent of SAPA. In the 1950s it was losing money, and more than once Christopher Chancellor, the general manager, offered to share the ownership with SAPA, or to sell out entirely. But the South Africans were uncertain whether to become involved, and no change was made. In 1968 SAPA at last offered to buy, but Reuters was no longer willing to sell. Revenue was now running at £100,000 a year, which provided a valuable £20,000 surplus. When in 1969 Stockmaster was introduced into South Africa, Michael Nelson, the RES manager, advised (25 March) against working in tandem with SAPA. 'An association with SAPA would be a drag on our business initiative.'

In contrast to Chancellor's willingness in the 1950s to sell the commercial side to SAPA, on the outward reporting side he was keen for Reuters to become less dependent. From 1938 SAPA had provided Reuters with all its coverage of South African news; but by 8 June 1949 Chancellor was suggesting gently to R. N. Horne, SAPA's general manager, that just as SAPA had its own correspondent in London, so Reuters might one day send its own man to Johannesburg. SAPA's susceptibilities were soothed by the appointment in 1952 of a roving correspondent for the whole African continent, not just for South Africa. Yet he was to be based in Johannesburg, ostensibly only because it constituted the best hub for air travel.

Chancellor assured Horne (8 October 1952) that the new arrangement 'would not disturb in any way the existing basic news coverage which is admirable'. This was not in fact the real opinion of Reuters. For reasons of economy, SAPA had come to depend heavily upon copy from reporters employed by its member newspapers. It did not necessarily report even big stories for itself. Government 'incitement' laws also affected the service, because the newspapers and SAPA sometimes chose to ignore sensitive stories. The Reuter roving correspondent appointed in 1952, Astley Hawkins, did his best to fill the gaps. From 1955 his stories were bylined. This protected SAPA from official blame; but it also highlighted any independent Reuter coverage.

Reuters was thus edging towards greater freedom of action in its relationship with SAPA. SAPA disliked this tendency, even though it was seeking greater freedom for itself. From 1954 the right of Reuters to exclusive copyright in SAPA news outside South Africa was ended.

In 1950 the Nationalist Government had appointed a Press Commission, which sat through the decade and did not report until 1962 and 1964. Its prolonged existence exerted an intimidating influence upon the South African press. The Commission's report described Hawkins's coverage of political and race relations as 'bad'. 'Hawkins is unilingual and appears to have made little contact with the Afrikaner.' The Commission found the reporting of his successor, Seaghan Maynes, to be even worse, 'blindly partisan for the demonstrators'. The Commission also complained strongly that SAPA's filing to Reuters on political and racial matters was faulty because the agency was too much dominated by the English-language press. It recommended a relaxation of the links between SAPA and Reuters when their existing contract expired in 1967. The Nationalist Government did not intervene to enforce this; but the fear of interference influenced SAPA, even though it remained technically a free agent.[17]

Incomplete coverage by SAPA of the Sharpeville massacre and of related events in March and April 1960 had damaged the reputation of Reuters. Although SAPA's first report of the massacre had accurately painted a picture of great bloodshed, the report did no more than imply that the police had been guilty of gross over-reaction:

> Johannesburg. March 21. Reuter—Fifty people were killed and 150 wounded in clashes south of here today when police opened fire on surging crowds of Africans demonstrating against South Africa's pass laws. Mangled bodies of men, women and children lay sprawled on the roadway in the square of Sharpeville African township, which had the appearance of a battlefield . . . The police seemed to be rather shocked themselves at the scene.

SAPA had taken its account from reporters for the *Rand Daily Mail* and the Johannesburg *Star*. They were South African citizens, and their reporting was necessarily conditioned by the need to observe the Nationalist Government's emergency regulations. The correspondents' self-censorship—doing no more than hint at police guilt—was not acceptable in a report for a world news agency.

Reuters became still more dissatisfied by SAPA's handling of the tense aftermath to Sharpeville. South Africa, claimed Cole on 8 April 1960, had become a 'transcendent story'. The world wanted to know what would happen next—a bloodbath, war between blacks and whites? Yet SAPA dare not report fully, for fear of being charged with incitement. Doon Campbell, the Reuter news manager, complained to Crosse on 7 April of SAPA's 'lack of interpretation and eyewitness descriptions'. David Friedmann, who in 1958 had returned from being SAPA correspondent in London to become editor, denied that SAPA was being too timid. He warned Campbell on 8 April about 'what might have happened if through the distribution by Reuters of some unsubstantiated reports, there was a censure in the Union Parliament today'. The problem was that SAPA dare not risk such censure, whereas Reuters (in the case of a 'transcendent' story) was prepared to do so.

In 1958 Alan Humphreys, the distinguished Reuter Second World War correspondent, who had joined SAPA, was seconded to oversee the file delivered to Reuters. Humphreys found that he had to spend much time simply rewriting what SAPA had collected. After Sharpeville, Reuters finally insisted upon assigning its own staff correspondents to Johannesburg, free to report regardless of SAPA. Sandy Gall, the first man appointed, later claimed that he was coolly received by Friedmann. Certainly, during the 1960s Friedmann was regarded by Reuters as almost hostile, and likely to prefer incoming AP copy.[18]

Reuters remained keen for SAPA to provide a file of South African news; but it wanted to shed the constraint of association with SAPA elsewhere in Africa, where black countries were achieving independence. Under the 1938 agreement, SAPA had been left to serve the newspapers of Rhodesia, Nyasaland, Angola, and Mozambique on behalf of Reuters. Significantly, however, after the Second World War Chancellor was reminding Horne (9 June 1949) of the Reuter rule that if newspapers anywhere objected to being served by a third party, Reuters must be free to deal with them directly. By the 1960s it was becoming clear that when the central and southern African colonies became independent they would not want to take their news through SAPA, which they regarded as compromised. This gave Reuters grounds for further relaxing its ties with SAPA. If Reuters had hesitated, the American agencies would have taken over. Seaghan Maynes of Reuters himself drafted a letter for President Kaunda of Zambia which asked for a direct news service from Reuters.

The South African Press Commission had recommended that the next contract between SAPA and Reuters should loosen the old bonds. In the event, Reuters was at least as ready as SAPA to make a fundamental change. Crosse warned Ralph Wilson, the SAPA general manager, on 13 June 1966 of 'our general feeling that the time has come to try to express the relationship between SAPA and Reuters in terms more consonant with reality than those of the 1938 texts'. A report to the Reuter board in July 1966 from Gerald Long gave a version of the historical background which left no doubt about his wish for a new beginning. Long explained that the failure of the post-war attempt to bring SAPA into the Reuter partnership had left a 'bitterness of feeling' which had overshadowed the successive renewals of the 1938 agreement. 'It was largely because of these complications', claimed Long, 'that the Reuter negotiators on each occasion avoided trying to rewrite the text of the agreement.' That text had conceded special access to the Reuter file, which may have been justifiable on historical grounds in 1938, but was no longer acceptable nearly thirty years later. SAPA could still order news reports directly from any Reuter bureau or correspondent. It also controlled the content and transmission of the southern Africa service, and it was entitled to inject its own material without check by Reuters. 'SAPA has exercised these powers with moderation and understanding', wrote Long diplomatically, 'but it is obvious that they cannot be allowed to continue.'

The old joint involvement was ended by a complicated piece of geographical surgery. Reuters and SAPA agreed that Zambia and Malawi would become exclusively Reuter territories; that in Mozambique and Angola, and in the British protectorates, Reuters might sell any service it wished, whereas the only Reuter news which SAPA might publish there would be the Reuter element within the southern Africa service. In Rhodesia the parties agreed that Reuters would be free to sell its services directly, except that the southern Africa service would be left in the hands of SAPA. In short, Africa's news supply arrangements were being carefully adjusted to match the changed political reality.

Long's summing up of the negotiations was coloured by a conscious sense of ending and beginning. He claimed to have retained the goodwill of the South African newspapers. 'Its continuance will now depend on the service we give against fair payment, and not on the survival of an anachronistic partnership on paper which did not and could not exist in fact.'

The same last stage of release from an imperial special relationship had been reached in India during the same decade. The paradox was that it was not the newspapermen of either South Africa or of India who felt the most relieved—not SAPA or PTI, but Reuters in London.

8

Reuters was conscious that it must now serve the press of independent black Africa with the same readiness as it had long served the English-speaking press of South Africa. In 1967 it promoted the writing of a 500-page handbook entitled *The New Africans, A Guide to the Contemporary History of Emergent Africa and its Leaders*. This book drew upon the African experience of some fifty Reuter correspondents. Under a cover of describing black African attitudes, the introduction contrived to imply sympathy for the ending of white rule:

> A factor likely to trouble the continent for some time is white domination of the southern part of Africa. *Apartheid* in South Africa and the rule of white minorities in Rhodesia and the Portuguese territories, where the Africans often outnumber the Europeans by as much as 30 to 1, continue as an affront to African nationalism and a disturbing element in the affairs of the continent as a whole.

Within less than a hundred years, noted the Reuter book, the wheel had turned full circle. 'The European colonisation of Africa, which lasted a relatively brief period, has tended to cause European influence upon the continent to be overstated.' Black Africa was becoming independent again. And Reuters, which had started as the servant of white imperialism inside Africa during the 1860s, was starting afresh with a very different attitude inside Africa a century later.

In this post-colonial spirit, Reuters gave vital support to many of the news agencies and broadcasting networks of the newly independent and developing countries. In particular, it provided editorial and technical training. The Ghana News Agency, started in 1957, was an early beneficiary. By 1979 Reuters had offered assistance—free, excluding hardware costs—to some forty infant media bodies, ranging far beyond the old British Empire. By way of return, Reuters hoped to form close trading links with them.[19]

In 1980 UNESCO published a report from a committee under the chairmanship of Sean MacBride, a former Irish Foreign Minister, entitled *Many Voices, One World*. Some third-world politicians and journalists, encouraged by the Communist bloc, were demanding the creation of a 'new information order'. Western news agencies, such as Reuters and AP, were alleged to be exercising a capitalist stranglehold over the news. Only bad news from the third world—disorder, corruption, famine—was said to receive much publicity in the West. There was some truth in this charge; but colourful news— rather than news of (say) African economic progress—was what subscribers in the developed world mostly wanted. Even so, Reuters did not concede that its news file was unbalanced. It did regularly report positive stories from the Third World; but, as Jonathan Fenby, a former editor of Reuters World Service, pointed out, it could not make western editors publish them: 'the agencies are judged on the basis of news choices made by their subscribers'.[20]

Reuters also rejected the contention, countenanced by UNESCO, that because the flow of world news was imperfect, it should in some way be controlled. At the 1979 annual meeting of the International Press Institute Long argued strongly against such interference. He noted that much of the clamour was coming from countries with authoritarian regimes which already censored their domestic news. At a Reuter dinner for media representatives in New York on 13 May 1980, he again spoke out bluntly:

> UNESCO's aims are clear: it seeks money from those countries that have developed technology of media communications, and which are for the most part committed to the view that information is an essential component of freedom, and makes plans to use that money to transfer media technology to the countries that do not have it, while encouraging them to use the technology to control information for the purposes of government. We are being asked to put up the money and to provide the technical, human, and operational resources to spread throughout the world that very view of information that is most repugnant to us.

Eventually, the clamour against the western international news agencies diminished. Reuters did not lose any contracts.

9

Relations with the British Government remained closer during the 1960s and 1970s than Reuters liked publicly to admit. By 1960 payments under the 1945 Radcliffe–Chancellor agreement were overdue for revision. Reuters was spending over three times as much on transmission in 1960 as in 1945— £271,219 compared with £84,200. Yet British Government payments had increased by only £2,500 during the same period, and Cole complained that the payments had become 'derisory and frankly do not bear scrutiny on any commercial basis'.[21]

Even while seeking large financial support from the British Government, Reuters always wanted to maintain the appearance of a commercial basis. Burgess assured the board in February 1961 that he would negotiate with the Government only for services rendered. He would never accept a block payment by way of grant-in-aid; 'and no payment was to be made by the

Government to Reuters which could not be thoroughly justified, nor should any strings be attached in any way to any payment'.

This sounded high-minded enough. Yet negotiations in the 1960s and 1970s were kept as quiet as possible both by Reuters and by the Foreign Office. All written exchanges took the form of personal letters. Such business, Burgess explained on 9 July 1963 to Leslie Glass of the Foreign Office Information Research Department, was handled within Reuters only by the chairman, general manager, and secretary: 'the files were kept separately.' Glass answered that his department was the only one in the Foreign Office with a separate registry, 'and whose files did not go into the archives'. Burgess expressed himself 'glad to hear this'.

The British Government expressly said (21 February 1961) that some of the money on offer was intended to sustain or to start non-economic services. 'Her Majesty's Government also note your Board's determination to continue to implement the paragraph in your Trust Deed stating: "That no effort shall be spared to expand, develop and adapt the business of Reuters in order to maintain in every event its position as the leading world news agency." ' This was piquant indeed. The Trust agreement—intended to proclaim the independence of Reuters—was being quoted by the Foreign Office in a paragraph relating to payments which amounted to subsidies.

By 1967 the Foreign Office was paying £123,480 per annum on behalf of the overseas departments, and £40,000 on behalf of the Central Office of Information (COI). Judah told Long on 7 July that the contract with the Foreign Office was regarded by both sides 'as a normal commercial one'. Consequently, the negotiations had been lengthy. The Treasury required a detailed analysis of Reuter cost increases to justify a claim for increased subscriptions. The Treasury was certainly being careful; but the original 1961 payments, now being periodically increased in line with rising costs, had contained an element of subsidy. That element was still being protected. In 1975, for example, the subscription from the Foreign and Commonwealth Office (FCO) and COI was increased from £239,000 to £387,000. The Government accepted that Reuters had suffered a 40 per cent rise in world reporting costs during the previous two years.

The readiness of Reuters to accept substantial indirect British Government help was strikingly illustrated by the continuing connection with the Arab News Agency (ANA). The ANA, which was subsidized through large subscriptions from the Foreign Office Information Research Department and the BBC, had collected and distributed news for Reuters in the Middle East since 1954. In 1963 its name was changed to Regional News Services

(Mid-East) Limited (RNS (ME)). Not until 1969 did Reuters end the connection, and then on still compromising terms.

Upon becoming general manager in 1963 Long had seemed content to continue what he described to the board in June as 'our very satisfactory association with this organisation'. Even when arguing at the end of 1968 for a resumption of direct Reuter operations throughout the Middle East, Long did so entirely on business grounds. Shahe Guebenlian, the sales manager for Africa, had conducted a survey which had shown that the Reuter annual trading surplus from the Middle East was over £50,000. Yet, argued Guebenlian, it could have been even more. RNS concentrated too much upon general news, and this was restricting potentially profitable expansion for the economic services in the Middle East.

An important meeting took place on 18 November 1968 between Horton and Judah for Reuters and Nigel Clive, head of the FCO's Information Research Department. They met to discuss how Reuters might best resume direct operations in the Middle East. Horton and Judah emphasized that, although wanting to end the connection with RNS, Reuters did not want to lose Government money.

The agreed record (marked 'secret' on every page) explained that Reuters had not yet been able to work out the extent, or the annual incidence, of the necessary compensating subsidy, 'diminishing at the end of five years to nil'. In the next paragraph the word 'subvention' took the place of 'subsidy'. Was this a belated attempt at delicacy in choice of word? If so, the substitution scarcely softened the indelicacy of what was being requested. In discussion, 'it was noted that RNS (ME) would become widely known as "bought out" by Reuters, and there might be dangers in its continuing to pay a large sum to Reuters for no apparent reason'. An alternative was adroitly found. 'Reuters representatives hoped that all the necessary subvention could be channelled through the External Services of the BBC.' These services were themselves funded by the Foreign Office. The idea for this manœuvre came from Charles Curran, director-general of the BBC.

Horton and Judah outlined the recent progress of Reuters in Africa, East Asia, and the United States. 'Reuters were backing themselves, and were asking HMG to back them, to achieve a similar success in both the Middle East and Latin America.' On 2 April 1969 Sir Denis Greenhill, the permanent under-secretary, assured Barnetson, the Reuter chairman, that the FCO wanted 'strong and independent' Reuter operations in the Middle East: 'this will be of value to British interests.' Reuters resumed direct distribution throughout the region from 1 July 1969.

The BBC External Services' subscription to Reuters was increased from

£20,000 in 1968 to £80,000 for 1969 and 1970, to £90,000 for 1971, and to £100,000 for 1972. These payments were fixed to rise in step with the planned run-down of RNS (ME). Formally, the BBC was paying for rights 'in such Reuter regional services as are available in London which the BBC may from time to time require'. The BBC did indeed use much Reuter material in its overseas broadcasting, and this had been fairly reflected in the £20,000 subscription for 1968. But the greatly increased payments in subsequent years amounted to a concealed subsidy.

Interviewed twenty years later, Judah emphasized that—whatever may have been the intention at earlier periods, especially before 1941—these payments were not now intended by the FCO to influence the content of news from Reuters. Because of this restraint, successive post-war general managers had convinced themselves that acceptance of generous payments for services to official outlets did not contravene the commitment to independence made in the 1941 Trust agreement. Nevertheless, in the *Oxford English Dictionary* sense of the word, the money certainly constituted a subsidy: 'financial aid furnished by a state or a public corporation in furtherance of an undertaking or the upkeep of a thing.'

Why was so much care taken to conceal the negotiations? Mainly because, claimed Judah in retrospect, outsiders might well have assumed that the British Government did indeed exert an influence over the Reuter news file. Looking back from retirement, Long confessed to much greater unease than Judah that such a close relationship with the British Government had continued under his management.

In 1976 Nelson prepared a paper for Long, dated 19 January, about Reuter contracts with governments, including the British Government. Nelson argued that the percentage of income derived from the governments of the home countries of the international news agencies ought not to exceed 2 per cent of revenue. This was the percentage received by Reuters at that date (see Table 13.3). Nelson calculated that AP and UPI derived respectively 2.2 and 1.6 per cent of their income from the United States Government.

The generous payments to Reuters from the BBC were adjusted during 1973–5 in line with rising reporting costs and currency fluctuations. But from 1976—paradoxically because of British Government pressure upon the BBC to curtail expenditure—full adjustment ceased. Finally, from 19 May 1980 the BBC gave up its External Service contract with Reuters entirely. Payment was then running at the rate of £250,000 per annum.

By the 1980s British Ministers and officials were fully aware that Reuters was seeking to be accepted as supranational in its approach; but the British Government was still ready to be supportive. Indeed, at the time of the

TABLE 13.3. British Government subscriptions to Reuters, 1965–75. (£000)

	1965	1970	1975
FCO/COI	134.0	118.0	368.8
COI special traffic	–	–	12.7
BBC External Service	20.0	80.0	156.1
International News Rights and Royalties Ltd—			
British Government subsidized	45.0	–	–
Miscellaneous	2.7	4.0	6.6
Total	201.7[b]	202.0[c]	562.2[d]

b 5% of total Reuter revenue of £4,051,000; *c* 2.9% of total Reuter revenue of £10,491,000; *d* 1.9% of total Reuter revenue of £29,921,000.

flotation of Reuters as a public company in 1984 the joint permanent secretary to the Department of Trade and Industry (Sir Anthony Rawlinson) went so far as to commend the 'integrity' of Reuters, even while lobbying on its behalf with the insurance companies on grounds of 'public interest'. Rawlinson wrote on 5 January 1984:

> The Secretary of State is of opinion that, as has been recognised in the past, Reuters is an undertaking involving special considerations of public interest, and that because of this factor it is desirable both that adequate safeguards should continue to sustain the integrity of the news service, and that the proposed share issue should be made in London, with substantial subscription by British institutions.

Did this attitude reflect a novel perception that the presence in London of a great supranational news and information agency benefited the host country?

In 1986 payments from the British Government were finally placed upon an unquestionably commercial basis. In that year the annual British Foreign and Commonwealth Office subscription was drastically cut from £296,000 to £20,000. The Government was keen to make economies, and the FCO had received offers from AP and other agencies to supply services for 'a four figure sum'. Sir Antony Acland, the permanent under-secretary, wrote to Glen Renfrew, the managing director, on 6 February emphasizing FCO preference for the Reuter services, but not at the old price: 'it could be argued that the historical links between us warrant an especially advantageous rate for the FCO.' In other words, Acland was wanting to turn the old financial relationship right round. The head of the FCO News and Information Department had earlier remarked that Reuter offices overseas now seemed to keep their distance from British embassies. Clearly, attitudes had changed on both sides.

To the surprise of some senior Reuter executives, who had earlier pressed the FCO for a continuing large payment, when Renfrew came into the negotiations he settled for £20,000 without much demur. He simply complained in passing to Acland (19 February) about 'American dumping and government-subsidised offerings from France'; and he required that the subscription should rise to £40,000 over three years.[22]

Early in 1976, Reuters had been angered by leaks from the proceedings of a United States Congressional Committee on intelligence activities. William Colby, outgoing director of the Central Intelligence Agency (CIA), was said to have testified that a number of Reuter correspondents had worked for the CIA, manipulating stories and inserting material. At a press conference on 26 January Colby denied that the CIA had ever tried to influence the news file from Reuters. Despite this denial, the allegation resurfaced at intervals.[23]

In a 1981 BBC programme about international intelligence activities a former CIA officer spoke of 'the general assumption of my colleagues that a Reuters journalist is more likely than not to be tied in with British intelligence in some way'. A number of Reuter journalists have since revealed in conversation how at various times in various places—especially in central Europe during the cold war—approaches were made to them by British embassy or other officials to undertake casual intelligence gathering. If any ever did so, they never admitted the fact even in retirement.

The Communist authorities in eastern Europe spied upon all western correspondents in the belief that they would reveal themselves to be intelligence agents and/or homosexuals. If the latter, there might be scope for blackmail. Michael Weigall, Reuter correspondent in Prague 1956–8, returned after the cold war to study his secret police file. He found that his flat had been bugged, with particular notice paid to his sexual relationships.[24]

10

The question of the cost, priority, and status of general news was an issue which received much attention within Reuters during the 1970s. In all previous decades the general news journalists had regarded themselves—and had been generally accepted—as superior to those who worked in the economic services. This attitude was becoming much harder to sustain as Reuters began to flourish thanks to the rapidly increasing profits made by RES.

The general news side had to bear the steeply rising costs of running a world network at a time when its revenue was increasing only slowly. The economic services, on the other hand, had the advantage of healthy revenue growth upon a relatively small cost base. In addition, capital was going into the Reuter Monitor services ahead of investment in improvements likely to improve efficiency in news handling. The resignation at the end of 1973 of Brian Horton as editor-in-chief was a clear sign that general news had lost the initiative.

The old underlying problem remained: general news could not make money overall, or even cover its costs. But this shortfall was aggravated by the fact that the British, Australian, and New Zealand newspaper proprietors— the owners of Reuters through the PA, NPA, AAP, and NZPA—were paying less and less in real terms for their news from Reuters. In 1978 their 'assessments' totalled only £619,865: to have maintained even its modest 1965 value, this figure ought to have been four times higher.

Long regretfully accepted that, instead of aiming at profitability, Reuters World Service—launched in 1974 as a cost centre—would have to concentrate upon cost-effectiveness and improved quality. How best to achieve this became the subject of a major inquiry within Reuters during the late 1970s. Known as 'the Media Study', it was conducted by Michael Neale, an experienced bureau chief, who was appointed media development manager in May 1977. As part of the media study, a reconstruction rearranged the figures to reveal what was called the 'GND gap'. This gap measured the losses which would have been recorded if the General News Division had continued to exist as a profit centre after 1973. The reconstruction found that these losses would have been huge and accelerating, totalling over £5.4 million for 1977. The forecast was for an unacceptable gap of well over £12 million by 1983. Clearly, further changes in management and structure were needed.

Michael Reupke was made editor-in-chief in 1978. He came to the post from being manager in Latin America, after experience as a correspondent in Africa and West Germany. Long respected his calm judgement, his attachment to principle, and his courtesy to all. Editor-in-chief was an old title, but this was a new post in the sense that Reupke was made responsible for all editorial operations. He oversaw the collection and distribution of news both for the media markets and for the economic services.[25]

In February 1979 Reupke called a meeting of Reuter senior editors at the Royal Automobile Club in London to prepare them for the changes which he had in mind. He wanted to remove the siege mentality which had grown up among many general news journalists. He also wanted to assuage grievances felt among the economic journalists. Many of them—working seemingly endless hours in London—felt unnoticed, and therefore unlikely to be thought suitable to become bureau chiefs.

Reupke—born in Germany but educated in Britain—also wanted to 'de-Londonize' attitudes. In the field the impression prevailed that the editorial floor at 85 Fleet Street was unaware of operational needs, and that the ultimate test of quality was still whether or not the London papers had printed a Reuter story.

The most important structural change resulting from the recommendations of the media study was the merging of the separate RWS and RES editorial operations into one all-embracing Reuters World Service. The logic behind this merger was clear, but the psychology of the situation was delicate. The merger therefore took some time for Reupke to push through. Nelson—now less of a partisan for the economic services than in earlier days—accepted the change, although with hesitation. He was influenced by Reupke's proposal that Manfred Pagel, the RES editor, should become editor of the combined service.

The new RWS began functioning from 1 January 1980, designated a cost centre. The North American editorial operation remained separate. Reupke had warned that Reuters would need to be careful not to dissipate the specialist knowledge which RES had accumulated. This was avoided. But there were other problems. The promotion of Pagel was seen by many as a threatening victory for RES. He was not a conciliator by temperament. Hans Ouwerkerk, the manager for Asia based in Hong Kong, wrote to Reupke on 21 November 1980 expressing the fears of some general news journalists that Reuters was 'progressively opting out of the news-gathering business'. Morale was said to be low. A few senior correspondents did leave. They had not foreseen that in the 1980s coverage of general news would be extended, not diminished. The prosperous new Reuters could afford to do this. Reupke might have been more definite in forecasting this expansion.[26]

A second major structural change followed in 1982. Editorial responsibility began to be shared between London, Hong Kong, and New York for eight hours each per day. Traditionally, ultimate editorial control had been in the hands of a team of journalists in London, working round the clock seven days a week. The new arrangement was intended to encourage greater responsiveness to regional needs, and to demonstrate both to staff and to outsiders that Reuters was now truly supranational. From 17 October 1982, for the period of the Hong Kong day and of the London night, Hong Kong took over; New York was brought in later. To give Hong Kong the status appropriate to such global responsibility, Reupke sent out Ian Macdowall, an especially skilful and respected newsman, as editor.[27]

I I

Writing in the budget and plan for 1981 about the years of his leadership, Long was able to claim a logical, although not inevitable, progression for Reuter market strategy since 1963. That strategy, he explained, had been:

1. to employ American technology in order to expand in Europe, and then to spread computerized retrieval services throughout the markets of the world.
2. to spend profits earned by the new services in Europe to help build a stronger base in the United States.
3. to use that United States base to produce technologically advanced services employing cable television.

This progression was clearer in retrospect than in progress. It had certainly not been easy to sustain, and the third objective—centring upon row-grabbing—had scarcely been attained. The whole movement might well have faltered, if Long had not been persistent with the board, and if he had not been fortunate in his senior colleagues.

The breakthrough into computerized information-retrieval services need not have been led by Reuters. The lead was more likely to have come from a new company based in the United States. Reuters in 1963 was an old company, reputable but not known for its daring. Yet by the time of Long's resignation in 1981 the success of the new Reuters was becoming apparent to all. The quadrupling of profits in that year, and their more than doubling again in 1982, signalled a novel prosperity. Interviewed in 1989 Nelson described the realization that the company had at last achieved financial ease as his most rewarding moment in Reuters.

Nelson was to be well rewarded financially as well as emotionally for his contribution. Long was not to be so fortunate. He resigned as managing director from 1 March 1981. His departure came suddenly. He had accepted an offer from Rupert Murdoch to become managing director of Times Newspapers; Murdoch was its new owner. Long had completed his main work at Reuters by the mid-70s, and had latterly shown signs of becoming bored. This left his eccentricities in greater prominence. His tendency to lapse from acceptable forthrightness into unacceptable rudeness intensified. When managers were required to organize Long's almost royal overseas tours down to the last restaurant, they felt driven (in the words of David Ure, who was one of them) by 'an electricity of terror'. Cole had struck his own kind of apprehension during such tours, but he had also done much business. Long was now doing less, either on tour or in London. 'It is the right moment for me to go and it will benefit the company.'[28]

This was true. Yet by leaving Reuters when he did, Long missed the chance to become a multi-millionaire—as his colleagues Renfrew, Nelson, and Judah soon did when, at Renfrew's insistence, they were allowed to acquire shares on easy terms in the booming company. In the opinion of one *New Statesman* reviewer, writing on 17 May 1985, this made Long the 'tragic hero' of the new Reuters. Both noun and adjective were perhaps too strong; but how much too strong? Long himself, his work done, professed to be un-troubled.[29]

FOURTEEN

Going Public

1981–1984

I

GERALD LONG was succeeded as managing director not by Michael Nelson, as many in the company had expected, but by Glen Renfrew. At a meeting of senior staff in London, called to hear the news, Long left no doubt that he had recommended Renfrew as his successor. Renfrew's knowledge of communications technology—'the lifeblood of Reuters'— was, claimed Long, unequalled outside the ranks of the specialists. This, Long believed, made Renfrew especially well qualified for the top job. Nearly two years later, Long explained his thinking more fully in a letter to Rupert Murdoch (18 November 1982):

> I had prepared the succession for Renfrew for many years, against the passive opposition of Barnetson, who thought Nelson would be safer. I thought he would be too safe, that, like me, he had given Reuters all he had to give, whereas Renfrew still had development potential, chiefly through his knowledge of computerised business services and his creative command of technology.

Long told Murdoch that he had previously wanted Renfrew to take charge of all Reuter communications; but that Renfrew had been unwilling to do so— partly because of his involvement in North America, partly because he did not want 'the fight with Nelson that would have ensued'.

Opinions about Renfrew within Reuters differed sharply, and continued to do so throughout the 1980s. His critics questioned whether his undoubted technological enthusiasm had always been tempered by sound judgement. In North America he had concentrated during the 1970s upon developing broad-band and satellite technology for row-grabbing services, aiming to blast out data to cheap terminals. Reuter Monitor Money Rates and Reuter Monitor Dealing had been developed under Nelson's control in London, and had interested Renfrew much less. Yet these expensive interactive products were the ones which were to make huge profits for Reuters. Renfrew's defenders answered that his pursuit of new technology had greatly improved

the image of Reuters in the United States, and had also prepared for the successful introduction of small-dish satellites in the 1980s.

Long's farewell remarks in 1981 gave the impression that he had virtually
nominated his own successor. This was not so. Long could do no more than
recommend Renfrew strongly to Sir Denis Hamilton, the chairman. A selec-
tion committee was appointed consisting of Hamilton plus Alan Hare of the
Financial Times and Christopher Dicks of the *Huddersfield Examiner* group.
The sub-committee looked no further than the two obvious candidates,
Renfrew and Nelson. At interview, as Dicks recollected some years later,
Renfrew came over as 'the hungrier of the two', full of ideas for the future.[1]

Renfrew was felt to have the right combination of personality and experience for the top job. Nelson had equally long experience, but there were
those within the company ready to denigrate him. Renfrew had even contrived during 1980 to steer RNA into apparent profitability. The directors,
some of them doubtful about the heightened involvement of Reuters in
North America, were relieved and impressed by this. Conversely, the Reuter
Dealing project, with which Nelson was closely associated, had been repeatedly delayed. Although destined for great success, it was still not launched
when Long announced his departure. Despite his disappointment, Nelson
stayed on as deputy managing director and general manager, and played an
important part until his retirement in 1989.

2

Renfrew was able to tell the board in November 1981 that profits for the third
quarter had 'left previous records far behind'. At £6,472,200 they were six
times more than budget, and ten times more than in the same quarter of the
previous year. During Long's last years as managing director Renfrew had
advocated a determined push into large profitability. Long had not disciplined
Reuters to take full advantage of its increasingly strong product and market
position, even though he had himself overseen the establishment of that position. Renfrew knew that the potential for a profit explosion was there, and as
soon as he took over he began vigorously to fuel such an explosion. He
brought new revenue down to the bottom line as never before. The year
1982—his first full year in charge—was much better than 1981 for profit
growth. Although revenue for the year increased by rather less than in 1981
(£41 million compared with nearly £49 million), 1982 pre-tax profits rose
by some £20 million compared with just over £12 million in the previous
year (see Appendix). This meant that nearly half of all new revenue was now

being brought down to the bottom line, whereas in 1981 little more than a quarter of new revenue had shown in this way. The 1981 proportion was again to be surpassed in 1983, 1984, 1988, and 1989.

Renfrew had become deeply impressed during the years of the joint venture with Ultronic by the American emphasis upon profitability and upon the need to show an adequate return upon capital. Revenue targets and financial forecasting, first introduced by Renfrew for the joint venture, had eventually spread to the whole company. As managing director he was to lay great emphasis upon the setting of targets. He was also to emphasize strongly that profitability depended not only upon adding to revenue, but also upon restraining costs even when revenue was buoyant. Equipment costs were reduced, notably by extending the use of cheaper IDR terminals. And the appetite of the technical staff for ever more resources was curbed; during the 1970s this had diminished the benefits of increased revenue. For 1980 profit before tax as a percentage of revenue was only 4.0 per cent; Renfrew told management (1 July 1981) that this was 'not good enough to guarantee the security of the company'. The percentage rose to 12 per cent in 1981, and Renfrew asked for 15 per cent by 1984. The figure actually achieved was a remarkable 23.7 per cent.

Renfrew had reported in November 1981 that Reuters World Service costs for the previous September were equivalent to only 14.4 per cent of revenue. This was the lowest such proportion on record, and was (Renfrew suggested) 'far below the level at which the costs of the news service might be seen as an excessive burden'. He was seeking to underline how much the new regime valued the contribution of the old-style journalists. A management circular on 1 July 1981 announced that 'the primary objective' was to achieve the highest possible standards in the news services. Renfrew rightly believed that the editorial dimension to the work of Reuters gave it a distinctiveness and an authority which set it apart from its computer-service competitors, which depended solely upon their technological expertise. From June 1982 the direct relationship between general news and economic information was continuously illustrated when news summaries were made available on Monitor screens.

For Renfrew the highest standards meant having not only the best but also the biggest. He launched a drive to open fresh reporting bureaux in many parts of the world, filling gaps which in the past would have had to be left unfilled. He told Lord Matthews (16 November 1983), a Reuter trustee, that editorial spending had risen by 85 per cent since 1981. Reuters, said Renfrew, now had 'many more *international* bureaux than any other agency'. He liked to compare the numbers of journalists posted by the main news agencies outside their respective headquarters countries. At the end of 1984 Reuters had 514 such journalists: AP/Dow Jones only 346, AFP 310. The hundredth Reuter bureau was opened in October 1984 in Oman.

Reuter staff numbers had reached 3,865 by 1984—2,085 in Europe; 817 in North America; 675 in the Middle East, Asia, and Australia; and 288 in Latin America. In the United Kingdom, however, Renfrew pushed through large staff reductions. He came fresh from his victory in the 1980 New York strike. General enabling agreements were negotiated with the unions at Reuters; these agreements introduced changes in working conditions, including the abolition of demarcations. Between 1980 and 1983 the number of London editorial staff fell from 387 to 271. Renfrew told the board briskly in November 1981 that the journalists 'now seem to have accepted that it is better to negotiate the future than to have it imposed on them'.

In 1981 Reuters had the chance to buy up its American competitor, UPI (United Press International), which had recently lost much ground. The opportunity was seriously considered, and Renfrew was at first inclined to favour buying. Nelson was against. He realized that such a purchase would put Reuters in head-on competition inside the American market with the largest United States agency, the Associated Press. As a national media co-operative, AP could call upon whatever resources were necessary to maintain its leading position. Reuters would have been fighting year by year a battle which it could never win. The decision not to buy UPI was a crucial negative decision.[2]

In June 1984, however, Reuters did buy the UPI news picture business outside the United States for the modest price of $5,760,000. A Reuter picture service was started from the beginning of 1985. This was an overdue addition, which quickly showed its worth. Reuter representatives, particularly in Asia and Latin America, had long complained about the lack of pictures to complement textual news, as AP and UPI did.

Back in 1960 Reuters had bought shares in Visnews, the television news-film agency. In 1968 the Reuter shareholding was increased from 11 per cent to 33 per cent, the same as the BBC's. By 1983 Visnews was employing 350 staff in London, plus a further fifty overseas; and it was able to draw upon the Reuter network of offices and communications worldwide. Nevertheless, Reuters felt Visnews to be under-capitalized and over-bureaucratized. Long had at one stage wanted to pull out entirely. Renfrew and Nelson were more enthusiastic, and in October 1985 Reuters took a 55 per cent shareholding, increased in 1992 to full ownership. Visnews was then renamed Reuters Television. The aim was to make Reuters as strong in newsfilm as it was in textual and still-picture journalism. From the first, Visnews photographers had been committed to objectivity. Their motto was said to be: 'We don't take sides, we just take pictures.'[3]

Renfrew believed strongly in decentralization. He was determined to appoint capable young overseas managers and to give them their heads. He made this policy public in a press interview (*Financial Weekly*, 25 September 1986):

> we restructured the management of Reuters into profit centres and gave our best executives bottom-line responsibility for geographical areas. We decentralised. For a long time I knew we needed geographical profit centres, because previously a lot of our costs were managed centrally. We did not combine responsibility for revenue growth and cost control with the same executive. That's basically wrong.

In other words, Renfrew was establishing everywhere the same combination of responsibility as he had insisted upon bearing when manager in North America.

From 1 May 1981 two new profit centres—Reuters Europe (RE), including the United Kingdom and Ireland; and Reuters Overseas (RO)—were established alongside the existing Reuters North America (RNA). The central management was placed in London. Andre Villeneuve became manager of Reuters Europe, and Peter Job manager of Reuters Overseas. Renfrew continued to manage RNA.

The decentralization process was completed when from the beginning of 1983 Reuters Overseas was split up. RO remained the profit centre for Africa and Latin America. A new Reuters Asia (RA) profit centre was created to cover Asia, Australia, and New Zealand. Job became its manager, based in Hong Kong. Villeneuve was transferred to become manager in North America. Ure succeeded him as manager of Reuters Europe.

These were the rising stars within Reuters. Job at 40 was the oldest of the group. He had joined Reuters in 1963 as a graduate trainee from Oxford University. He had steadily acquired all-round experience in journalism, marketing, and management, mainly in Asia and Latin America. In 1991 he was to succeed Renfrew as managing director.

3

Reuters in West Germany, which had developed a new dynamism in the 1970s, continued in the same spirit into the 1980s. In December 1980 Ingo Hertel—who had been the first German journalist hired for the new German-language service in 1971—was appointed editor of a German-language retrieval service for economic news. This was targeted at securities markets within German-speaking Europe. Reuters Europe was the company's most developed trading area. It generated the largest turnover, and it made the largest contribution to profits (see Table 14.1). Reuters North America was thus barely in profit for the year, and had slipped back into continuing monthly loss by the end. Nevertheless, American operations were expanding steadily, and this was accepted as necessary. A large new technical centre was opened in November 1982 at Hauppage, Long Island, forty miles from New York City. But two American competitors, Quotron and Telerate, were posing problems. Quotron held over half the United States market for financial information video systems. Telerate had the advantage of direct access to one of the big Wall Street brokers (Cantor Fitzgerald), which acted as a market-making intermediary for United States Government securities. This made Telerate a unique source for bond-price movements.

Reuters Asia was growing fast during the 1980s. Total revenue rose dramatically from £5 million in 1978 to over £240 million by 1989, with more than half of this coming from the Monitor Money Rates service. Peter Job had argued that Reuters would prosper best if the region were run by a single management team. 'Not one for Japan, and lots of others reporting back to London in different ways.' From 1983 he was given the task of running such a single management from Hong Kong.[4]

In Japan, the Monitor services had initially been distributed through Quotation Information Center (QUICK); but the distribution agreement was allowed to run out in May 1984. The received wisdom had been that foreign organizations always needed a partner to succeed in Japan. Job concluded that the Japanese had sufficiently liberalized their attitude to make this no longer essential. He assured Nelson on 30 August 1983 that the connection with QUICK had become an impediment. 'I do not mean that there are no non-tariff barriers, though many of them exist only in the minds of foreigners. There are such barriers. Ours has long been identified. It is KDD.' Kokusai Denshin Denwa was the Japanese telecommunications agency. It

TABLE 14.1. Turnover figures for 1983 by area. (£000)

	RE	RA	RO	RNA
Turnover	112,133	62,822	16,985	39,827
Profit contribution	33,585	24,360	2,204	226

had blocked the introduction of Monitor Money Rates into Japan until 1979; and Reuter Monitor Dealing was to be delayed until 1986.

In the previous year Reuters had introduced its first internal news product for Japan—the Reuters Japan Financial Service. This combined general news and financial market reports with real-time foreign exchange and money market rates. An editorial desk in Tokyo provided the news content. The service took its place within an expanding range of non-English-language services from Reuters—Arabic, French, German, and Spanish.

India was now entering a phase of major economic growth; and the Press Trust of India (PTI) belatedly agreed that more effort should be made to promote the economic services, for which it retained exclusive distribution rights. The Reuter Money Report began to be delivered by satellite to India in 1979, the revenue shared equally with PTI. And after prolonged negotiations and bureaucratic delays the Reuter Monitor Money Rates service became operational at Bombay from 1981, being subsequently extended to other cities. In that year, Reuter revenue from all services to India totalled only £262,000; five years later it had reached an annual rate of £2 million and rising. Reuter Monitor subscriptions became the largest single source of revenue for PTI itself. From 1987, through a joint venture with PTI, Reuters secured direct participation in the provision of its financial services within India. And from 1991 PTI finally allowed direct delivery of news from Reuters to the Indian media, PTI taking a half share of the revenue. After nearly fifty difficult transitional years, a relationship had at last been established with PTI which was entirely shaped by reasonable business practice.[5]

4

Reuters was operating one of the largest private communications networks in the world. The five primary computer-data centres were located in London, Hong Kong, New York, Frankfurt, and Geneva. The latest innovation had been direct satellite delivery by small dishes (SDS), introduced from October 1982. It was rated by Nelson as one of the major Reuter innovations—following upon the International Financial Printer, Stockmaster, and the Reuter Monitor Money Rates and Dealing services. SDS offered economies in equipment and transmission, while still allowing subscribers fast access to data. It started in the United States, and was extended in 1984 to Central America. Market data, textual news, and news pictures could all be received on the same satellite signal.[6]

Renfrew was fascinated by this technology. He was also strongly driven by a desire to make money—for Reuters and for his family. Upon becoming managing director, he quickly addressed the question of how to allow senior executives a stake in the company through a share-option scheme. Judah had been pressing for some such provision for years, but Long had always pro-crastinated. Renfrew by contrast was convinced that most people wanted to earn ever more money, and that this motivation could be harnessed to per-suade them to work more productively. During the early 1980s he therefore promoted various schemes which offered a stake in the company upon favourable terms—first to top executives, led by himself; then to other exec-utives; and then to all members of staff. 'It's human nature, it's just good busi-ness to give those responsible for success a share in that success. Then you get more success.'

In 1981 a new class of non-voting 'E' shares was introduced. The first ben-eficiaries were Renfrew, Nelson, and Judah. They ended up with 545, 361, and 306 'E' shares respectively. Such provision for senior executives was becoming widespread among British companies; but the trio were to be espe-cially fortunate as the value of their holdings grew remarkably. They were each allowed to buy one year's salary-worth of shares. Reuters in effect loaned them 90 per cent of the share valuation by issuing the shares 10 per cent paid, with the balance payable only on disposal. The shares were initially priced at £147. The company was valued on a price/earnings multiple of four. This was very low; but it had been fixed by the Inland Revenue Capital Office, which estimated the worth of the shares in open trading. When a dividend was paid by Reuters in 1982—the first for over 40 years—the multiple rose to eight. Subsequently it trebled again. As the company was bound to buy any 'E' shares which a holder wished to sell at current valuation, there was a safe market. For these various reasons, the holdings of Renfrew, Nelson, and Judah became extremely valuable. By September 1983, only two years after first issue, the 'E' shares were valued at £6,450 per share.

Nelson liked to quip that when he joined the company in 1952 the monas-tic virtues—poverty, chastity, and obedience—were necessarily observed, at least in the first and last instances. Now, poverty was no longer a part of Reuters. The 'E' share scheme was made available in stages to 124 other senior executives. The more senior received sixty-seven shares. Recipients were selected from all parts of the company, but complaints were heard that only sixteen editorial staff had been included. Some middle-ranking executives, who were offered 'E' shares in 1983, were already participating in an incen-tive cash bonus scheme which had been launched at the start of 1982. Bonuses were linked to achievement of profit targets.

Renfrew admitted in September 1983 that there was 'a sense of growing division between those staff who had benefits and those who did not'. To counter this, a share-savings scheme was introduced in June 1984, after the public flotation of Reuters. This scheme did not contain any element of reward, and was open to all who chose to join. Staff acquired non-transferable options to buy 'B' shares through saving for five years. Three principal schemes were devised, to suit employees in different parts of the world. Out of 3,342 eligible staff, 1,600 joined the scheme, a very high participation ratio. In addition, an employee and pensioner share offer was made at the time of the flotation in 1984. 3 million 'B' shares were made available at only 75p each; 3,335 employees bought 2,353,450 shares.[7]

Reuters could now afford to pay Renfrew, Nelson, and Judah the full market rate. New service contracts for the three men were drawn up at the time of the flotation in 1984. Renfrew's paid him £36,000 in respect of his duties within the United Kingdom and $148,000 in respect of duties elsewhere. On 1 June 1984 Sir Denis Hamilton wrote to Christopher Hogg, soon to be his successor as Reuter chairman, about the three top executives:

> I was convinced that our competitors would be poaching this year, and I have no regrets that already their expectations have gone to the stratosphere! But they made it all a success, Glen more than his predecessor Gerry Long, who went to The Times in 1981 and is crying his eyes out now, and taking the credit for what Glen and Mike Nelson fashioned . . . I am a great believer in motivating your leaders and technical experts—the human factor I learned as a CO on the D-day beaches 40 years ago . . . I am always open to serious argument based on facts, rather than the envy which fills the souls of some of our Board colleagues.

5

The flotation of Reuters as a public company in 1984 was described by *Time* magazine on 11 June as a saga that had everything: 'high-risk corporate strategies and fierce boardroom battles, missing heirs and angry workers, high technology and hard news.' There were four sets of interested parties:[8]

(1) The British, Irish, Australian, and New Zealand newspaper publishers who collectively owned Reuters, and amongst whom the British publishers wanted to take out some of the millions to which they now found themselves entitled.

(2) The three executive directors (Renfrew, Nelson, and Judah), who owned 'E' shares.

(3) The trustees, who sought to be the guardians of Reuters.

(4) The staff, who depended upon Reuters for their livelihoods.

The man charged with presiding over the discussions about whether to float Reuters as a public company was Sir Denis Hamilton (1918–88), Barnetson's successor as chairman. Hostile critics said that he was a man who had advanced in the newspaper industry beyond his abilities, chiefly by seeming to be 'a nice chap'. He had started as a reporter for Kemsley Newspapers in the north-east of England before the Second World War. He had enjoyed a 'good war' and eventually commanded a battalion, something to which he often referred. He was always conventionally well-dressed, and he relished his contacts with the great and the good. Hamilton was famous for his long silences, thoughtful without being a deep thinker. His greatest contribution was made as editor-in-chief of the *Sunday Times* from 1961 to 1967. He was editor-in-chief of Times Newspapers from 1967 to 1981. He had many cultural interests outside Fleet Street, and in 1976 he was knighted for his services to the arts.[9]

Hamilton joined the Reuter board in 1967, becoming chairman in 1979. By the time of the flotation discussions, advancing illness was allowing him to work only intermittently. To his credit, he tried to ensure that the revised Reuter Trust provisions were made as watertight as possible within the new public company, stronger than they had been under the old company. But Hamilton did not play the dominant overall part claimed in his posthumously published recollections.

The June 1984 Offer for Sale of shares in the new Reuters Holdings PLC explained why Reuters had become a public company. This prospectus adroitly linked the recent changes with the maintenance of the Reuter Trust principles:

> The guarantee of independence and integrity provided by the Reuter Trust Agreement has been a key factor in Reuters business. In 1983 the Directors of Reuters Limited decided that, by means of a corporate reorganisation, Reuters could obtain access to the public capital markets and thereby more readily achieve its business objectives and enable existing shareholders to realise part of their investment, while preserving the Reuter Trust Principles.

Why did Reuters not go public sooner? During 1977–8 Long had aired a scheme to float a new company—'Newco'—to handle all Reuter activities except media services. But the prospective financial benefit was not yet great enough to tempt the cautious directors from the PA. What changed the situation in the eyes of the owners of Reuters—first, the national newspapermen in the NPA, and then the provincials in the PA—was the dramatic growth in Reuter profits during the early 1980s. These quadrupled between 1980 and 1981, and then doubled again for 1982. Reuters even began to declare dividends: £1.9 million for 1981, £5.8 million for 1982.

Here was clear evidence to the four owning organizations that their holdings had taken on a vastly greater value. The NPA representative directors began to be much more interested in Reuters, while the PA representatives became much more assiduous. The PA and the NPA remained very different bodies—in terms of the personalities connected with them, and also in terms of status. The Press Association was a legal entity and a co-operative, and its members usually maintained a common front. The Newspaper Publishers Association, on the other hand, was no more than an organization which represented the national newspaper groups in labour negotiations, and for a few other common purposes. Its members remained fierce rivals in the newspaper market place. This rivalry was sometimes reflected in clashes at NPA council meetings.

These tensions became the more serious when the possibility of a public flotation of Reuters made it necessary for the NPA to establish the precise holdings in Reuters attributable to each member newspaper group. Down the years these groups had tried to minimize the size of their contributions towards the NPA 'assessment' payable to Reuters by having few shares. But when a flotation came into prospect each group suddenly wanted to lay claim to as many shares as possible (see Table 14.2).

TABLE 14.2. Total shareholdings in Reuters, May 1983.

	%	Stock	'E' shares
PA	40.8	37,500 ('A')	2,085
NPA	40.8	37,500 ('B')	2,085
AAP	13.6	12,500 ('C')	695
NZPA	2.7	2,639 ('C')	139
Executives	2.1	–	1,993

The Press Association, representing the provincial press, had a problem of finding owners for 1,800 derelict shares. Having been worth little for over a century, these shares were now worth millions. In January 1985 the PA launched a national advertising campaign to find the heirs of the original owners. Predictably, this led to a field-day for genealogists and lawyers. Some owners were never found.

6

The chief players among the directors and trustees during the discussion and implementation of the flotation were:

Directors	Trustees
Peter Gibbings (NPA/PA)	Lord Hartwell
Ian Irvine (NPA)	Lord Matthews
Rupert Murdoch (NPA)	Lord Rothermere
Mick Shields (NPA)	
Lyle Turnbull (AAP)	
Richard Winfrey (PA)	

Rupert Murdoch was the best-known newspaperman involved. He had joined the Reuter board in 1979 as an NPA representative—not (as was sometimes assumed) as a representative of AAP, in which at that time he held only a minor shareholding. The majority AAP shareholders—the *Melbourne Herald and Weekly Times*, and the John Fairfax Company, owners of the *Sydney Morning Herald*—regarded Murdoch with suspicion. His awareness of Reuters went back to his youth when his father, Sir Keith Murdoch, had been involved in bringing the AAP into the Reuter partnership in 1947. While studying at Oxford University, young Murdoch had sometimes stayed with the Chancellors.

By the early 1980s, branching out from Australia, Murdoch had gained control of the *News of the World*, the *Sun*, and (in 1981) of *The Times*. These London titles, owned together by News International, brought Murdoch the prospect, if Reuters became a public company, of a shareholding worth up to £100 million. How much did this colour his attitude during the flotation discussions? Murdoch's interest in Reuters was thought by some to be well-intentioned, strongly influenced by the memory of his father. But did such care rule out the possibility—perhaps even increase the possibility—that he might be nursing aspirations to take control? This suggestion was often made. Perhaps Murdoch was doing no more than keeping an open mind. Des Anderson, a senior accountant with the *Melbourne Herald*, reported back to Australia on 5 October 1983: 'Murdoch stated that he is leaving his options open with Reuters, but the concern is that he has a master plan to take control of Reuters shortly after it is floated.' Certainly, Murdoch took a close interest throughout the prolonged flotation discussions, and he rarely missed a Reuter board meeting.[10]

Ian Irvine was an accountant who became managing director of Fleet Holdings in January 1982. He knew that Fleet, which owned the *Daily Express*, was vulnerable. It needed assets to show in its books, and he quickly realized that Fleet's shareholding in Reuters might be valued at £100 million if the company were publicly floated. In retrospect, Irvine was to argue that such awareness was not greed—that Fleet was less interested in getting money from Reuters than in obtaining an authentic valuation of its holding. Although Fleet took out about £5.7 million from the flotation, it retained most of its 'B' shareholding. Irvine became an NPA member of the Reuter board at the beginning of 1984.

The chairman of Fleet Holdings was Lord Matthews, a self-made businessman and only recently a newspaper proprietor. He was a trustee of Reuters. Briefed by Irvine, Matthews was to play an active early part in pressing for Reuters to go public.

Lord Rothermere, another Reuter trustee, headed the third generation of the Harmsworth newspaper family. He was chairman of Associated Newspapers. Rothermere's *Daily Mail* was in fierce competition with Matthews's *Daily Express*. At meetings both of the NPA council and of the Reuter trustees, Rothermere clashed with Matthews over the flotation.

Like Matthews and Rothermere, Lord Hartwell served both as a member of the NPA council and as a trustee of Reuters. He came from the Berry newspaper family, and was chairman and editor-in-chief of the *Daily Telegraph*. 'Of all the proprietors', remarked another NPA council member, 'it was Hartwell who insisted on preserving Reuters' virginity.' Nevertheless, he became persuaded that a careful flotation need not violate the Reuter Trust principles.[11]

Another member of the NPA council who played an important part was Peter Gibbings, who also served on the PA board. He was chairman of the Guardian and Manchester Evening News plc. Gibbings and Mick Shields, the managing director of Associated Newspapers, were said by Irvine to be the only players, apart from Matthews and himself, who fully understood the financial complexities. Gibbings became an NPA director of Reuters at the beginning of 1984.

Richard Winfrey was managing director of East Midland Allied Press. He became a PA director of Reuters in 1981, and he was chairman of the PA during 1982–4. With Hamilton ill, he was made chairman of an unofficial working party of Reuter shareholders. Winfrey worked with great diplomatic skill to achieve agreement over the mechanics of the flotation.

Lyle Turnbull had served since 1974 as the AAP director on the board of Reuters. He was determined to maintain the independence and objectivity of the Reuter services; he was also keen to protect the advantageous business relationship of AAP with Reuters. He feared that many NPA members did not share his respect for the Reuter Trust, and he dealt with them watchfully.

7

Who first thought of pressing for Reuters to go public? The idea was not entirely new, but it seems to have acquired a new impetus early in 1982. An article by Maggie Brown in the *Guardian* of 10 June gave the first informed account in the press of how the owners of Reuters were realizing that they might gain access to large sums of money. By that date, flotation was being actively canvassed by Gibbings, and by Alan Hare, the chairman and chief executive of the *Financial Times*, who was an NPA director of Reuters.

Hare knew that PA support would be vital, and he sent a letter which was discussed at a special PA board meeting on 10 August 1982. In a similar letter of 23 July 1982 to Christopher Dicks—who was acting as Reuter chairman while Hamilton was absent ill—Hare had argued in favour of a flotation, so long as the Trust principles were maintained. He had talked to Murdoch and Renfrew, and he claimed that neither had been 'adverse to the idea'. However, at a Reuter board meeting on 8 September, which Hare was unable to attend, Renfrew gave the idea little encouragement. On the other hand, at a PA board meeting next day, Gibbings spoke in favour of a flotation.

Hare had circulated a study, dated 19 July, of the position and prospects of Reuters, 'which Lazards [the merchant bank] have done off their own bat'. This declared that the long history, excellent profit record, and 'exciting potential' of Reuters meant that there would be no difficulty in obtaining a listing on the London stock exchange. Hare wanted Lazards to be authorized to explore the matter further. Ian Fraser, Lazards chairman (once a Reuter correspondent), lobbied NPA members. But Renfrew told Winfrey on 3 November that he would always oppose any merchant bank 'digging into Reuters', except under the control of management. Hare said that he had expected Murdoch to contact the Australians. In view of Murdoch's poor relations with the AAP board, Max Suich, an AAP board member, commented that the idea was 'quite comical'. Murdoch, for his part, complained to Dicks on 20 September about the 'atmosphere of conspiracy' which was developing: 'all these discussions should be conducted openly at the board table.' Judah told Renfrew on 28 September that Hare was now admitting 'that he had presented the case very badly'.

Matthews and Irvine had their own reasons for wanting a flotation. The annual general meeting of Fleet Holdings was fixed for 13 October. Institutional shareholders needed to be persuaded to hold on to their Fleet shares. Matthews began to talk to journalists about the golden prospects for Reuters. Fleet revealed in September that it had received a Reuter dividend. In his speech as chairman at the Fleet annual meeting Matthews said nothing about Reuters; but one of the first questions from the floor concerned Fleet's Reuter shareholding. Matthews afterwards denied that he had planted the question. But he was ready with an encouraging reply, which received wide publicity in the press. 'Their profits are rising fairly dramatically. For many years we've been helping to prop them up. Now suddenly there is a new look about them. In the end it will mean a market quotation.' In another answer, Matthews added that he had been 'chivvying' Reuters towards such a quotation. 'I would imagine there would be two classes of shares. There would still have to be control. It could happen this year.'

Next morning, the *Wall Street Journal* duly noticed that Fleet Holdings, 'whose newspapers posted losses last year', might find its stake in Reuters a valuable asset. The *Journal* added that Murdoch was joining Matthews in moves towards a flotation. This was not correct. Brian Horton, formerly of Reuters and now on the staff of Murdoch's *Times*, phoned Matthews to say that Murdoch was 'very irritated' by what Matthews had said: 'he felt the whole affair should be allowed to simmer down now.' Immediately after Matthews had spoken, Nelson as general manager of Reuters had also tried to dampen down expectation by issuing a statement that the company had 'not authorised any action', nor any inquiry.

Matthews had spoken of possible developments before the end of the year. Rothermere let it be known within the NPA that he was opposed in principle to any public issue of Reuter shares. Most other NPA members, however, were keen for a flotation. And how long would it be before members of the PA decided that they too needed the money? Several provincial newspapers were in financial trouble, and most of them wanted to introduce new printing technology. Winfrey, the PA chairman, admitted to Renfrew on 3 November that pressure upon the PA board would probably increase. Winfrey also wondered if 'it might be best to find some way of letting NPA members have what they appear to want, and do it quickly rather than wait for pressure for action to build up'.

The staff of Reuters was growing understandably concerned about these rumours and manœuvres. The National Union of Journalists Reuter chapel sent a letter to *The Times* on 19 November; but it was not published. The letter feared that the independence of Reuters was being threatened, and asked for a strengthening of the powers of the Reuter trustees.

The Reuter board met on 8 December. Turnbull told his NPA and PA colleagues plainly that the AAP and NZPA had been 'somewhat disturbed' by the persistent talk of a flotation. The Australians saw great advantage in the existing company structure, which not only ensured the independence of Reuters, but also gave them access to the Reuters World Service on favourable terms, and influence within a global company. Max Suich, an AAP board member, later recalled his personal attitude at this point, in the light of Australian participation within the Reuter partnership since 1947. 'We felt that we had saved Reuters, and now for the first time some money was coming through. As soon as some money was coming through the Poms wanted to get hold of it.'

Why change? The AAP newspaper groups were pleased with the novel prospect of being paid increasingly large annual dividends. Some were less interested in making a capital gain from a share sale. In response to this Australian line, the Reuter board agreed to publish an announcement to staff and to the press. It declared that no proposal had been considered 'for any kind of change in Reuters ownership'. This was of course true—up to that point. The announcement also reaffirmed the board's commitment to the Reuter Trust principles.

Turnbull was not so naïve as to believe that this would be the end of the matter. In a memorandum for his fellow AAP board members written on 23 December 1982 he noted that the NPA wanted the question of going public to be raised again. Murdoch, in particular, had asked for further consideration.

8

By the spring of 1983, renewed calls for action were being heard. The *Financial Times* of 9 March quoted Ian Irvine as saying that if Reuters wanted to compete internationally, 'it is going to have to establish a much broader base for raising finance'. Renfrew replied tartly in a letter on 12 March that Reuters had been competing with success internationally for 132 years. 'It is financing its heavy capital investment programme entirely from its own resources and still has surplus cash balances.'

On 24 March *The Times* looked at 'the extraordinary rise and sudden desirability of Reuters'. The article noted that NPA members were squabbling over their respective stakes. An NPA council meeting on 26 April, according to leaks reaching Winfrey, was 'very stormy'. The members could not agree how to split the 1982 Reuter dividend.

The Reuter board met on 18 May 1983 in New York. Renfrew now submitted a management proposal for the issue of non-voting but marketable shares in Reuters. He admitted that two months earlier he had disagreed publicly with suggestions that the company needed to attract outside capital in order to compete internationally. But his appetite had been whetted by the 'impressive' success of recent Datastream and Telerate stock issues. Extra capital would enable Reuters to make major acquisitions. Telerate had gone public on a remarkable price/earnings ratio of 54: 'and is now in a stronger surplus cash position and better placed to make strategic investments than we are.' At a price/earnings ratio of between 25 and 40, continued Renfrew, an issue of 10 per cent of total Reuter stock would be worth between £125 million and £200 million.

Meanwhile, another proposal had been prepared for Matthews and Irvine to present to the NPA. This allowed NPA members to hold marketable ordinary Reuter shares directly; but it sought to protect the independence of Reuters through reserve powers attached to 'special voting shares'. These would carry the right to appoint 'special Reuter directors', who were to possess 'the absolute power' to veto any proposal contrary to the principles of the Reuter Trust. Ownership of the special shares would be through the NPA, PA, and AAP. But the ordinary shares would be vested in a new company— Reuters Holdings—and would be held by members separately.

Hartwell, an NPA council member speaking as a Reuter trustee, quickly dismissed this proposal. So also did Renfrew, when proposing the bonus share scheme to the May board meeting. He described the proposed system of two boards—and of two classes of directors within the Reuter board with different voting powers—as 'objectionable and probably unworkable'. Renfrew also argued that it would probably weaken the Trust safeguards. If, for example, the directors appointed by Reuters Holdings chose to cut back the news reporting network for short-term financial gain, the special voting directors 'would only have an ill-defined power of veto and could not force the Reuter board to take positive action'. These were unanswerable objections.

At the board meeting on 18 May Winfrey admitted that the PA membership was interested in raising capital from Reuters, even though the PA board had not yet supported this. Turnbull also now revealed AAP as ready to accept some change. He did not want to get out of step with the Reuter top management, led by Renfrew. Close collaboration with Reuters was necessary for the success of AAP's ambitious current development plans. Turnbull therefore supported Renfrew's proposal for a bonus share issue. Turnbull was pleased to find that the NPA view, as relayed by Hare and Murdoch, 'did accept that any change in the capital structure would be done only within the intentions of the Reuter Trust'. Discussion at the board rambled on without much shape until Murdoch suddenly exclaimed 'equity is *for ever*'. By this he meant that if Reuters went public, the resulting equity would have to be serviced by a dividend, and that 'City' considerations would influence policy. He contrasted this unfavorably with the existing private company status of Reuters, under which it was possible to take decisions which might reduce immediate profitability for the sake of long-term benefit.

The board agreed to make a final decision at its September meeting. A general order to staff on 14 July announced that Reuters had commissioned Binder Hamlyn, its auditors, to produce a report, 'following a management proposal that it should issue stock'. Staff were also told that the board had 'decided to study ways of enabling existing shareholders to put a value on their stock in Reuters'.

The press now had no doubts that the outcome would be a flotation. 'Reuters set to go public', announced *The Times* on 26 May 1983. 'Reuters is set for £1bn market float', proclaimed the *Sunday Times* on 12 June. Both Winfrey for the PA and Hamilton for Reuters issued statements denying that there was any commitment to go public. Hamilton's denial appeared on 10 June, the day of the yearly meeting of the Reuter trustees and of the annual general meeting. At the trustees' meeting Matthews tried to gather support for a flotation initiative. He was opposed by Rothermere, Hartwell, and others:

> Matthews: As Trustees we would not be opposed to a public flotation in some formal manner provided the safeguards of the Trust were there, and you suggested obviously that proposals have to be put forward. But by whom? Would it be improper for a Trustee to put them forward, or would we look to management to initiate that proposal, or otherwise we remain silent on it? There is a distinct feeling that, if everyone is rather shy of saying too much about it, I have a feeling that no one would be really opposed to it because obviously there is substantial money involved . . .
>
> Rothermere: I think the trustees only come into this at a considerable remove. Their fundamental duty is not to the shareholders and their profits but to uphold the objectives of the Trust, and I don't think in that connection that this Board of Trustees should take the initiative in anything. We should be fully informed, and we should contemplate and make our decision on whatever is put before us to ensure that it is in accord with the Reuter Trust . . .

Matthews: I would also suggest we have a responsibility not only for the trust
　　but for the shareholders as a whole. It is implied.
Rothermere: I don't think so.
Matthews: That is my view, that it is our duty to look after the Trust and the
　　shareholders.
Rothermere: I think that is the duty of the directors.

Rothermere was of course right.

Arguments continued within the NPA council about the points system
used to establish the sums payable by each paper towards the overall NPA
'assessment' for Reuters. The more points each group could claim the more
valuable would be its holding if Reuters went public. Dailies received six
points, London evenings three points, Sundays one point. These weightings
had been devised to reflect the likely usage of the Reuter news service by each
category of paper. But there were anomalies, and these gave room for argument; the *Sporting Life*, for example, had been counted as a daily, whereas the
Financial Times counted only as a Sunday.

9

A meeting of the board of the Australian Associated Press on 30 June 1983
considered the position at that date. The AAP board expressed its willingness
to support action, but with important qualifications:

> The board agrees in principle to a bonus issue of Reuter shares and to a public
> issue of non-voting shares provided AAP ownership rights are retained at not
> less than the present level, and provided also that the issued non-voting stock
> could not be converted to voting stock nor could it diminish the control of the
> management of Reuters by the present ownership, in order that all the provi-
> sions of the Reuter Trust are preserved.

This resolution was read out to the Reuter board on 13 July.

The two possible courses of action endorsed by the AAP—a bonus issue
and a public issue—were discussed throughout the summer of 1983. At the
13 July board Renfrew voiced concern that the bonus share issue for the benefit of the present shareholders seemed to be overshadowing the management
proposal to build up a capital fund. He was assured by Dicks and Hamilton
that the management's wishes were regarded by 'everybody' as 'the first priority'.

In August 1983 two Australian representatives, Des Anderson and Max
Suich, were sent by the AAP to London for consultations with the various

British parties. The AAP and the PA now decided to work together, and to present 'a united front on matters of control'. Both bodies also needed to overcome major tax difficulties before selling any of their holdings in Reuters. However, at a meeting of the Fairfax board on 15 September after his return to Australia, Suich was still far from certain that a Reuter flotation would happen at all. Although the shareholders had agreed in principle, two serious obstacles remained, said Suich. 'One was the disputation at board level, and the other was whether Mr. Renfrew would leave. There was no one adequate to take his place.' The fear was that Renfrew would cash in his 'E' shares and run.

The likely introduction of non-voting shares, devised to allow the existing owners to retain control, had brought a further difficulty. The British Insurance Association Investment Protection Committee and the National Association of Pension Funds let Reuters know that they firmly opposed the issue of equity capital without voting rights. They represented such major investors as Prudential Insurance, the largest sub-underwriter of United Kingdom issues.

S. G. Warburg, the merchant bank, had previously advised that non-voting shares would be acceptable to the market. Now, revealed Renfrew to the crucial Reuter board meeting on 14 September, Warburgs admitted that there would be opposition from the institutions. Nevertheless, management had instructed Warburgs to estimate the market available for non-voting shares. 'Non-voting shares', insisted Renfrew, 'represent the simplest way of raising money without changing the principles of the Reuter trust agreement.' Warburgs had concluded that there would be a market for non-voting shares of up to £200 million in the United Kingdom, and up to £300 million in the United States.

In general, Warburgs had been encouraging. They concluded in a report for the Reuter board circulated on 9 September 1983 that:

1. Reuters could be valued at between £1,000 million and £1,500 million, and would be attractive to a broad section of investors in both the United Kingdom and the United States.
2. a tax structure was designable which would avoid double taxation for the PA.
3. 'A flotation of the company is compatible with safeguards for control of Reuters.'

Protection against taxation difficulties would require the creation of a holding company above the existing Reuters Limited. This would necessitate the reinstatement of the Reuter Trust agreement in connection with the new company.

Rupert Murdoch had other ideas. He revealed them to the very meeting of the Reuter board on 14 September which received these Warburg proposals. He suggested that Reuters should be split into two companies. Reuters Limited would continue to sell general news on the existing basis:

> Into a new company would be put the business services, the economic services, the whole revenue flow and the whole costs which today produce the profit Reuters had overall. The continuing subsidy of the news services would be provided for by simply licensing the name Reuters to the new company which had an identical management and the same staff.

The idea of some such split was, of course, not new. Long had wanted it in his time as managing director, and had now recommended it to Murdoch.[12]

The Reuter top management came down very firmly against this suggestion. A management paper, dated 21 September, dismissed the idea of division as being based upon two false assumptions: first, that there was a clear separation between the services sold to the media and those sold to business subscribers; and secondly, that 'guarantees of independency and integrity' were only needed to protect the general news side and not the economic services. Both assumptions were not merely wrong but dangerous.

At Murdoch's suggestion, a working party was set up to consider four options:

1. a financial restructuring 'to separate editorial from trading activities'.
2. 'An issue of marketable non-voting shares'.
3. 'An issue of marketable shares with restricted voting rights, with the existing owners retaining 30 per cent of Reuters equity'.
4. 'An issue of marketable shares with restricted voting rights, with the existing owners retaining a minimal equity interest.'

Because some NPA members had objected to being represented by others, a first meeting of the working party on 20 September had to take the form of merely a discussion between interested parties and their advisers. The meeting was attended by Irvine and Shields from the NPA, Winfrey from the PA, Anderson from the AAP, and Renfrew and Judah from the management; Hamilton took the chair. The meeting soon decided that the first option, Murdoch's scheme for division, was not practicable. Renfrew spoke against it emphatically, describing it as 'disaster for the company'. The meeting also decided against option 2, an issue of non-voting shares. Such an approach was thought likely to limit substantially the number of shares which might be sold, and would reduce their price.

Discussion therefore concentrated upon options 3 and 4. Hamilton described option 3—an issue of marketable shares with restricted voting rights, and with the existing owners retaining 30 per cent of the equity—as 'a half-way house'. This formula was intended to preserve as far as possible the form of the existing structure, by keeping 'A', 'B', and 'C' shares and by entrenching the appointment of 'A', 'B', and 'C' directors.

Option 4—an issue of marketable shares with restricted voting rights, with the present owners retaining a minimal equity interest—involved the replacement of the existing control structure by a special share, 'the master share'. All the rest of the shares would be voting ordinary shares, and would be listed. The master share would carry the right in defined circumstances to cast sufficient votes on a poll at a general meeting to pass any ordinary resolution and to defeat any ordinary or special resolution. This master share would be held by the Reuter trustees, and a revised agreement of trust would set out the circumstances in which they would be able to wield it.

The NPA, as a body, was still unable to offer a united reaction to any proposals. But the PA was capable of doing so. At its board meeting on 13 October it came out strongly in favour of combining the idea of a master share with that of weighted voting.

Although a practicable scheme was now beginning to emerge in private, outside observers still feared that the good name of Reuters was about to be sacrificed to satisfy the greed of the press barons. This was the fear of many veteran Reuter figures—notably, Malcolm Graham (a director in 1941 when the Reuter Trust was created); Christopher Chancellor (the former general manager); and John Burgess (the former chairman). During the summer of 1983 they had variously expressed their concerns by letter and in person to Hamilton and Renfrew. Chancellor proved very difficult to calm down. Hamilton wrote to Burgess on 11 October 1983 about 'the wanderings, in every sense, of Christopher Chancellor'. Sadly, Chancellor's mind was growing enfeebled; but his contacts were extensive. Not least, his son Alexander—himself a former Reuter correspondent—was editor of the *Spectator*, the respected London weekly. The issue for 22 October contained a three-page article written by Alex Chancellor and Geoffrey Robinson, a barrister. It was entitled 'Reuters: The Price of Greed'. This article traced the history of Reuters as an agency selling general news, and noticed how the Reuter Trust had been formed in 1941 for its protection. Unfortunately, claimed the article, the great profits now being earned by the Monitor services had become a danger to the integrity of Reuters.

Nelson and Judah read the article and invited Alex Chancellor to lunch. One of their purposes was to explain that they, and Renfrew, had no personal interest in pushing for a flotation, since their 'E' shares had a high value whether or not Reuters went public. They would not countenance a reorganization of the company which did not respect the Reuter Trust principles. Alex Chancellor was persuaded of the integrity of the three top executives; but in a paragraph on 5 November he still spelt out what their holdings would be worth if Reuters went public at £1,000 million—Renfrew £5,450,000; Nelson, £3,610,000; Judah, £3,060,000. Paragraphs about Reuters appeared in the *Spectator* each week throughout November.

During the summer of 1983 Gibbings had used his overlapping position within both the NPA and PA to try to find a way forward towards a flotation. He called informal meetings at his office. One such meeting on 25 October brought together Hare, Irvine, and Shields from the NPA, and Dicks, Winfrey, and Donald Anderson from the PA. It proved very fruitful in giving firm shape to detailed proposals which came to be part of the final scheme. The note of the meeting included the following points:

> The structure of the new company should be kept simple and as near to the existing one as possible.

> There should be commercial reasons for a possible flotation, because 'the Revenue did not take kindly to artificially created schemes'.

> The present shareholders should retain the lowest possible economic interest consistent with retaining control. The PA suggested a 25 per cent interest with a 3–1 multiple. The NPA suggestion of 30 per cent was too high.

> The NPA members should control their shares individually, but under cover of a shareholders' agreement. The PA, AAP and NZPA should hold their control shares under a separate agreement.

> If voting control by present shareholders dropped below 50 per cent, then a 'Master Share, controlled by Trustees' should operate in specified circumstances.

> No one shareholder to hold more than 15 per cent.

> The new board to comprise up to 14 members—three PA; three NPA; two AAP; three Reuter executives; three directors from outside the newspaper industry.

The note concluded with the reminder: 'Agreed integrity of Trust re independence vital'.

At the Reuter board on 9 November Murdoch described weighted voting shares as an attempt to sell and yet to keep control:

> He thought it was a case of wanting to have one's cake and eat it, and really the decision ought to be whether one kept it as an entirely private company. He thought it 'a classic case of great British hypocrisy', at which Turnbull interjected that he thought 'it was more international than that'.

Murdoch emphasized that he was speaking personally, and not for the NPA. He would not press his opinion, as he was a director appointed to represent the NPA, which had now agreed to a flotation on the proposed terms. Alan Hare, another director from the NPA, afterwards described Murdoch's last-minute assertion that 'it would be better for Reuters to stay as it was', as 'pure theatre'—intended to demonstrate that he was not a greedy press baron. But Murdoch seems to have been saying the same in private to Gerald Long.

The AAP continued to act as a brake. With regard to possible reductions in holdings, Turnbull finally conceded that a reduction from 25 to 20 per cent of the equity could take place with only 75 per cent of the existing share-holders approving; but he insisted that for anything below 20 per cent approval would have to be unanimous. Three classes of shares were now envisaged. Ordinary 'B' shares in the new company were initially to form 25 per cent of the equity. 'A' shares were to have four votes per share. No person or group was to own more than 15 per cent of any shares. The master share was to be held by a separate company, with the Reuter trustees as directors. The board also agreed that the company should itself raise $100 million at the time of the flotation. This would create the capital fund wanted by management.

10

Hartwell now resolved the problem of the division of share interest in Reuters between the members of the NPA. He produced for the NPA council an analysis of the competing claims. His paper (8 November) amounted to a piece of *reductio ad absurdum*. It recommended adoption of a neutral plan devised by John Le Page, the NPA director. This was now accepted.

A press release after the Reuter board meeting of 9 November con-firmed—what had already become public knowledge—that the Reuter Trust agreement was in fact no more than a shareholders' agreement: the owners, acting unanimously, could repudiate it. Renfrew sought to reassure his staff and the public by emphasizing that the changes being envisaged would ensure that 'the principles of the present Trust Agreement would be maintained'.

The National Union of Journalists at Reuters responded by passing a reso-lution on 1 December which called upon the owners to strengthen the Trust 'in terms which would imply legal obligations'. The journalists were well aware that not all the NPA shareholders wanted to respect the Trust con-straints. Des Anderson reported on 5 October:

Fleet openly expresses the view that the Reuters Trust is no more than a share-holders' agreement based upon old-fashioned ideals which do not have a place in the commercial world of today. Fleet say that such things as Trusts and restrictions should not exist, as market forces will come into play and dictate the policy and future of Reuters.

James Callaghan, the former British Prime Minister, had been told by Christopher Chancellor about his fears for Reuters. Callaghan was interviewed on BBC television on 10 November and on BBC radio next day. He argued that since the Trust seemed to be in danger, the House of Commons should look into the position of Reuters, as it had done in 1941.

Even now, a flotation was not quite certain. The shareholders' working party met on 17 November and 6 December, under Winfrey's chairmanship. No AAP representatives were present, which was a pity. The AAP was becoming increasingly concerned at what it saw as attempts by various NPA newspaper groups to weaken the control function of the 'A' shares. The Australians demanded tight restrictions upon 'A' share ownership and sale, in order to provide a control element additional to that operating through the trustees—'belt and braces'.

The working party met again on 13 December, with Turnbull of the AAP present. In his report back to Australia on 20 December he described the meeting as 'difficult:

Both the NPA and PA representatives there (and their nine advisers from Warburgs and Rothschilds) sought to persuade me to change the AAP position so that there could be a less restricted float.

Specifically, they sought to change the previous decisions that we should maintain a minimum equity in Reuters after the minimum 3-year locked-in period; they also sought relaxation of other essential elements of the scheme, the consequence of which I thought would make inevitable our future loss of control of the company.

I denied their final claim that we were using a minority shareholder's veto to block the proper future development of the company. I told them this was humbug and the opposite of the truth; in fact, only AAP seemed to be interested in the purposes of the Trust and in a long-term commitment to Reuters.

Both the NPA and PA sought the right to drop below a 20 per cent equity in Reuters after three years with only a simple majority of shareholders agreeing; our position was that we should not go below 20 per cent (with a weighted vote ratio) unless with the unanimous consent of all shareholders. In the end, when things got blunt, I said their choice was whether they wanted to get the benefits of 80 per cent of something, or 100 per cent of nothing.

The transcript notes of the meeting confirmed the sharpness of some of the exchanges. Irvine charged Turnbull with advocating controls which would act against one of the Reuter Trust principles, the commitment to develop the business:

> Turnbull: You have got it back to front. I don't believe it is your intention to preserve the integrity, the trust of Reuters.
> Irvine: You have not answered the question.
> Turnbull: You are saying we are exercising a veto. We are just saying we wish to preserve the present.

The Reuter board meeting on 14 December proved to be even more contentious, although the formal minutes spoke only of 'full discussion'. Turnbull telexed an account of the proceedings back to Australia:

> An eight-hour meeting after much argument today agreed in principle to float Reuters in London and New York along lines of the scheme approved by us, that is weighted voting, media-controlled board plus founder share and trustee system. Murdoch tried to upset whole plan by arguing for an abandonment of the weighted voting system on grounds that Warburgs advice was that it would reduce market value of the float in London. We therefore had to argue all over again the principles already decided at yesterday's committee meeting.
>
> I said that we would not agree to a float except on our terms, and that in any case there was no time left to go back to square one and produce a new scheme if they wanted to get their money out next year. This was finally conceded.

In the background to these disputes about structure were doubts about the prospects for a flotation. Warburgs and Rothschilds, reported Turnbull, had told the board 'that our scheme was not popular in the City', and that there would be difficulty selling something which relied heavily upon weighted voting and controlled board membership.

In addition, there were differences about the future policy of the new company. Turnbull reported that Murdoch and Renfrew had 'clashed repeatedly' over this at the board on 14 December. According to Turnbull, Murdoch had argued against further investment in hardware, and also against acquisitions. He wanted Reuters to confine itself to the provision of services. The top executives, reported Turnbull, had told him privately that they were 'very grateful to us for the preservation of what they regarded as the proper future control of the company'.

After the board meeting of 14 December, a press release and a general order to staff announced that the board had decided to seek a public flotation of Reuters, 'and to submit a plan to the Reuter trustees for their comments'. It was noticed that the trustees were not being asked for their 'approval'. Two days later Renfrew had to issue another general order. 'I do want to assure staff, yet again, that preservation of the principles of the Reuter Trust Agreement has been the paramount consideration in all the discussions.'

Renfrew then attacked recent press comment, and criticized those who were seeking to bring the British Government and Parliament into the matter. Any connection with the Government or legislature of any country, wrote Renfrew, was 'simply not consistent with Reuters principles of independence'. This seemed to be confusing the wish of the British authorities to be reassured about the future independence of Reuters with a desire to interfere with that independence. In fact, the former ruled out the latter.

The benevolence of the interest being shown by the British Government was revealed early in January 1984. The Department of Trade and Industry tried to persuade the leading investment institutions to waive in the special case of Reuters their opposition to non-voting or weighted shares. On 5 January the permanent under-secretary, Sir Anthony Rawlinson, asked David Walker, the executive director of the Bank of England, to use his influence 'on grounds of public interest'. Walker was authorized to copy Rawlinson's letter to the chairmen of the relevant City of London institutions. The National Association of Pension Funds and the British Insurance Association both refused to give way. The chairman of the BIA suggested (20 January) that the master share safeguard would be sufficient to protect Reuters without need for weighted 'A' shares.

At the Reuter board meeting on 11 January 1984 the mechanics of flotation were discussed, including the feasibility of a joint offering in London and New York. This would be the first initial public offering made simultaneously in the two cities. David Scholey of Warburgs explained that this was desirable in order to demonstrate how much Reuters was a world-wide company. Scholey also said that it would be advantageous to add some non-press directors to the Reuter board. Murdoch asked him what sort of persons, and Scholey suggested that they might be bankers. 'We don't want to fill the board with a lot of City stiffs', answered Murdoch.

The House of Commons discussed the position of Reuters on 27 January, upon a motion from a Labour back-bencher, Austin Mitchell, himself a journalist. The board had authorized the briefing by Michael Nelson of Kenneth Baker, the Minister for Information Technology. Nelson talked to Baker on the phone. As in 1941, only a handful of members heard the Commons exchanges; but the fact that a discussion had taken place at all was a useful expression of concern for the maintenance of the Reuter Trust principles. One MP, Nicholas Soames, Churchill's grandson, still spoke in the old vein of 'a splendid British institution'; but Mitchell's opening remarks had recognized its international role. He asked for Government intervention to protect not British interests but 'the public interest worldwide'. In reply, the Minister reconciled the two different emphases by describing Reuters as 'a national asset' because it was a successful international company with its headquarters in Britain. And it was the more an asset, continued Baker, because it was unconnected with the British Government. He declared himself satisfied that the board and trustees of Reuters would preserve its independence after flotation.

At meetings of the Winfrey working party on 25 January and 7 February 1984 Irvine returned to the attack on the 'A' share restrictions because they would affect market value. Winfrey reminded the meeting on 7 February that the 'A' shares had been devised to reconcile the wish of the British owners to raise money with their wish to retain control. Des Anderson told the meeting forcefully that the AAP had already compromised over the percentage of equity to be retained by the holders of 'A' shares. 'Originally we suggested 51% for ever and a day. We have come now to 25% and 20%. We are certainly not prepared to go below that, and that is final.' And so it was.

The trustees had not become involved in the prolonged discussions of ways and means. They waited to be asked for their reaction to a particular scheme. Although their powers had been shown to depend only upon a shareholders' agreement, their moral authority remained strong. In particular, they were in a good position to comment upon any proposed new Trust agreement. Hartwell was especially active in collecting opinion. At a meeting on 21 February the Reuter trustees accepted the new trustee structure devised by the board. This centred upon the creation of a Founders Share held by a Founders Share Company. A deed of mutual covenant, agreed by the owners, was to convey to the Founders Share Company the right to enforce procedures for the preservation of the Reuter Trust principles. The 1941 statement of principles, as revised in 1953, was to be reaffirmed with updating amendments. The existing trustees were assured that the new trustees would be given sufficient powers:

(1) If any single Reuter Trustee believes that an interest group or faction has obtained or is seeking to obtain or maintain control of Reuters, then a majority of the Reuter trustees can ensure that the Founders Share rights are exercised to ensure compliance with the Reuter Trust Principles.

(2) If any attempt is made to vary the protective powers vested in the Founders Share, then any two Reuter Trustees can ensure that the Founders Share rights in the holding company are exercised to prevent this.

The necessary deed of mutual covenant was entered into by the owners on 9 May.

At their meeting on 21 February the Reuter trustees had expressed 'enormous satisfaction' with the proposed reorganization of the ownership of Reuters. This had involved considerable legal manœuvring. The taxation difficulties which had threatened the PA and AAP were circumvented; while the NPA was enabled to participate as a legal entity through a new body, NPA Nominees. A new public limited company, Reuters Holdings, acquired Reuters Limited. Reuters Holdings was initially given four classes of share capital:

(1) 'A' ordinary shares, representing 25 per cent of the equity, entitling holders to four votes on most matters and producing a voting majority for 'A' shareholders, with restrictions on share transfer.

(2) 'B' ordinary shares, representing 75 per cent of the equity, with one vote per share.

(3) One Founders Share, with a minimal economic interest but with overriding voting rights in defined circumstances.

(4) 'E' shares.

Three or four 'independent' 'D' trustees were to be added to the existing 'A', 'B', and 'C' trustees. These independent trustees were to have no connection with Reuters, and no financial interest in the newspaper industries of the United Kingdom, Ireland, Australia, or New Zealand likely to affect their independence. The first 'D' trustees eventually appointed were Kingman Brewster, a former United States Ambassador to the United Kingdom and a distinguished academic lawyer; John Freeman, chairman of London Weekend Television, once a Labour junior minister and subsequently Ambassador to the United States; Kenneth Morgan, director of the Press Council, an experienced journalist; and Lord McGregor, Professor of Social Institutions at London University, and chairman of the Royal Commission on the Press 1975–7.

Critics such as Callaghan and the Chancellors now expressed themselves satisfied. 'As an exercise in having one's cake and eating it', conceded the *Spectator* on 3 March, 'the restructuring of the company is to be admired.' In a private letter to Christopher Chancellor on 8 March Denis Hamilton summed up soothingly:

> I would have preferred that the structure of Reuters had been left alone, and we could have gone on building up reserves sufficient to develop our businesses still further . . . Anyhow, as we both know, people new to journalism see it as a heaven-sent opportunity to line their own pockets and develop their rather

fragile businesses. The only real sympathy I have for some of our Fleet Street friends is that they have been plundered by the unions and at last they will get something back, though I fear the printers will grab what they can, as they always have done. Michael Hartwell has been magnificent throughout all this, and I must tell you that Rupert Murdoch, himself, has played a constructive and statesmanlike role in memory of his father.

II

The offer of 'B' shares to the public took further time and discussion. Uncertainty persisted up to the last minute about just how many 'B' shares each owner would be prepared to offer for sale. This uncertainty caused friction at a meeting of Winfrey's working party on 12 March 1984. When Des Anderson suggested that every shareholder would be a seller, Winfrey answered that this would not be the case:

> Anderson: If we are going to have a cat and mouse game as to who is going to sell and who is not, I think our stand could well be that we won't sell any shares.
> Winfrey: A float gives value to the shareholding.
> Anderson: It should be equal. The purpose was to benefit the company. If those commercial reasons for the company are not there and it is only an exercise to benefit certain shareholders, we ought to know . . . If we are going to find the large shareholders are not going to sell, then we can say 'the float's off'.
> Irvine: The shareholders in the NPA have said that they would prefer not to sell shares. In order to establish a market they will be willing to sell shares.

Reuters Holdings was registered as a public limited company on 11 April 1984, and held its first board meeting on that same day. A new board was constituted, with Sir Denis Hamilton—as chairman of the old Reuters Limited—appointed chairman of the new company. At a board meeting on 8 May three new 'B' directors were appointed. These 'outside' directors were intended to introduce high-powered and international business experience into the direction of the new public company. The old board had decided that they should be drawn from the United Kingdom, continental Europe, and the United States. The individuals chosen were Christopher Hogg, chairman and chief executive of Courtaulds; Pehr Gyllenhammar, chairman of Volvo; and Walter Wriston, chairman of Citicorp.

The same board meeting on 8 May discussed the size of the 'B' share offering (106,800,000 shares), the likely valuation of the company (£708 million–£920 million), the minimum tender price (180p), and the consequences of a joint flotation in London and New York. Joint flotation prevented the usual fixed-price share offer. Instead, there had to be an auction by tender through Warburgs and Rothschilds. The suggested valuation range was considerably less than earlier estimates of £1 million or more: the institutional boycott had lowered the figure by perhaps £100,000. The valuation at sale was £770 million.

The seventy-two-page prospectus was one of the largest ever issued. It was advertised in full over nine pages in four British national newspapers. 'Roadshow' presentations by senior management were made in London and Edinburgh, and in cities across the United States and Europe. Up to 70 per cent of shares were thought likely to be sold to institutions. In the event, the response in the United States was less than expected, partly because share prices there had recently collapsed. Investors in New York were offered 49,800,000 'B' shares, but subscribed for only 39,000,000. The shortfall was made up in London, where investors took up 67,800,000, against an originally planned 57,000,000.

The choice of a striking-price had been a final matter of sharp contention. It was set too low. Despite the boycott by financial institutions, the British market could have absorbed the whole issue at over 200p per share. But in order to suit the reluctant American market, Merrill Lynch and Morgan Stanley, who were handling the New York offering, insisted upon a figure of 196p. The London *Times* commented on 5 June that the experiment of making simultaneous offerings was 'unlikely to be repeated in a hurry'.

TABLE 14.3. The main sellers of Reuter shares and their approximate proceeds.

	£m.	% of total
International Thomson	20.7	13.6
Associated Newspapers	14.9	9.8
Reed International (including Mirror Group)	11.7	7.7
United Newspapers	9.5	6.3
Daily Telegraph	6.7	4.4
S. Pearson (including *Financial Times*)	6.4	4.2
Fleet Holdings	5.7	3.8
Westminster Press	5.4	3.6
Eastern Counties Newspapers	5.4	3.6
Guardian and *Manchester Evening News*	5.1	3.4

Total proceeds for all newspaper groups amounted to £152 million. The table assumes capital gains tax deducted at 15%.
Source: *UK Press Gazette*, 11 June 1984.

Murdoch's News International finally decided not to offer any 'B' shares for sale, perhaps for tax reasons. Proceeds from the flotation of Reuters helped to finance the removal to new premises and the modernization of various British national and provincial newspapers (see Table 14.3). In this connection, however, the value of retained Reuter shareholdings mattered at least as much as any money taken out. Their shareholdings now enabled several newspapers to borrow heavily. For example, within a year the *Daily Telegraph* had raised £110 million for two new printing works.[13]

On the afternoon of 4 June Hamilton, Renfrew, Nelson, and Judah appeared on the floor of the London stock exchange, all looking suitably confident (Plate 57). The atmosphere turned out to be low-key—despite the previous questioning in Parliament and by the press, and even though the issue was over-subscribed 2.7 times in the United Kingdom. The trading-floor remained open after hours, and the price rose to 218p. But there was no great excitement. Reuters itself raised £53 million through the sale of new shares. This cash, plus marketable paper, was now available to finance acquisitions.

12

Not everyone was convinced that the flotation was right. Just under a year after the event *The Price of Truth: The Story of the Reuters Millions* was published, promising on its jacket 'a story of greed and intrigue surrounding Fleet Street and of how a small group of men broke a solemn undertaking in their efforts to unlock a treasure house'. The book was written by John Lawrenson, who had worked for Reuters between 1955 and 1971, assisted by Lionel Barber, a young financial journalist.

How valid was the charge that the owners of Reuters had broken their solemn undertaking? Under the original Trust agreement the PA and NPA had been committed to treating their ownership 'in the nature of a trust rather than as an investment'. These were high-sounding words, which were omitted from the restatement of Reuter Trust principles at the time of the flotation. Was this omission significant? Was it a tacit confession of guilt by the owners—about the money which they had just made, and about the money which they intended to continue to make?

Not at all. First, Reuters had now been floated publicly. Within the new public company these same newspaper groups—in their role as controlling 'A' shareholders—had accepted an obligation to the ordinary 'B' shareholders to seek profits. In such circumstances, the 1941 form of words was obviously inappropriate.

Secondly, even though the 1941 form of words had still been operative when the owners agreed to seek financial gain, they had a good defence against any charge of breach of faith. Their defence turned upon the wording of the limitation imposed upon them. Had the owners of the old private company really been excluded from seeking in any circumstances to make money out of Reuters? The question had not arisen for forty years because there had been no chance to make money. The language of the Trust agreement had been chosen by Haley in 1941 with deliberation: he was a careful writer. He had decided to describe the commitment of the owners as 'in the nature of a trust rather than as an investment'. He did not write 'in the nature of a trust *and not* [or *and never*] as an investment'.

In other words, Haley imposed a qualified and not a total negative. The chosen formula at least left open the possibility of the owners treating Reuters as an investment, so long as they did not infringe the Trust principles.

In 1984 the owners were able fairly to claim that in the process of taking money out of Reuters they had actually made the Trust much more secure. Its authority was no longer founded simply upon a shareholders' agreement, which could be overturned. Moreover, in order further to protect the company they had introduced weighted 'A' shares, even at the expense of reducing the market value of their own holdings.

Some of this was explained by Lawrenson and Barber, despite the hyperbole of their dust-jacket. Reviewing the book for *Reuters World* in August 1985 Kevin Garry, now an assistant general manager of Reuters, remarked that 'in the end the authors seem almost relieved not to find the villainy they lead their readers to expect'. The temptation to satisfy greed through breach of faith had certainly existed during 1982–4—for some more than others. The high-principled had coached the less-principled. Greed had been scaled down to merely healthy appetite.

FIFTEEN

The World's News
1945–1989

I

A T the coming of peace in 1945, the reputation of Reuters as a general
news agency stood high. In the succeeding decades the task of Reuter
journalists and managers was to maintain and to develop that reputation. 'Now the hard work begins', Cole had warned. By this, he meant that
the Second World War had been easy to report at least in one sense. It was
usually obvious which were the big war stories to follow, whereas in peacetime correspondents were required much more to seek out unanticipated and
preferably exclusive stories. Moreover, they were expected to do so without
official support, such as had been widely available during the Second World
War. Doon Campbell recalled 'how simple it all was with a uniform, an
accreditation, a movement order and a note to the Field Cashier . . .
Everything was laid on—transportation, accommodation, filing facilities,
spokesmen, conducting officers, interpreters, handouts and censorship guidance.' In contrast, after 1945, while reporting from many different parts of
Asia, Campbell remarked how he had suffered 'more headaches coping with
local conditions, currencies . . . climates, codes, conventions, cranks and censors than with the actual business of getting news and writing it'.[1]

Reuters, like the British press and the BBC, had felt no unease about supporting the Allied cause in wartime. Even so, the agency had been more careful than in the First World War to report only what it believed to be the truth.
And Seaghan Maynes was later to claim that he had never spoken of 'the
enemy', because he was aware that his stories were being read in many neutral countries.

Such awareness of the global market grew steadily within Reuters after
1945. The British Empire was fading away, and the old agency was straining
to compete in a changing world. At first, Reuters still gave most attention to
the United Kingdom, where it served the national and provincial papers and
the BBC; but it now began to recognize a need to serve its overseas markets
more carefully than in the past—to remove from its outward services that

blanket of 'Britishness' which, during a hundred years, the agency had never thought to question, and had indeed regarded as a virtue. Here was a major shift.

In this wider new spirit, on 18 May 1949 an important Reuter editorial note was given the comprehensive title of 'A World News Agency'. The note emphasized that Reuter news services reached newspapers in over fifty countries, and that for many of these papers Reuters was the only news source. Yet this, said the note, was not to be taken as a cause for complacency. On the contrary, it meant that Reuter correspondents and sub-editors 'must develop a world outlook'. Everything must be written 'as though it were intended for each one of those thousands of newspapers':

> What, for instance, do you suppose is the reaction of a newspaper editor in India when Reuters sends him this message?:
> 'Twenty-five Asiatics were injured in a bomb explosion in the native quarter early today.'
> Were they Indians, Chinese, or what? The generalisation is completely uninformative. Moreover, such a message reflects an out-of-date view that is actually insulting to Asian readers. It is the sort of message that a correspondent of an individual European, say British or French, newspaper might conceivably send to his own paper—meaning, in effect, 'there was a bomb explosion here today, but no Europeans (Britons, Frenchmen?) were hurt, only 25 Asiatics'. Nothing of the world outlook in that.

In 1906, as noticed in Chapter 4, the editorial instruction had been to ignore most mishaps affecting non-Europeans, whilst always noticing those involving Europeans, 'even an obscure missionary'. Forty years later Reuters was beginning to expect a very different attitude from its correspondents.

Regional news desks had been created in London by Cole. This targeted provision made it more than ever desirable not to take sides in disputes anywhere in the world, even where such sides were clear, which was not always the case. The decades after 1945 witnessed many bloody wars fought without frontlines or rules of engagement, waged by participants called 'terrorists' by some, 'freedom fighters' by others. In covering these conflicts Reuter correspondents were instructed to avoid either expression. When in 1980 the British Foreign Office suggested that Reuters should describe Irish Republican Army (IRA) activists as terrorists, Reuters refused to do so. In all such cases, correspondents were told to write of 'guerrillas', or (if appropriate) of 'gunmen' or 'bombers'.[2]

During 1947–8, Seaghan Maynes covered one of the first of these unstructured outbreaks—the confrontation between the British, the Arabs, and the Jews in Palestine. The situation was confused, and one temptation for correspondents in such circumstances has always been to impose a false clarity, perhaps by giving conscious or unconscious preference to one party. Maynes noted in his diary (15 May 1948) that he had been told on arrival in Jerusalem 'that if I wanted a good time I should contact [the] Jewish Agency, write favourable pieces occasionally, and everything would be laid on for a very pleasant time. Some people are obviously doing the favourable pieces without too much regard for impartial reporting.'

How then did Reuters come to define objectivity? Gerald Long, the managing director, explained to the British Foreign and Commonwealth Office on 8 December 1980 why objectivity did not mean neutrality. 'What we seek is not so much neutrality in the sense of evenhandedness between different sides in a conflict, but rather the absence of emotion in vocabulary, so that events may be judged dispassionately, at least as far as the account of them is concerned.' This definition of objectivity allowed room for informed comment by Reuter correspondents, so long as it helped to explain a story and did so without bias.

Reuters was chary of using words in its reports, especially adjectives, which might introduce value judgements without due consideration. This was illustrated during the brief Reuter career (1961–5) of Frederick Forsyth, who went on to write *The Day of the Jackal* and other best-selling political thrillers partly based upon his journalistic experiences. The qualities of high imagination and expression which were to make Forsyth's novels so gripping had scarcely recommended him to his superiors in Reuters. 'He views the world around him in rather unreal terms like a spectator at the cinema identifying himself with the larger-than-life characters and incidents depicted on the screen.' Such was one confidential assessment of Forsyth by David Sells, chief correspondent in Bonn, dated 22 April 1964. A few days later, when Forsyth filed that 'East Berlin seethed with East German troops in the small hours of today', Doon Campbell sent back a reprimand about his casual introduction of the verb 'seethed'. Forsyth had not realized that this military activity was merely in preparation for the annual May Day parade. Nor had he understood that his language was likely to cause alarm 'at deadline time in America'.

Successive Reuter style guides always emphasized the importance of sourcing. No story was complete without a source, reference to which also provided protection for Reuters. When Herman Goering committed suicide in his cell in 1946, just before he was to be executed as a war criminal, Reuters issued a wrong report that all the eleven condemned Nazis—by implication including Goering—had been hanged. The source was properly given as DANA (Deutsche Allgemeine Nachrichten-Agentur), the American-zone news service, but with the prudent addition 'So far the report is unconfirmed'. Reuters was thus doubly covered. The British national newspapers headlined the news without qualification, and then unfairly blamed Reuters when the unexpected truth became known.

Of course, mistakes were bound sometimes to occur, usually because of human error, and hoaxes were an ever-present risk. These could have an immediate impact upon trading markets. 'Be on guard against April Fool's Day hoaxes and all fantasia such as the birth of five-legged sheep.' So warned the internal *International Style Guide* in 1988. It also addressed the key question: 'What is news?' Its short answer was that what Reuters reported became news by the very fact of being reported: 'we give it the Reuter hallmark and it rises above the status of a mere report to that of news.'

Reuter correspondents were expected to concentrate upon news likely to be of interest to readers with some education and world awareness. This had been the practice ever since the first days of the agency. Cole told the 1948 Royal Commission on the Press that 'our criterion' was what suited *The Times, Manchester Guardian, Glasgow Herald*, and *Scotsman*. The assumption was that the more popular papers would edit Reuter material down to the level of their readers. Increasingly, however, Reuters was to bear in mind the expectations of overseas newspaper readers, and also of radio and television audiences in many countries.[3]

2

One problem for Reuters as it transformed itself into a supranational news agency was how to handle ideology, not least within 85 Fleet Street itself. Derek Jameson has written about the small left-wing cell on the editorial floor in the late 1940s, of which he was himself briefly a young member. If Reuters had ever been forced publicly to admit the existence of this group, its reputation for objectivity would have been tarnished. The left-wingers numbered perhaps a dozen, of whom only three or four were Communist Party members, the rest fellow-travellers. Their leading spirit was Lawrence Kirwan, who was one of the duty editors. A purge was instituted after Frances Wheeler, one of the group, was found to have omitted an important long reference to the cold war in a speech by President Truman. Was the omission politically motivated? According to Jameson, the left-wingers were careful not to let their politics influence their work; but others within Reuters were to say in retrospect that group members probably did sometimes manipulate the news. Called to explain herself, Wheeler revealed all about the cell. There were no sackings; but the main figures were removed from positions of responsibility, and gradually left Reuters. Several reappeared working for Tass and other Communist news organizations. The obligation upon all Reuter staff to maintain political non-commitment was underlined by Chancellor in a letter to Kirwan on 24 June 1950. Working for Reuters, wrote Chancellor, involved its staff 'in a form of self-discipline and self-abnegation. Those of you who feel strongly on political matters must be doubly careful in the position of trust which working for Reuters involves.'[4]

Chancellor's letter was written at the time of the Peet affair. John Peet (1915–88), the chief Reuter correspondent in Berlin—then divided between Western and Soviet sectors—had crossed into East Berlin on 12 June 1950, not as a journalist in search of news but as a suddenly revealed Communist sympathizer. Peet's posthumously published recollections—*The Long Engagement, Memoirs of a Cold War Legend* (1989)—described his Quaker pacifist family background, and then traced his varied career in journalism. His left-wing sympathies first emerged at school in York. On leaving, he became a junior reporter for a local paper, and briefly he was a member of the Communist Party. He next joined the Grenadier Guards with the purpose of subverting the British army; but when this proved too difficult, he bought himself out. His short experience of weapons' handling proved useful, however, when in 1937 he joined the left-wing English brigade fighting on the Republican Government side in the Spanish Civil War.

During the Second World War Peet served first in the Palestine police, and then as a news editor in the Public Information Office at Jerusalem under the British regime. This latter experience helped to secure him a job with Reuters in August 1945. The agency was very short of journalists capable of reporting from newly liberated Europe. On saying that he spoke fluent German, Peet was sent with little preparation to report from Vienna.

By 13 January 1948 Cole was congratulating Peet on his 'excellent news file'. He was then posted to Berlin—currently the world's most important place for news, where a third world war might well have been triggered. Such was Cole's confidence in Peet's judgement as a journalist and manager, that in 1949 he was promoted to bureau chief. No one in Reuters was aware of Peet's underlying feelings. He described these in his book:

Professionally I was doing very nicely, and apparently giving full satisfaction, but I began to anticipate difficult times ahead. Ever since my schooldays I had regarded myself, despite my somewhat erratic course, as a committed Marxist, agreeing in general with the political line of the international Communist movement, though I was reluctant to become a card-carrying Red . . . By reporting as impartially as possible the policies and actions of both sides in the emerging cold conflict on the confrontation line in central Europe, I had the vague hope that it might be possible to do at least something to redress the balance in the western media which by and large reflected the Anglo-American establishment view of the clash—'We have governments: they have regimes'.

In other words, Peet had always been pursuing a political purpose even while reporting stories from both sides of the Iron Curtain. He was not, as Reuters assumed, doing so in a spirit of objectivity—at least not as Reuters understood objectivity.

By 1950 Peet was losing all hope that he might contribute to the achievement of an understanding between East and West. His realization that the Western powers were planning to re-establish a German army shocked him. He became convinced that the West did not want peace. The final spur was provided by Western media coverage of the preparations for an East German youth rally in Berlin at Whitsun 1950. These were provocatively reported, said Peet, as if they might be preparations for a Communist incursion into West Berlin. He ignored the fact that the Russians had blockaded West Berlin during 1949, and that this made such a fear understandable. Peet claimed that he was reprimanded by Reuters for not expressing similar alarm in his coverage. He concluded that 'the time had come to decline to play the role of supplier of information to the warmongers'.[5]

On Sunday, 12 June 1950 Peet supervised the morning's bureau shift as usual, and then said that he would not be available for twenty-four hours. He drove his car through the Brandenburg Gate to a pre-arranged rendezvous in East Berlin with an official of the East German Information Office.

Peet's flight was, of course, a great coup for the Communists, and they were ready to give it maximum publicity. In the afternoon he held a press conference at the Information Office, attended by correspondents from both sides of the Iron Curtain. Peet explained himself at length, how he had found that his coverage was published only selectively in the West, with news favourable to East Germany 'suppressed by the newspapers'. Asked when he had joined the Communist party, Peet caused surprise by replying that he was 'non-party'.

In a last twist, Peet himself sent a crisp fifty-two-word report of his press conference to Reuters in London: 'Reuters chief correspondent in Berlin 34-year-old John Peet, today made a public declaration that he "could no longer serve the Anglo-American warmongers".' The report was not published. Others issued the story first, while Reuters pondered how to limit the damage. But after this initial hesitation Reuters reported the Peet affair fully until it faded as a story.

Yet how to explain what Peet had done? The reputation of Reuters was now at risk. One of its leading correspondents had been revealed as a covert left-wing activist. Could Peet be represented as curiously naïve? But, if naïve, why had the agency selected such a man for one of its top postings? And had he been acting alone, or was Reuters widely infiltrated by covert reds?

This last question was bound to be asked, especially in the United States, where the McCarthyite fever was growing. One explanation quietly put into circulation by Reuters was that Peet was a physically sick man, suffering from duodenal ulcers; also that he was upset because his second wife had left him. There had certainly been a separation, but it was amicable. And Peet's ulcers had been cured in the previous year.

The reality was that Reuters found itself baffled. Chancellor admitted this in a letter to Cole, who was visiting North America, written on the day of Peet's flight. 'The extraordinary thing about the Peet affair is that no one had the slightest inkling of his views beforehand and he was very popular, as you know, with the British officials in Berlin.' British intelligence in Berlin told Alfred Geiringer, who was sent in search of an explanation, that because of Peet's Spanish Civil War involvement, they had watched him, but had found no evidence of subversion. Nothing has ever suggested that Peet was a Communist agent.[6]

Cole acted quickly to assure American subscribers that Reuters had not gone Communist. The diversions about Peet's ill health and marital problems seem to have won credence. Cole cabled Chancellor three days after the flight: 'Everybody impressed our handling story generally regarded quote one of those things unquote and eye unworried.' It had been a 'twelve hour wonder', wrote Cole on the same day, 'and we did ourselves a lot of good in unpleasant circumstances by fully handling the story'. A week later the *Newspaper World* confirmed that the affair had 'not affected Reuter's reputation for balanced reporting'.

Peet worked as a political commentator and writer in East Germany until his death in 1988. He had committed no offence under English law, and visited Britain at intervals.

4

Even the best correspondents could be frustrated by censorship. A 'Report on World Censorship' from the Reuter statistical department on 16 June 1965 noted that relatively few countries were operating formal censorship in peacetime, 'in the sense of officials blue-pencilling press matter'. Only eleven countries attempted this for outgoing stories. A further eighteen had imposed restrictions on filing copy in certain emergencies. And thirty-six countries had adopted 'responsibility censorship'. This allowed the authorities to take action against correspondents who had filed copy which was not liked. Despite these impediments, Reuters preferred to maintain at least some presence under censorship, rather than no presence at all.

The situation was particularly difficult in Moscow. Correspondents there were required to submit all copy through the central telegraph office; and any hint of criticism about Soviet policies, or about the internal condition of the Soviet Union was disliked (Fig. 15). During the immediate post-war years, little was allowed out apart from official news; and nearly all that could be sent had already been picked up by Radio House from monitoring of Soviet or East European broadcasts. Partly in exasperation, and partly for reasons of economy, at the beginning of 1950 Reuters withdrew its full-time correspondent, Don Dallas, from Moscow. He was replaced by a locally engaged American journalist working part-time. Reuters eventually decided not to maintain any local stringers behind the Iron Curtain. As nationals of their

FIG. 16. Cartoon by Reuter correspondent Adrienne Farrell, 1946

respective countries, experience had shown how much they were exposed to arrest or to harassment, and how Reuters could not protect them.[6]

After Stalin's death in 1953 Reuters sent Sidney Weiland to Moscow. He was the only British correspondent in the Soviet capital at that period. His nickname within Reuters was 'sizzling Sid', because of his energy. The one-man Moscow assignment certainly needed both energy and stamina. Censorship at the central telegraph office continued, although copies of reports were now returned to correspondents to show them what had been removed before transmission. For example, in a sentence from Weiland about Soviet economic plans (6 January 1956) the words italicized were removed, thereby losing much of the point: 'In many cases, this has meant a readjustment of piecework rates, *so that workers must now work harder and produce more in order to get the same wages which they took home before the change.*'

Weiland served two terms in Moscow, 1953–6 and 1964–7. He gleaned much information from the Soviet press, subscribing to the few papers available to foreigners from the Soviet republics. These were scanned by a translator, who had been appointed by the Soviet authorities. Correspondents were allowed early copies of *Pravda* and *Izvestia*, obtained at the telegraph office usually after midnight.

On 11 February 1956 Weiland was invited with Richard Hughes of the *Sunday Times*, and representatives of Tass and *Pravda*, to witness the reappearance in public of Guy Burgess and Donald Maclean, the British diplomats who had defected five years earlier. In a Moscow hotel room the two men handed over a statement, and talked very briefly; but they refused to be interviewed, and the whole encounter lasted just five minutes. It was none the less a major story. A month later Reuters enjoyed an even greater success. On 16 March 1956 it published an account of a remarkable speech denouncing Stalin, delivered on 25 February by Nikita Khrushchev, the Soviet leader, to the 20th Communist Party Congress. There had been a fortnight's time lag. On 11 March Weiland first heard of the denunciation in a whispered conversation with a friendly Communist journalist at a Finnish Embassy reception. Moscow's diplomatic community had begun to buzz with excitement. Reuters had now assigned a second correspondent to Moscow, John Rettie; and it was Rettie who enterprisingly obtained a paraphrased but detailed account of the speech from a contact.[7]

Weiland and Rettie went for a walk in the street, away from bugging surveillance, to discuss whether they could trust the accuracy of the account; and also whether to break censorship by filing the story from outside the Soviet Union, something not done since before the Second World War. They knew that the *New York Times* correspondent was leaving the country; and once out, he could be expected to report what little he knew. This meant that, unless they acted quickly, Reuters would be beaten on the story, even though Rettie alone had secured a detailed version of the speech. They therefore decided that Rettie should fly to Stockholm, and from there telephone the story to London. To protect his position when he returned to Moscow the report was published under a Bonn dateline as coming from 'reliable Communist sources':

> Bonn, March 16—Nikita Khrushchev has bitterly accused Stalin of responsibility for massacre and torture during his 30 years as Russia's leader, according to reports from reliable Communist sources reaching here today . . .
>
> Mr. Khrushchev is said to have painted a vivid picture to the delegates of the regime of 'suspicion, fear and terror' through which Stalin ruled, especially in his last years . . .
>
> He is reported to have held Stalin responsible for Soviet failure in the early stages of the last war both by ignoring warnings by Sir Winston Churchill and by 'weakening' the country's morale and economy in the great pre-war purges . . .

The full text of this speech did not reach the West for another two months.

In 1961 the cold war took on physical expression with the erection of the Berlin Wall. The story broke on 13 August. Adam Kellett-Long, the Reuter correspondent in East Berlin, had received a tip-off from a member of the East German hierarchy that something was going to happen. But what? Rumours had been circulating for several days about drastic action to stop the exodus of East Germans to the West, via Berlin. Kellett-Long had reported these rumours to London with a report starting 'Berlin is holding its breath . . .' He was beginning to wonder whether he had overdone the story when at about 1 a.m. he received an anonymous phone call in German. A man's voice said only: 'I strongly advise you not to go to bed tonight,' and then rang off. Soon afterwards the East German agency teleprinter rattled out a Warsaw Pact communiqué from Moscow urging 'effective control' round West Berlin. Kellett-Long decided to hurry out to see what was meant by 'effective control'. He consequently became the first reporter to discover that the Brandenburg Gate crossing-point to the West was closed. The wall was about to go up.[8]

Reuters was eight minutes ahead with this major beat. Its impact was reinforced because Kellett-Long was able to follow quickly with a widely published eyewitness account:

> The streets were filled with lorry-loads of troops, police cars and motor-cyclists. Lights flicked on and people watched from their windows as I drove

to the main border crossing at the Brandenburg Gate. There I found steel barricades blocking the West-bound roads and a police cordon around the gate itself. When I tried to drive through a policeman stopped me and said: 'You are not allowed to go through'. Later I tried to approach another border point but a police cordon stopped me before the border was in sight. Black-uniformed railway police, some still buttoning their uniforms, were running towards the stations to control trains which now stop at the border . . . Violent arguments developed among the crowd, with Communist speakers apparently outnumbered. But the atmosphere was not so tense as it could have been. People were laughing at each other's arguments.

In March 1962 the Soviet Government leased a duplex teleprinter line to Reuters, which became the first Western news agency to be allowed such a direct connection with its headquarters. Reuter Moscow correspondents could now themselves transmit their dispatches to London, and they could receive Reuter news reports. AP, UPI, and AFP secured the same facilities two months later. Whereas a few years earlier correspondents of the four Western agencies had battled at the Central Telegraph Office for access to the single international phone, now at last Moscow had become linked to the global news network.

The Cuban missile crisis of 1962 saw the cold war nearly end in real war. The White House commended Reuters for providing the first available version of Khrushchev's crucial message of 27 October, proposing a 'deal'. This reached President Kennedy via his Reuter teleprinter. The report had come from a Reuter radio monitor in London, who had scribbled down the text in Russian while a colleague looked over his shoulder and dictated a rough English translation down an open telephone line to the Central Desk at 85 Fleet Street. A sub-editor there polished the English, and then dictated to an operator teleprinting directly into the circuit. The first intimation for Reuters in London that the crisis was ending came with a report received on the commodities desk. This told that Cuban sugar prices were firming on the rumour that Khrushchev had pulled back from the brink. Here was a notable instance of overlap between commercial information and general news.[9]

In 1964 Reuters mistakenly reported Khrushchev's death, attributing the news to DPA, the West German agency, citing Tass. In fact, Tass had published no such report, and Reuters had held back and only published the story after other agencies had used it. Campbell, regarded the Reuter report as an avoidable mistake, not excused by the inclusion of a source. He circulated an emphatic note on 'Fact and Rumour' (16 April 1964): 'For Reuters to lend its name to this report was sufficient guarantee for many subscribers to accept it as fact, even though pinned to another agency . . . The credit does not go to an agency which first reports a rumour. It goes to the agency which can first report the FACT.'

Although the Soviet authorities had allowed direct lines to be installed in foreign news agency offices, the subsequent 'responsibility censorship' was still oppressive. In 1964 Peter Johnson, the chief Reuter correspondent, was expelled after reporting an African student demonstration in Moscow. He had liked to dig deep as a reporter, and his pertinacity had provoked earlier official complaint. Reuters told the British Foreign Office that it did not want any formal representations about the expulsion to be made on its behalf, lest this implied that it was connected with the British Government. The Soviet Ambassador in London was called in, and told that in order to improve relations Soviet policy ought to be to remove impediments to the free flow of news, 'not to create new ones'. Sidney Weiland was sent back to Moscow for a second term in Johnson's place.[10]

In February 1968 Kellett-Long, Weiland's successor, was warned against publishing stories based upon contacts with private citizens. The most serious instance of pressure occurred, however, in June 1974, when a Soviet official told the chief correspondent that a Soviet citizen was claiming to have had homosexual relations with two other Reuter correspondents. The claim was an invention. On 30 July 1975 Gerald Long, the managing director, took the unprecedented step of addressing a letter to the Soviet Foreign Minister, Andrei Gromyko, asking him to put a stop to the harassment of foreign correspondents. Long received no reply.

5

Coverage by Reuters of the Korean War of 1950–3 was privately admitted to be inadequate. With a maximum of eight correspondents involved, it was heavily outmanned by AP and UP, which used saturation coverage. Cable costs were also high. And Reuters was often beaten on timings because many reports from Tokyo were cabled to the west coast of America, where the American agencies could feed material into their private lines, and so beat Reuters to New York by up to an hour. Reuters also accused UP of 'throwing forward' news, which meant reporting that places had been lost or captured before this had actually happened. Some American correspondents filed so many human interest stories about US servicemen that these swamped the reporting of significant developments. At least, Reuters could not afford to over-file in this way.[11]

The war was expensive for the Western media in lives as well as in money. As many as seventeen Western correspondents were killed, ten of them Americans. Derek Pearcy—an Australian on secondment to AAP–Reuter from the *Japan News*—was killed in May 1951 when his jeep ran over a land-mine.

The fact that the war was being fought on behalf of the United Nations meant that Reuter correspondents felt that they could take sides. The Chinese and North Koreans were called 'the enemy' without hesitation. The abandonment and burning of Seoul, the South Korean capital, was described in this partisan spirit by Warren White of Reuters on 4 January 1951. White also took care to notice the British troops involved. 'The Ulsters gave some ground, but promptly counter-attacked and regained it. The Northumberlands had a wedge driven into their lines by about a company of the enemy . . . communications were uprooted, and the capital died—with many "Welcome U.N. Forces" banners (put up three months ago) still flying.'

Mao Tse-tung's victorious Communists had expelled all Western corre-spondents and managers from China in the summer of 1949. The locally born veteran Tommy Aldeguer, the news editor, remained in charge for Reuters at Shanghai until September 1951 when he quit after much harassment. During the next five years coverage of the Chinese scene was left mainly to radio monitoring from Hong Kong. This remained important even after a Reuter correspondent was at last allowed back to Peking in April 1956. This was David Chipp. He spoke no Chinese, which may have been one reason why he was acceptable to the Communist authorities. In return, a correspondent from Xinhua, the Chinese news agency, was posted to London.[12]

Chipp engaged a translator, and started the Reuter service from his hotel room. He laid the foundations for a news exchange agreement with Xinhua, and for a commercial agreement between Comtelburo and the Chinese Government. Assiduous and engaging, Chipp developed good working rela-tions with the Communist authorities. Most of his stories were descriptive, telling about the condition of the people. He also reported major political speeches, and interviewed Premier Chou En-lai and other leaders, as well as Pu Yi, 'the last Emperor'. The fact that Reuters was still regarded by the Chinese as a semi-official news agency added to its status in their eyes; but this also meant that they might at any time attempt to pressure its correspondents for political purposes.

For two years Chipp was one of only two Western correspondents per-mitted to reside in China. American journalists were not allowed to open offices there for another twenty years. In consequence, direct and continuous coverage by Reuters was particularly welcomed by United States subscribers.

Chipp's successor, Jack Gee, stayed for only eight months in 1958. Chancellor reported to the board (Sept 1958) that Gee had 'given offence', and that there were three reasons why he should be quietly withdrawn. First, concern for his safety; secondly, the high importance of maintaining a Reuter presence in Peking; and thirdly, 'our £20,000 a year contract with Hsinhua'. Ronald Farquhar was sent in Gee's place. After his own return from China , Farquhar heard that one of his translators had been arrested. He wrote to Mason (24 January 1961) urging that Reuters should protest, even if to no purpose. 'Reuters didn't gain any prestige or face with the Chinese by pulling Jack out without demur as soon as they were asked to.'

The position of Reuter correspondents in Communist China had obviously been delicate. It became dangerous soon after Anthony Grey took over in March 1967. In July he was put under house arrest in retaliation for the imprisonment of Chinese Communist journalists after riots in Hong Kong. Grey was confined until October 1969. On one occasion he was attacked at his house by Red Guards, and for a time he was held in a tiny room.[13]

The Chinese Government presumably believed that action against Grey would force the British and Hong Kong Governments to free the journalists quickly. This did not happen. The prison sentence of the last Communist journalist was completed in September 1969, with remission for good conduct. This enabled the Chinese to release Grey on 4 October 1969 without loss of face. He had kept a secret diary, and this formed the basis for his best-selling book, *Hostage in Peking*, published in 1970. Grey left Reuters, and went on to become a successful writer of novels and other books.

A Peking presence by Reuters was resumed in September 1971, when James Pringle was appointed. He was soon joined by a second correspondent, partly to improve coverage but also to give moral support. The Chinese authorities still insisted upon regarding Reuters as a semi-official organization. Their attitude, the managing director told the board in July 1977, was therefore likely to fluctuate with shifts in Anglo-Chinese relations. A second Grey incident could not be entirely ruled out. Indeed, in April 1976 another Reuter correspondent, Peter Griffiths, had been manhandled, arrested, and fiercely interrogated for two hours. The Chinese authorities had objected to his interviewing people in Tiananmen Square during disturbances after the death of Premier Chou En-lai. Personal contact with ordinary Chinese was always difficult. Even though many later Reuter correspondents spoke fluent Chinese, the neighbourhood watch system kept them at bay.

REUTERS
INTERNATIONAL NEWS SERVICE

Office: Room 64, Nava Bldg., No. 4-6 General Post Office Lane. Bangkok Tel. 31216.
Receiving Station: 16 Soi Suphang (Soi 34) Sukhumvit Road. Telephone 912859

FOURTH EDITION

Sunday, April 9th., 1967

Item 70

CHINA - ARMY

By Anthony Grey

PEKING, April 9, --Reuter-- Mao Tse-Tung has ordered the army, now wielding wide powers across the country in the cultural revolution, to curb its heavy-handed treatment of the population, it was revealed here today.

Strict orders have gone out to nearly the three-million-strong Peoples Liberation Army forbidding troops to use arms against anti-Maoists or to carry out mass arrests.

They must restrict themselves to "political education work," the orders said.

This clamp down on the Army was made public in a ten-point edict from the Military Affairs Commission of the Party Central Committee pasted up on walls in Peking today. It bore the red seal of the Commission which is headed by Defence Minister Lin Piao, heir-apparent to Mao

Mao's approval was made clear by a heading which read "Comrade Lin Piao: this is an excellent document, it must be published. Mao Tse-Tung". --More

MX: 1900

FIG. 17.   Reuter report, Peking, 9 April 1967

During the 1970s, following the Chinese rapprochement with the United States, the number of foreign correspondents in Peking grew from about thirty to some 150. Vergil Berger (1964–7), who had preceded Grey, returned in 1987 as chief representative in charge of a much-enlarged operation. He now deployed four other Reuter correspondents, plus a photographer. Yet one thing remained unchanged. There had never been any formal censorship; but Western correspondents were still invited for 'little chats', and given 'serious warnings' when the authorities did not like what they had written.

6

The way Reuters reported the 1956 Anglo-French landings in the Suez Canal zone, and the subsequent brief occupation, demonstrated strikingly to the world that, after a century as a national and imperial institution, the old agency was ceasing to be the news agency of the British Empire. Its Suez reporting showed that Reuters no longer wanted to be a channel for writing the news from the 'British point of view', even while claiming to be objective; and that instead it was developing a supranational attitude.

At the start of the crisis the chief Reuter correspondent in Cairo was Gilbert Sedbon. In August 1956 he was joined there from Athens by Aleco Joannides, a Reuter staff correspondent who was a Greek citizen. Mason, the chief news editor, sent Joannides a long briefing letter which explained the 'world view' to which Reuters was now committed (9 August). In case of emergency, Joannides was told to maintain a Reuter presence by filing under Egyptian censorship. Mason emphasized that Reuter correspondents might well find themselves writing from opposite sides, but that they must not favour either side:

> the Reuter file on this particular story must under all circumstances be completely objective. The dispute about the Canal is an international one. It is likely to have serious repercussions in the Middle East and elsewhere, and in this matter many countries are concerned which have no particular sympathy for either Britain or France on the one hand or Egypt on the other ... This does not mean that we should not report all the facts as we know them, or that coverage should lack appropriate descriptive [*sic*] ... If any views are made expressing disagreement with either of the two sides mainly concerned in the dispute, they should be given. We must try to see the world point of view on this story.

Reuters, in short, must report with detachment, bearing in mind every news angle and every news market.

In this same spirit, when the Anglo-French invasion was beginning, Chancellor issued on 1 November 1956 the circular to staff already quoted in

Chapter 11. This noted that British opinion was divided; that Reuters 'does not represent the British Government'; and that the agency had a duty to supply an unbiased service 'to the many newspapers all over the world who rely on the Reuter service'.

Although the Egyptians expelled all Agence France-Presse correspondents—and also Sedbon of Reuters, a French Jew—Joannides, a Greek, was allowed to stay and to report for Reuters from Port Said. To protect his acceptability, Reuters deliberately did not ask for his accreditation as a war correspondent with the British forces, even after they had captured the town; nor were his stories bylined, as they would normally have been.[14]

Joannides reported the attack upon Port Said and its subsequent occupation with commendable coolness, both physical and mental:

> I was on the receiving end of RAF and French bombs in Port Said . . . Acting like surgeons British and French fighters knocked out one by one all the AA batteries of the Egyptians on the two days preceding the landing operation. I saw British fighters rocket-hit the emplacement of a 3.7 AA gun of the Egyptian Army placed below the Canal Company's main building. Some of the gun's crew were killed and one hopped away on one leg; the other had been cut off by the rocket.

Joannides continued to file from Port Said under the Anglo-French occupation (8 November):

> Egyptian officials have now resorted to passive resistance against the occupying forces . . . Port Said is now a town without a police force. I watched last Tuesday a central police station in Port Said when their chief told them to go home and stay there until further orders. One after the other the policemen discarded their uniforms and left the station for home in their underwear.

Here was a good example of a story likely to be read differently in different news markets. Anglo-French readers might find the undressing story laughable, whereas third world readers would probably read it as an example of enterprising protest. Joannides carefully made no comment. After the cessation of fighting, he was allowed by the Egyptians to return to report from Cairo, reaching there circuitously from Port Said via Athens.

Seaghan Maynes had volunteered to serve as a war correspondent with the Anglo-French invasion force. He did so, not out of British patriotism but because he was tired of editorial desk work in London. As a Roman Catholic Ulsterman, he found no difficulty in maintaining the desired non-British approach. Interviewed in retirement many years later, he commented that 'such events have bespattered English history since they first began to practise

it in Ireland seven or eight centuries ago. And there I was getting ready to
report the latest scandalous episode in the Middle East.'[15]

Maynes landed at Port Said with the first British troops; but his initial report
was delayed for two days, perhaps in order to allow the official communiqués
to dominate. Outward radio communications proved to be very unreliable;
and Maynes and others sometimes flew back to the cablehead at Cyprus—
from where Reuter coverage was being co-ordinated—to deliver stories
themselves.

Setting aside his personal opinions, Maynes wrote in suitably detached
terms for the world markets, and he also contributed the traditional home-
town pieces for the British press:

> British Front, Suez Canal, Nov. 14, Reuter—The 'Advance Man' of the British
> Army in Egypt is 20-year-old national serviceman Brian Williams, of Sutton-
> at-Hone, Dartford, Kent. He is dug in at a well-camouflaged slit trench on the
> side of the canal road, which is the furthest point of the British advance . . . He
> said he had not fired a single shot during three days of frontline duty but, pat-
> ting his Bren gun, he added: 'If they want to start trouble, we are ready'.

Maynes was here simply reporting a frontline human interest story as he
found it. He was tacitly accepting that the overall rights and wrongs of the
operation were not for him (or the soldiers) to discuss. Indeed, when General
Stockwell, the British commander, denounced the politicians for holding his
troops back, Maynes and other correspondents protected the General from
himself by not reporting his outbursts. Perhaps by not doing so, Maynes was
left open to a charge of unconscious pro-British bias.

The British Foreign Office kept a careful watch upon Suez reporting by
Reuters. For example, the British Embassy in Tel Aviv, the Israeli capital, was
contacted by the Foreign Office on 1 November 1956:

> The following Reuter message, timed 13.28 November 1, has been received
> from Tel Aviv:
>
> 'Israel Government tonight (presumably last night) called upon Egyptian forces
> in the Sinai to lay down their arms while there was still time, because they were
> nearly cut off and isolated and their Air Force was about to be put out of action
> as a result of Anglo-French-Israeli bombing.'
>
> 2. I assume that the last four words are attributable solely to Reuter's corre-
> spondent. If this is so, the correspondent has been grossly inaccurate and most
> unhelpful: you should reprimand him accordingly.
> 3. If the wording is that of any official Israeli statement you should protest
> strongly.
> 4. We are doing our best to counter the effect of this message.[16]

Clearly, the Foreign Office thought that Reuters was still in a special relationship, and that its correspondents overseas could be reprimanded upon
request. The Foreign Office News Department in London issued a repudiation: 'Suggestions that Her Majesty's Government are concerting military
action with Israel as well as with France are entirely false'. Yet there had
certainly been collusion with the Israeli Government, encouraging it to
attack Egypt so as to provide a pretext for separate Anglo-French military
intervention. The Reuter report was too close to the truth for Foreign Office
comfort.

Although for financial reasons Reuters remained ready during the 1950s
and 1960s to work with British Government-subsidized bodies such as the
Arab News Agency, and also to receive generous official subscriptions, it was
now unwilling to shape its news file to suit British interests. Earlier in his
career Christopher Chancellor had been ready enough to describe Reuters as
'British'; but by the end of his time as general manager, in a 1958 radio interview, he was stressing its global approach. 'Reuters is not just a British news
service; it is not an organ for presenting British news; it is not associated with
the British Government . . . It is an organisation to supply newspapers and
radio stations of every country of the world with a truthful and complete service of world news.'

John Pigott and others, reporting for Reuters from Egypt and the Sudan
during the 1880s, had not thought it necessary to be objective while describing the expansion of the British Empire. In contrast, Aleco Joannides and his
colleagues in Egypt during 1956–7 took a detached view of the disintegration
of that same empire. The world was changing, and Reuters was proving able
to change with it.

7

For thirty years, from the end of the war in the Pacific until the North
Vietnamese capture of Saigon in 1975, Indo-China—Laos, Cambodia, and
Vietnam—provided a running story of high international importance, and
Reuters assigned many of its best correspondents to report it. By 1967 Reuters
in Saigon was deploying three or four London-based correspondents, plus
two or more from Singapore and several local reporters. One of these locally
engaged men, Pham Xuan An, admitted in later years that, as well as working for Reuters and then becoming a correspondent for *Time* magazine, he
also worked for the Vietcong. He passed on military information which came
to him for Reuters; but he claimed that, in the other direction, he had never

fed Reuters with false reports: 'if I had I would have been sacked, and no one else was paying me.'[17]

In 1967 Reuters had broken its last links with the Associated Press, the American agency, and this meant that the Vietnam War was the first post-1945 conflict which Reuters covered without backup from any other news agency. Reporting out of Vietnam was costing as much as £40,000 a year by 1970, equal to about one-fifth of the company's overall annual profit. In part compensation, Reuters was able to earn good revenue by carrying newspaper correspondents' own reports as 'special traffic' on its recently improved telecommunications link with Singapore.

Nevertheless—as in the Korean War—AP and UPI could afford to spend much more than Reuters. The American agencies each maintained on the ground in Vietnam at least three times as many correspondents as Reuters. It partly offset this disadvantage by operating an informal news exchange arrangement with *Stars and Stripes*, the United States army newspaper. Its journalists were thereby favoured with speedy access to American military information.

In the early days Reuter correspondents showed a better understanding of the political background in Saigon than their American rivals, and also more knowledge of the National Liberation Front. Aware of the importance of such depth, the managing editor's report for May 1966 justified recent concentration upon Vietnam politics rather than upon the fighting for its own sake. 'It was not a story of troops locked in battle or waves of bomber aircraft but rather of internal division among the South Vietnamese themselves— opposition to the military junta which evidenced itself in bloody riots and horrifying acts of self-immolation by devout Buddhists prepared to martyr themselves for political convictions.'

In general, Reuters benefited throughout the Vietnam war from its international reputation for accuracy and depth. For example, an analysis from Reuters Japan explained on 26 March 1968 that Kyodo, the Japanese agency, had found the American agencies to be very fast and detailed on frontline stories, but thought that Reuters was more balanced: 'better out of Saigon on political developments, which they feel the Americans tend to neglect for the sake of the big action story.' Kyodo liked to wait for confirmation from Reuters of stories from AP or UPI, 'since we have what they call the built-in advantage of a reputation for reliability'.

The strain and danger of the Vietnam assignment meant that most Reuter correspondents stayed for only about a year. Two of them lost their lives. Ronald Laramy, an Englishman, Bruce Pigott, an Australian, and two other journalists, riding in a jeep in a Saigon suburb, were ambushed and killed by

Vietcong in May 1968. During the 1968 Tet (New Year) offensive the Reuter bureau had itself become exposed. It was located in a house midway between two prime Vietcong targets, the presidential palace and the United States embassy.[18]

In 1975, when the American evacuation had become inevitable, all Reuter staff with British or United States passports were withdrawn from Vietnam. Bernard Edinger, a Frenchman, was flown in to cover the final stages. He qualified for protection from the French Embassy in Saigon, which remained open. Edinger wrote the first story sent out under the new Communist regime.

8

After the liberation of Paris in 1944 Harold King was appointed chief correspondent for France. He remained in charge until his retirement in 1967. He developed wide contacts within the French political world; but most important of all, he was closer to General de Gaulle, in and out of office, than any other foreign journalist. King found time also to know the best restaurants in Paris, and the finest wines. In 1958 he was given the title of assistant general manager, still based in Paris. In 1971 he was made a Commander of the Légion d'Honneur, a rare honour for a foreigner.

King's weakness was that he was a poor manager of staff, irascible and demanding, even while sometimes indulgent with a few favourites. Only the toughest remained unperturbed when he screamed and even foamed at the mouth over alleged misdemeanours.

The fall of the French Fourth Republic in 1958 and the return to office of de Gaulle were stories particularly suited to King's talents. Throughout the crisis he spent up to sixteen hours each day sounding out opinion in the lobby of the national assembly. Once or more a day he met a representative from de Gaulle's private office in Paris.

Gerald Long was assigned to Paris at King's request to help cover the story. Upon King's death in 1990 Long claimed that King had never been prejudiced in his reporting, even though strongly prejudiced in his personal opinions. When a young diplomat in the press department of the French Foreign Office dared to suggest that King should give a particular slant to a report, he was answered with a fierce lecture about the freedom of the press, punctuated by the banging of King's umbrella on the desk. Admittedly, he was inclined to give de Gaulle ample space, and his critics less.[19]

The crucial message from de Gaulle, that he was 'prepared to assume the powers of the Republic', reached his Paris office on 17 May 1958. When King arrived there, scores of journalists were already milling around outside. King found the AFP representative, Jean Mauriac, who held a copy of the message in his hand. 'Take it', said Mauriac generously. The historic words were immediately phoned to the Paris office of Reuters, for rapid transmission to London.

King hurried to the Chamber of Deputies to collect reaction. He cabled London: 'General de Gaulle's record shows that nothing is further from his nature than to lust after a dictatorship. But most of the politicians inside and outside Parliament think that, whatever he declares beforehand, once back in power he will double-cross them by abolishing Parliament.' This was characteristic King. The emphasis favoured de Gaulle, and yet the report included criticism of him.[20]

Two days later, de Gaulle called a press conference. In preparation, King rented a bedroom on the same floor of the hotel where the gathering was to be held. This room became the base for King and his three reporting colleagues, Long, Sedbon, and a parliamentary stringer. King's secretary kept the telephone line open by reading continuously from the New Testament, a classic ploy. The four men came and went in turn to phone through de Gaulle's statement as it unfolded majestically, followed by his adroit answers to questions. Asked whether he would allow the politicians, if they now voted him into power, later to vote him out, de Gaulle replied that 'procedures become very flexible'. 'All is only too clear', commented one deputy afterwards to King. 'He wants to brush Parliament aside.'

9

The sudden death of a major world figure always tests the reaction of journalists. The assassination of Gandhi in 1948 was one such instance, over which Reuters did well.

Doon Campbell had already reported the coming of Indian independence on 15 August 1947. 'I saw more violence and slaughter in Delhi in the next few weeks', he wrote in his recollections, 'than I had seen in Europe at war.' In these tense circumstances, he instructed the local Reuter staff to be more than usually careful not to circulate rumours or to use emotional language; hard-sourced statistics were to be preferred. Twice daily, Campbell travelled round Delhi to count the corpses, starting at the very doors of his hotel.[21]

During this period Campbell was to suffer from one particularly bad example of a misrepresentation which all reporters fear—inaccurate rewriting by a sub-editor thousands of miles away from the event. Lord Mountbatten, the

Governor-General, told a press conference that a news agency, 'one that prided itself upon its international reputation for accuracy', had sent a lurid report about Old Delhi being engulfed in blood and flame, when in reality the violence there had been on a relatively small scale.

One of Mountbatten's staff showed Campbell the report, which had been attributed to Reuters in the *Chicago Tribune* and other American papers. Campbell was horrified, for he had sent no such story. He cabled Cole asking for publication of a repudiation. Unfortunately, the report had indeed been issued by the North American desk. A sub-editor had decided that Campbell's copy lacked colour, and had lifted an exaggerated piece from a London paper and issued it as a Reuter story. The culprit was sacked, and Cole sent a fulsome apology to the Indian authorities. Campbell, who had been at serious risk of expulsion, was allowed to stay.

He was still in India when Mahatma Gandhi was assassinated on 30 January 1948. P. R. Roy, a young Indian reporter, had asked permission to cover a prayer meeting in Delhi to be attended by Gandhi. Roy was told to telephone only 'hot' news. At 5.13 p.m. Campbell's desk telephone rang. 'A man has just fired four shots at Mr. Gandhi . . . don't know if he's dead . . . worst feared.' Campbell's immediate flash to London read: 'Man fired four shots at Gandhi pointblank range worst feared.' This gave Reuters a beat of seven minutes.

Campbell hurried to the scene, where Roy described what had happened. Campbell took the eyewitness account back to the office, while Roy stayed to wait for further news. Campbell's phone rang; 'Gandhi dead'. He immediately sent a flash to London, although this reached Fleet Street one minute behind a pick-up from All-India Radio, monitored at Radio House. UP and AP were respectively fourteen and fifteen minutes behind Reuters.

Radio House enjoyed many such successes at this period, but it failed badly over the death of Stalin. At 01.03 on 6 March 1953 a dictation-speed broadcast from Moscow for Soviet provincial newspapers announced the dictator's death. Unfortunately, Radio House was not listening to that channel. Exchange Telegraph heard the broadcast, and issued the news at 01.09. The first Reuter snap did not come until five minutes later, and then only at second-hand via New York: 'New York radio stations reported tonight that Stalin was dead.' Weak as this was, it was the only way for Reuters to break the dramatic news. The editorial report for the month admitted 'our worst defeat for many years'.

The death in a plane crash in 1962 of Dag Hammarskjöld, the United Nations Secretary General, proved particularly awkward for Reuters, because it tested under pressure the rule that certainty, not presumption, must be the basis for a statement of fact. Hammarskjöld had been flying across the Congo from Leopoldville to Ndola for talks with the Congolese leader Moise Tshombe. Gerry Ratzin, the Reuter correspondent in Elizabethville, had driven to Ndola to cover the talks. Some reporters there, using binoculars, saw a man, whom they presumed to be the Secretary-General, leaving an aeroplane at the far side of the heavily guarded airport. They wrongly reported the Secretary-General's 'arrival'. Prudently, Ratzin did not do so, because he had not himself identified Hammarskjöld. Regrettably, London editorial none the less issued a report from the South African Press Association saying that he had arrived. When this report came back on the teleprinter to Leopoldville, the Reuter correspondent there, Friedel Ungeheuer, who had seen Hammarskjöld leave, realized that he could not possibly have reached Ndola so quickly. Ungeheuer cabled his doubts to London. Campbell, the news manager, phoned Ndola and found that indeed the Secretary-General had not landed. Reuters immediately issued a correction. UPI and AP stuck by the 'arrival' story for several hours.

Meanwhile, the search for Hammarskjöld began on the ground. At first, Ratzin joined in; but fortunately he gave up, and instead phoned the Government spokesman in Ndola. The spokesman exclaimed that the plane with Hammarskjöld's body had been found less than eight miles away. 'I was the first journalist he had been able to tell, as the rest were out in the bush somewhere.' Ratzin's report for Reuters of how 'an African charcoal burner was the first man to spot the smouldering wreckage' won a thirty-eight minute beat in London.[22]

The assassination of President John F. Kennedy on 22 November 1963 was described ten days after the event by Pat Heffernan, chief correspondent in Washington, as 'the greatest story we are ever likely to report'. And yet the episode demonstrated how limited was the reporting capability of Reuters inside the United States; how great was its dependence upon AP, especially for early spot news. Kennedy was shot while being driven in a motorcade through Dallas, Texas. Because Reuters did not trail the President everywhere, it had no reporter at the scene. Its early coverage was necessarily taken entirely from AP. The American agency also supplied about half of the Kennedy-related material published by Reuters during the drama of the next few days. Aware, however, of the need to keep its file sufficiently distinctive, Reuter reporters were deployed to watch developments in Dallas and Washington. Reuters also monitored American radio and television. Overall, the story was handled as well as possible with the limited resources available. Within four years, as noticed in Chapter 12, the link with AP was to be broken, and Reuters was to develop its own separate news collection network across North America.

10

As many as eleven Reuter correspondents and cameramen were killed on duty during the half century of 'peace' after 1945. The deaths of Pearcy in Korea (1951), and of Laramy and Pigott in Vietnam (1968) have already been noticed. Others who died were Najmul Hasan in Iran (1983); Willie Vicoy in the Philippines (1986); Roberto Navas in San Salvador (1989); John Mathai in Addis Ababa (1991); Dan Eldon, Anthony Macharia, and Hos Maina together in Somalia (1993); and Adil Bunyatov in Azerbaijan (1995).

These eight Reuter deaths from the 1980s and early 1990s illustrate how the unstructured conflicts and tensions of the last quarter of the twentieth century have proved to be even more dangerous to correspondents than earlier conventional wars. One count, not claiming completeness, has listed 208 journalists killed in war zones between 1934 and 1981; in comparison, during the eight years between 1982 and 1989 at least 273 journalists are known to have lost their lives. Just 12 per cent of these deaths in the 1980s were accidental, in action or otherwise; 69 per cent were deliberate acts of revenge or deterrence.[23]

No Reuter correspondent has ever been killed deliberately, although in 1949 there was nearly one such instance. Graham Jenkins, one of the first AAP–Reuter correspondents, was arrested by the Nationalist Chinese, sentenced to death but finally released. In 1960 Sandy Gall was detained and nearly shot as a Belgian spy during the civil war in the Congo.[24]

The best correspondents have never pretended to be brave, even though prepared to risk danger. In July 1988 Helen Womack, a Moscow correspondent, described for *Reuters World* her feelings while covering the Soviet withdrawal from Afghanistan:

> Exhausted, ravenous, filthy, thirsty and dying for the toilet on the non-stop eight hour trip through scorching heat and dust, I had little room for thoughts of mortality. But on a later trip by military aircraft to the Soviet border, when I was well fed, watered and rested, I broke down for fear of Stinger missiles.

The experience of Bernd Debusmann, chief correspondent in the Middle East, was particularly testing. The high quality of his reporting made him particularly vulnerable. In April 1975 he was expelled from Addis Ababa for refusing to reveal his sources regarding a report about the execution of five Ethiopian army officers. After five hours of questioning the interrogating officer remarked: 'Our prisons are not very pleasant.' Fingering a gun, he added pointedly: 'You know accidents can happen.' In September of the following year Debusmann was wounded by gunfire while visiting Beirut's commercial sector. Most seriously of all, in June 1980 he was shot by a gun-man firing from a passing car in Beirut. Here was an Arab attempt at censor-ship by terror. This was the extreme; but throughout the unending Arab–Israeli confrontation, both sides have accused Reuters of favouring the other, and both have tried on occasion to impede honest reporting, either through censorship, cajolery, or threat. Israeli military censorship was criti-cized at intervals by Reuters for being not merely strict but also unpredictable; summed up as 'the Israeli Lottery'.

The editor-in-chief told the board in May 1985 that Reuters had chosen not to report fully about atrocities by Shiite militiamen and Lebanese army soldiers committed inside Palestinian refugee camps. 'Our local staff feared there was a serious danger the militia would attack them if we did.' AP and AFP did publish the story, but only to subscribers outside the Middle East. Reuter policy, explained the editor-in-chief, was against such self-censorship; its news must be made available 'to all subscribers or to none'. As for personal danger, the general rule has been that Reuter correspondents must never risk their lives for the sake of a story, an instruction reiterated at intervals ever since Julius Reuter's day. And yet there will always be some stories which, even though dangerous to report, are found too important to ignore.[25]

I I

The 1982 Falklands (Malvinas) War between Britain and Argentina was rightly called by Reuters World 'one of the world's more improbable wars'. It was conducted under conditions which mixed the atmosphere of a nineteenth-century colonial expedition with elaborate reporting restric-tions reminiscent of the two world wars. The handling of Falklands news became of particular significance in the history of Reuters. Put to the test of reporting a big running story in which the United Kingdom was a prin-cipal player, Reuters confirmed by its detached attitude that, although still keeping its headquarters in London, it had become a truly supranational organization.

In the nineteenth century Reuters would have reported the Falklands War from a British imperial angle. In contrast, by 1982 Michael Reupke, the edi-tor-in-chief, did not expect that any correspondent would write in pro-British terms. When Glen Renfrew, the managing director, asked if a circular should be sent to staff similar to that from Chancellor at the time of the 1956 Suez invasion, Reupke replied that to issue such a circular would to insult everyone's integrity.[26]

At the start of the conflict Reuters made it easier for the Argentinian authorities to allow continued coverage from Buenos Aires. Reuter staff with British passports were transferred to Montevideo in neighbouring Uruguay, while non-British staff were flown in as replacements. A full news file was circulated from Montevideo to Latin American subscribers outside Argentina. The file on the war in Spanish for Argentina was confined to official news from all quarters, often led by Argentinian material but balanced from other sources.

On 6 June 1982 Reupke explained to Ambassador Ros, the Argentinian representative at the United Nations, that Reuters was not a British news agency, and that only a relatively small part of its business was now conducted in the United Kingdom:

> Reuters takes no position, national or otherwise, in any situation or conflict, whether in the war between Iran and Iraq, the conflict between Israel and the Arab states, or the present conflict between Argentina and Britain . . . we have taken care to explain to the world the Argentinian position and the significance of the islands to the Argentinian people. We have in no different manner reported the position of the British Government.

Reuter correspondents, added Reupke, were drawn from forty-eight different nationalities. 'We take pride in that fact since it must help to ensure that no one national or partisan view can prevail in our reporting.'

The Argentinian authorities at least half accepted these arguments, although they refused to allow a Reuter correspondent to go with their forces. A similar request was made for a Reuter correspondent to accompany the British task force. This request was granted only belatedly, when Leslie Dowd was allowed on the liner *Canberra*, serving as a troopship, which sailed ten days behind the first warships.

The British Ministry of Defence had let the NPA allocate places for reporters with the task force, and the NPA had not recognized the claims of Reuters. On 5 April Reupke wrote adroitly to the British Defence Secretary, John Nott, explaining that he might find the file from 'the leading international news organisation' damagingly inadequate if Reuters were not allowed to report from the British side, particularly for its subscribers in the United States, Latin America, Europe, and elsewhere.

Dowd became subject to military censorship. But Reuters did not feel bound to take full account of the 'D notice' system in London. This was the arrangement originating from just before the First World War under which British editors voluntarily agreed to suppress news for the sake of national security or national interest. When the secretary of the 'D notice' committee,

Rear-Admiral William Ash, telephoned Manfred Pagel, the Reuter World Service editor, to complain because Reuters had reported the departure of the British fleet from Ascension Island, he was given a short answer. Ash had asked if Pagel was not concerned about the safety of 'our forces'. Pagel, whose German accent must have been noticed, replied that this was Ash's problem and not that of Reuters. 'I'm not British.' Reuters said that it was only pre-pared to hold back stories if their release might put lives in danger. This applied to lives on either side. In practice, only one report was delayed. But how could Reuters always be sure about the effects of its stories?

In general, Reuters did well with its Falklands coverage, both from the islands and from Buenos Aires, often being ahead of AP and UPI. But on 15 June the London bureau admitted to being 'comprehensively beaten' over the news of the final Argentine surrender. It lagged seventeen minutes behind UPI, and for 'no good reason'. Reuters was still sometimes fallible, even if it was now supranational.

12

The Reuter file was not all devoted to war or political news. The sports department was re-established under Vernon Morgan on 1 January 1945, even before the Second World War had ended. From then onwards, news of sport and adventure featured regularly in the Reuter news services.

An exclusive report about the conquest of Mount Everest in 1953 gave Reuters a story headlined throughout the world. The British Commonwealth expedition was under contract to *The Times*, and on 2 June the paper broke the news of Hillary and Tensing reaching the summit. The crucial message from *The Times* correspondent with the expedition, James Morris, had come down from the mountain in a plain language code which was deliberately misleading. It seemed to tell of failure: 'Snow conditions bad stop advanced base abandoned May twenty-nine stop awaiting improvement stop all well.' This coded message was shown by an Indian police radio officer to Peter Jackson, who was covering the expedition for Reuters. Jackson was given the chance to send a message of his own at the same time. Fortunately, he resisted the temptation to copy the apparently disappointing news: 'my suspicion of the veracity of Morris's report triumphed.' The words 'Snow conditions bad' in fact meant 'Everest climbed'.[27]

Instead, Jackson secured a notable follow-up beat. After a fourteen-day trek leading his own eleven-porter expedition, Jackson reached the Khumbu glacier, 18,000 feet up. He obtained the first interviews with Hillary and

Tensing, and sent his report back by a Sherpa messenger who had a 100-mile journey on foot over the mountains to Katmandu. A week later Jackson heard the story broadcast over the radio. His success had owed much to the Delhi correspondent, Adrienne Farrell, his future wife, who played a vital part in organizing the communications.

Everest was a story of man conquering nature, always fascinating to the public. Space travel provided an even greater challenge. On 12 April 1961 radio monitoring gave Reuters a two-minute beat in London with news of the first manned space flight by Yuri Gagarin, the Soviet cosmonaut. In 1969, filing directly from Houston mission control centre, Reuters was one minute ahead of AP with news of the first landing on the moon.

Competition over sports coverage was intense during the post-war years, particularly from AFP, the French agency. Reporting of the Olympic Games every four years required increasingly elaborate planning, with communications demanding great attention. The last major sporting event for which Reuters targeted the United Kingdom news market in particular was the Tokyo Olympics of 1964. Even then, full special reports were already being provided for world regional markets.

At the 1972 Munich Olympics Reuter journalists assigned to a sports story found themselves also covering a violent political episode. Palestinian guerrillas seized and killed Israeli hostages. Four Reuter reporters were on the perimeter of the Fürstenfeldbruck airbase when the final shoot-out occurred. Although themselves at a distance from the action, they collected good eye-witness accounts. But they failed to notice the Mayor of Munich leaving the base. He was buttonholed by the single AFP reporter, who secured a major beat with the news that all the hostages were dead.[28]

Four Olympics later, coverage of the 1988 Seoul Games cost Reuters £480,000; this compared with less than £10,000 for the 1952 Helsinki Games. Just under half of the 1988 cost was for news pictures, now an essential feature. Directly attributable revenue was only £80,000 because the coverage was included without extra charge in the basic Reuter news service. Once again AFP beat everyone on the main story; it was more than an hour ahead with news of drug traces being found in the urine of Ben Johnson, the winner of the 100 metres.

The *Reuter Sports Guide*, first published for internal circulation in 1988, provided a sport-by-sport survey of how to report everything from Alpine skiing to yachting. The Guide emphasized that the spread of computerized communications meant that Reuters no longer thought only in terms of media outlets. Retrieval figures showed that Monitor subscribers exhibited 'an enormous appetite for sports news, provided it is fast, clear and accurate'.

13

Economic news and information from Reuters had become increasingly important for the working of the international economy. As early as 1968 R. B. Maclurkin, the chief news editor, was urging general news journalists to show a wider awareness:

> We flounder frequently on treatment of economic events as general news stories. In the pre-war slump few of the people in the long dole queues took much interest in the actual mechanics of why they were unemployed and poor. The modern generations want to know why they are becoming richer or poorer and what their governments are doing about it. All of us as journalists must gain a bit more expertise on gold, monetary systems and the other technical aspects of trade and wealth.

Maclurkin was sensing that the old distinction between general news journalists and economic journalists was becoming outdated.

By January 1989 an analysis of agency play in ten leading world newspapers taking the Reuter service in English revealed that 58 per cent of their business news content came from Reuters, 21 per cent from AP, and 11 per cent from AFP. For other news, Reuters was only just ahead of AP—36 per cent against 33 per cent. So it was superiority with economic news and information for worldwide business users which gave Reuters its competitive edge. Well over half the total file now consisted of such material. And by the end of the 1980s about two-thirds of the journalists on the United Kingdom editorial staff were primarily economic journalists. Increasingly, however, recruits into reporting for Reuters were expected to become all-rounders, equally competent to cover markets or murders.

The 1987 world stock market crash was economic news in content which, because of its effects, quickly became also general news. It was tracked by Reuters minute by minute from financial centres all round the world. On 21 October, when the markets seemed to have settled down, Ian Macdowall, the chief news editor, congratulated the North American staff on its handling of the story. 'Its copy crackled with authority and energy, and was rich in initiative reporting.' He also emphasized the importance of related coverage from Europe and Asia. 'News is indivisible. Each region must guard the backs of the others . . . Think globally'.

In the United States the Reuter Business Report kept clients abreast of every development, starting in Washington at 08.36 on 14 October with figures of the United States trade deficit, which was down from a record $16.47 billion in July to $15.68 billion in August. By 11.19 Reuters Washington was reporting that the improvement 'in the crucial measure of U.S. trade world-wide was less than had been expected by market analysts . . . The news quickly undermined confidence in U.S. financial markets.' At 13.19 Washington was reporting from London that British share prices had 'ended sharply lower', and early next morning at 08.36 the same was being reported from Tokyo. Next day, Friday 16 October, Reuters New York saw the Dow-Jones index drop 100 points; and by 11.07 on the following Monday morning New York was indicating real trouble: 'Wall Street stocks nosedived again . . . in a wave of frantic selling that outdid even Friday's wild plunge.' The situation was still worse by 11.37: 'as investors around the world dumped their holdings, forc-ing the Dow Jones industrial average down a remarkable 200 points in early trading, losing 9 percent of its value in just 90 minutes.' Monitor and Row-Grabber screens could not keep up with the market; but the new Equities 2000 terminal did so, greatly assisting Reuter reporters and editors. At every 100-point drop a news snap was rushed out. On Tuesday Reuters was record-ing from London that share prices were taking 'new punishment round the globe'. Reports from Tokyo, Sydney, Paris, Zurich, Bonn, and elsewhere confirmed this. Then came a rebound, starting in New York, reported by Reuters at 18.02 on Wednesday, 21 October. The worst was over.[29]

The editorial report for October 1987 congratulated itself that economic and general news reporting had been 'impeccably integrated', while 'the regions tossed the ball back and forth between them with all the deftness of a pride of circus sealions':

> Economic and general reporters combined to produce a breadth of cover unmatched . . . by our competitors: concise market reports, reviews of the need for new techniques to cope with colossal moves in share prices, the strains placed on the stock exchange computer systems, the chances of a recession, the political implications for President Reagan and next year's presidential candi-dates, Treasury Secretary James Baker's man-in-the-middle role, the effect of Reaganomics, the losses at brokerage houses, colour pieces on the frenzy in the exchanges and brokerage houses, the atmosphere in Wall Street bars and the attitude of small investors.

14

The year 1989 was a turning-point in history, notable for the break-up of the Communist empire in Eastern Europe. The collapse of that empire had been foreshadowed and frustrated in Hungary in 1956 and in Czechoslovakia in 1968. In both countries, AP was first with the news of Russian intervention, but on each occasion Reuters had published some notable follow-up stories. One from Vincent Buist, the Reuter correspondent in Prague, received worldwide play:

> Crowds of Czechs, many of them students, roamed through the streets of the capital on foot or on lorries chanting support for party leader Alexander Dubcek, who had given them new freedom in defiance of the Kremlin, and hurling abuse at Soviet troops. Some people scrambled over Soviet tanks, arguing with the crews.
>
> One young girl banged on the barrel of a Soviet paratroop lieutenant's rifle and yelled: 'Go home, do you know where you are. You are in my country. Go away, you idiot'.

Buist also obtained an exclusive account, supplied by Czechoslovak contacts, of the abduction of Dubcek.

Reuters had been first with the news of the erection of the Berlin wall in 1961: it was first again in 1989 with the news that it was to come down. Such dominance of the continuing story out of East Germany was the reward for careful groundwork. Since the opening of the Reuter bureau in East Berlin thirty years earlier Reuters had maintained close contact with the East German Government through the official agency, Allgemeiner Deutscher Nachrichtendienst (ADN). From 1987, in anticipation of the story to come, Reuters had increased its staff numbers in Eastern Europe, and it assembled some of its best-qualified reporters in Berlin during the final days. The national angle was fully covered for the German-language service, while Reuter photographers and Visnews cameramen were present in force (Plate 65).[30]

The event which heralded the crumbling of Communist rule was the resignation of the Honecker Government on 7 November 1989. Reuters was nine minutes ahead even of ADN, which found the story hard to believe. When the wall was opened Reuters was ahead again in London. Martin Nesirky followed up with an eyewitness account from West Berlin on 10 November:

> Hundreds of East Berliners swarmed across checkpoint Charlie and West Berliners stood at the Berlin Wall on Friday as a divided city was reunited in a tumultuous embrace.
>
> Wide-eyed women clutched their faces, crowds hugged and cheered and East German border guards looked on in bewilderment.
>
> At the nearby Friedrichstrasse station crossing, a crowd of West Germans crossed to the East and staged a pro-reform protest, chanting: 'The Wall is down, the Wall is down'.
>
> At the Brandenberg Gate, two East German girls scaled the Wall, helped over into the West by young West Berliners.

The girls telephoned their startled mothers in East Berlin and told them they would be home after looking round the shops.

On 12 November Paul Mindus, a correspondent with a sense of history, for the first time put the unqualified dateline 'Berlin' on a report for Reuter. He told of the opening of the wall at Potsdamerplatz. 'For a brief moment, as the mayors of the two halves of the divided city clasped hands in the gap that East German troops had smashed through the wall, the city was one again and Berliners roared their approval.'

China was the country where the barriers did not come down. To report such a major and difficult story in such a huge country required large resources. About fifty-five staffers from Reuters and thirty from Visnews, among them nineteen Chinese-speakers, were involved in covering the demonstrations for democracy in 1989. Reuters in Peking patiently followed the story from the first student demonstrations in April until and beyond the Tiananmen Square bloodbath of 3–4 June. The square was watched day and night for both text and pictures. On 3 June Guy Dinmore, the chief correspondent in Peking, reported:

> Armoured troops crashed into the heart of Peking early on Sunday killing over 40 civilians and wounding hundreds more who tried to block their way.
>
> In Tiananmen Square, the focus of weeks of pro-democracy demonstrations that humiliated China's ageing leaders, crowds of students and workers huddled waiting for their fate.
>
> Doctors and witnesses at four hospitals said they knew that at least forty-two people had been shot dead and more than 200 wounded. There were unconfirmed accounts of at least 20 more deaths . . . 'It's a sheer massacre' a Chinese journalist said.[31]

15

Reuters was very successful in reporting the great events of 1989. Was it none the less unconsciously biased? In the internal editorial magazine, *Highlights*, for April 1990, Dinmore asked some searching questions from Peking, typical of the commendable self-examination to be found among Reuter journalists:

> Are we really a 'world information agency' as we rather pompously like to claim? Or, at least in its news coverage, is Reuters still very much a Western-based, Western-looking organisation? Whose views do we express?
>
> Watching events unfold in Eastern Europe, I couldn't help but sense sometimes that elation in our reporting had crossed that hazy boundary into glee . . .

It was inevitable that the 'collapse of communism in Eastern Europe' would be portrayed as just that. But does it, as our and other commentaries often imply, vindicate what is left in the West?

Dinmore then turned to recent coverage of his own territory, China: 'the end of seven weeks of celebration of people's power in Peking was a sobering experience.' He suggested that pro-Western bias had revealed itself in the form of too much optimism about the outcome:

> The sources we often quoted—diplomats or otherwise—were as much betrayed by their own wishful thinking as we were. Analyses we wrote at the time saying this must be the end of the Deng Xiaoping era were at least premature. I wish I could go back and insert a few more 'But on the other hand . . .'

In the December 1990 number of *Highlights* Macdowall answered Dinmore's question about pro-Western bias. It was, Macdowall argued, a matter not of bias but of writing for a market. Most Reuter subscribers were located in Western or Westernized countries. 'If we cater primarily for the West it should not be because of ethnic or cultural bias but because we pay most attention to the needs of those clients who pay us most for our services.' Nelson had once pointed out to the Pacific Board (13 June 1979) that there was 'a fairly consistent relationship' between the revenue received by Reuters and the Gross National Product of each country. And yet, emphasized Macdowall, Reuters did seek to supply news to the whole world. The agency must therefore strike a balance between commercial considerations and 'our ethical obligation to provide a news service whose values transcend colour, creed or religion'.

Additional national-language services were being introduced by Reuters during the late 1980s. These variously provided domestic or economic news; and as well as seeking profit, they sought to show the countries in question not simply that Reuters no longer gave the news a 'British' slant, conscious or otherwise, but even that Reuters could select so sensitively that its national-language services would not seem 'foreign' within each country. Paradoxically, Reuters was now so supranational that it could aspire to suit any nationality.

Was Dinmore measuring himself and his colleagues against an unattainable standard of perfection? Or against an unsuitable standard of neutrality? Gerald Long's warning against 'evenhandedness' was quoted early in the present chapter. The test was to be not neutrality but objectivity. Admittedly, objectivity is an absolute standard, and as such is unattainable in practice. Reuters has realized this, but it has still believed that the steady pursuit of objectivity in news collection and distribution is worth while.

Of course, all journalists are conditioned by their personal backgrounds, by their education and by their experience. Long admitted in a 1966 broadcast: 'nobody can be completely objective. That, however, isn't a reason why we shouldn't try.' And Long always insisted that because modern Reuter correspondents were constantly aware of the risk of unconscious bias, they usually got as close to objectivity as was humanly possible. Certainly, Reuters in 1989 was more nearly objective in its news reporting than in 1939, and much more so than in 1889.

SIXTEEN

Retrospect
1849–1989

I

By the late 1980s Reuters was very different from the often hard-pressed news agency of earlier times. It had embraced computer technology with great enthusiasm and with great reward.

Reuters had always tried to keep up with the latest innovations, but in the past the effect had been to modernize the company without really changing it. Such had been the consequence, for example, of the introduction of wireless services during the 1920s and 1930s. By contrast, the Reuter Monitor and other computerized products of the 1970s and 1980s did much more than keep Reuters up-to-date. Their introduction changed the shape of Reuters. They did so not because of the wonder of their technology—telegraphy and wireless had also been wonderful in their time—but because they produced a change of main market for the old agency. Revealingly, *Reuters. A Brief Description and Chronology*, issued in September 1991 by the corporate relations department, took this change of emphasis for granted. Its opening paragraph put the sale of news to the media not in first place but in second:

> Reuters is the world's leading electronic publisher. It serves the financial and business community in all the world's major markets and supplies news services for newspapers, magazines, broadcasters and news agencies.

The company profit and loss statement justified this order of priority. In 1989 Reuter revenue from media products totalled £78.4 million, compared with revenue from transaction products of £162.7 million, and from information products going to financial markets of £945.8 million. News and data from Reuters reached some 16,000 customers via more than 200,000 video terminals. Only 9 per cent of these customers worked in the media; some 60 per cent were finance houses; 25 per cent were business corporations; and 6 per cent were government bodies.

The collapse from the early 1970s of the Bretton Woods system of fixed exchange had left currency values fluctuating against each other, and dealers wanted to take advantage of slight but rapid changes to make profits. The Reuter Money Rates and other services spread the necessary real-time information worldwide—foreign exchange rates, stock exchange prices, major commodity prices, securities, and options.

The world's press, radio, and television were increasingly interested in economic information. The oil-price explosion of the 1970s was a striking instance of a commodity price trend which aroused general concern. Stimulated by daily exposure to television, this greater public awareness became continuous; and business pages or sections began to appear in many mass circulation newspapers.

Reuters was now contributing centrally towards the working of the global economy. This point was emphasized by Peter Job, the managing director, in a talk about the influence of Reuters to the Royal Institute of International Affairs in 1991:

> Periodic snapshots of economies at fixed exchange rates had to give way to a moving video . . . It was here that Reuters was the agent of change. Utilising computer technology harnessed to information flow, it was possible to give instant valuations of a country's exchange rate to a broad spectrum of users across the world . . . Using such systems the experts in the banking industry could take a real-time look at national pretensions, and by taking a speculative view of the future, start to use fast information flows to discount what might happen in the following hours, days, weeks or months. I think it is arguable that in this very specialised and highly focused area, we were amongst the first to exploit the freedom to alter and adjust the known values of the world.

An independent assessment of the part played by Reuters came from the American *Forbes* magazine (30 October 1989). From being, it wrote, 'a poor but proud ward of the British newspaper industry', Reuters had 'turned itself into nothing less than the world's leading supplier of computerized information'. Walter Wriston, a former chairman of Citicorp and a director of Reuters, graphically pictured the new situation:

> The world now operates on the information standard, which has replaced Bretton Woods and the gold standard. When the President goes out in the Rose Garden and says something, over 200,000 screens light up in the trading rooms of the world.[1]

In responding vigorously from the 1960s to this new opportunity Reuters was following the example set by Julius Reuter in the 1850s and 1860s. And in the process it remained committed to the standards which he had laid down—standards of accuracy, speed, and impartial distribution. A fourth standard—that of objectivity—had been harder for Reuters to approach dur-

ing its first hundred years, largely because of the pull of conscious or unconscious British 'patriotism', especially in wartime. Julius Reuter and his assistants had spoken simply of reporting the facts, as if such an approach was
bound to be objective. His Victorian contemporaries were great collectors of
facts. In *Hard Times* (1854), Dickens had caricatured those who wanted to
make the British entirely 'a people of fact, and of nothing but fact'. But late
twentieth-century media commentators—writing under the influence of
ideas of relativity—have expressed doubts, not only about the attainability of
objectivity but even about the finality of facts. One media practitioner turned
academic exclaimed in 1978: 'the journalist finds his "facts" vanish into opinions as he tries to take them across the frontiers of East and West. The clarity
of purpose which absorbed and concentrated the energies of English journalism at its peak a century ago has gone and will never return.'[2]

Where then has this left the journalists in Reuters? If objectivity must
always be unattainable, they cannot be blamed for falling short. On the other
hand, Reuters has never stopped aiming for objectivity, in the belief that by at
least making the attempt it can maintain a high standard. The 1956 Suez crisis marked a turning-point. When Chancellor, as general manager, exhorted
his staff not to take sides because British opinion was divided, he appeared to
be still assuming that Reuters was 'British'. Yet from the Suez period the
agency was increasingly to be credited with a supranational perspective.

Chancellor himself can be seen in retrospect as a transitional figure. While
serving as Far Eastern manager in the 1930s he had been an active representative of the old British imperial idea. Yet by the time of his resignation in 1959
he had started to claim that Reuters was 'not an organ for presenting British
news'. Even so, he had begun as a protégé of Roderick Jones, a lifelong imperialist, and both men had readily accepted offers of British knighthoods. In
contrast, two later chief executives, Long and Renfrew, were to receive no
British honours.

2

From 1984 Reuters was a public company. It soon had about 30,000 shareholders worldwide, although pension funds and institutions owned a large
majority of the shares. Might shareholder insistence upon the making of profits to pay dividends provoke a crisis if Reuters ever ran into serious financial
difficulties? Might institutional shareholders demand the pruning or sale of
some or all of the media services, if these were losing money? In a review of
The Price of Truth, Jonathan Fenby, a former editor-in-chief, pointed out that

there were historical grounds for this fear, going back to the time when Reuters was previously a public company:

> At the turn of the century, the company chairman regularly apologized to annual general meetings for the expenses involved in the news business. He assured shareholders that everything was being done to hold down the costs of foreign coverage and spoke warmly of the funds that were being devoted to more lucrative activities.

Fenby expressed the hope that the new chairman of Reuters would never have 'to sing the same song as his predecessor'.[3]

In answer to these fears, the Reuter management emphasized that the media services were an asset, financially and strategically. First, the availability of selected general news items on Monitor screens—chosen with the interests of economic service subscribers in mind and coming from a unified editorial operation—gave the non-media products an extra competitive edge. And secondly, the separate economic news services were highly successful, and yet their revenue was not included in the media products total.

In the budget and plan for 1985–7 Renfrew recognized the importance of shareholder expectations. He stated two basic objectives. The second was to secure the longer-term future of the company by 'aggressive development'. But the first was 'to sustain short and medium-term revenue and profit growth rates in line with high shareholder expectations' (see Table 16.1). After going public Reuters succeeded in satisfying the first of these objectives while vigorously pursuing the second. 'Aggressive development' led to the acquisition of nine companies in North America and the United Kingdom. The aim was to enable Reuters to offer a 'total package' of services. Renfrew assured the board in February 1985 that the purchase of Rich Inc. of Chicago for $58.5 million was justified because of the 'perfect strategic fit'. Rich manufactured trading room systems. Another acquisition was the purchase of Institutional Network Corporation [Instinet] for just over $100 million. It ran a computerized equities trading service. This acquisition ensured that Reuter

TABLE 16.1 Rise in revenue and profit figures after flotation in 1984. (£000)

	Revenue	Net Profit
1985	434,121	55,360
1989	1,186,910	182,863

customers in the securities market would be able to obtain information and deal through one keyboard, in the same way as those in the money markets. The image of Reuters in North America was much enhanced by this addition.

3

The biggest pessimists within Reuters during the 1980s were found among the old-style journalists. Many harked back to the camaraderie of the much smaller Reuters of the 1960s; some even enjoyed remembering their own poverty. Reuters, they complained, had become a business like any other. The sense of the special nature of Reuters, which had been so powerful a driving force throughout its history—and not least during the initial excursion into computerized products—was thought by many long-serving staff to have diminished during the 1980s. Certainly, in a 1989 interview, Mark Wood, the new editor-in-chief, dismissed the 'cradle-to-grave' approach as outdated. 'We can't be both a successful growing organisation and the Civil Service or the BBC.' Earlier in the century Roderick Jones had tried to measure Reuters against both these bodies. The management in the 1980s still encouraged a sense of the specialness of Reuters; but as a newly dynamic enterprise rather than as a 'family' business.[4]

The very rapid increase in staff numbers worldwide, resulting especially from acquisitions, inevitably threatened the old sense of oneness. World numbers grew from 3,865 at the end of 1984 to 10,071 five years later. By 1989 the 4,274 technical staff constituted much the largest category, compared with 1,640 in editorial. Another 1,768 worked in sales and marketing.

Since 1941 the Reuter Trust agreement had proclaimed that Reuters would work to remain 'the leading world news agency'. In fact, at that date Reuters was not in the leading position. The American agencies AP and UP led the way. By the 1980s, however, Reuters could fairly claim first place, if measured by numbers of journalists employed worldwide (although the figures available were not always strictly comparable) and by revenue earned. One count of full-time news agency correspondents engaged in foreign countries about 1990 gave Reuters 968; AP 617; AFP 550; Tass 150; and UPI 105. In terms of gross revenue, Reuters had passed UPI in 1975 and AP in 1978. In 1945 AP's revenue had been four times that of Reuters; half a century later that of Reuters was ten times that of AP (see Table 16.2).

In his 1986 book on *The International News Services* Fenby pointed out that AP and UPI were not international at all in terms of their priorities: 'the home

TABLE 16.2 News agency revenue, 1975–8

	1975	1976	1977	1978
		($000)		
Reuters	66,125	75,457	93,067	129,330
AP	90,891	97,392	101,624	112,097
UPI	62,372	63,405	67,372	74,307
AFP	45,811	46,462	50,575	60,774

market dominates their activities . . . their essentially American nature has been disguised by their worldwide organization and reach.' In 1977 Reuters was earning $78,356 in foreign revenue, compared with AP's $19,879 and UPI's $17,190. AP's foreign income amounted to only some 20 per cent of its revenue. Conversely, Reuters was earning only 16 per cent of its revenue from the United Kingdom.[5]

As a United States media co-operative, AP was bound to be essentially American, in contrast to Reuters which could strive to be less British. During the 1980s British predominance was reduced, at least in terms of proportionate staff numbers. The 10,071 staff at the end of 1989 were drawn from 160 nationalities, with ten nationalities achieving three-figure totals. The British (3,308) and the Americans (2,577) reached four figures.

Was Reuters then no longer a British-dominated company? Some said not. The best people, they thought, could rise regardless of nationality. This belief was strong among those who were themselves doing well in the United States. It perhaps reflected the fact that the Americans, as the second-largest group of employees, had the most to gain by playing down the Britishness of Reuters. Staff in continental Europe were much less likely to accept that Reuters had ceased to be British-dominated. If it had changed, said some, it was only because it was now dominated by the Anglo-Saxons together, British and American. Not all Europeans thought this a cause for complaint; many small-country nationals were glad to work for, or do business with, a British or Anglo-Saxon company of such high repute. In this spirit, Pehr Gyllenhammar of Volvo, the Swedish international businessman, told *Reuters World* in December 1997, upon his retirement after thirteen years as a director of Reuters, that 'the UK identity gives people a sense of security in dealing with Reuters. If one would claim that Reuters was something else, I would feel that was strange.'

Reuters remained male-dominated. A handful of women journalists had played significant parts during the twentieth century, but these women had been the exception. Even by 1991 there were comparatively few women in middle or senior management positions, only sixty-six out of 666.

If not a British or Anglo-Saxon company, then what? About 1980, the idea of moving the headquarters to Geneva had been considered. Job was to prefer a strong centre in London balanced by strong local organization. This, he suggested, might require the creation of more local subsidiary companies. These gave Reuters greater appeal to local staff, and circumvented the charge that Reuter products were 'foreign'. Such a structure also brought tax advantages.

Others in Reuters in the late 1980s were saying that its structure should reflect the fact that it was now product-led internationally. Certainly, one of the strengths of Reuters throughout the 1980s lay in its wide range of products and services. It had become market-sensitive, striving not simply to satisfy expressed customer needs but to anticipate them. To this end, Reuters invested heavily in research and development during the 1980s and beyond— £3.2 million in 1980, £59.7 million by 1989.

In the 1860s Julius Reuter had briefly acquired his own cables as part of his plan to dominate the international news scene. From the 1960s Reuters once more became deeply involved in communications on its own account. It developed the world's largest private communications network. The aim was to keep out competition by making comprehensive products available which gave Reuters control of client desktops. As in Julius Reuter's day, Reuters was aspiring not simply to compete but to dominate.

Even though profits were rising dramatically throughout the 1980s (see Appendix), Reuters could not afford to stand still. It was committed to continuous product development. Decision-makers in financial markets were undertaking more information analysis; and they were to become less and less satisfied with pre-composed price data, which was what the Monitor pages offered. They began to demand information not in analog form, but as a digital stream which they could analyse readily—drawing graphs, calculating ratios, predicting trends, identifying arbitrage opportunities, and so on.[6]

Towards the end of the 1980s Reuters therefore gave priority to the Integrated Data Network [IDN]. This was a global 'highway for data', intended gradually to replace the Monitor system. The aim was comprehensiveness and 100 per cent accuracy in databases, plus rapid retrieval times for subscribers (two seconds) and in changing data on display (one second). The first services on IDN, launched during 1987, were futuristically named Equities 2000, Commodities 2000, and Energy 2000. The difficulty was that large numbers of subscribers were reluctant to transfer to IDN because of the cost and upset to their systems. Ure admitted later that Reuters had underestimated the difficulty of swapping customers from Monitor. 'We were telling our customers, "Here's a new BMW. It's much more powerful, it consumes a lot more gas, you must drive 400 miles to pick it up, and—incidentally— your old BMW will self-destruct".' The Monitor services were gradually phased out during the 1990s under the direction of an uncompromisingly named 'Monitor End-of-Life Project Team'.[7]

Reuters was able to present its annual revenue figures either by product or by area. Such double measurement was intended to illustrate the broad strength of Reuters as a global organization with a growing product range (see Table 16.3).

TABLE 16.3. Revenue Figures in 1989. (£000,000)

	Revenue	% of Global product revenue
By product		
Real-time information	775.8	65
Historical information	44.4	4
Trading-room systems	129.1	11
Transaction products	159.2	13
Media products	78.4	7
By area		
Reuters Europe Middle East and Africa (REMA)	723.8	60
Reuters Asia (RA)	249.4	21
Reuters America (RAM)	234.9	19

4

Acquisitions had brought some outsiders straight into prominent positions. Were they all aware of the Reuter Trust principles? A reminder was thought desirable. 'Integrity, independence and freedom from bias', explained a 'Code of Conduct', dated 1 November 1988, 'must be demonstrable daily in the work and activity of all Reuter employees.'

The Reuter Trust had been greatly strengthened at the time of the flotation in 1984. The powers of the trustees were the strongest of the defences put in place at that time to protect Reuters against taint or takeover. A second defence was the limitation of any shareholder to a 15 per cent stake. In 1988 the effectiveness of this restriction was demonstrated when Rupert Murdoch increased his holding in AAP, thereby bringing his total number of Reuter 'A' shares to about 23 per cent. He disposed of the excess 8 per cent under the watchful eyes of the trustees and the chairman, Sir Christopher Hogg.

Robert Maxwell, the controversial chairman of Mirror Group News-papers, was a director of Reuters from 1986 to 1990. Hogg kept him under tight rein. On 28 July 1986 Maxwell was formally censured 'for a lack of due care and attention' in allowing, through oversight, some of his group's hold-ing of Reuter shares to be sold in contravention of the company code gov-erning such transactions. Maxwell was also reprimanded at intervals for non-attendance or late arrival at board meetings.

In 1989 the 'A' share structure was dismantled. It had been devised in 1984 as a third line of defence to ensure that the newspaper groups retained a built-in voting majority. After prolonged discussion among the interested parties, all the 'A' shares were now converted into ordinary shares for sale. This meant that the PA and NPA owners of the shares were finally relinquishing control. The trustees accepted that this was not dangerous, and was indeed desirable. It made Reuter shares more marketable by removing the two-tier structure, which in 1984 had provoked strong objections from some institutional investors.

The hope was expressed by Hogg and by Renfrew, the managing director, that in future the board of Reuters would function like that of any other pub-lic company, with less sectionalism. The expectation was also that there would be room for more executive directors. Job, Ure and Villeneuve joined the board in 1988; Wood in 1990.

During board discussions on 15 June 1988 Sir Richard Storey—the son of Samuel Storey, the chairman in 1941—had asked directly if the dismantling of the 'A' shares 'would put the integrity of Reuters at risk'. Renfrew replied that 'the Founders Share Company was quite capable of doing its job'. The careful scrutiny of the move by the trustees, whose powers derived from their control of the Founders Share, demonstrated that this was indeed the case.

A more elusive threat to the good name of Reuters resulted from the daily appearance of its name on video screens all over the world. Reuter products had become vital and visible tools of the capitalist system. Had Reuters unwit-tingly become a tool of the system in a second sense? Had it contributed to the rise of the materialistic 'yuppie' culture of the 1980s? In Sweden and else-where the yuppie condition was defined as possession of 'a fat salary, a red Porsche and a Reuter terminal' (Fig. 18). This was unfairly fixing guilt by asso-ciation. Even if the services supplied by Reuters had produced an effect which was social as well as commercial, Reuters deserved its commercial success.

The creation of the Reuter Foundation in 1982 demonstrated that, in its new affluence, Reuters was ready to accept an obligation to adopt a policy of constructive charity. Ever since Julius Reuter's day the agency had made occa-sional small charitable donations; but the Reuter Foundation was intended to

FIG. 18. The 'yuppie' dimension

operate with more system, upon a regular and generous basis. It was launched as a charitable trust with a grant from the company of £1 million. The aim was to help journalists from developing countries by offering fellowships— two at Oxford University, two at Stanford University, California, and one at Bordeaux University—to enable them to spend a sabbatical period in mid-career studying subjects beneficial to their work. This, wrote *Reuters World* (January 1983), would 'help narrow the gap between industrialised and developing countries in the use of information technology'. During the following years the Foundation was to extend its supportive activity into a variety of educational and humanitarian causes in different parts of the world. A publicity brochure explained that the Foundation was 'independent of Reuters business interests, but its guidelines are based on the founder's principles of accuracy, impartiality, reliability—and technical innovation. The Foundation aims to safeguard this tradition and pass it on to others.'

The Foundation had been started upon the recommendation of Michael Nelson. Looking back from 1996 Nelson, one of makers of the new Reuters, suggested four underlying reasons why it had done so well in his time. These had been the necessary preconditions for the creation of innovative products, headed by Monitor:[8]

(1) Recruitment of 'good and well-educated staff'.
(2) Training of such staff to high standards in their various fields.
(3) Concentration of effort within known spheres of activity, 'to grow, mostly organically, from that base'.

The other underlying success factor identified by Nelson was accidental:

(4) 'The fourth was not sought, but imposed upon Reuters. That was hunger. I do not think Reuters would have been such a focused company in the second half of this century if it had had financial resources. It had to be very selective because it had so little money.'

In the 1850s, Julius Reuter had likewise been focused by poverty. He had kept purposeful, in the belief that eventually his 'electric news' would find a market. And so it did. If he were to return at the end of the twentieth century he would not be surprised by the character of the company which bears his name. He would be pleased by its emphasis upon using the latest technology. He would be glad to find a continuing commitment to accuracy and speed, and to impartiality in distribution. He would welcome the integration of general and economic news, both of which he had sold from the start. He would be reassured to find Reuters so strong in his native Germany, where he had been frustrated by Bismarck. He would be interested in its future in Japan, and in Asia generally. He would be happy that it had at last achieved a truly worldwide presence, unencumbered by British imperial obligations which were never the whole of his vision. He would be intrigued by the end-of-century problem of 'information overload', and, not least, as a businessman in journalism, he would have been delighted that, after over a century of searching, Reuters had at last found the way to make large and continuing profits.[9]

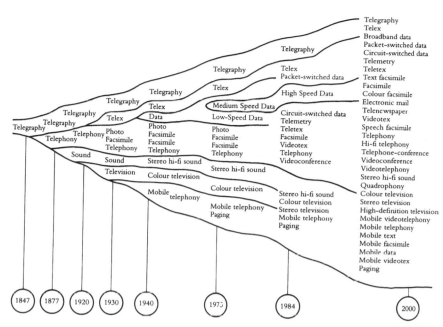

FIG. 19. Telecommunications: Prospects for the year 2000

APPENDIX

Comparison of Results 1952–1989 (£000)

Note: All figures (£000) are as originally reported in the group accounts for Reuters Limited (1952–83) and Reuters Holdings PLC (1984–9). Figures have not been restated to reflect subsequent events, e.g. changes of accounting policy, legislation, mergers.

	Revenue	% Increase	Profit/(Loss) before tax	% Increase/ (decrease)	Profit/(Loss) before tax as a % of revenue	Profit/(Loss) attributable to ordinary shareholders	% Increase/ (decrease)
1951	1,435.5		2.1		2.0	(7.5)	
1952	1,572.9	9.6	31.8	1,430.7	1.0	19.1	355.1
1953	1,667.2	6.0	15.9	(50.0)	0.0	10.5	(44.8)
1954	1,703.8	2.2	0.1	(99.1)	0.0	(10.2)	(197.2)
1955	1,788.6	5.0	11.8	8,346.4	0.7	6.7	165.2
1956	1,934.7	8.2	(19.6)	(265.5)	(1.0)	(18.8)	(381.6)
1957	2,042.2	5.6	38.3	295.9	1.9	27.2	244.9
1958	2,194.3	7.4	3.8	(90.2)	0.2	(6.0)	(122.1)
1959	2,270.3	3.5	35.9	854.8	1.6	18.1	401.2
1960	2,407.3	6.0	(18.5)	(151.6)	(0.8)	(25.8)	(242.5)
1961	2,706.8	12.4	70.9	482.7	2.6	39.6	253.4
1962	2,942.5	8.7	77.6	9.4	2.6	36.7	(7.3)
1963	3,155.8	7.2	53.3	(31.3)	1.7	26.8	(27.0)
1964	3,570.8	13.2	(57.1)	(207.0)	(1.6)	(51.0)	(290.3)
1965	3,992.9	11.8	60.6	206.2	1.5	71.4	239.9
1966	4,330.3	8.5	39.4	(35.0)	0.9	48.1	(32.6)
1967	4,840.0	11.8	(26.5)	(167.2)	(0.5)	(28.3)	(158.3)
1968	6,427.7	32.8	21.3	180.3	0.3	16.5	158.3
1969	8,826.9	37.3	213.7	904.9	2.4	209.6	1,171.5
1970	10,490.7	18.8	208.4	(2.5)	2.0	194.8	(7.1)
1971	11,896.6	13.4	306.5	47.1	2.6	284.9	46.2
1972	13,846.5	16.4	400.0	30.5	2.9	374.9	31.6
1973	17,494.6	26.3	1,023.3	155.8	5.8	798.9	113.1
1974	22,531.8	28.8	784.9	(23.3)	3.5	569.4	(28.7)
1975	29,921.0	32.8	1,124.0	43.2	3.8	1,026.0	80.2
1976	41,921.0	40.1	3,225.0	186.9	7.7	2,954.0	187.9

	Revenue	% Increase	Profit/(Loss) before tax	% Increase/ (decrease)	Profit/(Loss) before tax as a % of revenue	Profit/(Loss) attributable to ordinary shareholders	% Increase/ (decrease)
1977	53,487.0	27.6	3,218.0	(0.2)	6.0	2,892.0	(2.1)
1978	67,712.0	26.6	3,649.0	13.4	5.4	3,167.0	9.5
1979	76,309.0	12.7	3,515.0	(3.7)	4.6	3,100.0	(2.1)
1980	90,095.0	18.1	3,886.0	10.6	4.3	3,246.0	4.7
1981	138,804.0	54.1	16,681.0	329.3	12.0	13,994.0	331.1
1982	179,913.0	29.6	36,730.0	120.2	20.4	33,385.0	138.6
1983	242,630.0	34.9	55,253.0	50.4	22.8	11,907.0	(64.3)
1984	312,990.0	29.0	74,279.0	34.4	23.7	42,610.0	257.9
1985	434,121.0	38.7	93,562.0	26.0	21.6	54,312.0	27.5
1986	620,900.0	43.0	130,077.0	39.0	21.0	80,268.0	47.8
1987	866,875.0	39.6	178,754.0	37.4	20.6	108,831.0	35.6
1988	1,003,249.0	15.7	215,371.0	20.5	21.5	126,054.0	15.8
1989	1,186,910.0	18.3	283,059.0	31.4	23.8	180,634.0	43.3

PICTURE ACKNOWLEDGEMENTS

Agence France Presse (Plate 3); Alex (Fig 18); Australian War Memorial, Canberra (Plate 21); Bettman Archive, New York (Plate 65); British Library Newspaper Library, London (Fig 4, Plate 11): Lady Burgess (Plate 50); Canada Post Corporation (Plate 41); Canadian International Bank of Commerce (Plate 55); Deutsche Postmuseum, Frankfurt (Plate 4); *Financial Times*, London (Plate 56): Hulton Picture Company, London (Plates 35, 40); *Illustrated London News* (Plate 6); Imperial War Museum, London (Plates 20, 39); Gunilla Ingmar, *Monopol pa nyheter* (Uppsala, 1973), 24–5, trans. in Terhi Rantanen, *Foreign News in Imperial Russia* (Helsinki, 1990), 45 (Fig. 6); Liselotte Lenhart (Plate 5); Seaghan Maynes (Plate 38); National Army Museum, London, courtesy of the Director (Plate 9); *Online Magazine*, Mar. 1990, by permission of Online Inc. (Fig. 19); Postal Museum, Pretoria (Plate 19); Press Association Picture Library, London (Plate 34); *Punch* Library, London (Fig. 1); Reuters (Frontispiece, Plates 1, 2, 7, 8, 12, 13, 16, 17, 18, 22, 23, 24, 25, 26, 27, 28, 29, 30, 31, 32, 36, 42, 43, 44, 45, 46, 47, 48, 49, 51, 52, 53, 54, 57, 58, 60, 61, 62, 63, 64, Figs. 2, 3, 5, 7, 8, 9, 10, 11, 12, 13, 14, 15, 16, 17); Len Santorelli (Plate 59); Transvaal Archives, Pretoria (Plate 14); Turner Entertainment, USA (Plate 37).

GLOSSARY

beat	News delivered sooner than competitors: 'a beat'.
broadband	Communications channel with a band-width greater than a voice channel and therefore capable of higher-speed data transmission.
cable-ese	Method of word condensation and combination to save costs of transmission. Latin forms often used: e.g. CUMSPEED, ETBE, POSTDINNER.
copy	Generic term for all news reports and feature articles, general and economic, through from reporters' drafts to issued version.
copytaker	Clerk/telephonist who types copy telephoned through by reporters or other news suppliers.
copytaster	Senior sub-editor who scans incoming copy to decide its news value.
dateline	Place (and often also time) from which a message is sent. Verbal form: 'datelined'.
flash	Signal for highest-priority news of supreme urgency. Conveys the bare fact only, e.g.:
	FLASH
	WASHINGTON: NIXON RESIGNED—REUTER
kill	A news story already issued but found to be without foundation or even partly inaccurate has to be 'killed'. A substitute version may then follow.
lead	A new opening to a running news story.
multiplexing	Division of a transmission facility into two or more channels. Hence 'time-division multiplexing', allotting a transmission facility to different channels one at a time.
real time	In computer language a system which processes information at the time of input as opposed to storing for processing at a later date. The Reuter Monitor (ch. 12) is a notable example.
representation allowance	Extra payment for personifying 'Reuters', usually for managers or correspondents overseas.
scoop	An exclusive 'beat'.
service message	An instructional or administrative communication to a manager or correspondent.
situationer	A holdable story, suitable for supplementing the immediate news file, containing background and interpretation suitable for feature pages. Sent from overseas by mail.

snap	Signal used to break urgent news just below 'flash' value. Usually of one sentence.
spike	Unusable messages were put on a spike. Hence 'to spike'.
stringer	Part-time correspondent, paid by the word published, often a reporter from a local newspaper.
sub-editor	Journalist in the newsroom with responsibility for checking, tidying, and if necessary rewriting correspondents' copy.

REFERENCES

U NPUBLISHED British Government material cited here—with references 'CAB', 'C.O.', 'D.O.', 'H.O.', 'INF', F.O.', 'T', 'W.O'—is in the Public Record Office, London. The Reuters Archive holds photocopies of this material, and also clippings or photocopies of most of the Reuter-related newspaper and other external matter. The board minute books are complete (and indexed) from the formation of the first company in 1865; because of their obvious and continuous relevance, specific reference has not been thought necessary.

CHAPTER ONE
Julius Reuter: Before and After 1851

1. On Havas, see P. Frédérix, *Un siècle de chasse aux nouvelles* (Paris, 1959); A. Lefebure, *Havas, les arcanes du pouvoir* (Paris, 1992).
2. Early biographical material about Julius Reuter is patchy and contradictory, with no single main source. The Benfey family archive contains related genealogical material; photocopies are held in the Reuters Archive. Informative obituaries were published in *L'Eclaireur de Nice*, 26 Feb. 1899; *Riviera Daily*, 26 Feb. 1899; *The Times*, 27 Feb. 1899; *Jewish Chronicle*, 3 Mar. 1899; *Punch*, 8 Mar. 1899; *Leipziger Illustrierte Zeitung*, 16 Mar. 1899; *Annual Register, 1899, Chronicle*, p. 136. Other articles containing significant personal information appeared in *Notes & Queries*, 3 Nov. 1860, p. 346, 29 Dec. 1860, pp. 515–16; *Once A Week*, 23 Feb. 1861, pp. 243–6; *Vanity Fair*, 14 Dec. 1872, p. 191; *Monetary Gazette*, 7 Mar. 1877; *British Colonial Printer & Stationer*, 10 Feb. 1898; *Fortunes Made in Business* (1902), pp. 332–8; *B.L. am Mittag*, 26 May 1913, 10 Mar. 1916; *Kasseler Neueste Nachrichten* 5 May 1933; *Bad Nenndorf Badezeitung*, 2 Sept. 1934; *Bankers' Magazine*, Aug. 1937, pp. 237–7; *Koralle*, 21 Jan. 1941.
3. For background, see D. Sorkin, *The Transformation of German Jewry, 1780–1840* (Oxford, 1987).
4. H.O. 2/142, no.1627; St George's Lutheran Church marriage register, TH 8371/13 fo. 16 (Tower Hamlets Local History Library and Archives).
5. M. C. Gritzner, *Flüctlingsleben* (Zurich, 1867), ch. 11.
6. On the Wolff Bureau, see D. Basse, *Wolff's Telegraphisches Bureau 1849 bis 1933* (Munich, 1991).
7. L. Hymans, *Types et Silhouettes* (Brussels, 1877), pp. 181–6.
8. *Norddeutsche Allgemeine Zeitung*, 16 Mar. 1899; *Hannoverscher Courier*, 8 Aug. 1902; *Politisches Tageblatt* [Aachen], 28 Nov. 1906; H. Collins, *From Pigeon Post to Wireless* (1925), pp. 26–9.

9. XI/125/5A (Rothschild Archive, London).

10. Letter Book 2, fo. 34 (*The Times* Archive).

11. W. Siemens, *Inventor and Entrepreneur, Recollections of Werner von Siemens* (2nd. edn., 1966), p. 77.

12. H.O. 2/220, no. 2919, 20.

13. Letter Book 2, fo. 367; Letter Book 3, fo. 64 (*The Times* Archive).

14. Letter Book 3, fos. 224, 415; K. Marx and F. Engels, *Collected Works*, vol. 41 (1985), p. 122. For background, see R. E. Coons, *Steamships, Statesmen and Bureaucrats. Austrian Policy Towards the Steam Navigation Company of the Austrian Lloyd, 1836–1848* (Wiesbaden, 1975).

15. XI/125/5B (Rothschild Archive, London).

16. *T.P's Journal for Men and Women*, Nov. 1916, p. 23.

17. J. B. Atkins, *Life of Sir William Howard Russell* (1911), ii., p. 384; R. Furneaux, *The First War Correspondent* (1944), pp. 39–40.

18. G. T. Griffiths to A. E. Watson, 12 Dec. 1925 (MF 431, Reuters Archive).

19. P. C. Usoff, *Istorichesky Vestnik* [Memoirs] (St Petersburg, 1882), pp. 633–4.

20. H.O. 179/2403.

21. Zl. 498/1858; 2802/1859 (Staatsarchiv, Vienna).

22. F.O. 83/156; *History of The Times, The Tradition Established, 1841–1884* (1939), p. 272.

23. F.O. 83/166; Delane Correspondence, vol. 9, fo. 44 (*The Times* Archive).

24. For background, see A. J. Lee, *The Origins of the Popular Press in England, 1855–1914* (1976); and Lucy Brown, *Victorian News and Newspapers* (Oxford, 1985).

25. *The Times, The Tradition Established*, p. 272.

26. Usoff, [Memoirs], p. 634.

27. Letter Book 9, fos. 88, 97 (*The Times* Archive).

28. Ibid., fos. 167, 176, 596; *The Times, The Tradition Established*, pp. 272–3.

29. For background, see D. Beales, *England and Italy, 1859–60* (1961), pp. 36–7.

30. H. Barty-King, *The Baltic Exchange* (1977), pp. 130, 153–4, 174–6.

31. Letter Book 14, fo. 422 (*The Times* Archive).

32. Marx and Engels, *Collected Works*, vol. 41 (1985), pp. 121–2.

33. F. Scudamore, *A Sheaf of Memories* (1925), pp. 234–5. For Engländer's career, see Austrian police files, esp. Zl. 3899/1854, 498/1858 (Staatsarchiv, Vienna); *Jewish Chronicle*, 19 Dec. 1902; M. Palmer, 'L'Agence Havas et Bismarck, L'Echec de la Triple Alliance Télégraphique (1887–1889), *Revue d'Histoire Diplomatique*, 90 (1976), 321–57.

34. H. Heine, *Werke*, vol. 23 (Berlin, 1972), p. 181; vol. 26 (Berlin, 1975), pp. 315–16.

35. A. Herzen, *My Past and Thoughts* (1968), iii. 1200; Marx and Engels, *Collected Works*, vol. 17 (1981), p. 277; vol. 39 (1983), pp. 126, 548, 553; vol. 41 (1985), pp. 70, 121–2, 144.

36. Typescript 'Note from F. W. Dickinson' (MF 431, Reuters Archive).

37. Ethel C. Mayne, *Enchanters of Men* (1909), pp. 274–5.

38. For Heckscher, see *The Times*, 16 Sept. 1909; *Globe*, 16 Sept. 1909; *Daily Telegraph*, 17 Sept. 1909; *Jewish Chronicle*, 24 Sept. 1909.

39. For Williams, see G. V. Williams, 'The Late Mr. G. Douglas Williams & Reuters Agency' (MF 431, Reuters Archive); V. Williams, *The World of Action* (1938), chs. 1–4.

40. For Collins, see his published reminiscences, *From Pigeon Post to Wireless* (1925); *Australian Dictionary of Biography*, vol. 8 (1981), pp. 75–6.

41. For Bradshaw, see *North Middlesex Chronicle*, 8 May 1915; Sir Roderick Jones, *A Life in Reuters* (1951), pp. 82, 108–10, 141–3.

42. For Dickinson, see his typescript recollections (MF 431, Reuters Archive); his correspondence with Roderick Jones (Reuters Archive); *Reuter Service Bulletin*, May 1918, p. 6; June 1923, pp. 2–7; Oct. 1923, p. 28; *The Times*, 4, 7 Sept. 1922; Jones, A *Life in Reuters*, chs.9–26.

CHAPTER TWO

'The Great Reuter'

1. Marx and Engels, *Collected Works*, vol. 41 (1985), pp. 121–2.

2. *Fortunes Made in Business*, p. 334.

3. Williams, *World of Action*, p. 56.

4. George J. McCall to Reuters, 1 Jan. 1919 (MF 431); T. Cadogan, 'When Crookhaven Made News', *Cork Examiner*, 2 Sept. 1991; 'Clever Foreign Speculator Scoops American News', *Search. A Newsletter from the Reuter Archive*, no. 1 (Sept. 1991).

5. Sarah A. Wallace and Frances E. Gillespie (eds.), *The Journal of Benjamin Moran, 1857–1865* (Chicago, 1948), ii. 868–9, 887, 904, 911, 1018, 1075, 1213, 1214, 1219, 1302, 1313.

6. The Times, *The Tradition Established*, pp. 367–8.

7. Collins, *Pigeon Post to Wireless*, pp. 41–3.

8. *The Times*, 27, 29 Apr. 1865; *Morning Advertiser*, 27 Apr. 1865.

9. *Supplement to The City*, 5 May 1883, p. 10; Dickinson, typescript recollections, pp. 14–15.

10. W. G. Fitzgerald, 'The Romance of Our News Supply', *Strand Magazine*, 10 (1895), pp. 69–79; T. A. Jones, 'Our Network of News: The Press Association and Reuter', *Windsor Magazine*, 4 (1896), pp. 517–24; *Reuter Review*, Jan. 1938, p. 24. For background, see J. L. Kieve, *The Electric Telegraph* (Newton Abbot, 1973), ch. 3.

11. J. Grant, *The Newspaper Press* (1871), ii. 332–4; *Riviera Daily*, 26 Feb., 1899.

12. For the Press Association, see G. Scott, *Reporter Anonymous. The Story of the Press Association* (1968), pp. 13–55.

13. K. J. Fielding (ed.), *The Speeches of Charles Dickens* (Oxford, 1960), p. 339.

CHAPTER THREE

An Imperial Institution, 1865–1914

1. Wolff, typescript recollections, pp. 14–15, 18.
2. Kieve, *Electric Telegraph*, ch. 6.
3. *Beeton's Dictionary of Universal Biography* (2nd edn., 1870), p. 882.
4. Wolff, typescript recollections, pp. 27–8.
5. Ibid., pp. 19–26; Grant, *Newspaper Press*, ii. 337.
6. *Fortunes Made in Business*, p. 336. For background, see F. Stern, *Gold and Iron, Bismarck, Bleichröder, and the Building of the German Empire* (New York, 1977), pp. 263–8; H. J. Hohne, 'Nachrichtenagenturen unter Bismarcks Regie', *Publizistik Vierteljahreshefte für Kommunikationsforschung* (1981), pp. 104–10.
7. Grant, *Newspaper Press*, ii. 338–40.
8. *The Times*, 10 Aug. 1869; C. Bright, *Submarine Telegraphs* (1898), p. 107; *Annual Register, 1899*, Chronicle, p. 136.
9. R. A. Schwarzlose, *The Nation's Newsbrokers*, vol. 2 (Evanston, Ill., 1990), ch. 5.
10. For background, see P. M. Kennedy, 'Imperial Cable Communications and Strategy, 1870–1914', *English Historical Review*, 86 (1971), pp. 728–52; H. Barty-King, *Girdle Round the Earth. The Story of Cable and Wireless* (1979), chs. 1–6; J. Henry, 'A Century of Speeding the News by Printer', *Reuters World* (June 1983), pp. 14–15.
11. F.O. 371/166.
12. *Leipziger Illustrierte Zeitung*, 16 Mar. 1899.
13. *Bristol Times*, 27 Feb. 1899.
14. A. H. Kingston, typescript note on Reuters in India, 31 Mar. 1919 (MF 431, Reuters Archive); *Reuter Service Bulletin* July 1920, pp. 14–15; Collins, *From Pigeon Post to Wireless*, pp. 65–6.
15. Collins, *From Pigeon Post to Wireless*, p. 83.
16. Ibid., pp. 105–15.
17. Letters of L. Mackinnon to J. S. Johnston (Johnston Collection, Melbourne University); *Chambers's Journal*, 22 Dec. 1888, pp. 805–6; *A Century of Journalism, The Sydney Morning Herald, 1831–1931* (Sydney, 1931), pp. 276–80; R. B. Walker, *Yesterday's News: A History of the Newspaper Press in New South Wales* (Sydney, 1980), ch. 17; G. Souter, *Company of Heralds* (Sydney, 1981), p. 18.
18. For the New Zealand background, see J. Sanders, *Dateline NZPA. The New Zealand Press Association, 1880–1980* (Auckland, 1979), pt. 1.
19. Justine Taylor, 'General Survey of Reuters in Latin America', 25 May 1989, typescript.
20. G. C. Delany, typescript on 'Reuters Service in Egypt' (MF 431, Reuters Archive).
21. Atkins, *William Howard Russell*, ii. ch. 16; *The Times, The Tradition Established*, pp. 429–31.
22. *The Civilisation of Our Day* (1896), pp. 286–7.

23. Hausarchiv A I 28b K1 Nr, 36 (Bäyrische Staatsarchiv, Coburg).

24. F.O. 60/405–7; *Reuters World*, Dec. 1994, pp. 8–9. For background, see F. Kazemzodeh, *Russia and Britain in Persia, 1808–1914* (1968), ch. 2; G. Jones, *Banking and Empire in Iran. The History of the British Bank of the Middle East*, vol. 1 (1986), ch. 1; P. Avery *et al.* (eds.), *Cambridge History of Persia*, vol. 7 (Cambridge, 1991), pp. 187–9, 401, 593.

25. Dickinson, typescript recollections, p. 2.

26. D. Read, *The Age of Urban Democracy* (1994), pp. 63–7.

27. Dickinson, typescript recollections, pp. 5–12. See also on Baron Herbert, Williams, *World of Action*, pp. 79–82.

28. Wolff, typescript recollections, pp. 41, 50.

29. R. Williams, *The Long Revolution* (1965), p. 227.

30. Wolff, typescript recollections, pp. 16, 32–3, 40.

31. Ibid., pp. 50–2.

32. Ibid., pp. 46–7.

33. Ibid., pp. 47–9; Dickinson, typescript recollections, pp. 12, 30.

34. Ibid., p. 39.

35. *Reuters Bank Limited, Memorandum and Articles of Association*, 26 June 1913; Sir Roderick Jones, *A Life in Reuters* (1951), pp. 102–3

36. *The Times*, 25, 28, 29, 30 Oct., 3 Nov. 1913; 24 June 1914; Jones, *Life in Reuters*, p. 103.

37. F.O. 371/2012; A. M. Pooley, *Japan at the Crossroads* (1917), pp. 121, 138–9, 152–5; Jones, *Life in Reuters*, p. 103.

38. Palmer, 'L'Agence Havas et Bismarck', pp. 321–57.

39. S. Levy Lawson, 'Facts and Reminiscences within the Experience of the Present New York Manager', pp. 3–5 (MF 431, Reuters Archive); R. A. Schwarzlose, *The Nation's Newsbrokers*, vol. 2 (Evanston, Ill., 1990), chs. 5–7.

40. For Buck, see his typescript recollections, 11 Mar. 1919 (MF 431, Reuters Archive); *The Times*, 28 Apr., 1948.

41. *Collected Works of Mahatma Gandhi*, vol. 6 (Ahmedabad, 1961), p. 269; M. K. Gandhi, *An Autobiography* (Ahmedabad, 1966), pp. 126, 145–6.

42. Mathilde Rees to G.C. Delany, 28 Feb. 1919 [Recollections] (MF 431).

43. For background, see R .P. T. Davenport-Hines and G. Jones (eds.), *British Business in Asia since 1860* (1989), esp. ch. 7.

44. *Reuter Service Bulletin* (Jan. 1918), p. 16.

45. G. Bain, 'Of Baron Reuter and the Blue Jays', *Report on Business* (Dec. 1986), pp. 29–31.

46. Salisbury MSS 3M/A95/19.22 (Hatfield House Library); Zara S. Steiner, *The Foreign Office and Foreign Policy, 1898–1914* (Cambridge, 1969), pp. 36–7.

47. *Report of the British Committee of Inquiry into the Raid*, Blue Book 311 (1897), Q.4513; H. M. Hole, *The Jameson Raid* (1973), pp. 145–6.

48. Wasserfall to Jones, 11 Mar. 1926; J. S. Dunn, 'Notes for Mr. Graham Storey', 1950 (MF 431, Reuters Archive).

49. A. N. Porter, *The Origins of the South African War* (Manchester, 1980), pp. 115–16.

CHAPTER FOUR

The World's News, 1865–1914

1. G. W. Smalley, *London Letters* (1890), ii. 339–47. For background, see M. Sewell, ' "All the English-Speaking Race is in Mourning": The Assassination of President Garfield and Anglo-American Relations', *Historical Journal*, 34 (1991), pp. 665–86.

2. Collins, *Pigeon Post to Wireless*, pp. 78–80. For background, see R. T. Stearn, 'War Correspondents and Colonial War, *c.*1870–1900', in J. M. MacKenzie (ed.), *Popular Imperialism and the Military, 1850–1950* (Manchester, 1992), pp. 139–61.

3. Wolff, typescript recollections, pp. 28–9; Dickinson, typescript recollections, pp. 16–17.

4. Williams, *World of Action*, p. 34.

5. Dickinson, typescript recollections, p. 18.

6. *Reuters Service Bulletin* (July 1917), p. 10.

7. Add. MSS. 39015–18 (British Library, London); W. F. Monypenny and G. E. Buckle, *Life of Benjamin Disraeli, Earl of Beaconsfield*, vol. 6 (1920), p. 243.

8. For the Central News, see H. G. Hart, *The Central News Diamond Jubilee Souvenir* (1931); for the Exchange Telegraph, see J. M. Scott, *Extel 100. The Centenary History of the Exchange Telegraph Company* (1972).

9. Letter Books, 2nd ser., vol. 4 fos. 32, 528; vol. 5, fos. 84, 179; vol. 8, fo. 620; vol. 10, fos. 617, 629 (*The Times* Archive); Enid H. C. Moberly Bell, *Life and Letters of C. F. Moberly Bell* (1927), pp. 165–7.

10. Williams, *World of Action*, p. 84.

11. Letter Books, 2nd ser., vol. 17, fo. 241; vol. 18, fo. 447; vol. 20, fo. 413 (*The Times* Archive).

12. Sir F. Maurice, *Life of Lord Wolseley* (1924), p. 184.

13. *Graphic*, 6 June 1885; *The Times*, 18 June 1888.

14. G. C. Delany, 'Army up the Nile', *Reuter Review*, June 1938, p. 6.

15. Dickinson, typescript recollections, pp. 19–20; Bell, *Moberly Bell*, pp. 173–4; H. A. Gwynne, 'Adventures and Experiences in Pre-War Wars', in H. W. Nevinson (ed.), *Anywhere for a News Story* (1934), ch. 6.

16. The Times, *The Twentieth Century Test* (1947), p. 787.

17. Collins, *Pigeon Post to Wireless*, pp. 277–8.

18. A. 739/4.5.6 (State Archives, Pretoria).

19. MSS. 312, vol. 44, fos. 584–5 (Mitchell Library, Sydney).

20. D.O. 119/405; *Reuter Service Bulletin* (Oct. 1923), pp. 39–40.

21. Dickinson, typescript recollections, pp. 28–9. For background, see M. Palmer,

'Quand les agences rapportent l'événement: "l'actualité" russe, 1904–1906', in F. Almeida (ed.), *La Question médiatique* (Paris, 1997), pp. 205–19.
22. *Reuters Review*, Mar. 1978, pp. 8–9.

CHAPTER FIVE

Wartime Reconstruction, 1914–1918

1. *Despatches from His Majesty's Ambassador at Berlin Respecting an Official German Organisation for Influencing the Press of Other Countries* [Cd. 7595], Sept. 1914, esp. pp. 2–4.
2. F.O. 371/2220.
3. Dickinson, typescript recollections, pp. 29–32; *The Times*, 17, 20, 21, 23 Apr. 1915.
4. *The Times*, 20 Aug. 1919; *Reuter Service Bulletin* (Sept. 1919), pp. 1–4; Lord Oxford and Asquith, *Memories and Reflections* (1928), i. 58–9.
5. For Jones, see especially *A Life in Reuters* (1951); *The Times*, 24 Jan. 1962 [anonymous obituary by Haley]; Enid Bagnold, *Autobiography* (1969); J. Lees-Milne, *Another Self* (1970), pp. 122–31; W. Haley, 'Sir Roderick Jones', *Dictionary of National Biography, 1961–1970* (1981), pp. 598–9; Anne Sebba, *Enid Bagnold* (1986).
6. Jones, *A Life in Reuters*, p. 159.
7. Ibid., p. 156.
8. Frances Donaldson, *The Marconi Scandal* (1962), p. 276.
9. Jones, *A Life in Reuters*, p. 159.
10. Ibid., p. 169.
11. Ibid., ch. 20.
12. For background, see M. L. Sanders and P. M. Taylor, *British Propaganda During the First World War* (1982).
13. E. A. Perris to R. Donald, 11 July 1917 (INF 4/10).
14. F.O.371/2565. See also F. van Free, *Reuters in the Netherlands. De La Mar and the Reuters Amsterdam Branch* (Rotterdam, 1993).

CHAPTER SIX

War News, 1914–1918

1. W. L. Murray, 'Reuter and the Censorship', *Reuter Review*, Apr. 1938, p. 31.
2. *Reuter Service Bulletin* (Sept. 1918), p. 14; (Apr. 1919), p. 25; (Sept. 1919), p. 7; (July 1920), pp. 10–11; K. Fewster (ed.), *Gallipoli Correspondent* (Sydney, 1985), pp. 13, 165–70, 187.
3. Williams, *World of Action*, chs.20, 22. For background, see P. Knightley, *The First Casualty* (1975), ch. 5.

4. *Reuter Service Bulletin* (Sept. 1918), pp. 13–14; (July 1920), p. 10; *Western Morning News*, 27, 28 Mar. 1944.

5. Home Political A, Dec. 1914, nos. 230–1 (National Archive of India).

6. For Beringer, see F.O. 395/105–10, General Correspondence, News, Russia Files; Vestnik photocopies in Reuters Archive from TsGIA SSSR, St Petersburg, and TsGAOR (Central State Archive of the October Revolution), Moscow; *Reuter Service Bulletin* (Apr. 1919), pp. 11–12; (Feb. 1921), p. 24; *The Times*, 27 Jan. 1926: R. Pares, *My Russian Memoirs* (1931), pp. 114, 243, 407, 478.

7. H.O. 139/37/156.

CHAPTER SEVEN

The Autocracy of Roderick Jones, 1919–1934

1. 'Statement by Sir Roderick Jones, Chairman of Reuters, for the Foreign Office Committee appointed by the Secretary of State to consider the question of British publicity abroad and, in particular, the effect of the Leafield wireless service upon Reuters' business', 2 Apr. 1925, typescript; F.O. 395/403.407.408. For background, see P. M. Taylor, *The Projection of Britain. British Overseas Publicity and Propaganda, 1919–1939* (Cambridge, 1981).

2. F.O. 395/305; Taylor, *Projection of Britain*, pp. 58–60.

3. Taylor, *Projection of Britain*, pp. 60–1.

4. Ibid., pp. 62–3.

5. See Vestnik-Tass photocopies in Reuters Archive from TsGAOR (Central State Archive of the October Revolution), Moscow.

6. For Buchan and Reuters, see *Reuter Service Bulletin* (Oct. 1923), pp. 17–18, 21–2; *Reuter Review*, Jan. 1938, p. 2; Susan Tweedsmuir, *John Buchan by his Wife and Friends* (1947), pp. 82–5; Jones, *A Life in Reuters*, pp. 7, 170, 189, 234, 263–4, 356; A. Lownie, *John Buchan, The Presbyterian Cavalier* (1995), pp. 155–6.

7. For Jeans, see *Reuter Service Bulletin* (June 1923), pp. 9–10; (Oct. 1923), pp. 2–4, 20.

8. For Rickatson-Hatt, see Hatt to Jones, 17 Feb. 1930 [typescript c.v.]; *World's Press News*, 31 Mar. 1932; Jones, *A Life in Reuters*, pp. 248–9; *The Times*, 9, 15 Aug. 1966; *Daily Express*, *Daily Telegraph*, 9 Aug. 1966; *Evening Standard*, *Guardian*, 10 Aug. 1966; G. Mant, *A Cuckoo in the Bodyline Nest* (Kenthurst, New South Wales, 1992), pp. 43–5.

9. For Murray, see *Reuters Review*, Jan. 1938, pp. 5–6, Apr. 1938, p. 31; Jones, *A Life in Reuters*, pp. 151–2.

10. For Carter, see Jones, *A Life in Reuters*, p. 357.

11. Lees-Milne, *Another Self*, pp. 122–31.

12. *Observer*, 24 Jan. 1932; J. Willis, *Restless Quest* (n.d.), ch. 15.

13. *UK Press Gazette*, 21 Nov. 1966; *Reuters News Letter*, Jan. 1970, pp. 15–17; *Reuters World*, Apr. 1984, pp. 24–5, Mar. 1991, p. 25; June 1994, p. 4; *The Times*, 28 Apr. 1997.

14. *Reuter Service Bulletin* (Oct. 1923), pp. 15–24.

15. Scott, *Reporter Anonymous*, pp. 211–12; Lees-Milne, *Another Self*, pp. 122–3, 125.

16. Jones, typescript, 'Note for Mr. Burgess', 22 Apr. 1931.

17. *Titbits*, 5 Aug. 1933; *Reuters World*, June 1983, pp. 14–15.

18. *Reuter Service Bulletin* (Jan. 1920), pp. 3–6; (Feb. 1921), p. 16; *Reuter Review*, May 1938, pp. 12–13.

19. For Fleetwood-May, see typescript 'Personal Reminiscences by Mr. Fleetwood-May for Mr. Graham Storey', 21 June 1950; *The Times*, 15 Oct. 1971.

20. C. Fleetwood-May, 'Reuters . . . in the days of codes and pirates', *UK Press Gazette*, 13 Sept. 1971, pp. 8–9.

21. 'Reuters' Wireless Services', *Post Office Electrical Engineers' Journal*, 39 (1946), pp. 1–5; R. Gough, 'How Radio Helped Spread the Written Word', *Reuters World*, Feb. 1985, pp. 12–13.

22. R. W. Desmond, The Information Process. *The Press and World Affairs* (New York, 1937), pp. 114–15, 121–2; Barty-King, *Girdle Round the Earth*, ch. 8.

23. Jones, *A Life in Reuters*, p. 383.

24. Ibid., pp. 451–2; *Reuters News Letter*, Nov. 1972, pp. 16–17.

25. For Jones's version, see his *A Life in Reuters*, chs. 19–25, 28–34.

26. Scott, *Reporter Anonymous*, pp. 209–10.

27. E. W. Davies, 'A Short History of the Press Association, Prepared for the Confidential Information of the Board of Directors by the General Manager', rev. 1960, typescript, pp. 15, 42–3.

28. K. Bickel to K. Cooper, 16 Jan. 1943 (Cooper MSS. 11, Manuscript Collections, Lilly Library, Indiana University) [I owe this reference to Professor Terhi Rantanen]; Jones, *A Life in Reuters*, ch. 35.

29. C. McNaught, *Canada Gets the News* (Toronto, 1940), chs. 5, 6.

30. Jones, *A Life in Reuters*, pp. 349–51.

31. *South African Press Association. 50 Years Service to the News Media, 1938–1988* (Johannesburg, 1988). For Jones's version, see his *A Life in Reuters*, chs. 41–3.

32. For Delany, see *Reuter Service Bulletin* (Aug. 1922), p. 31; Lord Wavell, *Allenby in Egypt* (1943), p. 6; Jones, *A Life in Reuters*, ch. 33; *The Times*, 15 June 1974.

33. *Reuters World*, Oct. 1990, pp. 6–9; June 1994, p. 42; Dec. 1994, p. 46.

34. For Moloney, see *Reuter Review*, May 1938, pp. 10–11; typescript, 'Autobiographical Note by W.J. Moloney', 11 July 1944; Jones, *A Life in Reuters*, pp. 282–3; *The Times*, 20 Feb. 1968; Chancellor's printed address on 'W. J. Moloney', for St Bride's, Fleet St., memorial service, 15 Mar. 1968.

35. *The Times*, 8 Sept. 1931; G. N. S. Raghavan, *PTI Story* (Bombay, 1987), pp. 53–61. For background, see M. Israel, *Communications and Power, Propaganda and the Press in the Indian Nationalist Struggle, 1920–1947* (Cambridge, 1994), esp. ch. 2.

36. *The Times*, 19 June 1970.

37. Dorothy Newman (ed.), *Nehru. The First Sixty Years* (1965), p. 631; *Selected Works of Jawaharlal Nehru* (New Delhi, 1972), i. 37.

38. For William Turner, see *Reuter Service Bulletin* (Sept. 1919), pp. 5–6; Jones, *A Life in Reuters*, pp. 268–9, 385–6, 452, 474; *The Times*, 11 June 1965.

39. Jones, *A Life in Reuters*, pp. 377–81.

40. Ibid., pp. 385–6, 452, 474–5. For Chancellor, see also H. Cudlipp, *At Your Peril* (1962), pp. 10, 133, chs. 20–3; *Dictionary of Business Biography*, vol. 1 (1984), pp. 656–61; *The Times, Daily Telegraph, Independent*, 11 Sept. 1989; Harriet Sargeant, *Shanghai* (1991), ch. 4; D. Read, 'Sir Christopher Chancellor', *Dictionary of National Biography, 1986–1990* (1996), pp. 65–6.

41. Managing Director's Tour 1923–1924, Report No. 1, typescript.

42. Typescript minute, 'Special Meeting of the Board, June 20, 1933'; Kent Cooper, *Barriers Down* (New York, 1942), p. 9 and *passim*; Jones, *A Life in Reuters*, chs. 35–6; S. Iwanaga, *Story of Japanese News Agencies* (Tokyo, 1980), pp. 39–40, 42–3.

43. Scott, *Reporter Anonymous*, pp. 213–14; Iwanaga, *Japanese News Agencies*, pp. 54–6.

44. Cooper, *Barriers Down*, p. 247; Jones, *A Life in Reuters*, p. 389.

CHAPTER EIGHT

The Decline and Fall of Roderick Jones, 1934–1941

1. Jones, *A Life in Reuters*, chs. 39–40; Scott, *Reporter Anonymous*, pp. 200–1.

2. *Reuter Review*, June 1938, pp. 12–13; Apr. 1939, pp. 1–2. 11, 23; *Builder*, 12 Jan. 1940, pp. 43–7; *Architects' Journal*, 27 Mar. 1941, pp. 208–12; A. S. C. Butler, *The Architecture of Edwin Lutyens* (1950), iii. 33–4; N. Pevsner, *The Buildings of England, London*, vol. 1 (3rd edn., 1973), p. 356.

3. *Picture Post*, 13 Jan. 1940.

4. For Storey, see T. G. Moore, 'Our President—The Lord Buckton', 11 Oct. 1976, typescript; *The Times*, 19, 21 Jan. 1978. Storey's son, Sir Richard Storey, has most helpfully allowed me to use his father's relevant papers, even though our respective interpretations of some events and personalities differ significantly; for Sir Richard's view, see his careful analysis in a long letter to me, 24 Apr. 1996, copy in Reuters Archive.

5. For Haley, see *The Times, Guardian*, 8 Sept. 1987; *Dictionary of National Biography, 1986–1990* (1996), pp. 175–6. Haley's son, Donald, has kindly provided diary transcripts and other material, which I have used without restriction.

6. For Ewing, see *Glasgow Weekly Herald*, 26 May 1934; *The Times*, 29 Jan., 1960 [anonymous obituary by Haley].

7. F.O. 395/527.536; 595/46.

8. CAB 24/273, CP 301 (37); CAB 27/641 (37); F.O. 395/576; Jones, *A Life in Reuters*, ch. 45; Taylor, *Projection of Britain*, pp. 66–8, 208–11.

9. T 161 1036 S433550/2.

10. Jones, *A Life in Reuters*, pp. 474–5.

11. *Manchester Guardian* papers (John Rylands Manchester University Library).

12. T 161 1037 S433550/7.
13. Ibid. For the MOI background, see I. McClaine, *Ministry of Morale* (1979).
14. Jones, *A Life in Reuters*, pp. 464–5.
15. *Manchester Guardian* papers.
16. Jones, *A Life in Reuters*, pp. 491–2.
17. S. Underhill, typescript recollections, p. 147; Sebba, *Enid Bagnold*, pp. 131, 183.

CHAPTER NINE

News between the Wars, 1919–1939

1. For Bailey and BUP, see *The Times*, 20 Mar. 1939; *Newspaper World, The Press, 1898–1948* (1948), p. 104.
2. V. Bartlett, *This is My Life* (1937), pp. 62–6.
3. *Reuter Service Bulletin* (Sept. 1919), pp. 5–9; *Lord Riddell's Intimate Diary of the Peace Conference and After, 1918–1923* (1933), pp. 101–2; Bartlett, *My Life*, pp. 71–4.
4. H. Nicolson, *Some People* (1927), pp. 187–8.
5. *Reuter Service Bulletin* (Oct. 1923), p. 14; Jones, *A Life in Reuters*, p. 268.
6. *Reuter Service Bulletin* (June 1923), pp. 18–19; Williams, *World of Action*, ch. 26.
7. *The Times*, 22 Sept. 1931.
8. R28/169; R28/154/1 (BBC Written Archives, Caversham); F.O. 395/552; A. Briggs, *The Birth of Broadcasting* (1961), pp. 130–3, 172–4, 215, 262–7; and *The Golden Age of Wireless* (1965), 153, 372, 377, 383.
9. F.O. 395/578.
10. For Fleming and Reuters, see E. Lyons, *Assignment to Utopia* (1938), ch. 14; H. A. Zeiger, *Ian Fleming* (New York, 1965), pp. 30–61; J. Pearson, *Life of Ian Fleming* (1966), pp. 58–71; A. Lycett, *Ian Fleming* (1995), pp. 46–56, 62–3, 72–3.
11. R. Cockett, *Twilight of Truth, Chamberlain, Appeasement and the Manipulation of the Press* (1989), p. 17
12. Jones, *A Life in Reuters*, ch. 27; Sebba, *Enid Bagnold*, pp. 129–30.
13. K. Dickins, 'With Hitler in Munich', *London Magazine*, 35 (1995), pp. 40–1.
14. For Collins, see his typescript recollections; *The Times*, 23 Oct. 1956.
15. K. Anderson, typescript recollections, pp. 88, 173–4.
16. Williams, *World of Action*, pp. 62–3.
17. G. Orwell, *Collected Essays, Journalism and Letters* (1970), iii. 196.
18. For Holme, see *The Times*, 13 July 1991; C. Holme, 'The Reporter at Guernica', *British Journalism Review*, 6 (1995), pp. 46–51. Holme's poetry, including his poem on Guernica, was collected in *Portrait* (priv. printed, Oxford, 1992).
19. *Newspaper World*, 1 Aug. 1936.
20. For Barnes, see his autobiographies, *Half a Life* (1933) and *Half a Life Left* (1937); *The Times*, 29 Aug. 1955; King's College, Cambridge, *Annual Report, 1955*, pp. 2–3. For background, see R. Griffiths, *Fellow Travellers of the Right* (1980), ch. 1.

21. F.O. 395/533.
22. Barnes, *Half a Life Left*, chs. 16–17.
23. Ibid., pp. 185–9.
24. Ibid., pp. 254–6.
25. Knightley, *First Casualty*, pp. 206–9; Lefebure, *Havas*, p. 250.
26. C. Holme, 'The night the world ended', *Herald* (Edinburgh), 26 Apr. 1997. For a detailed analysis, see H. R. Southworth, *Guernica! Guernica!* (1977); for background, see H. Buckley, *Life and Death of the Spanish Republic* (1940).
27. For Sheepshanks, see *The Times*, 3, 4, 10 Jan. 1938; *Reuter Review*, Apr. 1938, pp. 5, 12–17; June 1938, p. 7; Nov. 1938, p. 14.
28. F.O. 371/21301.
29. C. Andrew and G. Gordievsky, *KGB* (1991), pp. 232–5; G. Borovnik (ed.), *The Philby Files* (1994), ch. 8.
30. For Clifford, see *Reuter Review*, Apr. 1938, p. 27; *Daily Mail*, 14 Mar. 1952; *The Times*, 15, 28 Mar. 1952.
31. F.O. 395/577; 'Report by Mr. A. T. Priest for Wireless Manager. Reuterian, Globereut and Globereuter Press', 22 Feb. 1940, typescript; Taylor, *Projection of Britain*, pp. 210–11.
32. 'Note by the Secretary, Report for Sir Roderick Jones, Hitler's Speech', 13 Sept. 1938, typescript.
33. 'How Reuter Covered The Crisis', *Reuter Review*, Nov. 1938, pp. 2–8.
34. E. W. Swanton, *Follow On* (1977), ch. 10; Mant, *Cuckoo in the Bodyline Nest*, esp. ch. 4, pp. 57, 96, 129.
35. Lord Birkenhead, *Walter Monckton* (1969), p. 128; P. Ziegler, *King Edward VIII* (1990), p. 278.
36. Ibid., pp. 367–8, 382–3.

CHAPTER TEN

War News, 1939–1956

1. For background, see Rear-Admiral G. P. Thomson, *Blue Pencil Admiral, The Inside Story of the Press Censorship* (n.d.).
2. Orwell, *Collected Essays*, ii. 138; P. M. Taylor, *Munitions of the Mind* (Manchester, 1995), pp. 213–14.
3. Hatt to Jones, 'Conference at Home Office', typescript, 30 Aug. 1939; 'Second Agency Conference at Home Office', typescript, 31 Aug. 1939; Viscount Templewood, *Nine Troubled Years* (1954), p. 392; Cockett, *Twilight of Truth*, pp. 119–20.
4. 'Memorandum by Mr. W. J. Haley', typescript, 16 July 1942, pp. 2, 5.
5. G. Young, *Outposts of War* (1941), ch. 3. A photocopy of Tighe's wartime diary is in the Reuters Archive.
6. For Sale, see *The Times*, 1, 2, 13 Oct. 1943.

7. A. Christiansen to Lord Beaverbrook, 28 Aug. 1942 (BBK H 112, House of Lords Record Office); A. E. Barker, 'Agency Monitoring of Radio News and Talks', typescript, 12 Feb. 1945 (R28/152/3, BBC Written Archives).

8. G. Imeson to D. Read, 1 Mar. 1991.

9. For King, see G. Waterfield, *What Happened to France* (1940), pp. 119–21, 137–8; *World's Press News*, 16 July 1942; *Newspaper World*, 9 Jan. 1943; King, typescript recollections, 'Chasing the News', photocopy in Reuters Archive; *Guardian*, 26 Sept. 1990; *The Times*, 27 Sept., 11 Oct. 1990; *Independent*, 12 Oct. 1990; *Reuters World*, Nov. 1990, p. 18.

10. King, 'Chasing the News', pp. 155–7; E. Radzinsky, *Stalin* (1997), p. 480.

11. King, 'Chasing the News', pp. 150–1; *Independent* 12 Oct. 1990.

12. For Humphreys, see *Reuters News Letter*, June 1973, pp. 27–8; *Reuters World*, June 1992, p. 20.

13. Orwell, *Collected Essays*, ii. 502–3. For background, see Knightley, *The First Casualty*, pp. 317–20; C. Buckley, *Norway, The Commandos, Dieppe* (1977), esp. pp. 264–5.

14. For Campbell, see his typescript recollections, photocopy in Reuters Archive.

15. For Maynes, see *Irish News*, 26 Mar. 1945; *Evening News*, 7 June 1969; *Irish Times*, 19 Feb. 1991; *The Times*, 18 Aug. 1998.

16. For Lynch, see his recollections, *You Can't Print That!* (Toronto, 1988).

17. Editorial Report, 'Reuters and the Second Front', typescript, n.d.

18. *Salisbury Times*, 16 June 1944; Campbell, typescript recollections, p. 79; Lynch, *You Can't Print That!*, pp. 54–7.

19. *Daily Telegraph*, 17 Aug. 1994; Lynch, *You Can't Print That!*, pp. 67–9.

20. Maynes to Mason, 2 Mar. 1951; *Daily Telegraph*, 4 Jan. 1991.

21. *Reuters Review*, May 1977, pp. 6–7, 21–3.

22. F.O. 371/24738; F.O. 371/24740; *The Times*, 30 July 1940; *Nippon Shuhe*, 15 Oct. 1954; Norman Macswan, *The Man Who Read the East Wind. A Biography of Richard Hughes* (Kenthurst, New South Wales, 1983), pp. 32–3; P. Elphick, *Far Eastern File. The Intelligence War in the Far East* (1997), pp. 187–8, 249–50.

23. L. Walters, 'Government Arrangements', 2 July 1941, typescript. For Graham-Barrow, see *Reuters World*, Aug. 1993, p. 28.

24. Carter to Messrs. Douglas Cox, Tyrie & Co. Ltd., 4, 22 Oct. 1945. For background, see G. Mant, *The Singapore Surrender* (Kenthurst, New South Wales, 1992).

25. Reuter circular, 'Sent to Trade Papers', 30 Oct. 1944, typescript.

26. Warner Brothers archives (University of Southern California, Los Angeles); film scripts by Valentine Williams and Milton Krims (Reuters Archive).

CHAPTER ELEVEN

'In the Nature of a Trust', 1941–1963

1. T 161 1037 S433550/7.
2. *Manchester Guardian* papers (John Rylands Manchester University Library).
3. I. McLaine, *Ministry of Morale. Home Front Morale and the Ministry of Information in World War II* (1979), pp. 239–41.
4. *Press Association Ltd., Report of the Extaordinary General Meeting Held at the Chief Offices . . . Friday, October 17, 1941*; Scott, *Reporter Anonymous*, pp. 224–9.
5. R 28/166 (BBC Written Archives, Caversham).
6. H. S. Underhill, 'Notes of conversation with G. Long of Reuters in London, Jan. 1976', handwritten photocopy.
7. 'Note for Mr. H. L. Howarth, Chairman of the Press Association, from Sir Christopher Chancellor, The Management of Reuters', typescript, 19 Feb. 1959. p. 1; *Independent*, 11 Sept. 1989.
8. F.O. 953/117; Lord Hartwell to N.L. Judah, 7 June 1989.
9. For Cole, see *The Times, Guardian, Scotsman, Chicago Daily Tribune*, 26 Jan. 1963; *Observer*, 27 Jan. 1963; Underhill, typescript recollections, pp. 149–51, 188; S. Gall, *Don't Worry About the Money Now* (1984), pp. 11–12, 105–6, 108, 175; D. Jameson, *Touched by Angels* (1989), pp. 96–8, 150, 152–3.
10. Gall, *Don't Worry*, p. 12.
11. T. Little to J. Burgess, 28 Jan. 1963.
12. Underhill, typescript recollections, pp. 46, 53–4.
13. 'Joint Standing Committee of Reuters and the Ministry of Information, Draft Minutes . . . 27th Jan. 1941', typescript, enclosing 'Note for Sub-Committee on Inclusion of Enemy Communiques'.
14. 'Meeting between the Reuter Board and Mr. Cyril Radcliffe, Director-General of the Ministry of Information, Jan. 27', typescript.
15. F.O. 953/117.
16. F.O. 371/36612.
17. F.O. 371/46022/2597.
18. F.O. 953/117; F.O. 953/118.
19. F.O. 395/417; F.O. 395/425; F.O. 395/434; F.O. 395/467; F.O. 395/645.
20. F.O. 371/30506; F.O. 371/33896; F.O.371/38195; F.O. 371/45010; F.O. 953/117; F.O. 953/118; F.O. 953/1898; F.O. 953/1954; G. Storey, *Reuters' Century, 1851–1951* (1951), p. 238; J. H. Henry, 'Reuters in Latin America', typescript.
21. For Cooper's version, see *Barriers Down*, chs. 31, 33.
22. *Chicago Daily Tribune*, 16 Feb. 1945; F.O. 953/1165.
23. Underhill, typescript recollections, pp. 100–3, 159–63.
24. Cooper, *Barriers Down*, p. 309.
25. *Time*, 11 Feb. 1946; C. Chancellor to J. R. Scott, 25 Mar. 1946 *(Manchester Guardian* papers); Storey, *Reuters' Century*, p. 250.

26. W. J. Haley, 'Mission to Australia (Dec. 1942–May 1943)', typescript.

27. 'Mr. [Cromarty] Bloom's report on Shanghai', typescript in board minutes 4 Nov. 1942.

28. G. Cromarty Bloom, 'Memorandum on Far Eastern Outports, October 14 1942', typescript.

29. C. Chancellor, *How Reuters Did Its Job Right Through The War* (reprinted from *World's Press News*, 13 Dec., 1945). pp. 5–10; E. Edbrooke to J. Entwisle, 15 Dec. 1985, enclosing T. H. Stockwell, typescript note, 29 Oct. 1964.

30. H. Martin to W. J. Haley, 25 June 1941, enclosure (*Manchester Guardian* papers).

31. For Mason, see *Managing Editor's Review*, 28 Apr. 1965; Underhill, typescript recollections, pp. 148–9, 156; Jameson, *Touched By Angels*, p. 99.

32. J. P[igg], 'Reuters Editorial Headquarters', 7 May 1946, typescript; *Royal Commission on the Press, Evidence*, 18th day (21 Jan. 1948), Cmd. 7379, questions 5806–15.

33. 'Reuters Editorial', typescript board paper, Jan. 1961; Underhill, typescript recollections, pp. 161–2; Jameson, *Touched by Angels*, pp. 151–4.

34. F.O. 371/41899; Storey, *Reuters' Century*, pp. 241–3.

35. F.O. 371/49094; F.O. 953/117; F.O. 953/118; *World's Press News*, 21 July 1949. For background, see H. Pigeat, *Nouveau désordre mondial de l'information* (Paris, 1987); J. Turnstall and M. Palmer, *Media Moguls* (1991), pp. 69–84; and J. Huteau and B. Ullmann, *A.F.P. une histoire de l'Agence France-Presse, 1944–1990* (Paris, 1992).

36. For Geiringer, see *The Times*, 10 Jan. 1996 [anonymous obituary by Nelson].

37. G. Long to D. Read, 6–13 Oct. 1989.

38. Jameson, *Touched by Angels*, p. 154.

39. Note by E. Edbrooke, Mar. 1989.

40. *Royal Commission on the Press*, qu. 5772.

41. F. Williams, *Transmitting World News* (Paris, 1953), pp. 43–5; 'Reuter Communications', typescript board paper, Nov. 1960.

42. Chancellor-Henderson correspondence (*Sydney Morning Herald* Archive, Box 200); Storey, *Reuters' Century*, pp. 252–6; G. Souter, *Company of Heralds* (Sydney, 1981), pp. 275–9; Lyall Rowe, typescript interviews with Chancellor (10 June 1983) and Henderson (18 June 1984). For the New Zealand view, see Sanders, *Dateline NZPA*, ch. 12.

43. For a Reuter overview, see 'Note by the General Manager, India—The History of the negotiations', typescript. For the Indian side, see V. K. Narasimhan, *Kasturi Srinivasan* (Bombay, 1969), chs. 12–13; and Raghavan, *PTI Story*, ch. 4, appendix 2.

44. Storey, *Reuters' Century*, pp. 258–63.

45. F.O. 953/117.

46. Janet Morgan (ed.), *The Backbench Diaries of Richard Crossman* (1981), p. 519; P. M. Williams (ed.), *The Diary of Hugh Gaitskell, 1945–1956* (1983), pp. 495–6; *Independent*, 11 Sept. 1989.

47. 'Note for Mr. H. L. Howarth, Chairman of the Press Association, from Sir Christopher Chancellor, The Management of Reuters', 19 Feb. 1959, typescript, p. 2.

48. For the Indian view, see Raghavan, *PTI Story*, pp. 102–18; for the Pakistani view, see M. Tajuddin, *Foundation of Associated Press of Pakistan* (Islamabad, 1952).

49. Narasimhan, *Kasturi Srinivisan*, pp. 109–11.

50. Raghavan, *PTI Story*, p. 8.

51. D.O. 35/5278; Gall, *Don't Worry*, pp. 28–31; D. Friedmann, typescript recollections, vol. 9, pp. 80–96.

52. Underhill, typescript recollections, p. 152.

53. For Jenkins, see J. Lawrenson and L. Barber, *The Price of Truth. The Story of the Reuters Millions* (1986), pp. 101–3; *Reuters World*, June 1997, p. 44.

54. For background, see *Comtelburo, Reuters Commercial Service* (1963); and 'Michael Nelson on the Development of Reuters, 1952–1989', Science Museum interview, 3 July 1989, transcript.

55. H. Lindley to Scott, 24 July 1957; Scott to Burgess, 29 July 1957; C. Chancellor to L. P. Scott, 6 Jan. 1959; King to Scott, 10 Jan. 1959 (*Manchester Guardian Archive*).

56. For Burgess, see *The Times*, 12 Feb. 1987.

57. For an overview, see Secretary [Judah] to General Manager [Long], 'BBC', 19 Mar. 1968, typescript.

58. For the Arab News Agency, see R. J. Fletcher, 'British Propaganda since World War II—A Case study', *Media, Culture and Society*, 4 (1982), pp. 97–109.

59. *Manchester Guardian* papers.

60. F.O. 953/2043.

61. For Crosse, see *Independent*, 22 June 1993; *The Times*, 25 June 1993; *Reuters World*, Aug. 1993, pp. 27–8; *Patrick Crosse 1916–1993, Recollections of a Very Special Man* (priv. printed, 1993).

62. Lawrenson and Barber, *Price of Truth*, pp. 107–8.

CHAPTER TWELVE

The Coming of the Reuter Monitor, 1963–1981

1. *Evening Standard*, 6 Mar. 1995.

2. J. Burgess to Sir W. Carr, 8 Feb. 1963; J. Burgess to R. R. Gleave, 8 Feb. 1963 (Burgess papers, DB 20/312, Cumbria Record Office, Carlisle).

3. For Long, see Underhill, typescript recollections, pp. 199–205; *Reuters News*, Feb. 1981, p. 3; K. Bringmann, '1946 Neuanfang: Leben in Düsseldorf' (Düsseldorf, 1986), pp. 224–5; H. Evans, *Good Times, Bad Times* (1983), esp. ch. 9; B. Mooney, typescript recollections, pp. 81–2, 114–17.

4. For retrospects by Long, see G. Long to Sir D. Hamilton, 24 Mar. 1981; G. Long to D. Read, 18 June 1990, enclosing typescript 'Notes on an Interview with

Michael Nelson on the development of Reuters, recorded at the Science Museum'; G. Long, 'Reuters & the British Government: The Question of Editorial Independence', *Intermedia*, 21/3 (1993), pp. 4–6; and G. Long to S. Somerville, 16 Nov. 1994, enclosing 'Reuters 1963–81: A Case History', typescript lecture.

5. For Judah, see G. Long to J. Burgess, 18 July 1967; *Reuters World*, July 1991, p. 22.

6. For Stockwell, see *Guardian*, 11 July 1989; G. Long, 'Brian Stockwell and Staff Policy in Reuters, 1963–1975', 15 July 1989, typescript; *Reuters World*, Aug. 1989, p. 14.

7. Associated Industrial Consultants Limited, 'Report No. 1, Head Office Location, Review of Staff Employment Considerations', Dec. 1969, typescript, p. 56.

8. NATSOPA, *Journal and Graphic Review*, Dec. 1974, pp. 1, 3; 'Minutes of Meeting with NGA Telegraphic Chapel Committee on 7 Mar. 1975', typescript; ibid., 3 Apr. 1975.

9. G. Long, 'Notes for an Address on: World-Wide Communications—The Role of the Press', 30 Apr. 1966, typescript; G. Long, 'Speech to Young Newspapermen's Association at Waldorf Hotel', 1 May 1969, typescript.

10. *Reuters World*, Aug. 1993, pp. 20–1; Dec. 1994, p. 5.

11. B. Horton, 'Reuter World Services, 1967–1973', 5 Dec. 1973, typescript; B. Horton to D. Read, 11 Dec. 1992; 27 Aug. 1993; *Reuters World*, Aug. 1993, pp. 20–1.

12. For Nelson, see Underhill, typescript recollections, pp. 212–13; *Reuters World*, May 1989, p. 18; 'Michael Nelson on the Development of Reuters, 1952–1989', Science Museum interview, 3 July 1989, transcript.

13. For Renfrew, see *Reuters News Letter*, Jan 1970, p. 24; *Wall Street Computer Review*, July 1988, p. 69; *Reuters World*, Mar. 1991, pp. 10–11, 28.

14. For the history of Stockmaster, see Nelson to Underhill, 3 Nov. 1976; 'Nelson on the Development of Reuters', pp. 12–19, 46–8; G. Renfrew, 'Notes on the Joint Venture', 'Persuading the P.T.T.s', 'The Battle of the Bourses', 25 Oct. 1991, typescripts. For background, see J. Fenby, *The International News Services* (New York, 1986), pp. 109–18; and Tunstall and Palmer, *Media Moguls*, ch. 3

15. For Taylor, see J. Ransom to D. Read, 19 May 1989.

16. For the history of Monitor, see *Reuters World*, Nov. 1981, pp. 1–5; M. Neale, 'The Reuter Monitor—The First Ten Years', 7 June 1983, typescript; 'Nelson on the Development of Reuters', pp. 20–30.

17. J. C. Parcell to D. G. Ure, 'Monitor Profit, 1973–83', 6 June 1983, typescript.

18. D. Bell, 'Communications Technology—For Better or For Worse', *Harvard Business Review*, May–June 1979, p. 22; 'Nelson on the Development of Reuters', p. 53.

19. *Financial Times*, 23 Feb. 1982; *Reuter Alert*, May 1984.

20. *FX Weekly*, 28 June 1991.

CHAPTER THIRTEEN

Achieving Worldwide Presence, 1963–1981

1. For Barnetson and Reuters, see G. Long to Sir D. Hamilton, 24 Mar. 1981; G. Long to R. Murdoch, 11 Oct. 1983; *Dictionary of National Biography, 1981–1985* (1990), pp. 27–8.
2. *Reuters News Letter*, May 1969, pp. 1–2; *Reuters Review*, Dec. 1976, pp. 16–17; Oct. 1977, pp. 11–12; Dec. 1979, p. 1.
3. P. Job, 'Reuters in Latin America, 1958–75', Oct. 1975, typescript; Lawrenson and Barber, *The Price of Truth*, pp. 106–7; Fenby, *International News Services*, pp. 206–12; Mooney, typescript recollections, ch. 2.
4. 'Nelson on the Development of Reuters', pp. 40–2. See esp. Long's retrospective board paper, 26 July 1968, typescript.
5. S. Underhill to G. Long, 24 Feb. 1967.
6. Underhill, typescript recollections, pp. 214–24.
7. J. W. Heffernan, 'Washington, Profile of a Bureau', *Reuters News Letter*, Apr. 1974, pp. 5–12.
8. *United States District Court, Southern District of New York, Robert Nagel, Plaintiff against Reuters Limited . . .* [New York, 1977].
9. 'Nelson on the Development of Reuters', pp. 30–3.
10. *Reuters World*, Nov. 1981, p. 1.
11. *Reuters News Letter*, June 1974, p. 14; D. F. Renwick, 'Guild Negotiations', 12 Sept. 1977, typescript; D. F. Renwick, 'Status of Guild Negotiations', 5 Mar. 1980, typescript; G. Renfrew, 'The Newspaper Guild of New York', Sept. 1980, typescript.
12. A. Kellett-Long, 'A New Reuter Service', *Reuters News Letter*, Dec. 1971, pp. 7–9; *Reuters World*, Apr. 1990, p. 19.
13. 'Memorandum by Reuters for the VWD Negotiating Committee', 27 June 1973, typescript; M. Pagel, 'RES in Germany', *Reuters News Letter*, Feb. 1974, pp. 3–4; *Financial Times*, 15 July 1980; *Frankfurter Allgemeine Zeitung*, 15 July 1980.
14. For the Indian view, see 'Foreign News, Feature and Other Services, Evolution of Policy 1947–1956', prepared for the Second Press Commission, 15 Oct. 1980, typescript; and Raghavan, *PTI Story*, pp. 116–17, 151.
15. K. Garry, 'Reuters and the Australian Associated Press', Oct. 1962, typescript; G. Long, 'Note to a Committee of the "A" and "B" Shareholders of the Reuter Board', 7 Apr. 1965, typescript; G. Long, 'Background Notes for Talks with the AAP', Dec. 1965, typescript; 'Notes of a Meeting to Discuss the AAP-Reuter Agreement of 1947' typescript.
16. A-F. H. Villeneuve, 'Pacific Board', 14 Mar. 1979, typescript.
17. For background, see Elaine Potter, *The Press as Opposition. The Political Role of South African Newspapers* (1975).
18. Gall, *Don't Worry*, pp. 106–11.

19. 'Reuters Help to National News Agencies of Non-Industrial Countries since 1958', [1979], typescript.
20. Fenby, *International News Services*, ch. 10. For background, see A. Smith, The *Geopolitics of Information* (1980); A van Dijk, *News Analysis, Case Studies of International and National News in the Press* (Hillsdale, NJ), 1988; O. Boyd-Barrett, *Contra-flow in Global News* (1992); and M. D. Alleyne, *News Revolution. Political and Economic Decisions about Global Information* (1997).
21. F.O. 953/2043. For discussion of relations betweeen Reuters and the British Government, see O. Boyd-Barrett, 'Subsidy and the Power of Reuters', *Intermedia*, 21/2 (1993), pp. 41–3; and G. Long, 'Reuters and the British Government: The Question of Editorial Independence', 21/3 (1993), pp. 4–6.
22. G. Hanson to Justine Taylor, 'FCO Renegotiation, 1985/6', 14 June 1991, typescript.
23. *Evening Standard*, 23 Jan. 1976; *The Times*, 30 Jan. 1976.
24. *Financial Times*, 5 Sept. 1994.
25. For Reupke, see 'Reuter profile number 1: Michael Reupke', *Byline*, 2nd quarter 1988, p. 4. For the Media Study, see Reupke's typescript notes for D. Read, 17 Nov. 1989.
26. Mooney, typescript recollections, pp. 74, 118.
27. *Reuters World*, Jan. 1983, p. 19.
28. *Reuters Review*, Feb. 1981, pp. 3, 6–7; Mooney, typescript recollections, pp. 114–17.
29. *Daily Mail*, 19 May 1984.

CHAPTER FOURTEEN

Going Public, 1981–1984

1. *Reuters Review*, Feb. 1981, pp. 3, 6–7.
2. G. Gordon and R. E. Cohen, *Down to the Wire. UPI's Fight for Survival* (New York 1990), pp. 47–8, 119–20, 166–9.
3. J. Crawley, 'The History of Visnews', Mar. 1977, typescript; A. Stanbrook, 'Today's News Today', *Sight & Sound*, winter 1986–7, pp. 24–9; *Broadcast*, 8 Oct. 1993.
4. *Evening Standard*, 6 Mar. 1995.
5. Raghavan, *PTI Story*, p. 151.
6. 'Nelson on the Development of Reuters', p. 34.
7. M. E. Nelson, 'Executive "E" Share Scheme', 22 Feb. 1984, typescript; *Reuters World*, Feb. 1985, p. 3.
8. For extensive documentation relating to the flotation, see the affidavits and other material collected in 1991–2 for the New South Wales tax appeal case between Reuters Investments (Australia) Pty. Limited [formerly the Australian Associated Press] and the Commissioner of Taxation. A book by J. Lawrenson and

L. Barber, *The Price of Truth, The Story of the Reuters Millions* (1985; rev. 1986) was an interim account from a former Reuter journalist, written without access to the above.

9. For Hamilton, see Evans, *Good Times, Bad Times*, esp. pp. 13–15; J. Grigg, *The History of The Times, The Thomson Years, 1966–1981* (1993), esp. pp. 6–11, 74–5, 166–8. Hamilton's recollections were published posthumously: *Editor-in-Chief* (1989).

10. On Murdoch and Reuters, see W. Shawcross, *Rupert Murdoch* (1992), pp. 47, 68, 237–40, 301, 320; R. Belfield *et al.*, *Murdoch. The Great Escape* (1994), pp. 74–6, 245, 284–7.

11. Lawrenson and Barber, *Price of Truth*, p. 127.

12. G. Long to R. Murdoch, 11 Oct., 28 Nov. 1983; 31 May 1984.

13. Lawrenson and Barber, *Price of Truth*, pp. 152–3; G. Taylor, *Changing Faces. A History of the Guardian, 1956–1988* (1993), pp. 295–8.

CHAPTER FIFTEEN

The World's News, 1945–1989

1. D. Campbell, 'Life in the World's Trouble Spots', *Inky Way Annual, 1947–48*, p. 131; Lynch, *You Can't Print That!*, p. 86.

2. G. Long to Lord Nicholas Gordon Lennox, 8 Dec. 1980; Editorial Report, July 1985, typescript; I. Macdowall, *Reuters Handbook for Journalists* (1992), pp. 147–8.

3. *Royal Commission on the Press*, qu. 5766.

4. Jameson, *Touched by Angels*, pp. 120–2.

5. *Literary Gazette*, 25 Aug. 1950, article by Peet, translated (F.O. 371/85097). For Peet, see *Daily Telegraph*, 2 July 1988; *Independent*, 6 July 1988; and his book, *The Long Engagement* (1989).

6. Peet, *Long Engagement*, p. 13 For background, see W. Bassow, *The Moscow Correspondents* (New York, 1988).

7. Bassow, *Moscow Correspondents*, pp. 179–80; *Moscow News*, 28 (1990), p. 16; 31 (1990), p. 16; G. Rettie to D. Read, 17 Feb. 1993.

8. D. Chapman, 'Berlin Border Closed!', *Reuters World*, Dec. 1988, pp. 12–13.

9. J. W. Heffernan to J. Entwisle, 6 July 1989; I. Macdowall to D. Read, 29 May 1990.

10. F.O. 371/177731.

11. F. L. Mott, *American Journalism, A History: 1690–1960* (3rd edn., New York, 1967), ch. 54.

12. For Chipp in China, see G. Searls, 'The Hong Kong Outpost', *New Republic*, 8 Apr. 1957, pp. 11–13; *Editor & Publisher*, 17 Aug. 1957, p. 12; E. J. Kahn, Jr., 'The Wayward Press, Waiting', *New Yorker*, 30 Nov. 1957, pp. 156–63.

13. For Grey, see his books: *Hostage in Peking* (1970); *A Man Alone* (1971); *Crosswords from Peking* (1975).

14. For Joannides, see his letter to Justine Taylor, 26 Aug. 1992, with enclosures (Reuters Archive).

15. For Maynes and others, see S. Gall, *Don't Worry About the Money Now* (1982), ch. 2; R. MacNeill, *The Right Place at the Right Time* (New York, 1990), pp. 30–5.

16. F.O. 371/121785; K.O. Morgan, *The People's Peace* (1992), pp. 150–1.

17. See. H. Lunn, *Vietnam. A Reporter's War* (St Lucia, Queensland, 1985). For Phan Xuan An, see M. Safer, *Flashbacks. On Returning to Vietnam* (New York, 1990), ch. 23; S. Karnow, 'Vietnamese Journalist's Divided Allegiance', *San Francisco Chronicle*, 30 May 1990; *Reuters World*, Aug. 1993, pp. 22–3; *International Herald Tribune*, 29 Apr., 1997.

18. For background, see F. Palmos, *Ridding the Devils* (Sydney, 1990).

19. For King in Paris, see E. Behr, *Anyone Here Been Raped and Speaks English?* (1981), pp. 85–7; *Guardian*, 26 Sept. 1990; *The Times*, 27 Sept.; 11 Oct. 1990; *Independent*, 12 Oct. 1990; Long on King, typescript for *Reuters World*, 9 Oct. 1990; *Reuters World*, Nov.1990, p. 18.

20. King, 'Chasing the News', pp. 248–71.

21. *UK Press Gazette*, 22 July 1985; Campbell, typescript recollections, pp. 152–76.

22. G. Ratzin to D. Read, 3 June 1991.

23. L. R. Sussman, 'Dying (and Being Killed) on the Job: A Case Study of World Journalists, 1982–1989', *Journalism Quarterly*, 68 (1991), pp. 195–9; M. D. Alleyne, *News Revolution, Political and Economic Decisions about Global Information* (1997), ch. 6.

24. S. Gall, 'The Bakwanga Incident', typescript, 15 Sept. 1960; Gall, *Don't Worry*, pp. 93–102; *Reuters World*, June 1997, p. 44.

25. *Highlights*, Dec. 1987, p. 3; *Jerusalem Post*, 24 Mar. 1995.

26. G. M. Williams, 'Falklands Crisis - Relations with M.O.D.', 22 Apr. 1982, typescript; *Reuters World*, June 1982, p. 20; Sept. 1982, pp. 4–7. For background, see D. Mercer *et al.*, *The Fog of War. The Media on the Battlefield* (1987).

27. For Jackson and Everest, see Jesus College, Cambridge, *Alumni News*, 1994. For background, see I. McDonald, *History of The Times*, vol. 5, *Struggles in War and Peace, 1939–1966* (1984), pp. 237–41.

28. R. Cooper, 'The Olympics—When Sports Reporters Became War Correspondents', *Reuters News Letter*, Sept. 1972, pp. 2–5.

29. 'The Shock Heard Round the World', *Reuter Business Report*, 14–21 Oct. 1987; *Highlights*, Dec. 1987, pp. 1–3.

30. 'Berlin Wall: Reuters from start to finish', *Byline*, 4th quarter 1989, p. 1; 'Opening the Curtain', *Byline*, 1st quarter 1990, pp. 1–4; *Highlights*, Jan.1990, pp. 1–5; *The Wall Comes Down*. Reuters videotape (1990).

31. *Reuters World*, July 1989, pp. 4–5; P. Eedle, 'Covering China's "Overwhelming moment of history" ', *Highlights*, Aug. 1989, p. 2.

CHAPTER SIXTEEN

Retrospect, 1849–1989

1. *Forbes*, 30 Oct. 1989, p. 146. See also W. B. Wriston, *The Twilight of Soveriegnty. How the Information Revolution is Transforming Our World* (New York, 1992).
2. A. Smith, 'The Long Road to Objectivity and Back Again: The Kinds of Truth We Get in Journalism', in G. Boyce *et al.* (eds.), *Newspaper History* (1978), pp. 153–71; A. Smith, *The Politics of Information. Problems of Policy in Modern Media* (1978), ch. 11; D. McQuail, *Mass Communication Theory* (2nd edn., 1991), pp. 130–2.
3. *Management Today*, July 1985.
4. *Reuters World*, Nov. 1988, p. 5; *UKI Herald*, Dec. 1996, p. 1.
5. O. Boyd-Barrett and M. Palmer, *Le Trafic des nouvelles. les agences mondiales d'information* (Paris, 1981), pp. 90, 688; Fenby, *The International News Services*, pp. 73, 123; M. D. Alleyne and Janet Wagner, 'Stability and Change at the "Big Five" News Agencies', *Journalism Quarterly*, 70 (1993), pp. 41–3; J. Tunstall, *Newspaper Power. The New National Press in Britain* (1996), p. 340; H. Pigeat, *Médias et déontologie. règles du jeu ou jeu sans règles* (Paris, 1997), pp. 76, 164–9.
6. P. Job, 'Plotting a Course through the Digital Highway', *News From Reuters*, 24 July 1996, p. 1. For independent overviews, see A. Dhebar, *Reuters Holdings PLC.* Harvard Business School Case Study 1–888–107 (Boston, 1988); and *Reuters Holdings PLC.* Harvard Business School Case Studies 9-595-113, 114, 115 (Boston, 1995); and Cheri Lofland, *Reuters: Analysis of its Administrative Heritage and Positioning for the Future*, London Business School (1995). See also W. Goldsmith and D. Clutterbuck, *The Winning Streak, Mark II* (1997).
7. *Reuters World*, May 1989, pp. 6–7; Dhebar, *Reuters Holdings*, 9–595–115, p. 1.
8. M. E. Nelson, 'Reuters and the World of News', Institute of Directors, Monaco, 15 Oct. 1996, typescript, pp. 5–6; Goldsmith and Clutterbuck, *The Winning Streak*, p. 70.
9. *Time*, 9 Dec. 1996. For Reuter-sponsored views of 'information overload', see *Dying for Information? An Investigation into the Effects of Information Overload in the UK and Worldwide*, Reuters Business Information (1996); *Glued to the Screen, An Investigation into Information Addiction Worldwide*, Reuters (1997).

SELECT BIBLIOGRAPHY

T HE main body of documentary evidence used in this book is to be found in the Reuters Archive, London. This Archive—managed by a professional archivist—is recognized as one of the best-organized journalism archives in the world. It contains not only the usual records of a great business (minute books, cash books, planning papers, etc.) but also a quantity of more personal material, including a notable series of video and audio interviews with veteran Reuter staffers. Also in the Archive are typescript copies of the unpublished recollections of some key members of staff, with memories ranging variously from the 1860s to the 1980s. There are, however, some unexpected gaps in the Archive holdings. For example, few news telegrams have survived from between 1881 and 1944. And although the voluminous office and private papers of Sir Roderick Jones—head of Reuters between the wars—cover more than half a century, there is little personal material relating to Jones's predecessors, Julius Reuter and his son, Herbert. Fortunately, during research for the present book, much Reuter-related material has been found in other collections both in Britain and overseas, and photocopies of all key documents found elsewhere have been placed in the Archive. From 1949, the typescript 'Reuters Chronology' (first compiled by J. H. Henry) brings together much useful factual information.

The Reuters Archive is not open to the public; but access for research purposes may be allowed by arrangement.

One previous history of Reuters has been published. To celebrate the centenary of Julius Reuter's start in London, the company commissioned Graham Storey, a young Cambridge academic, to write *Reuters' Century, 1851–1951* (1951). Storey did not have access to much material now available, especially for the twentieth century; but his readable account caught the spirit of Reuters up to the First World War. An unpublished typescript by Charles Marriott, 'Reuters, A History', is in the Archive. It is an ill-digested compilation, dating from 1919, largely based upon the recollections of a group of Reuter pioneers then still alive, many of whom had memories stretching back to Julius Reuter's day. Copies of these recollections survive upon microfilm, and are more readable than Marriott's text. This is surprising, since Marriott was himself a member of the Reuter editorial staff.

In writing about news agencies, the following secondary works are among the most helpful. Place of book publication is London, unless otherwise indicated.

Background Books and Articles

Ahvenainen, J., *Far Eastern Telegraphs* (Helsinki, 1981).
Alleyne, M. D., *News Revolution. Political and Economic Decisions about Global Information* (1997).

Bell, A., *The Language of News Media* (1991).

Blondheim, M., *News Over the Wires. The Telegraph and the Flow of Public Information in America, 1844–1897* (Cambridge, Mass., 1994).

Briggs, A., *The Birth of Broadcasting* (1961).

Bright, C., *Submarine Telegraphs* (1898)

Brown, F. J., *The Cable and Wireless Communications of the World* (1927).

Brown, Lucy, 'The Treatment of the News in Mid-Victorian Newspapers', *Transactions of the Royal Historical Society*, 5th ser., vol. 27 (1975), pp. 23–39.

—— *Victorian News and Newspapers* (Oxford 1985).

Cooper, K., *The Right to Know. An Exposition of the Evils of News Suppression and Propaganda* (New York 1956).

Desmond, R. W., *The Information Process. The Press and World Affairs* (New York, 1937).

—— *The Information Process. World News Reporting to the Twentieth Century* (Iowa City, Ia., 1978).

Dijk, T. A. van, *News Analysis. Case Studies of International and National News in the Press* (Hillsdale, NJ, 1988).

Evans, H., *Good Times, Bad Times* (1983).

Fletcher, R. J., 'British Propaganda since World War II—A Case Study', *Media, Culture and Society*, 4 (1982), pp. 97–109.

Grant, J., *The Newspaper Press* (1871).

Headrick, D. R., *The Invisible Weapon. Telecommunications and International Politics, 1851–1945* (New York 1990).

History of The Times. *The Tradition Established, 1841–1884* (1939).

Hohenberg, J., *Foreign Correspondence. The Great Reporters and Their Times* (New York, 1965).

Israel, M., *Communications and Power, Propaganda and the Press in the Indian Nationalist Struggle, 1920–1947* (Cambridge, 1994).

Kennedy, P. M., 'Imperial Cable Communications and Strategy, 1870–1914', *English Historical Review*, 86 (1971), pp. 728–52.

Kieve, J. L., *The Electric Telegraph* (Newton Abbot, 1973).

Barty-King, H., *Girdle Round the Earth. The Story of Cable and Wireless* (1979).

Knightley, P., *The First Casualty* (1975).

Lee, A. J., *The Origins of the Popular Press in England, 1855–1914* (1976).

Linton, D., *The Twentieth-Century Newspaper Press in Britain. An Annotated Bibliography* (1994).

McLaine, I., *Ministry of Morale. Home Front Morale and the Ministry of Information in World War II* (1979).

McNaught, C., *Canada Gets the News* (Toronto, 1940).

Mercer, D., *et al.*, *The Fog of War. The Media on the Battlefield* (1987).

Mills, J. Saxon, *The Press and Communications of the Empire* (1924).

Moberly Bell, Enid H. C., *The Life and Times of C. F. Moberly Bell* (1927).

Pigeat, H., *Le Nouveau Désordre mondial de l'information* (Paris, 1987).

Pigeat, H., *Médias et déontologie. règles du jeu ou jeu sans règles* (Paris, 1997).

Sanders, M.L., and Taylor, P. M., *British Propaganda During the First World War* (1982).

Sargeant, Harriet, *Shanghai* (1991).

Schudson, M., *Discovering the News. A Social History of American Newspapers* (New York, 1978).

Simonis, H., *The Street of Ink* (1917).

Smith, A., 'The Long Road to Objectivity and Back Again: The Kinds of Truth We Get in Journalism', in G. Boyce, *et al.* (eds.), *Newspaper History* (1978), pp. 153–71.

—— *The Politics of Information. Problems of Policy in Modern Media* (1978).

Souter, G., *Company of Heralds* (Sydney, 1981).

Stern, F., *Gold and Iron. Bismarck, Bleichröder, and the Building of the German Empire* (New York, 1977).

Taylor, P. M., *The Projection of Britain. British Overseas Publicity and Propaganda, 1919–1939* (Cambridge, 1981).

—— *Munitions of the Mind. A History of Propaganda from the Ancient World to the Present Day* (Manchester, 1995).

Thomson, Rear-Admiral G.P., *Blue Pencil Admiral. The Inside Story of the Press Censorship* (n.d.).

Tunstall, J. and Palmer, M., *Media Moguls* (1991).

Willert, *et al.*, Sir A., *The Empire in the World* (1937).

Williams, F., *Press, Parliament and People* (1946).

—— *Transmitting World News* (Paris, 1953).

Wriston, W. B., *The Twilight of Sovereignty. How the Information Revolution is Transforming Our World* (New York, 1992).

Books and Articles about News Agencies (including Reuters)

Alleyne, M. D., and Wagner, Janet, 'Stability and Change at the "Big Five" News Agencies', *Journalism Quarterly*, 70 (1993), pp. 40–50.

Basse, D., *Wolff's Telegraphisches Bureau 1849 bis 1933* (Munich, 1991).

Bloomberg, M., *Bloomberg by Bloomberg* (New York, 1997).

Boyd-Barrett, O., 'Market Control and Wholesale News: The Case of Reuters', in G. Boyce, *et al.* (eds.), *Newspaper History* (1978), pp. 192–204.

—— *The International News Agencies* (1980).

—— and Palmer, M., *Le Trafic des nouvelles. les agences mondiales d'information* (Paris, 1981).

—— *Contra-flow in Global News* (1992).

Cooper, K., *Barriers Down* (New York, 1942).

—— *Kent Cooper and the Associated Press. An Autobiography* (New York, 1959).

Dhebar, A., *Reuters Holdings PLC.* Harvard Business School Case Study 1-188-107 (Boston, 1988).

—— *Reuters Holdings PLC.* Harvard Business School Case Studies 9-595-113, 114, 115 (Boston, 1995).

Fenby, J., *The International News Services* (New York, 1986).

Frédérix, P., *Un siécle de chasse aux nouvelles* (Paris, 1959).

Frie, F. van, *Reuters in the Netherlands. De La Mar and the Reuters Amsterdam Branch* (Rotterdam, 1993).

Goldsmith, W., and Clutterbuck, D., *The Winning Streak, Mark II* (1997).

Gordon, G., and Cohen, R. E., *Down to the Wire. UPI's Fight for Survival* (New York, 1990).

Gramling, O., *A.P. The Story of News* (New York, 1940).

Haley, Sir W. J., 'Sir Roderick Jones', *Dictionary of National Biography*, 1961–1970 (1981), pp. 598–9.

Hart, H. G., *The Central News Diamond Jubilee Souvenir* (1931).

Höhne, H., *Reportüber Nachrichtenagenturen* 2 vols. (Baden, 1976; 1977).

Huteau, J., and Ullmann, B., *A.F.P. une histoire de l'Agence France-Presse, 1944–1990* (Paris, 1992).

Iwanaga, S., *Story of Japanese News Agencies* (Tokyo, 1980).

Kim, Soon Jim, *EFE. Spain's World News Agency* (Westport, Conn., 1989).

Kruglak, T., *The Foreign Correspondents* (Geneva, 1955).

Lefebure, A., *Havas. les arcanes du pouvoir* (Paris, 1992).

Lofland, Cheri, *Reuters: Analysis of its Administrative Heritage and Positioning for the Future*, London Business School (1995).

Morris, J. A., *Deadline Every Minute. The Story of the United Press* (New York, 1957).

Narasimhan, V. K., *Kasturi Srinivasan* (Bombay, 1969).

Palmer, M., 'De l'information etrangère dans la presse quotidienne française: les agences de presse et le journalisme anglo-saxon, 1875–1885', *Revue d'Histoire Moderne et Contemporaine*, 23 (1976), pp. 203–35.

—— 'L'Agence Havas, Reuters et Bismarck. l'echec de la triple alliance télégraphique (1887–1889)', *Revue d'histoire diplomatique*, 90 (1976), pp. 321–57.

—— 'The British Press and International News, 1851–1899. Of Agencies and Newspapers', in G. Boyce, *et al.* (eds.), *Newspaper History* (1978), pp. 205–19.

—— *Des petits journaux aux grandes agences: naissance du journalisme moderne* (Paris, 1983).

——'L'Information agencée, fin de siècle. visions du monde et discours en fragments', *Réseaux*, 75 (Jan.–Feb. 1996), pp. 87–109.

—— 'Quand les agences rapportent l'evenement: "l'actualité" russe, 1904–1906', in F. d'Almeida (ed.), *La Question médiatique* (Paris, 1997), pp. 205–19.

Raghavan, G. N. S., *PTI Story* (Bombay, 1987).

Rantanen, Terhi, *Foreign News in Imperial Russia. The Relationship between International and Russian News Agencies, 1856–1914* (Helsinki, 1990).

—— *Mr. Howard Goes to South America. The United Press Associations and Foreign Expansion* (Roy W. Howard Monographs, no. 2, Bloomington, Ind., 1992).

—— *Howard Interviews Stalin. How the AP, UP and Tass Smashed the International News Cartel* (Roy W. Howard Monographs, no. 3, Bloomington, Ind., 1994).

Rantanen, Terhi, 'The Globalization of Electronic News in the 19th Century', *Media, Culture & Society*, 19 (1997), pp. 605–20.

—— *After Five O'clock Friends, Kent Cooper and Roy W. Howard* (Roy W. Howard Monographs, no. 4, Bloomington, Ind., 1998).

—— and Vartanova, Elena, *From State Monopoly to Competition: The Changing Landscape of News Agencies in Russia* (Helsinki, 1993).

Read, D., 'Sir Roderick Jones and Reuters: Rise and Fall of a News Emperor', in D. Fraser (ed.), *Cities, Class and Communication* (1990), pp. 175–99.

—— 'War News from Reuters: Victorian and Edwardian Reporting', *Despatches*, 4 (1993), pp. 72–85.

—— 'Reuters: News Agency of the British Empire', *Contemporary Record*, 8 (1994), pp. 195–212.

—— 'Truth in News: Reuters and the *Manchester Guardian*, 1858–1964', *Northern History*, 31 (1995), pp. 281–97.

—— 'Reuters and South Africa: "South Africa is a country of monopolies" ', *South African Journal of Economic History*, 11 (1996), pp. 104–43.

—— 'Sir Christopher Chancellor', *Dictionary of National Biography, 1986–1990* (1996), pp. 65–6.

—— 'The Impact of "Electric News" 1846–1914. The Role of Reuters', in F. A. J. L. James (ed.), *Semaphores to Short Waves* (1998), pp. 121–35.

Renaud, J.-L., 'U.S. Government Assistance to AP's World-Wide Expansion', *Journalism Quarterly*, 62 (1985), pp. 1–16, 36.

Sanders, J., *Dateline NZPA. The New Zealand Press Association, 1880–1980* (Auckland, 1979).

Schwarzlose, R. A., *The Nation's Newsbrokers*, vol. 2 (Evanston, Ill., 1990).

Scott, G., *Reporter Anonymous. The Story of the Press Association* (1968).

Scott, J. M., *Extel 100. The Centenary History of the Exchange Telegraph Company* (1972).

South African Press Association, *50 Years Service to the News Media, 1938–1988* (Johannesburg, 1988).

Storey, G., *Reuters' Century, 1851–1951* (1951).

Tajuddin, M., *Foundation of Associated Press of Pakistan* (Islamabad, 1952).

Publications by Reuter Journalists (with Reuter-related Content)

Barnes, J. S., *Half A Life* (1933).

—— *Half A Life Left* (1937).

Bartlett, V., *This is My Life* (1937).

Behr, E., *Anyone Here Been Raped and Speaks English?* (1981).

Brooke, Lord, *An Eye-Witness in Manchuria* (1905).

Chancellor, C., 'The New Order in East Asia', *Journal of the Royal Central Asian Society*, 26 (1939), pp. 575–98.

—— 'How Reuters Did its Job Right Through the War', reprinted from *World's Press News* (13 Dec. 1945).

Clarke, B., *My Round of the War* (1917).

Collins, H. M., *From Pigeon Post to Wireless* (1925).

Dallas, D., *Dateline Moscow* (1952).

Dickins, K., 'With Hitler in Munich', *London Magazine*, 35 (1995), pp. 25–43.

Eldon, Kathy (ed.), *The Journey is the Destination. The Journals of Dan Eldon* (San Francisco, 1997).

Gall, S., *Don't Worry About the Money Now* (1982).

Grey, A., *Hostage in Peking* (1970).

—— *A Man Alone* (1971).

—— *Crosswords from Peking* (1975).

Gwynne, H. A., 'Adventures and Experiences in Pre-War Wars', in H. W. Nevinson (ed.), *Anywhere for a News Story* (1934), ch.6.

Hamilton, D., *Editor-in-Chief* (1989).

Hasan, N., *Reporting India and Her Neighbours* (New Delhi, 1989).

Holme, C., *Portrait* (Oxford, 1992)

James, L., *High Pressure* (1929).

Jameson, D., *Touched by Angels* (1989).

Jones, Sir Roderick, *Reuters* (School of Military Engineering, Chatham, 1928).

—— 'The Romance of Reuters', *Journal of the Institute of Journalists* (Dec. 1930), pp. 223–4.

—— *Reuters* (Cardiff Business Club, 1932).

—— *Property in News* (Empire Press Union, 1936).

—— *Transmission of News* (Empire Press Union, 1937).

—— *A Life in Reuters* (1951).

Lawrenson, J., and Barber, L., *The Price of Truth. The Story of the Reuters Millions* (1985; rev. 1986).

Lees-Milne, J., *Another Self* (1970).

Lunn, H., *Vietnam. A Reporter's War* (St Lucia, Queensland, 1985).

Lynch, C., *You Can't Print That* (Toronto, 1988).

Macdowall, I., *Reuters Handbook for Journalists* (1992).

MacNeil, R., *The Right Place at the Right Time* (New York, 1982).

Mant, G., *A Cuckoo in the Bodyline Nest* (Kenthurst, New South Wales, 1992)

—— *The Singapore Surrender* (Kenthurst, New South Wales, 1992).

Nelson, M., *War of the Black Heavens. The Battles of Western Broadcasting in the Cold War* (1997).

Newman, H., *A Roving Commission* (1937).

Peet, J., *The Long Engagement. Memoirs of a Cold War Legend* (1989).

Pooley, A. M., *Japan at the Crossroads* (1917).

Reuters, *The Wall Comes Down*. Reuters videotape (1990).

Savidge, I., *Hugo Manning, Poet and Humanist* (1997).

Sebba, Anne, *Enid Bagnold* (1986).

Tetley, B., *Mo. The Story of Mohamed Amin, Front-line Cameraman* (1988).

Waterfield, G., *What Happened to France* (1940).

Ward, E., *Number One Boy* (1969).
Williams, V., *The World of Action* (1938).
Willis, J., *Restless Quest* (n.d.).
Young G. (ed.), *Outposts of War* (1941).

INDEX

Entries for illustrations are shown in *italics*; *Pl.* indicates one of the plates grouped between pages 142–3 and 302–3; *Fig. (p.)* indicates a figure on that page. There are important entries under 'news' and 'objectivity'.